Patent Misuse and Antitrust Law

Empirical, Doctrinal and Policy Perspectives

Daryl Lim

The John Marshall Law School, USA

Edward Elgar
Cheltenham, UK • Northampton, MA, USA

Published by
Edward Elgar Publishing Limited
The Lypiatts
15 Lansdown Road
Cheltenham
Glos GL50 2JA
UK

Edward Elgar Publishing, Inc.
William Pratt House
9 Dewey Court
Northampton
Massachusetts 01060
USA

A catalogue record for this book
is available from the British Library

Library of Congress Control Number: 2013942206

This book is available electronically in the ElgarOnline.com
Law Subject Collection, E-ISBN 978 0 85793 018 7

ISBN 978 0 85793 017 0

Typeset by Servis Filmsetting Ltd, Stockport, Cheshire
Printed and bound in Great Britain by T.J. International Ltd, Padstow

Contents

Foreword

For much of the 20th century, the systems of U.S. antitrust law and patent law resided in largely separate domains. Academics, public officials, and practitioners formed two distinct communities, each with its own professional culture and training (many patent lawyers are engineers or scientists, and many antitrust lawyers regard mathematics and science with bewilderment). Individuals with deep knowledge of both the antitrust and patent regimes were rare. The absence of a widely shared interdisciplinary perspective obscured conceptual connections between the two disciplines and impeded recognition of complementarities between the antitrust and patent systems.

At times, outright antagonism reinforced the separation. From the 1940s through the 1970s, many expressions of U.S. antitrust policy regarded patents with suspicion. Antitrust lawyers developed the common habit of speaking of "the patent monopoly," as though the issuance of a patent automatically conferred substantial market power upon its owner. Antitrust courts and public enforcement agencies skeptically examined restrictions embodied in licensing agreements. Monopolization cases served as tools to resist what antitrust agencies regarded as overreaching by the patent system.

This gloomy history has taken a decided turn for the better. The past twenty years have witnessed an encouraging realignment of the relationship between U.S. antitrust law and patent law. Public enforcement policy has abandoned the former hostility to patents and patent licensing. Courts and enforcement agencies increasingly emphasize the complementary roles that competition and patent rights can play in promoting innovation that improves economic performance. The work of academics and professional societies reflects the need for a truly interdisciplinary approach to understanding the origins and content of antitrust and patent institutions and to facilitate the development of coherent doctrine and policy between the two fields.

Daryl Lim exemplifies the new generation of scholars whose work is dismantling barriers between the antitrust and patent regimes and spurring a transformation in the relationship between the two bodies of law and policy. In this volume, he not only provides the best study to date of the patent misuse doctrine, but he also sets a valuable foundation for integrating the study of antitrust law and patent law, generally.

Three major contributions stand out. First, *Patent Misuse and Antitrust Law* illustrates as well as any other work how to bridge the study of antitrust law and patent law, for Professor Lim displays mastery of both the technical details and broader policy considerations of the patent misuse doctrine and traces its origins in patent and antitrust law. In doing so, he reveals how concepts of antitrust policy informed judicial development of the patent misuse doctrine. Only a scholar proficient in both fields could illuminate important interactions between the two fields.

A second and related feature is Professor Lim's excellent use of historical narratives to show how patent misuse concepts have developed over time. He places doctrinal developments in their historical context and relates them to changes in law and policy. By this approach, he highlights the historical and intellectual forces that have shaped misuse principles over time. This provides a useful basis for anticipating how the law might unfold in the future, and what distinctive contributions misuse doctrine might make to resolve tensions that arise in determining which mix of policies are best suited to stimulate innovation.

A third impressive dimension of *Patent Misuse and Antitrust Law* is its powerful empirical orientation. Professor Lim is faithful to the cause of theory, and he skillfully sets out the conceptual framework for misuse doctrine. What he does next makes this volume special. Professor Lim combines a comprehensive examination of misuse cases with extensive interviews to demonstrate how theory meets practice. Painstaking empirical study, not mere theory-based intuition, supports Professor Lim's inquiry. He provides an unprecedented view of the jurisprudence and the forces that have determined outcomes in individual cases. The interviews supply rich interpretations of the cases and broader trends, as well as valuable insights about possible future directions for law and policy.

In these respects and others, *Patent Misuse and Antitrust Law* broadens and extends the emerging path of a refreshing new scholarship that links antitrust and patent law. Professor Lim supplies a model for future work, not only in what he has done but in how he has done it. In the years to come, as we benefit from the deeper intellectual integration of antitrust and patent law and policy, we will look back with gratitude at *Patent Misuse and Antitrust Law* for showing us the way.

William E. Kovacic
Global Competition Professor of Law and Policy
George Washington University Law School
Washington, D.C.
27 March 2013

Preface and acknowledgements

This study is testament to the marvel of technology and to the profound impact it has had on legal research. Twenty years ago, a study examining every reported case in a field of the law could scarcely have been imaginable. It would have taken many hundreds of hours of laborious searching, photocopying and indexing to even consolidate a body of cases to commence the research. To hunt down the literature perused in this study would likely have taken as long. Today, many processes, from searching to cross-referencing are nearly instantaneous. Technology has facilitated the statistical analysis of legal data and narrowed the socio-legal research gap. While there will always be an important place for doctrine and policy, empirical work like this reflects the kind of practical scholarship our increasingly complex and sophisticated society demands from those who research and teach the law.

Technology has also connected the world in a way previously unimaginable. It has reduced the opportunity cost of travel and telecommunications, making many of the interviews conducted for this study possible today in a way that simply could not otherwise have been done between other professional commitments. The interviews were at once the most demanding and rewarding aspect of this study. Interviews are a two-way process, and I have learnt that interviewers can be expected to contribute much more to the content of the discussion than merely asking the "right" questions. But done well, interviews provide a rich and stirring interaction that breathes life into dry numbers and doctrine. It was a great privilege to be able to speak with a most remarkable group of interviewees, who gave most generously of both their time and thoughts. Because the interviews were conducted on the condition of confidentiality, references to their contributions do not appear. The purpose of the interviews was to capture the perceptions of stakeholders of patent misuse in practice, both in relation to, as well as apart from my findings. The interviews are not meant to be a representative survey of all constituents.

This book is an invitation to join my journey to understand the contours of patent misuse and how it relates to antitrust law. Readers will quickly see that this book features more verbatim quotes than they may be used to seeing in a legal publication such as this. More like a photographer and less like a painter, I have tried to capture snapshots of how misuse has featured in real life into a scrapbook rather than present a projection of my own reality. The verbatim text as they left the minds of judges who wrote the opinions and the interviewees and commentators discussing them best represent the state of the world as they see it with as little distortion from my paraphrasing as possible. Those with even a passing knowledge of patent law or antitrust law will hear the echoes of many great minds who have given thought to issues intricately woven around each other to form and inform the doctrine of misuse within these pages.

The value of this enterprise revealed itself through the many interview sessions and subsequent presentation of my findings to experts in the field who were informed, engaged and entertained by the findings and how perceptions in practice deviated from case law and/or conventional wisdom. Indeed, the best moments came when one of them would remark—"Oh that's interesting, I didn't know this!" The study began in 2008 and was completed in 2012. The interviews were based on preliminary results whose trends remained the same over time. My hope as you read this book is that it will do for you what it has done for me and those I have shared snippets of it with—expanding your mind to look beyond conventional wisdom. Readers will also note the limited scope of this book. When it comes to an equitable doctrine like misuse, any book will reach its limits long before it exhausts its topic. This book is intended to be comprehensive but not exhaustive, and to be both exploratory and practical. With that said – welcome.

The pleasure of thanking those who have helped the writing process is a sweet one. I am grateful to Professor Hugh C. Hansen, Professor of Law, Director of the Fordham IP Law Institute and "IP provocateur", for his friendship, guidance and the many opportunities he made possible. He also generously shared his thoughts on improving the study. This book blossomed while I served as the Institute's inaugural Microsoft Teaching and Research Fellow. Teaching courses in patent law, copyright law and EU IP law refined the observations made in the book. I am also grateful to my supervisors at Stanford Law School: Professor Mark Lemley, Professor Deborah Hensler and Dr Moria Paz who guided the writing of my thesis on which this book is based. While at Stanford, I also benefitted from the guidance of Visiting Professor Barton Beebe, whose seminal work on fair use in copyright law provided the inspiration for the case content analysis model used in this book, as well as Professor David Victor, whose thoughts helped refine my empirical analysis. The journey started at Stanford but moved through a number of places as I interviewed people and wrote and presented the work along the way. It has finally settled at the John Marshall Law School, my new academic home. Here,

I take pleasure in thanking Deans John Corkery and Ralph Ruebner for their steadfast support for my scholarship. I also thank the faculty and staff of John Marshall for many hours of edifying conversations which helped make this work better, including Professors Doris Long, Bill Ford, Arthur Yuan and Ben Liu as well as Research Librarian Raizel Liebler. I would like to thank Nick Bartelt, Research and Conference Fellow at the Fordham IP Institute, for his careful comments on my draft manuscript. Mention must also be made of Jason Lunardi, Research Fellow at the Fordham IP Institute as well as Kimberly Reagan and Ali Abid, Research Fellows at the John Marshall Law School. In addition I would like to thank my Research Assistants Joseph Noferi, Michael Sullivan and William Gros and Adam Sussman who ably and cheerfully provided much assistance, and Sandra Sherman of the Fordham IP Center who helped bring this work to fruition.

Many individuals carefully read my draft and provided many insightful comments along the way. They have helped bring my scholarship to the very center of applied research—where theory is only as good as the insights it brings to practice. Naturally, any errors that remain are my responsibility alone.

This study would also not have been possible without the following people, who have individually and collectively inspired me along the path of patent misuse and antitrust scholarship with their thoughtful insights and personal encouragement: from the judiciary: Chief Judge Randall R. Rader (Court of Appeals for the Federal Circuit) (May 31, 2010–present), Chief Judge Paul Michel (Court of Appeals for the Federal Circuit) (December 25, 2004–May 31, 2010), Judge Richard Posner (Court of Appeals for the Seventh Circuit), Judge Kent Jordan (Court of Appeals for the Third Circuit), Judge T.S. Ellis III (District Court, Eastern District of Virginia), Judge Ronald M. Whyte (District Court, Northern District of California); from the government: Commissioner William E. Kovacic (U.S. Federal Trade Commission), Hon. Stanford McCoy (U.S. Trade Representative's Office) and James Toupin (U.S. Patent and Trademark Office); from academia: Professors Lawrence Friedman, Paul Goldstein, David Victor (Stanford Law School), Barton Beebe (Benjamin N. Cardozo School of Law), Herb Hovenkamp (University of Iowa College of Law), Hugh C. Hansen (Fordham University School of Law), Thomas Cotter (University of Minnesota Law School), Larry Franklin (Hong Kong University of Science and Technology Business School) and Joshua Walker (Stanford IP Litigation Clearinghouse); from legal practice: Nick Groombridge, Alan Weinschel and Jason Kipnis (Weil, Gotshal & Manges LLP), Robert Lipstein (Crowell & Moring) and John Richards (Ladas & Parry). The patient and enthusiastic assistance of members of the Stanford Law School's staff, particularly Lucy LaPier, Sonia Moss and George Wilson, as well as the friendship, advice and assistance of Lee Jyh-An and Stuart Loh are gladly acknowledged.

At Edward Elgar Publishing, many pairs of hands helped me make this journey from manuscript to print possible. It is to Elgar's credit that it has been able to attract such fine professionals. I am grateful to Tim Williams and his team which include Jane Bayliss, Rosemary Campbell, Tara Gorvine, Emma Gribbon and Laura Mann.

Economic theory teaches that the price one pays should reflect its market worth. It can only be hoped that the net present value of this work represents a fair return on its backers' investments. In this regard, I have been blessed to have received the Franklin Family Fellowship for my studies at Stanford Law School and the Ewing Marion Kauffman Foundation funding for my field research. The Law School also kindly supported me in attending the Fordham IP Conference at Cambridge University, UK, where the findings of this study was presented to the international IP community. I am also grateful to the Emily C. and John E. Hansen IP Institute and to the John Marshall Law School for their financial and administrative support. Finally, a book is always written at the expense of those closest to the author. They know who they are, and I thank them for their resigned but gracious tolerance.

The law is described as it appeared to me on December 31, 2012.

Prologue

This book explores the doctrine of patent misuse which was created and exists today to make sure patents are used in ways that are consistent with the purpose and intent of the law. There is probably more general debate about the purpose and intent of patent law now than there has ever been. A study of patent misuse, therefore, not only elucidates an important doctrine but also contributes to the ongoing debate about the role of patents.

This book looks at patent misuse through an historical and empirical lens. It discusses important doctrinal and policy issues. It also looks at patent misuse through the eyes of practitioners, judges and academics. This has never been done before. Hopefully, it will provide a resource for the curious, the expert and all those who are engaged in deciding what patent misuse means and should mean today.

Introduction

I. "THE METAPHYSICS OF PATENT LAW"

On April 18, 1951, Congressman Joseph R. Bryson of South Carolina introduced a new patent bill, the most significant revision of patent law in more than a century.[1] Like the start-up company Google nearly half a century later, the Patent Act of 1952 largely sprung from the ingenuity of two men—Pasquale Joseph Federico, Chief Examiner of the U.S. Patent Office, and Giles Sutherland Rich, patent attorney and President of the New York Patent Law Association.[2] Rich would become Chief Judge of the Court of Customs and Patent Appeals, and then later a judge of the newly created Court of Appeals for the Federal Circuit, the nation's patent court. Judge Rich was widely regarded as being one of the most influential individuals in patent law.[3] He remarked that if patent law was "the metaphysics" of the law, then patent misuse is the "metaphysics of patent law."[4]

Patent misuse finds its origins in the equitable doctrine of unclean hands, "whereby a court of equity will not lend its support to enforcement of a patent that has been misused."[5] In invoking the defense of misuse,

---

[1] H.R. 3760, 82nd Cong. § 1 *et seq.* (1951).

[2] *Giles Sutherland Rich*, WIKIPEDIA, http://en.wikipedia.org/wiki/Giles_Sutherland_Rich.

[3] Jon Thurber, *Judge Giles Rich; Patent Law Authority*, LOS ANGELES TIMES, June 14, 1999, http://articles.latimes.com/1999/jun/14/news/mn-46460 (noting that Judge Rich was "widely regarded as the century's preeminent lawyer, jurist and scholar in the patent field").

[4] See *Rohm & Haas Co. v. Dawson Chem. Co.*, 599 F.2d 685, 706 (5th Cir. 1979) *aff'd*, 448 U.S. 176 (1980) ("[P]atent cases are the only cases argued by professionals and decided by amateurs. We take some comfort in noting that any shortcomings of our effort can safely be laid to the difficulty of the subject matter. Mr. Giles S. Rich observed on several occasions during the hearings on section 271 that patent law is 'the metaphysics' of the law and that contributory infringement/patent misuse issues are the metaphysics of patent law"). Google was founded by Sergey Brin and Larry Page in 1998. Management Team, GOOGLE, http://www.google.com/about/company/facts/management/.

[5] See *B. Braun Med., Inc. v. Abbot Labs.*, 124 F.3d 1419, 1427 (Fed. Cir. 1997).

defendants accept that they have infringed another's patents whether by breach of a license agreement or some other form. At the same time, these defendants temerariously argue that justice requires the courts to aid them by tempering the letter of the law, because the patentees had by their own conduct reached beyond the boundaries of their patent grant in a manner contrary to public policy.[6] Patentees found guilty of misuse are punished by having the patent or patents in question rendered unenforceable until the effects of the misuse have been purged.[7] In policing patent misconduct, misuse therefore delineates the metaphysical boundary beyond which the patent grant, according to Thomas Jefferson, becomes "more embarrassment than advantage to society."[8] It acts as a public injunction against abuses of the privilege granted under patent law, and balances public and private interests.[9]

At the heart of misuse lies a delicate balance. The patent grant is based upon a constitutional privilege to "promote the Progress of Science and the useful Arts."[10] To fulfill this mandate, Congress allows patentees to exclude others, earn royalties, and set the terms of access for those benefitting from the use of technology protected by patents. This limited monopoly rewards innovators who take risks and invest in innovation and the commercialization of their inventions, incentivizing them to develop and market inventions that may not have been realized otherwise.[11] The

---

[6]   See *Mallinkrodt, Inc. v. Medipart, Inc.*, 976 F.2d 700, 704 (Fed. Cir. 1992).

[7]   *Morton Salt Co. v. G. S. Suppiger Co.*, 314 U.S. 488 (1942) ("Equity may rightly withhold its assistance from such a use of the patent by declining to entertain a suit for infringement, and should do so at least until it is made to appear that the improper practice has been abandoned and that the consequences of the misuse of the patent have been dissipated").

[8]   Letter from Thomas Jefferson to Isaac McPherson (Aug. 13, 1813), available at: http://press-pubs.uchicago.edu/founders/documents/a1_8_8s12.html.

[9]   *Syndicate Sales, Inc. v. Floral Innovations, Inc.*, 2012 U.S. Dist. LEXIS 140345, at *6–7 (S.D. Ind. Sept. 28, 2012) ("A patent is, therefore, appropriately viewed as a contract between the patentee and the public. Patent misuse occurs when the scope of an otherwise valid patent monopoly extends beyond the prescribed boundaries of the patentee's control," citing *Zenith Radio Corp. v. Hazeltine Res., Inc.*, 395 U.S. 100, 136, 89 S. Ct. 1562, 23 L. Ed. 2d 129 (1969)). *SmithKline Beecham Corp. v. Apotex Corp.*, 247 F. Supp. 2d 1011, 1046 (N.D. Ill. 2003). ("The core of that doctrine is the proposition that a patent may not be used to obtain more protection from competition than patent law contemplates").

[10]   U.S. CONST. art. I, § 8, cl. 8. The Intellectual Property Clause of the Constitution gives Congress the power "[t]o promote the Progress of Science and useful Arts, by securing for limited Times to Authors and Inventors the exclusive Right to their respective Writings and Discoveries," ibid.

[11]   It is worth mentioning at this early stage that such legal monopolies do not necessarily translate into economic monopolies which concern the antitrust laws.

lure of exclusive rights also attracts others into the inventive enterprise. It feeds into a virtuous ecosystem of innovation where each successive generation "stand[s] on the shoulders of Giants"[12] as new entrants, licensees, and competitors are enabled to build upon the patent owner's technology, which is disclosed in return for the monopoly protection.[13] When patent owners are overcompensated for their contributions, it disrupts the incentive system and results in inefficiency and reduced technological output.

Misuse typically arises in the context of licensing agreements, and is commonly associated with tying arrangements, where patentees sell one product (the tying product) but only on condition that the buyer also purchases a different (or tied) product, or in cases where patentees attempt to extend the life of the royalty period due under their patents through contracts. Agreements and conduct which offend competition policy invoke the other great theme of this book—the antitrust laws. Patentees may engage in conduct which amounts to antitrust violations and will not be able to restrain infringement by others, even if the patent is valid, because "[e]ven constitutionally protected property rights such as patents may not be used as levers for obtaining objectives proscribed by the antitrust laws."[14]

Misuse is not restricted to a closed category of "wrongful" practices, but "appl[ies] to whatever the form of the suit by the patent owner may be."[15]

As Judge Richard Posner explained "[a] patent confers a monopoly in the sense of a right to exclude others from selling the patented product. But if there are close substitutes for the patented product, the patent 'monopoly' is not a monopoly in a sense relevant to antitrust law." This important distinction has now formed a settled part of the IP-Antitrust canon. Thomas F. Maffei, *The Patent Misuse Doctrine: A Balance of Patent Rights and the Public Interest*, 11 B.C.L. REV. 46 (1969), available at: http://lawdigitalcommons.bc.edu/bclr/vol11/iss1/4 ("The term 'monopoly', however, must be used carefully in the antitrust and patent contexts because of its changing connotation"); Kevin J. Arquit, *Patent Abuse and the Antitrust Laws*, 59 ANTITRUST L.J. 739, 740 (1991) ("An often-neglected point, though critical, is that a patent monopoly does not invariably translate into a monopoly in what an antitrust lawyer would describe as a relevant market").

[12]   Letter from Isaac Newton to Robert Hooke (1676) ("What Descartes did was a good step. You have added much several ways, and especially in taking the colours of thin plates into philosophical consideration. If I have seen a little further it is by standing on the shoulders of Giants").

[13]   See 35 U.S.C. § 112, cl. 1 (1952) (requiring the patent applicant be fully in possession of the invention claimed and to disclose his invention in a manner which enables a person ordinarily skilled in the art to make and use the invention).

[14]   Joel R. Bennett, *Patent Misuse: Must an Alleged Infringer Prove an Antitrust Violation?*, 17 AIPLA Q.J. 1, 8 (1989).

[15]   *United States v. United States Gypsum Co.*, 124 F. Supp. 573, 594–95 (D.D.C. 1954).

Patentees guilty of misuse must purge their misconduct to the satisfaction of the court if they wish to realize the remedies they seek.[16] Purging requires patentees to show that they have completely abandoned the misconduct, and that their "baleful effects" have dissipated.[17] What amounts to a successful dissipation depends on the nature and extent of the misuse. Cancellation of an offending licensing clause may be sufficient.[18] Where the conduct involves a price-fixing conspiracy, the violation is presumed to continue until some affirmative act of termination or withdrawal is shown.[19] However, where misuse consists of "extensive and aggravated misconduct over several years," which "substantially rigidified the price structure of an entire market and suppressed competition over a wide area, affirmative action may be essential to effectively dispel the consequences of the unlawful conduct."[20] Abandonment may occur at any time, even after the filing of the suit in which the question of misuse is raised. If the misuse is in the terms of licenses, the patentee may simply cancel the licenses. The standard is an objective one, and the abandonment need not take the particular form desired by the defendant.[21] At the same time, "[t]here is no set time period for purging; the time will vary with the facts of each case," since "whether a purge has been accomplished is a factual matter and is 'largely discretionary with the trial court.'"[22] Additionally, successful defendants may recover expenses in defending the action in an award for damages.[23]

---

[16] See *In re Yarn Processing Patent Validity*, 472 F. Supp. 180, 183 (S.D. Fla. 1979) (noting that since the doctrine of misuse was developed based on "the strong public policy against allowing one who wrongfully uses a patent to enforce it during the misuse, the remedy of purge has developed, requiring that there be a showing that a dissipation or purge of the misuse has occurred, before the patentee may enforce his patent").

[17] *U. S. Gypsum*, 124 F. Supp. at 594–95 ("Because of the nature of patent grants and because of the nature of this equity doctrine, such owner may, as to *future* protection of his rights and after the baleful effects of the misuse have been fully dissipated, relieve himself of this impediment by ceasing the unlawful use. This is the doctrine of 'purge'").

[18] See *Berlenbach v. Anderson & Thompson Ski Co.*, 329 F.2d 782, 785 (9th Cir. 1964).

[19] *United States v. Consolidated Laundries, Corp.*, 291 F.2d 563, 573 (2d Cir. 1961).

[20] *Ansul Co. v. Uniroyal, Inc.*, 306 F. Supp. 541, 560 (S.D.N.Y. 1969) (citing *Preformed Line Prod. Co. v. Fanner Mfg. Co.*, 328 F.2d 265, 279 (6th Cir. 1964), cert. denied, 379 U.S. 846 (1964)).

[21] See *B. B. Chemical Co. v. Ellis*, 314 U.S. 495 (1942).

[22] *Jack Winter, Inc. v. Koratron Co., Inc.*, 375 F. Supp. 1, 71 (N.D. Cal. 1974) (quoting *Preformed Line Prod.*, 328 F.2d at 279).

[23] *Kearney & Trecker Corp. v. Cincinnati Milacron Inc.*, 562 F.2d 365, 374 (6th Cir. 1977) ("one who has established or is attempting to establish an illegal monop-

By "metaphysical," Judge Rich may have meant "difficult to understand." And it is so. Misuse lies at the crossroads of innovation and competition, overlapping messily with laws and doctrines which profess to do much the same things.[24] In particular, courts disagree whether misuse must first constitute an antitrust violation or whether it is different, and if so, how.[25] Further, as an equitable defense, misuse rests uneasily in the minds of judges who see commercial certainty as a better measure of justice than responses calibrated *ad hoc* to patent misdemeanors.[26] Finally, decades of cavalier assertions of misuse by defendants, and the unwillingness of courts to articulate and develop a framework for misuse has cast it into a state of dubious repute and vitality. In 1997, the *Harvard Law Review* published a note carrying the provocative title "Is the Patent Misuse Doctrine Obsolete?" The note observed that "[b]oth judges and commentators have argued that this equitable doctrine should be eliminated, primarily because they believe that the antitrust laws more adequately address the same concerns."[27] Without a clear and general theory for resolving the

---

oly by fraud on the Patent Office or misuse of a patent should not be permitted to further this goal by means of an infringement suit. When the antitrust violations are causally connected to the infringement action it is permissible to include the expenses of defending that action in the award of damages").

[24] The Supreme Court recently noted that: "different rules of law have supported challenges to tying arrangements. They have been condemned as improper extensions of the patent monopoly under the patent misuse doctrine, as unfair methods of competition under § 5 of the Federal Trade Commission Act, 15 U.S.C. § 45, as contracts tending to create a monopoly under § 3 of the Clayton Act, 15 U.S.C. § 14, and as contracts in restraint of trade under § 1 of the Sherman Act." *Illinois Tool Works Inc. v. Indep. Ink, Inc.*, 547 U.S. 28, 34 (2006). See, e.g., Kelly Hershey, *Scheiber v. Dolby Laboratories, Inc.*, 18 BERKELEY TECH L.J. 159, 161 (2003) ("The patent misuse doctrine was developed to regulate the intersection of the patent and antitrust laws."). See also *Mallinckrodt, Inc. v. Medipart, Inc.*, 976 F.2d 700, 706 (Fed. Cir. 1992) (discussing exhaustion and misuse).

[25] One court even mistakenly referred to an antitrust counterclaim as an affirmative patent misuse claim. See, e.g., *Bendix Corp. v. Balax, Inc.*, 471 F.2d 149, 158 (7th Cir. 1972).

[26] *USM Corp. v. SPS Technologies, Inc.*, 694 F.2d 505, 512 (7th Cir. 1982) ("If misuse claims are not tested by conventional antitrust principles, by what principles shall they be tested? Our law is not rich in alternative concepts of monopolistic abuse; and it is rather late in the day to try to develop one without in the process subjecting the rights of patent holders to debilitating uncertainty").

[27] See Note, *Is the Patent Misuse Doctrine Obsolete?*, 110 HARV. L. REV. 1922, 1922 (1997); see also James B. Kobak, Jr., *A Sensible Doctrine of Misuse for Intellectual Property Cases*, 2 ALB. L.J. SCI. & TECH. 1, 38 (1992) (suggesting, among other reforms, limiting misuse to those "attempts [by patent holders] to enforce offending provisions"); Mark A. Lemley, *The Economic Irrationality of Patent Misuse*, 78 CAL. L. REV. 1599, 1631 (1990) ("there is no reason to retain

problem of what practices should be viewed as appropriate exercises of the patentee's statutory patent rights, the ambiguity surrounding misuse will remain intractable, even if the doctrine itself lingers on.[28]

II.   WHY STUDY MISUSE?

Why study patent misuse? The most obvious reason is that it is a doctrine that has been a part of patent law at least since 1917. It also continues to feature in patent wars. Recently defendants Apple and LG alleged patent misuse based on the patentee's violation of a reasonable and non-discriminatory licensing ("RAND") agreement.[29] The District Court for the Southern District of California, in refusing to dismiss the misuse defense, noted that "several courts have held that a patentee's violation of its RAND obligations may in certain circumstances constitute patent misuse."[30]

But there is another reason. The study of patent misuse also reveals fault lines that are relevant not only for misuse cases but also for cases on what the scope of patent protection should be and also on the interface

---

specific parts of the patent misuse doctrine, and very good reason to abolish the entire defense"); but see Mark A. Lemley, *Beyond Preemption: The Law and Policy of Intellectual Property Licensing*, 87 CAL. L. REV. 111, n.188 (1999) ("I must here confess error in this debate. I now believe that there may be circumstances in which rules peculiar to patent law make it appropriate to apply the misuse doctrine but do not warrant invocation of antitrust law. So too with copyright law. The application of the patent (or copyright) misuse doctrines, however, should be coupled with a reasonable mechanism to link the harm charged with the remedy administered; on that point (the thesis of my earlier paper), I am resolute").

[28]   6 Donald S. Chisum, CHISUM ON PATENTS § 19.04 (2011) ("[I]t is clear that the courts lack a clear and general theory for resolving that inquiry. Thus, individual problems are resolved in a piecemeal fashion, and it is difficult to harmonize decisions in one area (such as price restrictions) with decisions in another (such as field-of-use restrictions)").

[29]   *MultimediaPatent Trust v. Apple Inc.*, 2012 U.S. Dist. LEXIS 167479, at *73–75 (S.D. Cal. Nov. 9, 2012). See also *UTStarcom, Inc. v. Starent Networks, Corp.*, 2008 U.S. Dist. LEXIS 98498 (N.D. Ill. Dec. 5, 2008) (finding that the patentee's failure to offer the defendant a license to the patents on reasonable, non-discriminatory terms prior to suit could be evidence supporting a finding of patent misuse.); *Apple, Inc. v. Motorola Mobility, Inc.*, 2011 U.S. Dist. LEXIS 72745, at *22–42 (W.D. Wis. Jun. 7, 2011) (finding accused infringer plaintiff had properly pleaded patent misuse based on the patentee's alleged violation of its RAND obligations).

[30]   *MultimediaPatent Trust*, at *79 (citing *Apple*, 2011 U.S. Dist. LEXIS 72745, at *40–42; *UTStarcom*, 2008 U.S. Dist. LEXIS 98498, at *6).

of antitrust law and patent law. It is no coincidence that the heyday of a narrow interpretation of patent law, vigorous antitrust oversight of patents and a vigorous view of patent misuse co-existed in the same period of time. Patent misuse is a doctrine whose scope will depend at least in part upon the courts' views of the role and value of patents, and the degree to which one can trust patent owners not to abuse or misuse the rights that they have.

The scope of misuse reflects the wider policy choices that the courts and government have to make about access and exclusivity. As the final arbiter on patent law, the Court's focus on these industries worries some patent practitioners, who think its recent decisions were based on a misaligned view of how these industries work.[31] It is not out of the question that the Court might take a position that is at odds with the Federal Circuit's current skeptical view of patent misuse,[32] which, itself, is at odds with the positive approach of earlier Supreme Court cases.[33]

A tighter rein on patents would defeat the incentives provided by their exclusivity. On the other hand, making it harder for defendants to allege misuse could encourage abusive conduct by patentees to the detriment of consumers and the "Progress of Science and the useful Arts". What is clear is that this is the beginning of a new normal for both the Federal Circuit and the Supreme Court. Conflicting views on innovation and competition are, and will continue to be, fought out in future cases.

III. THE STUDY

A. Through the Lens of Freakonomics

This book is a study of patent misuse. It combines doctrinal and policy discussion with empirical research. There is a fairly substantive volume of case law and literature on misuse. This may tempt some to lean on conventional wisdom as the sole and accurate guide to its past, present,

---

[31] See, e.g., Gene Quinn, *Killing Industry: The Supreme Court Blows* Mayo v. Prometheus, IP WATCHDOG (Mar 20, 2012), available at: http://www.ipwatchdog. com/2012/03/20/supreme-court-mayo-v-prometheus/id=22920/ ("It is shocking that all 9 Justices of the Supreme Court know so little about patent law, yet the collective fate of the industry rests on those with only a cursory understanding of patent law—and that is at best!").

[32] *Princo Corp. v. Int'l Trade Comm'n*, 616 F.3d 1318 (Fed. Cir. 2010) *cert. denied*, 131 S. Ct. 2480 (2011).

[33] See, e.g., *Morton Salt Co. v. G. S. Suppiger Co.*, 314 U.S. 488 (1942).

and future. But conventional legal doctrine, like conventional wisdom, derives from a small set of cases selected by case reporters and academics. Economist Kenneth Galbraith explains why people sometimes have tremendous difficulty unfettering themselves from conventional wisdom, even where it is misplaced:

> We associate truth with convenience, with what closely accords with self-interest and personal well-being or promises best to avoid awkward effort or unwelcome dislocation of life. We also find highly acceptable what contributes the most to self-esteem. ... But perhaps most important of all, people approve most of what they best understand. As just noted, economic and social behaviors are complex, and to comprehend their character is mentally tiring. Therefore we adhere, as though to a raft, to those ideas which represent our understanding. This is a prime manifestation of vested interest. For a vested interest in understanding is more preciously guarded than any other treasure. It is why men react, not infrequently with something akin to religious passion, to the defense of what they have so laboriously learned.[34]

Reflecting on Galbraith's observation, Stephen Dubner and Steven Levitt, authors of *Freakonomics*, conclude that "conventional wisdom in Galbraith's view must be simple, comfortable and comforting—though not necessarily true."[35] This book therefore seeks to present a systematic, comprehensive account of the recent history of case law and the current state of misuse and its relationship with antitrust law. Seminal patent cases have quoted Justice Holmes' quip that "a page of history is worth a volume of logic."[36] This study concurs, and seeks to provide the reader with an aerial view of misuse as well as focusing on its treatment in U.S. courts at every level. It is based on the use of the quantitative analysis of cases complemented by interviews.

B. Case Content Analysis

The study is based on a dataset consisting of all reported U.S. federal opinions that provided substantial analysis of patent misuse from January 1,

---

[34]   John Kenneth Galbraith, THE AFFLUENT SOCIETY 7 (1998).
[35]   Stephen Dubner & Steven Levitt, *Freakonomics: A Rogue Economist Explores the Hidden Side of Everything* 115 (2006).
[36]   See *eBay Inc. v. MercExchange*, L.L.C., 547 U.S. 388, 395 (2006) ("When it comes to discerning and applying those standards, in this area as others, 'a page of history is worth a volume of logic.' New York Trust Co. v. Eisner, 256 U.S. 345, 349 (1921) (opinion for the Court by Holmes, J.)"). In the copyright context, see *Eldred v. Ashcroft*, 537 U.S. 186, 200 (2003) ("To comprehend the scope of Congress' Copyright Clause power, 'a page of history is worth a volume of logic'").

1953, the effective date of the U.S. Patent Act, through December 31, 2012.[37] The result is a dataset spanning 60 years, with 368 cases coded into over 12,000 data points.

This portion of the study does not set out to analyze the doctrine contained in case law. Rather, cases are relevant to the quantitative analysis only to the extent that they reveal a feature of misuse case law that can be categorized and sub-categorized. For example, each of the various categories of misuse collectively form a category called "the categories of misuse" which is itself a category presented in the dataset.

Case content analysis lays the theoretical foundation and provides structure to the study. It identifies markers that facilitate forming informed hypotheses about factors driving case outcomes in practice. It will determine whether conventional wisdom on misuse has empirical support. It highlights key aspects of misuse, including the way it has been interwoven with antitrust principles. It "allows scholars to verify or refute the empirical claims about case law that are implicit or explicit in all branches of legal scholarship,"[38] by "selecting cases likely to provide information pertinent to the study, coding the content of the collected cases, and analyzing the coded content."[39]

This naturally raises the question of selection bias, because few disputes reach trial and even those which do may not result in a published opinion.[40] Further, the nature of case selection in a study of this kind is necessarily underexhaustive. Between 1983 and 2008, nearly 50,000

---

[37]   Act of July 19, Pub. L. No. 82-593, 66 Stat. 815, §4 (1952) ("This Act shall take effect on January 1, 1953 and shall apply to all applications for patent filed on or after such date and to all patents granted on such applications"). "Substantial analysis" refers to patent cases which both mention and analyze the two issues rather than merely citing them.

[38]   Mark A. Hal & Ronald F. Wright, *Systematic Content Analysis of Judicial Opinions*, 96 CAL. L. REV. 63, 67 (2008).

[39]   Lee Petherbridge et al., *The Federal Circuit and Inequitable Conduct: An Empirical Assessment*, 84 S.CAL L. REV. 1293, 1303 (2011).

[40]   Additionally, summary affirmances under FED. R. CIV. p. 36, while omitted are also not relevant to the study as they do not add statements of law or explanations to the facts. However, as others have noted, outcomes under Rule 36 decisions may be relevant because the appellate court may have applied the relevant doctrine, here misuse, to resolving the issue on appeal. See, e.g., Lee Petherbridge et al., *supra* note 39, at n. 41 (noting that Rule 36 dispositions may increase the size of a sample of case outcomes, but that "[t]he text of opinions—the evidence of the law cited in briefs and argued to courts—is unchanged."); see also Christian A. Chu, *Empirical Analysis of the Federal Circuit's Claim Construction Trends*, 16 BERKELEY TECH. L.J. 1075, 1128 (2001) (reporting the use of Rule 36 in 21% of patent cases).

patent cases were filed in the district courts alone.[41] At the same time, the impact of this aspect of the study on its veracity and worth should not be exaggerated. Case content analysis is a well accepted method of empirical legal research in patent law and elsewhere, and the data systematically and comprehensively collected flow from the same sources which legal professionals in every field continue to rely upon.[42] It represents the entire population of reported misuse cases during this period, and in the unlikely event it does not, it represents nearly the entire population that allows the study to make a practicably generalizable claim to statistical significance as a sample of a super-population.[43]

The content for the cases studied was then manually coded along 36 distinct variables capturing various facts of misuse, from the physical and legal characteristics of misuse cases (industries, case distribution by court level and circuit, posture, type of alleged misuse and related antitrust violations, cases outcomes, dissents and petitions for certiorari) to the policy undergirding misuse (patent or antitrust policy, bad faith), to how it relates with antitrust law (broader, different or coextensive), and how judges defined the proper scope of a patent (by its claims, in relation to time or product embodying the technology). In order to study trends over time, some arbitrary measures were selected, such as over 10-year periods, over 15-year periods (where 10-year periods would yield to closely bunched results), as well as before and after 1988, the year the Patent Misuse Reform Act was enacted. Sometimes, such as when studying trends in the industries in which misuse cases arose, the Act had nothing to do with the trends. The 1988 cut-off point, however, remains a useful

---

[41]   Christian E. Mammen, *Controlling the "Plague": Reforming the Doctrine of Inequitable Conduct*, 24 BERKELEY TECH. L.J. 1329, 1349 (2009).

[42]   See, e.g., Barton Beebe, *An Empirical Study of U.S. Copyright Fair Use Opinions, 1978–2005*, 156 U. PA. L. REV. 549 (2008); John R. Allison & Mark A. Lemley, *Who's Patenting What? An Empirical Exploration of Patent Prosecution* 53 VAND. L. REV. 2099 (2000); Christopher A. Cotropia, *Nonobviousness and the Federal Circuit: An Empirical Analysis of Recent Case Law*, 82 NOTRE DAME L. REV. 911, 941 (2007); Lee Petherbridge & R. Polk Wagner, *The Federal Circuit and Patentability: An Empirical Assessment of the Law of Obviousness*, 85 TEX. L. REV. 2051, 2070–71 (2007); David L. Schwartz, *Practice Makes Perfect?: An Empirical Study of Claim Construction Reversal Rates in Patent Cases*, 107 MICH. L. REV. 223, 237–38 (2008); R. Polk Wagner & Lee Petherbridge, *Is the Federal Circuit Succeeding? An Empirical Assessment of Judicial Performance*, 152 U. PA. L. REV. 1105, 1133–34 (2004).

[43]   See Lee Petherbridge et al., *supra* note 39, at 1308 (noting their endeavor to collect the entire population of written inequitable conduct analyses over the period studied, which are "by definition a statistically significant representation of the population").

broad-brush division that cuts the 60-year period into 35 years from the beginning period of the study and 25 years after, up to December 31, 2012.

Much of the coding was objective. However, some of it could not be so. One of the most challenging aspects of defining the variables was finding a way to effectively deconstruct the process of how a judge decides a case. As Judge Richard Posner of the Court of Appeals for the Seventh Circuit noted with regard to judicial reasoning:

> The published opinion often conceals the true reasons for a judicial decision by leaving them buried in the judicial unconscious. Had the intuitive judgment that underlies the decision been different, perhaps an equally plausible opinion in support of it could have been written. If so, the reasoning in the opinion in support of it is not the real cause of the decision, but a rationalization. This is not to denigrate the social value of published opinions but merely to indicate their limitations. They not only aid in catching the errors that are inevitable in intuitive reasoning about complex issues; they not only flag, if only by omission, any gap between the outcome and the capacity of a legalist analysis to generate it; they also facilitate the consistent decision of future cases. The first decision in a line of cases may be the product of inarticulate emotion or hunch. But once it is given articulate form, that form will take on a life of its own—a valuable life that may include binding the author and other judges of his court (along with lower-court judges) and thus imparting needed stability to law through the doctrine of precedent, though a death grip if judges ignored changed circumstances that make a decision no longer a sound guide.[44]

After reading through a few dozen cases, the rhetoric begins to settle into a discernable, though inconsistent pattern. Naturally, the cleaving of fluid legal analysis into discrete categories for statistical enumeration is liable to appear artificial, and often it is. The nature of empirical analysis, putting numbers on people and their behavior, is ultimately an artificial exercise, and the limits of the study in this respect must be readily acknowledged. For example, judges who write the opinons may present a strategic view of the facts or law to shape the doctrine. Litigants may also decide to emphasize aspects of the doctrine on appeal when other aspects may be more applicable.[45]

---

[44]   Richard Posner, How Judges Think 110–11 (Cambridge, 2008) ("At every stage the judge's reasoning process is primarily intuitive. Given the constraints of time, it could not be otherwise; for intuition is a great economizer on conscious attention. The role of the unconscious judge in judicial decision making is obscured by the convention that requires a judge to explain his decision in an opinion. The judicial opinion can best be understood as an attempt to explain how the decision, even if (as is most likely) arrived at on the basis of intuition, could have been arrived at on the basis of logical, step-by-step reasoning . . .").

[45]   See Lee Petherbridge, *supra* note 39, at 1304.

The objectivity of this aspect of the analysis was enhanced by subjecting the coding to independent verficiation by a research fellow at the Fordham University School of Law and two student research assistants at the John Marshall Law School. Where coding results differed, results were compared and corrections were made to the dataset. The statistical techniques used are largely simple descriptive statistics, including graphical representations that describe variables in histrograms or pie charts. These graphs allow the reader a quick and easy look at how different variables relate to each other, such as trends over time and how outcomes may be affected by characteristics such as the type of industry or category of misuse concerned. However, the value of empirical work like this is to articulate judicial decision-making in a systematic and comprehensible way.

C. Interviews

The second principal component of this book is to link both conventional wisdom and the unearthed data from the case content analysis to the larger socio-legal context through interviews. Law is an integral part of the broader society and culture. It is part of a complex web of factors, but it is not a seamless web unto itself.[46] The law is crafted to influence human behavior, and effective laws are hard to craft and implement.[47] At times, the law may fail those it governs, but human ingenuity supplements, and at times outperforms, what formal law can offer. At other times, it is human ingenuity that leads to suboptimal and occasionally tragic outcomes. The Law and Society perspective, the study of how humans relate to society in the context of laws, gives us both the means and the responsibility to better understand, and hence to improve, the world around us through invisible but integral threads that weave through misuse cases. Interviewees sometimes prefaced their answers with the caveat that their views straddle the narrow border between anecdotal observations and reasoned speculation. In attempting to unravel the contours of misuse, this study unearthed few definitive clues. While these clues provide some fodder for intuitive conclusions, this study accepts and echoes the prudence of the interviewees' caveat.

---

[46] See Lawrence M. Friedman, *Is there a Modern Legal Culture*, 7 RATIO JURIS 117, 118 (1994) (noting that legal culture refers to ideas, values, attitudes, and opinions with regard to law and the legal system).

[47] See Lawrence M. Friedman, THE LEGAL SYSTEM: A SOCIAL SCIENCE PERSPECTIVE (1979); Stewart Macaulay et al., LAW IN ACTION: A SOCIO-LEGAL READER 397 (2007) (factors include: the nature of the sanction and behavior controlled; the perceived risk and immediacy realizing the sanction; and the number and personality of the people affected).

The case content analysis spans 60 years and 368 opinions. The opinions are segmented into 36 variables coded quantitatively. In contrast, the interviews are contemporary, narrative and organic. The datasets therefore complement, rather than substitute for, each other. The sum of the findings present an empirical analysis of how federal judges employed the misuse doctrine, and how misuse is currently perceived by contemporary judges, academics, government officials, and lawyers. It also provides an indication of whether more in-depth research is required to unravel the nature and extent of the interaction between patent misuse and antitrust.

In line with the overarching goal of capturing stakeholders' views as accurately as possible, this study uses more direct quotations than usual in academic articles or treatises. The verbatim language in these carefully selected quotations conveys not only information and analysis, but the character and tone of those who make them. In this way, the legal consciousness of those who have discussed or decided cases involving patent misuse have their thoughts presented as a quilted fabric, and leave it to the reader to determine their veracity and persuasiveness. This last point underscores the living, dynamic, and interactive aspect of empirical work, which sets it apart from much of traditional legal scholarship.

The significant question for this study is not which view of patent misuse is best. Rather, the focus is on presenting the past and current state of the patent and antitrust communities through court opinions, commentary, and in-depth interviews with those in these communities. In this way the study attempts to draw out an objective measure against which to measure conventional wisdom. A judge who was interviewed noted that academic work is more valuable when it presents policy recommendations based on facts rather than opinions.[48] Perhaps the perception is that work based on personal bias is less useful than more verifiable data-based conclusions. Thus while this study may offer observations on the various views, and may identify questionable assertions found in the literature and opinions, it attempts to retain a measure of objectivity by discussing the collected data rather than by advancing a personal view of patent misuse.

A study of patent misuse gives rise to multifarious issues. While every effort has been made to chart and discuss the key facets of misuse, a study like this cannot cover everything, and should never pretend to. A number of notable issues and perspectives are missing in whole or in part. These

---

[48] On file with author. (Noting that "where the policy is in the eye of a commentator but it's not in the case law, I feel I have to be quite hesitant to not adopt some personal policy and then try to implement it in the case law. That's not a legitimate role, in my view, for an appellate judge. I'm not the policy arbiter. The Congress is the policy arbiter, or maybe the Supreme Court in certain instances".)

qualitative and quantitative indicia can then be examined, explained, and criticized. The exercise may seem contrived at times, but it is crucial to reaching an informed conclusion to the debate. The interpretations offered are the ones considered most likely in light of the data, and the study attempts to explain why this is so. However, other narratives might be developed from the results presented.

D.   Structure and Outline

The first chapter traces the roots of patent misuse to its origins in equity. It explains how equity features in other areas of patent law, and how this can inform misuse analysis. The chapter then provides a primer to antitrust law before transitioning, first to its interface with intellectual property law, and then to misuse. Drawing on recent empirical data, the chapter identifies a surprisingly disproportionate increase in the number of patent litigation cases compared to those cases asserting patent misuse as a defense. This finding sets the stage for an examination of the possible reasons for this in subsequent chapters.

The second chapter presents a brief history of misuse. It traces misuse to its earliest roots in 1917, when the Supreme Court refused to enforce a patent against providers of inputs to be used with the patented invention because to do so would be to allow the patentee to extend its rights beyond the statutory scope of the patent. From there, misuse became intertwined with the antitrust laws until the Supreme Court severed those cords in 1942. Subsequent cases, however, muddied the two. The growing importance of science and technology and divergent views on patent rights precipitated the establishment of the Federal Circuit in 1982 to harmonize federal patent law. Today the Federal Circuit's oversight of patent appeals from district courts has led to a novel formulation of misuse that is tied to a new antitrust rubric that remains inalterable by all but the Supreme Court. The chapter concludes by posing the question whether a specialist penultimate court is better placed than a generalist court of last resort to determine the correct formulation of the misuse doctrine.

The third chapter introduces the key forms of misuse. Weaving together case law and commentary, the chapter narrates how each of these forms of misuse has shaped the jurisprudential landscape. The most common forms featured in the literature are tying and time extensions. The former requires the licensee to purchase an unpatented product used in conjunction with the patented good from the patentee, to the exclusion of the patentee's other competitors. The latter requires the licensee to continue paying royalties beyond the date the patent has expired. Misuse, however, rapidly morphed beyond these prototypes. Misuse today includes royalty and restrictive obligations placed upon the licensee, patent pools, and trademark-related misuse. The chapter also examines how the wrongful procurement and enforcement of the patent right can also give rise to misuse.

The fourth chapter considers the three main objections to misuse—vagueness, lax standing requirements, and the risk of over-deterring would-be patentees. First, the study notes that the vagueness of misuse stems both from its nature as an equitable defense as well as a lack of a coherent theory about what misuse represents and the kinds of wrongdoings it should address. At the same time, it also notes a recent interest by courts and commentators in rethinking these fundamental points of jurisprudence in giving meaning to its roots in equity and patent policy. There are also views that misuse has no less potential to be administrable or effective than the antitrust laws. Second, it notes that those asserting that misuse provides overbroad standing requirements to vigilantes, who are not themselves harmed, may stem from ill-informed rhetoric. Case law states that misuse exists to protect the public interest and not the interests of the parties in suit. For this reason, misuse is unusual in allowing even infringers with unclean hands to assert the defense, because they serve as proxies to the public in bringing the patentees' conduct before judicial scrutiny. Further, the study reveals that licensees or competitors from nearly all of the cases studied alleged direct harm from the misuse. To the final argument that misuse is overly harsh in rendering the patent unenforceable to the world at large prior to the purge of misconduct, the study observes that this is firstly a corollary to the public harm potentially caused by the misuse, and secondly that courts have exercised their discretion in tailoring the defense, even at times refusing to give effect to it notwithstanding a finding of misuse in the interest of fairness between the parties.

The fifth chapter presents three specific areas where courts and commentators have expressed possible application of misuse, or have actually applied misuse: (1) standard-setting organizations, where patent owners entrap industries locked into a patented standard and then extort supernormal profits from "locked-in" users through deceptive conduct or collusive practices;[49] (2) settlement agreements by owners of patented

---

[49] See, e.g., Richard Li-dar Wang, *Deviated, Unsound, and Self-Retreating: A Critical Assessment of the* Princo v. ITC *En Banc Decision*, 16 MARQ. INTELL. PROP. L. REV. 51, 79 (2012) ("It is the author's hope that the Princo decision is an end to the beginning, not a beginning to end. Instead of substantially weakening the misuse doctrine, this decision could be an excellent stimulus and starting point for careful reflection on its function, foundation, and better configuration");

drugs with generic drug companies, where branded drug companies justify paying the generic drug companies to keep out of their markets on the basis of their exclusionary patent rights; and (3) providing a foundation for neighboring doctrines, such as copyright and trademark misuse.[50] It also looks briefly at the European Union, which has attempted to address similar problems to those arising under misuse in the United States.

The sixth chapter introduces the quantitative aspect of the study on misuse. Drawing upon case content analysis, it unveils the rich and varied landscape of misuse. It examines the distribution of misuse cases across time and courts across the nation. It identifies the most common forms of procedural postures in misuse cases, and their outcomes at trial and on appeal and applications for certiorari. In particular it examines the peculiar relationship between bench and jury trials in misuse cases. The chapter identifies the most influential judges in shaping misuse at the Federal Circuit. It studies misuse cases proceeding under equity compared with those under the antitrust laws. It exposes the surprising variety of industries misuse cases occur in, and scrutinizes conventional wisdom put forth by leading thinkers concerning the influence of industry on the nature of misuse cases. The chapter reveals the 11 categories of misuse and charts their developments over time, with a surprising revelation—the quintessential form of misuse today is starkly different from yonder years. Finally the chapter concludes by looking to the future by charting the willingness of courts to expand the categories of misuse.

The seventh chapter begins the qualitative phase of the study. It deconstucts patent misuse into its component parts as they exist in the minds

---

Christopher A. Suarez, *Look Before You "Lock": Standards, Tipping, and the Future of Patent Misuse After Princo*, 13 COLUM. SCI. & TECH. L. REV. 371 (2012) ("patent suppression agreements may still "leverage" existing patents in ways that unlawfully expand their scope"); Daryl Lim, *Misconduct in Standard Setting: The Case for Patent Misuse*, 51 IDEA 559 (2011).

[50] See, e.g., Alyssa L. Brown, *Modest Proposals for A Complex Problem: Patent Misuse and Incremental Changes to the Hatch-Waxman Act As Solutions to the Problem of Reverse Payment Settlements*, 41 U. BALT. L. REV. 583, 612–13 (2012) ("Given the varied nature of these settlements and the lack of information publicly available about them, as well as, the cost and time needed for the courts to determine whether agreements are anticompetitive or procompetitive under antitrust law, alternative solutions to the problem must be considered. . . . patent misuse represents one possible defense available to subsequent ANDA filers under the current system"); Cory J. Ingle, *Reverse Payment Settlements: A Patent Approach to Defending the Argument for Illegality*, 7 I/S: J. L. & POL'Y FOR INFO. SOC'Y 503 (Winter, 2012) ("While patent misuse is similar to antitrust analysis, the policy issues underlying patent misuse make it more sympathetic to the view of restricting suspicious reverse payment settlements").

of judges. Modern-day misuse requires that the defendant show that the patentee has impermissibly broadened the "physical or temporal scope" of the patent grant with anticompetitive effect.[51] The chapter begins by examining what factors go into determining when patentees exceed the scope of their rights. Specifically, it attempts to deconstruct the analytical process judges employ, and articulates the policies driving misuse that have been obscured by rhetoric in the opinions. It finds that judges employ a surprisingly diverse array of perspectives in resolving the fundamental question of whether a patent right has been exceeded.

The appendices at the end of the study provide the interested reader with substantially more detail than is required to follow the discussion. These details were included so that the study could be as comprehensive as possible. Appendix I briefly discusses the methodology employed as well as the general limitations of this study. Appendix II presents the list of interviewees and Appendix III presents the interview protocol. A glossary of terms and details of key statutes appear in Appendix IV. Appendix V presents the coding form. Appendix VI contains a table of Supreme Court and Federal Circuit misuse cases and the judges presiding over the courts at each point in its history. The complete dataset containing the cases may be found on Edward Elgar's website at http://goo.gl/hUcly.

---

[51] *Windsurfing Int'l, Inc. v. AMF, Inc.*, 782 F.2d 995, 1001 (Fed. Cir. 1986). The courts generally follow a rule of reason approach with a few per se misuse exceptions. See *Va. Panel Corp. v. MAC Panel Co.*, 133 F.3d 860, 869 (Fed. Cir. 1997); *Mallinckrodt, Inc. v. Medipart, Inc.*, 976 F.2d 700, 708 (Fed. Cir. 1992) (establishing rule of reason analysis for patent misuse where conduct at issue is neither per se misuse nor exempt from misuse consideration by section 271(d) of the Patent Act).

1.   Misuse and antitrust

I.   CHILD OF EQUITY

Like other areas of the law, situations arise in patent law where adherence to the letter of the law would create formalistically correct but unjust outcomes.[1] In these situations judges invoke equity in an attempt to guide the case to an outcome that is fair and just to all parties concerned as well as to the public at large. Equity in patent law functions as both a sword and shield. Equity enables patentees, through the doctrine of equivalents, to strike at those who "make unimportant and insubstantial changes and substitutions in the patent which, though adding nothing, would be enough to take the copied matter outside the claim, and hence outside the reach of the law."[2]

Equity also functions as a shield, coalescing around infringers when patentees abuse their rights, and in so doing makes it unjust to allow them to insist on asserting their rights. One such defense is inequitable conduct.[3] Patentees are permanently prevented from asserting their patents if those patents were obtained through their owners' deceptive conduct in omitting material information while prosecuting their patents at the Patent Office.[4] The patent system relies on the honesty of applicants, because patents are granted with neither public scrutiny nor scientific or commercial proof

---

[1]   Traditional notions of equitable relief apply with equal force in the context of patents. See *eBay Inc. v. MercExchange*, LLC, 547 U.S. 388, 393–94 (2006) (holding that a categorical rule of granting an injunction to a prevailing patent holder abrogates a district court's discretion in granting equitable relief and runs afoul of traditional principles of equity).

[2]   See *Graver Tank & Mfg. Co. v. Linde Air Prod. Co.*, 339 U.S. 605, 607 (1950).

[3]   *Kingsdown Med. Consultants, Ltd. v. Hollister Inc.*, 863 F.2d 867, 876 (Fed. Cir. 1988) ("the ultimate question of whether inequitable conduct occurred is equitable in nature"); *Aventis Pharma S.A. v. Hospira*, 675 F.3d 1324 (Fed. Cir, 2012) (concluding concluded that inequitable conduct can be still be found under the heightened standards for materiality and specific intent enunciated in *Therasense, Inc. v. Becton, Dickinson and Co.*, 649 F.3d 1276, 1288 (Fed. Cir. 2011)).

[4]   See *Therasense, Inc.* ("Unlike validity defenses, which are claim specific, . . . inequitable conduct regarding any single claim renders the entire patent unenforceable. . . . Unlike other deficiencies, inequitable conduct cannot be cured by reissue").

that they have enriched the public. Patentees, however, may be tempted by the potentially vast rewards that accompany the grant of patent rights to withhold from the examiner information adverse to their applications.[5] Inequitable conduct thus protects the public from patentees who intentionally fail to disclose material information, or who submit false information to the Patent Office and thereby obtain their patents illegitimately.[6]

Yet even patents that were legitimately obtained can nonetheless be illegitimately misused. The gaze of equity reaches to such abuses just as a sentinel at the guardhouse continues his watch over a visitor who, while having received permission to enter the compound, nonetheless remains under a duty to act civilly towards others in the compound, and indeed to the compound itself. Perhaps the best known of these is patent misuse.

In determining misuse, courts acknowledge the doctrine's equitable nature and its role in keeping patentees within the metes and bounds of their patent rights.[7] It arises out of the doctrine of "unclean hands."[8] Unclean hands applies:

> whenever a party, who as actor, seeks to set the judicial machinery in motion and obtain some remedy, has violated conscience, good faith, or other equitable principal, in his prior conduct, then the doors of the court will be shut against him *in limine*; the court will refuse to interfere on his behalf, to acknowledge his right, or to award him any remedy.[9]

Misuse thus prevents wrongdoing. However, unlike the doctrine of unclean hands which requires a direct nexus to the wrongdoing and the

---

[5] Martin Adelman et al., Cases and Materials on Patent Law 558 (3d ed. 2009) ("Experiences teaches, however, that application obligations of candor may be tempered by the great incentive they possess not to disclose the information that might deleteriously impact their prospective patent rights. Thus the concept of inequitable conduct: the intentional failure to disclose material information brings about the unenforceability of the resulting patent"). For a discussion on purging inequitable conduct, see *Rohm & Haas Co. v. Crystal Chem. Co.*, 722 F.2d 1556, 1572 (Fed. Cir. 1983).

[6] See *Therasense, Inc.*, 649 F.3d at 1285.

[7] See, e.g., *United States v. U. S. Gypsum Co.*, 124 F. Supp. 573, 594–95 (D.D.C 1954) ("This rule is applicable where the owner of patent rights seeks to extend those rights beyond the limits of his patent monopoly. This is the doctrine of 'misuse' of patents").

[8] The 1952 Patent Act codified the defense of unclean hands. See 35 U.S.C. § 282, cl. 1(1) (1952) (providing that "unenforceability" is a defense to an infringement action); P.J. Federico, *Commentary on the New Patent Act*, 75 J. Pat. & Trademark Off. Soc'y 161, 215 (1993) (explaining that paragraph (1) includes "equitable defenses such as laches, estoppel and unclean hands").

[9] 2 Pomeroy's Equity Jurisprudence § 397 (1941).

subject of the infringement claim, misuse is based on a subversion of public policy and applies even though the patentee's misconduct was ancillary to the subject of the claim.[10] A judge finding misuse has the discretion to withhold damages or injunctive relief, which patentees typically seek, even if the patents themselves have not yet been enforced.[11] One court explained that "[t]he inchoate threat which these circumstances engender hangs in the air and we may doubt that that threat is without its effect in a highly competitive market."[12] Courts have also been willing to infer misuse from the facts.[13] Misuse can thus be a valuable tool for judges seeking to enforce equity.

There has been a continuing debate about the proper role and scope of misuse.[14] A principal reason for this debate stems from the overlap between misuse and the antitrust laws as well as doctrines within patent law itself. Justice Sandra Day O'Connor noted that "the Patent Clause itself reflects a balance between the need to encourage innovation and the avoidance of monopolies which stifle competition without any concomitant advance in the 'Progress of Science and useful Arts.'"[15] It is perhaps unsurprising

---

[10]   Roger Arar, *Redefining Copyright Misuse*, 81 COLUM. L. REV. 1291, 1298 (1981).
[11]   See, e.g., *United Shoe Mach. Corp. v. United States*, 258 U.S. 451, 458 (1922) ("The power to enforce them [tying restrictions] is omnipresent, and their restraining influence constantly operates upon competitors and lessees. The fact that the lessor in many instances forbore to enforce these provisions does not make them any less agreements within the condemnation of the Clayton Act").
[12]   *Berlenbach v. Anderson & Thompson Ski Co.*, 329 F.2d 782, 785 (9th Cir. 1964) (quoting *F. C. Russell Co. v. Consumers Insulation Co.*, 226 F.2d 373, 376 (3d Cir. 1955)).
[13]   For example, the Ninth Circuit found misuse because the patentee refused to sell patented parts except with the device as a whole, despite the fact that the patented parts represented only 10% of the invention. *Stearns v. Tinker & Rasor*, 252 F.2d 589, 603 (9th Cir. 1957) ("we hold that on the basis of Stearns' testimony, the alleged existence of a market for the patented parts, the fact that the patented parts represented only 10% of the cost of the complete detector, and the admitted policy of Stearns of not selling the patented articles alone, the trial court properly could draw a reasonable inference that the practices followed by D. E. Stearns Company were being employed to expand the scope of the patent monopoly and restrain competition").
[14]   Ibid. at 600 ("The doctrine of patent misuse is today one of the most important and unsettled aspects of patent law. This has been brought about by inconsistent decisional law and statutory enactment"). Patricia Martone, *The Patent Misuse Defense—Does It Still Have Vitality?*, 832 PLI/PAT 145, 201 (2005) ("The debate over whether the patent misuse doctrine is justified and, if so, what the scope of the doctrine should be, is not new").
[15]   *Bonito Boats, Inc. v. Thunder Craft Boats, Inc.*, 489 U.S. 141, 146 (1989).

then that misuse involves some shade of anticompetitive effect. Robert Hoerner observed that there are two types of patent misuse.[16] The first "is a violation of the antitrust laws to which the patent in suit significantly contributed". The second involves an "extension of the monopoly" where patentees attempt to reach beyond the patent "whether by way of geographical scope, temporal scope, channels of distribution beyond the first authorized sale, or scope beyond the coverage of the claims."[17]

The stream of applicable circuit precedent then depends on the type of misuse alleged. According to Hoerner, "the substantive source of 'extension of the monopoly'-type patent misuse law is Article 1 Section 8, Clause 8 of the Constitution and Title 35 of the United States Code."[18] One reason for the overlap between misuse and antitrust relates to how they feature in litigation. Misuse counterclaims frequently resemble antitrust claims in their economic rubric more than patent validity and infringement and are therefore tried separately.[19] Another reason is the fact that misuse cases tend to arise out of patent licensing agreements. Such agreements affect market competition, and courts have expanded misuse to include antitrust standards to address market distortions.[20] Even between the close cousins, however, significant differences exist.

---

[16] Robert J. Hoerner, *Patent Misuse: Portents for the 1990s*, 59 ANTITRUST L.J. 687, 688 (1991). See also Joel R. Bennett, *Patent Misuse: Must an Alleged Infringer Prove an Antitrust Violation?*, 17 AIPLA Q.J. 1, 8 (1989) ("There are two distinct types of patent misuse conduct. First, if a patentee engages in an antitrust violation sufficiently related to the patent in suit, he is deprived of the aid of the Court to restrain an alleged infringement by one who is a competitor, even if the patent is valid. . . . The second type of patent misuse is the so-called "extension of the monopoly" doctrine. What this means is that the patentee has acted in some way to obtain more than the patent laws and patent grant awarded him. This type of patent misuse "requires that the alleged infringer establish that the patentee has impermissibly broadened the physical or temporal scope" of the patent grant").

[17] Robert J. Hoerner, *supra* note 16.

[18] Ibid. at 689.

[19] *Hunter Douglas, Inc. v. Comfortex Corp.*, 44 F. Supp. 2d 145 (N.D.N.Y. 1999) (Holding that antitrust and patent misuse would be heard separately from the infringement claims).

[20] Thomas F. Maffei, *The Patent Misuse Doctrine: A Balance of Patent Rights and the Public Interest*, 11 B.C.L. REV. 46, 52 (1969), available at: http://lawdig italcommons.bc.edu/bclr/vol11/iss1/4 ("Because the subject matter of the licensing agreement and the manner in which it is obtained effect directly the maintenance of a competitive economy, the existence of licensing abuses has necessitated the application of antitrust principles to patent law. Although the patent misuse doctrine as originally developed was grounded solely on a violation of the patent laws, the existence of anticompetitive licensing practices has caused the courts to expand the doctrine to include antitrust standards where the patentee's conduct tends to

II.   ANTITRUST LAW: "MAGNA CARTA OF FREE ENTERPRISE"

The antitrust laws balance vigorous marketplace competition against restrained interference with the free market so that investment incentives, such as those from patentees, are protected. The antitrust laws, unlike patent law, were authorized under the Commerce Clause, which gives Congress the power to regulate interstate and foreign commerce.[21] The Supreme Court heralded the antitrust laws as "the Magna Carta of free enterprise." It explained that the antitrust laws "are as important to the preservation of economic freedom and our free enterprise system as the Bill of Rights is to the protection of our fundamental personal freedoms. And the freedom guaranteed to each and every business, no matter how small, is the freedom to compete."[22]

A.   Principle Statutes

The principal antitrust statutes are the Sherman and Clayton Acts, which are jointly administered by the U.S. Department of Justice ("DOJ") and the Federal Trade Commission ("FTC").[23] Private plaintiffs, a powerful and controversial force, can also invoke these antitrust statutes in shaping the contours of antitrust law. With regard to this, Professor Herbert Hovenkamp notes that "[a] great deal of unwarranted expansion in antitrust during the middle part of the 20th Century occurred as a result of private-plaintiff actions."[24]

---

restrain trade or lessen competition in a patented or unpatented item. Thus, a patent misuse may be grounded on a violation of the antitrust laws, or, the defense may be invoked where, absent any antitrust violation, the conduct of the patent owner violates the patent laws").

[21]   U.S. CONST. art I, § 8 cl 3.

[22]   *United States v. Topco Assocs.*, 405 U.S. 596, 610 (1972).

[23]   J. Thomas Rosch, Comm'r, Fed. Trade Comm'n, Remarks at the USC Gould School of Law 2010 Intellectual Property Institute: Promoting Innovation: Just How "Dynamic" Should Antitrust Law Be? (Mar. 23, 2010), available at: www. ftc.gov/speeches/rosch/100323uscremarks.pdf ("The Federal Trade Commission, the Department of Justice, and the private plaintiffs bar all have authority to bring claims under Sections 1 and 2 of the Sherman Act in federal district court"). However the FTC, unlike the DOJ, does not have explicit statutory authority to enforce the Sherman Act.

[24]   Herbert Hovenkamp, *The Federal Trade Commission and the Sherman Act*, 62 FLA. L. REV. 871, 878 (2010). The history of antitrust is a checkered and tumultuous one. Just like patent law, antitrust law is a battleground of different ideologies and persuasions, economic, social and political. See, e.g., U.S.

Section 1 of the Sherman Act reaches "[e]very contact, combination [and] . . . conspiracy" among firms acting in "restraint of trade"[25] and "virtually any practice that has the effect of reducing output and raising price—or those activities that are 'anticompetitive' under the ordinary definitions of neoclassical economics."[26] Section 2 of the Sherman Act prohibits firms from monopolizing or attempting to monopolize.[27]

Section 3 of the Clayton Act covers abuses falling under both Section 1 and 2 and has largely been regarded as co-extensive with the two.[28] The governing principle is that "in order for a contract to violate Section 3 of the Clayton Act, competition foreclosed by it must constitute a substantial

---

Dep't of Justice, Competition and Monopoly: Single Firm Conduct Under Section 2 of the Sherman Act 129 (2008), http://www.justice.gov/atr/public/reports/236681.htm (issued under the administration of Republican President George W. Bush which was disavowed by the Federal Trade Commission in 2008 and withdrawn by the Department of Justice in 2009 under the administration of Democrat President Barak Obama); see also J. Thomas Rosch, Comm'r, Fed. Trade Comm'n, Remarks at the Conference on Antitrust and Digital Enforcement in the Technology Sector: Some Thoughts on the Role of Intellectual Property in Innovation Market Cases and Refusals to License (Jan. 31, 2011), available at: www.ftc.gov/speeches/rosch/110131technologysector.pdf ("Since the withdrawal, neither the courts nor the antitrust agencies have reached a consensus on how to evaluate that conduct if more than a *mere* refusal to deal is involved").

25 15 U.S.C. § 1 (2006).
26 Hovenkamp, *supra* note 24, at 874.
27 15 U.S.C. § 2 (2006).
28 *Tampa Elec. Co. v. Nashville Coal Co.*, 365 U.S. 320, 335 (1961) (holding that since the contract did not fall within the broader proscription of Section 3 of the Clayton Act, it was likewise not forbidden by Section 1 or Section 2 of the Sherman Act either). "Since the standard utilized in determining the proper relevant market for a Section 3 Clayton Act violation is the same as a Section 2 Sherman Act violation, the defendants' allegations that the plaintiffs violated Section 3 of the Clayton Act also fail by reason of the Court's definition of the relevant market and the lack of any relevant evidence regarding the plaintiffs' share of said market", *Mercantile Nat. Bank of Chicago v. Quest, Inc.*, 303 F. Supp. 926, 934–35 (N.D. Ind. 1969) *aff'd*, 431 F.2d 261 (7th Cir. 1970); 2 William C. Holmes, Intellectual Property and Antitrust Law § 20:2 (2010) ("More recent decisions draw no distinction between the two statutory provisions and state that the per se standard for illegal tying agreements is the same under either statute. Some older decisions, however, took the position that in a case brought under Clayton Act § 3, as opposed to Sherman Act § 1, the last two elements were alternatives to one another, so that the plaintiff need only prove either the presence of sufficient 'economic power' in the tying market or a 'not insubstantial' amount of affected commerce in the tied market . . . the more recent view treating the two standards alike seems by far the better reasoned one").

share of the relevant market." Section 7 of the Clayton act prohibits merger activity that has the potential to substantially lessen competition.[29]

Recent years have also seen a resurrection of interest in Section 5 of the FTC Act, which allows the FTC to prosecute "unfair methods of competition" that patent owners might undertake—authority that overlaps both with the Sherman and Clayton Acts.[30] In *FTC v. Brown Shoe Co. Inc.*, the Supreme Court rejected the lower court's decision that the FTC was required to show competitive harm, but instead allowed the FTC to apply Section 5 so as to "arrest trade restraints in their incipiency."[31] Professor William Kovacic and Marc Winerman note that Section 5 also allows the FTC to implement equitable relief that could include equitable defenses of nonenforceability.[32]

B. The Interface between IP and Antitrust Law

At a sufficiently high level of abstraction, the goals pursued by both the antitrust and intellectual property laws are similar.[33] Similarly, both

---

[29]   15 U.S.C. § 18.

[30]   See *FTC v. Sperry & Hutchinson Co.*, 405 U.S. 233, 239–44 (1972) (holding that Section 5 enables the FTC to address conduct covered by the letter and spirit of other antitrust laws and even some that violates neither); 1 Louis Altman & Malla Pollack, Callmann on Unfair Comp., Tr. & Mono. § 4:57 (4th ed., 2010) ("In addition, if the misuse of a patent is an 'unfair method of competition' the Federal Trade Commission can issue a cease and desist order under the Federal Trade Commission Act").

[31]   *F.T.C. v. Brown Shoe Co.*, 384 U.S. 316, 322 (1966).

[32]   William E. Kovacic and Marc Winerman, *Competition Policy and the Application of Section 5 of the Federal Trade Commission Act*, 76 Antitrust L.J. 929, 930–31 (2010) ("Congress intended Section 5 to be a mechanism for upgrading the U.S. system of competition law by permitting the FTC to reach behavior not necessarily proscribed by the other U.S. competition statutes, including the 1890 Sherman Act and the Clayton Act. Section 5 would be applied by an expert administrative tribunal which had power to impose prospective equitable relief (not damages or criminal sanctions), whose decisions interpreting Section 5 would not have collateral effects in private litigation and whose work would be reviewed by appellate courts under a deferential standard").

[33]   U.S. Dep't Of Justice & Fed. Trade Comm'n, Antitrust Enforcement And Intellectual Property Rights: Promoting Innovation And Competition 1–8 (2007), available at: www.ftc.gov/reports/innovation/ P040101PromotingInnovationandCompetitionrpt0704.pdf ("Over the past several decades, antitrust enforcers and the courts have come to recognize that intellectual property laws and antitrust laws share the same fundamental goals of enhancing consumer welfare and promoting innovation. This recognition signalled a significant shift from the view that prevailed earlier in the twentieth century, when the

misuse and the antitrust laws seek to restrain the myriad of ways that a patentee's exclusive right can be exploited.[34] At their core, the antitrust laws promote vigorous competition in the marketplace so that consumers benefit from a variety of goods and services at competitive prices.[35] They rest on the assumption that markets generally work well, and provide symptomatic relief when they do not to reset the balance. They thus sharply contrast with patent law, which assumes that market failure resulting from free-riding would result in a suboptimal level of innovation to the detriment of society.[36] Legal intervention is thus the rule for society that, while recognizing that the altruistic inventor may exist, is not prepared to forgo the contributions from those who would be otherwise deterred.[37]

---

goals of antitrust and intellectual property law were viewed as incompatible: intellectual property law's grant of exclusivity was seen as creating monopolies that were in tension with antitrust law's attack on monopoly power. Such generalizations are relegated to the past. . . . [A]ntitrust and intellectual property are properly perceived as complementary bodies of law that work together to bring innovation to consumers: antitrust laws protect robust competition in the marketplace, while intellectual property laws protect the ability to earn a return on the investments necessary to innovate. Both spur competition among rivals to be the first to enter the marketplace with a desirable technology, product, or service").

[34] See *Dawson Chem. Co. v. Rohm & Haas Co.*, 448 U.S. 176, 221 (1980) ("The policy of free competition runs deep in our law. It underlies both the doctrine of patent misuse and the general principle that the boundary of a patent monopoly is to be limited by the literal scope of the patent claims").

[35] U.S. Dep't Of Justice & Fed. Trade Comm'n, *supra* note 34 ("Antitrust laws, in turn, ensure that new proprietary technologies, products, and services are bought, sold, traded, and licensed in a competitive environment. In today's dynamic marketplace, new technological improvements are constantly replacing those that came before, as competitors are driven to improve their existing products or introduce new products in order to maintain their market share. Antitrust laws foster competition by prohibiting anticompetitive mergers, collusion, and exclusionary uses of monopoly power").

[36] See, e.g., Christina Bohannan & Herbert Hovenkamp, *IP and Antitrust: Reformation and Harm*, 51 B.C. L. Rev. 905, 921 (2010) ("market failure is the starting point for IP laws, and it is market failure that gives rise to the need for legal entitlements").

[37] Kelly Hershey, *Scheiber v. Dolby Laboratories, Inc,*.18 Berkeley Tech L.J. 159, 160–61 (2003) ("The patent system encourages investment in the creation of a good that otherwise would not be on the market by allowing monopoly control for a period of years. Antitrust analyses compare consumer welfare under monopoly control versus competitive conditions. Thus, the patent and antitrust laws handle two different market phases, so to speak: patent law facilitates entry of new products into the market, and antitrust law advocates a competitive environment for production of a good once the inventor has been sufficiently rewarded for her invention").

As with rights in tangible real property, courts have been willing to use antitrust laws to rein in abuses of patent rights, even if properly obtained. In *United States v. Microsoft*, the Court of Appeals for the D.C. Circuit rejected Microsoft's argument that it had "an absolute and unfettered right to use its intellectual property as it wishes," stating, "[t]hat is no more correct than the proposition that use of one's personal property, such as a baseball bat, cannot give rise to tort liability."[38] Some, therefore, see antitrust and patent law as quite different, and in some cases as inherently in conflict. Invoking cases from the early era, some courts observed that "there is an obvious tension between the patent laws and the antitrust laws" since "[o]ne body of law creates and protects monopoly power while the other seeks to proscribe it."[39] Other courts, while recognizing that "[t]he patent and antitrust laws serve the public in different ways," have held that they are "complementary, the patent system serving to encourage invention and the bringing of new products to market by adjusting investment-based risk, and the antitrust laws serving to foster industrial competition."[40] Yet according to Louis Kaplow, "[t]he intersection of antitrust law and patent policy has proved to be a source of perpetual confusion and controversy since the passage of the Sherman Act nearly a century ago."[41] It is a view that continues to resonate today.[42]

C. Misuse and Antitrust

A number of differences exist between misuse and antitrust. First, misuse is an affirmative defense; antitrust laws state a federal cause of action. Second, unlike antitrust plaintiffs who need to show evidence of an antitrust injury, infringers asserting misuse need not prove direct harm from the misuse. Third, whereas misuse results in unenforceability of the patent, antitrust provides for a host of remedies, including a devastating

---

[38]   *United States v. Microsoft Corp.*, 253 F.3d 34, 63 (D.C. Cir. 2001). See also *In re Indep. Serv. Orgs. Antitrust*, 203 F.3d 1322, 1325 (Fed. Cir. 2000) (as the Federal Circuit succinctly stated: "Intellectual property rights do not confer a privilege to violate the antitrust laws").

[39]   *United States v. Westinghouse Elec. Corp.*, 648 F.2d 642, 646 (9th Cir. 1981) (citing *E. Bement & Sons v. Nat'l Harrow Co.*, 186 U.S. 70, 91 (1902)).

[40]   *Intergraph Corp. v. Intel Corp.*, 195 F.3d 1346, 1362 (Fed. Cir. 1999).

[41]   Louis Kaplow, *The Patent-Antitrust Intersection: A Reappraisal*, 97 HARV. L. REV. 1813, 1815 (1984).

[42]   See e.g., Bruce D. Abramson, THE SECRET CIRCUIT: THE LITTLE-KNOWN COURT WHERE THE RULES OF THE INFORMATION AGE UNFOLD 290–304 (2007) (noting that the controversy and confusion has continued through today and that the conflict may be inevitable).

nondiscretionary trebling of damages by a court.[43] Fourth, while the policies have some similarities, there are also differences. As Professors Areeda and Hovenkamp observe:

> [Misuse] has additional concerns that antitrust does not capture, or at least that it does not capture very effectively. One of these concerns is with protection of the public domain, even if nonmonopolistic. Another is with practices that restrain rather than promote innovation. Of course, one might say that "foreclosure" of the public domain is an antitrust concern. Further, antitrust is also concerned as much with dynamic as with static competition, and thus innovation is always important to its analysis. While both of these things are true, antitrust takes a much more cautious and restrictive approach to these problems than IP policy does. Price and output competition and performance are relatively "well behaved" in the sense that capacity construction, consumer demand, and new entry with existing technology are all rather predictable. As a result, antitrust has always been able to insist upon strict proof of causation and harm and has tended to abhor speculation.[44]

In contrast to matrices for competition, innovation is radically indeterminate, often producing results that are entirely unexpected. The result of these differences is that economic models of innovation are much more varied and less robust than economic models of static competition. More importantly, while the elements of effective competition enjoy a broad consensus, the design of optimal patent policy is subject to very wide dispute. While antitrust is concerned almost exclusively with foreseeable consequences, patent policy must somehow manage a policy for consequences that are unforeseeable. Patent policy, which is entirely a creature of intellectual property law, can take some of these consequences into account where antitrust policy cannot.[45]

III.   RISING LITIGATION, FALLING MISUSE?

Patent litigation in America is rising, nearly tripling in the last ten years (Figure 1.1). With the proliferation of technology in corporate America, the number of patent filings and grants has risen. Figure 1.1 shows the

---

[43]   Note, *Is the Patent Misuse Doctrine Obsolete?*, 110 HARV. L. REV. 1922, 1924 (1997).

[44]   10 Philip E. Areeda & Herbert Hovenkamp, ANTITRUST LAW ¶1781(2d ed. 2004).

[45]   Ibid.

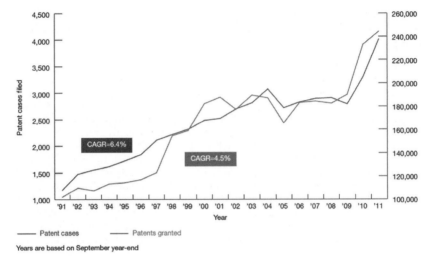

Source: PWC Report (2012).[46]

Figure 1.1   Patent case filings and grants

strong correlation between the spike in litigation and patent grants. Each patent represents a potential landmine that may trigger a lawsuit. In the software, hardware, and semiconductor industries the likelihood of firms treading on each other's patents is high. A core microprocessor chip, for example, comprises thousands of components, which can read on as many patents, and it is unclear what these patents cover and what they do not.[47] More recently, antitrust lawyer David Balto observed that:

> The smartphone wars are emblematic of the patent system's dysfunction and the impact on antitrust, competition, and consumers. There are too many

⁴⁶   Chris Barry et al., *Litigation continues to rise amid growing awareness of Patent Value 6* (Sep 2012) PricewaterhouseCoopers LLP. See also ibid at 30 ("To study the trends related to patent decisions, PwC identified final decisions at summary judgment and trial recorded in two WestLaw databases, Federal Intellectual Property – District Court Cases (FIP-DCT) and Combined Jury Verdicts and Settlements (JV-ALL), as well as in corresponding Public Access to Court Electronic Records (PACER) system records. The study focuses on 1,751 district court patent decisions issued from 1995 to 2011.).

⁴⁷   See James Beseen & Michael Meurer, PATENT FAILURE: HOW JUDGES, BUREAUCRATS AND LAWYERS PUT INNOVATORS AT RISK 190 (2008).

patents; many of which probably should not have been granted because they are either obvious, trivial, incremental, abstract, indefinite, mathematical laws of nature, or have only been theorized but not demonstrated.[48]

Perhaps unsurprisingly, patent misuse has also been raised here.[49]

Another factor fuelling the high rate of litigation may be the high payoff to the plaintiff from a successful suit. A PricewaterhouseCoopers study published in 2012 reveals that the annual median damage award ranged from $1.9 to $16.1 million between 1995 and 2011.[50] Conventional wisdom suggests that patent misuse cases tend to arise from disputes over existing license agreements.[51] As the number of issued patents increase, companies anxious to avoid patent thickets contribute to a higher frequency of licensing agreements and therefore a higher likelihood that misuse might precipitate from these greater numbers.[52] Conceivably, increased litigation risks should lead to more defendants invoking misuse. Indeed, one commentator warned that "it's *per se* malpractice to fail to advise a client who is considering an intellectual property infringement suit that he must be prepared to litigate any manner of crazy antitrust or misuse counterclaim—or misuse defense."[53] However, the opposite has proven to be true.

Swept by a rising tide of litigation, the number of misuse cases on the whole has also risen over the years (Fig. 1.2). Misuse featured in 20 appel-

---

[48] David Balto, *Why An Antitrust Lawyer Cares About Patent Reform*, ANTITRUSTCONNET BLOG (Nov. 16, 2012), http://antitrustconnect.com/2012/11/16/why-an-antitrust-lawyer-cares-about-patent-reform/.

[49] See e.g. *MultimediaPatent Trust v. Apple Inc.*, 2012 U.S. Dist. LEXIS 167479, at *73-75 (S.D. Cal. Nov. 9, 2012).

[50] Chris Barry et al., *2012 Patent Litigation Study: Litigation Continues Amid Growing Awareness of Patent Value*, PRICEWATERHOUSECOOPERS LLP, 5 (2012), available at: http://www.pwc.com/en_US/us/forensic-services/publications/assets/2012-patent-litigation-study.pdf [hereinafter "PWC Report"].

[51] Robert P. Merges, PATENT LAW AND POLICY 911 (1992) ("patent misuse [is] concerned with ancillary activities, activities done at the periphery of the patent grant"). Yet the data shows that they may also arise in non-licensing cases such as patent hold-ups, reverse payments and traditional infringement cases where the defendant pleads vexatious litigation or some other form of extra-licensing misconduct.

[52] Marshall Leaffer, *Patent Misuse and Innovation*, 10 J. HIGH TECH. L. 142, 142 (2010) ("As the number of issued patents skyrocket, companies more frequently enter into arrangements with competitors 'not only to recover their investment from creating patented products but also to avoid the patent landmines that line the path of innovation'").

[53] U.S. Dep't of Justice & Fed. Trade Comm'n, *supra* note 34 (quoting Abbott B. Lipsky).

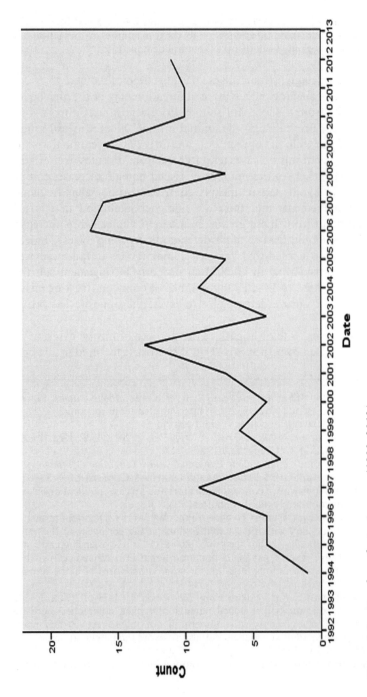

Figure 1.2　Number of misuse cases (1993–2012)

late level cases between 1991 and 2012. To give some context to this figure, it is useful to consider another equitable defense—inequitable conduct. Inequitable conduct featured in about 300 appellate level cases in the same period.[54] Since the facts that give rise to inequitable conduct also give rise to misuse,[55] it is surprising that misuse is not alleged every time an allegation of inequitable conduct is raised.[56] The foregoing suggests that misuse should have occurred more frequently in case law over the years. The incongruity of the sparing use and an increasing need of defendants for a defense like patent misuse makes for a curious conundrum.

Today, between the flagships of patent and antitrust laws stands a vast and murky ocean of misuse case law containing statements of allegiance to both without articulating where the boundaries of misuse end and those of antitrust law begin.[57] Some courts have viewed misuse as a broader wrong than antitrust violations, so that while the nature of the offense may be similar, misuse may arise if the degree of the offense does not warrant attention under the antitrust laws.[58] In affirming this sentiment,

---

[54] Christian E. Mammen, *Controlling the "Plague": Reforming the Doctrine of Inequitable Conduct*, 24 BERKELEY TECH. L.J. 1329, 1333 (2009) ("The Federal Circuit has issued over 600 cases since 1983 that mention 'inequitable conduct.' Over 300 of those cases substantively address, and contain a ruling on, an issue of inequitable conduct" [citations omitted]).

[55] See discussion in Chapter 3.

[56] See, e.g., *Power Integrations, Inc. v. Fairchild Semiconductor Int'l, Inc.*, No. 08-309-JJF-LPS, 2009 U.S. Dist. LEXIS 118383, at *29 (D. Del. Dec. 18, 2009) ("Power relies for its patent misuse defense on the same 'facts and allegations' on which it bases its inequitable conduct allegations").

[57] See Kelly Hershey, *Scheiber v. Dolby Laboratories, Inc.*, 18 BERKELEY TECH L.J. 159, 162 (2003) ("It is difficult for a patentee to know which behaviors patent misuse will punish that antitrust law will not"); Marshall Leaffer, *Engineering Competitive Policy and Copyright Misuse*, 19 U. DAYTON L. REV. 1087, 1099 (1994) ("The misuse doctrine is derived from a basic assumption that the patent monopoly is restrictive on a free economy. The doctrine is applied because of a perceived necessity and a deeply ingrained perception about the patent system. ... Although it governs competitive practices addressed by the antitrust laws, the misuse defense has retained a separate identity, albeit uncertain").

[58] See *Zenith Radio Corp. v. Hazeltine Research, Inc.*, 395 U.S. 100, 140–41(1969) (The Supreme Court noted that "if there was such patent misuse, it does not necessarily follow that the misuse embodies the ingredients of a violation of either § 1 or § 2 of the Sherman Act, or that Zenith was threatened by a violation so as to entitle it to an injunction under § 16 of the Clayton Act"); see also *Raychem Corp. v. PSI Telecomms*, No. C-93-20920, 1995 U.S. Dist. LEXIS 22325 (N.D. Cal. March 6, 1995) ("Although the contours of this doctrine are vague, patent misuse claims are generally tested by conventional antitrust principles"); see, e.g., *Windsurfing Int'l, Inc. v. AMF, Inc.*, 782 F.2d 995, 1001 (Fed. Cir. 1986)

Professor Hovenkamp et al. noted that the "modern view of some courts and commentators [is] that effect on competition is the only legitimate concern of patent misuse doctrine."[59] Other have noted it that may be one of the most frequently discussed and least frequently upheld defenses in patent law.[60] Other courts have treated misuse as essentially coextensive with antitrust.[61]

To the extent that misuse overlaps with antitrust law, it can provide a basis for a treble damages claim.[62] One reason for this is that the open-ended nature of the antitrust statutes enables courts to interpret them so as to embrace potentially every suspect form of commercial conduct, including conduct that could fall within the ambit of patent misuse. Section 5 of the FTC Act adds to the overlap. Another example is the overlap between misuse and the doctrine of exhaustion, which prohibits patentees from controlling the aftersales market.[63] If this spaghetti bowl of laws were not complex enough, sometimes internal and external overlaps can also

---

(the Federal Circuit required "that the alleged infringer show that the patentee has impermissibly broadened the 'physical or temporal scope' of the patent grant with anticompetitive effect," and that "a factual determination must reveal that the overall effect of the license tends to restrain competition unlawfully in an appropriately defined relevant market").

[59]   1 Herbert Hovenkamp et al., IP AND ANTITRUST, § 3.2b, §§ 3-8.1–3-9 (2002).

[60]   Joe Potenza et al., *Patent Misuse—The Critical Balance, A Patent Lawyer's View*, 15 FED. CIR. B.J. 69 (2005).

[61]   See, e.g., *Linzer Prods. Corp. v. Sekar*, 499 F. Supp. 2d 540, 552 (S.D.N.Y. 2007) ("Patent misuse, which developed long before the advent of antitrust law, has largely merged with antitrust law. 'Misuse is closely intertwined with antitrust law, and most findings of misuse are conditioned on conduct that would also violate the antitrust laws'").

[62]   The Seventh Circuit, in dismissing the patentee's plea to the contrary, held that "[t]here is no merit in HRI's contention that the misuse of its patents, including the one in suit, furnishes no basis for an award of treble damages. The requisite anti-competitive effect is presumed where the tying product is patented. Zenith's expenses in defending the infringement suit brought pursuant to HRI's antitrust violations are a proper subject of threefold recovery," *Hazeltine Research, Inc. v. Zenith Radio Corp.*, 388 F.2d 25, 35 (7th Cir. 1967). Misuse can also attract compulsory licensing as a remedy. *American Cyanamid Co. v. F.T.C.*, 363 F.2d 757, 771–72 (6th Cir. 1966) ("Compulsory licensing of patents by the courts for patent misuse is a permissible remedy in anti-trust cases") (citing *Hartford-Empire Co. v. United States*, 323 U.S. 386 (1945)).

[63]   *Monsanto Co. v. McFarling*, 302 F.3d 1291, 1298 (Fed. Cir. 2002) ("As a second ground for challenging the agreements, Mr. McFarling states that the contractual prohibition against using the patented soybeans to produce additional seeds for planting by the farmer violates the doctrines of patent exhaustion and first sale, and that the parties could not enter into an enforceable contract that has this effect").

occur in the same case, as they did in *Hartford Empire*, where the Supreme Court found that conduct in violation of the exhaustion doctrine also attracts an antitrust violation.[64] Following this track, the Seventh Circuit in *Hazeltine Research* awarded treble damages against the patentee on finding misuse.[65]

Yet others have acknowledged that while misuse dovetails in part of their analysis with antitrust laws, the policies pursued by each are different.[66] One stream of development sees misuse as a useful response to new developments in patent practice that might be outside the reach of antitrust laws, and are in conflict with important patent innovation policies. For example, Judge Richard Posner noted that:

> When the advance of science . . . enables a form of patent misuse that is new but is well within the conceptual heartland of the doctrine, the boundaries of the doctrine can expand modestly to encompass it. . . . It would be inappropriate to confine patent misuse, as is sometimes suggested, to practices that violate antitrust law, for in that event the doctrine would be superfluous.[67]

Tentative steps in innovation leave society languishing in a suboptimal state of advancement. If indeed misuse is an anachronism with the potential to become "an open-ended pitfall for patent-supported

---

[64]   *United States v. Arnold, Schwinn & Co.*, 388 U.S. 365, 382 (1967) ("Once the manufacturer has parted with title and risk, he has parted with dominion over the product, and his effort thereafter to restrict territory or persons to whom the product may be transferred—whether by explicit agreement or by silent combination or understanding with his vendee—is a per se violation of § 1 of the Sherman Act").

[65]   *Hazeltine Research, Inc. v. Zenith Radio Corp.*, 388 F.2d 25, 35 (7th Cir. 1967) *aff'd* in part, *rev'd* in part, 395 U.S. 100 (1969) ("There is no merit in HRI's contention that the misuse of its patents, including the one in suit, furnishes no basis for an award of treble damages").

[66]   See *Clayton Mfg. Co. v. Cline*, 427 F. Supp. 78, 79 (C.D. Cal. 1976 ("We reject the view that any violation of patent law necessarily violates the antitrust laws. From some abuses of patent policy may flow consequences not drastic enough to meet antitrust prerequisites of effect on competition. In addition, many patent abuses are more effectively curbed by simply denying equitable relief as a matter of *patent policy*") (emphasis added) (citing the REPORT OF THE ATTORNEY GENERAL'S NATIONAL COMMITTEE TO STUDY THE ANTITRUST LAWS 254 (1955)).

[67]   See *Smithkline Beecham Corp. v. Apotex Corp.*, 247 F. Supp. 2d 1011, 1047 (N.D. Ill. 2003); see also Dan L. Burk & Mark A. Lemley, *Biotechnology's Uncertainty Principle*, 54 CASE W. RES. L. REV. 691, 741 (2004) ("The patent misuse doctrine can play a powerful role in deterring anticompetitive efforts to extend patent rights beyond the scope a rational pharmaceutical patent policy would give").

commerce,"[68] then it should be exorcised by Congress or the courts—the sooner the better. If, however, misuse has vitality—whether as a part of a quasi-antitrust doctrine or apart from antitrust considerations—then Congress and the courts should give guidance as to their endorsement of the doctrine, as well as making the bounds of the doctrine's administration principled and predictable. However, unless and until the central issue—whether misuse has vitality apart from antitrust—is clarified, new cases will not have a firm foundation to develop into sound precedents themselves. Vague rules are also bad precedent, open to misinterpretation and misapplication by other courts. Some, like Professor Robin Feldman, observe that this has already happened, resulting in "a confusing tangle of doctrine that distorts both patent misuse and antitrust."[69] Others observe that while the Supreme Court has found misuse "in whole or in part" in 12 out of 16 cases, the Federal Circuit "has found misuse only a few times since its creation, and has rejected misuse claims on more than twenty occasions."[70] The last Supreme Court case finding misuse was in 1980 and it has not made a holding on it since.

---

[68]   *C.R. Bard Inc. v. M3 Sys., Inc.*, 157 F.3d 1340, 1373 (Fed. Cir. 1998).

[69]   Robin C. Feldman, *The Insufficiency of Antitrust Analysis for Patent Misuse*, 55 HASTINGS L.J. 399, 401 (2003). ("the Federal Circuit . . . has changed patent misuse by inserting an antitrust test. Current Federal Circuit opinions note that patent misuse is aimed at practices that do not necessarily violate the antitrust laws but then proceed to test for patent misuse by applying antitrust rules. In particular, as the general rule for testing patent misuse, current cases require application of the antitrust Rule of Reason. The result is a confusing tangle of doctrine that distorts both patent misuse and antitrust").

[70]   1 Hovenkamp et al., *supra* note 60, at §3.2 ("the Supreme Court decided 16 patent misuse cases between 1917 and the present. Of those 16 cases, the Court found misuse in whole or in part in 12 cases, and refused to find it in only four cases. By contrast, the Federal Circuit has found misuse only a few times since its creation, and has rejected misuse claims on more than twenty occasions. Further, it is worth noting that the Supreme Court last considered a misuse issue in 1980, and refused to find misuse in that case. The last Supreme Court decision to find misuse was in 1969. This pattern seems to represent a fundamental shift away from misuse doctrine in the past 30 years, though it is worth noting that the Supreme Court has never spoken on the Federal Circuit's jurisprudence in this area"). The 16 Supreme Court cases were: *Motion Picture Patents Co. v. Universal Film Mfg. Co.*, 243 U.S. 502 (1917); *Carbice Corporation of America v. American Patents Development Corporation*, 283 U.S. 27 (1931); *Leitch Mfg. Co. v. Barber Co.*, 302 U.S. 458 (1938); *Morton Salt Co. v. G. S. Suppiger Co.*, 314 U.S. 488 (1942); *B. B. Chemical Co. v. Ellis*, 117 F.2d 829, 834–35 (1st Cir. 1941), *aff'd*, 314 U.S. 495 (1942); *Mercoid Corp. v. Minneapolis-Honeywell Regulator Co.*, 320 U.S. 680 (1944); *Mercoid Corp. v. Mid-Continent Inv. Co.*, 320 U.S. 661 (1944); *Precision Instrument Mfg. Co. v. Auto. Maint. Mach. Co.*, 324 U.S. 806, 817 (1945);

The conflicting calls both for the eradication of an anachronism and a neo-classical renaissance of misuse remains at the fringes, their respective advance stunted by the paucity of empirical data to shepherd the debate towards a meaningful resolution.[71] Misuse continues to be a steady feature in both patent litigation and academic discussion. However, the debate has largely generated more heat than light. Case law generally neglects current perceptions in the relevant legal community of what the courts are doing. If, as one commentator argued, other laws that have developed since its inception have rendered misuse "superfluous," then Congress and the courts should say what those laws are and what they do. Moreover, the uncertainty as to the nature and future of misuse is undesirable. Indeterminate defenses discourage bold, strategic moves by patentees, licensees, or related third parties in asserting and defending their rights.[72]

Casual observers looking at the considerable amount of attention given to misuse might assume that the issue should already have been comprehensively discussed and resolved.[73] If so, then they would be deceived. In

---

Transparent-Wrap Mach. Corp. v. Stokes & Smith Co., 331 U.S. 837 (1947); *United States v. Line Material Co.*, 333 U.S. 287 (1948); *United States v. U.S. Gypsum Co.*, 333 U.S. 364 (1948); *Automatic Radio Mfg. Co. v. Hazeltine Research*, 339 U.S. 827 (1950); *U.S. Gypsum Co. v. National Gypsum Co.*, 352 U.S. 457 (1957); *Brulotte v. Thys Co.*, 379 U.S. 29 (1964); *Zenith Radio Corp. v. Hazeltine Research, Inc.*, 395 U.S. 100 (1969); *Dawson Chemical Co. v. Rohm and Haas Co.*, 448 U.S. 176 (1980).

[71] See Vincent Chiappetta, *Living with Patents: Insights from Patent Misuse*, 15 MARQ. INTELL. PROP. L. REV. 1, 5 (2011) ("In the prevailing market efficiency paradigm, the doctrine's limitations on exploitation of patent rights are not only superfluous, but affirmatively harmful. ... Antitrust law draws more appropriate balances between maximizing patent incentives while minimizing undue interference with market operation and innovation. Inequitable conduct, abuse of process, antitrust sham litigation, and Walker Process liability more effectively control abuses of the patent prosecution process and improper assertions of patent rights").

[72] See also Christina Bohannan & Herbert Hovenkamp, *supra* note 37, at 991–92 ("On the accused infringer's side, reliable predictions about what does and does not constitute an infringement will also greatly facilitate the incentive to make efficient investments").

[73] Patent misuse has enjoyed more attention in the last decade than in any other period in its history. A Lexis search revealed that 111 law review articles mentioned patent misuse and antitrust since 2000, compared to 105 articles from 1990 to 1999 and 31 articles from 1980 to 1989. There have been more federal cases since 2000 than at any other period in its history. There were more cases mentioning or discussing "patent misuse" from 2003 to 2008 (296) than in the 1990s (246), or the 1980s (182).

2010, this lack of clarity might have changed for a while as misuse was for the first time considered by an *en banc* Court of Appeals for the Federal Circuit, America's *de facto* patent court, in *Princo Corp. v. ITC*.[74] The Federal Circuit is the nation's patent court, principally responsible for articulating the scope of American patent law. *Princo* was also the first time in 30 years that an appellate court ruled on misuse.[75] Nevertheless, the *Princo* court offered three distinct points of view in the majority opinion, concurrence, and dissent.[76] These deeply split opinions represent the polarized view of misuse, and form a corpus of substantial discussion later in the book.[77]

These opinions attracted equally polarized responses from the legal community. The National Law Journal reported that the American Antitrust Institute found the ruling "very disappointing" because the majority "put 'formalism before substance' by requiring that patent misuse must involve extending the physical or temporal scope of the patent," when "it's an improper use of the patent right to force the market to accept a standard devised by two companies."[78] In contrast, the American IP Law Institute was "content with the outcome" and found the majority ruling "a vindication of the traditional antitrust analysis in cases like this . . . The court clearly declined to expand the categories of action or activity which constitute patent misuse."[79]

Hence the reason for this book. It is hoped that the spectrum of doctrinal and policy perspectives, together with the empirical data on misuse will improve the ability of judges, lawyers, policymakers and others to participate more meaningfully in the debate encouraged by the Federal Circuit's *en banc* reconsideration of the parameters of misuse.

---

[74] *Princo Corp. v. Int'l Trade Comm'n*, 616 F.3d 1318 (Fed. Cir. 2010) *cert. denied*, 131 S. Ct. 2480 (2011). The *en banc* decision capped a trilogy of Federal Circuit decisions arising out of an International Trade Commission patent infringement litigation. See *U.S. Philips Corp. v. Int'l Trade Comm'n*, 424 F.3d 1179 (Fed. Cir. 2005); *United States Philips Corp. v. Princo Corp.*, 173 Fed. Appx. 832 (Fed. Cir. 2006).

[75] See *Dawson Chem. Co. v. Rohm & Haas Co.*, 448 U.S. 176 (1980) (being the last Supreme Court decision on patent misuse).

[76] The *en banc* majority opinion was authored by Judge Bryson and joined by Chief Judge Rader and Judges Newman, Lourie, Linn, and Moore. The concurrence was authored by Judge Prost and joined by Judge Mayer. The dissent was authored by Judge Dyk and joined by Judge Garjasa. *Princo Corp.*, 616 F.3d 1318.

[77] See *infra* Chapter 2.

[78] Sheri Qualters, *Full Federal Circuit Narrowly Applies Patent Misuse Doctrine*, NAT'L L. J. (Sep. 2, 2010).

[79] Ibid.

More importantly, it is hoped that by presenting conventional wisdom alongside the qualitative and quantitative facets of misuse, the book will allow misuse to at last receive a fair trial in the court of public opinion, and its fate will be decided according to merit and reason rather than misunderstanding and rhetoric.

2. A brief history of patent misuse

I. INTRODUCTION

The history of patent misuse in America spans nearly a century. While its past is rooted in patent law, its present is intertwined with antitrust law. The passage of time usually helps define the contours of a doctrine, but not so with misuse. While the formulaic statement for misuse at each point in its history may have been tolerably clear, its application has been muddied both by the shifting views of patents and the policies underlying both the patent and antitrust laws. Hence, it is perhaps the best known but least understood defense in patent law.

Some say that the modern doctrine of patent misuse began with *Morton Salt v. G.S. Suppiger Co.*, a 1942 Supreme Court decision.[1] Justice Harlan Fiske Stone, writing for a unanimous court, invoked the Court's equitable powers to prevent a violation of patent policy through the improper expansion of patent grant. The patent right, the Court declared, could not be enforced until the effects of the misuse had been purged.[2] But the roots of misuse go back further yet—to the Court's 1917 decision in *Motion Picture Patents Co.*[3] There, the Supreme Court first declared that

---

[1] *Morton Salt v. G.S. Suppiger Co.*, 314 U.S. 488, 490 (1942); see *Lasercomb Am., Inc. v. Reynolds*, 911 F.2d 970, 975 (4th Cir. 1990) ("Although a patent misuse defense was recognized by the courts as early as 1917, most commentators point to Morton Salt Co. v. G.S. Suppiger as the foundational patent misuse case"); Christina Bohannan & Herbert Hovenkamp, CREATION WITHOUT RESTRAINT: PROMOTING LIBERTY AND RIVALRY IN INNOVATION 261, 254 (2011) ("Strictly speaking, MPPC did not create the misuse doctrine as we know it today. It was first and foremost a first-sale case. . . . The modern expression of misuse doctrine came in the Morton Salt case"); Robert J. Hoerner, *The Decline (And Fall?) of the Patent Misuse Doctrine in the Federal Circuit*, 69 ANTITR. L J. 669, 669 (2002) ("The 'misuse of the patent' doctrine was originated by name in Morton Salt Co. v. G.S. Suppiger Co."); see also Raymond T. Nimmer & Murali Santhanam, *The Concept of Misuse in Copyright and Trademark Law: Searching for a Concept of Restraint, in Patents, Copyrights, Trademarks and Literary Property Handbook Series*, 524 PLI/PAT 397, 404 (1998) ("The first express recognition ofmisuse [sic] law in patent licensing was the decision of the Supreme Court in Morton Salt Co. v. G.S. Suppiger Co. . . .").

[2] *Morton Salt*, 314 U.S. 488 at 493.

[3] *Motion Picture Patents Co. v. Universal Film Mfg. Co.*, 243 U.S. 502 (1917).

patent policy did not allow patentees to control economic activity beyond the scope of their patents. But to truly understand the genesis of misuse, the inquiry must go further back still—to the days following the civil war, when patentees' rights were nothing short of sacrosanct.[4]

II. 1914–1941: THE MOTION PICTURE PATENTS CO. YEARS

In the wake of the Civil War, corporate monopolies dominated the American marketplace. Companies formed monopolies and cartels, which fixed prices and outputs in order to dampen price depressions flowing from the oversupply of goods. These monopolies and cartels were controlled through trusts. In 1890, Senator John Sherman spearheaded Congressional efforts to outlaw cartels and monopolies.[5] The climate was, however, still a sweet one for patentees. Professor Christopher Leslie observed that "[i]n the early days after the passage of the Sherman Act, antitrust law did little to affect the supremacy of intellectual property rights."[6] He attributed this to the separate evolution of the antitrust and IP laws, leading to court affording "little weight to the idea that anticompetitive effects of intellectual property rights could implicate antitrust concerns."[7] Accordingly in *E. Bement Court & Sons v. National Harrow*, the Supreme Court held:

> the general rule is absolute freedom in the use or sale of rights under the patent laws of the United States. The very object of these laws is monopoly, and the rule is, with few exceptions, that any conditions which are not in their very nature illegal with regard to this kind of property, imposed by the patentee and

---

See *Princo Corp. v. Int'l Trade Comm'n*, 616 F.3d 1318, 1326 (Fed. Cir. 2010) ("The doctrine of patent misuse has its origins in a series of Supreme Court cases, beginning with the 1917 decision in Motion Picture Patents Co. v. Universal Film Manufacturing Co."); see also Nimmer & Santhanam, *supra* note 1, at 404 ("The Supreme Court in 1917 recognized concepts related to the defense of misuse for the first time in (*Motion Picture Patents Co*) . . . [but] the Court did not use the word 'misuse' in any part of its judgment").

[4] Alan J. Weinshel, *Intellectual Property and the Antitrust Laws*, in ANTITRUST ADVISOR 5–6 (Irving Scher ed., 2006) (noting that courts "treated a patentee's exclusive rights to make, sell, and use the patented invention as virtually sacrosanct").

[5] Robert Bradley Jr., *On the Origins of the Sherman Act*, 9 CATO J 737, 737–38 (1990).

[6] Christopher Leslie, ANTITRUST LAW AND INTELLECTUAL PROPERTY RIGHTS 39 (2011).

[7] Ibid.

agreed to by the licensee for the right to manufacture or use or sell the article, will be upheld by the courts. The fact that the conditions in the contracts keep up the monopoly or fix prices does not render them illegal.[8]

This view of patent rights allowed a generous amount of latitude in how patentees chose to exploit their patents. They can condition licenses on buying from the patentee anything used in conjunction with the invention. Using other inputs voided the license and turned users into direct infringers. It also made knowing suppliers of those unpatented inputs contributory infringers.[9] For example in *Henry v. A.B. Dick*, the defendant Sidney Henry, who sold unpatented ink used with the patented mimeograph machine was held to be liable for patent infringement.[10] This was because "[the Court] had thought well of the patentee's system of selling a machine at practically cost and making its entire profit from the sale of supplies because the intention was thereby made widely available to the public."[11] The Supreme Court in a later case explained that "[t]he traditional remedy against contributory infringement is the injunction. And an inevitable concomitant of the right to enjoin another from contributory infringement is the capacity to suppress competition in an unpatented article of commerce."[12]

To Congress, however, the Court had gone too far and *A.B. Dick* catalyzed the introduction of new federal laws in 1914. The Clayton Act expressly prohibited price discrimination, tying and exclusive dealings, mergers and interlocking directorates, while differing from the Sherman Act in that it was civil rather than criminal in nature. Congress also introduced the Federal Trade Commission Act that year, creating a complementary federal agency to the Antitrust Division of the Department of Justice, and which would curtail "unfair methods of competition" and "unfair or deceptive acts or practices".[13] The FTC was created in response to Congressional recognition that judges may have been reticent to give

---

[8]   *E. Bement & Sons v. Nat'l Harrow Co.*, 186 U.S. 70, 91 (1902).

[9]   *Heaton-Peninsular Button-Fastener Co v. Eureka Specialty Co.*, 77 Fed. 288 (6th Cir. 1896).

[10]   The Court held that use of a competitor's ink in violation of a condition of the agreement—that the rotary mimeograph "may be used only with the stencil, paper, ink and other supplies made by A.B. Dick Company"—constituted infringement of the patent on the machine. *Henry v. A.B. Dick*, 224 U.S. 1, 26 (1912).

[11]   *Rohm & Haas Co. v. Dawson Chem. Co.*, 599 F.2d 685, 693 (5th Cir. 1979), *aff'd*, 448 U.S. 176 (1980).

[12]   *Dawson Chem. Co. v. Rohm & Haas Co.*, 448 U.S. 176, 197 (1980).

[13]   Federal Trade Commission Act § 5, 15 U.S.C. § 45 (1914).

effect to the harsh consequences of the Sherman Act and to establish administrative procedure.

Subsequent to these Congressional acts, the Supreme Court in *Motion Pictures Patents Co.* confined patentees' rights to only what was in the patent grant itself. Those rights could no longer be extended contractually to unpatented inputs. As in *A.B. Dick*, the patentee *in Motion Picture Patents* relied on its patents to require licensees of its projectors to incorporate its patented film projector to show its films. The Court regarded its decision in *A.B. Dick* as being overruled by the Clayton Act and emphasized that the scope of a patent was limited to its claims and that patent policy's bias was toward the public over the inventors.[14] The Court reasoned that the inventor's reward was based on the entire invention and that "he should not be permitted by legal devices to impose an unjust charge upon the public in return for the use of it."[15] Patent law was meant to encourage innovation and, while "inventors shall be fairly, even liberally, treated,"[16] patentees could not "extend the scope of its patent monopoly by restricting the use of it to materials necessary in its operation."[17] In contrast to the modern form of misuse, the Court implicitly confined non-enforceability to the infringer in suit.[18] Yet while recognizing that the Clayton Act was "a most persuasive expression of the public policy of [America] with respect to the question before [it],"[19] the Court found that resorting to the Clayton Act was unnecessary.[20]

Instead, the Court held that there was no infringement to start with, because the patentee sought to enforce rights which were not granted by his patent.[21] Because of the patentee's dominance of the

---

[14] See *Motion Picture Patents Co. v. Universal Film Mfg. Co.*, 243 U.S. 502, 517–18 (1917) (explaining that, in light of § 3 of the Clayton Act, *A.B. Dick* "must be regarded as overruled").

[15] Ibid. at 513.

[16] Ibid. at 511.

[17] Ibid. at 516.

[18] Ibid. at 508 (Affirming "that the limitation on the use of the machine attempted to be made by the notice attached to it after it had been sold and paid for, was invalid, and that the [defendants], had an implied license to use the machine as it had been used").

[19] Ibid. at 517–18.

[20] Ibid. at 517; Clayton Antitrust Act, Pub.L. 63-212 § 3, 38 Stat. 730 (1914) (codified in 15 U.S.C. § 12(a)).

[21] *Rohm & Haas Co. v. Dawson Chem. Co.*, 599 F.2d 685, 693 (5th Cir. 1979), *aff'd*, 448 U.S. 176 (1980); see Christina Bohannan & Herbert Hovenkamp, CREATION WITHOUT RESTRAINT: PROMOTING LIBERTY AND RIVALRY IN INNOVATION 261, 254 (2011), at 262 ("the Court did not base its concern with monopolies on antitrust law or policy. Rather, it relied on the public interest underlying federal patent law to

film-projector market, users had to use the patent holder's films and there would be little or no incentive for others to produce films.[22] If the infringement action were upheld, Professors Herbert Hovenkamp and Christina Bohannan note that there "would have been an impoverished film market in which consumers had access to far fewer films than they would have had otherwise. This was an innovation problem as much as a competition problem."[23] Motion Pictures, said antitrust attorney Geoffrey Oliver, "marked the beginning of an extended period of development and fairly aggressive application of the patent misuse doctrine."[24]

While representing a high watermark for the misuse doctrine, *Motion Pictures* did little to actually deter misconduct. As William Nicoson ruefully observes, "the business practices spawned by judicial sanction during the period did not vanish gracefully."[25] Instead, patentees "clung to old, now bad, habits with what proved to be unfortunate tenacity."[26] Still the die had been cast. In 1931, the Court in *Carbice Corp of America v. American Patents Development Corp* affirmed a strong misuse doctrine— that a patentee could not use its patent to exclude a supplier of unpatented peripherals, unpatented dry ice to be used with the patented refrigerated transport packages, from competing with the patentee in what was essentially a secondary market for the invention, one outside the scope of the patent grant.[27] While the patentee could "prohibit entirely the manufacture, sale, or use of such packages," or "grant licenses upon terms consistent with the limited scope of the patent monopoly" and "charge a royalty or license fee" it could "not exact as the condition of a license that unpatented materials used in connection with the invention shall be purchased only from the licensor."[28] Indeed, "this limitation, inherent in

---

forbid patent holders from obtaining control over additional products not covered by the patent grant. As such, the Court recognized a *patent law* policy in favor of encouraging competition and innovation in the markets for unpatented products").

[22]   Ibid. at 275.

[23]   Ibid. at 267.

[24]   Geoffrey D. Oliver, Princo v. International Trade Commission: *Antitrust Law and the Patent Misuse Doctrine Part Company*, 25 ANTITRUST 62, 62–63 (Spring 2011).

[25]   William J. Nicoson, *Misuse of the Misuse Doctrine in Infringement Suits*, 9 UCLA L. REV. 76, 80 (1962).

[26]   Ibid.

[27]   *Mercoid Corp v. Mid-Continent Inv. Co.*, 320 U.S. 661, 677 (1944). (Alluding to *Carbice*, Justice Frankfurter noted that "if there is not infringement of a patent there can be no contributory infringer.")

[28]   *Carbice Corporation of America v. American Patents Development Corporation*, 283 U.S. 27, 30–31 (1931).

the patent grant, is not dependent upon the peculiar function or character of the unpatented material or on the way in which it is used."[29]

Also during this period, antitrust enforcers continued to loosely enforce the antitrust laws, relying instead on misuse to keep patentees in check. The markets boomed and there appeared to be little reason for intervention. In the early years of the New Deal, business practices flourished and were even encouraged through the stock market crash in 1929. In 1935, the Supreme Court struck down legislation initiated by President Franklin D. Roosevelt. The legislation coordinated industry-wide output and pricing which radically affected New Deal-era policy. In 1938, the Court was presented with a twist.

Leitch Mfg v. Barber Co. concerned a patented process of laying bituminous emulsion over cement roadways.[30] The patentee allowed any contractor who bought his emulsion to use his process, but the parties never entered into an actual license agreement. The defendant sold the emulsion to a contractor who did not buy from the patentee. Unlike the earlier misuse cases, the third party in *Leitch* was supplying a direct infringer. The Court found that an actual license was unnecessary to finding infringement. The patentee simply could not extend the scope of his right and force a finding of infringement. Misuse was raised not as a defense to infringement, but as a demarcation of the patent grant to preclude the finding of infringement. Nicoson notes "[t]he language used, however, was so sweeping as to convey the misleading impression that the plaintiff, due to his misconduct, was being denied relief which would otherwise have been available."[31] Some lower courts saw *Leitch* as creating a new doctrine which immunized infringers,[32] and "without the judicial climate these cases created, the courts would never have taken the radical step of engrafting a new exception upon statutory patent rights in order to engraft an additional sanction upon statutory antitrust remedies."[33] The foundation laid down in these early years led to the development of the 'modern' doctrine of misuse, which would soon follow in *Morton Salt*.

---

[29] Ibid. at 33.

[30] *Leitch Mfg. Co. v. Barber Co.*, 302 U.S. 458 (1938).

[31] Nicoson, *supra* note 25, at 82.

[32] See, e.g., *American Lechithin Co v. Warfield Co.*, 105 F.2d 207, 211 (7th Cir. 1939), *cert denied*, 308 U.S. 609 (1939) (holding that "the defense of attempted extra-legal monopolization" prevented recovery, citing *Motion Picture Patents Co., Carbice* and *Leitch*).

[33] Nicoson, *supra* note 25, at 82.

III. 1942–1981: THE *MORTON SALT* YEARS

The period spanning the 1940s through the early 1980s was a period in which monopolies, including those created through the grant of exclusive rights conferred by patent were treated with deep suspicion by the antitrust agencies. Under Thurman Arnold who served as chief competition attorney in the Justice Department, the Department would issue its infamous Nine No-Nos. The Nine No-Nos would make agreements which involved tying arrangements, resale price maintenance, vertical non-price restraints and horizontal agreements to divide markets or designate customers as *per se* illegal.[34] As the Fifth Circuit noted "there is no inquiry into purity of heart vs. bad motive, or market impact, or matters of what may seem to be essential fairness—a *per se* violation of the Sherman Act is deemed such a monopolistic action that the patentee is barred from enforcing the limited and special monopoly given him by the patent laws."[35] These reflected government views about the actions that patentees could not take without drawing the attention of the Antitrust Division. As Christopher Leslie noted, "[t]he Nine No-Nos' were part and parcel of a larger antitrust regime that treated almost all business relationships with suspicion."[36] *Per se* violations made the administration of antitrust laws easier because parties need not present evidence of anticompetitive effects, and courts did not have to weigh such factors.

The Supreme Court also regarded markets as susceptible to abusive conduct by firms and correctable by antitrust intervention in order to achieve socio-political rather than economic goals. Under the leadership of Chief Justice Earl Warren, the Court aggressively crushed conduct which it deemed harmful.[37] For example in *United States v. Loew's Inc.*,

---

[34]   See Bruce B. Wilson, Deputy Assistant Attorney Gen., Remarks before the Fourth New England Antitrust Conference, Patent and Know-How License Agreements: Field of Use, Territorial, Price and Quantity Restrictions (Nov. 6, 1970).The "Nine No-Nos" were: (1) tying the purchase of unpatented materials as a condition of the license; (2) requiring the licensee to assign back subsequent patents; (3) restricting the right of the purchaser of the product in the resale of the product; (4) restricting the licensee's ability to deal in products outside the scope of the patent; (5) a licensor's agreement not to grant further licenses; (6) mandatory package licenses; (7) royalty provisions not reasonably related to the licensee's sales; (8) restrictions on a licensee's use of a product made by a patented process; and (9) minimum resale price provisions for the licensed products.

[35]   *Hensley Equip. Co. v. Esco Corp.*, 383 F.2d 252, 263-64 (5th Cir. 1967), *judgment amended, reh'g denied*, 386 F.2d 442.

[36]   Leslie, *supra* note 6, at 42.

[37]   See, e.g., *Brown Shoe v. United States*, 370 U.S. 294, 346 (1962) (holding that

the Court noted that "[s]ince one of the objectives of the patent laws is to reward uniqueness . . . the existence of a valid patent on the tying product, without more, establishes a distinctiveness sufficient to conclude that any tying arrangement involving the patented product would have anticompetitive consequences."[38] Patent misuse, however, was to move in a different trajectory from antitrust law. And the decision that formulated that approach was *Morton Salt*.

A. *Morton Salt*: **Patent Policy Beginnings**

In 1942, the Supreme Court decided *Morton Salt* which represented an important shift toward grounding misuse analysis in policy considerations aside from antitrust concerns. The patentee was a canning company with a wholly owned subsidiary devoted to making and leasing a patented salt tablet depositing machine.[39] The subsidiary's business was primarily based on the sale of tablets used with the machine. The patentee leased the machines and required its licensees to use only its salt tablets, which were unpatented. The patentee sued a competitor that was leasing similar machines and sold salt tablets used with those machines. Chief Justice Stone writing for a unanimous court framed the question as to whether a court of equity would aid a patentee using its patent to restrain competition. While competition was its concern, the Court expressly held that violation of the antitrust laws was not. Instead, the public policy informing the Court's exercise of its equitable discretion was drawn from the patent statute and based on the doctrine of "unclean hands" and patent policy to exclude everything not embraced in the invention. Chief Justice Stone explained:

> The grant to the inventor of the special privilege of a patent monopoly carries a public policy adopted by the Constitution and laws of the United States, 'to promote the Progress of Science and the useful Arts, by securing for limited Times to . . . Inventors, the exclusive Right. . . .' But the public policy which includes inventions within the granted monopoly excludes from it all that is not embraced in the invention.[40]

---

the fact that two merging firms held 5 percent of total market output did not preclude application of the Clayton Act); see also *United States v. Arnold Schwinn*, 388 U.S. 365, 391–92 (1967) (holding that vertical restraints which placed restrictions on territorial or customer restrictions were *per se* illegal and that such condemnations "without inquiry into actual market conditions" are "only appropriate if the existence of forcing is probable").

38   *United States v. Loew's, Inc.*, 371 U.S. 38, 46 (1962).
39   *Morton Salt v. G.S. Suppiger Co.*, 314 U.S. 488 (1942).
40   Ibid. at 492.

An additional consequence of the ruling is that not only did patentees find themselves without remedy against those whose conduct was outside the scope of its patent, the patent itself became unenforceable even against those whose conduct was within that scope.[41] Nicoson stated that "[t]he reason behind the rule is that such extension tends to undermine the basic purpose of the patent grant 'to Promote the Progress of Science and useful Arts' by destroying incentives for further invention."[42]

The Court's basis for unenforceability lay not in precedent, but in policy. It was the policy inherent in patent law that prevented the patentee from "claim[ing] protection of his grant by the courts where it is being used to subvert that policy."[43] As with *Motion Picture Patents Co.*, the Court found it "unnecessary to decide whether [the patentee] had violated the Clayton Act, for [it] concluded that in any event the maintenance of the present suit . . . [was] against public policy"[44] Commentators note that the Court wanted to draw "parallels from other areas like copyright and trademarks to reiterate the appropriateness of its holding premised on public policy."[45] Later, in reflecting on the lower court's holding that the patentee's misuse was predicated on an antitrust violation which the Supreme Court reversed in *Morton Salt*, Judge Rich noted that:

> Misuse and antitrust law violation are two separate issues governed by separate criteria, as that court failed to recognize. The field of misuse, as such, lies in between the sphere of the patent monopoly and the sphere of the antitrust statutes and violation of the latter has never been a condition precedent to a finding of misuse. This is so notwithstanding findings of both misuse and antitrust law violation in some cases. Misuse has been predicated on the *policy inherent in the antitrust laws*, not on a violation of those laws. The Supreme Court made this clear in reversing the Seventh Circuit Court of Appeals in the *Morton Salt* case . . .[46]

---

[41]   Bohannan & Hovenkamp, *supra* note 21, at 264 ("Thus developed the highly draconian remedy that if a patentee's license agreement constitutes 'misuse,' the patentee loses its right to enforce that patent against *anyone*").

[42]   Nicoson, *supra* note 25, at 84 ("If simply by contract or other business devices an inventor may gain patent advantages for unpatented property, what need has he to invent anything new? If private business were permitted to 'function as its own patent office' the underlying purpose of the patent system would be subverted, the system itself destroyed").

[43]   Morton Salt 314 U.S. at 494.

[44]   Ibid.

[45]   See Raymond T. Nimmer & Murali Santhanam, *The Concept of Misuse in Copyright and Trademark Law: Searching for a Concept of Restraint*, in Patents, Copyrights, Trademarks and Literary Property Handbook Series, Order No. G4-4037, 524 PLI/PAT 397 (1998).

[46]   Giles S. Rich, *Infringement Under Section 271 of the Patent Act of 1952*, 14 FED. CIRCUIT B. J. 117, 133 (2005) (emphasis in original).

Morton Salt was decided together with *B.B. Chemical*.[47] In that case, the patentee owned a process for reinforcing shoe soles. The defendant sold unpatented components used in the process which had no substantial noninfringing uses. The Court found that the patentee was not using its patent to monopolize the market for the unpatented product because there were no substantial noninfringing uses, and therefore the patentee was not guilty of misuse.

B.   The Mercoid Cases and §271(d) of the Patent Act

Yet only two years after the *Morton Salt* judgment decision separating misuse and antitrust doctrine, patent misuse became infused with antitrust analysis in the *Mercoid* decisions.[48] Misuse gradually melded with antitrust jurisprudence as courts began to hold that conduct that represented patent misuse also violated the antitrust laws. As courts attempted to balance IP rights and antitrust concerns, antitrust interests often prevailed. Against this backdrop, interviewees noted that throughout the 1960s and 1970s, the judiciary was active in expanding the scope of patent misuse. One practitioner interviewed noted that "In the 1970s, we were very active, being concerned about overbroad interpretations of patents . . ."[49] Commentators like William J. Nicoson attribute this development to the controversial decision in *Mercoid Corp. v. Minneapolis-Honeywell Regulator Co.* (*Mercoid II*).[50] *Mercoid II* and *Mercoid v. Mid-Continent Investment Co.* (*Mercoid I*) were related decisions.[51]

---

[47]   *B.B. Chemical Co. v. Ellis*, 314 U.S. 495 (1942).

[48]   Ibid. ("Almost immediately applications of the misuse doctrine became suffused with antitrust considerations"). Raymond Nimmer and Jeff Dodd note that: "Even though *Morton Salt* stated that it was not using antitrust principles, subsequent cases blend or equate competition law with the policies flowing from property law," Nimmer & Santhanam, *supra* n.45.

[49]   On file with author.

[50]   *Mercoid Corp. v. Minneapolis-Honeywell Regulator Co.*, 320 U.S. 680 (1944) (hereinafter "*Mercoid II*"). See Nicoson, *supra* note 25, at 85 (" . . . the Supreme Court seemed to confirm this intrusion of antitrust policy as the controlling element in applications of the patent misuse doctrine by its decision in *Mercoid Corp v. Minneapolis-Honeywell Regulator Co.*"). Roger Arar, *Redefining Copyright Misuse*, 81 COLUM. L. REV. 1291, 1298–302 (1981) ("Subsequent to *Morton Salt*, the relevance and applicability of antitrust principles in implementation of the patent-misuse defense was badly confused. A prime source of this confusion lay in a comment by Justice Douglas in *Mercoid Corp. v. Minneapolis-Honeywell Regulator Co.*, in which the Court seemingly grounded the patent-misuse doctrine on antitrust principles").

[51]   *Mercoid II*, 320 U.S. at 681. *Mercoid v. Mid-Continent Investment Co.*, 320 U.S. 661 (1944) (hereinafter "*Mercoid I*").

The dispute involved a patent held by Mid-Continent over a domestic heating system. Mid-Continent entered into an exclusive license with Honeywell. Royalties to Mid-Continent were based on the non-patented switches used in the system which it sold. These switches had no substantial noninfringing uses. Mid-Continent only licensed to those who bought switches from Honeywell. Mercoid made unlicensed switches, and its customers were accused of directly infringing Mid-Continent's patent. Mercoid was found to knowingly supply its customers with the switches and was found guilty of contributory infringement by the district court and the Seventh Circuit on appeal. Certiorari was granted in both cases.

In *Mercoid I*, the Court assumed that Mercoid was a contributory infringer but barred Mid-Continent from enforcing the patent because its licensing system constituted an attempt to extend the grant of the patent to unpatented devices. The Court could see no difference between parts with and without substantial noninfringing uses.[52] In *Mercoid II*, the Court went further and ruled that the antitrust laws, rather than patent law determined whether an attempt to bring unpatented goods within the protection of the patent was misuse.[53]

The *Mercoid* decisions were problematic for a number of reasons. The foremost of these was the basis for misuse. According to William Nicoson, uncertainty as to the exact basis upon which relief for infringement was denied "stems from the same failure throughout the opinion to separately identify the issues of misuse and antitrust violation."[54] As a stark example, the Court opined that "[t]he legality of any attempt to bring unpatented goods within the protection of the patent is measured by the antitrust laws not by the patent law."[55] Was the Court referring to the antitrust claim made by the infringer, or was it based on the infringement claim by the patentee? A clue may be found in the Court's observation that:

> the effort here made to control competition in this unpatented device plainly violates the antitrust laws ... It follows that [the infringer] is entitled to be relieved against the consequences of those acts. It likewise follows that [the patentee] may not obtain from a court of equity any decree which directly or

---

52   Ibid. at 667 (It was irrelevant whether the stoker switch was "the heart of the invention" or the "advance in the art," since the separate element had not been claimed as the invention, it is not protected by the patent monopoly "when dealt with separately").

53   *Mercoid II*, 320 U.S. at 684 (holding that attempts to control competition in the unpatented switch plainly violated the antitrust laws).

54   Nicoson, *supra* note 25, at 86.

55   *Mercoid II*, 320 U.S. at 684.

indirectly helps it to subvert the public policy which underlies the grant of its patent.[56]

Thus, it appears that the answer is "both." Nicoson points out that the opinions of the dissenting four Justices in *Mercoid II* may hint at "their misgivings at the antitrust tenor" of the case.[57] Indeed, Justice Roberts, wrote in his partial dissent that the patentee's inability to recover was "a pure question of the extent of the right of exclusion conferred by the patent statute. It nowise involves the antitrust acts."[58] Further, Professors Areeda and Hovenkamp observe that the use of "power" and "monopoly" in antitrust and misuse very likely contributed to the virtual merger of misuse law into antitrust law in the 1940s. When the antitrust laws spoke of unlawful "extension" of power they were concerned with greater amounts of economic monopoly power. By contrast, patent misuse doctrine was more concerned with the appropriate boundaries and uses of the patent.[59]

The second controversial aspects of the *Mercoid* decisions lay in their virtual extinguishing of the contributory infringement doctrine. The Court later summarized its decisions in the *Mercoid* cases as holding that "any attempt to control the market for unpatented goods would constitute patent misuse, even if those goods had no use outside a patented invention."[60] Until the *Mercoid* cases, the law had condemned suits against those who dealt in goods with substantial noninfringing uses, such as the salt tablets in *Morton Salt* or the dry ice in *Carbice*. None had involved an unpatented component integral to the functioning of the patented system, with consequently no substantial noninfringing uses. The *Mercoid* Court, however, refused to distinguish the two. Patentees, in its view, could not use contracts to circumvent the limitations placed upon

---

[56]   Ibid. at 681.

[57]   Nicoson, *supra* note 25, at 87.

[58]   *Mercoid I*, 320 U.S. at 674.

[59]   10 Philip E. Areeda & Herbert Hovenkamp, ANTITRUST LAW ¶1781 (2d ed. 2004).

[60]   *Dawson Chem. Co. v. Rohm & Haas Co.*, 448 U.S. 176, 195 (1980), *citing Mercoid I*, 320 U.S. 661. Tom Arnold & Louis Riley, *Contributory Infringement and Patent Misuse: The Enactment of §271 and its Subsequent Amendments*, 76 J. PAT. & TRADEMARK OFF. SOC'Y 357, 358–59 (1994) ("By the early 1940s the roller-coaster began its rapid descent when the defense of patent misuse reared its head and spread like an epidemic virus. Misuse became the alleged infringers' preferred defense to the claim of contributory infringement. Patent misuse trumped contributory infringement without fail. Indeed, merely filing suit for contributory infringement constituted misuse of a patent which rendered the patent unenforceable").

patent rights.[61] The Court saw the Mid-Continent's conduct as a contest "solely over unpatented wares which go into the patented product", rather than a struggle to protect its rights in the combination patent.[62] Mid-Continent's patent was being used impermissibly to protect the market for a device on which no patent had been granted. Irrespective of whether the stoker switch was "the heart of the invention" or the "advance in the art," since the separate element had not been claimed as the invention, it was not protected by the patent monopoly "when dealt with separately."[63]

In the wake of the *Mercoid* cases, there was disagreement whether patentees should be allowed to control the sale of non-patented goods. Even amongst those who allowed patentees to control those sales, there was disagreement whether a line should be drawn between staple goods, which could be used in ways unconnected with the invention, and non-staple goods, for which there was no substantial noninfringing use. At that time, the scales were weighed heavily in favor of antitrust plaintiffs, leading Justice Stewart to observe that the "sole consistency that I can find is that . . . the Government always wins."[64] This debate turned upon where one saw the scope of the patent to end. The *Mercoid* decisions, along with the Antitrust Division of the Department of Justice at that time, took the view it ended with the invention itself.[65] Competition in the submarket for nonstaple goods was destroyed.

---

[61]   *Mercoid I*, 320 U.S. at 666 ("When the patentee ties something else to his invention, he acts only by virtue of his right as the owner of property to make contracts concerning it and not otherwise. He then is subject to all the limitations upon that right which the general law imposes upon such contracts. The contract is not saved by anything in the patent laws because it relates to the invention. If it were, the mere act of the patentee could make the distinctive claim of the patent attach to something which does not possess the quality of invention. Then the patent would be diverted from its statutory purpose and become a ready instrument for economic control in domains where the anti-trust acts or other laws not the patent statutes define the public policy").

[62]   Ibid. at 666.

[63]   Ibid. at 667.

[64]   *United States v. Von's Grocery Co.*, 384 U.S. 270, 301 (1966).

[65]   See, e.g., *Rohm & Haas Co. v. Dawson Chem. Co.*, 599 F.2d 685, 695–706 (5th Cir. 1979) ("T. Hayward Brown, Chief of the Patent Litigation Unit, showed especial opposition to paragraph (d), which the Justice Department deemed a major and controversial change from then current misuse principles and, as such, inappropriate for inclusion in a codification"), *aff'd*, 448 U.S. 176, 207 (1980) ("In addition, Roy C. Hackley, Jr., Chief of the Patent Section, Department of Justice, made an appearance on behalf of the Department. He took the position that statutory clarification of the scope of contributory infringement was desirable, but he warned Congress against using language that might 'permit illegal extension of the patent monopoly.' 1948 Hearings, at 69. On this ground he opposed the portion

This was a sign of the times, for the 1940s also saw a period where the Court began to hold that market power was presumed from the mere existence of a patent right.[66] The *A.B. Dick* court took the view that it encompassed everything connected with the use of the patent. Justice Douglas, who wrote the *Mercoid* opinions was described by C. Paul Rogers III as believing that "'big is bad' and that the Sherman Act was designed to make illegal significant concentrations of economic power, no matter how attained."[67] With respect to patents, Justice Douglas was "quite distrustful of the monopoly power granted a patent holder and favored a quite restrictive view of the patent holders rights" and "his concern was with the effect of the patent monopoly on small businesses."[68]

Others, such as Giles Rich and others like him, recognized that the view in *Mercoid* created an anti-patent environment which was not conducive to innovation, and took the middle ground, allowing the patentee some control over those unpatented or unpatentable goods that would be used to infringe the patent.[69] Rich recognized that while some courts limited *Mercoid* to factually similar license agreements, others took a more expansive view, so that that even the filing of an action for contributory infringement, by threatening to deter competition in unpatented materials, could

---

of the proposed bill that included language substantially similar to what is now § 271(d)").

[66] See, e.g., *Int'l Salt Co. v. United States*, 332 U.S. 392 (1947).

[67] C. Paul Rogers III, *The Antitrust Legacy of Justice William O. Douglas*, 56 CLEV. ST. L. REV. 895, 896, 936 (2008).

[68] Ibid. (Early in his tenure, Douglas was in the mainstream of the New Deal Court in limiting the scope of the patent privilege. He voted with a unanimous Court in *Ethyl Gasoline Corp. v. United States*, which outlawed a scheme of patent holders fixing resale prices of their product throughout the country. Then, two years later, Douglas voted with a still-united Court in three patent-antitrust cases, writing the opinion in *United States v. Masonite Corp.* There the Court found unlawful price fixing arising from a patent holder's uniform licensing agreements to so-called del credere agents authorized to sell the patented product. Douglas wrote that "Since patents are privileges restrictive of a free economy," the rights of patent holders "must be strictly construed . . . ")

[69] *Rohm & Haas Co.*, 599 F.2d at 699–700. Citing to Patent Law Codification and Revision: Hearings on H.R.3760 Before Subcomm. No. 3 of the House Comm. on the Judiciary, 82d Cong., 1st Sess. (1951) at 157–59 (Giles Rich, the chief draftsman of the contributory infringement provisions explained "that the statutory solution was designed to avoid restricting competition in items that were staples, while at the same time allowing patentees to deal in certain materially important unpatented elements and to sue competitors therein without being thrown out of court on grounds of misuse").

supply evidence of patent misuse.[70] This uncertainty made it difficult for patent attorneys to advise clients on the legality of their licensing agreements. They recognized that if both misuse and contributory infringement doctrines are to coexist, each had to have some a sphere of operation with which the other does not interfere. Legislation was needed to restore some scope to contributory infringement.[71] It was this aspect of the decision, which evoked a legislative reversal by Congress when it passed the 1952 Patent Act.

Judge Rich's view carried the day and was eventually adopted in the 1952 Patent Act after advancing his proposal in three successive Congresses as 35 U.S.C. § 271(d).[72] As Professor Christopher Leslie notes, "Congress responded to the *Mercoid* opinion by codifying the patent misuse defense and by specifying circumstances that do not constitute misuse."[73] The thinking was that patentees exploiting their inventions within their claimed scope should be allowed to fully reap profits which would have accrued to them since no separate market exists for nonstaple goods other than for use with the patented product or process.[74] Further

---

[70]   See, e.g., *Stroco Prods., Inc. v. Mullenbach*, 67 U.S.P.Q. 168, 170 (S.D. Cal. 1944).

[71]   *Rohm and Haas Co.*, 599 F.2d at 698. (Intriguingly, the Fifth Circuit in *Dawson* record that

"There was apparently no debate on the House floor regarding the 1952 codification and scant public debate in the Senate. An interchange in the Senate shortly before the bill was passed has often been cited as evidence that section 271 did not overturn the result in *Mercoid*. In response to a question by Senator Saltonstall about the purpose of the bill, whether it changed the law in any way or merely codified it, Senator McCarran, Chairman of the Judiciary Committee that had been in charge of the bill in the Senate, stated: 'It codifies the present patent laws,' 98 Cong. Rec. 9323 (July 4, 1952). The force of this exchange is mitigated, however, by Senator McCarran's introduction a few moments later of a short prepared statement that in part states: 'In view of the decisions of the Supreme Court and others as well as trial by practice and error there have been some changes in the law of patents as it now exists and some new terminology used.'")

[72]   See *Dawson Chem. Co. v. Rohm & Haas Co.*, 448 U.S. 176, 204-12, 100 S. Ct. 2601, 2617-21, 65 L. Ed. 2d 696 (1980). Section 271(d) statutorily exempts from misuse three types of conduct by the patentee: allowing patentees to make and sell nonstaple goods used in connection with his invention, licensing or otherwise allowing another to perform otherwise infringing acts, and bringing suit without fear that his doing so will be regarded as an unlawful attempt to suppress competition.

[73]   Leslie, *supra* note 6, at 57.

[74]   Giles Rich in the 1949 hearings remarked that "It is crystal clear, when you have thoroughly studied this subject, that the only way you can make contributory infringement operative again as a doctrine, is to make some exceptions to the

as the Court later observed, the article may be 'unpatented' only because of the technical rules of patent claiming.[75] Allowing patentees latitude to claim against contributory infringers simply places the commercial value of an invention in its proper real-world context. In the case of non-patented staple, allowing the patentee to leverage its exclusive rights into the market for the unpatented staple would foreclose competition.[76]

Despite the passage of the 1952 Act, the *Mercoid* decisions remain good law in other aspects. As the District Court in *Rohm & Haas Co. v. Dawson Chem. Co., Inc.* noted:

> Neither the Supreme Court nor the United States Court of Appeals for the Fifth Circuit has construed § 271(d) to overrule the result in the *Mercoid* decisions. Although neither of these Courts has confronted this question in the precise context of a *Mercoid*-type misuse, both have continued to cite the *Mercoid* decisions as good authority. Certainly the enactment of § 271 quelled the broad dictum in the *Mercoid* decisions. However, if it likewise overruled the result in *Mercoid*, it is incongruous that Mercoid is nevertheless still cited as good law.[77]

The Supreme Court's *Dawson* decision is the leading case on the effects of the 1952 Act on Mercoid.[78] It stands for the proposition that "although patent misuse remains a viable defense, a patentee is not *per se* guilty of misuse merely because he extends his patent to cover unpatented goods."[79] Section 271(d) protected patentees from allegations of misuse where suing contributory infringers would result in an otherwise objectionable anticompetitive effect in the market for nonstaple goods. As the Court held: "the provisions of § 271(d) effectively confer upon the patentee, as a lawful adjunct of his patent rights, a limited power to exclude others from competition in nonstaple goods. A patentee may sell a nonstaple article

---

misuse doctrine and say that certain acts shall not be misuse. Then contributory infringement, which is there all the time, becomes operative again. Hearings on H.R. 3866 before Subcommittee No. 4 of the House Committee on the Judiciary, 81st Cong., 1st Sess., 11 (1949) at 13–14.

[75]   *Dawson Chemical Co. v. Rohm & Haas Co.*, 448 U.S. 176, 198 (1980).

[76]   *Rohm & Haas Co.*, 599 F.2d at 695–706.

[77]   *Rohm & Haas Co. v. Dawson Chem. Co., Inc.*, No. 74-H-790, 191 U.S.P.Q. 691, 704 (S.D. Tex. 1976).

[78]   Tom Arnold & Louis Riley, *Contributory Infringement and Patent Misuse: The Enactment of § 271 and its Subsequent Amendments*, 76 J. PAT. & TRADEMARK OFF. SOC'Y 357, 375 (1994) ("The leading case in the area of 1952 Patent Code contributory infringement, patent misuse and its effects on Mercoid is Rohm & Haas").

[79]   Ibid. at 375–76.

himself while enjoining others from marketing that same good without his authorization."[80]

This explains why cases studied in this book continue to cite the *Mercoid* cases controlling precedents for the proposition that "the policy underlying the misuse doctrine is designed to prevent a patentee from projecting the *economic* effect of his admittedly valid grant beyond the limits of his legal monopoly" despite its apparent demise in the halls of Congress.[81] However, returning to the relationship between misuse and antitrust after the *Mercoid* cases, lower courts and later Supreme Court decisions relied upon antitrust policy almost exclusively.[82] With each successive case in that era, the equitable essence of misuse became calcified in antitrust law, and the defense of misuse became subsumed into an antitrust counterclaim.[83] By the 1950s, an antitrust violation itself became a defense to infringement without having to consider the defense misuse.[84] In 1957, the Supreme Court once again considered misuse in *United States Gypsum Co. v. National Gypsum Co.*[85] The United States government had earlier charged the parties in the suit with conspiracy to restrain commerce under the Sherman Act. U.S. Gypsum stopped receiving royalties, something later modified by decree. U.S. Gypsum sued in an Iowa district court against its codefendants, including National Gypsum, to recover royalties lost during that period. The district court's opinion was appealed to the Supreme Court, which found that violation of the Sherman Act during that period would have barred recovery on the infringement claim.[86] Nonetheless, some courts continued to apply *Morton Salt*, eschewing a

---

[80]   *Dawson Chem. Co. v. Rohm & Haas Co.*, 448 U.S. 176, 201 (1980).

[81]   See *Panther Pumps & Equip. Co. v. Hydrocraft, Inc.*, 468 F.2d 225, 231 (7th Cir. 1972); see also *Compton v. Metal Prods.*, Inc., 453 F.2d 38, 46 (4th Cir. 1971) ("The patent law does not give Joy this power, and we think that any attempt to control unpatented augers would run afoul of the antitrust laws").

[82]   See, e.g., *Automatic Radio Mfg. Co. v. Hazeltine Research Inc.*, 539 U.S. 827 (1950).

[83]   Nicoson, *supra* note 25, at 88 ("Particularly in cases involving antitrust counterclaims, separation of misuse concepts from proven antitrust violations appear superficially to be the proper concern only of purists").

[84]   See, e.g., *Baker-Commack Hoisery, Mills Inc.v. Davis Co.*, 181 F.2d 550, 568–73 (4th Cir. 1950); *Hazeltine Research Inc. v. Superior Moire Co.*, 237 F.2d 283, 290–94 (3d Cir. 1956); *Kobe Inc. v. Dempsey Pump Co.*, 198 F.2d 416, 418 (10th Cir. 1952) *cert. denied*, 3324 U.S. 837 (1952).

[85]   *United States Gypsum Co. v. National Gypsum Co.*, 352 U.S. 457 (1957).

[86]   Ibid. at 472. ("The only patent misuse that has ever been established in this long-drawn-out litigation is concerted price fixing under the former patent licenses ... the 1950 holding of this court was not an adjudication of other violations.")

requirement that the defendant show anticompetitive effects in order to raise a misuse defense.[87]

Beginning in the mid-1970s, interviewees for this study observed that a movement away from finding misuse was precipitated by a shift in economic thinking toward less judicial intervention and a greater reliance on the free market to iron out anticompetitive kinks caused by patent rights. This shift occurred during the time when the high-technology and entertainment industries, which were IP dependent, became a considerable focus of the economy.

This trend continued during the Reagan Administration when the Antitrust Division under William Baxter began a purposeful reform of the treatment of IP rights.[88] Baxter argued that IP owners should get maximum legitimate rewards for their efforts, and the pro-competitive benefits of licensing needs to be properly considered. He also suggested that Congress should curtail the ability of courts to find IP licenses as *per se* illegal. But perhaps most relevantly, he argued that there was a need to define the contours of misuse in order to mitigate danger that courts may vent hostility toward IP and chill innovation. At the same time, political conservatism in the 1980s compounded the Supreme Court's doctrine of nonintervention. The Reagan Administration reduced the resources available to the FTC and Department of Justice. The Supreme Court had also begun to retreat from a *per se* approach to vertical non-price restraints. Since many of the items of the "Nine No-Nos" list were vertical non-price restraints, the "Nine No-Nos" became inconsistent with antitrust law as interpreted by the courts and were gradually replaced by the rule of reason approach. Further, the Supreme Court raised evidentiary requirements for antitrust injury. For example in *Matsushita Electrical Industrial Co. v. Zenith Radio Corp* 475 U.S. 574 (1986), the Court demanded economically rational evidence of harm, rather than circumstantial evidence. In *Leegin Creative Leather Products, Inc. v. PSKS Inc.* 551 U.S. 877, 895 (2007), the Supreme Court while recognizing that *per se* rules "decrease administrative costs", acknowledged that they can also increase costs by "prohibiting procompetitive conduct the antitrust laws should encourage", "promoting frivolous suits against legitimate practices" if applied to practices that were not "manifestly anticompetitive."

---

[87]   *Berlenbach v. Anderson & Thompson Ski Co.*, 329 F.2d 782, 784 (9th Cir. 1964) ("In view of the history and policy of the defense of patent misuse we find no merit in appellant's contentions that the proof of substantial lessening of competition is a prerequisite to finding patent misuse. Neither do we feel that the cases cited in the margin overrule the Morton Salt case, as appellant suggests").

[88]   Christopher Leslie, ANTITRUST LAW AND INTELLECTUAL PROPERTY RIGHTS 42 (2011) at 42.

Robert H. Bork, Richard Posner and others from the Chicago School influenced the Court and caused it to re-evaluate its attitudes toward vertical non-price restraints in the 1970s. In *Continental TV v. GTE Sylvania*, the Court held that such restraints should be considered under the rule of reason rather than a *per se* approach. Over time, the antitrust laws themselves were reformulated with the express mandate to protect competition and not competitors. Hence, all antitrust plaintiffs both public and private would have to show an injury to market competition. This paradigm shift meant that conduct that led to firms exiting the marketplace could be justified by gains in economic efficiency.

C. USM: Misuse as Antitrust

Professor Robert Merges commented that "[t]he thinking [was] that antitrust has evolved a 'precise' methodology for ascertaining when improper market leverage is being used by a patentee . . . and that the relatively imprecise 'equitable' doctrine of misuse only adds confusion and uncertainty to the scene."[89] Perhaps the most vocal proponent of a rule of reason type analysis has been Judge Richard Posner. In 1981 the Seventh Circuit in *USM Corp. v. SPS Technologies, Inc.* had to consider whether a patentee who included a differential royalty rate in the license agreement had misused its patent.[90] In refusing to find misuse, Judge Posner wrote that "[t]he patentee who insists on limiting the freedom of his purchaser or licensee—whether to price, to use complementary inputs of the purchaser's choice, or to make competing items—will have to compensate the purchaser for the restriction by charging a lower price for the use of the patent."[91] In a well-known passage, he wrote:

> The [misuse] doctrine arose before there was any significant body of federal antitrust law, and reached maturity long before that law (a product very largely of free interpretation of unclear statutory language) attained its present broad scope. Since the antitrust laws as currently interpreted reach every practice that could impair competition substantially, it is not easy to define a separate role for a doctrine also designed to prevent an anticompetitive practice—the abuse of a patent monopoly. One possibility is that the doctrine of patent misuse, unlike antitrust law, condemns any patent licensing practice that is even trivially anticompetitive, at least if it has no socially beneficial effects. . . . But apart from the conventional applications of the doctrine we have found no cases

---

[89]   See Robert P. Merges, *Reflections on Current Legislation Affecting Patent Misuse*, 70 J. PAT. & TRADEMARK OFF. SOC'Y 793, 795 (1988).

[90]   *USM Corp. v. SPS Technologies, Inc.*, 694 F.2d 505, 510 (7th Cir. 1982).

[91]   Ibid.

where standards different from those of antitrust law were actually applied to yield different results.[92]

Judge Posner then turned to the patent misuse defense, which he concluded "must be evaluated under antitrust principles."[93] This movement toward reduced government intervention in the economic activities of patentees in misuse cases is reinforced by the embracing of a dynamic rather than static view of antitrust law by courts and antitrust enforcers.[94] The static view of antitrust analysis focuses on price competition and short run-consumer welfare, and tends to promote a more interventionist approach to antitrust oversight of the commercial strategy of patentees. In contrast, the dynamic analysis tends to focus on long-term protection from competitive pressures in order to preserve the incentive to innovate. In three cases, *General Dynamics Corp.*, *Aspen Skiing* and *Microsoft* the courts considered both static and dynamic dimensions of antitrust law, favoring a dynamic approach in its decisions.[95] Critics contend that patent misuse is therefore an "anachronism".[96]

But Judge Posner's arguments beg the question why could courts not simply have relied upon preexisting antitrust laws? The Sherman Act, after

---

[92] Ibid. at 511.

[93] Ibid. at 512.

[94] *Data Gen. Corp. v. Grumman Sys. Support Corp.*, 36 F.3d 1147, n. 64 (1st Cir. 1994) *abrogated* on other grounds by *Reed Elsevier, Inc. v. Muchnick*, 130 S. Ct. 1237 (2010) ("Wary of undermining the Sherman Act, however, we do not hold that an antitrust plaintiff can never rebut this presumption, for there may be rare cases in which imposing antitrust liability is unlikely to frustrate the objectives of the Copyright Act"); see generally 10 Areeda & Hovenkamp, *supra* note 59, at ¶2100.

[95] *United States v. General Dynamics Corp.*, 415 U.S. 486, 506 (1974) (noting that an assessment of concentration and market shares had to take into account indicia that change over time.); see, e.g., *United States v. Microsoft Corp.*, 253 F.3d 34, 59, 76 (D.C. Cir. 2001) (*en banc*) (observing that "Evidence of the intent behind the conduct of a monopolist is relevant to the extent it helps us understand the likely effect of the monopolist's conduct" and finding that documents authored by senior executives, which showed that "Microsoft's ultimate objective" was to thwart Java's threat to Microsoft's monopoly power in the market for operating systems, were probative of Microsoft's liability); *Aspen Skiing Co. v. Aspen Highlights Skiing Corp.*, 472 U.S. 585, 610 (1985) (observing that the defendant "elected to make an important change in a pattern of distribution that had originated in a competitive market and had persisted for several years" and that such conduct "support[ed] an inference that [the defendant] was not motivated by efficiency concerns and that it was willing to sacrifice short-run benefits and consumer goodwill in exchange for a perceived long-run impact on its smaller rival).

[96] Note, *Is the Patent Misuse Doctrine Obsolete?* 110 HARVARD L. REV. 1922, 1924 (1997).

all, was enacted in 1890, and by 1914, the Clayton Act, which the lower court of appeals in *Motion Picture Patents Co.* relied on to reach the same result was also available to the courts. It is possible that courts were unwilling to employ the antitrust laws, which were relatively new at that time. The debilitating remedy of treble damages and conviction as a felon were harsh outcomes for an antitrust violation. On the other hand, non-enforcement simply places the parties roughly in the position that they would have been in but for the misuse.[97] Professors Hovenkamp et al. have criticized the limited view of misuse Judge Posner proposed in *USM*. They note that:

> Judge Posner's concerns are legitimate from an economic standpoint. They do not fully reflect the law today, however. In part this is because patent misuse is not only about "monopolistic abuse," but also serves as an internal constraint on efforts to expand the patent system beyond its bounds. One might question whether the patent law needs such a constraint, but it seems clear that the courts intend to apply misuse doctrine to at least some sorts of conduct antitrust law would not reach.[98]

More fundamentally, it may be a leap of logic to conclude that just because old Supreme Court precedent employing the *per se* approach fell out of favor, it automatically means that old misuse precedent is also bad because courts during that time often used similar rhetoric when talking about patent "monopolies." Joel Bennett observed that "Judge Posner, in the foregoing analysis, ignored a long line of Supreme Court cases holding that there was no need to establish substantial anticompetitive effects in order to prove patent misuse."[99] A leading commentary notes that the two bodies of law come from different sources and are concerned about different things.[100] Antitrust policy is concerned about economic monopoly power and of patentees using that power to raise prices and stifle output.[101] In contrast, misuse is concerned about the appropriate boundaries of the patent itself and the public domain.[102] However, the line between them is not a rigid one. Inappropriate extensions that violate patent policy can

---

[97]   *Am. Soc. of Mech. Engineers, Inc. v. Hydrolevel Corp.*, 456 U.S. 556, 575–76 (1982) ("It is true that antitrust treble damages were designed in part to punish past violations of the antitrust laws. But treble damages were also designed to deter future antitrust violations. Treble damages 'make the remedy meaningful by counterbalancing "the difficulty of maintaining a private suit" under the antitrust laws'").

[98]   See 1 Herbert Hovenkamp et al., IP AND ANTITRUST §3.2 (2010).

[99]   Joel R. Bennett, *Patent Misuse: Must an Alleged Infringer Prove an Antitrust Violation?*, 17 AIPLA Q.J. 1, 11–12 (1989).

[100]   See 10 Areeda & Hovenkamp, *supra* note 59, at ¶1781.

[101]   Ibid.

[102]   Ibid.

harm market competition which causes there to be cases where antitrust and misuse coexist. Similarly, antitrust is also concerned with dynamic efficiency, and dynamic efficiency is all about innovation. Antitrust takes a more cautious approach and requires strict proof of causation and harm and robust economic models. On the other hand, patent policy is concerned with how to manage a system that incentivizes the creation and dissemination of innovation. Innovation is difficult to quantify and the consequences of a patentee's actions can be difficult to predict, because while innovation can only be understood backwards; it must be lived forwards. This set-up means rewarding a lot of inventions which have no economic value because at the time the decision to patent is made, the value of that patent is uncertain. If patent examiners required the proof of commercial success that antitrust does, then the cotton gin, the electric light bulb or the Google search engine might not have been patentable.

One consequence of the changes resulting from antitrust-based thinking on the misuse landscape was that the influence of special interest groups has accelerated the influence of antitrust on misuse further. Professors Bohannan and Hovenkamp argue that "influence of special interests depends on the relative robustness of the model under which democratic policymakers work" and "when an area of enterprise is not well understood, lawmakers are more vulnerable to special interests."[103] Here they observe that: "[t]he history of competition and innovation policy shows more consensus about the nature of traditional competition than about the nature of innovation."[104] This is because "the basic outline of the requirements for competition [has] been well known for more than a century and claim a broad professional and policy consensus."[105] In contrast:

> When we ask instead what government policy will encourage the optimum amount of innovation, the answers become far less determinate and go much more to the extremes. To this day, the economics of innovation has no equivalent to formulations such as the robust, broadly applied neoclassical rule that under perfect competition price equals marginal cost. . . . About the best we can say is that the primary goal of IP policy should be to maximize net gains from innovation after all transaction costs have been paid. As such, it must balance the incentive value of exclusion against that of access to the developed technology and ideas of others. This may or may not require different decisions about patent term and scope in different industries.[106]

---

[103] Christina Bohannan & Herbert Hovenkamp, *IP and Antitrust: Reformation and Harm*, 51 B.C. L. Rev. 905, 924 (2010).
[104] Ibid.
[105] Ibid.
[106] Ibid. at 923–24.

In this landscape, they describe how pro-IP advocates were also getting better organized and better able to articulate their views persuasively to Congress and shape the governing laws as well as the attitude of those interpreting and enforcing those laws. One example is the detail in which the IP statutes have been written. All were carefully crafted with significant input from lobby groups. In contrast, they note than the antitrust statutes had far less detail, relaying only broad Congressional intent to the courts and leaving them to flesh out the contours of the law.[107] The sweeping trend of discarding old Supreme Court precedent and the advent of intensive lobbying by industries dependent on strong IP rights paled in comparison to another development which would radically change the doctrine of patent misuse. It was a new kind of court, an experimental court created especially for the adjudication of patent rights, the first of its kind anywhere in the world.

IV.   1982–PRESENT: *THE WINDSURFING* YEARS

A.   The Secret Circuit

In *The World is Flat: A Brief History of the Twenty-First Century*, *New York Times* columnist Thomas Friedman observed the positive correlation between IP protection and America's prosperity:

> We in the U.S. are the lucky beneficiaries of centuries of economic experimentation, and we are the experiment that has worked . . . the quality of American IP protection . . . further enhances and encourages people to come up with new ideas. In a flat world, there is a great incentive to develop a new product or process, because it can achieve global scale in a flash. But if you are the person who comes up with that new idea, you want your IP protected. No country respects and protects IP better than America . . . and as a result, a lot of innovators want to come here to work and lodge their IPs.[108]

---

[107]   Ibid. at 920 ("Congress apparently did not want to get involved in articulating a specific definition of competition or in determining which practices might promote or undermine it. Rather, it enacted a few general principles derived from the common law, and then left it largely to the courts to determine what practices violate them. By contrast, both the Patent Act and the Copyright Act are lengthy codes, describing in detail the kinds of rights they create and the remedies that are available to enforce them. Patents in particular are the subject of heavy regulation, mainly through the U.S. Patent and Trademark Office (the 'PTO')").

[108]   Thomas Friedman, THE WORLD IS FLAT: A BRIEF HISTORY OF THE TWENTY-FIRST CENTURY 246 (2005).

This sentiment, echoing from the halls of Congress to universities, company boardrooms and the living rooms of ordinary Americans seems almost trite today. In the last century, America led the world to higher levels of IP protection through multilateral and bilateral agreements.[109] Not coincidentally, it is also the world's greatest exporter of IP-protected products and services.[110] The belief that stronger rights facilitate the production of more works is deeply etched in the minds of Congress and the courts. Congress saw stronger patent rights as being directly linked to technological progress, and commentators saw a swing toward an "unabashed admiration of the property rights principles embodied in intellectual property systems."[111]

The Federal Circuit established in 1982, is unique among appellate courts in that its jurisdiction is determined by subject matter rather than geographical location. The Federal Circuit's case portfolio covers a number of areas including federal claims, veterans' claims, international trade dispute claims, and federal employment claims. It is, however, perhaps best known as the nation's patent court, with Congress conferring upon it exclusive appellate jurisdiction for patent infringement cases, including issues relating to misuse.[112] The Federal Circuit has also been dubbed "The Secret Circuit" because in the words of former Chief

---

[109] See Peter Yu, *The Global Intellectual Property Order and its Undetermined Future*, 1 WIPO J. 1, 28–29 (2009) ("Strong actors, in particular the US, but also the EU and Japan, are offering favourable market conditions to specific trading partners against concessions in the field of IP. . . . Apart from the possibly detrimental effects ensuing for individual countries, the tendency to move ahead on a bilateral level might also be a mere foreplay to a further turn of the spiral moving upwards to more and stronger protection: once a substantial portion of trading partners have agreed to observe the same standards as those enshrined in present US (or EU) legislation, there is no way back to a meaningful reduction of what appears as widely accepted standards").

[110] Aaron Schwabach, INTERNET AND THE LAW: TECHNOLOGY, SOCIETY, AND COMPROMISES 55 (2005).

[111] Charles F. Rule, *Patent-Antitrust Policy: Looking Back and Ahead*, 59 ANTITRUST L.J. 729, 729 (1991).

[112] See Federal Courts Improvement Act of 1982, Pub. L. No. 97–164, 96 Stat. 25, §§ 37–39 (codified as amended at 28 U.S.C. §1295 (2000)); Thomas F. Cotter, *Misuse*, 44 HOUS. L. REV. 901, 912 (2007) ("In 1982, Congress established the U.S. Court of Appeals for the Federal Circuit and charged that court with, among other things, hearing all appeals from federal district court judgments involving claims for patent infringement. The Federal Circuit therefore has taken the leading role in recent years in refining the contours of the patent misuse doctrine"). See Adelman et al., CASES AND MATERIALS ON PATENT LAW 15–17 (3d ed. 2009) (providing a comprehensive introductory history of the Federal Circuit).

Judge H. Robert Mayer "[t]he Court has been a relatively secret gem in the judiciary until recently. No other court permits judges to work only on matters of significance with an absolute minimum of tedium and routine."[113]

Perhaps more than any other appellate circuit court, the Federal Circuit sees itself as having a mandate for facilitating a market for patent rights. Throughout the 1980s there was a need for a unified approach to the nation's patent law. It had to draw upon disparate strands of prior case law to create an eclectic brand of patent law guided by the need for the commercial certainty so integral to a robust system of rights. It had to "[i]nject enough stability and certainty into the patent law for investors to see patents as reliable tools of business strategy,"[114] since, as Judge Newman articulately put it, "uncertainty is the enemy of innovation."[115] Reflecting on the development of the Federal Circuit, Professor John R. Thomas noted that:

> In its salad days, the Federal Circuit addressed this mandate by attempting to resolve inconsistencies in the nation's collective patent jurisprudence. Now that the initial housecleaning has come to a close, the court's mission has a different flavor. Certainty and predictability have become the watchwords of the day. Today it is quite clear that an antitrust claim at the Federal Circuit will fail,

---

[113] H. Robert Mayer, Foreword to Kristin L. Yohannon, THE UNITED STATES COURT OF APPEALS FOR THE FEDERAL CIRCUIT: A HISTORY 1990–2002, xxi–xxii (2004). See also Bruce D. Abramson, THE SECRET CIRCUIT: THE LITTLE KNOWN COURT WHERE THE RULES OF THE INFORMATION AGE UNFOLD 1 (2007) ("This book is about a court—the United States Court of Appeals for the Federal Circuit. . . . The very existence of such a court raises many questions: Why does it exist? What does it do? What goals should we ask it to achieve? How does it further the needs of a liberal society on the cusp of the information age? How can we assess its performance? Why don't we hear more about it? And perhaps above all: Why is it such a secret?").

[114] Abramson, ibid note 113, at 34 ("Though the Federal Circuit is more than just the 'patent court,' it is indeed the patent court. The court's founders assigned it several tasks, but its central mission was clear: Strengthen the patent system. Inject enough stability and certainty into the patent law for investors to see patents as reliable tools of business strategy."); Adelman et al., *supra* note 112, at 17 ("Since its creation, the Federal Circuit has sought to bring uniformity and predictability to patent law.").

[115] *In re Bilski*, 545 F.3d 943, 977, 995 (Fed. Cir. 2008) ("Although this uncertainty may invite some to try their luck in court, the wider effect will be a disincentive to innovation-based commerce. For inventors, investors, competitors, and the public, the most grievous consequence is the effect on inventions not made or not developed because of uncertainty as to patent protection. Only the successes need the patent right.").

that few innovations will fail to comprise patentable subject matter, and that a plaintiff-patentee basing his or her infringement theory solely on the doctrine of equivalents ought to reconsider its case. The Federal Circuit's continuing drive for doctrinal stability within the patent law has been advanced largely through the mechanism of adjudicative rule formalism.[116]

The Federal Circuit's views of refusals to license and injunctive relief show that it is willing to stand apart from the other circuits, even where its jurisdictional mandate is unclear. One example where the Federal Circuit for uncertainty may be seen is in its view of refusals to license. The position in the First and Ninth Circuits is that while patentees may have legitimate business justifications for refusing to license their patents, that presumption is certainly rebuttable.[117] In contrast, the Federal Circuit's position is that the patentee's refusal to license could never amount to an antitrust violation regardless of the reason for the refusal, even if the refusal has an anticompetitive effect, "so long as that anticompetitive effect is not illegally extended beyond the statutory patent grant."[118] This would only happen in the case of fraud on the patent office, sham petitioning or extending its patent beyond the scope of the grant in some other way.[119] A joint report by the FTC and DOJ reported panelists criticizing the Federal

---

[116] John R. Thomas, *Formalism at the Federal Circuit*, 52 AM. U. L. REV. 771, 794 (2003).

[117] See *Data Gen. Corp. v. Grumman Sys. Support Corp.*, 36 F.3d 1147, 1187, n.64 (1st Cir. 1994) (holding that a unilateral refusal to license does not violate Section 2, except possibly in "rare cases" in which the antitrust plaintiff can rebut a presumption that the defendant was motivated by a valid business justification); see also *Image Technical Servs. v. Eastman Kodak Co.*, 125 F.3d 1195, 1218–20 (9th Cir. 1997) (holding that the defendant had lacked a legitimate business justification for its refusal, and therefore was liable under Section 2).

[118] *In re Independent Serv. Org. Antitrust Litig.*, 203 F.3d 1322, 1327 (Fed. Cir. 2000). By comparison, the FTC and DOJ's position is that while "mere" refusals to license patents were not prohibited, conditional refusals to license by firms with monopoly power were subject to antitrust scrutiny. U.S. Dep't of Justice & Fed. Trade Comm., ANTITRUST ENFORCEMENT AND INTELLECTUAL PROPERTY RIGHTS: PROTECTING INNOVATION AND COMPETITION 30 (2007).

[119] *In re Indep. Serv. Orgs. Antitrust Litig*, 203 F.3d at 1325–28. See also *Intergraph Corp. v. Intel Corp.*, 195 F.3d 1346, 1356–62 (Fed. Cir. 1999) (holding that Intel's refusal to license proprietary information with Intergraph did not violate the essential facilities doctrine, constitute an unlawful refusal to deal, or violate Section 2 in any other way); *SCM Corp. v. Xerox Corp.*, 463 F. Supp. 983, 1010–15 (D. Conn. 1978) (refusing to impose damages liability upon the defendant for lost profits because of its refusal to license), *aff'd*, 645 F.2d 1195, 1206 (2d Cir. 1981).

Circuit's decision in CSU which "narrowly construed the circumstances of antitrust liability can arise for a refusal to license. These circumstances— illegal tying, fraud on the U.S. Patent and Trademark Office, and sham litigation—provided little guidance, according to panelists, because they are independent bases for antitrust liability."[120] Similarly, former FTC Chairman Robert Pitofsky was vocally concerned that the Federal Circuit's approach to antitrust law "could be read to say that the invocation of IP rights settles the matter, except in [some exceptional] narrow situations . . . regardless of the effect of the refusal to deal on competition . . . [which] has disturbing implications for the future of antitrust in high-technology industries".[121]

More recently the Federal Circuit held that its own law controls the grant or denial of preliminary injunctions exclusively.[122] The panel opinion reversed the lower court on the basis that it had applied a higher "clear and substantial" likelihood of success on the merits standard as required under the Second Circuit law rather than the Federal Circuit's lower standard of a preponderance of the evidence.[123] In criticizing the opinion, Professor Dennis Crouch concludes that "*eBay* places this notion in serious question" because "[a] major element of *eBay* is the Supreme Court's suggestion that the law of injunctive relief in patent cases should be the same law that is applied in other areas of law."[124]

It seems reasonable to surmise that some judges at the Federal Circuit may display an institutional predilection toward stronger and more certain patent rights, and that this view may cause them to eschew defenses like misuse, which circumscribe those rights. For example in *Princo*, the dissent noted that:

---

[120]   U.S. Dep't of Justice & Fed. Trade Comm., *supra* note 118, at 5.

[121]   See Robert Pitofsky, *Challenges of the New Economy: Issues at the Intersection of Antitrust and IP*, remarks at the American Antitrust Institute's conference: An Agenda for Antitrust in the 21st Century (June 15, 2000), available at: http://www.ftc.gov/speeches/pitofsky/000615speech.shtm.

[122]   *Revision Military, Inc. v. Balboa Mfg. Co.*, 700 F.3d 524 (Fed. Cir. 2012).

[123]   Ibid. at 526. ("Substantive matters of patent infringement are unique to patent law, and thus the estimated likelihood of success in establishing infringement is governed by Federal Circuit law. Revision need not meet the Second Circuit's heightened 'clear or substantial likelihood' standard, but rather the Federal Circuit's standard of whether success is more likely than not.")

[124]   Dennis Crouch, *Federal-circuit-ism: Defining the Relationship between the Federal Circuit and its Regional Sister Courts*, PATENTLY-O (Nov 29, 2012), available at: http://www.patentlyo.com/patent/2012/11/federal-circuit-ism-defining-the-relationship-between-the-federal-circuit-and-its-regional-sister-courts.html.

The majority declines to give the patent misuse doctrine significant scope because it "is in derogation of statutory patent rights against infringement." Evidently the majority thinks it appropriate to emasculate the doctrine so that it will not provide a meaningful obstacle to patent enforcement. . . . Indeed, the majority goes so far as to suggest that the misuse doctrine be eliminated entirely.[125]

This view may also have informed the majority's analysis in *Princo* that misuse is only found when "the conduct in question restricts the use of that patent and does so in one of the specific ways that have been held also to be outside the otherwise *broad* scope of the patent grant."[126] Professors Hovenkamp et al. observe that:

More recently, the creation of the United States Court of Appeals for the Federal Circuit in 1982 has reduced the importance of patent misuse doctrine. In a series of important cases, the Federal Circuit cut back on the scope of patent misuse. The court imposed substantial new hurdles on accused infringers seeking to demonstrate misuse, and confined its findings of misuse primarily to conduct that also violated the antitrust laws.[127]

The Federal Circuit's attempt to cabin misuse is consistent with Professor Thomas' observation that:

Patent lawyers prefer rules. Patent lawyers draft the exclusionary rules that are patent claims, and then subject those rules to high-stakes litigation. They also bear the consequences when the rules are imprecise or of inappropriate scope. No wonder, then, that the patent bar has long demanded more rules and fewer standards in judicial decision-making.[128]

Bruce Abramson has also suggested that the Federal Circuit's institutional bias toward robust and certain patent rights may make it less suitable than other appellate courts to apply antitrust analysis to the exercise of patent rights. Judge Lourie in *Nobelpharma* created "Federal Circuit antitrust law" when he held that Federal Circuit law applied where the case involved patent issues within its exclusive jurisdiction, and that antitrust claims arising as counterclaims in patent infringement cases would be

---

[125]   *Princo Corp. v. Int'l Trade Comm'n*, 616 F.3d 1318, 1342 (Fed. Cir. 2010) *cert. denied*, 131 S. Ct. 2480 (2011).

[126]   See *Princo*, 616 F.3d at 1329 (emphasis added).

[127]   1 Hovenkamp et al., *supra* note 98, at §3.2.

[128]   John R. Thomas, *Formalism at the Federal Circuit*, 52 Am. U. L. Rev. 771, 794–96 (2003).

determined by Federal Circuit law rather than the law of regional circuits as well.[129] Abramson voiced his concern over this development, noting that:

> Scholars could only wonder, though whether Lourie's announcement was tantamount to a fox announcing that it would guard the henhouse. The Federal Circuit's raison d'être was the strengthening of patent rights. Did we really want a court widely perceived as the champion of patents refereeing potential conflicts between patent law and antitrust law? That might have sounded like a good idea in the Chicagoan heyday, but by 1998 that day had come and gone. Was it still a good idea? . . . The Federal Circuit seemed mired in a 1980s Chicago School view of the world: Patentees may use valid patents as they see fit.[130]

A court's view of patents based on a property of liability rule informs its view of patent misuse in another way. The refusal to grant an injunction has been viewed as a form of compulsory license.[131] Judges with this view are conceivably more concerned with the effects of finding patent misuse than the refusal to grant an injunction. By rendering a patent unenforceable, patent misuse makes the patent owner even worse off because the owner does not even get a shot at the reasonable royalties or damages that would accrue to a successful patent plaintiff in lieu of an injunction. The Federal Circuit seems to think of patent rights through the lens of property rules, rather than liability rules.[132] Under the lens of property rules, the patent owner is entitled to deny access to its technology. Liability rules, in contrast, "confer a lesser degree of protection that is akin to tort law: the right to collect damages caused by another's intrusion."[133] As the majority noted, the concern was that:

> In the licensing context, the doctrine limits a patentee's right to impose conditions on a licensee that exceed the scope of the patent right. Because patent

---

[129]   *Nobelpharma AB v. Implant Innovations*, 141 F.3d 1059, 1061–63. (Fed. Cir. 1998). See also Abramson, *supra* note 113, at 296, 298.

[130]   Abramson, *supra* note 113, at 296, 298.

[131]   See Mark A. Lemley, *The Economic Irrationality of Patent Misuse*, 78 CAL. L. REV. 1599, 1619 (1990) ("In effect, the patent misuse doctrine creates a scheme of royalty-free compulsory licensing where a patentee is guilty of misuse"). Judges such as Chief Judge Rader have thumbed down even the use of on-going royalties rather than lost profits because the former would amount to a compulsory license. *Paice LLC v. Toyota Motor Corp.* 504 F.3d 1293, 1316 (Fed. Cir. 2007) ("calling a compulsory license an 'ongoing royalty' does not make it any less a compulsory license").

[132]   See generally Guido Calabresi & A. Douglas Melamed, *Property Rules, Liability Rules and Inalienability: One View of the Cathedral*, 85 HARV. L. REV. 1089 (1972) (discussing the distinction between property and liability rules).

[133]   Adelman et al., *supra* note 112, at 840.

misuse is a judge-made doctrine that is in derogation of statutory patent rights against infringement, this court has not applied the doctrine of patent misuse expansively.[134]

To be sure, many on the Federal Circuit view patents more as a real property right than a privilege. Bruce Abramson notes that:

> When issues like patent misuse and antitrust *force* the court to consider behavioral effects and the underlying policy implications, the Federal Circuit mouths suitable analytic inquires and balancing tests. When it applies those tests, however, all of its rulings seem to fall on one side of the scale. Why? Perhaps because rulings that recognize patents as property and protect the rights of property owners surely fall within the Federal Circuit's bailiwick, while rulings that restrict the rights of property owners under certain circumstances risk injecting impermissible policy considerations into the law. Only the latter set *may* overstep the court's legitimate boundaries. Why risk it? Better to play it safe whenever an institutional boundary comes into view.[135]

In contrast, the Supreme Court in *eBay v. MercExchange*, seems to lean more toward viewing patent rights through the lens of liability rules. In the context of granting enjoining patent infringements, the Court noted that:

> According to the Court of Appeals, this statutory right to exclude alone justifies its general rule in favor of permanent injunctive relief. 401 F.3d, at 1338. But the creation of a right is distinct from the provision of remedies in violations of that right. . . . Just as the District Court erred in its categorical denial of injunctive relief, the Court of Appeals erred in its categorical grant of such relief.[136]

A possible reason for the Supreme Court's caution was suggested by Guido Calabresi and Doug Melamed who observed that, "[i]f we were to give victims a property entitlement not to be accidentally injured we would have to require all who engage in activities that may injure individuals to negotiate with them before an accident."[137] In an environment where firms have to navigate through a plethora of patent thickets to commercialize their inventions, business efficacy demands that patent law avoid imposing expensive and inefficient tollbooths on the highways of innovation. Rendering an entire patent unenforceable would amount to over-deterrence where it would suffice merely to render the offending condition

---

[134] *Princo Corp. v. Int'l Trade Comm'n*, 616 F.3d 1318, 1321 (Fed. Cir. 2010).
[135] Abramson, *supra* note 113, at 345.
[136] *eBay Inc. v. MercExchange, L.L.C.*, 547 U.S. 388, 394 (U.S. 2006).
[137] Guido Calabresi & A. Douglas Melamed, *supra* note 132, at 1108.

unenforceable. Alternatively, if rendering an entire patent unenforceable appears "too onerous, the penalty paradoxically may deter too little, due to reluctance to invoke it."[138]

While reasonable minds may differ as to which is better, it seems fair to suggest their views would profoundly affect how they also view an equitable defense like misuse. First, finding misuse in "a broad range of cases" will diminish the value of patent rights and discourage investment in innovation. Licensees lose out if they are deprived of licensing options that, while appearing onerous, may provide better financing options. Similarly, "the patent applicant has made an irrevocable but valuable disclosure, to the benefit of the public, in his patent application, and that he should be regarded as having a *property right* to enforce it."[139] In reformulating misuse, the Federal Circuit has taken the leading role in strengthening the rights of patentees and, as Professor Dan Burk suggests, may have correspondingly narrowed the instances where misuse can be found.[140]

If some members of the Federal Circuit do indeed have this predilection, they are certainly not alone and this may even be expected. In the *Princo* case, for example, the New York Intellectual Property Law Association and the Intellectual Property Owners Association filed briefs *amici curiae* supporting Philips, the patent owner in the case.[141] The American Antitrust Institute, in contrast, filed a brief *amicus curiae* supporting Princo.[142] While the American Intellectual Property Law Association and the U.S. Federal Trade Commission filed briefs in support of neither party, a closer scrutiny of the contents of their briefs shows the respective parties urging the court toward non-intervention and intervention.[143]

---

[138]   Cotter, *supra* note 112, at 960.

[139]   Hoerner, *supra* note 1, at 684–85.

[140]   Dan L. Burk, *Anticircumvention Misuse*, 50 UCLA L. REV. 1095, 1118–19 (2003) ("This patent fervor has, in part, been fueled by the creation of the U.S. Court of Appeals for the Federal Circuit, a body invested by Congress with exclusive appellate jurisdiction over patent cases, and with a perceived mandate to produce a uniform body of U.S. patent law").

[141]   Eugene L. Chang et al., *Princo Corp. V. ITC*, 4 LAW 360 (2010), available at: http://www.law360.com/ ("At one end of the spectrum, the NYIPLA argued that the agreement in issue is vertical, procompetitive, and presumptively lawful. At the other end of the spectrum, the AAI argued that such an agreement is horizontal, 'inherently suspect' and presumptively unreasonable").

[142]   Brief of Amicus Curiae American Antitrust Institute On Rehearing En Banc in Support of Appellants and Reversal of Underlying ITC Decision at 3-5, *Princo Corp. v. ITC*, 616 F.3d 1318 (No. 337-TA-474) (Fed. Cir. 2010).

[143]   Brief of Amicus Curiae Federal Trade Commission on Rehearing En Banc Supporting Neither Party at 4-5, *Princo Corp. v. ITC*, 616 F.3d 1318 (No. 337-

B. Windsurfing: Adding "Anticompetitive Effect"

The first misuse case to come before the Federal Circuit was *Windsurfing Int'l Inc. v. AMF, Inc.*[144] The patentee there sued its licensees alleging infringement of its patent on the hinging mechanism used on a windsurfing board. The licensees responded that the license required them to recognize the validity of, and refrain from using the patentee's registered trademarks and that license term amounted to patent misuse. The district judge below found the marks had become generic and the patentee had improperly leveraged its patents to keep licensees from using words which were in the public domain.

Chief Judge Howard Markey wrote the opinion for the panel. The panel first cabined the expansion of the *per se* approach, holding that "to sustain a misuse defense involving a licensing arrangement not held to have been *per se* anticompetitive by the Supreme Court a factual determination must reveal that the overall effect of the license tends to restrain competition unlawfully in an appropriately defined relevant market."[145] It therefore required the infringer to prove that the practice was unlawful *per se*, or that the patentee who has market power in the market for the patented product was acting in a way that produced anticompetitive effects.[146] Hoerner notes that "[t]his was a genuinely startling pronouncement because existing case law, including controlling Supreme Court precedent, had never held that a relevant market finding or a finding of an anticompetitive effect had been required to support a finding of extension of the monopoly-type patent misuse."[147] Intriguingly, Chief Judge Markey also noted that "[r]ecent economic analysis questions the rationale behind holding any licensing practice *per se* anticompetitive."[148] The Chicago view of antitrust law, which advocated minimal intervention, was transcendent. Indeed, the careful reader may detect echoes of *USM Corp.* resonating within *Windsurfing*'s holding.

Chief Judge Markey through his opinion in *Windsurfing* fashioned an

---

TA-474) (Fed. Cir. 2010). (Explaining that an agreement between competitors to suppress a nascent competing technology is prohibited without proof that such technology necessarily could have been commercialized. Such agreements are inherently suspect and the burden is on the patent holder to prove that the agreement was reasonably necessary to achieve the procompetitive efficiencies of the pool collaboration.)

[144] *Windsurfing Int'l Inc. v. AMF, Inc.*, 782 F.2d 995 (Fed. Cir. 1986).
[145] Ibid. at 1001–1002.
[146] Ibid. at 1001.
[147] Hoerner, *supra* note 1, at 697.
[148] Ibid.

"antitrust-lite" version of misuse. Unlike antitrust, the focus was on the scope of the invention and not market demand. At the same time, the defendant had to show an "anticompetitive effect," a requirement whose criteria seems difficult to fathom given that the showing of market power through market definition is typically a necessary precursor to showing an anticompetitive effect has resulted from the antitrust defendant's conduct. Commentators have noted that "the Federal Circuit pulled out of thin air the additional 'anticompetitive effect' requirement for a finding of patent misuse."[149] Chief Judge Markey cited *Blonder-Tongue Laboratories, Inc. v. University of Illinois Foundation*, a Supreme Court case for the proposition that misuse requires the infringer to "show that the patentee has impermissibly broadened the 'physical or temporal scope' of the patent grant *with anticompetitive effect*."[150] However, Robert Hoerner points out, the words "anticompetitive effected" added in *Windsurfing* were "the *only* source of the entire Federal Circuit jurisprudence requiring an anticompetitive effect to support extension of the monopoly-type misuse" and that the *Windsurfing* analysis involving a misreading of *Blonder-Tongue*. Hoerner further observes that:

> It is possible that courts would engraft onto the extension of the monopoly misuse defense a requirement that the underlying conduct or offending license clause be shown to restrain competition unreasonably, as was suggested in *Windsurfing*, but it is difficult to see how any court other than the United States Supreme Court could take such action in view of the square contrary holding in *Morton Salt*.[151]

Indeed, Chief Judge Markey himself seemed to have had second thoughts. In *Senza-Gel Corp. v. Seiffhart* he noted commentary and criticism of Supreme Court decisions in light of "recent economic theory," but nonetheless acknowledged the Federal Circuit was "bound, however, to adhere to existing Supreme Court guidance in the area until otherwise directed by Congress or by the Supreme Court".[152] He then

---

[149] Brett Aaron Mangrum, *Patent Misuse – A Questionable Permission of Licensing Arrangements that Tie Down the Equitable Scales*, 60 SMU L. Rev. 307, 309 (2007).

[150] *Virginia Panel Corp. v. MAC Panel Co.*, 133 F.3d 860, 868–69 (Fed. Cir. 1997).

[151] Hoerner, *supra* note 1, at 704.

[152] See ibid. at 673–74 (emphasis added in source). See also Adelman, *supra* note 112, at 814 ("Should the Federal Circuit adopt the policy that no conduct will be labeled a misuse unless there is Supreme Court authority squarely holding that the challenged conduct is misuse, or alternatively, that the conduct is anti-

reiterated the Supreme Court's admonition that: "the patentee's act may constitute patent misuse without rising to the level of an anti-trust violation."[153] He distinguished antitrust and misuse law, holding that:

> The law of patent misuse in licensing need not look to consumer demand (which may be non-existent) but need look only to the nature of the claimed invention as the basis for determining whether a product is a necessary concomitant of the invention or an entirely separate product. The law of antitrust violation, tai-lored for situations that may or may not involve a patent, looks to a consumer demand test for determining product separability.[154]

Chief Judge Markey's retreat in *Senza-Gel*, however, was not followed by later cases, which tagged the requirement for anticompetitive effect to the successful showing of patent misuse. For example, one court noted that "[a]nticompetitive effects are a critical element of any patent misuse case that is evaluated under *this 'rule of reason' approach.*"[155] Others have read the Federal Circuit's stance as one where "the body of misuse law and precedent need not be enlarged into an open-ended pitfall for patent-supported commerce",[156] and have consciously construed patent misuse narrowly.[157] For example, Judge Whyte observed in *Hynix Semiconductor* that "[t]he Federal Circuit has cautioned that the defense not be read broadly to capture any generally-alleged 'wrongful' use of patents. . . . Rather, the defense is generally directed towards conduct that 'affect[s] competition in unpatented goods or that otherwise extend[s] the eco-

---

competitive and therefore violates the antitrust laws? Beyond the *Mallinckrodt* decision, the Federal Circuit may have adopted this view in *Windsurfing International.* However, in *Senza-Gel* the court appears to have stepped away from it").

[153]   *Senza-Gel Corp. v. Seiffhart*, 803 F.2d 661, 668 (Fed. Cir. 1986).

[154]   Ibid. at n. 14. Similarly in *B. Braun Medical, Inc. v. Abbot Labs*, the Federal Circuit held that "the patent misuse doctrine, born from the equitable doctrine of unclean hands, is a method of limiting abuse of patent rights separate from the antitrust laws." *B. Braun Med., Inc. v. Abbott Laboratories*, 124 F.3d 1419, 1426 (Fed. Cir. 1997).

[155]   *Diamond Heads, LLC v. Everingham*, No. 8:07-cv-462-T-33TBM, 2009 WL 1046067, at *7 (M.D. Fla. Apr. 20, 2009).

[156]   *C.R. Bard Inc. v. M3 Sys., Inc.*, 157 F.3d 1340, 1373 (Fed. Cir. 1998).

[157]   See *Hearing Components, Inc. v. Shure, Inc.*, No. 9:07-CV-104, 2009 WL 815526, at *1 (E.D. Tex. 2009) ("The Federal Circuit has cautioned that the doctrine should be construed fairly narrowly . . . ('the body of misuse law and precedent need not be enlarged into an open-ended pitfall for patent-supported commerce.')").

nomic effect beyond the scope of the patent grant.'"[158] Indeed, one court in 2011 arguably narrowed the *Princo* majority's formulation of misuse still further when it noted that "[t]he *Princo* court confined the patent misuse doctrine to licensing agreements that either have 'the effect of extending the life of the patent beyond the statutory period,' or contain 'tying' requirements." [159] Patent misuse today either is *per se* illegal or else evaluated under the rule of reason approach. Professor Thomas Cotter explains that:

> Per se misuse includes, among other things, conditioning the use of the patent upon the defendant's agreement to pay post-termination royalties (as per Brulotte v. Thys), as well as tying. Per se lawful practices include . . . asserting a claim for contributory infringement based upon the defendant's sale of a nonstaple item, or merely refusing to license the patent to the defendant.[160]

The practice is then either allowed or prohibited outright. If not, the court must then determine if the conduct was reasonably within the patent grant and again if not, whether there was an unjustified anticompetitive effect.[161] Other cases also require that there must be some anticompetitive effect directly connected to the "patent-in-suit" even if it may have contributed to that end result.[162] Opponents of this restricted view point to the fact that the public interest function which misuse was created to serve allows defendants to assert misuse even if they were not

---

[158] *Hynix Semiconductor Inc. v. Rambus Inc.*, 609 F. Supp.2d 988, 1030 (N.D. Cal. 2009).

[159] Order Granting Motion to Dismiss the First Amended Complaint with Leave to Amend at 8, *Samsung Elec. Co., Ltd. v. Panasonic Corp.*, No. C-10-03098 JSW (N.D. Cal. Aug. 25, 2011).

[160] Cotter, *supra* note 112, at 913.

[161] Virginia Panel Corp. v. MAC Panel Co., 133 F.3d 860, 869 (Fed. Cir. 1997); Cotter, *supra* note 112, at 914 ("Using this approach, the Federal Circuit has held that practices such as threatening to void or limit warranties if third parties did not agree to purchase certain unpatented products from the patent owner, or requiring the licensee to acknowledge the validity of and avoid using the patentee's trademarks, did not constitute misuse because they did not broaden the scope of the patent claims. Other practices, such as grantbacks and field-of-use restrictions, are evaluated, if at all, under the rule of reason."); J. Dianne Brinson, *Patent Misuse: Time for a Change*, 16 RUTGERS COMPUTER & TECH. L.J. 357, 372 (1990) ("The misuse cases emphasize the anticompetitive nature of the patentees' misuse of their patents.").

[162] *McCullough Tool Co. v. Well Surveys, Inc.*, 395 F.2d 230, 238-39 (10th Cir. 1968) ("This principle has been applied in patent cases by allowing the defense of patent misuse only where there had been a misuse of the patent in suit"); *Princo Corp. v. Int'l Trade Comm'n*, 616 F.3d 1318, 1333 (Fed. Cir. 2010).

personally harmed by the misuse, such as when they were not in privity to a contract with the patentee containing the clause giving rise to the alleged misuse.[163]

In *Princo*, a recent and significant misuse decision, the majority of the Federal Circuit sitting *en banc* rejected the patent defendant's invitation to overrule the requirement to show anticompetitive effect.[164] It stated that it had "consistently adhered to that requirement," and that this position was "consistent with the traditional characterization of the defense of patent misuse by the Supreme Court."[165] In support of its position, the majority cited the Supreme Court's opinion in *Illinois Tool Works* which in its view "describe[ed] the patent misuse as applying 'when a patentee uses its patent "as an effective means of restraining competition with its sale of an unpatented good.""' The majority also cited two appellate decisions—*County Materials Corp v. Allan Block Corp.* from the Seventh and Ninth Circuits to support its proposition.[166] Finally, it pointed to the 1988 amendments to section 271(d) of the Patent Act as making it clear that Congress intended to limit patent misuse to practices having anticompetitive effects.[167] Each will be examined in turn.

C. The Patent Misuse Reform Act of 1988

In 1988, Congress enacted the Patent Misuse Reform Act, amending the Patent Act to eliminate the market power presumption in patent misuse cases for cases involving patentees who tied the purchase of their patented inventions to unpatented goods. The relevant provision reads:

> (d) No patent owner otherwise entitled to relief for infringement or contributory infringement of a patent shall be denied relief or deemed guilty of misuse or illegal extension of the patent right by reason of his having done one or more of the following: . . . (5) conditioned the license of any rights to the patent or the sale of the patented product on the acquisition of a license to rights in another

---

[163]   *Morton Salt Co. v. G.S. Suppiger Co.*, 314 U.S. 488, 494 (1942) ("It is the adverse effect upon the public interest of a successful infringement suit in conjunction with the patentee's course of conduct which disqualifies him to maintain the suit, regardless of whether the particular defendant has suffered from the misuse of the patent").

[164]   *Princo Corp. v. Int'l Trade Comm'n*, 616 F.3d 1318, 1334 (Fed. Cir. 2010).

[165]   Ibid.

[166]   *County Materials Corp v. Allan Block Corp.*, 502 F.3d 730 (7th Cir. 2007) and 616 F.2d 1133, 1141 (9th Cir. 1980).

[167]   *Princo Corp.*, 616 F.3d, at 1131.

patent or purchase of a separate product, *unless, in view of the circumstances, the patent owner has market power in the relevant market for the patent or patented product on which the license or sale is conditioned.*[168]

With the Patent Misuse Reform Act, the patent and antitrust bars had to deal with two questions. First, did the Act prescribe the scope of misuse or merely circumscribe situations where Congress determined that there would be no misuse? Second, was the requirement of market power in tying cases a Congressional indication that: (a) patent misuse as a whole was to be analyzed by antitrust rules; (b) a more limited application to conduct proscribed by Section 271; or (c) as Judge Posner suggested in *USM*, an indication that patent misuse should be subsumed completely into antitrust law?

To the first question, it is interesting to note that when writing for an earlier case, it was Judge Bryson, the author of the majority opinion in *Princo*, who noted that the 1988 amendments codified patent misuse inversely and acknowledged that they were safe harbor provisions which did not otherwise alter misuse.[169] Indeed, at a later part of the opinion, he acknowledged that "instead of saying what patent misuse is, Congress has said what it is not."[170] *Illinois Tool Works* advanced a similar characterization of section 271(d)(5), stating that "Congress included a provision in its codification that excluded some conduct . . . from the scope of the patent

---

[168]   35 U.S.C. § 271(d)(5) (2006) (emphasis added).

[169]   See *Princo*, 616 F.3d. at 1330 ("Congress enacted section 271(d) [of the Patent Act] not to broaden the doctrine of misuse, but to cabin it"). Cf. *U.S. Philips Corp. v. Princo Corp.*, 173 Fed. Appx. 832, 834 (Fed. Cir. 2006) ("The district court interpreted section 271(d)(5) not as a safe harbor provision, but as a definition of patent misuse in the context of tying arrangements . . . That interpretation of section 271(d)(5) is inconsistent with the proper construction of the statute, which provides a safe harbor for certain conduct, not a comprehensive definition of patent misuse"); with *U.S. Philips Corp. v. Int'l Trade Com'n*, 424 F.3d 1179, 1186 (Fed. Cir. 2005) ("Although section 271(d)(5) *does not define* the scope of the defense of patent misuse, but merely provides a safe harbor against the charge of patent misuse for certain kinds of conduct by patentees, the statute makes clear that the defense of patent misuse differs from traditional antitrust law principles in an important respect, as applied to tying arrangements involving patent rights. In the case of an antitrust claim based on a tying arrangement involving patent rights, this court has held that ownership of a patent on the tying good is presumed to give the patentee monopoly power. Section 271(d)(5) makes clear, however, that such a presumption does not apply in the case of patent misuse. To establish the defense of patent misuse, the accused infringer must show that the patentee has power in the market for the tying product" (emphasis added)).

[170]   *Princo*, 616 F.3d at 1329.

misuse doctrine."[171] Both 271(d)(5) and *Illinois Tool Works* have thus been erroneously read for the proposition that patent misuse substituted for antitrust intervention in the early days and now merely tracks antitrust policy developments.[172]

To the *Princo* majority's assertion that the 1988 amendments cabined the patent misuse doctrine to a small number of cases involving leveraging, the dissent, however, responded that:

> While the misuse cases cited by the majority refer to patent leveraging, that is simply because leveraging of the patent—in tying and patent term extension cases—is a necessary part of the antitrust violation. Those cases do not suggest that leveraging is a necessary element where there is an agreement not to compete with the asserted patent.[173]

The dissent pointed to the Supreme Court's *Univis Lens* opinion which stated that "the particular form or method by which the monopoly is sought to be extended is immaterial."[174] The dissent's view is supported by Professor Hovenkamp et al., who note that "the Misuse Reform Act does not purport to be a general catalog of all actions that can no longer constitute misuse. Rather . . . the statute subtracted from the judge-made law of patent misuse five practices that should no longer be held to constitute misuse, leaving everything else intact."[175]

The distorting effects of *Princo* on misuse have already trickled down to the lower courts, and it appears that misuse has been distorted even further. On October 17, 2011, the U.S. District Court for the Northern District of California handed down its decision in *Samsung Elec. Co. v. Panasonic Corp.*[176] The patents in that case concerned memory cards using

---

[171] Illinois Tool Works Inc. v. Indep. Ink, Inc., 547 U.S. 28, 41 (2006).

[172] See Lemley, *supra* note 131, at 1624 ("This section clearly reverses existing patent misuse law in the case of tying arrangements and *brings that law into rough conformity with antitrust law*, which also requires proof of market power in tying cases" [emphasis added]); see also Abramson, *supra* note 113 (commenting on the Supreme Court's decision in *Indep. Ink, Inc. v. Illinois Tool Works, Inc.*, 396 F.3d 1342 (Fed. Cir. 2005): "On behalf of a unanimous court, Justice John Paul Stevens announced that from this point forward, antitrust law would adopt the patent law rule that only some patents define relevant antitrust market, thereby *moving patent misuse a step closer to antitrust tying*.") (emphasis added).

[173] *Princo*, 616 F.3d at 1349.

[174] Ibid. at 1346 *citing* United States v. Univis Lens Co. 316 U.S. 241, 251–52 (1942).

[175] 10 Areeda & Hovenkamp, *supra* note 59, at ¶1781.

[176] *Samsung Elec. Co., Ltd. v. Panasonic Corp.*, No. C-10-03098 JSW (N.D. Cal. Aug. 25, 2011).

the Secure Digital Memory (SD) Card technology, accounting for over 80 percent of global sales of flash-memory cards used in devices like mobile phones and digital cameras. Samsung asserted that the patentee misused its patent by requiring royalties to be paid based on the net sales price of the SD card, which contained both patented and unpatented components. Samsung relied on *Zenith Radio Corp v. Hazeltine Research*, which found misuse for requiring the licensee to pay a royalty on all sales of products regardless of whether the products were covered by the patents. The court relied on *Princo* for the proposition that misuse was limited to time extension and tying. It also distinguished *Zenith* on the basis that the SD card practiced the technologies despite the fact that it contained unpatented components. The court also found probative the fact that it was industrial practice to base royalty payments on total sales rather than the licensed technology alone.

Many interviewees for this study acknowledged that the 1988 amendments expressly affected only two forms of misuse, tying and refusals to license. At the same time, interviewees from the bar and the bench both generally shared the view that Congress was attempting to coordinate patent and antitrust policy through the Act. While the 1988 amendments were limited to tying and refusals to license, the message was clear that misuse as a whole should be read in light of antitrust principles and the Federal Circuit was acting in a manner consistent with that policy direction, so that, as an academic put it during an interview, the 1988 amendments had the effect of "animating patent misuse with antitrust policy." Commentators agree, noting that "[s]ince the Act's passage, the Federal Circuit has taken a more lenient view of licensing agreements in some cases."[177] Interviewees observed that the Federal Circuit itself may have been influenced by the 1988 amendments. It is conceivable that judges may feel that bright line rules do more justice for the parties before them when using robust antitrust policy compared to vague doctrines of equity, whether or not the result may really be just. Thus a judge noted that the uncertainty as to the implications of unenforceability has led to the sentiment that patent misuse and antitrust should overlap.

To the second question, whether and to what extent 271(d)(5) endorses the *Windsurfing* standard of misuse, Professor Vincent Chiappetta argues that the answer is "no". According to Professor Chiappetta, "Section

---

[177] See Brett Frischmann & Dan Moylan, *The Evolving Common Law Doctrine of Copyright Misuse: A Unified Theory and its Application to Software*, 15 BERKELEY TECH. L.J. 865, n. 31 (2000).

271(d)(5) clearly did not affirmatively adopt the Federal Circuit's much broader anticompetitive effects requirement. Commentators argue that by failing to enact a contemporaneous Senate bill which would have expressly required an antitrust violation to find misuse, Congress intended to preserve the doctrine's independence."[178] Instead, it listed practices that would not constitute misuse, including tying, refusals to license and lawful actions to enforce patents. On this basis, several commentators argue that Congress implicitly agreed that misuse allegations should be judged by looking to patent policy in addition to antitrust considerations.[179] For example, Joel Bennett commented that:

> By refusing to require proof of an antitrust violation in all instances, Congress preserved the central policy of the patent laws to limit the scope of a patentee's claims to the temporal and physical boundaries of the invention. It has long been recognized that conduct that does not have an anticompetitive effect upon competition in a separate and distinct relevant market, in the antitrust sense, may still violate critical public policies relating to patents.[180]

---

[178] Vincent Chiappetta, *Living With Patents: Insights From Patent Misuse*, 15 MARQ. INTELL. PROP. L. REV. 1, 22 (2011). There was a bill in the Senate, S.1200, that would have limited the patent misuse defense to cases in which an antitrust violation existed, but this was not adopted. See 134 Cong. Rec. S14, 434-03 (daily ed. Oct. 4, 1988) (statement of Sen. Leahy); 134 Cong. Rec. H10, 646-02 (daily ed. Oct. 20, 1988) (statement of Rep. Kastenheimer); 134 Cong. Rec. S17,146-02 (daily ed. Oct. 21, 1988) (statement of Sen. Leahy). Thus, the patent misuse doctrine should only be limited as much as Congress intended to limit it. See *In re Recombinant DNA*, 850 F. Supp. 769, 774 (S.D. Ind. 1994). S. 438 contained the following language: "No patent owner otherwise entitled to relief for infringement or contributory infringement of a patent shall be denied relief or deemed guilty of misuse or illegal extension of the patent right by reason of his or her licensing practices or actions or inactions relating to his or her patent, unless such practices or actions or inactions, in view of the circumstances in which such practices or actions or inactions are employed, *violate the antitrust laws*" (emphasis added).

[179] See Bennett, *supra* note 99, at 2 ("The Senate version of the Patent Misuse Reform Act, if passed, would have required proof of an antitrust violation in order to establish patent misuse. However, the House refused to acquiesce in this sweeping requirement. The compromise version of the Act imposed antitrust standards in only one situation, *i.e.*, tie-ins"); Richard Calkins, *Patent Law: The Impact of the 1988 Patent Misuse Reform Act and* Noerr-Pennington *Doctrine on Misuse Defenses and Antitrust Counterclaims*, 38 DRAKE L. REV. 175, 196 (1988); Jere M. Webb & Lawrence A. Locke, *Intellectual Property Misuse: Developments in the Misuse Doctrine*, 4 HARV. J.L. & TECH. 257, 266–67 (1991).

[180] Bennett, *supra* note 99, at 5–6.

One example of a case that illustrates the Federal Circuit's extra-Congressional extension of antitrust analysis beyond the bounds of Section 271 was *Mallinckrodt v. Medipart*.[181] There the Federal Circuit required antitrust analysis in a patent misuse case that did not fall within Section 271. In that case, the patentee sold a medical device meant for single use. The defendant reconditioned used devices for resale.[182] The district court prohibited Mallinckrodt from enforcing its use restriction based on "a strong public interest in not stretching the patent laws to authorize restrictions on the use of purchased goods," and "the interest in preventing restraints on use is stronger than the opposing interest in permitting a patent owner to use his monopoly to increase sales of his invention."[183] Writing for the Federal Circuit panel, Judge Newman reversed, adopting the position that, as one commentator put it, "if the Supreme Court has not ruled a particular use restriction *per se* illegal, then the Federal Circuit will decide allegations of patent misuse by looking solely to antitrust principles."[184] *Mallinckrodt* thus not only required more than market power, but also added the requirement to patent misuse across the board.[185] The *Mallinckrodt* opinion cited *Windsurfing* as the *Senza-Gel* precedent for patent misuse without expressing awareness of precedent that decoupled patent misuse from a compulsory showing of antitrust policy or the legislative history of the 1988 amendments.[186] *Mallinckrodt* also eviscerated the first sale doctrine, concluding that it did not justify use contrary to contractual prohibitions.[187]

---

[181]   *Mallinckrodt, Inc. v. Medipart, Inc.*, 976 F.2d 700 (Fed. Cir. 1992).

[182]   *Mallinckrodt, Inc. v. Medipart, Inc.*, 15 U.S.P.Q.2d (BNA) 1113, 1119 (N.D. Ill. 1990).

[183]   Ibid. at 1119.

[184]   Note, *supra* note 95, at 1928; Mallinckrodt, 976 F.2d at 706 ("Restrictions on use are judged in terms of their relation to the patentee's right to exclude from all or part of the patent grant . . . and where an anticompetitive effect is asserted, the rule of reason is the basis of determining the legality of the provision").

[185]   Note, *supra* note 95, at 1930 ("there is some resistance to the idea that the Federal Circuit had the authority to modify the misuse doctrine in this fashion").

[186]   See Robin C. Feldman, *The Insufficiency of Antitrust Analysis for Patent Misuse*, 55 HASTINGS L.J. 399, 426 (2003) ("The opinion showed no awareness of Judge Markey's subsequent retreat from Windsurfing in Senza-Gel, in which he acknowledged that the Federal Circuit did not have the authority to require an anti-trust analysis without Congressional or Supreme Court action. Nor did the opinion show any awareness of Congress' failure to pass the Senate proposal which would have required an antitrust analysis. The fact that Congress failed to approve requiring an antitrust analysis left the Federal Circuit still lacking the authority to alter the doctrine in this way, yet that is precisely what the court did in Mallinckrodt").

[187]   See Cotter, *supra* note 112, at 915–16 ("The court's reasoning therefore

Cases such as *Mallinckrodt* have led commentators like Katherine White to note that the Federal Circuit has: "narrowed the scope of patent misuse beyond the level Congress dictated. This limitation has allowed courts to aid and abet patentees in expanding the rights under their patents beyond that legally allowed under prior case law, even taking into account legislative changes."[188] By limiting the misuse defense to those use restrictions that violate antitrust principles, some commentators assert that the Federal Circuit has impermissibly contradicted *Morton Salt* where the Supreme Court explicitly looked to patent policy to judge alleged patent misuse.[189] The legislative history of Section 271 also points toward a misuse whose existence lies apart from antitrust laws. As Joel Bennett notes:

> On October 4, 1988, the Senate passed the Intellectual Property Antitrust Protection Act of 1988. This law, if enacted . . . would have prohibited a finding of patent misuse unless the alleged infringer established that the patentee had violated the antitrust laws. . . . On October 20, 1988 the House considered and amended the Senate version of H.R. 4972. This amendment deleted the provisions of Title II relating to . . . the requirement that an alleged infringer establish that the patentee has violated the antitrust laws.[190]

Section 271(d)(4) was added to specify that unilateral unconditional refusals to license would not be misuse. Section 271(d)(5) was added to require courts to determine whether patentees possessed sufficient market power in the relevant market in tying cases to be liable for misuse.[191]

---

appears to indicate that the Federal Circuit views the first-sale doctrine as merely a default rule—that is, it applies only when the patentee has made an unrestricted sale of an article incorporating the patented invention").

[188] See Katherine E. White, *A Rule for Determining When Patent Misuse Should be Applied*, 11 FORDHAM INTELL. PROP. MEDIA & ENT. L.J. 671, 674 (2001).

[189] See Robert J. Hoerner, *supra* note 1, at 704 ("It is possible that courts would engraft onto the extension of the monopoly misuse defense a requirement that the underlying conduct or offending license clause be shown to restrain competition unreasonably, as was suggested in *Windsurfing*, but it is difficult to see how any court other than the United States Supreme Court could take such action in view of the square contrary holding in *Morton Salt*").

[190] Bennett, *supra* note 99, at 3–4.

[191] Patent Misuse Reform Act of 1988, Pub. L. No. 100-73, 102 Stat. 4674 (codified at 35 U.S.C. § 271(d)). The addition to Section 271 provides that "(d) No patent owner otherwise entitled to relief for infringement or contributory infringement of a patent shall be denied relief or deemed guilty of misuse or illegal extension of the patent right by reason of his having done one or more of the following: (1) derived revenue from acts which if performed by another without his

The label it carries may however be a misnomer. Kenneth Burchfiel explains that:

> The adoption of an antitrust standard to govern patent misuse is explained by the curious evolution of the misuse provision. The patent misuse tying amendment proceeded neither directly from concern related to patent misuse, nor from ties of patents to staples. Instead, it was engendered by the desire of computer manufacturers to tie sales of computer hardware to copyrighted operating system software. Statutory immunity was sought primarily due to the fears of antitrust liability on the part of computer manufacturers employing such tying arrangements.[192]

Like the *Princo* majority, some commentators have pointed to the Supreme Court's decision in *Illinois Tool Works* as evidence that the Court implicitly endorsed the Federal Circuit's interpretation of misuse, since it did not disapprove of it.[193] As an initial matter, it must therefore be clarified that while the Court examined the history of section 271(d) (5), the issue before it was "whether the presumption of market power in a patented product should survive as a matter of antitrust law despite its demise in patent law."[194] Because the case was decided solely as a matter of antitrust law, it would be tenuous to infer a definition, or redefinition, of misuse from the Court's silence. The Court reviewed the history of misuse and determined that early misuse cases presumed market power by

---

consent would constitute contributory infringement of the patent; (2) licensed or authorized another to perform acts which if performed without his consent would constitute contributory infringement of the patent; (3) sought to enforce his patent rights against infringement or contributory infringement." See generally, Richard Calkins, *supra* note 179, at 175 (providing a detailed discussion of the 1988 Patent Misuse Reform Act and noting that the primary effect of Patent Misuse Reform Act is to eliminate the presumption that a tie-in license involving a patent is *per se* misuse).

[192]   Kenneth J. Burchfiel, *Patent Misuse and Antitrust Reform: "Blessed Be The Tie?"*, 4 HARV. J. LAW & TECH. 1, 21–22 (1991).

[193]   Abramson, *supra* note 113, at 324 ("The Supreme Court considered patent misuse in 2006, when it reviewed Independent Ink's claims against Trident. Though the issue at stake there was not quite the one that earned the Federal Circuit Hoerner's ire, it was close enough to open the door for a truly irate Supreme Court. Were even a single justice as incensed as Hoerner about the overall doctrinal development of the patent-misuse doctrine in the Federal Circuit's hands, there probably would have been at least a concurring opinion. The absence of even a snide dictum suggests that the Supreme Court is less troubled by the Federal Circuit's narrowing of the patent-misuse doctrine than is Hoerner").

[194]   *Illinois Tool Works Inc. v. Indep. Ink, Inc.*, 547 U.S. 28, 31 (2006).

possession of a patent.[195] This presumption was later exported to antitrust law.[196] Later, when the 1988 amendments required a showing of market power for tying cases, it seemed sensible to the Court that that requirement should also be required for antitrust violations involving patent ties.[197] William Holmes, in commenting on *Illinois Tool Works*, noted that "[t]he antitrust standard for claims of patent tying was, thus, brought into line with the 'patent misuse' rule relied upon by the Court in its analysis."[198] Correctly read, *Illinois Tool Works* was thus silent on the scope of misuse.

D. Patent Misuse in other Circuits and the Supreme Court

Patent misuse cases have in a few isolated instances been considered by regional appellate circuits after the Federal Circuit was established. *County Materials* was a Seventh Circuit case decided by Judge Diane Wood, known for her expertise in antitrust law.[199] In that case, the patentee granted exclusive rights to the licensee to make its patented concrete block. In return, the licensee agreed not to sell competing products for 18 months if it stopped making the patentee's product. *County Materials* held that "[t]he *Windsurfing* standard for patent misuse necessarily considers whether progress and innovation have been stymied and allows courts concretely to answer the vague question whether progress has been slowed."[200] Under the Seventh Circuit's view, *Windsurfing*'s antitrust rubric therefore incorporates both static price-output considerations as well as dynamic efficiency considerations—seamlessly melding patent and antitrust policy into one doctrine. This view of misuse potentially inserts

---

[195]   Ibid.

[196]   Ibid. at 29 (noting, "The presumption that a patent confers market power arose outside the antitrust context as part of the patent misuse doctrine, and migrated to antitrust law in *International Salt Co. v. United States*").

[197]   Ibid. at 28 (2006) (holding that market power could not be presumed because of the existence of patent rights, relying on 35 U.S.C. § 271(d)(5) which eliminated any presumption of market power for patent misuse claims and the virtual consensus among economists, DOJ/FTC, and the *IP Guidelines*).

[198]   2 William C. Holmes, INTELLECTUAL PROPERTY AND ANTITRUST LAW § 20:2 (2010).

[199]   Kristina Moore, *Nominee Analysis: Judge Diane Wood*, SCOTUS BLOG (May 20, 2009 5:08 PM), http://www.scotusblog.com/2009/05/nominee-analysis-judge-diane-wood/ ("With an academic background primarily in antitrust law and international finance, she might assist the Court as it answers legal questions emerging from the global economic crisis and the Department of Justice's increased efforts at antitrust enforcement").

[200]   *County Materials Corp. v. Allan Block Corp.*, 502 F.3d 730, 736 (7th Cir. 2007).

the missing perspective of patent policy established by *Morton Salt* but absent from other courts' interpretation of *Windsurfing*. No court before or after *County Materials* has articulated a similar view of *Windsurfing*. Rather courts usually formulaically regurgitate *Windsurfing*'s ratio and proceed under the rubric of antitrust law.

Carpet Seaming was a Ninth Circuit case wherein the antitrust plaintiff accused the patentee of violating Section 2 of the Sherman Act by "attempting to monopolize and conspiring to monopolize the manufacture and sale of hot-melt thermoplastic carpet seaming tapes."[201] The Court stated that "[i]n this circuit, a prima facie case of attempt to monopolize requires proof of three elements: (1) specific intent to control prices or destroy competition with respect to a part of commerce; (2) predatory or anticompetitive conduct directed to accomplishing the unlawful purpose; and (3) a dangerous probability of success." In this context, the Court held that "[t]o show misuse, a patentee must have the purpose of exercising anticompetitive power outside the lawful scope of that granted by the patent,"[202] and found that in this case there was no misuse amounting to an antitrust violation. The Court also considered whether "wrongful assertion and enforcement of the pooled patents [was] a ground for violation of the antitrust laws and misuse."[203] It held that "to amount to an antitrust violation or patent misuse, such attempted enforcement must be in bad faith," and found that the "trial court did not mention, much less give adequate consideration, to the requisite element of bad faith, the presumption of good faith, or the appropriate high burden of proof on this issue."[204] It is clear from the foregoing that *Carpet Seaming* was an antitrust case. It should therefore be unsurprising that the court was focused on finding anticompetitive effects from the exercise of the patentee's rights. *Windsurfing*, on the other hand, was a pure patent misuse defense. *Carpet Seaming* therefore does not support the *Princo* majority's view that misuse is premised on a finding of anticompetitive effects.

V.   CONCLUSION

If antitrust law during the *A.B. Dick* years was characterized by deference to patentees, and the *Morton Salt* years by debilitation, then the

---

[201]   *Carpet Seaming Tape Licensing Corp. v. Best Seam Inc.*, 616 F.2d 1133, 1141 (9th Cir. 1980).

[202]   Ibid. at 1141–42.

[203]   Ibid. at 1143.

[204]   Ibid.

Windsurfing years would be characterized by deliberation of the beneficial effects of conduct alleged to be misuse.[205] An academic interviewed summed up his views on the history of misuse:

> I think it seems pretty clear that, most notably in the 1940s, patent misuse had a life of its own independent of antitrust law, not only in cases like *Morton Salt*, but *Carbice*—cases that expanded the role of patent misuse in policing contributory licensing claims, for example. I think part of the point of the 1952 act and passing Section 271(d) was to rein in specific examples where patent misuse had gone beyond antitrust. Then I think probably again in the 1960s and 1970s there was some expansion of patent misuse. The 1988 statutory changes also, I think, were designed to rein in—they didn't make it exactly coextensive with antitrust, but they were clearly designed to limit expansion of patent misuse beyond antitrust principles in particular ways. But I think that since that time there have been only a very limited number of cases in which patent misuse has plausibly been asserted that don't involve antitrust. The Federal Circuit's current formulation of the test, which is expansion of a patent beyond its scope, with the anticompetitive effect, I think brings up—it's not exactly parallel in the antitrust law. One difference is the standing requirements. But it ends up meaning that the theories of harm that animate patent misuse tend to be antitrust areas of harm.[206]

The Federal Circuit has exclusive jurisdiction over patent appeals. It has both the experience and expertise in patent law. It has determined that patents rights should be robustly protected, and that clear rules rather than standards are the best way to fulfill the constitutional mandate to promote technological progress. The Supreme Court remains the ultimate interpreter of the patent statute and its equitable doctrines. A difficulty that some have, despite these apparently sound reasons for the *Windsurfing* formulation is that Supreme Court decisions are binding on the lower courts and if the Supreme Court holds that "'an anticompetitive effect' is not required for a finding of . . . misuse, by what warrant does the Federal Circuit ignore such holdings?"[207]

---

[205] Jerrad T. Howard, *When Concerted Conduct Leads to Misuse: An Examination of the Federal Circuit's* En Banc *Holding in* Princo, 100 KY. L.J. 687, 696-97 (2012) ("What is missing from the Supreme Court's jurisprudence is the Federal Circuit's "leveraging" requirement—a requirement that the defendant show the patent in suit has been leveraged in some manner to extend the scope of his monopoly. In fact, Supreme Court precedent indicates that this leveraging requirement is not required to establish misuse. . . . The doctrine should continue to be applied as the Supreme Court intended and not in the emasculated form into which the Federal Circuit has forced it").

[206] On file with author.

[207] Abramson, *supra* note 113, at 324.

The concern is that cases in other circuits percolate upwards to their appellate courts and differences between them provide an opportunity for reconsideration and reconciliation by the Supreme Court. Not so with patent cases. Few courts in the world have been entrusted with as much as the Federal Circuit. And where institutional checks are weaker, doctrinal ones, whether for the patentee or infringer, must be more carefully scrutinized and equally balanced.

However, the infrequency with which a certain type of case reaches the Supreme Court as well as the Court's preoccupation with policy can sometimes infuse its judgments with a debilitating tentativeness which makes such judgments useless as precedent. The Court's controversial opinion in *Bilski v. Kappos* stands in contrast to the Federal Circuit's conscious attempt to create the bright-line rules needed to guide commercial conduct.[208] As Chief Judge Rader noted at a Patent Law Institute event in 2012, businesses efficacy demands such rules, and businesses cannot wait for every case to be litigated before they get an answer to what the rule is.[209] As a matter of precedent, vague opinions full of policy pontifications fail to give the guidance that lower courts need, particularly district court judges who may find it challenging to sift through such judgments and find meaningful points of application to the facts of cases before them. Indeed, both the case content analysis and interviews for this study point to the Federal Circuit's decision in *Windsurfing* as being the dominant view of misuse in modern times.[210]

It also appears as if the Federal Circuit's framing of misuse within antitrust has even been accepted by the antitrust agencies. That the Federal Trade Commission embraced a rule of reason view of patent misuse in *Princo* is a signal that the Interface may be a step closer toward a unified approach being taken by federal institutions.[211] It is also the formulation

---

[208] *Bilski v. Kappos*, 130 S. Ct. 3218 (2010).

[209] Gene Quinn, *Chief Judge Rader Takes on Lobbying White House and SCOTUS*, IP WATCHDOG (Feb 21, 2012), http://www.ipwatchdog.com/2012/02/21/ chief-judge-rader-takes-on-lobbying-white-house-and-scotus/id=22364/ ("Rader explained that this is the world he lives in, the obvious implication being that the Supreme Court does not live in or understand the real world as it pertains to the business of innovation and the monetization of intellectual property").

[210] See *infra* Chapter 6.

[211] Brief of Amicus Curiae Federal Trade Commission on Rehearing En Banc Supporting Neither Party at 1-2, *Princo Corp. v. ITC*, 616 F.3d 1318 (Fed. Cir. 2010) (No. 337-TA-474) ("This Court's precedents establish that, apart from the realm of per se patent misuse, application of the patent misuse doctrine is to be informed by antitrust principles. The FTC accepts this principle as a given, and expresses no view on whether differences between antitrust law and the patent

of misuse that has taken root in the legal consciousness of litigants.[212] The infusion of a rule of reason analysis into patent misuse analysis has allowed market actors more latitude to impose restraints on competition.[213] Professor Carl Shapiro suggests that one reason for this relaxation is "[b]ecause the purpose of patent protection is to provide incentives for innovation, measures that permit a patentee to capture more fully the value of its patent may lead to a more efficient level of innovation,"[214] One reason for infusing antitrust analysis into patent misuse analysis is that it allows the development of such analysis to benefit from a large pool of antitrust cases and commentary. But even laying aside the problem of stare decisions, can the Federal Circuit bridle the antitrust chimera it created? As FTC Commissioner Thomas Rosch cautions:

> I'm not sure the rule of reason is all it's cracked up to be. Professor Hovenkamp (one of the principal champions of a full-blown rule of reason) may know how to "weigh" anticompetitive effects and precompetitive effects, but I sure don't. The Supreme Court rarely applies the rule of reason and provides no guidance on how to weigh rule of reason considerations more generally—a fact that is underscored by the appellate courts' own disarray. Indeed, even the D.C. Circuit's decision in *Microsoft*—arguably the most sophisticated Section 2 decision on the books—didn't explain very well how to weigh anticompetitive effects against procompetitive effects or how to decide which prevails. So, to put it bluntly, I'm not persuaded that applying the rule of reason to all conduct by innovators—simply because they are innovators—would result in anything more than additional discord (as opposed to certitude) for the business community.[215]

As the nation's patent court, the Federal Circuit perhaps is best placed to tweak patent policy levers rather than encumber already costly patent

---

misuse doctrine may warrant different approaches in some cases, or in this particular case").

[212] Brief for Intervenor U.S. Philips Corporation on Rehearing En Banc at 10, Princo Corp. v. ITC, 616 F.3d 1318 (Fed. Cir. 2010) No. 2007-1386 ("Under both antitrust and misuse law, '[t]he "rule of reason" is the prevailing standard of analysis'").

[213] See 1 Hovenkamp et al., *supra* note 98, at §§ 3.2d–e ("By relying on the language and doctrine of antitrust cases, the court [in *Virginia Panel*] presumably meant to invoke the considerable legal and economic structure that has been developed in substantive antitrust rule of reason cases").

[214] See U.S. Dep't Of Justice & Fed. Trade Comm'n, *supra* note 118, at 118.

[215] J. Thomas Rosch, Comm'r, Fed. Trade Comm'n, *Intel, Apple, Google, Microsoft, and Facebook: Observations on Antitrust and the High-Tech Sector FTC* (November 18, 2010), available at: http://www.ftc.gov/speeches/rosch/101118fallforum.pdf.

litigation with antitrust analysis. The Federal Circuit is the only specialist patent court in America, and one of few in the world staffed by judges whose decisions are informed by the research of law clerks and arguments of patent attorneys who have at least college-level technical backgrounds. One survey of patent attorneys, for example, showed that more than 30 percent of patent attorneys in the biological field had a PhD, while more than 25 percent of those in the chemical field had a PhD.[216] Even in the electrical, mechanical and computer engineering fields, where the number of PhDs is significantly lower, practitioners had technical undergraduate degrees.[217] Having a good understanding of the technology, at least in theory, allows practitioners and law clerks to better brief the panel on the sector specific technological landscape, enabling the panel to better appreciate both whether the conduct question crosses the misuse threshold as well as the potential consequences of finding misuse. Yet despite this body of expertise, as Professors Dan Burk and Mark Lemley note, however, the Federal Circuit has been reluctant to robustly use these levers.[218] Additionally, while an argument might be made that patent misuse may be replaced by other policy levers in patent law, Tom Cotter has observed that the converse, that misuse replace other policy levers, would be met with resistance:

> Perhaps "misuse" could serve a backup role by enabling courts to render unenforceable patents on inventions that qualify as nonobvious under the applicable nonobviousness criteria, but that nevertheless should be unenforceable due to a perceived surplus of social costs over social benefits in a particular case. As so described, however, the doctrine would probably have few advocates, conferring as it would such unfettered discretion upon judges that it would lead to unpredictable and inconsistent results. Moreover, given that Congress has seen

---

[216]   Dennis Crouch, *Patent Attorneys and Agents: Years of Hands-On Technical Experience Before Focusing on Patent Law*, PATENTLY-O (August 26, 2010), available at: http://www.patentlyo.com/patent/2010/08/index.html.

[217]   Ibid.

[218]   Dan L. Burk & Mark A. Lemley, *Policy Levers in Patent Law*, 89 VA. L. REV. 1575, 1664–65 (2003) ("Patent misuse similarly has the potential to serve as a powerful micro policy lever in a variety of contexts . . . While patent misuse has the potential to serve as a policy lever, its use by the Federal Circuit to date has been minimal, and seems to have diminished over time. The court has seemed more concerned with strictly cabining patent misuse and its cousin antitrust within strict limits than it has with engaging in detailed determinations of the facts and characteristics of given industries. The antitrust/misuse inquiry into competitive effects is necessarily industry-specific, however, and could serve as a policy lever designed to ensure that patents are given no more than their appropriate scope").

fit to create patent and copyright rights subject to various criteria it might seem to conflict with rule-of-law virtues for the courts to undo that bargain on the basis of their own seat-of-the-pants second-guessing. And intuition might seem to suggest that if there is to be a misuse doctrine of some sort, misuse should rest upon a finding of misconduct and not simply the assertion of possibly welfare-reducing, but lawfully procured, IPRs.[219]

While the Federal Circuit has expertise in patent law and policy, it is no better skilled at antitrust analysis than other appellate courts. And compared to antitrust policy, patent policy is likely to be more readily understood by district judges than appellate judges. This is so even though the theoretical distinctions there may be more settled, such as those relating to price effects. Both as an equitable doctrine and a defense to patent infringement, it is more familiar and more easily administrable by district judges, who would likely welcome the opportunity to avoid having to contend with complex economic considerations under the antitrust matrix, in addition to those inherent in any patent infringement trial. Given that the rule of reason-type analysis will feature in patent misuse jurisprudence for the foreseeable future, it is worth noting Judge Walker's advice that because many generalist judges lack training in economic analysis, evidence should be comprehensibly communicated to a generalist in a manner consistent with other evidence.[220] It has also been observed that the Federal Circuit seems to have struggled in articulating the different factors that need to be considered in a patent misuse analysis aside from the antitrust starting point.[221] One judge interviewed noted that it was important that patent misuse devised remedies that were clearly seen to be distinct from antitrust remedies, and that the remedies for each be shown to complement it in achieving the goals of antitrust or patent policy. The judge further commented that the choice of forum has as much a role to play in determining the future shape of patent misuse as any other factor—for example, a forum that recognizes that patentees are self-interested individuals with incentives to sue even on shaky grounds, and who recognize that PTO capabilities are limited will be more receptive to expanding patent misuse. Conversely, a forum that favors commercial certainty and strong patent

---

[219]   Cotter, *supra* note 112, at 935–36.

[220]   Vaughn R. Walker, *Merger Trials: Looking for the Third Dimension*, in 5 COMPETITION POLICY INT'L 1 (2009).

[221]   See Joe Potenza, Phillip Bennett & Christopher Roth, *Patent Misuse—the Critical Balance, A Patent Lawyer's View*, 15 FED. CIRCUIT B.J. 69, 97 (2005) ("This struggle has led to criticism by some commentators suggesting that the Federal Circuit body of patent misuse law fails to clarify what behavior will and won't be held to be patent misuse").

rights or antitrust policy would be less inclined toward arguments based on allegations of patent misuse.

The prevailing zeitgeist is in favor of certainty and against the desta-bilizing influence of policy levers like antitrust and patent misuse. Until the Supreme Court decides to speak further on misuse, *Windsurfing* will likely remain the controlling precedent on the law of misuse.[222] As a practical matter, it may be that the Federal Circuit, being the specialist court dealing more closely with stakeholders, has a better sense than the Supreme Court of delivering the rules that facilitate business efficacy. That is, however, an empirical assertion, and one which will be validated by future studies or by history. As a matter of doctrine, what *Windsurfing* really stands for will have to be clarified by the Federal Circuit. If it stands as a paler shade of antitrust then it begs the question how a form of misuse that is simply broader than antitrust law plays any meaningful role apart from the latter. As Professor Cotter notes:

> Absent market power on the part of the IP owner, though, it's not clear to me how a court can be confident that the condition at issue poses any serious threat to future innovation. By definition, a lack of market power would seem to imply that adequate substitutes for the IP rights in question exist, which in turn means that the prospective licensee could turn to other sources for the technology it needs to build its own innovations.[223]

Windsurfing as interpreted by *County Materials* reconciles *Morton Salt* with *Windsurfing*'s requirement of finding "anticompetitive effects" by requiring the court to take into account both static and dynamic factors, the latter capable of incorporating patent policy factors as well. The Supreme Court earlier hinted at this possibility in *Zenith Radio Corp* when it noted that misuse did not have to "embod[y] the ingredients of a viola-tion of either s 1 or s 2 of the Sherman Act."[224]

As noted earlier, however, *County Materials* stands alone in expressly mentioning that patent policy plays a meaningful role within the "anti-competitive effects" rubric of *Windsurfing*. On the other hand, if antitrust and patent policies are really concerned about two different things, this will mean that *Windsurfing* may be contrary to Supreme Court prec-edent and, if so, it should be abrogated or modified. If nothing else, the history of misuse shows how complex and controversial the doctrine is.

---

[222] See *infra* Chapter 6.
[223] Thomas F. Cotter, *IP Misuse and Innovation Harm*, 96 IOWA L. REV. BULL. 52, 59–60 (2011).
[224] *Zenith Radio Corp. v. Hazeltine Research, Inc.*, 395 U.S. 100, 140 (1969).

Understanding where misuse came from is, however, only the first step. It is equally important to examine how and why misuse has evolved from its quintessential form in tying cases to encompass a remarkable variety, nearly a dozen distinct forms, of misconduct today. It is to this discussion that we now turn.

3. The anatomy of a defense

I. INTRODUCTION

This chapter introduces the key forms of misuse, the ones found in the leading cases and discussed in the legal literature. Some are more important than others but they all derive from courts' attempts to determine what is "wrong" about patentees' conduct within the context of the facts before them. This *ad hoc* approach not surprisingly has led to some differences in results and philosophical approaches to misuse.

They all derive at least in part, however, from the general principle stated by Judge William Bryson of the Federal Circuit, writing for the *Princo* majority, who stated "the basic rule of patent misuse: that the patentee may exploit his patent but may not 'use it to acquire a monopoly not embraced in the patent.'"[1] That basic rule is the golden thread that has essentially been woven into patent misuse in every case from the beginning.[2] But this rule can hide more than it reveals. Courts face the real challenge of applying it to multifarious conjurations from the fertile minds of patent attorneys, and they must determine in each instance whether the patentee's conduct indeed amounts to actionable misuse.

To illustrate how complex this inquiry can be, one need only look to the Biblical commandment against stealing.[3] If to "steal" is to "to take (another person's property) without permission or legal right and without intending to return it,"[4] we can easily recognize that robbery, housebreaking, and pickpocketing are its illegitimate progeny. But what of streaming, rather than downloading movies off the Internet,[5] or piggybacking off of

---

[1]   *Princo Corp. v. Int'l Trade Comm'n*, 616 F.3d 1318, 1327 (Fed. Cir. 2010) (quoting *Transparent-Wrap Mach. Corp. v. Stokes & Smith Co.*, 329 U.S. 637 (1947)).

[2]   See *supra* Chapter 2.

[3]   *Exodus* 20:15 ("Thou shalt not steal").

[4]   See New Oxford American Dictionary 1705 (3d ed. 2010) (defining steal).

[5]   Jason Mick, *U.S. Senate Proposes Prison Time for Illegally Streaming Movies, TV*, Daily Tech (June 17, 2011, 9:38 AM), http://www.dailytech.com/US+Senate+Proposes+Prison+Time+for+Illegally+Streaming+Movies+TV/article21929.htm.

someone else's Wi-Fi signals,[6] or buying an e-book off Kindle after browsing it thoroughly in a bricks-and-mortar bookstore?[7] To some extent the answer as to whether each circumstance is lawful depends on whether one can convincingly extend notions such as "taking," "property," and "wrongful" that are embedded in the definition of "steal" to these acts.

The situation is even more difficult with regard to misuse, a concept that is amorphous and subjective. Any doctrine based on the "misuse" of a legal right will first be applied liberally, then challenged and confined to await the next cycle of the judicial zeitgeist.

With regard to patents, some might see every type of exploitation of a patented work as rightfully within the grant. Others might see even aggressive enforcement of the patent as misuse as a tool to intimidate potential competitors and receive more protection than is properly within the patent grant.

Courts, of course, are not immune to these conceptual and application problems. Yet they must try to craft a consistent law that adequately addresses both the rights of patentees and considerable concerns for users and competitors. Moreover, they need to decide whether to take a bright-line approach which creates more certainty as opposed to an ad hoc approach that might provide less certainty but more leeway in reaching the right result in a particular case. This chapter considers the five main forms of misuse and how courts have rationalized the theory of misconduct in each case. Each section is summarized below.

The first type of misuse case involves licensing related misuses: product or patent ties, time extensions, restrictions, and royalties. A patent tie occurs when "the sale of the patented product is conditioned on the purchase of the unpatented product."[8] The latter is normally an input of the former, such as salt tablets, ink, or paper. The earliest misuse cases all involved some form of tying. Cases such as *Carbice, Morton Salt*, and *Mercoid* represent classic forms of tying.

The second type of misuse case takes the form of agreements which extend the licensees obligation to pay royalties beyond the life of the

---

[6]   Mike Elgan, *Why It's OK to 'Steal' Wi-Fi*, Computerworld (June 19, 2008, 12:41 PM), http://blogs.computerworld.com/why_its_ok_to_steal_wi_fi; Lev Grossman, *Confessions of a Wi-Fi Thief*, Time (June 12, 2008), http://www.time.com/time/magazine/article/0,9171,1813969,00.html.

[7]   See, e.g., Mark Coker, *How Ebook Buyers Discover Books*, The Digital Reader (Sep 26, 2011), http://www.the-digital-reader.com/2011/09/26/how-ebook-buyers-discover-books/ (finding that 4% of respondents made ebook purchasing choices through browsing in bricks-and-mortar stores first).

[8]   U.S. Dep't of Justice & Fed. Trade Comm'n, Antitrust Enforcement and Intellectual Property Rights: Promoting Innovation and Competition 107 (2007).

patent, perhaps best exemplified by the controversial case of *Brulotte*. In other words, the misuse is a time extension of the patent. Tying and time extensions are the only two types of misuse cases that the Federal Circuit has condemned as *per se* illegal.[9]

The third type of misuse case involves licensing restrictions, which include covenants not to compete, obligations against reuse or resale, field of use restrictions, and territorial restrictions.

The fourth type of misuse cases come from those involving royalty obligations—royalties based on total sales of patented or non-patented goods, pre-grant royalties, excessive pricing claims, and price restraints.[10]

The fifth type of misconduct, "bad faith" litigation, while not as pervasive a form of patent misuse compared to licensing misuse, remains a significant consideration for defendants. This form includes vexatious litigation, enforcement of a fraudulently procured patent and abuse of judicial or regulatory processes. "Bad faith" litigation has increased dramatically over the years, a trend which Chapter 7 takes up in more detail and which will no doubt play a more significant role in the landscape of misuse in the future if current trends continue. Other categories of misuse, such as grantbacks and patent pools, which do not easily fit into these categories, are discussed in the conclusion to this Chapter.

II.   TYING AND RELATED CONDUCT

Tying first arose in antitrust law in the context of patent litigation.[11] Commentators differ on the number of types of tying claims and how they

---

[9]   1 Herbert Hovenkamp et al., IP AND ANTITRUST §3.3 (2010) ("Besides tying, the only category of conduct the Federal Circuit has specifically identified as constituting misuse per se is extending the patent beyond its expiration date or the date on which it is held invalid").

[10]   Strictly speaking, post-expiration royalties would also fall within this wide category of misconduct. However, to examine cases which have followed Brulotte over the years, this category of royalty agreements has been carved out and so will also be treated separately here as well as in Chapter 6 where the cases are tagged and numbered.

[11]   *Illinois Tool Works Inc. v. Indep. Ink, Inc.*, 547 U.S. 28, 33 (2006) ("American courts first encountered tying arrangements in the course of patent infringement litigation").

should be categorized. Some put the figure at three, others at four.[12] These are: (1) requiring the licensee to purchase patented and unpatented products; (2) suing contributory infringers; (3) package licensing of patents; and (4) "tie-outs." The first two types are classic examples of ties and they overlap significantly. They are therefore considered here. The first form of tying occurs when patentees force licensees to take products in a different market not covered by the patent. For example in *Morton Salt*, the patentee coerced its customers to buy salt, a separate product, from which they wished to lease the salt deposit machines. However, it appears that merely proposing to enter into a tying arrangement does not trigger misuse.[13] The second form, suing contributory infringers, occurs where the patentee sues those providing inputs from the patentee. Section 271(d)(3) generally exempts patentees from this form of misuse because "[a] logical corollary to the patentee's right to control nonstaple products is its right to file and prosecute lawsuits against those who infringe its patents, either directly or by inducing or contributing to infringement."[14] However, patentees could be found guilty of misuse where patentees attempted to expand the scope of its rights to preclude permissible repair of the patented device.[15]

The third form of tying is package licensing, where multiple patents are included in a single license or in a group of related licenses. The fourth, "tie-outs," are really non-compete clauses by another name, and are therefore more appropriately discussed in the context of licensing

---

[12] Robert S. Chaloupka, *Antitrust Concerns in Intellectual Property Licenses*, in CORP. COUNSEL'S GUIDE TO INTEL. PROP. § 15:13 (2012) ("Common types of conduct that can amount to patent misuse include tying arrangements, enforced package licensing, price restrictions, and extended royalty terms").

[13] *Virginia Panel Corp. v. MAC Panel Co.*, 133 F.3d 860, 871 (Fed. Cir. 1997) ("Finally, VP's proposal to ASCOR was not a consummated tying arrangement and for that reason was not *per se* patent misuse").

[14] 1 Hovenkamp et al., *supra* note 9, at §3.3.

[15] Arthur J. Gajarsa et al., *How Much Fuel to Add to the Fire of Genius? Some Questions About the Repair/Reconstruction Distinction in Patent Law*, 48 AM. U. L. REV. 1205, 1229 (1999) ("Similarly, a patentee's attempt to contract out of the repair/reconstruction doctrine could be seen as an attempt to secure, by contract, what is not permitted by law, or it could fall into a category of patent doctrines that one could limit by contract"). As a leading commentary notes: "[a] misuse claim might arise if patent law exhaustion principles treated a transaction as an unrestricted sale, but the patentee nonetheless conditioned the sale or license of the patented product on an agreement not to repair the product. In this situation, the question for misuse purposes would be whether such a condition served to 'impermissibly broaden the "physical or temporal scope" of the patent grant with anticompetitive effect.' Broadening the patent right is precisely the effect of such an agreement"); 1 Hovenkamp et al., *supra* note 9, at §3.3.

restrictions.[16] This study also considers refusals to license in this section. While refusals to license may be a patentee's retaliatory response to the licensee's rejection of any of its terms, this study has found that it has occurred exclusively in the context of tying cases.[17]

A. Theory of Harm

The concern common to the various forms of tying is the foreclosure of the market which could lead to stagnation of competition and innovation in the marketplace.[18] This could occur by forcing out rivals in the tied product. One example that commentators have given occurs when a patentee exercises its market power in the incumbent technology to require consumers to purchase both the incumbent and competing incipient technologies.[19] This tie allows the patentee to leverage on its market power to delay the development of the competing incipient technology. For example, the theory of harm in *Microsoft* was that by tying its Internet browser program to its operating system through intermingling of code and default installations, it made it more difficult for developers of rival browsers to convince consumers to switch to them.[20]

---

[16] James B. Kobak Jr., *Misuse Defense and Intellectual Property Litigation*, 1 B.U. J. Sci. & Tech. 25, 28 (1995) ("Tie-outs: Agreements not to develop or market goods that compete with those of the patent owner").

[17] See *infra* Chapter 6.

[18] 54 Am. Jur. 2d, Monopolies and Restraints of Trade § 88 (2d ed. 2012) ("Except where employed by a small company in an attempt to break into a market, tying arrangements can rarely be harmonized with the strictures of the antitrust laws. Tying arrangements flout the policy of the Sherman Act that competition rules the marketplace. Where they are successful, tying arrangements inevitably curb competition on the merits with respect to the tied product, as they deny competitors free access to the market for the tied product, not because the party imposing the tying requirements has a better product or a lower price, but because he or she has sufficient power or leverage in another market").

[19] Ibid. at §21.3 ("A more plausible and potentially anticompetitive version of leverage arises when the monopolies at issue are consecutive rather than simultaneous").

[20] *United States v. Microsoft Corp.*, 87 F. Supp. 2d 30 (D.D.C. 2000). As Professor Hovenkamp et al. explain: "The reason such theories are plausible, while the general leverage theory is not, is that the monopolies are successive rather than simultaneous. First the defendant obtains a monopoly in the prior technology; then it uses the tie-in to leverage a second monopoly in the successor technology. At any single instant there is only one relevant monopoly, and thus only one profit-maximizing price. As a result, this version of the leverage theory has some force whenever the threat is that the defendant will use tying in order to protect its monopoly position as technology A gives way to technology B. The anticompeti-

Foreclosure also restricts consumer choice in the market for the tied product. For example, the tying of a media player to an operating system would make it more difficult for rival media player providers to convince consumers to switch or to pay the higher prices the developers would be forced to charge in order to cover their development costs. This would make the patentee's media player more attractive even though it may be technologically inferior. Another form of tying identified by commentators is one that requires competitors to enter two markets rather than one.[21]

B. Antitrust Law and Tying

Antitrust law finds ties illegal where the patentee exerts its market power in the market for the tying product in order to coerce sales in the market for its tied product.[22] In the past, the antitrust laws both assumed market power from ownership of a patent and regarded patent ties as *per se* illegal.[23] Over the years the evolution of economic theory has changed the way that courts treat tying arrangements. First, antitrust agencies today regard tying arrangements as being capable of resulting in "significant efficiencies and pro-competitive benefits."[24]

Those from the Chicago School of Economics argue that tying cannot extend market power because consumers view the package as a whole, and

---

tive result is not higher monopoly prices at any given instant, but rather a longer duration for the defendant's monopoly position. 1 Hovenkamp et al., *supra* note 9, at §21.3 ("For example, consider the fishing rod monopolist that requires all of its buyers to take its fishing reels as well. As a result, the fishing reel market dries up and alternative fishing reel makers abandon it. At that decrease point, a firm wishing to manufacture fishing rods will not be able to find a free seller of reels, so it will have to make reels as well as rods. The illustration suggests that tying can increase entry barriers into either the rod market or the reel market, or effectively require that any competitive entry occur at both levels")

[21] 9 Philip E. Areeda & Herbert Hovenkamp, ANTITRUST LAW ¶1722 (2d ed. 2004).

[22] *N. Pac. Ry. Co. v. United States*, 356 U.S. 1 (1958).

[23] See *Illinois Tool Works Inc. v. Indep. Ink, Inc.*, 547 U.S. 28, 38–39 (2006) ("The presumption that a patent confers market power migrated from patent law to antitrust law in *International Salt Co. v. United States*, 332 U.S. 392, 68 S.Ct. 12, 92 L.Ed. 20 (1947). In that case, we affirmed a District Court decision holding that leases of patented machines requiring the lessees to use the defendant's unpatented salt products violated § 1 of the Sherman Act and § 3 of the Clayton Act as a matter of law"). Ibid. at 39.

[24] U.S. Dep't of Justice and Fed. Trade Comm'n, FTC ANTITRUST GUIDELINES FOR THE LICENSING OF INTELLECTUAL PROPERTY, Sec. § 5.3 (1995).

the patentee must reduce the price of the tying product to convince consumers to accept the tied product.[25] From the patentee's point of view, its "net level of monopoly profits stays the same; it is simply spread across two different markets when there is a tying arrangement."[26] Instead, Chicago School proponents argue that tying is pro-competitive because it allows patentees to meter usage through price discrimination, allowing patentees to charge a higher price to consumers who are willing to pay more and a lower price to those who value the product less.[27] Further, not all ties may be bad as a matter of IP policy either. Some ties result in lower prices and benefit consumers without restraining innovation. For example, price discrimination results in higher prices for heavy users but brings savings to lighter users. Manufacturers of photocopiers, for example, tend to sell the machines more cheaply and charge a higher price for the paper used with the machine. Such ties "generally increase output, and condemning outputting increasing practices under antitrust law is a fool's errand, unless the signs of competitive harm are particularly clear."[28] Courts have also largely rejected the theory that patentees can leverage their patents to obtain monopoly profits from both markets.[29] In view of the foregoing, commentators surmise that:

---

[25] See Christopher Leslie, ANTITRUST LAW AND INTELLECTUAL PROPERTY RIGHTS 135 (2011).

[26] Ibid.

[27] Ward Bowman, PATENT AND ANTITRUST 117–18 (1973); see also Byron A. Bilicki, *Standard Antitrust Analysis and the Doctrine of Patent Misuse: A Unification Under the Rule of Reason*, 46 U. PITT. L. REV. 209, 234–38 (1984) ("Metering allows the patentee to charge the licensee an amount that is closer to the actual value of the patent than would be attainable by other less direct or more costly means. As a result, the low-volume users of the invention can purchase the patent license at a lower royalty. Secondly, a patentee engaged in a price discrimination scheme will have an incentive to increase output. Provided the patentee prices the right to use his patented invention above his marginal cost, an increase in the number of low-volume users who decide to purchase the patent license will translate into an increase in the patentee's total revenue. Lastly, implementation of a price discrimination mechanism will increase competition in the market for the tied product. A patentee will be able to lower his marginal cost by lowering the price charged for the tied product. This decrease in marginal cost can be passed on to potential licensees in the form of royalty price reductions which will enable more low-volume users to purchase the patent license. Because any increase in output will necessarily increase total revenue, the patentee has every incentive to keep the market for the tied product as competitive as possible").

[28] Christina Bohannan & Herbert Hovenkamp, CREATION WITHOUT RESTRAINT 274 (2011).

[29] Raymond A. Atkins, *Economic Model of Tying: Obtaining a First-Mover Advantage*, 5 Geo. Mason L. Rev. 525, 526 (1996–1997) ("Various alternative

[T]ying law has generally developed in an aggressive manner that has condemned virtually all instances of truly anticompetitive ties, in addition to many
instances where anticompetitive effects were presumed or even imagined. As a
result, there is little warrant for concluding that an expansive doctrine of intellectual property misuse by tying is needed to repair lacunae in the coverage of
the tying laws . . . [I]f tying law is sufficiently broad to recognize anticompetitive ties, then any application of a "misuse" doctrine to condemn arrangements,
that tying law would not condemn, necessarily upsets arrangements that have
little or no anticompetitive effect. Given that tying arrangements are often
efficient and in the interest of consumers, such a misuse doctrine would be
counterproductive. The best defense of a doctrine of "misuse" by tying in the
absence of any antitrust violation is that a simple finding of misuse does not
ordinarily occasion the antitrust law's treble damages or attorney's fees. Once a
court finds misuse, it ordinarily refuses to enforce license restrictions embodying or implementing the misuse. According to this argument, when the penalties
are less, the dangers of overdeterrence are smaller and one can pursue more
marginal competitive harms.[30]

Commentators have argued that because some anticompetitive effect
is required under antitrust law as well as Federal Circuit misuse jurisprudence, the patent defendant alleging misuse should also show some form
of foreclosure by way of the patentee leveraging its market power into
the market for the tied good.[31] In this view, the tying arrangement must
affect the tied product market, which is the appropriate area of competition scrutiny. According to these commentators, market power is rarely
a concern when the tied good is a staple because it is "readily duplicated
from common inputs."[32] In their opinion, "such a requirement would
doom a case like *Morton Salt*."[33]

There are, however, several problems with this view. First, there has
never been a requirement to show market power in the market for the
tied good. Under misuse law, Section 271(d)(5) requires the person
making the allegation to show market power in the market for the tying

---

explanations have been offered for the popularity of tying, some having anticompetitive effects and some not, but the assumption at the core of the leverage theory
has been discredited").

[30] 1 Hovenkamp et al., *supra* note 9, at § 3.3.

[31] Kurt A. Strasser, *Atnitrust Policy for Tying Arrangements*, 34 Emory L.J.
254 (1985) ("In the typical case, then, the inquiry concerns whether the tying
product has sufficient market power to permit an inference of anticompetitive use
of leverage from the existence of the tie").

[32] Ibid. at §21.3.

[33] Ibid. at §3.3 ("Depositing salt into canned goods accounts for only a small
percentage of the many uses of salt. It is implausible to think that Morton could
use such a lever to gain control of the entire salt market, particularly given the low
barriers to entry and the lack of market concentration at the time").

product. It does not require a showing of market power in the market for the tied good. Second, while it is true that analysis under an antitrust rubric requires some showing of anticompetitive harm, the *Morton Salt* court made clear that it based its finding on patent policy rather than anticompetitive harm. While tying was regarded as a *per se* antitrust violation, it is nonetheless misleading to say that economic analysis was irrelevant. For example in *International Salt*, the Supreme Court did not consider the substitutability of other goods or the actual effect of the tying arrangement on competition as modern courts would. At the same time, it relied on the patentee's patent right to establish market power in the market for the tying product and the dollar volume of business in the tied product market to establish the anticompetitive effect.[34] In *Morton Salt*, the Court was aware of the economic matrices had it chosen to adopt them in analyzing the market effects of the tying arrangement. Indeed, if it had relied on the anticompetitive impact on the tied market for salt, it might well have rejected the claim of misuse altogether, since the patentee could not have any realistic way of monopolizing that market given the ready availability of alternative sources for the salt. The fact that the *Morton Salt* opinion did not rely on the anticompetitive impact points to the Court's determination to forge a brand of misuse focusing on distortions to the patent regime independent of antitrust law. Commentators have also observed that:

> Many of the decisions that have extended misuse doctrine beyond antitrust principles have either not involved ties at all, or else have involved additional practices that served either to restrain the innovation of rival products or else to sequester information or technology that rightfully belonged in the public domain. . . . The concern in these cases reaches beyond the tying up of commodities or other goods where foreclosure is unlikely; rather, they concern attempts to cut off access to alternative avenues of innovation or deny access to the public domain. These are appropriate concerns of intellectual property

---

[34] See also Leslie, *supra* note 25, at 138 ("The per se rule against tie-ins is nominal because: 1) it requires the plaintiff to prove that the defendant has market power over the tying product; 2) it requires the plaintiff to demonstrate that a not insubstantial dollar volume of commerce in the tied product is affected; and 3) it permits the defendant to argue that she has a legitimate business justification for imposing a tie-in. Some circuits even require that the plaintiff prove the actual anti-competitive effects of the tie-in under a per se test. . . . These elements and defenses negate the per se label because when an antitrust violation is truly per se illegal, the plaintiff does not have to demonstrate the defendant's market power or to prove anticompetitive effect; both are presumed as a matter of law. Nor is the defendant allowed to proffer a business justification for its conduct when per se rules are strictly applied").

even though the facts may not meet the technical requirements of an antitrust violation.[35]

Second, despite the substantial overlap between tying under misuse and the antitrust laws, courts have distinguished between tying as it exists under the two regimes. Under antitrust law, it matters whether the market demand for the items are linked. It requires a forced combination or bundle between different products or services by patentees with market power in the tying market that affects a substantial volume of commerce in the tied-product market.[36] Under misuse, it is the functional relationship between them that is relevant, and may be found using a lower standard.[37] Another difference between the two forms of tying is that tying under misuse is tied to the notion that it is inequitable to deprive the consumer of choice, a conclusion not based on market effects, but on free choice. Thus, those who focus on whether market leverage favors patentees maintain that tying arrangements extend market power from the market for the tying product to the tied product, and in so doing deprives consumers of independently choosing the source and nature of the tied good. As the Supreme Court noted in *Times-Picayune Pub. Co. v. United States*:

> By conditioning his sale of one commodity on the purchase of another, a seller coerces the abdication of buyers' independent judgment as to the "tied" product's merits and insulates it from the competitive stresses of the open market. ... the effect on competing sellers attempting to rival the "tied"

---

[35]   10 Areeda & Hovenkamp, *supra* note 21, ¶1781.

[36]   Ibid. at ¶1702.

[37]   *Jefferson Parish Hosp. Dist. No. 2 v. Hyde*, 466 U.S. 2, 19 (1984) ("the answer to the question whether two products are involved turns not on the functional relationship between them, but rather on the character of the demand for the two items"); *Senza-Gel Corp. v. Seiffhart*, 803 F.2d 661, 670 (Fed. Cir. 1986). As the Federal Circuit in *Senza-Gel* noted that the "effort to equate the determination of product separability for misuse purposes with product separability for antitrust purposes must fail in light of Ninth Circuit and Supreme Court law, which requires that 'consumer behavior' (market demand) be examined to determine the separability of products in determining whether there is a tying arrangement for antitrust purposes". It explained that "[t]he law of patent misuse in licensing need not look to consumer demand (which may be non-existent) but need look only to the nature of the claimed invention as the basis for determining whether a product is a necessary concomitant of the invention or an entirely separate product" ibid. at 670 n. 14. On the facts, it found "no conflict in the district court's holding that there are two products sufficient to sustain a defense of patent misuse, and its determination that a genuine issue of material fact exists on whether there are two products for antitrust purposes," ibid. at 670.

product is drastic: to the extent the enforcer of the tying arrangement enjoys market control, other existing or potential sellers are foreclosed from offering up their goods to a free competitive judgment; they are effectively excluded from the marketplace.[38]

Similarly, the Third Circuit held that "[w]hatever may be the asserted reason or justification of the patent owner, if he compels a licensee to accept a package of patents or none at all, he employs one patent as a lever to compel the acceptance of a license under another. Equity will not countenance such a result."[39] In sum, whether a court views a particular tying case as primarily an antitrust case or as a patent misuse case, and whether the court examines the facts by looking at the effect on the market for the tied product or the leverage exerted by the patentee, significantly affects the determination as to whether a patentee engaged in misconduct by tying.

C. Package Licensing

Package licensing raises foreclosure concerns when licensees want only one or a few items.[40] Package licensing can enhance efficiency when multiple licenses would otherwise be required to manufacture a product. At the same time, package licensing may impose several costs to competition and innovation.

The key theory of harm for package licensing was established in two Supreme Court cases, *Automatic Radio Mfg. v. Hazeltine Research* and *Zenith Radio Corp. v. Hazeltine Research*.[41] In both cases, the patentee,

---

[38] *Times-Picayune Pub. Co. v. United States*, 345 U.S. 594, 605 (1953).

[39] *Am. Securit Co. v. Shatterproof Glass Corp.*, 268 F.2d 769, 777 (3d Cir. 1959) ("We conclude that the court below committed no error in finding that the defense of misuse asserted by Shatterproof is a valid one").

[40] *Int'l Mfg. Co. v. Landon, Inc.*, 336 F.2d 723, 729–30 (9th Cir. 1964) (The Ninth Circuit explained that "[t]he evil of mandatory package licensing in that case was that the prospective licensee, in order to obtain a license under one patent, would be compelled to accept licenses under patents that were not necessarily needed. The same evil does not arise in mandatory package licensing of blocking patents. In such a case, the prospective licensee is being compelled to accept no more than he would, in any event, have to obtain in order to make worthwhile a license under any of the patents"); see also *Am. Securit Co.*, 268 F.2d at 777 ("Whatever may be the asserted reason or justification of the patent owner, if he compels a licensee to accept a package of patents or none at all, he employs one patent as a lever to compel the acceptance of a license under another. Equity will not countenance such a result. We conclude that the court below committed no error in finding that the defense of misuse asserted by Shatterproof is a valid one").

[41] *Automatic Radio Mfg. Co. v. Hazeltine Research, Inc.*, 339 U.S. 827, 834

Hazeltine Research, granted blanket licenses and based its royalty charge on the total price of the products embodying the technology. The Court in *Automatic Radio* found that such royalty provisions did not create another monopoly because "[s]ound business judgment could indicate that such payment represents the most convenient method of fixing the business value of the privileges granted by the licensing agreement."[42] In *Zenith Radio* the Court came to a different conclusion on the facts before it. It found that the license was due for renewal and that the licensee was being coerced into having to pay for royalties for items which did not embody the technology.[43] In addition to antitrust violation, the Court held that:

> Patent misuse inheres in a patentee's insistence on a percentage-of-sales royalty, regardless of use, and his rejection of licensee proposals to pay only for actual use. . . . There is nothing in the right granted the patentee to keep others from using, selling, or manufacturing his invention which empowers him to insist on payment not only for use but also for producing products which do not employ his discoveries at all.[44]

At the same time, the Court reiterated the limits to this rule set down in *Automatic Radio*, that is, a licensee cannot escape payment where a lump sum or percentage-of-sales royalty was bargained for by the licensee.[45] In

---

(1950); see also *Zenith Radio Corp. v. Hazeltine Research, Inc.*, 395 U.S. 100, 138–40 (1969).

[42] *Automatic Radio*, 339 U.S. at 827, 834; see also *Zenith* 395 U.S. at 138–40 ("It could easily be, as the Court indicated in *Automatic Radio*, that the licensee as well as the patentee would find it more convenient and efficient from several standpoints to base royalties on total sales than to face the burden of figuring royalties based on actual use. If convenience of the parties rather than patent power dictates the total-sales royalty provision, there are no misuse of the patents and no forbidden conditions attached to the license").

[43] *Zenith*, 395 U.S. at 138–40 ("But we do not read *Automatic Radio* to authorize the patentee to use the power of his patent to insist on a total-sales royalty and to override protestations of the licensee that some of his products are unsuited to the patent or that for some lines of his merchandise he has no need or desire to purchase the privileges of the patent. In such event, not only would royalties be collected on unpatented merchandise, but the obligation to pay for nonuse would clearly have its source in the leverage of the patent").

[44] Ibid.

[45] Ibid. It noted that "if the licensee bargains for the privilege of using the patent in all of his products and agrees to a lump sum or a percentage-of-total-sales royalty, he cannot escape payment on this basis by demonstrating that he is no longer using the invention disclosed by the patent." Moreover, "[A] licensee cannot expect to obtain a license, giving him the privilege of use and insurance against infringement suits, without at least footing the patentee's expenses in dealing with him. He cannot insist upon paying on use alone and perhaps, as things

comparing the Court's decisions in *Automatic Radio* and *Zenith*, Thomas Maffei notes that:

> The *Zenith* opinion is not contrary to the holding in *Automatic Radio* but clarifies it by indicating that the latter applies only to the narrow situation where no coercion exists and the parties, bargaining as equals, freely agree that such a royalty base will serve the convenience of both. In discussing the antitrust effect of the royalty base formula, the Court in *Automatic Radio* distinguished the cases involving tie-in arrangements by noting that such a base does not require the purchase of any goods nor does it restrict the licensee's right to manufacture or sell any other product not covered by the patent.[46]

The two cases created a touchstone for misuse based on the voluntariness of the dealing, which commentators like Professors Hovenkamp et al. have criticized as being "untenable."[47] They argue that:

> While in theory such a distinction might make sense, as a "tie" results only from a coercive connection, in practice it is likely to prove difficult if not impossible to distinguish voluntary from involuntary agreements. . . . [it] encourages self-serving testimony by both parties long after the fact of the agreement itself. Further, it encourages strategic behavior by licensors, who may be expected to include "voluntariness" clauses in contracts.[48]

Although those concerns may persist, the difficulty of making a voluntariness determination may, however, be overstated. Indeed, subsequent courts have devised and applied standards to determine voluntariness in patent misuse cases. In *Leesona Corp. v. Varta Batteries*, the U.S. District Court for the Southern District of New York looked "to see whether the license condition was the result of good-faith bargaining between the parties or was imposed on the licensee by the patent holder and whether the licensee raised objections that were overridden by the licensor."[49]

---

turn out, pay absolutely nothing because he finds he can produce without using the patent. If the risks of infringement are real and he would avoid them, he must anticipate some minimum charge for the license—enough to insure the patentee against loss in negotiating and administering his monopoly, even if in fact the patent is not used at all."

[46]   Thomas F. Maffei, *The Patent Misuse Doctrine: A Balance of Patent Rights and the Public Interest*, 11 B.C.L. Rev. 46 (1969).

[47]   1 Hovenkamp et al., *supra* note 9, at §3.3 ("The result of these cases was to create an untenable distinction between 'voluntary' and 'involuntary' package licensing deals").

[48]   1 Hovenkamp et al., *supra* note 9, at §3.3.

[49]   *Leesona Corp. v. Varta Batteries*, 522 F. Supp. 1304, 1341 (S.D.N.Y. 1981) (citing *Glen Mfg. Inc. v. Perfect Fit. Indus., Inc.*, 420 F.2d 319, 321 (2d Cir. 1970).

More recently in *Applera Corp. v. MJ Research* the U.S. District Court for the District of Connecticut examined a license arrangement in which the patentee charged a per-unit licensing fee and found no misuse because the licensee arrangement was reasonably within the scope of the patent grant.[50] Additionally, sham litigation in both misuse and antitrust law enquires into whether the litigation was entered into with improper purpose. Outside of patent law, contract law has well-established rules to enquire into instances of duress.[51]

Be that as it may, in U.S. *Philips Corp. v. International Trade Commission*, the Federal Circuit rejected the "hornbook law" that mandatory package licensing was patent misuse as "not supported by precedent or reason."[52] It held that package licenses did not prevent licensees from using alternative technology offered by a competitor to the patentee.[53] Commentators have, however, criticized the opinion because "*Philips* makes no effort to distinguish *Zenith* . . . even though it seems flatly to reject their voluntariness analysis."[54] Further, it ignored the fact that when "the licensee takes the nonessential patents for free [this] at least raises the risk that competition in that technology will suffer."[55]

Another key theory of harm in package licensing is the foreclosure effect it has in secondary markets. Patentees who are required to remove inessential patents have no incentive to reduce the price charged for the package, and can foreclose competition in the secondary market because "it forces a rival to compete against a price of zero, which of course rivals cannot do."[56] This is because, as U.S. District Court for the District of Columbia in *Microsoft* found, when licensees can use packaged technology at no

---

[50] *Applera Corp. v. MJ Research*, 349 F. Supp. 2d 314, 318 (D. Conn. 2004). In making its determination, the court cited a similar case before the Federal Circuit. In that case, the Federal Circuit held that "royalties may be based on unpatented components if that provides a convenient means for measuring the value of a license." *Engel Indus., Inc. v. Lockformer Co.*, 96 F.3d 1398, 1407–08 (Fed. Cir. 1996).

[51] 1 Arthur Linton Corbin, CORBIN ON CONTRACTS §28.02 (Desk ed., 2011).

[52] *Philips Corp. v. Int'l Trade Comm'n*, 424 F.3d 1179, 1187 (Fed. Cir. 2005) ("[A] package licensing agreement that includes both essential and nonessential patents does not impose any requirement on the licensee. It does not bar the licensee from using any alternative technology that may be offered by a competitor of the licensor. Nor does it foreclose the competitor from licensing his alternative technology; it merely puts the competitor in the same position he would be in if he were competing with unpatented technology").

[53] Ibid. at 1189–90.

[54] Hovenkamp et al., *supra* note 9, at §3.3.

[55] Ibid.

[56] Hovenkamp & Bohannan, *supra* note 28, at 278.

incremental cost, they are less likely to purchase a competing technology unless the benefit brought by that improvement overcomes the switching cost.[57] Following *Automatic Radio*, courts will scrutinize the substance of the parties' dealings and determine whether a particular license stemmed from coercion or deceit, or whether it bore the marks of mutual convenience.[58] For example, package licenses are permitted as long as the patentee can show it was willing to license any or all patents under reasonable, negotiated terms.[59] Reasonableness does not depend on the relative importance of the patents. Rather, the licensee's freedom of choice in taking the patent alone or in combination with other patents is the controlling factor.[60]

As a form of tying, package licensing is covered by Section 271(d)(5) and requires the one alleging misuse to show that the patentee had market power in the tying market. When examining the anticompetitive effect of such ties under *Windsurfing* or antitrust law where all the patents cover different aspects of the same product, both the tied and tying patents exist on the same market. In this case, the anticompetitive effect of the tie on the tied market may be difficult to discern. In *International Mfg. v. Landon, Inc.*, the evidence showed that the patents licensed were necessary to make the product, and that they had no use except in connection with each other. They were thus blocking patents. The Ninth Circuit rejected the misuse claim, pointing out that "the prospective licensee is being compelled to accept no more than he would, in any event, have to obtain in order to make worthwhile a license under any of the patents."[61]

Finally, it appears that licensees have a self-help remedy to objectionable package licensing arrangements. The Supreme Court's decision in *Lear, Inc v. Adkins* gives licensees the right to refuse to pay licensing fees on the basis that the patent is invalid. Robert Hoerner argues that *Lear*

---

[57]   *United States v. Microsoft Corp.*, 87 F. Supp. 2d 30, 51, n.6 (D.D.C. 2000) (finding commingling of Windows platform and Internet Explorer browser code anticompetitive because Windows customers received Internet Explorer automatically and had little incentive to install a second Web browser).

[58]   See *Automatic Radio Mfg. Co. v. Hazeltine Research, Inc.*, 339 U.S. 827 (1950) (noting that if the license agreement was for the convenience of the parties in measuring the value of the license, then the agreement cannot constitute patent misuse).

[59]   See *Well Surveys, Inc. v. Perfo-Log, Inc.*, 396 F.2d 15, 18 (10th Cir. 1968) ("In the case at bar, the affidavits submitted by WSI show a willingness to license any or all patents under reasonable, negotiated terms").

[60]   See ibid. ("The relative importance of patents has no significance if a licensee is given the choice to take a patent alone or in combination on reasonable terms").

[61]   *Int'l Mfg. v. Landon, Inc.*, 336 F.2d 723, 730 (9th Cir. 1964).

could be read to allow licensees to renounce it on a patent-by-patent basis in the context of a package license. This provides the licensee with "a self-help remedy for compulsory package licensing, at least if the royalty base is defined to be the coverage of the claims of licensed patents. He can simply renounce the license as being inapplicable to unwanted patents or patents believed to be invalid."[62]

III.   REFUSALS TO LICENSE

The antitrust agencies the U.S. Department of Justice and the Federal Trade Commission have indicated that unconditional refusals to license will not be pursued.[63] At the same time, the law is clear that "[t]he fact that a patentee has the power to refuse a license does not mean that he has the power to grant a license on such conditions as he may choose."[64] Despite the apparent *carte blanche* granted by Congress under section 271(d)(4) which immunizes patentees from "misuse or illegal extension of the patent right by . . . reason of his having . . . refused to license or use any rights to that patent. . . ."[65] the antitrust agencies have noted in their 2007 report that:

> [C]ourts have held that section 271(d)(4)'s companion provision, section 271(d) (5), does not immunize patentees from antitrust liability for the conduct it governs – conditioning a license, or sale of a patented product, on the purchase of some other product or the taking of some other license – and it would seem anomalous to read the phrase 'illegal extension of the patent right' to immunize patentees from antitrust liability for their refusal to license, but not for such conditioning of licenses.[66]

Drawing upon misuse case law, the report elaborated by discussing the Supreme Court's decision in *Motion Picture Patents Co. v. Universal Film Manufacturing Co.*[67] Summarizing the decision, the report concluded that

---

[62]   Robert J. Hoerner, *Patent Misuse: Portents for the 1990s*, 59 ANTITRUST L.J. 687, 704–11 (1991).

[63]   U.S. Dep't of Justice & Fed. Trade Comm'n, *supra* note 8, at 6 ("antitrust liability for mere unilateral, unconditional refusals to license patents will not play a meaningful part in the interface between patent rights and antitrust protections").

[64]   *Transparent-Wrap Mach. Corp. v. Stokes & Smith Co.*, 329 U.S. 637, 643 (1947).

[65]   35 U.S.C. § 271(d)(4) (2006).

[66]   U.S. Dep't of Justice & Fed. Trade Comm'n, *supra* note 8, at 26.

[67]   U.S. Dep't of Justice & Fed. Trade Comm'n, *supra* note 8, at 30–31. The report analyzed the decision:

"[c]onduct going beyond a mere refusal . . . may merit scrutiny under the antitrust laws."[68]

Additionally, as a jurisdictional matter, where an allegation of refusal to license is raised can hold significant consequences for the parties. The Ninth Circuit and Federal Circuit were faced with cases with similar facts—the patentee offered its machine on the condition that its customers purchased their services in the aftermarket as well.[69] While the Federal Circuit acknowledged that tying could attract antitrust liability, the issue was not raised. In contrast, the Ninth Circuit expressed concern that the patentee could have been tying its products and using its patent rights as a pretext for refusing to license,[70] leading commentators like Professors Herbert Hovenkamp, Mark Janis, and Mark Lemley to suggest that it might have condemned tying rather than the refusal to license.[71]

IV.   EXTENSIONS BEYOND THE PATENT TERM

A.   Brulotte and its Progeny

Royalty arrangements past the patent expiration date without reduction in royalty rates are *per se* misuse because that arrangement expands the scope of the patent beyond the temporal limits granted under patent law. Perhaps the best-known precedent addressing time extensions as a type of patent misuse is the Supreme Court decision in *Brulotte v. Thys Co.*[72] Commentators have noted that "[w]hile *Brulotte* itself did not invoke the

---

"[T]he Supreme Court rejected the theory that 'since the patentee may withhold his patent altogether from public use he must logically and necessarily be permitted to impose any conditions which he chooses upon any use which he may allow of it.' The Court explained that the 'defect in this thinking springs from the substituting of inference and argument for the language of the statute and from failure to distinguish between the rights which are given to the inventor by the patent law and which he may assert against all the world through an infringement proceeding, and rights which he may create for himself by private contract which, however, are subject to the rules of general [law] as distinguished from those of the patent law'" ibid. (quoting *Motion Picture Patents Co. v. Universal Film Mfg. Co.*, 243 U.S. 502, 514 (1917)).

   [68]   Ibid. at 30.
   [69]   See *Image Tech. Servs. v. Eastman Kodak*, 125 F.3d 1195 (Fed. Cir. 1997); *In re Indep. Serv.*, 203 F.3d 1322 (Fed. Cir 2000).
   [70]   *Image Technical Servs.*, 125 F.3d at 1218–20.
   [71]   Herbert Hovenkamp et al., *Unilateral Refusals to License*, 2 J. COMP. LAW & ECON. 1, 26–27 (2006).
   [72]   *Brulotte v. Thys Co.*, 379 U.S. 29 (1964).

patent misuse doctrine, merely speaking of the unenforceability of the royalty agreement itself, term extension has been accepted into the canon of patent misuse."[73]

At its simplest, the rule in *Brulotte* prohibits agreements that project beyond the expiration date of the patent without regard to the reason for that projection.[74] However, a closer reading shows the Court's sensitivity toward balancing the need to allow parties to contract freely and that their agreement under which the licensee pays royalties for a period longer than the life of the patent, presumably in the consideration of a lower rate, should be enforceable while prohibiting patentees from leveraging their patents to require payment of royalties after they expire.[75]

The patents in question were related to hop-picking machines. Licensees were requred to continue paying royalties to the licensor even after the patent expired. The Supreme Court found two provisions in the agreement to be evidence of abuse flowing from the patent: first, royalty payments remained unchanged before and after the patent expired; and second, the licensee could not assign or remove machines incorporating the patented technology after the patent expired.[76] The Court drew on the fact that the Constitution prescribed exclusive rights to inventors for "limited times," as well as Section 154 of the Patent Act which provided a fixed period, which at that time was 17 years.[77] It quoted with approval its own earlier

---

[73] Hovenkamp et al., *supra* note 9, at §3.3 (citing *Rocform Corp. v. Acitelli-Standard Concrete Wall*, 367 F.2d 678 (6th Cir. 1966); *B. Braun Med. v. Abbott Labs.*, 124 F.3d 1419 (Fed. Cir. 1997); *Mallinckrodt, Inc. v. Medipart, Inc.*, 976 F.2d 700 (Fed. Cir. 1992)).

[74] *Brulotte*, 379 U.S. at 32 ("we conclude that a patentee's use of a royalty agreement that projects beyond the expiration date of the patent is unlawful per se").

[75] Ibid. at 32 (noting that the patentee made no attempt to distinguish between the patent and post-patent periods, and the arrangement was a "bald attempt to exact the same terms" for the patent and post-patent periods, leaving the Court "unable to conjecture what the bargaining position of the parties might have been" had the patentee not exerted its leverage).

[76] *Brulotte*, 379 U.S. at 31 ("The royalty payments due for the post-expiration period are by their terms for use during that period, and are not deferred payments for use during the pre-expiration period. Nor is the case like the hypothetical ones put to us where non-patented articles are marketed at prices based on use. The machines in issue here were patented articles and the royalties exacted were the same for the post-expiration period as they were for the period of the patent. That is peculiarly significant in this case in view of other provisions of the license agreements. The license agreements prevent assignment of the machines or their removal from Yakima County after, as well as before, the expiration of the patents").

[77] Ibid. at 30 ("The Constitution by Art. I, s 8 authorizes Congress to secure 'for limited times' to inventors 'the exclusive right' to their discoveries. Congress exercised that power by 35 U.S.C. s 154 which provides in part as follows: 'Every

opinion in *Scott Paper Co. v. Marcalus Mfg. Co.*, where it was held that any attempted reservation or continuation in the patentee or those claiming under him of the patent monopoly, after the patent expires, whatever the legal device employed, runs counter to the policy and purpose of the patent laws.[78] The Court held that the license in *Brulotte* was unlawful because the patent had already entered the public domain.[79] These were not mere contractual restrictions but license terms which affected the public interest.[80] Analogizing the term extension to tying, it held that the license was "an attempt to tie the period of patent protection to the period after the period had expired, and did no further inquiry into the procompetitive justifications of the royalty arrangements."[81]

Subsequent cases following *Brulotte* have involved permutations on the fact pattern in that case.[82] For example, in *Rocform Corp. v. Acitelli-Standard Concrete Wall, Inc.*, the Court of Appeals for the Sixth Circuit expressly acknowledged:

> We do not deal here (as did the Supreme Court in *Brulotte v. Thys Co*) with the sale of a piece of machinery which incorporated a number of patents. Rather we deal with a licensing arrangement where one important patent (about to expire) is grouped with others of longer duration for "leverage."[83]

---

patent shall contain a short title of the invention and a grant to the patentee, his heirs or assigns, for the term of seventeen years, of the right to exclude others from making, using, or selling the invention throughout the United States, referring to the specification for the particulars thereof").

[78]   *Scott Paper Co. v. Marcalus Mfg. Co.*, 326 U.S. 249, 256 (1945).

[79]   *Brulotte*, 379 U.S. at 33 ("The exaction of royalties for use of a machine after the patent has expired is an assertion of monopoly power in the post-expiration period when, as we have seen, the patent has entered the public domain").

[80]   Ibid. at 32 ("The sale or lease of unpatented machines on long-term payments based on a deferred purchase price or on use would present wholly different considerations. Those arrangements seldom rise to the level of a federal question. But patents are in the federal domain; and 'whatever the legal device employed' . . . a projection of the patent monopoly after the patent expires is not enforceable" (citations omitted)).

[81]   Ibid. at 33 ("to use that leverage [provided by the patent grant] to project those royalty payments beyond the life of the patent is analogous to an effort to enlarge the monopoly of the patent by tieing [sic] the sale or use of the patented article to the purchase or use of the unpatented ones").

[82]   See *Rocform Corp. v. Acitelli-Standard Concrete Wall, Inc.*, 367 F.2d 678, 681 (6th Cir. 1966); see also *Meehan v. P.P.G. Indus., Inc.*, 802 F.2d 881, 885 (7th Cir. 1986); *Boggild v. Kenner Prods.*, 776 F.2d 1315, 1319 (6th Cir. 1985); *Pitney Bowes, Inc. v. Mestre*, 701 F.2d 1365, 1371 (11th Cir. 1983); *Leesona Corp. v. Varta Batteries, Inc.*, 522 F. Supp. 1304, 1342 (S.D.N.Y. 1981).

[83]   *Rocform Corp.*, 367 F.2d at 681; see also *Leesona Corp.*, 522 F. Supp. at 1342 ("A 'patentee's use of a royalty agreement that projects beyond the expiration

Nonetheless, citing *Brulotte* as precedential, the court had no difficulty concluding that "a contract, when it contains no diminution of license fee at the expiration of the most important patent and contains no termination clause at the will of the licensee, constitutes, in effect, an effort to continue to collect royalties on an expired patent."[84]

Later, in *Boggild v. Kenner Products*, the Sixth Circuit again applied *Brulotte*, this time to license provisions developed in anticipation of patent protection.[85] The patentee invented a toy extruder, but did not apply for any patents for the extruder at the time when the license agreement was executed.[86] However, the agreement required the patentee to apply promptly for patents on the extruder and for the licensee to make royalty payments for 25 years, regardless of whether the patents issued.[87] The Sixth Circuit held that *Brulotte* precluded enforcement of the license which required royalty payments beyond the life of the patent and did not contain provisions for reduction of post-expiration royalties.[88] Because the use restrictions on the extruder were the same in the post-expiration and pre-expiration periods, they were held unlawful *per se*.[89]

The Seventh Circuit in *Meehan v. PPG Indus., Inc.*, similarly reasoned that "[e]ven when an inventor has not yet applied for a patent, the right to apply for and obtain those protections is valuable. Such a right places the inventor in a strong bargaining position. It is that abuse of that leverage over which the Supreme Court expressed concern in *Brulotte*."[90] Elaborating on this reasoning, the court found that the leverage was "apparent from the terms of the agreement."[91] The parties anticipated an early patent application and required the defendant "to remain technical advisor to and provide information assistance" to the patentee in making

---

date of the patent is unlawful per se.' [quoting *Brulotte*] The use of such an arrangement constitutes patent misuse even in the absence of evidence demonstrating that the patent holder used the leverage of the patent coercively to impose an extended term on the licensee"); *Pitney Bowes, Inc.*, 701 F.2d at 1371; *Boggild*, 776 F.2d at 1319; *Meehan*, 802 F.2d at 885.

[84]   *Rocform*, 367 F.2d at 681.
[85]   *Boggild*, 776 F.2d 1315.
[86]   Ibid. at 1316–17.
[87]   Ibid. at 1316–17.
[88]   Ibid. at 1321.
[89]   Ibid. at 1319–21. The court reasoned that "the same violations of patent law arising from abuse of the leverage attached to a pending or issued patent can arise from abuse of the leverage afforded by an expressly anticipated application for a patent," ibid. at 1320.
[90]   *Meehan v. PPG Indus., Inc.*, 802 F.2d 881, 884-86 (7th Cir. 1986).
[91]   Ibid. at 886.

the patent application.[92] Further, one clause required the defendant "to pay royalties for only 10 years if no patent issued but for over 17 years (the life of the patent) if a patent issued."[93]

Further, following *Brulotte*, the Seventh Circuit determined in *Meehan* that where a license agreement covers both inventions subject to a patent or patent application as well as trade secrets, "there must be some provision that distinguishes between patent royalties and trade secret royalties."[94] Where the rate of royalty payments remains constant in the post-expiration period, patent leverage has been abused and the agreement is unlawful *per se* because the terms of the agreement demonstrate that the plaintiff used his right to obtain a patent to project his monopoly power beyond the patent period.[95] This decision came after the Supreme Court suggested in dicta that this rule might not apply where there was no issued patent.[96]

The Court held that absent an issued patent, federal patent law will not preempt state contract law.[97] Had the patent issued, enforcement of the royalty beyond the life of the patent would have been precluded.[98] In *Prestole Corp. v. Tinnerman Prods., Inc.*, the license excluded a device covered by patents, one of which had already expired when the agreement was signed.[99] The Sixth Circuit held that the condition extended a monopoly in an expired patent, and

> [t]he fact that the general public, other than [the licensee], was not thereby forbidden the use of this then unpatented device and that [the licensee] might employ it

---

[92] Ibid.

[93] Ibid.

[94] Ibid. at 886; see also *Brulotte v. Thys Co.*, 379 U.S. 29, 31–33 (1964).

[95] *Brulotte*, 379 U.S. at 31–33.

[96] *Aronson v. Quick Point Pencil Co.*, 440 U.S. 257, 265 (1979). Before concluding that "[t]his case does not require us to draw the line between what constitutes abuse of a pending application and what does not," the Court noted that: "No doubt a pending patent application gives the applicant some additional bargaining power for purposes of negotiating a royalty agreement. The pending application allows the inventor to hold out the hope of an exclusive right to exploit the idea, as well as the threat that the other party will be prevented from using the idea for 17 years. However, the amount of leverage arising from a patent application depends on how likely the parties consider it to be that a valid patent will issue. Here, where no patent ever issued, the record is entirely clear that the parties assigned a substantial likelihood to that contingency, since they specifically provided for a reduced royalty in the event no patent issued within five years," ibid. at 265.

[97] Ibid. at 262.

[98] Ibid. at 263–64.

[99] *Prestole Corp. v. Tinnerman Prods., Inc.*, 271 F.2d 146, 155 (6th Cir. 1959).

in manufacturing equipment not containing the invention of the licensed patents does not, in our opinion, exonerate [the licensor] from a charge of attempting to extend, for its own purposes, a monopoly in an expired patent.[100]

More recently, as agreements were drafted with *Brulotte* in mind, courts have reached differing conclusions as to whether to expand *Brulotte*. In *Hull v. Brunswick Corp.*, the agreement did not require royalty payments to continue after the time that the patents used had expired. Instead, it required the licensee to pay the full royalty rate on a bundle of licenses until the last patent expired. This represents a cross between package licensing discussed in the earlier section and time extensions. The court found that such an agreement was valid and "does not violate the letter or spirit of *Brulotte*, as it does not require payment for expired patents."[101] The licensee's obligation however, may not be in the form of continued royalty payments, but instead take the form of a continued obligation to purchase goods or services from the patentee. This is a hybrid form of tying-time extension type of patent misuse. An example of this hybrid form was litigated in *Hearing Components, Inc. v. Shure, Inc.*[102] In this case the license agreement required the licensee to continue purchasing foam tips for earphones for five years after the patents expired.[103] The court pointed out that the defendant had not cited "any case in which a post-expiration supply obligation was found to be patent misuse *per se*," and was unwilling to expand *Brulotte* to cover it.[104] The court held that section 271(d) (5) required the alleged infringer to show market power in the relevant market in order to prove the requisite anticompetitive effect.[105] In order to show that a continued obligation to pay royalties amounts to misuse, the accuser needs to show some element of coercion.[106] Robert Hoerner

---

[100]   Ibid.

[101]   *Hull v. Brunswick Corp.*, 704 F.2d 1195, 1202 (10th Cir. 1983); see generally *Brulotte v. Thys Co.*, 85 S. Ct. 176, 179 (1964) (stating that the continued payment on package license when some but not all patents have expired is permissible, even when payment is based on sales of items that may employ no patents at all).

[102]   *Hearing Components, Inc. v. Shure, Inc.*, No. 9:07-CV-104, 2009 U.S. Dist. LEXIS 25050, at *24–25 (E.D. Tex. Mar. 26, 2009), *rev'd in part on other grounds by* 600 F.3d 357 (Fed. Cir. 2010).

[103]   Ibid.

[104]   Ibid.

[105]   Ibid. ("Shure also put forth little, if any, evidence that HCI had the type of market power envisioned under Section 271(d)(5) that would make a tying agreement of this nature statutory patent misuse. In short, there is insufficient evidence that these practices extended HCI's patent rights with anti-competitive effect").

[106]   *Well Surveys, Inc. v. Perfo-Log, Inc.*, 396 F.2d 15, 17 (10th Cir. 1968) ("The lack of diminution in royalty rate for the use of Peterson without Swift and the

has suggested that the reason why courts find against such agreements is because "it is impossible for them to rewrite the agreement to determine what the 'right' rate is for the know-how when the patent(s) disappear from the picture as valid consideration."[107] The problem is not intractable and "yields itself to careful drafting".[108] For example:

> it is very probable that a court would uphold a hybrid agreement where the know-how was licensed at, say, four percent, with the royalty obligation to continue for so long as the license continued using the know-how, and with the patent (or application) licensed at, say, eight percent until it expired (or, say, five years had passed and the application had still not ripened into a patent) but with the royalty due under the know-how license creditable against the royalty due under the patent license.[109]

In sum, though license agreements have adapted to comply with *Brulotte*, the decision remains a strong precedent for courts that encounter apparent patent misuse in the form of time extensions.

B.   Criticism

Brulotte has principally received criticism for not recognizing the intention of parties to amortize payments over time. In the Seventh Circuit's decision in *Scheiber v. Dolby Laboratories, Inc.*, Judge Posner alluded to past criticism of *Brulotte* while adding that "*Brulotte* involved an agreement licensing patents that expired at different dates, just like this case; the two cases are *indistinguishable*."[110] He reasoned that "[t]he duration of

---

provisions for termination do not of themselves establish coercion. The question is whether the licensee was forced to enter into a package arrangement").

[107]   Robert J. Hoerner, *supra* note 62, at 704–11.
[108]   Ibid.
[109]   Ibid.
[110]   *Scheiber v. Dolby Labs.*, 293 F.3d 1014, 1017 (7th Cir. 2002) (emphasis added). ("The decision has, it is true, been severely, and as it seems to us, with all due respect, justly, criticized, beginning with Justice Harlan's dissent, and continuing with our opinion in *USM Corp. v. SPS Technologies, Inc.* . . . The Supreme Court's majority opinion reasoned that by extracting a promise to continue paying royalties after expiration of the patent, the patentee extends the patent beyond the term fixed in the patent statute and therefore in violation of the law. That is not true. After the patent expires, anyone can make the patented process or product without being guilty of patent infringement. The patent can no longer be used to exclude anybody from such production. Expiration thus accomplishes what it is supposed to accomplish. For a licensee in accordance with a provision in the license agreement to go on paying royalties after the patent expires does not extend the duration of the patent either technically or practically, because, as this case

the patent fixes the limit of the patentee's power to extract royalties; it is a detail whether he extracts them at a higher rate over a shorter period of time or a lower rate over a longer period of time."[111]

Judge Posner's *carte blanche* dismissal of *Brulotte* is troubling. Contrary to his observation, there were significant differences between the two cases. First, in *Brulotte* the patentee's terms were part of a standard agreement entered into by Brulotte, requiring him to pay royalties on patents covering technology which would have expired before the license agreement.[112] In *Scheiber*, it was the licensee who suggested the terms because "it hoped [to] pass on the entire royalty expense to its sublicensees without their balking at the rate. Scheiber acceded to the suggestion and the agreement was drafted accordingly, but Dolby later refused to pay royalties on any patent after it expired, precipitating this suit."[113] The majority in *Brulotte* recognized that parties were free to allocate their risks and rewards based on metering of usage, but that the binding force of those agreements should come from contracts rather than patent leverage.[114]

Second, Judge Posner in *Scheiber* concedes that his criticisms of *Brulotte* would be unjustified had *Brulotte* relied on the Constitution or statute rather than a "misplaced fear of monopoly."[115] However, in *Brulotte*,

---

demonstrates, if the licensee agrees to continue paying royalties after the patent expires the royalty rate will be lower.")

[111]   Ibid.

[112]   *Brulotte*, 379 U.S. at 30. ("All but one of the 12 expired prior to the expiration of the license agreements. The exception was a patent whose mechanism was not incorporated in these machines.")

[113]   Scheiber, 293 F.3d., at 1016.

[114]   *Brulotte*, 379 U.S. at 32 ("Those restrictions are apt and pertinent to protection of the patent monopoly; and their applicability to the post-expiration period is a telltale sign that the licensor was using the licenses to project its monopoly beyond the patent period. They forcefully negate the suggestion that we have here a bare arrangement for a sale or a lease at an undetermined price based on use. The sale or lease of unpatented machines on long-term payments based on a deferred purchase price or on use would present wholly different considerations. . . . The same provisions as respects both use and royalties are applicable to each. The contracts are, therefore, on their face a bald attempt to exact the same terms and conditions for the period after the patents have expired as they do for the monopoly period. We are, therefore, unable to conjecture what the bargaining position of the parties might have been and what resultant arrangement might have emerged had the provision for post-expiration royalties been divorced from the patent and nowise subject to its leverage").

[115]   Ibid. ("These criticisms might be wide of the mark if Brulotte had been based on an interpretation of the patent clause of the Constitution, or of the patent statute or any other statute; but it seems rather to have been a free-floating product of a misplaced fear of monopoly . . . that was not even tied to one of the antitrust

the Court expressly based its theory of actionable misuse on the "limited times" requirement under the Constitution.[116] Interestingly, in 2003, Judge Posner was perhaps an unlikely advocate of patent misuse doctrine based on his later decision in *Scheiber*.[117] In *SmithKline Beecham Corp. v. Apotex Corp.*, he concluded it would be a "travesty of equity" to permit the plaintiff an extension of its patent beyond the patent term.[118] In so doing, Judge Posner was effectively reaching the same result as if he had found misuse and refused to enforce the patent against Apotex since it had already expired. Indeed, Judge Posner noted that "[a]nother way to explain SmithKline's disentitlement to an injunction is in terms of the doctrine, classically equitable—an aspect of the historic doctrine of 'unclean hands'—of patent misuse."[119]

Third, courts such the U.S. District Court for the Eastern District of Texas in *Shure*, continue to recognize that *Brulotte* remains good law.[120] In another case, Amazon.com accused Cordance of misusing its patent by improperly extending the effective term of its patents through an exclusive license agreement with a third party, XDI.ORG.[121] The agreement granted access to its patents in order to create an open Internet standard necessary for widespread adoption. In exchange, Cordance received a 15-year contract to become the primary operator of global name registry services. Amazon argued that because a number of Global services had yet to be implemented as of February 2009, the exclusive contract to provide those services extends well beyond the expiration of Cordance's patents in 2016. The court found that this provided sufficient evidence for a colorable allegation of misuse, which led to the court denying Cordance's motion for summary judgment.[122] While the lingering presence of *Brulotte*

---

statutes. The doctrinal basis of the decision was the doctrine of patent misuse, of which more later").

[116]   Ibid. at 30.

[117]   *SmithKline Beecham Corp. v. Apotex Corp.*, 247 F. Supp. 2d 1011, 1046–47 (N.D. Ill. 2003) (Judge Posner sitting by designation).

[118]   Ibid.

[119]   Ibid. at 1046.

[120]   *Hearing Components, Inc. v. Shure, Inc.*, No, 9:07-CV-104, 2009 U.S. Dist. LEXIS 25050, at *30–32 (E.D. Tex. Mar. 26, 2009) ("There is some support for the position that licensing an expired patent can still extend the patentee's rights with anti-competitive effect, even when the general public is not prohibited from using the device covered under the patent").

[121]   *Cordance Corp. v. Amazon.com, Inc.*, 631 F. Supp. 2d 484, 495–97 (D. Del. 2009).

[122]   Ibid. at 497 ("Based on the evidence presented, and giving all reasonable inferences to the non-movant (Amazon), the court cannot determine, as a matter of law, that Cordance's agreement with XDI.ORG is not patent misuse").

does not necessarily validate its relevance or correctness in modern times, the burden may well lie on its critics to prove otherwise.

V.   RESTRICTIONS AND ROYALTIES

The basic premise underlying the attitude that courts take toward restriction and royalty arrangement stems from their view on the patentee's right to refuse to license its technology. American patent and antitrust laws impose no requirement that patentees use their inventions.[123] The law also gives patentees the right to refuse to license that technology to others, even for the offer of a reasonable royalty.[124] Section 271(d)(4) thus allows patentees to keep inventions solely to themselves and decide whether and to whom to license. Lawrence Sullivan suggests two rationales for this deference to patentees: encouraging others to invent around patented technology, as well as encouraging challenges to the patent validity, thus "freeing the mistakenly confined technology."[125]

A refusal to license is deemed unimpeachable, even if it is constructive, in the sense that the patentee prices the technology beyond what the licensee can reasonably be expected to pay. The Third Circuit explained that this was "not appreciably different from a refusal to license upon any terms", but justified because "[t]he right to refuse to license is the essence of the patent holder's right under the patent law which rewards invention disclosure by the grant of a limited monopoly in the exploitation of the invention."[126]

---

[123]   *United Shoe Mach. Corp. v. O'Donnell Rubber Prods. Co.*, 84 F.2d 383, 386 (6th Cir. 1936) ("Whatever may be the policy of patent laws elsewhere, it has long been settled that, in the United States, exclusion of competitors is the very essence of the right conferred by a patent, and it is the privilege of any owner of property to use or not to use it without question of motive").

[124]   James B. Kobak, Jr., *Antitrust Treatment of Refusals to License Intellectual Property*, Licensing J. (January 2002), available at: http://www.hugheshubbard.com/ArticleDocuments/Kobak%20Licensing.pdf ("A widely accepted first premise of our intellectual property laws is that an intellectual property owner is under no obligation to license that property to others. This principle is generally held to be true even when a firm has achieved a monopoly position in a market as a result of its ownership of intellectual property. Indeed, this principle is recognized by the Department of Justice/Federal Trade Commission *Guidelines for the Licensing of Intellectual Property* issued in 1995. Section 2.2 of the Guidelines explicitly states that an intellectual property owner has no general duty to license its intellectual property").

[125]   Lawrence Sullivan, Handbook of the Law of Antitrust 526 (1977).

[126]   *W. L. Gore & Assocs., Inc. v. Carlisle Corp.*, 529 F.2d 614, 622–23 (3d Cir. 1976).

From the basic premise that patentees can choose not to license their patents, courts have derived the corollary reasoning that they should generally be allowed to set the terms for access to their technology.[127] The latitude given to patentee is, however, not absolute. The law is clear that "[t]he fact that a patentee has the power to refuse a license does not mean that he has the power to grant a license on such conditions as he may choose."[128] Robert Hoerner explains that the alternative would mean that "Section (d)(4) will come close to swallowing up the entirety of the patent misuse defense, for a patent owner can always say that it was exercising its (d)(4) right to refuse to license unless the licensee agreed to the challenged clause."[129]

Antitrust policy treats licensing generally as pro-competitive, as it affords some competition in producing an otherwise exclusive product. This may explain why courts guided by antitrust policy may have taken a lighter touch where licensing is involved, as well as why courts have confined misuse to a limited set of antitrust-like conduct.[130] At the same time, several categories of patent misuse, such as non-metered royalties and resale field-of-use limitations, do not constitute antitrust violations unless they amount to monopolization or attempted monopolization of the tied product by a defendant with market power.[131] But proof of market power traditionally has not been necessary to prove patent misuse.[132]

---

[127]   Robert J. Hoerner, *supra* note 62, at 697 ("The lesson to be learned from *Windsurfing* is probably that prohibitions in license agreements are rarely, if ever, held to be misuse unless they have the effect of constituting patent-like restrictions on the ability of the licensee to make, use, or sell a product or process, which prohibition goes beyond either the scope of the claims or the scope of the rights granted by Title 35").

[128]   *Transparent-Wrap Mach. Corp. v. Stokes & Smith Co.*, 329 U.S. 637, 643 (1947).

[129]   See Hoerner, *supra* note 62, at 708.

[130]   See *Raychem Corp. v. PSI Telecomms.*, No. C-93-20920, 1995 U.S. Dist. LEXIS 22325, at *9 ("Application of the doctrine has been confined to a small number of specific anticompetitive acts, such as tying arrangements coupled with market power, covenants not to deal, and mandatory package licensing").

[131]   Non-metered royalties require payment irrespective of the extent of use. Package licenses often contain such clauses. See, e.g., *Automatic Radio Mfg v. Hazeltine Research*, 339 U.S. 827 (1950). A resale field of use limitation limits the scope that licensees can use the patent for upon resale of the article.

[132]   Robin Feldman, Rethinking Patent Law 139 (2012) ("A finding of market power is not required under traditional patent misuse doctrine, but it is required for establishing an antitrust violation. Thus, a finding of patent misuse does not necessarily mean that the patent holder has committed an antitrust violation").

More importantly, a defendant need not show injury to competition to prove patent misuse, as is required to show an antitrust violation. As a result, courts have refused to find that proof of misuse necessarily proves an antitrust violation.[133]

A. Restrictions

Licensing restrictions take a number of forms. Some require that "licensees refrain from either dealing in a competitor's goods or developing competing alternatives itself."[134] The starting point to understanding why licensing restrictions may constitute misuse comes from the principle of exhaustion. In *B. Braun Medical, Inc. v. Abbott Laboratories*, the Federal Circuit explained that "unconditional sale of a patented device exhausts the patentee's right to control the purchaser's use of the device thereafter," since "in such a transaction, the patentee has bargained for, and received, an amount equal to the full value of the goods."[135] Similarly, under antitrust law such restrictions have been held to violate the Sherman Act. Case law in this area has been sparse. The Fifth Circuit explained that post-sale restrictions were illegal because "to permit this would sanction franchising and confinement of distribution as the ordinary instead of the unusual method which may be permissible in an appropriate and impelling competitive setting, since most merchandise is distributed by means of purchase and sale."[136] Hence, "such restraints are so obviously destructive of competition that their mere existence is enough."[137]

According to the Federal Circuit, however, the exhaustion doctrine does not apply to an expressly conditional sale or license. In such a circumstance, "it is more reasonable to infer that the parties negotiated a price that reflects only the value of the 'use' rights conferred by the patentee."[138] Accordingly, "express conditions accompanying the sale or license of a patented product are generally upheld."[139] One court has held that there is no obligation on the patentee's part to renegotiate terms—

---

[133]   See *Laitram Corp. v. King Crab, Inc.*, 245 F. Supp. 1019, 1020 (D. Ak. 1965) ("[The] doctrine of misuse of patents does not necessarily include a violation of the antitrust laws").

[134]   Hovenkamp & Bohannan, *supra* note 28, at 280.

[135]   *Medical, Inc. v. Abbott Labs.*, 124 F.3d 1419, 1426 (Fed. Cir. 1997).

[136]   *Hensley Equip. Co. v. Esco Corp.*, 383 F.2d 252, 263–64 (1967).

[137]   Ibid.

[138]   *B. Braun Med., Inc. v. Abbott Laboratories*, 124 F.3d 1419, 1426 (Fed. Cir. 1997). The conditional sales doctrine is controversial and has been subject to challenge. See *Bowman v. Monsanto Co.*, 133 S. Ct. 420 (2012).

[139]   Ibid.

"[t]here is no legal compulsion to negotiate individual rates in the first instance and there is no legal compulsion to renegotiate them later upon demand."[140] While courts can limit the terms of agreements and redress oppressive agreements, they will not "reform an agreement merely to suit the present desires of one of the parties."[141] Such "oppressive agreements" include instances where "the refusal to negotiate individualized rates was merely a sham that forced the purchaser to accept unwanted patents in order to secure desired patents, that refusal could constitute patent misuse."[142]

As a general rule, restrictions are evaluated under a rule of reason analysis.[143] In *County Materials Corp. v. Allan Block Corp.*, the Seventh Circuit swiftly rejected the antitrust plaintiff's contention that the patentee's inclusion of a convent not to compete in the license was *per se* misuse.[144] On the facts, the Court found that the antitrust plaintiff having the non-compete obligation was reasonable condition for access to the patented technology, the patentee's trademarks, and support services.[145] The reason

---

[140]   *Hull v. Brunswick Corp.*, 704 F.2d 1195, 1200–1202 (10th Cir. 1983) ("The law does not force a patentee to renegotiate any specific terms within the framework of an existing agreement").

[141]   Ibid.

[142]   Ibid. (citing *American Securit Co. v. Shatterproof Glass Corp.*, 268 F.2d 769 (3d Cir. 1959); noting mandatory, coercive package licensing is misuse).

[143]   U.S. Dep't of Justice & Fed. Trade Comm'n, *supra* note 24 ("In the vast majority of cases, restraints in intellectual property licensing arrangements are evaluated under the rule of reason").

[144]   *County Materials Corp. v. Allan Block Corp.*, 502 F.3d 730, 734 (7th Cir. 2007) ("County Materials essentially claims that the inclusion of the covenant not to compete in the patent license here was *per se* unlawful patent misuse and the improper result of patent leverage. While at one time this argument might have had traction, in certain circumstances, it is at least disfavored today, if not entirely rejected").

[145]   Ibid. at 737 ("County Materials received significant benefits, starting with the right to use the patented technology for the manufacture of the concrete blocks, and continuing with the right to use Allan Block's trademark and the right to receive supporting technical, marketing, and strategic services from Allan Block. In return, County Materials had to promise to pay royalties to Allan Block and to devote significant efforts to the exploitation of Allan Block's patent. If County Materials had been free to pick and choose among all potentially competing products on the market, Allan Block may have signed over the rights to use its patent and know-how for little or nothing in return. Allan Block's services alone have considerable value for any company undertaking the manufacture and sale of these products (or so the parties could have concluded), whether or not they are tied to a patented product. Nothing in these facts suggests that Allan Block needed or used any kind of leverage made possible by the patent to secure County Materials's promise to refrain from working with all but the designated two com-

is that "[t]hese agreements pose clear competitive risks, because they allow a patentee to reduce innovation by competitors and may help to facilitate a cartel."[146] Non-compete clauses are, however, generally regarded with suspicion under misuse law.[147] Robert Hoerner highlights an exception: "[e]xcept where the licensor has granted an exclusive license and is dependent upon the good faith, best efforts of the licensee to obtain income from his patent, it has been and probably will continue to be a patent misuse for the patent owner to forbid a non-exclusive licensee from utilizing competitive non-patented technology."[148]

Similarly, in *Mallinckrodt*, the patentee restricted licensees from reusing a medical device. Such restrictions were justified on the basis of safety or the operational effectiveness of the device.[149] Professor Christina Bohannan, however, has criticized this as a "resource-costly way of metering downstream use by requiring a royalty on each use . . . because the patentee cannot measure the number of downstream uses, it simply limits

---

peting products, or its promise to refrain from using other products for 18 months after the expiration of the Agreement").

[146] Hovenkamp et al., *supra* note 9, at §3.3 ("As an example, suppose that companies *A* and *B* compete in the sale of a variety of computer-related devices, including cell phones, laptops, and desktop computers. Company *A* possesses a patent essential to the making of a particular type of laptop. *A* is entitled to prevent *B* from making that type of laptop, or to license *B* to make infringing laptops in exchange for a royalty. *A* is not, however, entitled to license *B* the right to make infringing laptops only on the condition that it will not make competing cell phones that are outside the scope of the patent. At least where *A* and *B* have a significant share of the market, the effect of such an agreement would be to foreclose competition outside the scope of the patent").

[147] See *Berlenbach v. Anderson & Thompson Ski Co.*, 329 F.2d 782 (9th Cir. 1964); see also *Compton v. Metal Prods.*, 453 F.2d 38, 44 (4th Cir. 1971); see also *Nat'l Lockwasher Co. v. George K. Garrett Co.*, 137 F.2d 255 (3d Cir. 1943); see also *Krampe v. Ideal Indus., Inc.*, 347 F. Supp. 1384 (N.D. Ill. 1972).

[148] Hoerner, *supra* note 62 at 704 (1991).

[149] *Mallinckrodt, Inc. v. Medipart, Inc.*, 976 F.2d 700, 708–709 (Fed. Cir. 1992) ("[Where] there are anticompetitive effects extending beyond the patentee's statutory right to exclude, these effects do not automatically impeach the restriction. Anticompetitive effects that are not per se violations of law are reviewed in accordance with the rule of reason. Patent owners should not be in a worse position, by virtue of the patent right to exclude, than owners of other property used in trade. Compare Tripoli Co. v. Wella Corp., 425 F.2d 932, 936–38 (3d Cir. 1970) (en banc) (holding in a non-patent action, restriction on resale of certain potentially dangerous products does not violate antitrust laws where motivation was prevention of injury to public and protection against liability risk), with Marks, Inc. v. Polaroid Corp., 237 F.2d 428, 436, 111 USPQ 60, 66 (1st Cir. 1956) (holding a single use only restriction based on safety concerns not patent misuse, and enforceable by suit for patent infringement)").

that number to one and licenses a new article for each use."[150] Framing the restriction as one on re-use, according to Professor Bohannan, is better because "[o]nce the first use is exhausted, the user is free to purchase elsewhere, and indeed, the single-use restriction may induce the user to do so. As a result, any general case for condemning single-use restrictions on foreclosure grounds is very weak."[151]

In any event, she notes that because *Mallinckrodt* involved a sale, it has been overruled by the Supreme Court's decision in *Quanta Computer, Inc. v. LG Elecs., Inc.*, which held such reach-through royalties to be unenforceable.[152] Another example of patent restrictions involves using the seeds produced by plants bearing patented traits. In *Monsanto Co. v. McFarling*, the Federal Circuit acknowledged the case was one of first-impression.[153] The court concluded that the patent read on seeds from the first and subsequent generations. Thus the restrictions that prohibited replanting of those seeds did not extend the patent rights beyond their permissible scope.[154] As with *Mallinckrodt*, the authority of *Monsanto* has been cast into doubt. Professors Hovenkamp et al. note that:

---

[150]   Christina Bohannan, *IP Misuse As Foreclosure*, 96 Iowa L. Rev. 475, 522 (2011).

[151]   Ibid.

[152]   Ibid. at 522 ("Insofar as *Mallinckrodt* involved a sale, it has now been overruled by the Supreme Court's decision in *Quanta*, which reinstated a strict patent 'exhaustion' (first-sale) rule against post-sale restraints. Because the first transaction in *Mallinckrodt* was a sale, under *Quanta*, the patentee did not have the right to impose any further restrictions on the device. More recently, a district court held that it could be patent misuse for a printer manufacturer to limit its printer cartridges to a single use").

[153]   *Monsanto Co. v. McFarling*, 363 F.3d 1336, 1343 (Fed. Cir. 2004). The court explained: "Our case law has not addressed in general terms the status of such restrictions placed on goods made by, yet not incorporating, the licensed good under the patent misuse doctrine. However, the Technology Agreement presents a unique set of facts in which licensing restrictions on the use of goods produced by the licensed product are not beyond the scope of the patent grant at issue: The licensed and patented product (the first-generation seeds) and the good made by the licensed product (the second-generation seeds) are nearly identical copies. Thus, given that we must presume that Monsanto's '435 patent reads on the first-generation seeds, it also reads on the second-generation seeds . . . . *See* '435 patent, col. 165, l. 12 (claiming '[a] seed of a glyphosate-tolerant plant')," ibid. (footnote omitted).

[154]   Ibid. ("Thus, given that we must presume that Monsanto's '435 patent reads on the first-generation seeds, it also reads on the second-generation seeds. *See* '435 patent, col. 165, l. 12 (claiming '[a] seed of a glyphosate-tolerant plant')").

[*Monsanto*] may be suspect after *Quanta v. LG*, however, because the ordinary use a farmer makes of soybean seeds is to plant them in the ground and grow new seeds. If a court were to find Monsanto's rights exhausted by the first sale, the door would be open to an argument that attempting to prevent seed saving by contract constituted patent misuse.[155]

Courts have considered a variety of other restrictions in license agreements and have found, or declined to find, patent misuse. First, the U.S. District Court for the District of Colorado summarized the Tenth Circuit's holdings in a series of cases by saying that where "unpatented operations were used to determine the royalty base only, the license agreements were voluntary on the part of the licensees, there was no evidence of economic coercion" and no attempt to extend the patent monopoly beyond the scope of the patent, there was no evidence of misuse.[156] However, a clause prohibiting a licensee from selling articles in competition with the patented articles can constitute misuse.[157] One example where such scrutiny resulted in a finding of misuse was *Compton v. Metal Products, Inc.*, in which the Fourth Circuit found that the agreement between the parties restricting the licensee from engaging in any business relating to the manufacture or sale of the type of licensed screw conveyors was an unreasonable restraint of trade amounting to patent misuse.[158] However, courts are generally unsympathetic to licensees who attempt to use the threat of a misuse claim to force patentees to the negotiating table, stating simply that if they were unhappy, they could end the agreement.[159]

Similarly, licensors cannot abuse their leverage by threatening licensees

---

[155] 1 Hovenkamp et al., *supra* note 9, at §3.3.

[156] *Valmont Indus., Inc. v. Yuma Mfg. Co.*, 296 F. Supp. 1291, 1298 (D. Colo. 1969).

[157] *Nat'l Lockwasher Co. v. George K. Garrett Co.*, 137 F.2d 255, 257 (3rd Cir. 1943) (holding that such a clause was "enough to show that the plaintiff was using its patent to suppress competition with it by non-patented articles"); see also *Berlenbach v. Anderson & Thompson Ski Co.*, 329 F.2d 782, 783 n.1 (9th Cir. 1964) (quoting the anticompetitive clause at issue: "It is understood and agreed that during the term of this agreement, or any extension thereof, Second Party shall not manufacture or distribute in the United States and Canada any other safety type or automatic releasing ski binding other than that manufactured by First Party, together with any improvements developed by First Party and approved by Second Party").

[158] *Compton v. Metal Products, Inc.*, 453 F.2d 38, 42 (4th Cir. 1971) (noting the extension of patents beyond their expiration in holding that the plaintiff engaged in patent misuse).

[159] See, e.g., *Hull v. Brunswick Corp.*, 704 F.2d 1195, 1200–1201 (10th Cir. 1983) ("If Brunswick became dissatisfied with its arrangement with Hull, it could end that arrangement within the terms of the agreement").

with discontinuing supply of the patented technology or dealing with distributors unless the licensees comply with the restrictions. In *Ansul Co. v. Uniroyal, Inc.*, the patentee threatened to discontinue dealing with distributors "who persisted in price-cutting or in selling outside of designated area, and price-cutting dealers were caused to be blacklisted."[160] This conduct was found to be a *per se* violation of the Sherman Act.[161] Even after the patentee relaxed its policing activities, however, the court found that the anticompetitive effects of its conduct had not dissipated because it did not take "affirmative steps that would convince distributors that they were free to engage in market competition. . . ."[162] Another license restriction alleged to be patent misuse is restricting "the classes of consumers to whom manufacturer-licensees could sell."[163] The Seventh Circuit found such restrictions valid,[164] but elsewhere the position is less clear. A restriction on the sale of an unpatented product made by a patented process that survived an antitrust attack in the D.C. Circuit was found to be misuse in a later case in that same circuit.[165] This schism has led one commentator to note that "patent misuse based on resale restrictions will be with us for as long as 'extension of the monopoly'-type misuse remains viable."[166] Overall, courts have examined a variety of restrictions while, in keeping with the rule of reason analysis, remaining attentive to each unique dispute as a whole, specifically, evidence of the conduct and intentions of the parties.

B. Excessive Royalties

Courts are not sympathetic to allegations of excessive royalties.[167] Even in the heyday of vigorous enforcement, case law made it clear that "[a] patent

---

[160] *Ansul Co. v. Uniroyal, Inc.*, 306 F. Supp. 541, 548, 557-59 (7th Cir. 1967).
[161] Ibid.
[162] Ibid. at 561.
[163] *Armstrong v. Motorola, Inc.*, 374 F.2d 764, 774 (7th Cir. 1967).
[164] Ibid.
[165] Cf. *United States v. Studiengesellschaft Kohle, m.b.H.*, 670 F.2d 1122 (D.C. Cir. 1981) with *Robintech, Inc. v. Chemidus Wavin, Ltd*, 450 F. Supp. 817 (D.D.C. 1978).
[166] See Hoerner, *supra* note 62, at 710.
[167] Ibid. ("A license clause which has no effect other than arguably increasing the amount of royalties which the patent-owning licensor receives should be held proper, whatever the amount"); *Verizon Commc'ns Inc. v. Law Offices of Curtis V. Trinko, LLP*, 540 U.S. 398, 407 (2004) ("The opportunity to charge monopoly prices—at least for a short period—is what attracts 'business acumen' in the first place; it induces risk taking that produces innovation and economic growth").

empowers the owner to exact royalties as high as he can negotiate with the leverage of that monopoly."[168] Indeed, royalty rates well of up to 30 percent have been upheld.[169] The patent system is premised on a belief that patentees should be able to charge as much as the market will pay for its invention and that such pricing schemes will not amount to misuse or an antitrust violation. They may be "[b]ased upon any convenient measure of the business value of a patent license, even if it includes royalties on items not embodying the patented invention or royalties on a percentage of the licensee's total sales."[170] The question is not whether royalties are paid on unpatented goods, but whether "the mutual convenience or efficiency of both the licensor and the licensee results in a royalty base which includes the licensee's total sales or sales of non-patented items."[171]

One reason for this approach is simply that parties should be free to decide what the value of the deal is worth to them. Thus under antitrust law, the position has been that prices are not subject to regulatory oversight. Another reason for the reluctance of courts to intervene is that it is too complicated and speculative a venture, even in the case of discriminatory pricing which arguably might provide a better common dominator for comparison. In *Laitram Corp v. Depoe Bay Fish Co.*, the U.S. District Court for the District of Oregon had to consider what an appropriate royalty rate would be with respect to shrimp-peeling technology.[172] In rejecting the allegation of misuse based on uniform pricing, the court found that "postpeeling yields vary greatly," and accordingly, discriminatory pricing would be untenable for the patentee's business, with which the court was reluctant to interfere.[173]

At the same time, royalty clauses in licensing agreements have been

---

[168]   *Brulotte v. Thys Co.*, 379 U.S. 29, 33 (1964).

[169]   See, e.g., *W. L. Gore & Assocs., Inc. v. Carlisle Co.*, 529 F.2d 614, 623 (3d Cir. 1976) (30% Royalty).

[170]   *Magnavox Co. v. Mattel, Inc.*, No. 80 C 4124, 1982 U.S. Dist. LEXIS 13773 (N.D. Ill. July 29, 1982).

[171]   Ibid.

[172]   *Laitram Corp. v. Depoe Bay Fish Co.*, 549 F. Supp. 29 (D. Or. 1982).

[173]   Ibid. at 35. The court analyzed the trial evidence: "postpeeling yields vary greatly, even in the Northwest. A wide variety of factors affect the yield, which varies from place to place even in the defendant Pacific Pearl's area of operations. ... The defendants would have the patent declared unenforceable because a uniform rate is charged. If Laitram were to adjust its royalty rate to account for the generally lower yields of the Northwest, it could also be required to adjust its rate for higher quality shrimp which command a higher price in the marketplace, or where higher fuel costs make it more expensive to produce a pound of peeled shrimp," ibid.

regarded as amounting to misuse because they violate both antitrust and patent policies. Antitrust law frowns upon clauses that result in static inefficiencies, as they do when they raise prices and result in lower market outputs.[174] Similarly, percentage-of-sales royalty provisions may amount to misuse. The Supreme Court in *Zenith Radio Corp. v. Hazeltine Research, Inc.* found two "undesirable consequences" of such provisions.[175] First, they "reduce the licensee's incentive to substitute other, cheaper 'inputs' for the patented item in producing an unpatented end-product."[176] This will "cause the price of the end-product to be higher and its output lower than would be the case if substitution had occurred."[177] Second, it "may enable the patentee to garner for himself elements of profit, above the norm for the industry or economy, which are properly attributable not to the licensee's use of the patent but to other factors which cause the licensee's situation to differ from one of 'perfect competition,' and that this cannot occur when royalties are based upon use."[178]

Another type of royalty misuse comes from reach-through royalty clauses. In this case, royalties are based not on using the patented technology but rather on dealing in products resulting from that technology. Patents over-research tools—reagents and laboratory equipment are the classic examples of these. These royalties meter usage and are used as price discrimination devices. Patent exhaustion does not affect these restrictions where the license is not attached to the sale of the good, and in any case can be imposed contractually. Reach-through licenses can be harmful because they can extend royalty payments beyond the patent term. In addition, the patentee may dampen the incentive of subsequent inventors by increasing the transaction costs through royalty stacking and fragmentation into a minefield of patent rights. On the other hand, such royalty agreements allow smaller firms who may not be able to pay royalties upfront to defer payment until the commercial potential of the invention is reached. The practice of collecting royalties from two different parties on the same products and patents at two different stages of production has been held

---

[174] *Glen Mfg., Inc. v. Perfect Fit Indus., Inc.*, 299 F. Supp. 278, 282 (S.D.N.Y. 1969) ("By requiring royalties on all toilet tank covers manufactured or sold by defendant whether or not the toilet tank covers come within the scope of United States Patent No. 2652874, plaintiff is guilty of a patent misuse. This royalty structure has the effect of raising the cost of non-patented, competing toilet tank covers, thereby restraining their output and tending to lessen competition in the toilet tank cover industry").

[175] *Zenith Radio Corp. v. Hazeltine Research, Inc.*, 395 U.S. 100, 145 (1969).

[176] Ibid.

[177] Ibid.

[178] Ibid.

to amount to misuse.[179] Commentators explained that this circumvents the exhaustion doctrine and expands the grant of a patent.[180] At the same time, where "the claim is based on the patentee's deception in doing so; presumably a license agreement with both licensees that clearly disclosed the royalty collected at each stage would not be considered misuse."[181]

C. Discriminatory Royalties

Some commentators are of the view that discriminatory royalty licensing provisions will not amount to patent misuse.[182] According to Robert Hoerner, "[c]harging one licensee more than another does not extend the 'monopoly' of the licensed patent; only the dollar amount of royalties is at issue."[183] Further, such discriminatory royalties do not amount to a violation of the antitrust laws.[184] However, recently companies have taken to holding patentees who have given that undertaking to license on reasonable and non-discriminatory terms where an industry standard reads on their patents. For example, Motorola Mobility sued Apple for patent infringement in Europe over its 3G UMTS technology, which Apple has called an industry standard. According to Apple, Motorola was obliged to license the patents on reasonable and non-discriminatory terms and failure to do so would attract scrutiny under the antitrust laws.[185] In such

---

[179] *PSC, Inc. v. Symbol Techs.*, 26 F. Supp. 505 (W.D.N.Y. 1998).

[180] 2 William C. Holmes, INTELLECTUAL PROPERTY & ANTITRUST LAW Appendix C (2012) ("panelists asserted that the collection of royalties on a patent that is beyond its statutory term or scope could amount to an antitrust violation or patent misuse").

[181] Ibid.

[182] See Hoerner, *supra* note 62, at 711 (1991) ("this writer predicts that discriminatory royalties will not again be the basis for a finding of patent misuse (unless the discrimination is found to be an element of a Section 2 violation, in which case an antitrust-type misuse holding would be possible). . . . The Supreme Court has never found royalty discrimination to be a patent misuse and it is to be doubted that the CAFC ever will either").

[183] Ibid. ("No reason appears why the patent owner has any more duty to put his licensees on a competitively equal footing with each other than he has to put them on a competitively equal footing with himself. The disfavored licensee can practice the full scope of the patent without restraint; as a disfavored licensee, he has more rights than if he were not a licensee at all").

[184] Ibid. ("Royalty discrimination does not violate the Robinson-Patman Act and the FTC Act is not one of the antitrust laws").

[185] Florian Mueller, *Apple Brought Formal EU Antitrust Complaint against Motorola Mobility over FRAND Abuse*, Foss PATENTS (Feb. 18, 2012, http://www.fosspatents.com/2012/02/apple-brought-formal-eu-antitrust.html.

instances, patentees who charge discriminatory royalties risk opening themselves up to allegations of misuse as well as antitrust violations. While most of the activity in this area has taken place in Europe, there are no major differences in the law in America which would preclude similar allegations from taking root here as well.

VI.   BAD FAITH: FRAUDULENT PATENT PROCUREMENT, VEXATIOUS LITIGATION AND ABUSE OF PROCESS

A.   Introduction

Bad faith cases largely fall into three categories. The first category stems from fraudulent or deceitful conduct, which includes the improper procurement of a patent and the patentee's subsequent attempt to enforce that patent, false marking and misrepresentations in the standard setting process. In *C.R. Bard, Inc. v. M3 Systems, Inc.*, the defendant accused the patentee of misrepresentations and omissions while prosecuting its patent.[186] The Federal Circuit held that "[t]o amount to an antitrust violation or patent misuse, such attempted enforcement must be in bad faith", and further, "infringement suits are presumed to be in good faith, a presumption which can be rebutted only by clear and convincing evidence."[187] It acknowledged that this was a "high burden of proof".[188] The second category of bad faith cases find their form in vexatious litigation. In order to establish misuse based on a patent infringement action, "there must be bad faith and improper purpose in bringing the suit."[189] "A purpose is improper if its goal is not to win a favorable judgment, but to harass a competitor and deter others from competition, by engaging in the litigation process itself, regardless of the outcome."[190] Such instances include imposing collateral pressure on the licensee's customers and group boycotts. The third category of bad faith cases arises from abuses of the court system through procedural delays or gaming regulatory processes through filing continuations or

---

[186]   *C.R. Bard, Inc. v. M3 Sys., Inc.*, 157 F.3d 1340, 1364–65 (Fed. Cir. 1998).

[187]   *Carpet Seaming Tape Licensing Corp. v. Best Seam Inc.*, 616 F.2d 1133, 1143 (9th Cir. 1980).

[188]   Ibid.

[189]   *Glaverbel Societe Anonyme v. Northlake Mktg. & Supply, Inc.*, 45 F.3d 1550, 1558 (Fed. Cir. 1995).

[190]   Ibid.

using the drug approval process to extend the duration of the patent monopolies.

Bad faith appears to be the "wild card" in the defendant's deck. Federal Circuit precedent recognizes that bad faith strips the patentee of the immunity that patent law generally provides.[191] Indeed, the results of the study presented herein show that where courts were convinced that the patentee had abused its patents in bad faith, they were comfortable with concluding that there was misuse without applying tests relating to patent scope relevant to a particular period in its history.[192] On appeal, panels reviewing the decisions of the lower courts will scrutinize them to see if this element has been sufficiently considered. The Ninth Circuit in *Carpet Seaming Tape Licensing Corp. v. Best Seam Inc* observed that "[t]he trial court did not mention, much less give adequate consideration, to the requisite element of bad faith, the presumption of good faith, or the appropriate high burden of proof on this issue."[193] Finally, just as bad faith is incriminating, good faith is exculpatory; both are relevant considerations in the misuse analysis.[194]

As an initial matter when evaluating an allegation of bad faith, it is useful to consider the role of intent. It seems logical to surmise that conduct motivated by bad faith is only meaningful if animated by some bad intent. Yet there is controversy between the courts over whether knowledge is sufficient to impute bad faith or whether some deliberate conduct is needed. Some courts have held that intent is irrelevant. The Federal Circuit in re *Indep. Serv. Organizations Antitrust Litigation* held that regardless of the anticompetitive effect, intent was only relevant if the defendant can show that the patentee had exceeded the scope of its grant through tying, *Walker Process* fraud or sham litigation.[195]

---

[191] *Zenith Elecs. Corp. v. Exzec, Inc.*, 182 F.3d 1340, 1343 (Fed. Cir. 1999); see also *Carpet Seaming Tape Licensing Corp. v. Best Seam Inc.*, 616 F.2d 1133, 1143 (9th Cir. 1980) ("To amount to an antitrust violation or patent misuse, such attempted enforcement must be in bad faith").

[192] See *infra* Chapter 6.

[193] *Carpet Seaming Tape Licensing Corp.*, 616 F.2d at 1143.

[194] Louis Altman & Malla Pollack, *The Patent Monopoly and the Antitrust Laws—Misuse of Patent Rights*, in 1 CALLMANN ON UNFAIR COMP., TR. & MONO. § 4:57 (4th ed., 2010) ("The patentee's good faith can rebut the charge of misuse").

[195] *In re Indep. Serv. Orgs.*, 203 F.3d 1322, 1327–28 (Fed. Cir. 2000) The court stated: "We see no more reason to inquire into the subjective motivation of Xerox in refusing to sell or license its patented works than we found in evaluating the subjective motivation of a patentee in bringing suit to enforce that same right. In the absence of any indication of illegal tying, fraud in the Patent and Trademark Office, or sham litigation, the patent holder may enforce the statutory right to

This position is puzzling and one may question if it adds anything meaningful at all: intent is irrelevant in proving tying and already an established element of *Walker Process* fraud and sham litigation. Antitrust law also normally regards intent as irrelevant. As the Court of Appeals for the District of Columbia noted in *Microsoft*, "our focus is upon the effect of that conduct, not upon the intent behind it. Evidence of the intent behind the conduct of a monopolist is relevant only to the extent it helps us understand the likely effect of the monopolist's conduct."[196] In contrast, the role of knowledge is significant in the Federal Circuit's opinion in *Windsurfing*.[197] In declining to find misuse, the panel found that "AMF failed to show that WSI granted the licenses or enforced its rights in the marks with knowledge that they were or had become a common descriptive name, and AMF failed to show that WSI should have had that knowledge."[198] Furthermore, under antitrust law, the Ninth Circuit in *Image Technical Services, Inc. v. Eastman Kodak Co.* rejected the patentee's argument that subjective intent was irrelevant in determining whether unilateral refusal to license amounted to an antitrust violation.[199] It found intent probative of a pretext upon which the Court rested its finding that a violation had indeed taken place. Accordingly, intent, while not determinative, should be considered when evaluating bad faith.

---

exclude others from making, using, or selling the claimed invention free from liability under the antitrust laws. We therefore will not inquire into his subjective motivation for exerting his statutory rights, even though his refusal to sell or license his patented invention may have an anticompetitive effect, so long as that anticompetitive effect is not illegally extended beyond the statutory patent grant. It is the infringement defendant and not the patentee that bears the burden to show that one of these exceptional situations exists and, in the absence of such proof, we will not inquire into the patentee's motivations for asserting his statutory right to exclude," ibid.

[196] *United States v. Microsoft Corp.*, 253 F.3d 34, 59 (D.C. Cir. 2001); see also *Aspen Skiing Co. v. Aspen Highlands Skiing Corp.*, 472 U.S. 585, 603 (1985); *Chicago Bd. of Trade v. United States*, 246 U.S. 231, 238 (1918) ("knowledge of intent may help the court to interpret facts and to predict consequences").

[197] *Windsurfing Int'l v. AMF, Inc.*, 782 F.2d 995 (Fed. Cir. 1986).

[198] Ibid.

[199] *Image Tech. Servs., Inc. v. Eastman Kodak Co.*, 125 F.3d 1195, 1219 (9th Cir. 1997) ("Evidence regarding the state of mind of Kodak employees may show pretext, when such evidence suggests that the proffered business justification played no part in the decision to act. Kodak's parts manager testified that patents 'did not cross [his] mind' at the time Kodak began the parts policy").

B. Improper Procurement

The theory of misconduct underlying improper procurement is the breach of the duty of candor and good faith that the patent applicant owes to the Patent Office during the prosecution process. The Patent Office does not conduct adversarial proceedings to determine patentability it relies heavily on the submissions of patent applicants. Self-interested competitors who would normally play a role in weeding out applications failing patent requirements are absent. With the changes introduced by the America Invents Act allowing post-grant opposition and *inter partes* review, this situation is ameliorated but not eliminated since bad patents may not be identified or even if identified might not be commercially worthwhile to challenge in the early stages of the technology's life.[200]

From the basic premise of a breach of that duty spring inequitable conduct and *Walker Process* fraud, two doctrines which police breaches of that duty. The court in *Analytichem International Inc. v. Har-Len Associates Inc* explained that:

> abuse of a patent consists of seeking economic gain by persuading or coercing the purchasing public to believe that a patent right exists when in fact and in truth it does not. The situation is akin to a private individual, like the legendary Captain from Kopenick, pretending to be a tax collector authorized by law to exact tribute when in fact he is an impostor without authority.[201]

Inequitable conduct focuses on conduct which takes place before the patent issues. Inequitable conduct occurs when the applicant has breached its duty of candor to the Patent and Trademark Office when applying

---

[200] Leahy-Smith America Invents Act, Pub. L. 112-29, 125 Stat. 284 (2011). Under the new patent law, third parties can challenge a patent on any statutory grounds within nine months of the patent's issuance by filing a petition with the Patent Office. The new law also replaces the old *inter partes* reexamination procedure with an *inter partes* review. Like the old system, the review is limited to using patents and printed publications as prior art under sections 102 and 103. Under this new system, the standards have changed from whether the cited art presents a substantial new question of patentability as to whether the petition shows that there is a reasonable likelihood that the petitioner will prevail with respect to at least the claim of the challenged patent. Further, the review will be heard by a Patent Trial and Appeal Board rather than a patent examiner.

[201] *Analytichem Int'l, Inc. v. Har-Len Assoc.*, Inc., 490 F. Supp. 271, 275 (W.D. Pa. 1980).

for its patent,[202] and has been called "a form of patent misuse."[203] In the Federal Circuit's recent *en banc* decision in *Therasense v. Becton, Dickenson & Co.*, the court determined that the patentee must have acted with specific intent to deceive the Patent Office by misrepresenting or omitting to provide evidence which would otherwise have resulted in a denial of the patent grant.[204] Previously, parties alleging inequitable conduct were required to meet a lower standard, an intentional misrepresentation or omission to the Patent Office of a matter that a reasonable patent examiner would have considered important in deciding whether to allow a claim. One commentator deemed this standard as "appropriate as a defense in patent enforcement cases because the litigant is seeking only to render a patent unenforceable, a considerably less severe remedy than the treble damages available in *Walker Process* fraud cases."[205] With *Therasense* raising the standard to the standard required to prove *Walker Process* fraud, there appears to be little room left for finding an independent existence for an inequitable conduct standard.[206] However, more

---

[202]   *Landers v. Sideways, LLC*, No. 4: 00CV-35-M, 2004 WL 5569335, at *23 (W.D. Ky., 2004) ("An applicant has the duty of candor with the PTO when applying for a patent. To successfully assert a breach of the duty of candor, otherwise known as inequitable conduct, based on a patent applicant's submission of untrue statements to the PTO, the person making the allegations must 'demonstrate by clear and convincing evidence that (1) the false information was material to the patent examiner's decision to issue the patent; and (2) the patentee intended to mislead the examiner'").

[203]   Vincent Chiappetta, *Living with Patents: Insights from Patent Misuse*, 15 MARQ. INTELL. PROP. L. REV. 1, n. 241 (2011). See also ibid. at n. 240 ("Misuse applied to behavior that results in an invalid patent claim, at most, only adds the deterrent downside of rendering all the patent's claims unenforceable. When the patent is entirely invalid there is no downside at all, making the attempt to mislead 'worth the risk.' Inequitable conduct's unenforceability remedy suffers from the same short-coming, leading advocates for its reform to argue for financial penalties instead. Adding the ability to affirmatively assert the improper conduct and claim damages rather than merely raise it as a defense to infringement, a serious flaw in misuse as well, would also go far toward resolving the issue.").

[204]   *Therasense v. Becton, Dickenson & Co.*, 593 F.3d 1289, 1319 (2010).

[205]   Kevin J. Arquit, *Patent Abuse and the Antitrust Laws*, 59 ANTITRUST L.J. 739, 742–43 (1991).

[206]   Katherine E. White, *There's a Hole in the Bucket: The Effective Elimination of the Inequitable Conduct Doctrine*, 11 J. MARSHALL REV. INTELL. PROP. L. 716, 743 (2012) ("With *Therasense* tightening the standards to prove inequitable conduct and the AIA limiting the enforcement remedies for misconduct before the PTO, the doctrine's effectiveness has essentially been eliminated. . . . It is important to finally have discussions about what is required to preserve the integrity of the patenting process now that one of the levers to maintain that process has been weakened").

recently, with a successful allegation of inequitable conduct in *Aventis Pharma S.A. v. Hospira* commentators have opined that "the inequitable conduct defense is still alive albeit more difficult to prove."[207]

Walker Process fraud is an antitrust violation where market competition has been harmed as a result of patentees enforcing a fraudulently procured patent.[208] The antitrust plaintiff must prove that the patentee made a material omission or misstatement to the Patent Office with a specific intent to deceive, and that its enforcement or threatened enforcement of the patent enabled the defendant to acquire market power.[209] As the Supreme Court in *Walker Process* pointed out, "[w]hile one of its elements is the fraudulent procurement of a patent, the action does not directly seek the patent's annulment. . . . but must answer under that section and § 4 of the Clayton Act in treble damages to those injured by any monopolistic action taken under the fraudulent patent claim."[210] A finding of fraud can "of itself render the patent unenforceable, and when accompanied by the elements of violation of the Sherman Act . . . can incur additional consequences."[211]

To establish fraud for purposes of antitrust violation the defendant "must make a greater showing of scienter . . . [and] materiality" than when seeking unenforceability based on conduct before the Patent Office.[212] This is because "the road to the Patent Office is so tortuous and patent litigation is usually so complex, that 'knowing and willful fraud' as the term is used in *Walker* can mean no less than clear, convincing proof of intentional fraud involving affirmative dishonesty, 'a deliberately planned and carefully executed scheme to defraud . . . the Patent Office.'"[213] A defendant who cannot establish *Walker Process* fraud and sham litigation

---

[207] *Aventis Pharma S.A. v. Hospira Inc.*, 675 F.3d 1324 (Fed. Cir, 2012) (concluding that inequitable conduct can still be found under the heightened standards for materiality and specific intent enunciated in *Therasense, Inc. v. Becton, Dickinson and Co.*, 649 F.3d 1276, 1288 (Fed. Cir. 2011). See Gene Quinn, *Industry Insiders Reflect on Biggest Moments in IP for 2012* (Dec 27, 2012), available at: http://www.ipwatchdog.com/2012/12/27/industry-insiders-reflect-on-biggest-moments-in-ip-for-2012/id=31924/ (quoting patent attorney Stephen Kunin.)

[208] *Walker Process Equip., Inc. v. Food Machinery & Chemical Corp.*, 382 U.S. 172 (1965).

[209] Ibid. at 176.

[210] Ibid.

[211] *C.R. Bard, Inc. v. M3 Sys., Inc.*, 157 F.3d 1340, 1364 (Fed. Cir. 1998); see *Nobelpharma AB v. Implant Innovations, Inc.*, 141 F.3d 1059, 1069–70 (Fed. Cir. 1998); *Norton v. Curtiss*, 433 F.2d 779, 792–94 & n. 12 (CCPA 1970) (citing W. Prosser, LAW OF TORTS §§ 100–105 (3d ed.1964)).

[212] 6 Donald S. Chisum, CHISUM ON PATENTS § 19.03[6][e] (1993).

[213] *Handgards, Inc. v. Ethicon, Inc.*, 601 F.2d 986, 996 (9th Cir. 1979).

may nonetheless succeed in establishing misuse, since the latter requires a lower standard of pleading.[214] Often the facts giving rise to misuse are identical to those giving rise to improper procurement.[215] In such instances, the outcome for both will be the same, though in both instances the sanctions imposed clearly overshadow the usual sanction of temporary unenforceability upon a finding of misuse.[216]

One danger posed by improper procurement type cases is the risk of collusion. This occurs when the incentives of the patentee and defendant in an infringement suit have their interests aligned. Kevin Arquit notes that:

> A would-be monopolist faced with the prospect of litigation over fraud or inequitable conduct with respect to its patent may prefer the economic rents of a cartel shared with the would-be challenger to no patent at all. It may attempt to avoid litigation by offering a licensing agreement in which the would-be challenger pays royalties that are insignificant in relation to the value of the patent.[217]

Should such a situation arise, "since the private interest that may be relied upon in the *Walker Process* situation to vindicate the public interest is inhibited by the licensing agreement, only the antitrust enforcement agencies remain as the safeguard against the anticompetitive use of the patent system."[218]

The risk of collusion has been a longstanding issue in pharmaceutical

---

[214] *Netflix, Inc. v. Blockbuster, Inc.*, No. C 06-02361 WHA, 2006 U.S. Dist. LEXIS 63154 (N.D. Cal. Aug. 22, 2006) ("Given that Blockbuster adequately alleged *Walker Process* fraud and sham litigation for purposes of surviving dismissal, it follows that Blockbuster has satisfied the lower standard for pleading patent misuse").

[215] See, e.g., *Unitherm Food Sys., Inc. v. Swift-Eckrich, Inc.*, 375 F.3d 1341, 1356 (Fed. Cir. 2004) ("The Supreme Court itself noted the policy consistency between penalizing patent misuse and stripping antitrust immunity from patentees who defraud the PTO"); *Power Integrations, Inc. v. Fairchild Semiconductor Int'l, Inc.*, Civ. No. 08-309-JJF-LPS, 2009 U.S. Dist. LEXIS 118383 (D. Del. Dec. 18, 2009) ("Power relies for its patent misuse defense on the same 'facts and allegations' on which it bases its inequitable conduct allegations. (D.I. 149 at 20) It follows that the inequitable conduct allegations that I have found to be deficient do not provide an adequate predicate for Power's patent misuse defense").

[216] *In re Gabapentin*, 649 F. Supp. 2d 340, 349 (D.N.J. 2009) ("Because Purepac's allegations of patent misuse rest on Warner-Lambert's allegedly inequitable conduct during the prosecution and procurement of the '482 Patent, if Purepac ultimately proves that Warner-Lambert engaged in the conduct alleged, this Court would have full discretion to declare the '482 Patent unenforceable").

[217] Arquit, *supra* note 205 at 741–43.

[218] Ibid.

patent litigation, which is discussed in more detail in Chapter 5.[219] Perhaps for this reason, Professors Christina Bohannan and Herbert Hovenkamp argue that antitrust law has an important role to play because the economic decision process is left entirely in private hands.[220] As a matter of law, patent misuse has elements of both *Walker Process* fraud and inequitable conduct. First, with all three types of allegations of bad faith, the patentee may rebut such allegations by showing good faith.[221] And both misuse and *Walker Process* fraud focus on the patentee's post-grant activity.[222]

Second, like antitrust plaintiffs alleging *Walker Process* fraud, defendants alleging misuse need not wait for the filing of a threatened suit by the patentee but may proceed via a declaratory judgment.[223] Misuse is

---

[219] See infra, Chapter 5.

[220] Christina Bohannan & Herbert Hovenkamp, *IP and Antitrust: Reformation and Harm*, 51 B.C. L. REV. 905, 931 (2010) ("Thus, the antitrust violation concerns post-issuance conduct, such as the filing of an infringement action, the threat to file such an action, or threats to customers or other business relations. All of these can occur many years after a patent has been issued. Antitrust law should stand aside when a government agency is an active regulator, but not when economic decision making is left entirely in private hands. As a result, antitrust rightfully has a place when the anticompetitive conduct occurs subsequent to patent issuance").

[221] *Walker Process Equip., Inc. v. Food Mach. & Chem. Corp.*, 382 U.S. 172, 177 (1965) ("Food Machinery's good faith would furnish a complete defense. This includes an honest mistake as to the effect of prior installation upon patentability-so-called 'technical fraud'").

[222] *Ectro Source, LLC v. Nyco Techs., Inc.*, No. CV 01-10825 DT (BQRx), 2002 U.S. Dist. LEXIS 28436, at *37 (C.D. Cal. Apr. 15, 2002) (Patent misuse involves the subsequent enforcement of a knowingly invalid or otherwise unenforceable patent to preclude competition, or the material misrepresentation of the scope of a patent for the same purpose. Inequitable conduct, on the other hand, is the wrongdoing alleged in Defendants' prosecution of the Patents-in-Suit, prior to their issuance. Inequitable conduct relates to the means of obtaining a patent, and deems any patent obtained by such means unenforceable. Patent misuse relates to the enforcement of a patent after it has been obtained").

[223] *Walker Process Equip., Inc.*, 382 U.S. at 176 ("In fact, one need not await the filing of a threatened suit by the patentee; the validity of the patent may be tested under the Declaratory Judgment Act. At the same time, we have recognized that an injured party may attack the misuse of patent rights. To permit recovery of treble damages for the fraudulent procurement of the patent coupled with violations of s 2 accords with these long-recognized procedures. It would also promote the purposes so well expressed in Precision Instrument, supra, 324 U.S. at 816, 65 S.Ct. at 998:'A patent by its very nature is affected with a public interest. . . . [It] is an exception to the general rule against monopolies and to the right to access to a free and open market. The far-reaching social and economic consequences of a patent, therefore, give the public a paramount interest in seeing that patent

also like inequitable conduct in that the remedies are both equitable in nature and the result is unenforceability of the patent. At the same time, the effect of finding misuse is less severe than both *Walker Process* fraud and inequitable conduct. As the court in *ResQNet.com, Inc. v. Lansa, Inc.*, noted, "misuse renders the patent unenforceable during the period of misuse only, and may be cured so that the patent is again enforceable. Inequitable conduct, on the other hand, renders the patent unenforceable permanently, and involves concealing facts or being dishonest in the procurement of the patent."[224] Besides the treble damages, *Walker Process* fraud also differs from misuse because the former requires the showing of market power and anticompetitive harm.[225] For these reasons, courts have decisively distinguished between patent misuse and inequitable conduct and *Walker Process* fraud.[226] A practitioner interviewed for this study noted that in his experience, patent misuse arose most frequently in connection with a *Walker Process* or inequitable conduct claim based on prior art that had been disclosed abroad in a corresponding application, but not to the USPTO. It is also worth noting that some case law suggests that as long as a patent has been properly procured, assertion of that patent cannot be patent misuse.[227] More recent case law, such as *Therasense*, suggests a discomfort with the current standards governing inequitable

---

monopolies spring from backgrounds free from fraud or other inequitable conduct and that such monopolies are kept within their legitimate scope'").

[224]   *ResQNet.com, Inc. v. Lansa, Inc.*, No. 01 Civ. 3578 (RWS), 2004 U.S. Dist. LEXIS 13579, at *10–12 (S.D.N.Y. July 21, 2004).

[225]   *Walker Process Equip., Inc.*, 382 U.S. at 177–78 ("Without a definition of that market there is no way to measure Food Machinery's ability to lessen or destroy competition. It may be that the device—knee-action swing diffusers—used in sewage treatment systems does not comprise a relevant market. There may be effective substitutes for the device which do not infringe the patent. This is a matter of proof, as is the amount of damages suffered by Walker").

[226]   See, e.g., *Rohm & Haas Co. v. Brotech Corp.*, 770 F. Supp. 928, 934 (D. Del. 1991) ("Unlike claims that a patent holder misused a patent to expand a patent monopoly in violation of the antitrust laws, such claims of fraud on the PTO directly implicate issues of patent law, and stem from the same 'roots' as infringement claims"); *Skil Corp. v. Lucerne Prods., Inc.*, 489 F. Supp. 1129, 206 U.S.P.Q. 792, 799 (N.D. Oh. 1980) ("While it is difficult to clearly define the outer boundaries of patent misuse, one difference between it and fraud on the Patent Office is that the patent misuse may be purged, after which the patent may once again be enforced, whereas fraud on the Patent Office infects the initial grant of the patent, thus is not capable of being purged").

[227]   See *C.R. Bard v. M3 Sys.*, 157 F.3d 1340, 1373 (Fed. Cir. 1998) ("It is not patent misuse to bring suit to enforce patent rights not fraudulently obtained, nor is otherwise legal competition such behavior as to warrant creation of a new class of prohibited commercial conduct when patents are involved").

conduct.[228] As with patent misuse, inequitable conduct has been accused of imposing uncertain disclosure and intent requirements which promote over-submission of prior art,[229] with some urging that it, like patent misuse, be abolished altogether.[230]

With respect to pleading requirements, inequitable conduct needs to be "pled with particularity."[231] If the defendant has a case of bad faith which nevertheless fails to meet these legal standards, then the proper route according the courts is to turn to Rule 11 of the Rules of Civil Procedure and not misuse.[232] Rule 11 allows courts to "impose an appropriate sanction on any attorney, law firm, or party that violated the rule or is responsible for the violation" as when cases are "presented for any improper purpose, such as to harass, cause unnecessary delay, or needlessly increase the cost of litigation."[233]

Finally, it is worth noting that different circuits place different emphasis on the question of whether the patent has been fraudulently procured, as well as whether the resultant enforcement was illegal. In *Dippin' Dots, Inc.*

---

[228]   *Therasense, Inc. v. Becton, Dickinson & Co.*, 593 F.3d 1289 (Fed. Cir. 2010).

[229]   Brief For The United States as Amicus Curiae on Rehearing *En Banc* in Support of Neither Party, Therasense, Inc. v. Becton, Dickinson & Co., 593 F.3d 1289 (Fed. Cir. 2010) (Nos. 2008-1511, -1512, -1513, -1514, and -1595), at 17 ("Because applicants are unclear what information to submit to the PTO, they all too often file mounds of information with questionable materiality").

[230]   See, e.g., Nat'l Research Council of the Nat'l Acads., A PATENT SYSTEM FOR THE 21ST CENTURY 123 (Stephen A. Merrill et al. eds. 2004), available at: http://www.nap.edu/catalog/10976.html ("[i]n view of its cost and limited deterrent value the committee recommends the elimination of the inequitable conduct doctrine or changes in its implementation").

[231]   See *Ferguson Beauregard/Logic Controls v. Mega Sys.*, LLC, 350 F.3d 1327, 1344 (Fed. Cir. 2003) ("inequitable conduct, while a broader concept than fraud, must be pled with particularity"); *Agere Sys. Guardian Corp. v. Proxim, Inc.*, 190 F. Supp. 2d 726, 733–34 (D. Del. 2002) ("Although the Federal Circuit has not ruled on whether Rule 8(a) or Rule 9(b) applies to allegations of inequitable conduct, a majority of federal courts have found that allegations of inequitable conduct (i.e. fraud before the Patent Office) in patent cases, like other allegations of fraud, are subject to the requirements of Rule 9(b)").

[232]   *Tech. Licensing Corp. v. Gennum Corp.*, No. C 01-04204 RS, 2007 U.S. Dist. LEXIS 35521, at *79 (N.D. Cal. May 4, 2007) ("The remedy for frivolous lawsuits is Rule 11 or, in appropriate instances, malicious prosecution suits, not patent misuse doctrine").

[233]   FEDERAL RULES OF CIVIL PROCEDURE 11. In *Q-Pharma, Inc. v. Andrew Jergens Corp*, the court looked at its previous order denying Rule 11 sanctions which "implicitly held that, at a minimum, Q-Pharma's actions in filing and maintaining the law suit were not objectively baseless," *Q-Pharma, Inc. v. the Andrew Jergens Corp., Inc.*, No. C01-1312P, 2002 U.S. Dist. LEXIS 27222, at *19–25 (W.D. Wash. Nov. 18, 2002).

v. Mosey, the Federal Circuit applied the same rubric used to determine inequitable conduct, examining whether there was actual fraud on the PTO based on a raised threshold of materiality and intent.[234] In contrast, the Seventh Circuit in a case decided after the establishment of the Federal Circuit, focused on the market effects of the fraud. In a nod toward the Court's strong Law and Economics jurisprudential bent, Judge Posner noted that the patent "must dominate a real market."[235] He reasoned that "[i]f a patent has no significant impact in the marketplace, the circumstances of its issuance cannot have any antitrust significance."[236]

In contrast, a court more concerned about the integrity of the patent system might have been more willing to impose liability, as the Supreme Court in *Singer* did. In that case, the Supreme Court was concerned that the patentee had colluded with a potential competitor, who had earlier challenged its patent in an interference proceeding, to exclude a mutual threat in the form of a Japanese company that offered superior technology in sewing machines.[237] The majority held that the antitrust laws would not permit such shenanigans, which "went far beyond the claimed purpose of merely protecting" the patentee's machine.[238] Justice White, in his concurrence emphasized the role of antitrust law in protecting the public domain. He noted that:

> Whatever may be the duty of a single party to draw the prior art to the Office's attention, clearly collusion among applicants to prevent prior art from coming to or being drawn to the Office's attention is an inequitable imposition on the Office and on the public . . . The patent laws do not authorize, and the Sherman Act does not permit, such agreements between business rivals to encroach upon the public domain and usurp it to themselves.[239]

Ultimately, collusion, like other forms of misconduct, is viewed unfavorably by courts, though some courts will defer to the market and business decisions of the parties at the time when the contract was entered into.

C. Vexatious Litigation

Vexatious litigation cases include bad faith enforcement of a patent, collateral pressure and group boycott. Vexatious litigation under patent

---

[234]   *Dippin' Dots, Inc. v. Mosey*, 476 F.3d 1337, 1345 (Fed. Cir. 2007).
[235]   *Brunswick Corp. v. Riegel Textile Corp.*, 752 F.2d 261, 265 (7th Cir. 1984).
[236]   Ibid.
[237]   *United States v. Singer Mfg. Co.*, 374 U.S. 174, 175 (1963).
[238]   Ibid. at 194.
[239]   Ibid. at 200.

misuse is similar to sham litigation under the antitrust laws in that the theory of misconduct flows from patentees coercing and intimidating defendants into submission despite having weak or invalid patents by saddling defendants with litigation costs.[240] One court has treated misuse based on vexatious litigation similarly to sham litigation.[241] The basis for liability under misuse differs from antitrust law, however, and is not based on the *Noerr-Pennington* doctrine.[242] Instead misuse is based on "bad faith and improper purpose in bringing the suit, in implementation of an illegal restraint of trade."[243] As the court in *International Motor Contest Ass'n* noted "affirmative defenses do not attempt to impose liability . . . for anything; rather, they attempt to raise certain kinds of inequitable conduct . . . as shields to . . . infringement claims. Thus, these affirmative defenses simply do not run afoul of *Noerr-Pennington* immunity from liability."[244]

Antitrust plaintiffs asserting vexatious litigation need to overcome the immunity provided to patentees under the *Noerr-Pennington* doctrine.[245] This doctrine allows patentees to enforce their patent without fear of antitrust liability unless the defendant can show by clear and convincing evidence that the infringement suit was "a mere sham to cover what is actually nothing more than an attempt to interfere directly with the business relationships of a competitor."[246]

The test for sham litigation under antitrust law comprises of two parts:

---

[240] See Guido Calabresi, THE COSTS OF ACCIDENTS: A LEGAL AND ECONOMIC ANALYSIS 26, 135–73 (1970) (arguing that imposing liability on the party best able to choose between accident and safety costs maximizes the efficiency in accident cost reduction).

[241] *Moore U.S.A., Inc. v. Standard Register Co.*, 139 F. Supp.2d 348, 362 (W.D.N.Y., 2001) ("it appears that SRC can state a patent misuse claim to the extent that it alleges that Moore NA, Toppan Printing and Moore Canada have engaged in sham litigation. In other words, the same facts that could support a finding of sham litigation (and an antitrust violation) could also support a finding of patent misuse. . . . In light of the Federal Circuit's decision in *Galverbel*, SRC's ninth counterclaim survives this motion to dismiss for the same reasons that SRC's antitrust counterclaims survived").

[242] 1 Hovenkamp et al., *supra* note 9, at §3.3 ("The rationale is not based on *Noerr-Pennington* antitrust immunity, which shields litigation conduct from liability but not from affirmative defences such as misuse").

[243] *Glaverbel Societe Anonyme v. Northlake Mktg. & Supply, Inc.*, 45 F.3d 1550, 1558 (Fed. Cir. 1995).

[244] *Int'l Motor Contest Ass'n, Inc. v. Staley*, 434 F. Supp. 2d 650, 663 (N.D. Iowa 2006).

[245] See *E. R.R. Presidents Conference v. Noerr Motor Freight, Inc.*, 365 U.S. 127(1961); *United Mine Workers of Am. v. Pennington*, 381 U.S. 657 (1965).

[246] *Noerr Motor Freight, Inc.*, 365 U.S. at 144.

first showing that the suit had no legal viability, and second, showing that it had no economic viability.[247] Accordingly "[t]o establish bad faith, the defendant must prove by clear and convincing evidence that the claims asserted were objectively baseless. Infringement allegations are objectively baseless when 'no reasonable litigant could reasonably expect success on the merits.'"[248] Only if challenged litigation is objectively meritless can a court examine the litigant's subjective motivation. Under this second part, the court focuses on whether the baseless lawsuit conceals "an attempt to interfere directly with the business relationships of a competitor," through the "use [of] the governmental process—as opposed to the *outcome* of that process—as an anticompetitive weapon."[249] In *Q-Pharma, Inc. v. Andrew Jergens Corp.*, the court held that the intent and actions of the patentee's attorneys prior to and during the suit were irrelevant.[250] The relevant evidence included the patent and the prosecution history.[251] It found that the claim language supported a broad range. While the prosecution history revealed that the phrase "effective amount" was changed to "therapeutically effective amount" in order to overcome a prior art objection, the exact quantity that constitutes therapeutic effectiveness is not specified.[252] In particular, given that another claim covered amounts of the drug down to 0.0001 percent by weight and that this claim was accepted by the Patent and Trademark Office, the Court presumed that the phrase "therapeutically effective amount" includes concentrations at least as low as 0.0001 percent by weight.[253] It concluded that it was neither unreasonable nor baseless to conclude that a product touting the therapeutic effects of the drug would contain concentrations as high as those specified in the patent's dependent claims.

After the two-part test is satisfied, the antitrust plaintiff must still

---

[247] *Prof'l Real Estate Investors, Inc. v. Columbia Pictures Indus., Inc.*, 508 U.S. 49, 60–61 (1993).

[248] See *Am. Med. Sys., Inc. v. Laser Peripherals*, LLC, 712 F. Supp. 2d 885, 923 (D. Minn. 2010) (quoting *Dominant Semiconductors SDN. BHD v. Osram GMGH*, 524 F.3d 1254, 1260, 1263–64 (Fed. Cir. 2008)); See also *In re Indep. Serv. Org.*, 85 F. Supp. 2d 1130, 1169 (D. Kan. 2000) (citing *Prof'l Real Estate Investors, Inc. v. Columbia Pictures Indus., Inc.*, 508 U.S. 49, 60–61 (1993); finding the filing of an infringement claim does not constitute misuse "unless the claim is (1) objectively meritless and (2) brought in an attempt to interfere directly with the business of a competitor").

[249] *Prof'l Real Estate Investors, Inc.*, 508 U.S. at 50.

[250] *Q-Pharma, Inc. v. Andrew Jergens Corp.*, No. C01-1312P, 2002 U.S. Dist. LEXIS 27222, at *19–25 (W.D. Wash. Nov. 18, 2002).

[251] Ibid. at 23–24.

[252] Ibid. at 23.

[253] Ibid. at 24.

show that anticompetitive harm resulted from the patentee's exercise of its market power.[254] In *Grip-Pak*, Judge Posner explained the intuition behind this test: "[m]any claims not wholly groundless would never be sued on their own sake; the stakes, discounted by the probability of winning, would be too low to repay the investment in litigation."[255] In such cases, the court can infer that "the plaintiff wants to hurt a competitor not by getting a judgment against him, which would be a proper objective, but just by the maintenance of the suit, regardless of its outcome."[256]

From the outset, the deck is stacked against anyone alleging sham litigation. As a general rule, Section 271(d)(3) immunizes patentees from misuse where it seeks to enforce its rights against patent infringement. The Supreme Court noted that the threshold was "probable cause to institute legal proceedings".[257] This "probable cause" requires only a reasonable belief "that there is a chance that [a] claim may be held valid upon adjudication."[258] Courts have noted that "Acquisition of enforcement of a patent do not in and of themselves constitute patent misuse."[259] Infringement suits are presumed to be in good faith, and it is a presumption which can be rebutted only by clear and convincing evidence.[260] According to empirical research, about 35 percent of patent claims are reversed on appeal.[261] This potentially provides every patentee with a basis to argue "that there was such a colorable similarity between the

---

[254] Ibid. "Of course, even a plaintiff who defeats the defendant's claim to *Noerr* immunity by demonstrating both the objective and the subjective components of a sham must still prove a substantive antitrust violation. Proof of a sham merely deprives the defendant of immunity; it does not relieve the plaintiff of the obligation to establish all other elements of his claim." *Prof'l Real Estate Investors, Inc. v. Columbia Pictures Indus., Inc.*, 508 U.S. 49, 61 (1993).

[255] *Grip-Pak, Inc. v. Illinois Tool Works*, 694 F.2d 466, 472 (7th Cir. 1982).

[256] Ibid.; *see also* Arquit, *supra* note 205, at 747 ("I am not sure that *Grip-Pak* always offers a workable rule of law. After all, measuring a party's subjective assessment of the discounted present value of a disputed claim at one point in time may often be infeasible. Nonetheless, I think that *Grip-Pak* gives us another useful tool in approaching *Noerr* cases").

[257] *Prof'l Real Estate Investors, Inc. v. Columbia Pictures Indus., Inc.*, 508 U.S. 49, 62–63 (1993).

[258] Ibid.

[259] *Eastman Kodak Co. v. Goodyear Tire & Rubber Co.*, 114 F.3d 1547, 1558 (Fed. Cir. 1997).

[260] *Handgards, Inc. v. Ethicon, Inc.*, 601 F.2d 986 (9th Cir. 1979).

[261] Kimberly A. Moore, *Markman Eight Years Later: Is Claim Construction More Predictable?*, 9 LEWIS & CLARK L. REV. 231, 239 (2005) ("After a de novo appeal, the Federal Circuit held that 34.5% of the terms were wrongly construed by the district court. In the 651 cases, the Federal Circuit held at least one term was wrongly construed in 37.5% of the cases").

defendant's device and the plaintiff's device as to give reasonable ground for plaintiff to believe that its patent was being infringed," and a difficult burden for the defendants to discharge.[262] Professors Christina Bohannan and Herbert Hovenkamp comment that the "uncertainty" created by the ambiguous boundaries of a patent makes it "impossible to say that no reasonable person would have brought a particular infringement suit to enforce a patent."[263] John T. Delacourt ruefully concludes that:

> The 'objective baselessness' prong of the *PRE* test, as interpreted by some courts, has transformed the 'sham' exception into an almost insurmountable hurdle. It is no longer accurate to describe the 'sham' exception as an analogue to Rule 11 or other standards governing the misuse of process. Rule 11 petitions occasionally succeed. The 'sham' exception, in contrast, is an endangered species, and rumors of its extinction abound.[264]

In *W. L. Gore & Associates, Inc. v. Carlisle Corp.*, the defendant accused the plaintiff of attempting to coerce it to accept a license to use the patent.[265] The district court agreed and held that "this threat was an attempt by the plaintiff to use its purchasing power in the conductor wire market to gain an unfair advantage in the sale of PTFE cable and constituted an attempt by it to engage in unlawful reciprocal dealing," which evinced an intent to monopolize the relevant market and a dangerous probability it would succeed, thereby violating section 2 of the Sherman Act and amounted to a misuse of the patent.[266] The Court of Appeals for the Third Circuit reversed. It held that patentees can choose who they transact with.[267] Nor does suing a customer of the licensee amount to misuse. The court found that this was "a natural consequence of the latter's infringing activities and does not suggest conduct coercive of the defendant."[268]

In determining where the boundaries of reasonableness lie, it is useful to

---

[262] *Bolt Assocs. v. Rix Indus.*, No. 49321, 1973 U.S. Dist. LEXIS 14060, at *16 (N.D. Cal. Apr. 12, 1973).

[263] Bohannan & Hovenkamp, *supra* note 220, at 929.

[264] John T. Delacourt, *Protecting Competition by Narrowing Noerr: A Reply*, 18 ANTITRUST 77 (2003–2004).

[265] *W. L. Gore & Assocs., Inc. v. Carlisle Corp.*, 529 F.2d 614, 623–25 (3d Cir. 1976) ("It surely cannot be the law that a patent holder must continue to do business with a wilful infringer, thereby possibly contributing financially to the ability of the latter to defend against and possibly defeat his infringement suit. To hold otherwise would be to require a plaintiff to assist the defendant in its defense against the assertion of the plaintiff's valid patent claim").

[266] Ibid.

[267] Ibid. at 624.

[268] Ibid. at 625.

consider how courts regarded various practices by patentees. For a start, sending "cease and desist" letters to alleged defendants is reasonable. The Federal Circuit in *Mallinckrodt* held that patentees with "a good faith belief that its patents are being infringed violates no protected right when it so notifies infringers."[269] Indeed, sending such notices are part and parcel of judicious dispute resolution, for "a patentee must be allowed to make its rights known to a potential infringer so that the latter can determine whether to cease its allegedly infringing activities, negotiate a license if one is offered, or decide to run the risk of liability and/or the imposition of an injunction."[270] For the same reason, notices to customers of the alleged infringer also do not constitute misuse.[271] In fact, the rule is so broad that even notices to government contractors who cannot be subject to liability or enjoined from practicing the invention do not constitute misuse.[272] Courts justify this generous approach because Section 271(d)(3) of the Patent Act provides that "[n]o patent owner otherwise entitled to relief from infringement or contributory infringement of a patent shall be . . . deemed guilty of misuse . . . by reason of his having . . . sought to enforce his patent rights against infringement or contributory infringement."[273]

Threats to void the warranty on patented inventions sold to the offending customer also do not constitute misuse.[274] While "threats to limit or void warranties presumably reflect a patentee's unwillingness to extend free repair or replacement services to usage of its product that it cannot control", courts have held that "voiding a warranty, or threatening to do so, does not constitute use of a patent to control unpatented products.

---

[269] *Mallinckrodt, Inc. v. Medipart, Inc.*, 976 F.2d 700, 709 (Fed. Cir. 1992); see also *Virginia Panel Corp.*, 133 F.3d, at 869. ("That VP sent infringement notices to various government contractors, even notices that threatened suit and injunctions, did not indicate that VP attempted to broaden its patent monopoly").

[270] *Viskase Companies, Inc. v. World PAC Int'l AG*, 710 F. Supp. 2d 754, 756 (N.D. Ill. 2010) (citing *Globetrotter Software, Inc. v. Elan Computer Group, Inc.*, 362 F.3d 1367, 1374 (Fed.Cir. 2004); see *Loctite Corp. v. Ultraseal Ltd.*, 781 F.2d 861, 877 (Fed. Cir. 1985) (noting "the public policy of erecting a barrier against thwarting patentees from asserting legitimate patent rights").

[271] *Virginia Panel Corp.*, 133 F.3d, at 870. ("VP's threats to seek injunctions against MAC's customers, whether in the form of an infringement notice or in direct negotiations, did not constitute patent misuse because VP had a good faith belief that those it notified were using a device that infringed the '005 patent").

[272] Ibid. ("That applies even to warning a company like MAC, that, at least in its role as a supplier to the United States, could not be subject to liability or enjoined from practicing the claimed invention").

[273] Ibid. (citing 35 U.S.C. § 271(d)(3) (2006)).

[274] Ibid. ("VP also asserts that its threats to void or limit warranties did not constitute patent misuse, much less anti-competitive conduct. We agree").

Voiding a warranty is not use of a patent at all."[275] Nor can it be a form of tying because "the purchaser is not deciding whether to buy a product. As for future sales, the threat is not to refuse to license, but only to limit a warranty, which is a matter of contract law between buyer and seller having no misuse implications."[276]

Despite the apparent carte blanche in favor of patentees, courts do apply a rule of reason analysis. For example, in *Virginia Panel* the Court found that the patentee "adopted its warranty policy based on the legitimate business purpose of protecting the integrity" of its invention.[277] It found that "damage may result when ATE components from different suppliers are mixed, and that determining which component caused the damage would be virtually impossible."[278] Under antitrust law, the result is the same. The court in *Virginia Panel* held that "antitrust laws do not preclude patentees from putting suspected infringers on notice of suspected infringement. Rather, they are designed to promote competition to the advantage of consumers, not for the protection of competitors."[279]

Kevin Arquit identifies that at the core of vexatious litigation is the question "whether the action is being pursued because its very maintenance, regardless of ultimate disposition, will harm a competitor."[280] In reflecting on the case law, Professors Bohannan and Hovenkamp have identified the Federal Circuit's role in shaping the difficult landscape for defendants to traverse:

> [T]he problem is exacerbated by the fact that the Federal Circuit itself is willing to overlook fairly outrageous patent assertions. In its 2007 decision, *Dippin' Dots, Inc. v. Mosey*, for example, the court refused to impose antitrust liability on a patentee who obtained a patent by deceiving the PTO. The court acknowledged that the patent applicant knowingly lied in a sworn statement that there had been no sales more than one year prior to the application. In fact, some 800 such sales had occurred. That such sales would have rendered the product unpatentable was indisputable because of the statutory on-sale bar. The Federal Circuit held that although the omission rendered the patent unenforceable, it was insufficient to create antitrust liability.[281]

---

275   Ibid. at 870–71.
276   Ibid.
277   Ibid. at 871.
278   Ibid.
279   Ibid. at 873–74.
280   Arquit, *supra* note 205, at 747.
281   Bohannan & Hovenkamp, *supra* note 220, at 929 (footnote omitted).

While the burden is a difficult one to discharge, it is not insurmountable. In *CMI, Inc. v. Intoximeters*, the District Court for the Western District of Kentucky found that the claims patentees made were on "patent infringement and patent scope which were outrageous and insupportable" and were made "without investigation or reasonable belief as to their truth."[282] In *Kobe, Inc. v. Dempsey Pump Co.*, the Court of Appeals for the Tenth Circuit affirmed a finding by the lower court that the patentee's suit intended to eliminate its rival and amounted to patent misuse.[283] In *Grip-Pak, Inc. v. Illinois Tool Works, Inc.*, Judge Posner held that a suit brought to impose litigation costs on the other party may satisfy the "sham" exception to the *Noerr-Pennington* Doctrine.[284] He explained that such conduct used litigation as a tool for suppressing competition and becomes a matter of antitrust concern, "even where there is probable cause for the litigation."[285] In *Rex Chainbelt, Inc. v. Harco Prods., Inc.*, the Ninth Circuit held that patent litigation brought to further a tying scheme may violate the antitrust laws.[286] Thus, though successfully asserting a claim of vexatious litigation may be difficult, courts have been receptive to such claims where a party is abusing patent and antitrust law to achieve an anticompetitive effect.

---

[282] *CMI, Inc. v. Intoximeter, Inc.*, 866 F. Supp. 342, 347–48 (W.D. Ky. 1994) ("Among other things, Defendant made claims about CMI's use of nickel in the Intoxilyzer 5000, which Defendant did not fairly investigate, and which it could never substantiate. It made claims to the scope of its patent which were unfair and insupportable—that its patent included methods which the inventor had specifically or impliedly disclaimed. Finally, it made claims, which are not supported by any evidence at this time, about the adsorbent qualities of extruded aluminum and, by direct implication, the veracity of the Intoxilyzer 5000 results. The impact of this conduct was highly anti-competitive").

[283] *Kobe v. Dempsey Pump Co.*, 198 F.2d 416, 425 (10th Cir. 1952) ("We have no doubt that if there was nothing more than the bringing of the infringement action, resulting damages could not be recovered, but that is not the case. The facts as hereinbefore detailed are sufficient to support a finding that although Kobe believed some of its patents were infringed, the real purpose of the infringement action and the incidental activities of Kobe's representatives was to further the existing monopoly and to eliminate Dempsey as a competitor").

[284] *Grip-Pak, Inc. v. Illinois Tool Works*, 694 F.2d 466 (7th Cir. 1982).

[285] Ibid. at 472; see also *Brunswick Corp. v. Riegel Textile Corp.*, 752 F.2d 261, 271–72 (7th Cir. 1984) ("harassing competitors by litigation that can fairly be described as malicious prosecution or abuse of process can violate the antitrust laws"); *Premier Elec. Constr. Co. v. Nat'l Elec. Contractors Ass'n., Inc.*, 814 F.2d 358, 372 (7th Cir. 1987) ("the costs the litigation will impose on a rival . . . may be treated as a sham").

[286] *Rex Chainbeld, Inc. v. Harco Prods., Inc.*, 512 F.2d 993 (9th Cir. 1975).

D.   Abuse of Process

Abuse of process claims include procedural delays, filing continuations, and collusive settlements. One example of an alleged collusive settlement took place in *M. Eagles Tool Warehouse, Inc. v. Fisher Tooling Co.*, in which the competitor argued that the patentee's settlement agreement with a counterclaim defendant was *per se* misuse.[287] In denying the patentee's request for summary judgment, the court noted that "the agreements effectively restrain the licensees' . . . ability to 'purchase, use or sell, or not to purchase use or sell, another article of commerce not within the scope of [the patentee's] patent monopoly.'"[288]

In *San Marino Elec. Corp. v. George J. Meyer Mfg. Co.*, the Court found that a patentee's filing of continuation application did not constitute misuse since it was merely exercising legal rights.[289] This was so even though the purpose of application may have been to broaden patent and cover the machine made by a competitor.[290] Likewise, the institution of patent interference with a competitor's application was a reasonable attempt to retain the value of an invention by obtaining patent protection against another's machine and was not misuse.[291] In *Taltech Ltd. v. Esquel*

---

[287]   *M. Eagles Tool Warehouse, Inc. v. Fisher Tooling Co., Inc.*, No. 97-1568-(JAG), 2007 U.S. Dist. LEXIS 23636 (D.N.J. Mar. 30, 2007).

[288]   Ibid. See also *Blount, Inc. v. Peterson*, Civil No. 06-3980AA, 2007 U.S. Dist. LEXIS 44007, at *9–10 (D. Or. June 13, 2007) ("The parties have not identified, nor has this court found, any case that supports finding a settlement payment plan to constitute patent misuse, especially when, as here, the agreement provides the defendant with the ability to satisfy the outstanding debt at any time. Similarly, the court has not located any authority that patent misuse may be found on the basis of a reporting requirement enabling a patentee to guard against continued infringement and monitor compliance with the Settlement Agreement and the Consent Decree. Particularly where, as here, the reporting requirement terminates upon expiration of the patents and therefore by its express terms does not extend beyond the life of the patents").

[289]   *San Marino Elec. Corp. v. George J. Meyer Mfg. Co.*, 64-1421-WPG, 155 U.S.P.Q. 617 (C.D. Cal. Oct. 9, 1967); see also *Revlon, Inc. v. Carson Prods. Co.*, No. 82 Civ. 4326, 1985 U.S. Dist. LEXIS 22237 (S.D.N.Y. Feb. 27, 1985) (finding that continuation-in-part applications did not constitute patent misuse).

[290]   *San Marino Elec. Corp.*, 155 U.S.P.Q. at 626 ("The Court concludes that Mr. Calhoun and the defendant were exercising their legal rights in filing a continuation application and, even if the purpose of the application may have been in part to broaden the patent and to cover the bottle inspection machine which Mr. Wyman developed and was marketing through Industrial Automation Corporation, the filing of such a continuation application does not constitute patent misuse or unclean hands").

[291]   Ibid.

Enters., the defendant accused the patentee of misuse by waiving royalties to the patentee's competitor in return for abandoning a competing patent application. It argued that the patentee "used the power of its patents to keep from the public eye [prior art] which would have alerted the public to the fact that [the patentee's] patents were very suspect."[292] The Court applied a rule of reason analysis and found that the competitor's application was abandoned on the grounds of lack of true inventorship. It also found that the defendant provided no evidence of anticompetitive harm.[293]

Abuse of process claims have also arisen in connection to false marking.[294] False marking requires proof of four elements: "(1) a marking importing that an object is patented; (2) falsely affixed to; (3) an unpatented article; (4) with intent to deceive the public."[295] In *Hearing Components, Inc. v. Shure, Inc.*, Shure argued that "requiring licensees to mark expired patent numbers on their products" amounted to misuse.[296]

The Court found that:

> this practice 'clearly injures' the 'important public interest in permitting full and free competition in the use of ideas which are in reality a part of the public domain' because the act of false marking misleads the public into believing that a patentee controls the article in question (as well as like articles), external-izes the risk of error in the determination, placing it on the public rather than the manufacturer or seller of the article, and increases the cost to the public of ascertaining whether a patentee in fact controls the intellectual property embodied in an article.

Nonetheless, the court was hesitant to accept Shure's invitation to find misuse without precedent that was on point.[297] It found that the licensing

---

[292] *Taltech Ltd. v. Esquel Enters. Ltd.*, No. C04-974Z, 2006 U.S. Dist. LEXIS 69463, at *4 (W.D. Wash. Sept. 15, 2006).

[293] Ibid. at *6.

[294] See, e.g., *Sperry Prods., Inc. v. Aluminum Co. of Am.*, 171 F. Supp. 901 (N.D. Ohio 1959) (holding that listing "'manufactured under one or more of the following patents,' where some devices include some patents whose inventions are not embodied in devices was not misuse where the alternative would be to make separate and different name plates for each device sold").

[295] *Clontech Labs., Inc. v. Invitrogen Corp.*, 406 F.3d 1347, 1352 (Fed. Cir. 2005) (interpreting 35 U.S.C. § 292(a)).

[296] *Hearing Components, Inc. v. Shure, Inc.*, No. 9:07-CV-104, 2009 U.S. Dist. LEXIS 25050, at *10 (E.D. Tex. Mar. 26, 2009) ("Specifically, Shure suggests that because the license agreements do not provide for the removal of expired patent numbers, continued marking of a licensee's products after expiration of the '076 and/or '151 patents is patent misuse due to false marking").

[297] Ibid. at *6–7 ("It is somewhat unclear whether false marking is patent misuse at all, much less patent misuse per se").

agreements required that the phrase "and International Equivalents" be included in the marking licensees place on their products.[298] Since the false marking statute, "only prohibits the marking of articles that are not subject to either foreign or domestic patent protection," the fact that foreign equivalents of the patents remained in force meant that those markings were not false.[299] It also found that it was "somewhat unclear whether a patent holder can even be liable for patent misuse if the licensing provisions complained of were not enforced in the United States."[300]

If one analogizes licensing agreements and tying arrangements in anti-trust law to patent law, several early cases might imply that it is immaterial whether a contract provision purporting to increase a patent monopoly was ever actually enforced in the United States, because the key is that the patent holder had the power to do so under the contract. The scope of false marking has been diminished by the America Invents Act which relegates false marking claims to *qui tam* actions by the government and instances of anticompetitive harm.[301] However, because anticompetitive harm is one of the main issues or else the main issue misuse is concerned about, misuse issues surrounding false marking remain live ones. More generally, it remains unclear what the precise standard for misuse is relative to antitrust law. As recently as 2001, commentators have noted that sham litigation is difficult to provide and "the full impact on patent/antitrust issues is still unresolved."[302]

VII.   OTHER FORMS OF MISUSE

A.   Grantbacks

Grantback provisions require licensees to grant improvements on licensed patented technology back to the licensor. These may amount to misuse where they "divest the licensee of all incentives to innovate."[303] Grantback clauses, which require the licensee to assign improvements it made to the

---

[298]   Ibid. at *14.

[299]   Ibid.

[300]   Ibid. at *15.

[301]   Leahy-Smith America Invents Act, Pub. L. 112-29, 125 Stat. 284 (2011).

[302]   James R. Atwood, *Securing and Enforcing Patents: The Role of Noerr/ Pennington*, 83 J. PAT. & TRADEMARK OFF. SOC'Y 651, 657 (2001) ("*PRE* reads *Noerr* very broadly and its sham exception very narrowly, and the full impact on patent/antitrust issues is still unresolved").

[303]   Hovenkamp & Bohannan, *supra* note 28, at 286.

licensed invention, may amount to misuse or an antitrust violation because it diminishes the incentive of the licensee to innovate.[304] Moreover, grantback clauses could also be used to systematically regiment an industry as the patentee acquires the use of improvements, and "perpetuate his control over an industry long after the basic patent expired. Competitors might be eliminated and an industrial monopoly perfected and maintained."[305] One example of when such coercion could occur is when market conditions do not allow a licensee other alternative forms of technology. But where "there were many competitive, alternative methods of subterranean foundation construction, some of which were available as alternatives," there courts are likely to find no misuse.[306] This is because the licensee could elect to use either the patented method or alternatives, "and in most instances these alternative methods were chosen because of economic considerations."[307]

In *Hull v. Brunswick Corp.*, the licensee argued that a grantback provision "inhibited it from inventing improvements that would increase the efficiency or desirability of the product or eliminate patented features of the product that would reduce the price to the consumer."[308] Such a clause, according to the court, "served as consideration for the license: the licensor gave the licensee the right to use the licensor's patents, and in exchange the licensee gave the licensor the right to collect royalties on his patents."[309] Further, the licensor had not claimed royalties on improvements made by parties other than the licensee and had previously agreed to the provision's elimination. On these facts, the Court required the defendant to show plausible instances where the "clause could inhibit Brunswick's ability to 'invent around' the patents."[310] It concluded that because "Brunswick never established any instance in which innovation

---

[304] *Transparent-Wrap Mach. Corp. v. Stokes & Smith Co.*, 329 U.S. 637, 645–48 (1947) ("Since the primary aim of the patent laws is to promote the progress of science and the useful arts, an arrangement which diminishes the incentive is said to be against the public interest"); *Duplan Corp. v. Deering Milliken, Inc.*, 444 F. Supp. 648, 666 (D.S.C. 1977) (finding that a grantback clause broader than the claims of a patent amounted to misuse).

[305] *Transparent-Wrap Mach. Corp.*, 329 U.S. at 647 ("Through the use of patents pools or multiple licensing agreements the fruits of invention of an entire industry might be systematically funneled into the hands of the original patentee").

[306] *Santa Fe-Pomeroy, Inc. v. P&Z Co., Inc.*, 569 F.2d 1084, 1101 (9th Cir. 1978).

[307] Ibid. ("It thus cannot be said that BARTD contractors were coerced into agreeing to the grant-back provision").

[308] Ibid.

[309] *Hull v. Brunswick Corp.*, 704 F.2d 1195, 1201–02 (10th Cir. 1983).

[310] Ibid.

was actually inhibited. In light of Hulls nonenforcement and relinquishment of the provision, we think the trial court properly held that it did not relieve Brunswick of its royalty obligation under the contract."[311] Overall, in determining the reasonableness of the grantback clause, courts will look to the duration and scope of the obligation.

On the other hand, Professors Hovenkamp et al. point out that grantback clauses can benefit competition by allowing the patentee and its licensee "to share the risks and rewards of subsequent innovation. Further, in markets where standardization is important, grantback clauses can benefit competition by ensuring that all licensees of the original patent get the benefit of the improvements, and therefore that the standard is not spilt by incompatible changes in subsequent product generations."[312] In *Transparent Wrap*, the patentee granted an exclusive license to its licensee in return for an assignment of improvements the licensee made to the machine. The licensee sought to invalidate the restriction on the basis that it amounted to misuse. The Supreme Court held that the clauses were not *per se* illegal.[313] Instead it held that those terms were to be analyzed under the rule of reason.[314] It was moved by the fact that the licensee did not have to pay for any improvement patents used. More broadly, the agreement facilitated the use of the improvement, with each use accruing royalties for the licensee.[315] Following from the enactment of Section 271(d)(5), those alleging misuse need to show market power.[316]

B.   Patent Pools

Patent pooling occurs when patentees cross-license their patents relating to a particular technology. This arrangement allows companies to

---

[311]   Ibid.

[312]   1 Hovenkamp et al., *supra* note 9, at §3.3.

[313]   *Transparent-Wrap Mach. Corp. v. Stokes & Smith Co.*, 329 U.S. 637, 645–48 (1947) ("We only hold that the inclusion in the license of the condition requiring the licensee to assign improvement patents is not per se illegal and unenforceable").

[314]   Ibid. (holding that "the inclusion in the license of the condition requiring the licensee to assign improvement patents is not *per se* illegal and unenforceable."); see also *Hull*, 704 F.2d at 1201–02 ("we believe that the conclusion of the *Transparent-Wrap* Court that the provision is not per se illegal but should be analyzed in the context of its application remains a valid one . . .").

[315]   *Transparent-Wrap Mach. Corp.*, 329 U.S. at 645–48 ("The agreement thus serves a function of supplying a market for the improvement patents").

[316]   2 William C. Holmes, INTELLECTUAL PROPERTY & ANTITRUST LAW § 17:4 (2012).

develop technological standards, overcome "blocking patents" and reduce the possibility of infringement.[317] Whether the pooling arrangement is proper therefore turns on whether the patents were actually blocking, and whether it was necessary to preempt infringement. Whether the pooling arrangement serves as a pretext for price-fixing, the law will be quick to condemn it. As the Supreme Court held in *United States v. U.S. Gypsum Co*:

> [There is] no support for a patentee, acting in concert with all members of an industry, to issue substantially identical licenses to all members of the industry under the terms of which the industry is completely regimented, the production of competitive unpatented products suppressed, a class of distributors squeezed out, and prices on unpatented products stabilized. ... it would be sufficient to show that the defendants, constituting all former competitors in an entire industry, had acted in concert to restrain commerce in an entire industry under patent licenses in order to organize the industry and stabilize prices. That conclusion follows despite the assumed legality of each separate patent license, for it is familiar doctrine that lawful acts may become unlawful when taken in concert.[318]

In *Princo Corp. v. Int'l Trade Comm'n*, the Federal Circuit had to consider allegations of tying and royalty over products that did not use the teaching of the patent arising from a patent pooling arrangement. The court found that package licensing "also has potential to create substantial procompetitive efficiencies" such as clearing possible blocking patents, integrating complementary technology, and avoiding litigation.[319] Where the package license was necessary to enable the practice of the technology, it "is not tying of the type that patent misuse doctrine seeks to prevent."[320] The court found that it was reasonable for a licensee to believe that the package license was necessary to practice the industry standard, and because "one of the major potential efficiencies of package licensing in the context of innovative technology is the avoidance of 'uncertainty that could only be resolved through expensive litigation,'" the court ruled that the "inclusion of the Lagadec patent in the patent pool did not give rise to an illegal tying arrangement."[321] The court found that at the time the package licenses were executed, "it appeared that [the patent] reasonably

---

[317] Camille Barr, Comment, *License to Collude: Patent Pools, the Patent Misuse Doctrine, and Princo*, 45 U.C. Davis L. Rev. 629, 641 (2011).
[318] *United States v. United States Gypsum Co.*, 333 U.S. 364, 400–401 (1948).
[319] *Princo Corp. v. Int'l Trade Comm'n*, 563 F.3d 1301, 1308 (Fed. Cir. 2009).
[320] Ibid.
[321] Ibid. at 1310–11.

might be necessary to manufacture Orange Book compact discs," the panel concluded that "it cannot fairly be said on these facts that a royalty is paid on products which do not use the teaching of the [patent]."[322]

C. Trademark-related

Allegations of misuse arise in the context of patent licenses involving obligations to usually use trademark in a certain way. This is related but distinct from trademark misuse, which does not concern a patent licensee. One court wrote that "there should not be a trademark misuse doctrine of the same type as the patent misuse doctrine, and where there are no unclean hands, the claim of trademark misuse should not constitute a defense."[323] It explained that:

> the foundations of the claims are different. Patent law derives from the Constitution which states that the purpose thereof is to secure for a limited time to inventors the right to exclusive use of their inventions. On the other hand, trademark law under the federal statute is not limited by such Constitutional statements of purposes, for the federal trademark law is based on the Commerce clause.[324]

In *Windsurfing Int'l Inc. v. AMF, Inc.*, the Federal Circuit considered whether misuse could be from "a provision in a patent license agreement requiring the licensee to acknowledge the validity of registered trademarks, and to avoid their use."[325] The lower court had found that the patentee had misused its patent by extracting from its licensees an agreement that the terms "Windsurfer," "Windsurfing" and "Wind Surf" were valid trademarks, as those terms were generic and were used by the public in those forms.[326]

In reversing the lower court, the Federal Circuit held that there was no patent misuse because "[i]t is not an uncommon precaution when licensing a product sold by the licensor under a trademark to prohibit the licensee from using the licensor's trademark on the licensee's product. That is but a matter of business prudence and in no manner misuses the patent right."[327]

---

[322] Ibid. at 1312–13.
[323] *Waco-Porter Corp. v. Tubular Structures Corp. of Am.*, 222 F. Supp. 332, 333 (S.D. Cal. 1963).
[324] Ibid.
[325] *Windsurfing Int'l, Inc.*, 782 F.2d at 1002 (Fed. Cir. 1986).
[326] *Windsurfing Int'l, Inc. v. Fred Ostermann GmbH*, 613 F. Supp. 933, 953 (S.D.N.Y. 1985).
[327] *Windsurfing Int'l, Inc.*, 782 F.2d at 1002 (Fed. Cir. 1986).

On the facts, the court found that "the license agreement provision merely asserted and recognized" the patentee's rights under trademark law.[328] Since the "assertion of trademark rights can have procompetitive effects," "under only the most rare of circumstances could such assertion, separately or as a provision in a patent license agreement, form in itself the basis for a holding of inequitable conduct such as that labeled 'patent misuse.'"[329] The fact that the trademarks were found to be generic after trial was irrelevant. Registered trademarks enjoyed a statutory presumption of validity. In order to provide misuse, the defendant had to show that the patentee "granted the licenses or enforced its rights in the marks with knowledge that they were or had become a common descriptive name."[330]

Jack Winter, Inc. v. Koratron Co., Inc. represents an instance where the court did find misuse.[331] In that case, the patentee required that garment maker licensees affix its trademark to all garments made by them under the license. This trademark tie constituted a *per se* violation of Section 1 of the Sherman Act and a misuse of the patent.[332] Another type of trademark issue arising in patent misuse concerns licenses requiring the assignment of the trademarks developed by the licensee during the period it licensed the patent. This, it has been argued without success, amounts to a form of patent misuse by tying the trademarks to the patent.[333]

D. Combinations

Apart from the main species of misuse described above and their permutations, there may also be combinations of two or more of the above. One example is discriminatory royalty tying, which involves charging more for

---

[328] Ibid.

[329] Ibid.

[330] Ibid.

[331] *Jack Winter, Inc. v. Koratron Co.*, 375 F. Supp. 1, 71-72 (N.D. Cal. 1974) ("Considering all the facts in this case, the Court finds that Koratron has misused its patent in that it violated § 1 of the Sherman Act of tying the use of unpatented Koratron-trademarked products to the granting of a license to utilize the '432 patent and also by tying the rights under '432 to the use of Koratron's trademark. Second, these tying arrangements, as well as the Dan River agreement and Swede consent decree, have been held to constitute an attempt to monopolize in violation of § 2 of the Sherman Act. As such, they also constitute patent misuse"). See also *Koratron Co., Inc. v. Lion Unif., Inc.*, 409 F. Supp. 1019, 1022 (N.D. Cal. 1976).

[332] *Jack Winter, Inc.*, 375 F. Supp. at 73.

[333] *Riker Labs., Inc. v. Gist-Brocades N. V.*, 636 F.2d 772, 776 (D.C. Cir. 1980) (acknowledging, without deciding, the trademark misuse claim raised by the appellant, as jurisdiction needed to first be established).

a license where the licensee refuses to buy an unpatented input from the patentee. Because the patentee is not withholding the license but merely penalizing the licensee with higher royalty rates, courts have held that this does not amount to misuse unless it amounts to a pretext for some form of abuse.[334] In all these cases, commentators noted, "a determination of intellectual property 'misuse' must rest either on a policy judgment of competitive harm or else on a finding that a practice is contrary to the relevant intellectual property provision."[335]

E. Overall Scheme

Courts also look to the overall facts in each case to determine whether there is cumulative evidence of misuse. For example, in *Kobe, Inc. v. Dempsey Pump Co.*, the Tenth Circuit found that the patentee engaged in a series of acts amounting to a scheme of misuse.[336] This scheme involved "the accumulation of patents relating to hydraulic pumps; obtaining covenants not to compete from those from which it purchased the patents; publicizing its infringement suits throughout the industry, and threatening suit against anyone trading with the infringer."[337] The Court concluded when the infringement action was considered in light of a larger "monopolistic scheme," then the litigation "may be considered as having been done to give effect to the unlawful scheme."[338] In reflecting on the case, Lawrence Sullivan noted that:

> Where, as in *Kobe*, the pattern of conduct as a whole has a "feel" about it which leads to the intuition that the patent-holder has been acting too aggressively, will it not often be possible, upon analysis, to make out a plausible cause of abuse on quite conventional grounds? A firm possessing patents can act unfairly and in ways tending to be excessively exclusionary in the enforcement of those patents, particularly if it possesses an aggregation of patents which bracket a technology. If a firm possesses monopoly power, such conduct will provide the additional element needed to establish monopolization; if a firm does not possess such power, but by its actions threatens to attain it, such conduct constitutes an attempt to monopolize.[339]

---

[334] *Carter-Wallace v. United States*, 449 F.2d 1374,1386 (Ct. Cl. 1971) (holding that resale restrictions are not misuse if, by paying more, the licensee enjoys unrestricted rights); *Urquhart v. United States*, 109 F. Supp. 409 (Ct. Cl. 1953).

[335] 1 Hovenkamp et al., *supra* note 9, at §21.3.

[336] *Kobe, Inc. v. Dempsey Pump Co.*, 198 F.2d 416, 425 (10th Cir. 1952).

[337] Joel R. Bennett, *Patent Misuse: Must an Alleged Infringer Prove an Antitrust Violation?*, 17 AIPLA Q.J. 1, 16 (1989).

[338] *Kobe, Inc.*, 198 F.2d at 425.

[339] Sullivan, *supra* note 125, at 522.

Other cases have also recognized that misuse of a patent may be inferred from the totality of patentees' conduct.[340] In *Berlenbach v. Anderson and Thompson Ski Co.*, the Ninth Circuit held that patentees who precluded the licensee from making or distributing competing equipment were guilty of misuse even though the patent was pending and the clause was unenforced.[341] Similarly, a license offered with onerous or unreasonable terms may also provide ammunition to those alleging a specific intent to monopolize.[342] In *Ansul Co. v. Uniroyal, Inc.*, the Second Circuit affirmed the trial court's refusal to enforce the patent against the defendant.[343] It agreed that the patentee's conduct violated the antitrust laws and amounted to misuse. As Joel Bennett noted, "[s]ignificantly, the fact that the patent played a role in the success of the product provided the only nexus required. The court specifically refused to require the existence of an express license agreement to find patent misuse."[344] In such cases, the

---

[340] See *Transitron Elec. Corp. v. Hughes Aircraft Co.*, 487 F. Supp. 885, 892 (D. Mass. 1980); *United States v. Telectronics Proprietary, Ltd.*, 607 F. Supp. 753, 754–57 (D. Colo. 1983); *Duplan Corp. v. Deering Milliken, Inc.*, 444 F. Supp. 648, 695 (D.S.C. 1977); see generally *Compton v. Metal Prods., Inc.*, 453 F.2d 38 (4th Cir. 1971) and *F.C. Russell Co. v. Comfort Equip. Corp.*, 194 F2d 592 (7th Cir. 1952).

[341] *Berlenbach v. Anderson & Thompson Ski Co.*, Inc., 329 F.2d 782 (9th Cir. 1964).

[342] See Sullivan, *supra* note 125, at 522 ("If a patent program, and all of its aspects and manifestations, seems greedy, overreaching and excessive, if would-be competitors seem cast in the role of victims, we may expect the policy to be vulnerable to antitrust attack. Of course, this is not to say that in counseling or predicting litigation outcomes one can rely on such vague, less than plenary indications; that is a luxury to be left to the courts . . . where, as in Kobe, the pattern of conduct as a whole has a "feel" about it which leads to the intuition that the patent-holder has been acting too aggressively, will it not often be possible, upon analysis, to make out a plausible cause of abuse on quite conventional grounds? A firm possessing patents can act unfairly and in ways tending to be excessively exclusionary in the enforcement of those patents, particularly if it possesses an aggregation of patents which bracket a technology. If a firm possesses monopoly power such conduct will provide the additional element needed to establish monopolization; if a firm does not possess such power, but by its actions threatens to attain it, such conduct constitutes an attempt to monopolize," ibid.).

[343] *Ansul Co. v. Uniroyal, Inc.*, 448 F.2d 872, 879 (2d Cir. 1971). The Second Circuit found that "where the patent plays a major role in enabling its holder unlawfully to restrain trade, public policy against abuse of the limited lawful monopoly requires that its enforcement against infringers be stayed until the effects of the restraint have been purged or dissipated. . . . Application of the doctrine . . . depends on whether the patent itself significantly contributes to the unlawful antitrust practice," ibid., 448 F.2d at 879.

[344] Bennett, *supra* note 337, at 17.

burden of establishing that the infringement action is part of an overall scheme is by a preponderance of the evidence—a lower threshold than clear and convincing evidence. [345] Accordingly, where a party engages in a larger scheme to circumvent patent misuse or antitrust law, courts are willing to look beyond the specific doctrine to hold parties accountable where their overall actions contradict the policies of patent and antitrust law.

VIII.   CONCLUSION

This initial foray into the landscape of misuse may surprise some with the varieties of misuse that courts have encountered over the years. It also illustrates how the doctrines which arise in misuse cases may overlap substantially with doctrines more commonly encountered in antitrust law, such as tying or *Walker Process* fraud. It also shows how the Federal Circuit has tried to shoehorn misuse completely into an antitrust standard, as in the case of inequitable conduct and vexatious litigation. Licensing-related misuse cases, such as misuse related to royalty and restriction clauses, are largely assessed within the *Windsurfing* rubric. However, one trend has become apparent: courts over the years seem to have become more hostile toward allegations of misuse. The next chapter delves into the most common reasons advanced by the fiercest critics of misuse, and considers whether, and to what extent, these criticisms might be addressed by the courts.

---

[345]   Ibid. at 19.

4. Key objections

I. GENERAL PROGNOSIS

One judge interviewed for the study acknowledged that "the defense must have more potential than has been realized by litigators" but suggested that it might be an "economic consideration" to favor stronger defenses or that "the client just doesn't want to bother".[1] An academic remarked "my advice to clients is to consider the patent misuse issues, but I think they are probably not collectively the strongest defense. It's a defense you have if you don't have another one."[2] Yet only a few of the interviewees thought that patent misuse had no future and should either be abolished or completely subsumed into antitrust.[3]

The rest perceived, in differing degrees, a role distinct from antitrust. Some viewed the doctrine as broader than antitrust law in requirements for standing and proof, but as essentially addressing the same issues. As one lawyer noted, the current misuse doctrine was developed at a time when licensing practices were different. Because patent misuse has not evolved since, it is seen as largely irrelevant to modern situations and "sits out there as a trap for the unwary." Others viewed misuse as addressing forms of misconduct that antitrust does not. One judge who was interviewed stated that courts would be willing to find patent misuse "where the facts support it." Another judge expressed willingness and, in some cases, even enthusiasm at the prospect of developing misuse to deal with new and creative attempts to stretch patent rights beyond their

---

[1] On file with the author. ("I think the defense must have more potential than has been realized by litigators. I don't know all the reasons why they don't litigate it more imaginatively and energetically. Maybe it's an economic consideration, because they have other defenses that they think are stronger, or the client just doesn't want to bother. I have no knowledge of those kinds of things.")

[2] Ibid.

[3] For example, one judge interviewed said "I don't really have any very distinct impressions about patent misuse as a doctrine. It's seldom raised. It's seldom discussed in any depth in court opinions, particularly here at the Federal Circuit. It seems to be quite unclear whether the patent use defense extends significantly beyond areas of fact covered by antitrust law."

constitutional mandate. Commentators too recognize that while the shift from a *per se* antitrust analysis to a rule of reason analysis has diminished the applicability of misuse precedent from that era, it remained viable. Others echo that despite criticism in recent years, the doctrine of patent misuse remains viable in preventing the unlawful expansion of the patent monopoly.

For misuse to be regarded seriously interviewees and commentators agree that those advocating revitalizing misuse need to convincingly address the concerns of detractors, so that it "does not dissolve into some sort of free-floating 'get out of jail free' card."[4] Many interviewees shared a common view that misuse should have adequate guidance in order for it not to become a runaway train. Once this condition has been met, the categories of misuse may be reviewed and incrementally expanded by "feeling the stones." Just as important as knowing where to go, however, is knowing where not to go, and why. This study therefore identifies three key areas which the harshest critics of patent misuse have converged upon. Simply put, the three key areas are as follows. First, misuse is an inherently vague concept and detracts from the commercial certainty parties require in order to determine their rights and liabilities. Second, misuse allows those not harmed by the patentee's misconduct to benefit when a court renders the misused patent unenforceable. Third, unenforceability is too harsh a consequence for a finding of misuse.

II. VAGUENESS

The Federal Circuit warned that "[a]lthough the law should not condone wrongful commercial activity, the body of misuse law and precedent need not be enlarged into an open-ended pitfall for patent-supported commerce."[5] Roger Arar argues that public policy concerns make the predictable application of misuse complicated and elusive. According to him it also creates "an undesirable *in terrorem* effect" because patentees

---

[4]   Thomas F. Cotter, Misuse, 44 Hous. L. Rev. 901, 936 (2007).

[5]   *C.R. Bard, Inc. v. M3 Sys., Inc.*, 157 F.3d 1340, 1373 (Fed. Cir. 1998); see Joseph P. Bauer, *Refusals to Deal With Competitors by Owners of Patents and Copyrights: Reflections on the Image Technical and Xerox Decisions*, 55 DePaul L. Rev. 1211, 1235 (2005–2006) ("The scope of the patent and copyright 'misuse' doctrine is imprecise and shifting. Neither the patent nor the copyright statutes have explicit provisions defining misuse, much less any that set forth the consequences of that behaviour").

have to assess their conduct or licensing agreements for their potential for subverting "ill-defined policy."[6]

It appears that at least one district court viewed the open-ended nature of misuse as a quagmire. In *Control Components, Inc. v. Lexmark International, Inc*, the court was faced with the novel question of whether patentees whose patents covered single use toner cartridges could restrict the use of any given cartridge after its patent rights in that cartridge has been exhausted even without licensing agreements containing post-sale reuse restrictions.[7] The court first observed that "[t]he Supreme Court has never addressed a situation like this."[8] Left with inadequate guidance on how to proceed, it found that there was no anticompetitive effect of the kind required under *Windsurfing*, and that it could not, as a "matter of law," find misuse even though it agreed that Lexmark was "doing something 'wrong' in a vague sense."[9] The discomfort with implementing a form of misuse that runs with the judge's sense of justice as opposed to a more objective inquiry was articulated by William Ridway. He argued that the discretionary nature of misuse "essentially invites judges to implement their own, often idiosyncratic, appraisal of the intellectual property system."[10] According to Ridway, this results in "a jumbled mix of platitudes and reprimands" and "encourages critics to attack the doctrine for lacking coherence and predictability, which, they charge, ultimately undermines the value of intellectual property rights."[11]

One judge interviewed explained that patent policy was a vague

---

[6]   Roger Arar, *Redefining Copyright Misuse*, 81 COLUM. L. REV. 1291, 1310-11 (1981).

[7]   *Static Control Components, Inc. v. Lexmark Int'l, Inc.*, 487 F. Supp. 2d 830, 854 (E.D. Ky. 2007).

[8]   See ibid. at 854; see also *Kolene Corp. v. Motor City Metal Treating, Inc.*, 440 F.2d 77, 84 (6th Cir. 1971) ("Motor City urges on appeal, however, that the patent and servicemark are so interrelated that, even accepting the finding of the District Court, there is still patent misuse. This theory presents a novel issue for which we can find no case directly on point"); *Bela Seating Co. v. Poloron Prods., Inc.*, 438 F.2d 733, 738 (7th Cir. 1971) ("Poloron poses the issue on this aspect of the appeal as one of first impression for this court: whether injunctive relief against future infringement should be 'withheld from a patent owner who seeks to discriminate in royalty rates charged to undifferentiable competitors under the patent'").

[9]   *Lexmark Int'l*, 487 F. Supp. 2d at 854–55 ("Without a finding by the jury that Lexmark's practices during the remanufacture of Regular domestic cartridges 'unreasonably restrain competition,' there can be no misuse").

[10]   William E. Ridgway, *Revitalizing the Doctrine of Trademark Misuse*, 21 BERKELEY TECH. L.J. 1547, 1565–66 (2006).

[11]   Ibid.

navigational tool for judicial decision making.[12] He said that judges were aware of policies as they were articulated in case law and statutes, but that the work of a judge is to implement policy and not to sit as patent policy reformer, since to do so would infuse too much subjectivity into the process.[13] The core challenge for misuse, as Professors Hovenkamp and Bohannan observed, is that it is "suffering from an identity crisis."[14] That identity crisis stems from a lack of a "coherent basis in IP policy" and "lacks unifying principles for determining which practices should be condemned and why."[15] Professor Donald Chisum concurs that the predictability of misuse is hindered because "courts have failed to adopt a general theory as to the proper limitations on the exploitation of the patent monopoly."[16] Patent law is guided by a constitutional mandate to promote technological progress. As one zooms into determining the means of achieving that goal, however, coherent jurisprudence vanishes into an ideological morass. Does that right stem from the noneconomic theories espoused by G.W.F. Hegel or John Locke?[17] Or does it stem from economic theories espoused by Edmund Kitch or Josef Schumpeter?[18]

---

[12]   On file with the author. ("I think the patent policy is a very vague navigational tool. It seems to be something that's in the eye of the beholder all too often. Obviously there are policies embedded in certain case-law decisions. Obviously there are policies embedded in different provisions in the patent statute. Sometimes they are quite clear. Other times you have to do a lot of discernment and read implications into it.")

[13]   Ibid. ("I'm supposed to implement the policies that are handed to me in authority, whether it's amendment to the statute or case-law development. I have to follow precedent. I have to follow authority. I don't really consider myself much of a patent policymaker. So I'm wary of an approach that talks about 'Well, we've got to make the case law conform to good, coherent patent policies,' because a hundred people in a room would have a hundred different views of what good, coherent patent policy is. What kind of a guide is that? It's way too subjective, way too indefinite, in a lot of instances.")

[14]   Herbert Hovenkamp & Christina Bohannan, CREATION WITHOUT RESTRAINT 258 (2011).

[15]   Ibid.

[16]   See 6 Donald S. Chisum, CHISUM ON PATENTS § 19.04[f][3] (2005).

[17]   See generally G.W.F. Hegel, THE PHILOSOPHY OF RIGHT (T.M. Knox trans., 1967) (arguing that property results from the expression of individual will); John Locke, THE SECOND TREATISE OF GOVERNMENT ¶27 (Thomas P. Peardon ed., 1952) (1690) (arguing that all individuals have a common right except to the labour of one's body which is one's own, subject to leaving enough in the "common for others").

[18]   See generally Edmund W. Kitch, *The Nature and Function of the Patent System*, 20 J.L. & ECON. 265, 278 (1977) (arguing that the patent system promotes efficiency by awarding exclusive, publicly recorded ownership in techno-

In comparison, Professors Hovenkamp and Bohannan note that "[t]he history of competition and innovation policy shows more consensus about the nature of traditional competition than about the nature of innovation."[19] They point to rivalry amongst firms in the same market and market entry as forming "the basic outline of the requirements for competition [which] have been well known for more than a century and claim a broad professional and policy consensus." [20] In contrast, determining "the optimum amount of innovation" is "far less determinate and go[es] much more to the extremes."[21]

Moreover, there appears to be a better alternative to misuse in antitrust law. Professor Robert Merges points out that "antitrust has evolved a 'precise' methodology for ascertaining when improper market leverage is being used by a patentee," and that "the relatively imprecise 'equitable' doctrine of misuse only adds confusion and uncertainty to the scene." The rule of reason analysis within antitrust law, its advocates argue, is supple enough to take into consideration innovation policy.[22] According to Professor Robin Feldman, advocates of an antitrust-centered misuse defense point to "a larger and more fully developed body of law than patent misuse" in their argument that "[a]pplying antitrust rules could provide greater clarity in patent misuse doctrine and eliminate a source of confusion at the intersection of patent and antitrust law."[23]

---

logical "prospects" shortly after their discovery); Josef Schumpeter, CAPITALISM, SOCIALISM, AND DEMOCRACY 81–110 (Harper & Row, 2d ed. 1947) (arguing that monopoly conditions promotes innovation and growth more effectively than competition, pointing to economic advances brought about by big business rather than fragmented competitive industries).

[19] Christina Bohannan & Herbert Hovenkamp, *IP and Antitrust: Reformation and Harm*, 51 B.C. L. REV. 905, 923 (2010).

[20] Ibid. at 923–24.

[21] Ibid. ("To this day, the economics of innovation has no equivalent to formulations such as the robust, broadly applied neoclassical rule that under perfect competition price equals marginal cost. ... No one knows what the optimal duration of patent or copyright protection should be, or whether there should be different periods of protection in different areas of enterprise. Some even doubt whether we need any protection at all").

[22] See Note, *Is the Patent Misuse Doctrine Obsolete?*, 110 HARV. L. REV. 1922, 1922 (1997) ("More importantly, there is no reason why the courts cannot use the rule of reason from the antitrust laws to achieve this same end, even if the rule of reason has, in the past, arguably failed to take adequate account of innovation, which patent law intends to encourage").

[23] Robin C. Feldman, *The Insufficiency of Antitrust Analysis for Patent Misuse*, 55 HASTINGS L.J. 399, 400 (2003–2004) (arguing that this assumption is unfounded, as "[a]ntitrust law is designed to address only particular types of harm, and it cannot reach everything that patent policy addresses. Thus, applying

Cast in this light, the clinical efficiency antitrust offers has the appeal of an automatic dishwasher to an overworked homemaker on Thanksgiving night. The countervailing view that the vagueness inherent in misuse is both justified and administrable may be presented in two parts to address both points.

A. The Nature of Equity

While reasonable minds may differ on the rubric misuse should proceed upon, there is general consensus that it is an equitable defense in patent law created by the Supreme Court to preserve policy underlying the grant of a patent right.[24] But what does it mean for misuse to be an equitable defense? Equity is known for two things: flexibility and justice.[25] When confronted with the assertion that patent misuse is vague, judicial opinions, commentary, and interviewees provided two main responses.

First, misuse serves as an insurance policy against unanticipated roughish behavior from patentees. A number of interviewees, notably judges, observed that they had no problems with the inherent vagueness of misuse. Interviewees opined that vague formulations are to be expected when dealing with equity. Doctrines meant to cover situations not defined in advance had no way but to be vague. The ingenuity of patentees to devise ways of abusing their patent rights is matched only by the potential malleability of patent misuse. As one judge noted there was no way that case law or statutes could cover every factual situation where there might be abuse.[26] Professor Marshall Leaffer adds that "[o]f course equitable

---

antitrust rules to test for patent misuse would ignore significant concerns under patent policy"). See also Thomas F. Cotter, *Misuse*, 44 Hous. L. Rev. 901, 935 (2007) ("Determining whether specific conduct violates the antitrust laws is hardly a trivial undertaking, to be sure, but there is a vast body of precedent and commentary to guide the inquiry in most instances").

[24] See *infra* Chapter 2.

[25] 7 West's Encyclopedia of American Law 160 (2000) (defining maxim as "[a] broad statement of principle, the truth and reasonableness of which are self-evident"); American Heritage Dictionary 1083 (4th ed. 2000) (defining maxim as "[a] succinct formulation of a fundamental principle, general truth, or rule of conduct").

[26] On file with the author ("Q: Does it bother you, though, that the doctrine is as vague as it is, and even if it comes before the court, it's hard, really, for the court to get a handle on defining with certainty where the boundaries of the doctrine lie, how it should be applied? A: No. Because it's meant to cover unusual, egregious situations, which can't be defined in advance. It's necessarily vague. I'm not bothered by its vagueness because it's unavoidably vague. I don't see any way it could be made more specific").

doctrines, like patent misuse, are messy by their very nature. However, they do allow for a needed flexibility for judicial determination."[27] As another judge interviewed emphatically put it, it was an empirical question whether the vagueness has impaired the rights of patentees, and the burden was on those making the claim to prove it.[28]

A survey of patent law reveals that judges routinely deal with doctrines that are at least as murky as patent misuse. For example, it seems no easier to determine the existence of non-literal infringement under the doctrine of equivalents than whether the limitations on the doctrine of equivalents apply. One such limitation is prosecution history estoppel, where a patentee who had previously allowed the narrowing of his claim could nonetheless succeed in ensnaring the accused product within its claims.[29] The Supreme Court prefaced its opinion by acknowledging the Federal Circuit's concern over uncertainty in its "flexible-bar rule", "because this case-by-case approach has proved unworkable. In the [Federal Circuit]'s view a complete-bar rule, under which estoppel bars all claims of equivalence to the narrowed element, would promote certainty in the determination of infringement cases."[30] The Court, however, went on to observe that:

> It is true that the doctrine of equivalents renders the scope of patents less certain. It may be difficult to determine what is, or is not, an equivalent to a particular element of an invention. If competitors cannot be certain about a patent's extent, they may be deterred from engaging in legitimate manufactures outside its limits, or they may invest by mistake in competing products that the patent secures. In addition the uncertainty may lead to wasteful litigation between competitors, suits that a rule of literalism might avoid. These concerns with the doctrine of equivalents, however, are not new. *Each time the Court has considered the doctrine, it has acknowledged this uncertainty as the price of ensuring the appropriate incentives for innovation, and it has affirmed the doctrine over dissents that urged a more certain rule.*[31]

---

[27]   Marshall Leaffer, *Patent Misuse and Innovation*, 10 J. HIGH TECH. L. 142, 157 (2010).

[28]   On file with the author. ("The question, though, I think, is an empirical question. Unless he can show me data where it has actually impaired patentees, then he's simply making an intuitive judgment about whether that's true or not.")

[29]   *Festo Corp. v. Shoketsu Kinzoku Kogyo Kabushiki Co.*, 535 U.S. 722, 741 (2002) ("The equivalent may have been unforeseeable at the time of the application; the rationale underlying the amendment may bear no more than a tangential relation to the equivalent in question; or there may be some other reason suggesting that the patentee could not reasonably be expected to have described the insubstantial substitute in question").

[30]   Ibid. at 730.

[31]   Ibid. at 732 (emphasis added).

In the Court's opinion, the right balance between the two was struck by placing the burden on the patentee to show that the previously surrendered patent scope was unforeseeable at the time of application.[32]

Similarly, in the Federal Circuit's *en banc* decision in *Therasense* concerning inequitable conduct, Judge Kathleen O'Malley noted in her concurrence that "clear guidelines," while practical, are sometimes inappropriate "when dealing with the application of equitable principles and remedies [where] the law is imprecise by design."[33]

In achieving the right balance, Supreme Court precedent is clear that it is the flexibility to "mold each decree to the necessities of the particular case" that allows equity which provides the fine-tuning to the broad brush of legislation and governmental policy.[34] In the same way, could some of the sting from patent misuse's open-endedness be mitigated by placing a burden on the defendant? One approach is to require the defendant to show cognizable harm either to the competitive process or to incentives to innovation under the general analysis that animates patent law cases.

---

[32]   Ibid. at 740 ("In Warner-Jenkinson we struck the appropriate balance by placing the burden on the patentee to show that an amendment was not for purposes of patentability: 'Where no explanation is established, however, the court should presume that the patent application had a substantial reason related to patentability for including the limiting element added by amendment. In those circumstances, prosecution history estoppel would bar the application of the doctrine of equivalents as to that element.' When the patentee is unable to explain the reason for amendment, estoppel not only applies but also 'bars the application of the doctrine of equivalents as to that element.' These words do not mandate a complete bar; they are limited to the circumstance where 'no explanation is established.' They do provide, however, that when the court is unable to determine the purpose underlying a narrowing amendment—and hence a rationale for limiting the estoppel to the surrender of particular equivalents—the court should presume that the patentee surrendered all subject matter between the broader and the narrower language").

[33]   *Therasense, Inc. v. Becton, Dickinson & Co.*, 649 F.3d 1276, 1296 (Fed. Cir. 2011) (O'Malley, J. concurring) ("Patent practitioners regularly call on this court to provide clear guidelines. They seek to know under precisely what circumstances governing principles will be applied, and precisely how they will be applied. While precision may be in the nature of what patent practitioners do, and the desire for defining rules in the scientific world understandable, the law does not always lend itself to such precision").

[34]   See, e.g., *Weinberger v. Romero-Barcelo*, 456 U.S. 305, 312 (1982) ("The essence of equity jurisdiction has been the power of the Chancellor to do equity and to mould each decree to the necessities of the particular case," quoting *Hecht Co. v. Bowles*, 321 U.S. 321, 329 (1944);"'[f]lexibility rather than rigidity has distinguished' equitable jurisdiction" quoting *Weinberger*, 456 U.S. at 312); *Holmberg v. Armbrecht*, 327 U.S. 392, 396 (1946) ("Equity eschews mechanical rules; it depends on flexibility").

Once defendants successfully do this, Marshall Leaffer proposes that "the burden should shift to the patent owner to demonstrate a business justification for having insisted on the restrictive licensing practice, or as the case may be, a strategic use of the patent grant exceeding its scope and contrary to patent policy."[35] This makes intuitive sense. The party best able to produce information to explain the situation to the court should be made to bear the burden. Sometimes it will be the defendant. Other times, it will be the patentee. If a licensing clause is on its face onerous, or litigation vexatious, it seems logical that the patent owner should explain why it nonetheless has good reason to prevail. In either case, misuse is an instrument which may be developed or dismembered by the judiciary alone. In this regard, the Tenth Circuit cited with approval a report by the Attorney General's National Committee to study the Antitrust Laws that misuse was "basically a problem of judicial control," and recommended "that the courts should make full use of their powers to curb such attempts to defeat justice."[36] It is thus, as Chief Justice Marshall noted so long ago in *Marbury v. Madison*, that "[i]t is emphatically the province and duty of the judicial department to say what the law is. Those who apply the rule to particular cases must, of necessity expound and interpret the rule."[37]

Second, as the Supreme Court in *Morton Salt* held, "[e]quity may *rightly* withhold its assistance from such a use of the patent by declining to entertain a suit for infringement."[38] If, as the Court notes, a sense of "rightness" directs equity, does that suggest that misuse is more than a judicial contraption in a misuse case created for merely mechanical economic analysis? Judge Posner, in recounting the history of equity, noted that:

> The doctrine of 'unclean hands'—colorfully named, equitable in origin, and reflecting, in its name at least, the moralistic background of equity in the decrees of the clerics who filled the office of lord chancellor of England during the middle ages, nowadays just means that equitable relief will be refused if it would give the plaintiff a wrongful gain.[39]

But that begs the jurisprudential question of why should the law concern itself with barring patentees from "wrongful" gains, unless there is also some measure of what is "right"? The English jurist Lord Alfred

---

[35]   Leaffer, *supra* note 26, at 159.
[36]   *McCullough Tool Co. v. Well Surveys, Inc.*, 395 F.2d 230, 240 (10th Cir. 1968).
[37]   *Marbury v. Madison*, 5 U.S. 137, 177 (1803).
[38]   *Morton Salt Co. v. G. S. Suppiger Co.*, 314 U.S. 488, 493 (1942) (emphasis added).
[39]   *Scheiber v. Dolby Labs., Inc.*, 293 F.3d 1014, 1021 (7th Cir. 2002).

Denning suggests an answer. He starts with the premise that legal positivism cannot be an end in itself:

> The judge says with calm detachment that the law is an end in itself. They regard law as a series of commands issued by a sovereign telling the people what to do or what not to do: they regard it as a piece of social engineering designed to keep the community in good order. Lawyers with this cast of thought draw a clear and absolute line between law and morals, or what is nearly the same thing, between law and justice. Judges and advocates are, to their minds, not concerned with the morality or justice of the law but only with the interpretation of it and its enforcement.
>
> That is a great mistake. It overlooks the reason why people obey the law. . . . People will respect rules which are intrinsically right and just and will expect their neighbours to obey them, as well as obey the rules themselves: but they will not feel the same about rules which are unrighteous or unjust.[40]

What is "unrighteous or unjust" may appear starker to the observer in cases involving due process or criminal law. The loss of life or liberty is naturally more viscerally felt than infringement of an abstract right framed by obtuse technical jargon. And yet justice remains the overaching goal in the outcome of each case. Every judge in America swears or affirms to administer justice "without respect to persons, and do equal right to the poor and to the rich, and that I will faithfully and impartially discharge and perform all the duties incumbent . . . under the Constitution and laws of the United States."[41] It is the creed of a nation who decided that "Equal Justice under Law" was worth writing in stone in its highest court.[42]

Misuse and antitrust law today are both based on economic analysis, with the sole purpose of maximizing efficiency.[43] There are fundamental

---

[40]   Alfred Denning, THE ROAD TO JUSTICE 2–3 (1955). See ibid. at 4 ("Thence I ask the question. What is Justice? . . . All I would suggest is that justice is not something you can see. It is not temporal but eternal. How does man know what is justice? It is not the product of his intellect but of his spirit. The nearest we can get to defining justice is to say that it is what the right-minded members of the community—those who have the right spirit within them—believe to be fair").

[41]   28 U.S.C. § 453 (2006).

[42]   *The Court and Constitutional Interpretation*, SUPREME COURT OF THE UNITED STATES, accessed at http://www.supremecourt.gov/about/constitutional.aspx (last visited Oct. 23, 2012) ("'EQUAL JUSTICE UNDER LAW'—These words, written above the main entrance to the Supreme Court Building, express the ultimate responsibility of the Supreme Court of the United States. The Court is the highest tribunal in the Nation for all cases and controversies arising under the Constitution or the laws of the United States. As the final arbiter of the law, the Court is charged with ensuring the American people the promise of equal justice under law").

[43]   See John B. Kirkwood & Robert H. Lande, *The Fundamental Goal of Antitrust: Protecting Consumers, Not Increasing Efficiency*, 84 NOTRE DAME L.

problems with this perspective when applied to misuse. It may be said that matters arising under patent law are matters of economic analysis or innovation policy, matters which closely approximate rational scientific enquiry of legal issues. Turning the argument for scientific rationality on its head, Lord Denning demurred:

> the law cannot afford to be a 'lawless science' but should be a science of law. Just as the scientist seeks for truth, so the lawyer should seek for justice. Just as the scientist takes his instances and from them builds up his general propositions, so the lawyer should take his precedents and from them build up his general principles. Just as the propositions of this scientist fail to be modified when shown not to fit all instances, or even discarded when shown to be in error, so the principles of the lawyer should be modified when found to be unsuited to the times or discarded when found to work injustice.
>
> Many a lawyer will dispute this analogy with science. 'I am only concerned', he will say, 'with the law as it is, not with what it ought to be.' For him the rule is the thing. Right or wrong does not matter. That approach is all very well for the working lawyer who applies the law as a working mason lays bricks, without any responsibility for the building which he is making. But it is not good enough for the lawyer who is concerned with his responsibility to the community at large. He should ever seek to do his part to see that the principles of the law are consonant with justice. If he should fail to do this, he will forfeit the confidence of the people. The law will fall into disrepute; and if that happens the stability of the country will be shaken. The law must be certain. Yes, as certain as may be. But it must be just too.[44]

Thus seen, the law is not merely an instrument to promote business efficacy but also must be right—the bulwark for this is constructed through the accumulation and refinement of case law over the years. Elaborating on the importance of Lord Denning's argument, Justice Andrew Phang of the Supreme Court of Singapore noted that "the entire enterprise becomes a contradiction in terms: for the law should not be undermined if justice, the very object of the law itself, is to be achieved."[45] It is an issue that deserves some attention. Justice Phang, in the context of contract law, noticed a debilitating trend toward "rationalism and individualism" as a

---

REV. 191, 192 (2008) ("The conventional wisdom in the antitrust community today is that the antitrust laws were passed to promote economic efficiency"); *Princo Corp. v. Int'l Trade Comm'n*, 616 F.3d 1318, 1335 (Fed. Cir. 2010) *cert. denied*, 131 S. Ct. 2480(U.S. 2011) (assessing misuse based on a weighing of efficiencies involved in joint ventures).

[44]   Alfred Denning, THE DISCIPLINE OF LAW 292–93 (1979).

[45]   Andrew Phang, *The Natural Law Foundations of Lord Denning's Thought and Work*, 14 DENNING L. J. 159, 176 (1999).

result of the secularization of the law.[46] Thus, "courts have been unable to mediate objectively the tension . . . between both certainty and technicality on one hand and fairness on the other."[47] Justice Phang does not advocate that the law functions as some kind of moral police. At the same time, both judges emphasize that it should not be devoid of notions of fairness and justice either.

Courts desiring to reclaim the heart of equity in misuse cases surely must also employ their intuitive sense of fair play and properly grounded sensibilities in economic efficiencies and the constitutional mandate inherent in the grant and exercise of patent rights. Perhaps it is precisely the need to do justice that allows courts to look beyond the form of a misuse to its effect. This gap-filling role of misuse was authenticated by the Federal Circuit in *Mallinckrodt, Inc. v. Medipart, Inc.*, which offered a rationale in support of the district court's ruling, pointing out that: "[t]he concept patent misuse arose to restrain practices that *did not in themselves violate any law*, but that drew anticompetitive strength from the patent right, and thus were deemed to be contrary to public policy," and noting that "[t]he policy purpose was to prevent a patentee from using the patent to obtain market benefit beyond that which inheres in the statutory patent right."[48]

An interviewee noted that "handled properly", patent misuse can be a "valid" doctrine.[49] According to the interviewee, the district court's ability to broker a settlement remains potent even in the face of adverse Federal Circuit precedent, giving patent misuse more vitality than it would appear to have. [50] He gave an example of how judges, particularly ones that are respected, could use a misuse claim to push parties toward settlement by allowing additional discovery in what they deem to be a colorable case of misuse.[51] The opacity of the judicial

---

[46]   Ibid. at 166.

[47]   Ibid. (noting that "a return to the objective religious foundations will enable a new (and more coherent) theory of contract law to be developed").

[48]   *Mallinckrodt, Inc. v. Medipart, Inc.*, 976 F.2d 700, 704 (Fed.Cir. 1992) (emphasis added).

[49]   On file with the author.

[50]   Ibid. ("Even if you have a Federal Circuit, which is strong and has these other things, there's room for a district court judge to manoeuvre, wiggle room, to talk the talk in a way that could lead to a settlement, rather than have—because they get it wrong—I mean, right now I have this little guy . . . But they'll get him out of the picture, because yes, the chances are that the Federal Circuit is going to go my way, but who knows what panel will be in the Federal Circuit, what they can do?").

[51]   Ibid. ("It doesn't need a lot of decided cases. As long as it's there and judges say those words—'to me, Mr Jones, this looks like a patent misuse case. That's the

deliberative process makes it risky for a patentee to litigate the case to its conclusion at the district court.[52] Indeed, if that patentee won, the interviewee notes, judges on the Federal Circuit may hold starkly different views of misuse, and one of its randomly constituted panels might choose to uphold the district court, even if its decision was on shaky ground under current precedents.[53] In any case, even if the risk of loss is low, the harm from a loss might lead the patentee not to take even a low risk. The specter of unenforceability, according to the interviewee, makes the impetus for the patentee to settle for a controllable outcome a compelling one.[54]

In the interviewee's opinion, patentees may therefore choose to settle in a way that is more favorable for the defendant.[55] In this sense, the vitality of patent misuse doctrine is not to be judged just by decided cases alone.[56] The danger, the interviewee warns, is that strategic thinking by judges and parties might mean that "patentees are settling things that shouldn't be settled," and that may harm incentives to innovate.[57]

This study also shows that there are indeed judges who have expressed a willingness to expand the categories of misuse, sometimes at the expense of abandoning their earlier hostility toward misuse.[58] One example, surprisingly, is Judge Richard Posner. In earlier cases, he was a strident advocate for subsuming misuse into antitrust analysis. More recently, however, he noted that:

> When the advance of science well illustrated by the products in this case enables a form of patent misuse that is new but is well within the conceptual heartland of the doctrine, the boundaries of the doctrine can expand modestly to encompass it. . . . It would be inappropriate to confine patent misuse, as is sometimes

---

way I'm going here. I just want you to know that. And I'm going to allow even more discovery into that aspect of the case'—those words are going to be, I would say, nine out of ten times, leading to a settlement that's much better for that party in a way that they are going to do all right. We don't see that in just-decided cases. So that has that vitality").

52   Ibid.

53   Ibid.

54   Ibid. ("The dire consequences of losing a patent are such that it can have vitality even if you're pretty sure it won't succeed ultimately in the district court or on appeal. To that extent, it has vitality in causing, I think, settlements").

55   Ibid. ("So they won't have this horrible penalty, but this other guy is going to get a nice break in settlement").

56   Ibid.

57   Ibid. ("Now, the danger of that is patentees may be settling things that shouldn't be settled, and that's going to backfire on incentives and other things").

58   See *infra* Chapter 6.

suggested, to practices that violate antitrust law, for in that event the doctrine would be superfluous.[59]

Another example comes from the U.S. District Court of New Jersey in *F.C. Russell v. Consumers Insulation*, which found that "the particular form or method by which the patent monopoly is sought to be extended is immaterial."[60] In such instances, Lord Denning's view that equity's strength and utility may lie precisely in its ability to fluidly fill the gaps left by the common law and temper outcomes that are formalistically correct but nonetheless unjust.[61] A judge interviewed for this study enthused that patent misuse plays a valuable role because it appeals to our sense of right and wrong, and exists to arrest misconduct not made illegal under existing laws "even at the cost of more vagueness in the doctrine".[62] The reluctance to rely on equity may thus be a reflection of society's dependence on mechanical rationality rather than human intuition as to what is right or wrong.[63] One lawyer interviewed noted that as an equitable doctrine, misuse retained a suppleness that is not afforded to courts relying on statutory or common law rules, putting it thus: "the more you codify, the less you are about to scratch the right itch."[64]

---

[59] *SmithKline Beecham Corp. v. Apotex Corp.*, 247 F. Supp. 2d 1011, 1047 (N.D. Ill. 2003).

[60] *F. C. Russell Co. v. Consumers Insulation Co.*, 119 F. Supp. 119, 122 (D.N.J. 1954).

[61] See *Solle v. Butcher*, [1950] 1 K.B. 671 (Eng. C.A.) ("[Equity's] role is to prevent [a party] from insisting on his strict legal rights when, owing to his behaviour, it would be unconscionable or inequitable to allow him to do so").

[62] On file with author. ("There are aspects of the patent arena that are such that a government-granted right to exclude might be a powerful enough tool that it warrants somewhat broader control by the courts, since the capacity of people to come up with ways to misuse things is probably endless and extends to the limits of the creativity of man. The principles of equity that originally gave rise to the patent misuse doctrine probably warranted being given a little greater flexibility, even at the cost of more vagueness in the doctrine.")

[63] But see Richard Posner, How Judges Think 110 (2008) ("At every stage the judge's reasoning process is primarily intuitive. Given the constraints of time, it could not be otherwise; for intuition is a great economizer on conscious attention. The role of the unconscious judge in judicial decision making is obscured by the convention that requires a judge to explain his decision in an opinion. The judicial opinion can best be understood as an attempt to explain how the decision, even if (as is most likely) arrived at on the basis of intuition, could have been arrived at on the basis of logical, step-by-step reasoning").

[64] On file with the author.

B. The Itch

What then is that itch? Case law is clear that "[a]lthough the defense of patent misuse indeed evolved to protect against 'wrongful' use of patents, the catalog of practices labeled 'patent misuse' does not include a general notion of 'wrongful' use."[65] Instead, the defense is anchored to the "type of harm" which misuse is designed to prevent.[66] The harm, as one court put it, is that:

[a] patentee, as the beneficiary of a public policy "to promote the Progress of Science and useful Arts", does not have the right to use the special privilege of a patent monopoly to secure rights not granted by the patent and that are contrary to public policy. . . . The doctrine of patent abuse is equitable in nature. Accordingly, "it is the adverse effect upon the public interest of a successful infringement suit in conjunction with the patentee's course of conduct which disqualifies him to maintain the [infringement] suit, regardless of whether the particular defendant has suffered from the misuse of the patent."[67]

This harm is, essentially: a patentee that is granted privileges for an invention because it promotes progress may then misuse its monopolistic privileges by bringing an infringement action and thereby undermine the very same public policy underlying the patentee's privilege—promoting the progress of science and the useful arts.[68] Further, the "equities" in

---

[65] *Eng'd Prods. Co. v. Donaldson Co.*, 313 F. Supp. 2d 951, 995 (N.D. Iowa 2004).

[66] *Tech. Licensing Corp. v. Gennum Corp.*, No. C 01-04204 RS, 2007 U.S. Dist. LEXIS 35521 at *81 (N.D. Cal. May 4, 2007) ("Because patent misuse is an equitable doctrine, Gennum would not necessarily need to show that the facts here fit precisely into the mold of situations in which it has been previously applied. Nevertheless, because the *type of harm* that patent misuse doctrine is designed to prevent is not present here even under Gennum's characterization of what occurred, its patent misuse defense fails").

[67] *Windsurfing Int'l, Inc. v. Fred Ostermann GmbH*, 613 F. Supp. 933, 952 (S.D.N.Y. 1985) (citing *Morton Salt Co. v. G.S. Suppiger Co.*, 314 U.S. 488, 491, 494 (1942)).

[68] *Ibid.*, at 952. The court explained: "A patentee, as the beneficiary of a public policy to promote the progress of science and useful arts, does not have the right to use the special privilege of a patent monopoly to secure rights not granted by the patent and that are contrary to public policy. . . . The doctrine of patent abuse is equitable in nature. Accordingly, '[i]t is the adverse effect upon the public interest of a successful infringement suit in conjunction with the patentee's course of conduct which disqualifies him to maintain the infringement suit, regardless of whether the particular defendant has suffered from the misuse of the patent,' ibid.

misuse cases are not merely confined to the parties in the case, but the protection of the public at large. The Supreme Court in *Mazer v. Stein* found the public policy goals of patent law to be promotion of public welfare.[69]

Indeed, the entire basis for misuse is directed toward the goal of ensuring that patentees obtain a right commensurate, and not more than, the services they render. With inequitable conduct, the public is not privy to the process of the grant and the fact that the PTO does not have the facilities to verify the claims made by applicants on the patentability of their inventions imposes a duty of candor on the latter to ensure that any exclusive rights eventually granted are justified because the public is thereafter affected. So, with the exercise of those same rights, misuse imposes a duty on patentees to conduct themselves so that they further (or at least refrain from contravening) the patent and antitrust policies embodied in the grant of patent rights. And where the equities favor neither party, the law is clear that the balance should be struck in favor of a broader rather than a narrow use of that technology, or in other words, the policy of public use should outweigh the monopolistic privilege of a patentee. As the Supreme Court noted, in holding that no infringement occurred:

> in light of this Nation's historical antipathy to monopoly . . . [w]e would require a clear and certain signal from Congress before approving the position of a litigant who, as respondent here, argues that the beachhead of privilege is wider, and the area of public use narrower, than courts had previously thought.[70]

C. Antitrust is more Administrable than Misuse

Conventional wisdom teaches that antitrust is a more a precise and less messy scaffold for cases falling under the ambit of misuse. But is antitrust law truly more administrable than misuse? Antitrust statutes are vague because "Congress apparently did not want to get involved in articulating a specific definition of competition or in determining which practices might promote or undermine it. Rather it enacted a few general principles derived from the common law, and left it largely to the courts to determine

---

(quoting *Morton Salt Co. v. G.S. Suppiger Co.*, 314 U.S. 488, 494 (1942)) (citations omitted).

[69] *Mazer v. Stein*, 347 U.S. 201, 219 (1954). The Court stated: "The economic philosophy behind the clause empowering Congress to grant patents and copyrights is the conviction that encouragement of individual effort by personal gain is the best way to advance public welfare through the talents of the authors and inventors in 'Science and useful Arts.' Sacrificial days devoted to such creative activities deserve rewards commensurate with the services rendered," ibid.

[70] *Deepsouth Packing Co. v. Laitram Corp.*, 406 U.S. 518, 531 (1972).

what practices violate them."[71] Commenting on the state of antitrust policy in the 1960s, Alan Greenspan observed that "[t]he entire structure of antitrust statutes in this country is a jumble of economic irrationality and ignorance. It is the product of (a) a gross interpretation of history, and (b) of rather naïve, and certainly unrealistic, economic theories."[72] This in part may have been because while the articulated goal of modern antitrust is the promotion of market efficiency, the antitrust laws were used for socio-political goals such as promoting small business interests.[73]

The potential vulnerability of antitrust to capricious judicial temperaments makes the assertion that it can provide a clearer and more stable vehicle than misuse suspect. At hearings conducted by the FTC in 2008, it was revealed that there was a lack of clarity and a deep concern over rules governing Section 2 liability.[74] Panelists surveyed for the study were also concerned with the chilling effect of treble damages and attorney fees.

One judge interviewed noted that while patent law was bound more strictly by detailed statutory provisions, antitrust law gave judges more room to maneuver because antitrust legislation was extremely vague and terse.[75] The tributaries of antitrust law are carved out and filled in by the

---

[71] Bohannan & Hovenkamp, *supra* note 18 at 920.

[72] Alan Greenspan, Chairman and President, Townsend-Greenspan & Co., Inc., *Antitrust* at the Antitrust Seminar of the National Association of Business Economists (Sept. 25, 1961).

[73] Bohannan & Hovenkamp, *supra* note 18, at 906 ("In the middle of the twentieth century, antitrust policy lost much of its concern with economic competition and started protecting less efficient small businesses from the lower costs of larger firms"). See 1 Phillip E Areeda & Herbert Hovenkamp, ANTITUST LAW ¶111, at 102–103 (3d ed. 2006).

[74] See, e.g., *Sherman Act Section 2 Joint hearing Before the Fed. Trade Comm'n & Dep't of Justice*, 46 (Feb. 13. 2007) (statement by Ron Stern), available at: http://www.justice.gov/atr/public/hearings/single_firm/docs/224623.htm (in-house counsel stressing that "it is important to have clear, administrable, and objective rules"); ibid. at 94 (statement by Patrick Sheller) (in-house counsel noting the desirability of clear rules that paint "brighter lines for the client"); ibid. at 126 (statement by Sean Heather) ("Firms do want to obey the rules of the road, but discerning and applying those rules is becoming increasingly difficult").

[75] On file with the author. ("The antitrust field developed very differently. Over the decades, judges made all sorts of antitrust law—just made it up out of nowhere. The Robinson-Patman Act, the Clayton Act, the Sherman Act are extremely vague, extremely terse. The courts just made it up. I don't know whether they did a great job or a so-so job or a mixed job or a terrible job, however one might evaluate it. But they did it. Patent law hasn't developed in that kind of free-wheeling way, where the law is basically being written, not by the Congress, but by appellate judges. The patent law has been, in my view, a little more modest—a

ideologies flowing from the well-spring deep within the recesses of the judge's own views of patents, economic monopolies, and market competition in general. As discussed in Chapter 1, the two main dichotomies animating antitrust law jurisprudence take the form of the static/dynamic and Chicago/post-Chicago camps. Those favoring visible competition from rivals advocate antitrust intervention to dilute the patent owner's influence on the relevant market, whereas those who favor protecting the incentives of IP owners resist the incursion of antitrust law's reliance on the market and internal regulation to correct any imbalances. While people generally agree that a competitive market structure fosters competition in product markets, "[t]here is not yet a universally accepted consensus as to the kind of market structure that best facilitates innovation."[76] As FTC Commissioner Thomas Rosch notes:

> If you were to get together a group of antitrust and patent experts, everyone would likely agree broadly that antitrust and intellectual property are complementary in that both areas of law seek to protect and encourage innovation. When it comes to antitrust law, however, promoting innovation is good in theory, but hard in practice.[77]

Dynamic analysis is less developed and more difficult to measure than static considerations, which requires more time and effort to articulate, and it is difficult to build a convincing case for or against dynamic efficiencies.[78] One reason for this could be because "[i]nnovation market definition is a speculative venture that often defies precision where one is forced to define relevant assets and close substitutes with limited information."[79] While adopting the dynamic perspective in place of the static perspective gives patentees more latitude to exploit their rights, that shift removes the

---

lot more modest. It has tried to carefully follow the policies that are discernibly embedded in the statute and in amendments to the statute and, of course, in Supreme Court authority, which, of course, we have to follow and we do follow.")

[76] Ronald W. Davis, *Innovation Markets and Merger Enforcement: Current Practice in Perspective*, 71 ANTITRUST L.J. 677, 681 (2003–2004).

[77] J. Thomas Rosch, Comm'r, Fed. Trade Comm'n, Promoting Innovation: Just How "Dynamic" Should Antitrust Law Be?, Remarks at USC Gould School of Law 2010 Intellectual Property Institute 2 (Mar 23, 2010), available at: http://www.ftc.gov/speeches/rosch/100323uscremarks.pdf.

[78] Ibid. at 4–5.

[79] Leaffer, *supra* note 26, at 158 ("Antitrust has engaged in analysis of innovation markets but has not had a particularly good track record in its application. It is not hard to see why. Innovation market definition is a speculative venture that often defies precision where one is forced to define relevant assets and close substitutes with limited information").

measureability of antitrust policy goals as competitive prices and outputs are replaced by new forms of innovation. Professor Christopher Leslie suggests that the antitrust community has a "natural bias" toward static analysis because it is more measurable.[80] Commissioner Rosch agrees that, "[t]he antitrust community—both lawyers and economists—has far greater familiarity and comfort with static analysis than dynamic analysis."[81] Ilan Charnelle explains that:

> Antitrust analysis relies on static single-period models that do not account for innovation and its effect on consumer welfare. In static single-period models, an investment is assumed to last for a set time period and the focus is on two possible fixed values at the end of that time period. The investment can go up or down, usually on a percentage basis. These models do not take into account fluctuations in value that occur between the start of the investment and the end of the investment. In order for innovation and creativity to occur, these fluctuations must be examined.[82]

Elaborating on why antitrust law falls short in these markets, Ramsey Hanna notes that in contrast to "copyright and patent law [which] recognize the importance of encouraging socially beneficial innovation," antitrust law "lacks similar sensitivity to the central role of innovation."[83] Hanna attributes this to "a dearth of economic literature dealing with determinants, mechanics, and dynamic effects of innovation"[84] as well as "the difficulty in defining markets in industries with differentiated but highly substitutable goods."[85]

Early antitrust case law showed remarkable sensitivity to IP policy.

---

[80] Transcript, *The Antitrust Marathon Part II: The Role of a Consumer Harm Test in Competition Policy*, 20 Loy. Consumer L. Rev. 151, 163 (2008) (remarks of Christopher Leslie: "[The] problem [is that] . . . static price analysis appears to be so precise. It gives this illusion of a precise quantifiable answer that you can see on a graph. But there's just no way that you can easily put quality, innovation, and consumer choice on that graph. Even when you try to have a balance between these two things, our natural bias is to give more weight to the thing that looks measurable").

[81] J. Thomas Rosch, Cmm'r of Fed. Trade Cmm'n, Remarks at Fifth Annual In-House Counsel Forum on Pharmaceutical Antitrust, 4–5 (Feb 18, 2010), available at: http://www.ftc.gov/speeches/rosch/100218pharmaantitrust.pdf.

[82] Ilan Charnelle, *The Justification and Scope of the Copyright Misuse Doctrine and its Independence of the Antitrust Laws*, 9 UCLA Ent. L. Rev. 167, 197 (2001–2002).

[83] Ramsey Hanna, *Misusing Antitrust: The Search for Functional Copyright Misuse Standards*, 46 Stan. L. Rev. 401, 422 (1993–1994).

[84] Ibid.

[85] Ibid. at 431–32.

In *United States v. Singer Mfg.*, the Supreme Court found an antitrust
violation on the basis that two patent applicants, one American and the
other German, attempted to subvert interference proceedings at the PTO
in order that the German applicant with the broader claims might obtain
that patent and assign it to the American company who would then use
it to exclude Japanese competitors from the American market, thereby
protecting both companies from competition.[86] As Justice White noted in
his concurrence:

> There is a public interest here which the parties have subordinated to their
> private ends—the public interest in granting patent monopolies only when the
> progress of the useful arts and of science will be furthered because as the con-
> sideration for its grant the public is given a novel and useful invention. When
> there is no novelty and the public parts with the monopoly grant for no return,
> the public has been imposed upon and the patent clause subverted. Whatever
> may be the duty of a single party to draw the prior art to the Office's attention,
> clearly collusion among applicants to prevent prior art from coming to or being
> drawn to the Office's attention is an inequitable imposition on the Office and
> on the public. In my view, such collusion to secure a monopoly grant runs afoul
> of the Sherman Act's prohibitions against conspiracies in restraint of trade—if
> not bad per se, then such agreements are at least presumptively bad. The patent
> laws do not authorize, and the Sherman Act does not permit, such agreements
> between business rivals to encroach upon the public domain and usurp it to
> themselves.[87]

However, as rule of reason analysis based on economic modeling replaced
rules in antitrust law, as well as the Federal Circuit hearing almost all
patent patents, antitrust analysis in patent cases has become a hybrid
of antitrust-patent rules applied by a specialist patent court without too
much regard for the antitrust principles and their nuances which underlie
those principles.

To the extent that advocates of antitrust law lord it over their opponents
on the basis of antitrust law's ability to balance the economic effects of the
alleged misuse against competing considerations, courts have also read
rule of reason analysis into the misuse doctrine. For example, in 2009
the court in *In re Gabapentin*, held that "[u]nder a rule of reason, patent

---

[86] *United States v. Singer Mfg.*, 374 U.S. 174 (1963).

[87] Ibid. at 199–200; see also *United States v. Paramount Pictures*, 334 U.S. 131,
158 (1948) (quoting Chief Justice Hughes in *Fox Film Corp. v. Doyal*, 286 U.S.
123, 127 (1932) "The copyright law, like the patent statutes, makes reward to the
owner a secondary consideration. . . . 'The sole interest of the United States and
the primary object in conferring the monopoly lie in the general benefits derived by
the public from the labors of authors'").

misuse can be found where the patentee's conduct violates the public policies addressed by the patent laws."[88] Intriguingly, it cited *Morton Salt, Blonder-Tongue* and *C.R. Bard* for the policy interests in keeping patent monopolies limited and equitable as well as the proposition that "[t]he concept of patent misuse arose to restrain practices that did not in themselves violate any law, but that draw anticompetitive strength from the patent right, and thus were deemed contrary to public policy."[89] However, the application of patent misuse informed by antitrust analysis suffers from accusations of vagueness as well. And the effect of licensing on net welfare is ambiguous at best. The *Harvard Law Review* noted that:

> Although a case for retaining the misuse doctrine can be made on the basis of both efficiency and pragmatic considerations, applying the doctrine to prevent the patent holder from obtaining excessive rewards is extremely difficult. Courts understandably have shied away from the view of the misuse doctrine that relies on patent policy because it is difficult to judge how patent scope affects innovation. Antitrust courts may have overlooked innovation concerns for this same reason.[90]

Professor Merges agrees that the antitrust rule of reason approach is by no means clearer than misuse because:

---

[88] *In re Gabapentin*, 648 F. Supp. 2d 641, 652–55 (D.N.J. 2009).

[89] Ibid.

[90] See Note, *supra* note 21, at 1935; see also ibid. at 1936, n. 86 ("The present lack of sufficient empirical findings makes arguing for either default rule problematic, however, because one does not know whether, on average, a particular type of licensing practice adds to or subtracts from net welfare. Consequently, one cannot structure the default rule to increase the chance that courts will preserve efficient restrictions and invalidate inefficient ones. Moreover, even trying to categorize different types of licensing practices may not increase the chance of a court reaching the most efficient result, because the optimal level of reward is highly context specific—it will vary for each patent, each licensee, and the other restrictions that are permitted"); see also ibid. at 1930–31 ("despite the *Mallinckrodt* court's specific instructions for evaluating use restrictions, the workings of the test remain unclear. For example, the court gave no guidance on how to determine, in general, whether the use restriction is 'reasonably within the patent grant' and, in particular, whether the use restriction in *Mallinckrodt* itself satisfied this first prong of the inquiry. More specifically, immunizing a licensing practice from further legal scrutiny because it falls 'reasonably within the patent grant' begs the question of which licensing practices should be allowed. The restriction in *Mallinckrodt* involved the patented device, but does such a connection, without more, make the use restriction 'reasonably within the patent grant' and therefore legal?").

Not only is [it] a notoriously difficult standard for an antitrust plaintiff to meet, it is also a standard that is very difficult to apply. Thus it is ironic indeed that advocates of greater certainty in the law of patent misuse would propose a unified rule of reason approach when this is arguably one of the least certain legal rules ever propounded.[91]

Congress twice considered and rejected revisions to a patent misuse law which would have required a successful showing of an antitrust violation, despite the law's proponents arguing that antitrust law provided greater certainty.[92] Others, however, view the "anticompetitive effects" doctrine as workable, allowing practitioners "to evaluate conduct under both patent misuse and antitrust law, confident that the analysis and result were likely to be consistent. Indeed, so similar were the methodologies of analysis that, in the absence of antitrust precedent, practitioners often relied upon patent misuse decisions as indicative of likely results under the antitrust laws."[93]

1. Filling the Gap

An antitrust plaintiff needs to show that the patentee has caused injury "of the type the antitrust laws were intended to prevent and that flows from that which makes the defendants' acts unlawful."[94] In contrast, a

---

[91]   See Robert P. Merges, *Reflections on Current Legislation Affecting Patent Misuse*, 70 J. Pat. & Trademark Off. Soc'y 793, 794 (1988).

[92]   See The Patent Misuse Reform Act of 1988, Pub. L. No. 100-703, § 201(a), 102 Stat. 4676 (1988) (patent ownership is not presumptive of market power); S. 1200, 100th Cong. (1st Sess. 1987) ("[N]o patent owner . . . shall be . . . deemed guilty of misuse . . . unless such practices . . . violate the antitrust laws"); Merges, *supra* note 90, at 793 (S. 1200 tests "all alleged patent misuse offenses under antitrust standards"); see also Kenneth J. Burchfiel, *Patent Misuse and Antitrust Reform: "Blessed Be the Tie?"*, 4 Harv. J.L. & Tech. 1, 25–26 (1991) ("It is equally clear that the House rejected any suggestion of a 'rule of reason' analysis in patent misuse determinations. Representative Fish explained that in response to concerns raised about the breadth of the original Senate bill, the amended version of S. 438 eliminated the detrebling provisions and does not require 'the application of the rule of reason to intellectual property arrangements.' Even the stronger Senate provision rejected by the House would have preserved the per se rule once market power was shown, avoiding consideration of the tying arrangement under the rule of reason. Furthermore, permitting business justification defenses would eliminate any cogent distinction between the 'threshold' market power requirement inserted by the House and the 'antitrust' standard for misuse which the House rejected").

[93]   Geoffrey D. Oliver, *Princo v. International Trade Commission: Antitrust Law and the Patent Misuse Doctrine Part Company*, 25 Antitrust 62, 65 (2011).

[94]   *Cargill, Inc. v. Monfort of Colorado., Inc.*, 479 U.S. 104, 109 (1986) (quoting *Brunswick Corp. v. Pueblo Bowl-O-Mat, Inc.*, 429 U.S. 477, 489 (1977)).

defendant to an infringement action can invoke patent misuse even if the defendant was unaffected by the misuse.[95] Professor Thomas Cotter offers an explanation for this discrepancy. He argues that:

> The only plausible reasons to have a misuse doctrine in addition to antitrust law, if the substantive content of the two is the same, would be (1) to permit someone who does not have antitrust standing or cannot prove antitrust injury to challenge the conduct at issue, or (2) to create an additional penalty (such as unenforceability of the IPR) in addition to the antitrust sanction.[96]

The Seventh Circuit, however, could find no precedent for extending the patent misuse doctrine beyond the antitrust laws.[97] The *en banc* majority in *Princo* was similarly unpersuaded that patent misuse is particularly relevant where antitrust law does not avail itself to victims of anticompetitive conduct. It did not address the objection squarely, but noted that the remedies provided by antitrust law were sufficiently "robust," and "as to the doctrinal limitations that apply to antitrust plaintiffs generally, such as the standing requirement, there is no reason to believe those limitations are inappropriate simply because a party is seeking relief against a patentee."[98] Others like Professor Vincent Chiappetta note that "[f]illing the gap by prohibiting these transactions through an independent misuse constraint does not prevent market harms. It interferes with an assessment mechanism specifically designed to ensure the law advances the overall net improvement goal."[99]

Yet, without the gap-filling role played by misuse, cases could arise, as the dissent in *Princo* acknowledged, which cry out for a just resolution unsatisfied by the application of antitrust law to misuse cases. The

---

[95] See *Transitron Elec. Corp. v. Hughes Aircraft Co.*, 487 F. Supp. 885, 892–93 (D. Mass. 1980).

[96] Cotter, *supra* note 22, at 935.

[97] See *USM Corp. v. SPS Techs., Inc.*, 694 F.2d 505, 516 (7th Cir. 1982) (finding that the patentee did not commit patent misuse by including a differential royalty schedule in the income agreement entered into as part of the settlement of parts of her suit for patent infringement).

[98] *Princo Corp. v. Int'l Trade Comm'n*, 616 F.3d 1318, 1333 n.6 (Fed. Cir. 2010) ("The dissenters argue that antitrust law is not adequate to protect victims of anticompetitive conduct by patentees and that the doctrine of patent misuse must be interpreted expansively to fill that gap. Antitrust law, however, provides robust remedies including both public and private enforcement. An accused infringer can raise a Sherman Act claim as a counterclaim in an infringement action or as an affirmative claim, and is eligible for treble damages and attorney's fees").

[99] Vincent Chiappetta, *Living With Patents: Insights From Patent Misuse*, 15 MARQ. INTELL. PROP. L. REV. 1, 31 (2011).

dissent in *Princo* comments on this blind spot, noting that the majority's narrow view of misuse does not address the instances when nascent competing technology is suppressed by an agreement between parties in a patent pool.[100] The *Princo* dissent details the difficulties defendants in patent misuse cases encounter, and the anticompetitive implications of the current legal regime:

> The antitrust laws also provide no adequate remedy for the suppression of competition. Private enforcement of the antitrust laws in this context is virtually impossible. Potential purchasers of the alternative product have no remedy. The ability of even a competitor to sue for damages is highly problematic given the early stage of development of the Lagadec technology. And injunctive relief at the request of a competitor is unlikely to take effect in a time frame that would allow for the development of an alternative technology given likely litigation delays. The difficulty of securing a misuse determination with respect to the suppressed patent or traditional antitrust relief underscores the importance of applying the doctrine of patent misuse to the protected patents. Unless the protected patents are held unenforceable, there will be no adverse consequence to the patent holder for its misconduct nor will the patent misuse be remedied.[101]

In such instances, patent misuse may offer parties harmed by a patentee's conduct the only remedy available: treble damages. However, this form of recourse, or litigation tactic, has concerned commentators and judges alike. Professor William Kovacic and Marc Winerman observe that federal courts since the 1970s have been concerned with limiting antitrust liability to avoid creating "unwarranted, disproportionate, and unavoidable treble damage liability for behaviour that was either legitimate or was improper only by a narrow margin."[102] Commissioner Rosch concurs,

---

[100]   *Princo Corp.*, 616 F.3d at 1350. The Court notes: "There is no realistic prospect of securing a misuse determination with respect to the suppressed patent. This is because there is no need for Philips to assert the Lagadec patent and open itself to a misuse defense. The mere threat of an infringement suit is typically sufficient to prevent a potential competitor from devoting the resources necessary to develop an alternative technology; the technology is thus suppressed at the outset. So too a potential competitor (wishing to secure an advance determination of invalidity) has no remedy by way of declaratory judgment to secure a determination that the patent for the alternative technology is unenforceable given our jurisprudence demanding a showing of a concrete plan to enter the market as the condition for testing patent validity and enforceability," ibid.

[101]   Ibid. at 1350.

[102]   See William E. Kovacic & Marc Winerman, *Competition Policy and the Application of Section 5 of the Federal Trade Commission Act*, 76 ANTITRUST L.J. 929, 938 (2009–2010); see also *NYNEX Corp. v. Discon, Inc.*, 525 U.S. 128, 136–37 (1998) ("To apply the per se rule here . . . would transform cases involving business

noting that recent Supreme Court precedent has "shown a disdain for the private class action bar."[103] This, Commissioner Rosch notes,

> has manifested itself in cases that relate to the procedural components of anti-trust law—the pleading of an antitrust claim in *Twombly* and the standard for preemption of an antitrust claim in *Credit Suisse*. In both of these cases, the thrust of the Court's concern was the same: the threat of treble damages available for Sherman Act violations combined with the difficulty generalist district court judges and/or lay juries have in drawing lines between procompetitive and anticompetitive behavior created real risks that antitrust defendants would suffer severe financial consequences for conduct that did not harm competition. This same concern militates in favor of the Commission using Section 5 in cases where there is a pronounced risk that collateral consequences will cause the very outcomes that Congress and, more recently, the Supreme Court have collectively sought to avoid.[104]

An interviewee for this study agreed with this view, noting that private enforcement in antitrust law, coupled with treble damages, presented a danger of over-penalizing patentees.[105] Because judges could not change the remedy, they focused on raising the doctrinal bar for finding an antitrust violation. One example of this cited by an interviewee is the Supreme Court's decision in *Twombly*, where the Court held that

---

behavior that is improper for various reasons, say, cases involving nepotism or personal pique, into treble-damages antitrust cases").

[103]   J. Thomas Rosch, Promoting Innovation, *supra* note 76, at 19.

[104]   Ibid. at 19; see also Daniel A. Crane, *Antitrust Antifederalism*, 96 CAL. L. REV. 1, 41 (2008) (observing that private litigation has negative spillover effects for public enforcement because "[t]he content of these liability rules is shaped by concerns peculiar to private litigation, such as abusive competitor suits, the risk that treble damage awards will chill vigorous competition, and the fear that setting the bar too low will encourage litigiousness. . . . at least in recent years, courts have often established sharply underinclusive liability norms in private antitrust cases" even though "[l]ogically, the liability rules might very well be less stringent in public litigation where those limiting concerns are absent").

[105]   On file with author. ("A typical fundamental difficulty in the system of competition law is that in private suits the chief means of imposing sanctions is to automatically treble damages and to try these suits in front of juries, to do all of the things that the system of private rights in the U.S. has done, and, in the eyes of our courts at least, that has raised great questions about the sensibility of a private right of action. So I think that finding a policy instrument that can provide a better, and maybe more discriminating, fit between the theory of harm and the correct choice of sanctions, be it equitable relief or some measure of damages that doesn't involve automatic trebling, I think would be the optimal approach. . . . There is a great deal of concern about how antitrust should intervene, even when the party pursuing the matter is a public agency that's not seeking treble damages.")

even in pleading a horizontal conspiracy the "[f]actual allegations must be enough to raise a right to relief above the speculative level."[106] He observed that precedents made during private litigation had the effect of making it more difficult for the Federal Trade Commission and Department of Justice to enforce antitrust law. European competition authorities, he observed, did not face the same guardedness from the courts because enforcement was still very much state-driven. Coupled with this is the deferential nature of antitrust toward the exercise of monopoly rights. In *Trinko*, Justice Antonin Scalia suggested that monopoly power was "an important element of a free market system," because it is "what attracts 'business acumen' in the first place . . . [and] induces risk taking that produces innovation and economic growth."[107] Commentators have also noted this phenomenon. Professor Marshall Leaffer observed:

> antitrust law has become too permissive, enabling those who abuse licensing practices to escape liability. The reason is that it is exceptionally difficult, if not impossible, to prove that a patent holder possesses market power at an early stage in the evolution of a market that the holder is nonetheless destined ultimately to control. In addition, antitrust is not sensitive to situations where a patent holder has leveraged its power into neighboring markets and where

---

[106]   *Bell Atlantic Corp. v. Twombly*, 550 U.S. 544, 545 (2007); see also Kovacic & Winerman, *supra* note 101, at 939 ("Public agencies now must meet liability tests that the courts have set to cope with what is perceived to be disproportionate treble damage exposure. In bringing their own Section 2 cases, public agencies today must satisfy liability standards that have been set to deal with overdeterrence hazards that the public agencies do not pose").

[107]   *Verizon Commc'ns Inc. v. Law Offices of Curtis V. Trinko, LLP.*, 540 U.S. 398, 407 (2004); see also Rosch, Promoting Innovation, *supra* note 76, at 11 ("The problem with Justice Scalia's assessment, however—apart from the fact that it was completely unnecessary to resolve the issue at hand—is that it goes way too far. While it is true that anticipated financial rewards certainly drive innovation and competition, the observation that monopolies incentivize a monopolist to engage in innovation is meaningless in the Section 2 context so long as it is divorced from the effects that monopolies have on rivals. If the *net* effect of a monopoly is less innovation in the relevant market, whether or not the *monopolist* engages in innovation is beside the point. Indeed, this thinking was the thrust behind many of the government's most prominent recent Section 2 cases, including both *Microsoft* and *Rambus*, where the DOJ and the FTC, respectively, argued that the exclusionary conduct by a monopolist impeded a rival's access to key inputs or to the post-innovation market and thereby reduced the possibility that an industry *in the aggregate* would successfully engage in innovation").

those acts would not constitute an antitrust violation, such as attempted monopolization.[108]

A heightened requirement to show anticompetitive effects under antitrust law also suggests that the number of patent misuse cases based on a finding of anticompetitive effects will be few and far between. Professor Kovacic and Winerman, in advocating the reinvigoration of Section 5 of the FTC Act to curb such conduct within the framework of antitrust law note that "[t]he FTC's institutional features, including Section 5, might supply a means of avoiding the pitfalls that judges associate with the litigation of private antitrust disputes in the federal courts."[109] For example, an FTC survey shows that private parties account for a "vast majority" of Section 2 enforcement activity under antitrust law, and most involve claims asserted against competitors.[110] Intriguingly, plaintiffs won

---

[108] Leaffer, *supra* note 26, at 158–59.

[109] See Kovacic & Winerman, *supra* note 101, at 947–48 (noting that "[t]his rationale could be presented front and center as a basis for applying Section 5, and it might be premised on two broad aspects of the FTC Act: The Commission's expertise, and the relatively limited implications of a Section 5 violation (at least under Federal law). The challenge is to identify specific problems with private litigation—the Supreme Court has been quite explicit in citing some—and to explain why, in a particular case, administrative enforcement should trouble a reviewing court less than would private litigation"). One government interviewee spoke about Section 5: "Initially, it was thought that the Sherman Act and the Clayton Act would be limited to a very small zone of operation and that this was a necessary element of elasticity. Particularly because of the 1940s', 1950s', and 1960s' interpretations of the Sherman Act and Clayton Act standards, the elasticity wasn't seen as necessary because the courts were saying the Sherman Act and Clayton Act would encompass a broader and broader array of behavior. In the last thirty years, that circle has been shrinking. Now you have Section 5 out there as a potentially useful tool. What has happened in cases is that courts have had a tendency to say, 'Yes, yes, in theory that's right, but you did not prove it here.' Or, 'Of course you have the power to do this, but . . . ' In laying out what you have to do there has been a tendency to establish specifications that resemble the demands that you would have to establish to satisfy or prove a Sherman Act case. In fact, what they have done is they have said, 'It's concepts, right? It's beyond the interpretations of the antitrust laws. But we have to say something about what you have to show to do that.' In defining that there has been a tendency to use criteria that tend to resemble what you see in Sherman Act jurisprudence. I suppose a consequence of that is that this could be a mirage, that this could be a bit of blue on the horizon, and the Commission will chase it," on file with the author.

[110] William F. Adkinson, Jr. et al., *Enforcement of Section 2 of the Sherman Act: Theory and Practice*, 14 (Working Paper, 2008), available at: http://www.ftc. gov/os/sectiontwohearings/docs/section2overview.pdf.

just 2 percent of all cases.[111] In nearly 60 per cent of all cases, defendants eliminated Section 2 claims in pretrial motions.[112] Section 5, however, may be limited to cases where a party's conduct causes anticompetitive effects in the form of price increases, output reductions and reduction in consumer choice.[113]

2. Recent views

Antitrust analysis may not address the questions which patent policy cares about. Professors Hovenkamp and Bohannan note that "[t]he antitrust approach undervalues the fact that the roots of misuse doctrine lie in IP policy, not in antitrust policy, and IP policy has its own reasons for limiting overreaching."[114] According to them, "[e]ven on antitrust's own rationale for misuse, namely to prevent anticompetitive conduct, the antitrust definition has focused too much attention on market power in the patented or copyrighted product or technology, and too little on the foreclosure of rival products or technologies."[115]

The patent grant is not a property right as such but a privilege conferred by the patent office to promote technological progress. If one needs support in more recent precedent, one need only look to the Supreme Court's treatment of injunctions in *eBay*, which noted that unlike real property rights, "the Patent Act itself indicates that patents shall have the attributes of personal property '[s]ubject to the provisions of this title.'"[116] Thus while antitrust law purports to be able to take into account dynamic efficiencies including innovation concerns inherent in patent policy, commentators like Professor Leaffer are concerned that "the rule of reason does not adequately consider how licensing and other practices affect innovation."[117] Professor Lemley adds that, "activities constituting

---

[111]   Ibid. at 15.

[112]   Ibid.

[113]   Rosch, Promoting Innovation, *supra* note 76, at 13 ("To my mind, that includes not only conduct that causes an increase in price or a reduction in output (as the Sherman Act case law requires), but also conduct that causes a reduction in consumer choice, which occurs when a firm's conduct impairs the choices that free competition brings to the marketplace"); see also Robert H. Lande, *Revitalizing Section 5 of the FTC Act Using "Consumer Choice" Analysis*, 8 ANTITRUST SOURCE 3 (2009); see also Robert H. Lande, *FTC v. Intel: Applying the "Consumer Choice" Framework to "Pure" Section 5 Allegations*, 2 CPI ANTITRUST J. 1 (2010).

[114]   Hovenkamp & Bohannan, *supra* note 13, at 260.

[115]   Ibid.

[116]   *eBay Inc. v. MercExchange, L.L.C.*, 547 U.S. 388, 392 (2006).

[117]   Leaffer, *supra* note 26, at 153.

patent misuse can (and often do) diverge from those activities constituting antitrust violations."[118]

These fundamental differences in policy explain why different or additional elements may be required to prove an antitrust violation from a case of patent misuse. This is perhaps the intuition behind Professor Robin Feldman's observation that antitrust law is "designed to address only particular types of harm, and it cannot reach everything that patent policy addresses"[119] and she cites as examples the following: preventing economic loss that occurs in defensive research activities in patent circumvention; the negative effects on innovation caused by an excess of patent rights, and the impediments to innovation from awarding patents to early-stage inventors at the expense of late-stage inventors.[120] Professors Julie Cohen, Brett Frischmann, Dan Moylan and a number of others agree, and have argued that misuse provides a more relevant answer to harms to market innovation.[121] Patent misuse could also be used to counterbalance pro-patent doctrines such as the doctrine of equivalents that effectively extended patent rights.[122]

Professors Hovenkamp and Bohannan also argue that misuse should be found when a patentee's practice "threatens unreasonable foreclosure

---

[118] See Mark A. Lemley, *The Economic Irrationality of Patent Misuse Doctrine*, 78 CAL. L. REV. 1599, 1611 (1990).

[119] See Feldman, *supra* note 22, at 400; Leaffer, *supra* note 26, at 157 ("Patent policy is involved with expansions of patent rights that impede system-wide innovation; even if those expansions do not create the kind of consequences that the antitrust law takes into account. The basic problem is that antitrust focuses on competition in defined markets and in so doing tends to disregard, and may even be blind to, activities that undermine the overall effectiveness of the patent system").

[120] Feldman, *supra* note 22, at 400.

[121] See Julie E. Cohen, *Reverse Engineering and the Rise of Electronic Vigilantism: Intellectual Property Implications of "Lock-Out" Programs*, 68 S. CAL. L. REV. 1091, 1192–94 (1995) (arguing that the misuse doctrine may be better tailored than antitrust to address harm to innovation); Brett Frischmann & Dan Moylan, *The Evolving Common Law Doctrine of Copyright Misuse: A Unified Theory and its Application to Software*, 15 BERKELEY TECH. L.J. 865, 927–30 (2000) (arguing that misuse doctrine should come into play in some cases in which restraints undermine public policy, such as by unduly inhibiting innovation, even if they fall short of violating antitrust law); Ramsey Hanna, *supra* note 82, at 423–25 (arguing antitrust does not sufficiently account for harm to long-term innovation, but the misuse doctrine can); see Note, *supra* note 21, at 1934–36 (arguing potential harm to innovation markets may justify the application of patent misuse in some cases, but noting the difficulty of applying this insight in practice).

[122] Hovenkamp & Bohannan, *supra* note 13, at 288.

of competition, innovation, or access to the public domain."[123] They note that once the infringer shows a *prima facie* case of misuse, whether or not there is market power, the burden shifts to the patentee to show "good reason for the challenged practice and the absence of less restrictive alternatives."[124] The remedy, they conclude, should be "tailored to the wrong," with the court opting between unenforceability when foreclosure has happened or is likely on one hand, and where foreclosure is less likely, to refrain from making an order of unenforceability but simply refuse to invalidate a particular license or infringement action.[125] Bruce Abramson concurs that "[t]he very nature of a balancing test creates uncertainty", but that over time cases will provide market participants with "data with which to gauge the propriety or impropriety of their behavior." [126]

III.   LAX STANDING REQUIREMENTS

The second criticism of misuse is that alleged infringers can act as "private attorney generals," invoking misuse where they have not been harmed by any misconduct. [127] Courts have determined that "[a]s a limit on the misuse doctrine, it can be stated generally that the misconduct must be connected with the matter in litigation, and the defense is not available to a party with whom the misconduct is of no concern."[128] While "it is not personal in the sense that the misuse must be directed at the infringement suit

---

[123]   Ibid. at 289.

[124]   Ibid.

[125]   Ibid. at 288.

[126]   Bruce D. Abramson, THE SECRET CIRCUIT: THE LITTLE KNOWN COURT WHERE THE RULES OF THE INFORMATION AGE UNFOLD 311 (2007). See also ibid., at 348 ("As with any flexible system, abuse is possible. The correct response to abuse is to improve guidelines, increase oversight, and stiffen penalties. Guidelines emerge from a combination of legislative statutes and judge-made law; the antitrust rule of reason is a prime example").

[127]   Adelman et al., CASES AND MATERIALS ON PATENT LAW 815 (3d ed. 2009) ("Misuse releases one wrongdoer (the infringer) from responsibility because the victim (the patentee) may have also wronged third parties (the anticompetitive activity) in ways unrelated to the specifics of this infringement action"); *Scheiber v. Dolby Labs., Inc.*, 293 F.3d 1014, 1021 (7th Cir. 2002) ("Dolby is in effect a private attorney general, charged by *Brulotte* with preventing Scheiber from seeking to 'extend' his patent and being rewarded for this service to the law by getting out of a freely negotiated royalty obligation").

[128]   *Kolene Corp. v. Motor City Metal Treating, Inc.*, 440 F.2d 77, 85 (6th Cir. 1971) ("[W]e find that Motor City has no cause to complain of the alleged misconduct of Kolene. Motor City is not a party to the allegedly illegal contracts . . . ").

defendant; however, it cannot be based on 'misuse in the air.' The misuse must be of the matter in litigation, to wit, misuse of the patent in suit."[129]

This, however, has not stopped commentators from criticizing misuse's apparently lax standing requirement as encouraging infringement that "give[s] rise to fishing expeditions with respect to one's assertion of IPRs vis-à-vis third parties."[130] Some may invoke it simply to get out of commercial deals which had been freely negotiated earlier. Others go further, arguing that misuse "pays the sanction as a windfall to an unrelated third party, thereby encouraging infringement while failing to compensate those actually injured."[131] Such concerns have led opponents of misuse to argue that its standing requirements should be circumscribed.[132] One judge interviewed expressed concern that patent misuse was the only area in patent law where the patentee loses all possibility of redress against the infringer because he or she may have harmed some third party with no relation to the underlying suit.[133] He stated further that some appellate courts have broadly defined a patentee's rights, thereby limiting the scope of patent misuse, giving the example of *Studiengesellschaft* which has been read for the proposition that "the patentee begins with substantial rights under the patent grant."[134]

A. Who are the Third Parties?

As an initial matter it is useful to peel away the rhetoric and identify the defendants in cases where misuse was successfully alleged. The history of

---

[129] *Skil Corp. v. Lucerne Prods., Inc.*, 489 F. Supp. 1129, 1162 (N.D. Ohio 1980).

[130] See Cotter, *supra* note 95, at 963.

[131] Lemley, *supra* note 117, at 1600.

[132] See Katherine E. White, *A Rule for Determining When Patent Misuse Should be Applied*, 11 FORDHAM INTELL. PROP. MEDIA & ENT. L.J. 671, 679 n. 56 (2000–2001) ("Patent misuse is a doctrine that could benefit from having a standing requirement that the misuse must directly affect the party raising the affirmative defense. Historically, there has been no standing requirement. This has caused substantial concern that the patent misuse doctrine is overbroad and overreaching").

[133] On file with the author.

[134] *Princo Corp. v. Int'l Trade Comm'n*, 616 F.3d 1318, 1328 (Fed. Cir. 2010); *United States v. Studiengesellschaft Kohle, m.b.H*, 670 F.2d 1122, 1127–28 (D.C. Cir. 1981) (holding that a patentee has "the right to suppress the invention while continuing to prevent all others from using it, . . . to license others, or to refuse to license, and to charge such royalty as the leverage of the patent monopoly permits." Excluding competitors and charging a high royalty are "at the core of the patentee's rights").

misuse reveals two different premises for misuse: the *Morton Salt* standard, which is more concerned about abuses of the patent system, and the
Windsurfing standard, which is more concerned about anticompetitive
effects measured through the rubric of the antitrust laws. Antitrust law has
made clear for at least 40 years that it is interested in protecting market
competition and not the competitor.[135] So unless the defendant can show
market harm, there is no misuse under the Federal Circuit's formulation.
As the Seventh Circuit noted: "[i]f no consumer interest can be discerned
even remotely in a suit brought by a competitor—if, as here, a victory
for the competitor can confer no benefit, certain or probable, present or
future, on consumers—a court is entitled to question whether a violation
of antitrust law is being charged."[136]

In a recent case involving standard-setting organizations, the District
Court for the Southern District of California denied the patent owner's
motion for summary judgment, accepting misuse as a plausible defense
against infringement claims by a holder of a standard essential patent.[137]
The Court found that the defendants, Apple and LG, presented plausible
evidence that the patent owner's "predecessors-in-interest were members
of the standards setting bodies ... [and] ... promised these standards
bodies that they would license the patents-in-suit on RAND terms, and
that MPT's damages request might violate its RAND obligations."[138]
While Apple and LG were neither licensees nor competitors, the court
implicitly accepted that misconduct in the standards-setting process warranted its further attention nonetheless.[139] This indicates that courts recognize misuse as a "system integrity check" to ensure that the mechanism
Congress had put in place to promote innovation and competition are not
compromised.

From an empirical perspective, the inquiry turns to what interviewees
and the data revealed. One attorney interviewed remarked that he had not
"seen patent misuse really raised except in conjunction with the infringed
patent. I think, more broadly, the courts have been fairly skeptical of
standing rights to raise arguments, unless they are directly affected by

---

[135]   *Brooke Group Ltd v. Brown & Williamson Tobacco Corp.*, 509 U.S.
209, 224 (1993) (quoting *Brown Shoe Co. v. United States*, 370 U.S. 294, 320
(1962)).
[136]   *Brunswick Corp. v. Riegel Textile Corp.*, 752 F.2d 261, 266–67 (7th Cir.
1984).
[137]   *Multimedia Patent Trust v. Apple Inc.*, 2012 U.S. Dist. LEXIS 167479 at
*80 (S.D. Cal. Nov. 9, 2012).
[138]   Ibid.
[139]   Ibid.

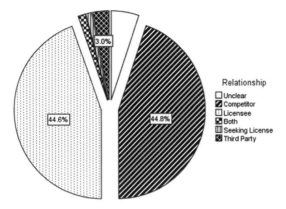

Figure 4.1   Relationship between patentees and infringers

the conduct at issue."[140] This study shows that the defendants invoking misuse were mostly either competitors or licensees or both; 44.8 percent were competitors and 44.6 percent licensees and about 1.4 percent were both competitors and licensees (see Figure 4.1). Only in 3 percent of the cases was the defendant an unrelated third party. To the extent that conventional wisdom teaches that misuse allows those not harmed to benefit from the defense, that wisdom may be misleading since competitors and licensees are plausibly "harmed" by the patentee's misconduct. Whether they can prove the ingredients of the doctrine are a separate matter.

B.   The Public Interest

Assuming *arguendo* that the defendants have only a colorable claim to being harmed or they were not "harmed", is there still value in extending standing to them? In *Compton v. Metal Products, Inc.*, the invention was a method of manufacturing screw conveyors used in coal mining. The patentee, Compton, granted an exclusive license with Polan Industries.[141] Polan then entered into an agreement with Joy Manufacturing extending the license beyond the patent term. Metal Products used a similar method and were found to directly infringe Compton's patents.[142] Metal argued that the Joy-Polan agreement amounted to a misuse because it extended the Compton patent beyond the scope granted under patent law. In

---

140   On file with the author.
141   *Compton v. Metal Prods., Inc.*, 453 F.2d 38, 44–45 (4th Cir. 1971).
142   Ibid. at 40–41.

particular, Metal Products argued that the license prevented Compton from manufacturing or selling equipment "of the type licensed."[143] The Court found that the word "type" indicated that the restriction was not limited to the specific machines embodying the licensed patents.[144] Further, the restriction extended to a time period when the patents would have expired. The Court concluded that the agreement amounted to misuse.[145] It did not matter that Metal Products was not a party to the agreement.

What was material was that "[t]he public, in a system of free competition, is entitled to have the competition of other devices with a patented device and here it is against that public's interest to use the patent to suppress such competition."[146] Thus it is not to some unidentifiable class of busybodies that misuse extends a flirtatious hand as an invitation to mischief. Rather, like the unclean hands doctrine it is, as the Tenth Circuit put it:

> based upon conscience and good faith, and is confined to misconduct in relation to or in all events connected with the matter in litigation so that it in some manner affects the equitable relations of the parties to the suit. It does not extend to misconduct which is unconnected with the matter in litigation, and with which the party who asserts the maxim as a defense to his wrong has no concern.[147]

It is the adverse effect upon the public interest of a successful infringement suit, in conjunction with the patentee's course of conduct, which

---

[143] Ibid. at 44.

[144] Ibid.

[145] Ibid. at 44–45 ("The agreement falls outside the limited monopoly granted by the patent laws, because in exclusively licensing his patents, the patentee himself could neither require non-competition beyond the term of the patents nor as to items not covered by the patents. We think that by agreeing to restrictions on his own competition which he could not compel of others, the patentee has extended the monopoly granted by the patent laws beyond its legal bounds, and that this extension constitutes a misuse of the patent").

[146] Ibid. (citing *McCullough v. Kammerer Corp.*, 166 F.2d 759, 762 (9th Cir. 1948)).

[147] *McCullough Tool Co. v. Well Surveys, Inc.*, 395 F.2d 230, 238 (10th Cir. 1968) ("This principle has been applied in patent cases by allowing the defense of patent misuse only where there had been a misuse of the patent in suit"); see also *Stewart v. Motrim, Inc.*, 192 U.S.P.Q. 410 (S.D. Ohio 1975) (quoting *Dubuit v. Harwell Enter.*, Inc., 336 F. Supp. 1184 (W.D.N.C. 1971))"The Court does not agree with plaintiff's assertion that such a defense is not available to one who is a party to the agreement. The defense of patent misuse 'is fully available, not only to one under license with the patentee but to all parties who are sued for infringement'").

disqualifies him or her from maintaining the suit regardless of whether the particular defendant has suffered from the misuse of the patent.[148] It was a conscious decision made by the Supreme Court in the earliest days of misuse to favor the promotion of the public interest over the private fortunes of those involved on both sides of the infringement suit.[149] And this decision resonated with courts at all levels.[150] At the same time equity requires that the defendant raising misuse come to the court with clean hands.[151] For example, royalty extensions beyond the life of a patent may be procompetitive in allowing parties to structure their agreements to suit their economic capabilities. At the same time, consumers end up paying the trickle down costs of those royalties. This policy rationale is what prompted the court in *Petersen v. Fee International, Ltd.*, to find that "[i]t

---

[148]   See *Petersen v. Fee Int'l, Ltd.*, 381 F. Supp. 1071, 1081 (W.D. Okla. 1974) ("It is not material that Plaintiffs were not a party to any of the various agreements and assignments between Space Tool, Colquitt and Defendants. In their 'ball of wax' is patent misuse with an adverse effect upon the public which disqualifies Defendants from claiming infringement of [the patent]."); see also *Touchett v. E Z Paintr Corp.*, 150 F. Supp. 384, 388 (E.D. Wis. 1957) ("The doctrine of Misuse of patents involves public policy. It involves more than the contracting parties. It is for the protection of the public"); Marcello D. De Frenza, *Vertical Territorial Restrictions as Patent Misuse*, 61 S. Cal. L. Rev. 215, 219 (1987) ("Since the patent misuse doctrine protects the public at large, an accused infringer need not prove individual harm from the plaintiff's misuse").

[149]   See *Motion Picture Patents Co. v. Universal Film Mfg. Co.*, 243 U.S. 502, 519 (1917) (refusing to enforce the patent against contributory infringers because "it would be gravely injurious to [the] public interest," which it deemed "more a favorite of the law than is the promotion of private fortunes").

[150]   The Sixth Circuit in *Kolene Corp. v. Motor City Metal Treating, Inc.* explained that misuse should be actionable even by "one who is not a competitor" because an infringement suit "is a powerful aid to the maintenance of the attempted monopoly of the unpatented article, and is thus a contributing factor in thwarting the public policy underlying the grant of the patent," *Kolene Corp. v. Motor City Metal Treating, Inc.*, 440 F.2d 77, 84 (6th Cir. 1971). And the United States District Court for the Eastern District of Wisconsin wrote "[t]he doctrine of Misuse of patents involves public policy. It involves more than the contracting parties. It is for the protection of the public, *Touchett*, 150 F. Supp. at 388.

[151]   *Texas Instruments, Inc. v. Hyundai Electronics Indus., Co. Ltd.*, 49 F. Supp. 2d 893, 917 (E.D. Tex. 1999) ("Patent misuse is an equitable defense. As such, Hyundai must be equitably entitled to invoke that defense"). See also *Keystone Driller Co. v. General Excavator Co.*, 290 U.S. 240, 244(1933) "'It is one of the fundamental principles upon which equity jurisprudence is founded, that before a complainant can have a standing in court he must first show that not only has he a good and meritorious cause of action, but he must come into court with clean hands'" (quoting Story's Equity Jurisprudence § 98 (14th ed. 1918).

is not material that Plaintiffs were not a party to any of the various agreements and assignments . . . In their 'ball of wax' is patent misuse with an adverse effect upon the public which disqualifies Defendants from claiming infringement of [the patent]."[152]

Misuse is not the only doctrine to allow unrelated third parties to sue. Antitrust law also allows those not directly harmed to bring antitrust suits. A leading commentary explains that "[i]f a patent owner improperly exploits his patent by violating the antitrust laws or extending the patent beyond its lawful scope, the courts will withhold any remedy for infringement, even against an infringer who is not harmed by the abusive practice."[153] This is because competitors can stand in as proxies for consumer harm, since consumers "do not realize they are victims of monopolistic practices, or if they do may lack incentives to bring suit because the harm to an individual consumer may be tiny even though the aggregate harm is immense."[154] In *Ritz Camera Image LLC v. Sandisk Corp*, the Federal Circuit itself recently recognized that even a party not threatened with an infringement suit "clearly had standing" to bring an antitrust claim against the patent owner.[155] In *Ritz*, a retailer which directly purchased patented flash memory chips brought an antitrust action against the patentee alleging that the patents were fraudulently procured by the owner to obtain and preserve a monopoly.[156] The patentee argued that the retailer lacked standing to assert the antitrust violation since it faced no threat of a patent infringement action and had no other basis for challenging the validity of the patents.[157] The panel found that the retailer had standing notwithstanding the fact that it would have been precluded from pursuing invalidity claims through a patent declaratory judgment action. It also rejected the patentee's assertion "that granting standing to direct purchasers would trigger a flood of litigation and stem innovation", citing Supreme Court precedent rejecting the argument.[158]

---

[152]   *Petersen*, 381 F. Supp. at 1080–81.

[153]   6 Donald S. Chisum, Chisum on Patents §§ 19.01 (2012).

[154]   *Brunswick Corp. v. Riegel Textile Corp.*, 752 F.2d 261, 266–67 (7th Cir. 1984).

[155]   *Ritz Camera & Image, LLC v. Sandisk Corp.*, 2012 U.S. App. LEXIS 23950 (Fed. Cir. Nov. 20, 2012).

[156]   Ibid. at *4.

[157]   Ibid. at *4–5.

[158]   Ibid at *11. ("As the Court explained, Walker Process claims 'deal only with a special class of patents, i.e., those procured by intentional fraud,' *id.*, and 'cannot well be thought to impinge upon the policy of the patent laws to encourage inventions and their disclosure,' *id.* at 180 (Harlan, J., concurring). Particularly in

This is not a feature peculiar to misuse or antitrust law. It is true that Article III of the Constitution has been interpreted to require plaintiffs to have a "personal stake in the outcome or controversy."[159] This rule operated to "[prevent] a multitude of claims arising out of one unlawful act and yet would ensure the vindication of the rule of law because the greatest incentive to challenge unlawful conduct lay with those economically affected."[160] At the same time, the Supreme Court recognized in *United States v. Students Challenging Regulatory Agency Procedures* that the wrong alleged by an interested party "was shared in equal measure by other members of the community at large, thereby demonstrating that public values can be the concern of the individual litigant; indeed the case all but suggests that a 'private attorney-general' can maintain an action to vindicate the public interest."[161]

A judicial interviewee noted that even a rogue infringer does the public a service by exposing a patentee's egregious conduct that did not cause anticompetitive harm. He remarked:

> People aren't just running around bringing actions for patent issues. Nobody has the time or inclination to do that that I know of. The only time you ever see it is as a distraction from an infringement battle, in my limited experience. There are real incentives to bring in—the fact that maybe when it's raised, it's often not a—"often" is the wrong word to use here—it's sometimes not raised properly. It's sort of a throw-everything-against-the-wall-and-see-what-sticks approach by some infringer scrambling to avoid liability. Sometimes you get an infringer who is actually doing the public a service by pointing out a genuine patent misuse. In those circumstances the fact that maybe the infringer has its own issues—there's not an unclean hands defense to patent misuse, as far as I know. That reflects an understanding that if we know somebody is using a grant from the government and using it wrongfully, we should be happy to know about it. In that respect, it's different from antitrust law, because it's not purely competitive behavior of a private party. It's somebody who has received something from the government and they are doing something wrong with it. We should be happy to know about it and stop it.[162]

If infringers should attempt to exploit this, courts can easily dismiss unmeritorious misuse defenses early in the litigation and prevent infringers

---

light of the demanding proof requirements of a Walker Process claim, we are not persuaded by SanDisk's 'flood of litigation' argument").

[159]   *Baker v. Carr*, 369 U.S. 186, 204 (1962).

[160]   Barry Hough, *Access to the US Federal Courts: Only Interested Parties Need Apply?*, 1 DENNING L.J. 85, 88 (1986).

[161]   Ibid. at 90 (quoting *United States v. Students Challenging Regulatory Agency Procedures*, 412 U.S. 669 (1973)).

[162]   On file with the author.

from illegitimately holding up patentees. Other judges who were interviewed generally agreed.[163] Another lawyer observed that it was good to uncouple patent misuse from antitrust, and that patent misuse has value as a safety valve that prevents harmful conduct by patentees not caught by antitrust law.[164] Professor Leaffer echoes this sentiment, noting that "[r]equiring parties to show antitrust injury would dramatically restrict judicial inspection of patent practices."[165] Seen in this light, there appears to be good reasons for the broad standing allowed under misuse. It allows the court as the proxy of the public interest to consider and reject frivolous allegations of misuse brought mostly by competitors or licensees while extending their equitable jurisdiction to arrest abuses of the patent right in appropriate cases. But this begs the question—assuming that is misuse, what is the appropriate response?

IV. OVER-DETERRENCE

The final objection to misuse is that it over-deters patentees because the sanction is unrelated to the magnitude of the injury. Critics are concerned that judges have no discretion to calibrate the remedy once misuse has been found.[166] While the unenforceability is lifted upon a purging of the relevant misuse, critics maintain that the burden of purging the misuse may well be greater than the benefits of pursuing the infringement, and will thus deter patentees from enforcing legitimate rights.[167] This gives

---

[163] Ibid.

[164] Ibid.

[165] Leaffer, *supra* note 26, at 158.

[166] For example, Professor Mark Lemley notes that: "despite its roots, the patent misuse doctrine is not one of 'equitable discretion'; indeed, it does not involve judicial discretion at all. An infringer who proves misuse is entitled to have the court refuse to aid the patentee. Thus, any 'discretion' the court may possess is only in finding the misuse," Lemley, *supra* note 117, at 1618 n.121 (citations omitted).

[167] See Sean Michael Aylward, *Copyright Law: The Fourth Circuit's Extension of the Misuse Doctrine to the Area of Copyright: A Misuse of The Misuse Doctrine?—Lasercomb America, Inc. v. Reynolds*, 17 U. DAYTON L. REV. 661, 694 (1991–1992) ("Although the Fourth Circuit states that this decision in no way invalidates the copyright holder's copyright, in many cases the burden of purging the misuse will be greater than recovering for the infringement. In many cases, the failure to purge will lead to the inability of a copyright to protect the rights provided by the Copyright Act"); Cotter, *supra* note 22, at 960 (noting the possible negative effects of nonenforceability: "one likely effect is that IPRs will become less valuable and IP owners less willing to 'push the envelope' by extracting bor-

rise to concerns around over-deterrance. As Professor Lemley states, that "because the bar on infringement suits continues until the wrongful consequences have been dissipated fully, a finding of misuse essentially gives a green light to infringers of that patent for the foreseeable future."[168]

Allowing the misuse defense to exist separately from the antitrust laws affords the infringer a dual recovery. As a result, "the cost of a false positive then becomes very high."[169] A successful antitrust plaintiff recovers damages related to the injury sustained.[170] In contrast, once a defendant proves misuse, the remedy of unenforceability is "set without regard for injury to the infringer or to society."[171] In addition, a defendant who succesfully asserts misuse is theoretically entitled to file an antitrust counterclaim. Thus, "[a]ny benefit an infringer receives from proving patent misuse and blocking an infringement action would be in addition to its antitrust remedies based on injury."[172] As Professor Chiappetta notes "by putting patent owners at a disadvantage relative to other market participants (who would only be subject to antitrust constraints), misuse unnecessarily undermines the value of patents and the innovation policies pursued by the regime."[173]

A. Deterrence

First, it is helpful to remember that misuse was designed to have a deterrent effect. Judge Giles Rich noted that: "[t]he misuse doctrine was a special form of punishment devised for over-reaching patentees who were using their patents to monopolize something other than the invention."[174] Similarly a judge interviewed remarked:

---

derline concessions. . . . Alternatively, if courts perceive the penalty for misuse as being too onerous, the penalty paradoxically may deter too little, due to reluctance to invoke it").

[168] *See* Lemley, *supra* note 117, at 1619–20 ("Overdeterrence imposes substantial costs on protected activity that might mistakenly be construed as misuse, both because of uncertainty over the exact scope of the law and because of risk aversion").

[169] Cotter, *supra* note 95, at 959.

[170] 15 U.S.C. § 15 (1988). A successful antitrust plaintiff can receive treble damages plus attorney's fees. See ibid. ("and shall recover threefold the damages by him sustained").

[171] See Lemley, *supra* note 117, at 1617.

[172] Ibid.

[173] Chiappetta, *supra* note 98, at 37.

[174] Giles S. Rich, *Infringement Under Section 271 of the Patent Act of 1952*, 14 FED. CIR. B.J. 117, 133 (2005).

I don't think that the doctrine is without use, because at the very least it would be a way of punishing patentees who engaged in egregiously bad behavior that might not be covered by all the other defenses, like invalidity or inequitable conduct, in front of the panel. So it gives the court one more instrument for preventing serious injustice or serious abuse. I think that's very useful. There's no way that rules from case law or rules derived from the statute can cover every factual situation. That's the value of equity-based doctrines like patent misuse.[175]

As the District Court for the Northern District of Indiana recently affirmed, patentees do not have to "actually obtain an improper market benefit for there to be actionable patent misuse claim."[176] Distinguishing the rule under antitrust law that "an improper market benefit is a prerequisite to the success of a rule of reason analysis under antitrust law", it found "no such holding in a non-antitrust case" and concluded that "as a matter of law, actual improper benefit is not a prerequisite to a claim of patent misuse."[177] The lower threshold for actionable misuse and therefore higher standard to which patentees are called to indicates the law's intention to penalize patentees for their misconduct.

Those arguing for penalizing patentees only with the aim to restoring defendants to a position where they would have been "but for" the misuse miss the point. While, as will be seen below, proportionality has guided the application of misuse, that penalty must nonetheless be severe enough to serve as a signal to deter similar conduct. These observations are consistent with the role of equity in general, for it was noted long ago that "[a] country can put up with laws that are harsh or unjust so long as they are administered by just judges who can mitigate their harshness or alleviate their unfairness."[178] Courts have also, upon finding misuse, decided not to enjoin the defendant rather than render the patent unenforceable. Indeed, a court that regards the upper limit of unenforceability as too harsh for patentees in close cases could factor the misuse into the balancing in determining whether to grant an injunction instead.[179]

---

[175] On file with the author.

[176] *Syndicate Sales, Inc. v. Floral Innovations*, Inc., 2012 U.S. Dist. LEXIS 140345, 16-17 (S.D. Ind. Sept. 28, 2012).

[177] Ibid.

[178] Denning, *supra* note 39, at 7.

[179] *Mallinckrodt Inc. v. Masimo Corp.*, No: 00-6506 MRP (AJWx), 2004 U.S. Dist. LEXIS 28518 at *106 n. 34 (C.D. Cal. July 12, 2004) ("Courts have frequently denied injunctions in cases of patent misuse, because granting the injunction would give the patent holder a monopoly that extends beyond the scope of the patent. Patent misuse has not been alleged in this case and this Court does not

An academic who was interviewed concurred with the observation that judges were unwilling to find misuse in marginal cases because of the perceived harshness of the doctrine.[180] Another way of looking at misuse is as a factor in determining whether a court should exercise its equitable powers in granting an injunction.[181] Patentees guilty of misuse could still have legal relief, but not equitable relief.[182]

B. Judicial Sensitivity

Judges are sensitive to the potentially harsh impact of unenforceability. As the court in *Kolene* noted, "*Morton Salt* itself makes it clear that the doctrine there enunciated is not to be taken as dogmatic and its application automatic. Denial of remedy against an infringer is a harsh remedy, a species of forfeiture."[183] Parsing the cases makes it readily apparent that courts have exercised their discretion, even upon finding misuse not to impose the remedy of unenforceability where the impact would be "too drastic."[184] For example in *Cordance Corp. v. Amazon.com, Inc.*, the court found that:

> even assuming that Cordance's contractual agreements did constitute patent misuse *per se* under *Brulotte*, it does not follow that the court need render the '710 patent unenforceable in its entirety. The court might invalidate only the post-expiration passive royalties. And here, any final extension that would put

---

assume that any misuse has occurred. Nevertheless, this case is analogous to patent misuse cases in that the injunction Masimo proposes would, because of the nature of the oximetry market, expand its monopoly beyond the monopoly to which its patents give Masimo a right").

[180]   On file with the author.

[181]   See *Polysius Corp. v. Fuller Co.*, 709 F. Supp. 560 (E.D. Pa. 1989), *aff'd* by 889 F.2d 1100 (Fed. Cir. 1989); *aff'd sub nom. Fuller Co. v. Krupp Polysius A.G.*, 889 F.2d 1100 (Fed. Cir. 1989) (refusing to grant an injunction where the patent license contained an objectionable clause).

[182]   Robert J. Hoerner, *Patent Misuse: Portents for the 1990s*, 59 Antitrust L.J. 687, 702–704 (1990–1991).

[183]   *Kolene Corp. v. Motor City Metal Treating, Inc.*, 307 F. Supp. 1251, 1270 (E.D. Mich. 1969) *aff'd*, 440 F.2d 77 (6th Cir. 1971); see also *Morton Salt Co. v. G.S. Suppiger Co.*, 314 U.S. 488, 492–94 (1942) (noting that judges may exercise their discretion in refraining from considering a claim under antitrust law once it has made a determination of unenforceability under use); see also *B. B. Chem. Co. v. Ellis*, 314 U.S. 495 (1942).

[184]   *Ethyl Corp. v. Hercules Powder Co.*, 232 F. Supp. 453, 458 (D. Del. 1963) ("Although Ziegler attempted to do that which he was incapable of legitimately doing, the application of the doctrine of misuse is too drastic").

the GSP Agreement beyond the term of the '710 patent has not yet been and might never be exercised.[185]

Commentators also observe that "misuse is an equitable judge-made doctrine that can have a suitably tailored judge-made remedy . . . If the misuse remedy is limited to nonenforcement of offensive provisions that do not have a good efficiency explanation, then an error in estimating foreclosure will not be exclusively costly."[186]

Secondly, it also bears remembering that the defense is temporary in its effect. Once patentees purge their misuse, they regain all rights to enforce their patents.[187] If the conduct or contractual provision were improper, its cancellation before suit qualifies the plaintiffs to maintain their suits.[188] In some cases, the boundaries of unenforceability need to be calibrated. One way is to distinguish between "transactional and litigation misuse," with the patent being rendered unenforceable only in the latter case, while the former case results only in the unenforceability for the offending contractual provision.[189] Professor Cotter has suggested retaining unenforceability for vexatious litigation-type misuse, while rendering only the offending clauses of patent licenses void in order to better retain a sense of proportionality in the effects of misuse. As he explains:

> [I]n cases involving transactional misuse, the penalty should be limited to nonenforceability of the challenged provision; this reform would impose a standing requirement that is, by most accounts, absent from the current system and would in effect merge misuse with preemption analysis. For litigation misuse . . . the unenforceability penalty may continue to be one, though

---

[185] *Cordance Corp. v. Amazon.com, Inc.*, 727 F. Supp. 2d 310, 336 (D. Del. 2010).

[186] Hovenkamp & Bohannan, *supra* note 13, at 279; see also Hoerner, *supra* note 181, at 704–11 ("It is reasonably predictable that future courts will, as the Second Circuit has done, adopt the technique of holding such a clause unenforceable rather than holding the patent unenforceable. Indeed, careful reading of *Brulotte* suggests that it was not a patent misuse case at all, but was itself simply a case which held a clause requiring payments beyond the life of the licensed patent to be unenforceable").

[187] See, e.g., *Preformed Line Prod. Co. v. Fanner Mfg. Co.*, 328 F.2d 265 (6th Cir. 1964); see also *Carter-Wallace, Inc. v. Davis-Edwards Pharm. Corp.*, 443 F.2d 867 (2d Cir. 1971); see also *Virginia Panel Corp. v. MAC Panel Co.*, No. 93-0006-H, 1996 WL 335381 (W.D. Va. May 29, 1996).

[188] See *Morton Salt Co. v. G.S. Suppiger Co.*, 314 U.S. 488 (1942).

[189] Cotter, *supra* note 95 at 903 ("Only the latter should result in unenforceability of the patent or copyright for the duration of the misuse; the former should result only in unenforceability of the offending contractual provision—and whatever other sanctions, if any, are appropriate as a matter of antitrust or other law").

perhaps not the only, option available to deter abusive litigation. So reformed, misuse would continue to play a modest, but useful, role in copyright and patent litigation.[190]

This view has judicial support. The Supreme Court in *Carbice* was concerned that the patent licensor honor the conditions of its license and "not exact as the condition of a license that unpatented materials used in connection with the invention shall be purchased only from the licensor."[191]

Thirdly, courts retain their full discretion in whether to allow a compounding of misuse and antitrust against the patentee. In *Koratron Co., Inc. v. Lion Unif., Inc.*, the court noted that "when the Court decides whether misused patent rights can again be enforced, either by way of an action for infringement or by way of an action for unpaid royalties, it sits in equity and is vested with considerable discretion in evaluating the actions of the patentee."[192]

In *Ansul Co. v. Uniroyal, Inc.*, the Court found that denying the patentee "recovery on the ground of misuse is a sufficient vindication of antitrust policy, at least where the patentee is no longer actively engaging in antitrust violations at the time he brings his suit."[193] On the facts, while the *effects* of the patentee's violations had not been dissipated, it had ceased "actively engaging in at least its most objectionable antitrust violations."[194] Under those circumstances, the infringer was denied treble damages for the costs of defending the patentee's suit.[195] A judge interviewed remarked:

> If you're suing somebody for infringement and they counterclaim, they might defend on patent misuse and they might also counterclaim saying that it's an antitrust violation. If they succeed on the patent misuse, they will win on the infringement. If they succeed on antitrust, they will get treble damages. I don't see that as getting hit twice. It's getting hit for two different things. One gives you a defense to infringement. The other gives you a remedy for a violation of a statute.[196]

Fourthly, courts are also sensitive to common-sense arguments for restrictions alleged to be misuse. In *Marks v. Polaroid Corp.*, the Court of Appeals for the First Circuit affirmed the lower court's finding that

---

[190]   Ibid. at 963–64.
[191]   *Carbice Corp. of Am. v. Am. Patents Dev. Corp.*, 283 U.S. 27, 31 (1931).
[192]   *Koratron Co. v. Lion Unif., Inc.*, 409 F. Supp. 1019, 1022 (N.D. Cal. 1976).
[193]   *Ansul Co. v. Uniroyal, Inc.*, 448 F.2d 872, 883 (2d Cir. 1971).
[194]   Ibid.
[195]   Ibid.
[196]   On file with the author.

the license restrictions were justified because "reuse by the public generally might spread eye infection for which perhaps it might be held liable, and in the case of the temporary viewers, that after one use they were likely to become bent or dirty and hence lose some it not all of their effectiveness."[197] This was so, even though the court recognized that "the restrictions if observed guaranteed an expansion of Polaroid's business."[198]

Courts retain an aerial view of the entire litigation. The fact that parties not directly harmed by the misuse can bring allegations is merely a mechanism to enhance the discovery of misuse. Courts, however, are cognizant of their attenuated interest in the outcome compared to another defendant who may have been directly harmed. This factor weighs against a finding of misuse. Courts, in the misuse inquiry, take into account the fact that the patents concerned do not "significantly contribute" to the allegedly wrongful practice, or that they do not produce the anticompetitive effects antitrust or patent policy are concerned about.[199] If a vast majority of the patentee's business conduct did not involve that improper use, courts will also take that into account in determining whether the patent should be rendered unenforceable and what impact that might have on the patentee's business as a whole. Courts also look to how the patentee treated other actual or potential licensees in determining if there were justifications for the patentee's conduct.[200]

---

[197] *Marks v. Polaroid Corp.*, 237 F.2d 428, 436 (1st Cir. 1956).
[198] Ibid.
[199] *Princo Corp. v. Int'l Trade Comm'n*, 616 F.3d 1318, 1331 (Fed. Cir. 2010) ("What that requires, at minimum, is that the patent in suit must 'itself significantly contribute[ ] to the practice under attack'").
[200] See, e.g., *Kolene Corp. v. Motor City Metal Treating, Inc.*, 440 F.2d 77, 85 (6th Cir. 1971) ("Applying these principles to the instant case, we find that Motor City has no cause to complain of the alleged misconduct of Kolene. Motor City is not a party to the allegedly illegal contracts, and a realistic analysis does not show that the patent in suit 'itself significantly contributes to the practice under attack.' This realistic analysis includes considering the fact that 98 per cent of Kolene's business does not involve the alleged misconduct. Moreover, it is only when someone wants to use the process in connection with Kolene's registered servicemark (at which time Kolene's reputation goes on the line) that they are required to purchase salts from Kolene. The record shows that Kolene is willing to license its process to heat treaters without the allegedly illegal tie-in but only when the licensee refrains from use of Kolene's servicemark. This offer was made to Motor City in the present case. Neither the right to use the servicemark, nor the sale of salts is tied to the right to practice the invention of the patent. Hence, the patent is not a lever used to extend a legal monopoly").

V. CONCLUSION

There is strong consensus that patent misuse needs to be better calibrated to respond to the concerns of its critics—first, so that egregious conduct brings the owner outside the boundaries of fair play envisioned by an exercise of the patentee's rights within the scope of the patent, or because the conduct has anticompetitive effect; and second, the unenforceability may be confined to products compliant with the standard, and thus more equitably aligned with the underlying breach of the duty to the sanction.[201]

At the same time, it is important to recognize that misuse is an affirmative defense, which prevents it from becoming a tool of unscrupulous third parties masquerading as roving avengers of the public interest. Because misuse is reactionary, only those whose actions have been challenged by patentees may present their allegations of misuse to the court.[202] Recent scholarship has noted that infringers may choose to settle and pay royalties rather than defend an infringement suit and challenge the validity of the patent.[203] Patent misuse gives affected downstream licensees an interest in addressing the misuse to sue. Those worried about the floodgates argument should be mollified by the chorus of judges interviewed, who note that the only people to use the defense are those who have been sued for infringement. Both the scope of unenforceability as well as the discretion the judge has in deciding whether patent misuse exists, should serve as a check against frivolous claims. As a matter of judicial economy, one commentator noted that:

> The parties are always already in court when an alleged infringer accuses the patent holder of misuse; therefore adjudicating such a defense should add incrementally less ... [and] courts can dismiss unmeritorious misuse defenses early in the litigation, because the party alleging misuse must, under the rule of reason, show that a restriction has an anticompetitive effect for the defense to survive a motion to strike. This requirement should help to prevent parties from illegitimately holding up their competitors via the misuse defense.[204]

---

[201] See generally *Qualcomm Inc. v. Broadcom Corp.*, 548 F.3d 1004, 1026 (Fed. Cir. 2008).

[202] Chiappetta, *supra* note 98, at 18 ("Neither those whose actions have not been challenged by the patent owner nor the government have standing to affirmatively attack possible patent owner over-reaching").

[203] See Joseph Farrell & Robert P. Merges, *Incentives to Challenge and Defend Patents: Why Litigation Won't Reliably Fix Patent Office Errors and Why Administrative Patent Review Might Help*, 19 BERKELEY TECH. L.J. 943 (2004).

[204] *See* Note, *supra* note 21, at 1938–39.

Misuse is also a judicial tool, and interviews with judges show that they are open to using the doctrine where the circumstances warrant it. One judge remarked that "misuse is routinely and carelessly alleged in a lot of cases and the not seriously pursued", while at the same time recognizing that:

> It's all a question of what the litigators present. If it's well tried, with evidentiary support below, it will be taken seriously. If it's not well tried below and well presented on appeal, it probably won't get much traction. It seems to me it's entirely the choice and ability of the litigators, not some attitudinal posture by one or more judges.[205]

The ultimate goal of the patent system is to promote the public good by providing a proper incentive to innovate and disclose. The antitrust laws, in contrast, are aimed at fostering competition in a free market society by preventing monopolies and unreasonable restraints of trade. If patent misuse is seen as being predicated on a finding of antitrust then there would never be a role for patent misuse because once antitrust fails, so too would a misuse doctrine that is coupled to antitrust.[206] Because of its roots in patent and antitrust policies, patent misuse offers itself as an alternative to antitrust law though which judges may consider the societal implications of both the alleged misconduct and the estoppel on innovation. Because of its antitrust fixtures, patent misuse allows the court to apply a rule of reason analysis to also weigh the effect of both the alleged misconduct and the estoppel on the competitive process. It allows, but does not require, complex economic analysis. It reacts to misconduct, but imposes no threat of litigation unless the patentees themselves choose to provoke its application. It imposes no fines or damages, but instead acts as a guardian of fair play in the patent arena by suspending the enforcement of the patent.

A recent study on inequitable conduct by Professors Lee Petherbridge, Jason Rantanen and R. Polk Wagner serve as a cautionary tale to advocates of abolishing discretionary defenses, even when they reach "plague" status.[207] The authors found that "patents held unenforceable have clear

---

[205]   On file with the author.

[206]   See Cohen, *supra* note 120, at 1191, n. 488 ("In a sense, this view is based wholly on wishful thinking: If the criteria for invoking the misuse doctrine were tightened to require antitrust injury for a finding of misuse, then the misuse doctrine would be redundant. Otherwise, the misuse doctrine will often be invoked by those to whom no antitrust recovery is available").

[207]   Lee Petherbridge et al., *Unenforceability* (University of Penn Law School, Public Law Research Paper No. 12-28, 2012), available at: http://papers.ssrn.com/sol3/papers.cfm?abstract_id=2167417.

hallmarks of risky prosecution behavior, such as longer pendency and fewer disclosures of prior art as compared to all other types we studied," and conclude that "the doctrine is likely to be operating better than the conventional wisdom would suggest."[208]

One refrain arising from the discussion in the last chapter is that as new forms of misconduct emerge, misuse can play a meaningful role in addressing them. It is a view which resonates within the courts themselves. For example, in *Sanitation Equipment, Ltd. v. Thetford Corp.*, the patentees argued that the claim of misuse raised by the alleged infringer "should be dismissed because the conduct alleged does not fit into traditional categories of patent misuse listed in a major treatise."[209] The Court responded that "courts recognize that the patent misuse doctrine subsumes a broad spectrum of wrongful conduct involving the improper exploitation of patent rights." [210] Similarly in *United States v. Univis Lens*, the Supreme Court held that in cases of patent misuse amounting to an antitrust violation, "the particular form or method by which the monopoly is sought to be extended is immaterial."[211] It then bears asking what forms of misconduct would be suitable candidates to bring under the umbrella of misuse and why. It is to these questions that we now turn in the next chapter.

---

[208] Ibid.

[209] *Sanitation Equip., Ltd. v. Thetford Corp.*, No. 83 C 3221, 1984 U.S. Dist. LEXIS 15444, at *3 (N.D. Ill. June 28, 1984) (citing *Riker Labs., Inc. v. Gist-Brocades N.V.*, 636 F. 2d 772, 777 (D.C. Cir. 1980)).

[210] Ibid.

[211] *Princo Corp. v. Int'l Trade Comm'n*, 616 F.3d 1318, 1346 (Fed. Cir. 2010) (quoting *United States v. Univis Lens Co.*, 316 U.S. 241, 251–52 (1942)).

5. Rethinking the future of patent misuse

I. INTRODUCTION

Judge Richard Posner famously asserted that it is "rather late in the day" to develop misuse and rather one should turn to antitrust law to solve the issues currently addressed or addressable under misuse.[1] While some courts are willing to apply misuse to new categories of misconduct, others are more reluctant to do so.[2] It is not at all obvious why a cohesive doctrine of misuse cannot be developed and applied to new fact patterns.[3] This study identified four areas where misuse either had an impact or could have an impact. The first area is with standard essential patents. When an industry standard coalescences around patents held by a patentee, it gives that patentee an ability to distort the competitive process beyond what inheres to the patent right. That ability may be obtained by deception or it may be properly obtained by improper exercise. The second area is in

---

[1] *USM Corp. v. SPS Tech., Inc.*, 694 F.2d 505, 512 (7th Cir. 1982), *cert. denied*, 462 U.S. 1107 (1983) ("If misuse claims are not tested by conventional antitrust principles, by what principles shall they be tested? Our law is not rich in alternative concepts of monopolistic abuse; and it is rather late in the day to develop one without in the process subjecting the rights of patent holders to debilitating uncertainty").

[2] Cf. *UTStarcom, Inc. v. Starent Networks, Corp.*, 2008 U.S. Dist. LEXIS 98498 (N.D. Ill. Dec. 5, 2008) (finding that the patentee's failure to offer the defendant a license to the patents on reasonable, non-discriminatory terms prior to suit could be evidence supporting a finding of patent misuse.); with *Syndicate Sales, Inc. v. Floral Innovations, Inc.*, 2012 U.S. Dist. LEXIS 140345, at *9–10 (S.D. Ind. Sept. 28, 2012) (noting that courts "have been reluctant to apply the patent misuse per se doctrine broadly. Instances where the doctrine has been recognized and permitted include '"tying" arrangements. . . . arrangements in which a patentee effectively extends the term of its patent by requiring post-expiration royalties'. . . .. 'any attempted reservation or continuation in the patentee or those claiming under him of the patent monopoly, after the patent expires' and preventing competition by uncontrolled resale prices").

[3] Ramsey Hanna, *Misusing Antitrust: The Search for Functional Copyright Misuse Standards*, 46 STAN. L. REV. 401, 445–48 (1993–1994).

pay-for-delay settlements, where brand pharmaceutical companies pay off actual or potential generic competitors to refrain from challenging the validity of their patents and delay entering the market. The result is that consumers end up paying considerably more because they are forced to purchase from the brand company, and do not have the option of purchasing from the generic company. The theory of misuse is that while patents may be used to exclude, it is a misuse of that patent to use it as a pretext to pay off challengers. The third area is copyright and trademark misuse. As with patent rights, these rights also give the respective rightsholder a right to exclude, and consequently the potential to harm market competition and innovation. Finally, the study also looked beyond misuse in America and briefly examines approaches taken by the European Union on patent abuses.

II. MISCONDUCT IN STANDARD SETTING[4]

A. Standards and Holdups

Modern life rests on an intricately interwoven web of technological networks bridged by uniform standards.[5] Formal standards ensure that products with multiple inter-working components operate as planned and interoperate as needed with other products. Properly structured standards allow different technologies to combine into a single solution and create a result that is greater than the sum of its parts. Standardization amplifies the rate that a particular technology is adopted through network effects catalyzed by a common standard.[6] Standards thus facilitate the dissemination of new technologies and promote competition among manufacturers

---

[4]   This section is based in part on an earlier work: Daryl Lim, *Misconduct in Standard Setting: The Case for Patent* Misuse, 51 IDEA 559 (2011).

[5]   See Jonathan L. Rubin, *Patents, Antitrust, and Rivalry in Standard-Setting*, 38 RUTGERS L.J. 509, 509 (2006–2007) ("Digital networks are polymorphic, so the need for digital interfaces (and the compatibility standards that make them work) increases as network functionality, the installed base of digital devices, and the volume of stored data enlarges").

[6]   See Robert P. Merges & Jeffrey M. Kuhn, *An Estoppel Doctrine For Patented Standards*, 97 CAL. L. REV. 1, 4–5 (2009) ("Standardization spurs network effects because a program that interoperates with a variety of programs and files is more valuable than one that works only in isolation. Standardization also results from network effects because adopting a technology already widely used often makes more sense than opting for a relatively untried technology without an 'installed base' of adopters").

practicing the standard in the downstream product market because consumers can select and transition between better products within the standard.[7] In this way, standardization improves consumer welfare and technological progress. As high-tech markets proliferate, the interoperability of their technologies, even from different vendors, will continue to grow.[8]

Many standards are based on technologies that qualify for patent protection. There are at least two reasons for this. First, the upward spiral of sophistication in consumer demand spurs a corresponding growth in the demand for platforms which comprise state of the art technology—technology which is almost always patented.[9] Second, without exclusive control to recoup patent-related investments, an optimal level of research and development may not occur.[10] Widespread adoption of a patentee's technology incentivizes the patentee to develop complementary products or provide support for creators of complementary products to implement the standard. Standards are selected through consensus and compromise. A standard today may consist of a myriad of patented inventions and

---

[7] See Mark A. Lemley, *Intellectual Property Rights and Standard-Setting Organizations*, 90 CAL. L. REV. 1889, 1896–97 (2002) ("Further, in markets for complementary products, companies will often gear their production to work with a product that is an industry standard, rather than a product that has only a small market share. For example, software vendors are more likely to write application programs that are compatible with Microsoft's operating system than with other operating systems, because there are more consumers for such a product. This in turn reinforces the desire of consumers to buy the product everyone else buys—a phenomenon known as 'tipping'. In network markets, then, standardization may well be inevitable, and certainly carries substantial consumer benefits").

[8] See Janice M. Mueller, *Patent Misuse through the Capture of Industry Standards*, 17 BERKELEY TECH. L.J. 623, 631–32 (2002) ("For example, one or more hardware or software standards govern virtually every aspect of using a computer or connecting to the Internet. . . . Beyond computing, standards exist in all industries, including 'safety and health, telecommunications, information processing, petroleum, [and] medical devices'").

[9] See Letter from Dan Bart, Vice President, Elec. Indus. Ass'n /Telecomm. Indus. Ass'n, to Fed. Trade Comm'n, at 4 (Jan. 22, 1996) ("Standards in . . . high-tech industries must be based on the leading-edge technologies. Consumers will not buy second-best products that are based only on publicly available information"); see also Janice M. Mueller, *Patenting Industry Standards*, 34 J. MARSHALL L. REV. 897, 916 (2000–2001).

[10] See David Friedman, *Standards as Intellectual Property: An Economic Approach*, 19 U. DAYTON L. REV. 1109, 1122 (1993–1994) ("the availability and quality of the standard may depend greatly on the reward provided, or not provided, by intellectual property law").

it is common for multiple companies to own patents covering different aspects.[11] Firms place high value on having their patents cover essential features, in part to strengthen their bargaining position vis-à-vis others who own essential patents. This leads to standards that read on the patents of many firms.[12]

Before a standard is adopted, the industry may be able to adjust to avoid relying on certain patents with unfavorable condtitions attached by using functional substitutes. Once a specific standard has been adopted, however, switching costs may become prohibitive. If manufacturers have begun selling products that comply with the initial standard, switching to a non-infringing design can be commercially unfeasible.[13] It can be extremely costly, or even impossible as a practical matter, to redesign a product standard to avoid infringing a patented technology. Manufacturers and developers thus become "locked-in" to the standard and become reliant on the patented technology.[14]

Patent holdups occur when patentees attempt to extract more value for its technology from users only because of that "lock-in," rather

---

[11] See Mark A. Lemley, *Ten Things to Do About Patent Holdup of Standards (and One Not To)*, 48 B.C. L. Rev. 149, 149 (2007) ("A central fact about the information technology sector is the multiplicity of patents that innovators must deal with. Indeed, hundreds of thousands of patents cover semiconductor, software, telecommunications, and Internet inventions. Because of the nature of information technology, innovation often requires the combination of a number of different patents").

[12] See Timothy S. Simcoe, *Explaining the Increase in Intellectual Property Disclosure* (Joseph L. Rotman School of Mgmt., Univ. of Toronto, Working Paper, Dec. 8, 2005), available at: http://www.rotman.utoronto.ca/timothy.simcoe/papers/SSO_IPR_Disclosures.pdf (documenting a dramatic increase over the past 15 years in the number of essential patents disclosed to standard setting organizations).

[13] *Am. Soc'y of Mech. Eng'rs, Inc. v. Hydrolevel Corp.*, 456 U.S. 556, 571 (1982) (cautioning that "a standard-setting organization . . . can be rife with opportunities for anticompetitive activity," which can give members "the power to frustrate competition in the marketplace" and harm competitors).

[14] See Deborah Platt Majoras, Chairman, Fed. Trade Cmm'n, Recognizing the Procompetitive Potential of Royalty Discussions in Standard Setting Prepared for Standardization and the Law: Developing the Golden Mean for Global Trade 3 (Sept. 23, 2005), available at: http://www.ftc.gov/speeches/majoras/050923stanford.pdf ("before lock in [of the new standard]—or 'ex ante'—technologies compete to be the standard, and no patent-holder can demand more than a competitive royalty rate. After lock in—or 'ex post'—the owner of the chosen technology may have the power to charge users supra-competitive royalty rates—rates that may ultimately be passed on to consumers in the form of higher prices").

than because of the value of the technology or standardization.[15] With very high redesign costs, the threat of an injunction can lead to large royalty overcharges, especially for weak patents.[16] The unanticipated royalty burden may make it unprofitable for the affected firms to conduct research and development and incur other costs necessary to develop the product. Alternatively, firms may not find it worthwhile to develop some versions of the product if the royalty burden prevents it from selling enough units at a large enough margin to recoup the additional development costs associated with those versions. Standards are commonly administered by Standard Setting Organizations (SSOs) which are often comprised of companies in the same industry where the patents are being pooled. According to the New York IP Law Assoication: "The rational and considered application of patent law at its interface with antitrust law and patent misuse doctrine is critically important to future economic growth in the burgeoning area of industry pooling and SSOs."[17]

In recent years, the courts have been confronted with allegations of hold-ups that take two forms. The first form usually involves a single patentee. By disclaiming or limiting the enforcement of certain patents,[18] the patentee may be able to assuage industry fears that it will charge high

---

[15] See Mark A. Lemley & Carl Shapiro, *Patent Holdup and Royalty Stacking*, 85 Tex. L. Rev. 1991, 2010–17 (2006–2007) (arguing that patent holdup and royalty stacking are serious problems, and that legislators or courts should limit the circumstances in which a patent holder may avail itself of the existing statutory right to enjoin the infringer's use of the patent—essentially only if the patent protects an input that represents a significant portion of the final value of the product).

[16] See *eBay Inc. v. MercExchange, L.L.C.*, 547 U.S. 388, 396 (2006) (Kennedy, J., concurring) ("an injunction, and the potentially serious sanctions arising from its violation, can be employed as a bargaining tool to charge exorbitant fees to companies that seek to buy licenses to practice the patent").

[17] Brief for New York Intell. Prop. Law Ass'n as Amicus Curiae on Rehearing En Banc in Support of Intervenor U.S. Philips Corporation in Favor of Affirmance of the Underlying ITC Decision, at 2, *Princo Corp. v. Int'l Trade Comm'n*, No. 2007-1386 (December 7, 2009), available at: http://www.nyipla.org/images/nyipla/Documents/Amicus%20Briefs/PrincovITC-3-2007-1386.pdf.

[18] See Merges & Kuhn, *supra* note 6, at 11–12 ("For example, some patentees offer a general promise that the relevant patents are 'dedicated to the public' or will otherwise never be enforced. Other patentees grant royalty-free licenses to developers of free and non-commercial software. Still other patentees claim to own no patents that cover a standard. Finally, a patentee may guarantee a particular royalty scheme to assuage fears that it would hike the rates once the industry adopted a standard").

rents after the industry is locked into the standard.[19] This may facilitate widespread adoption of a standard that might otherwise receive only a lukewarm reception. Once the industry has adopted its technology, the patentee either unveils its previously hidden patent and threatens litigation if appropriate royalties are not paid, or it reneges on its earlier undertaking not to enforce its patent. The key controversy involves finding the best way to address misconduct in standard setting.

The second form of hold-up occurs when two or more patentees with rival technologies agree on a common standard built on the patented technology that one of them developed. In return for compensation, the rival agrees that it will refuse to license the competing technology to third parties. The competing technology is suppressed and cuts off an avenue for third parties wishing to build upon the rival technology to offer a family of products and services that build on the alternative standard. This was the key controversy presented to the Federal Circuit sitting *en banc* in *Princo* which will be discussed in detail later in this chapter.

B. Unilateral Conduct

1. Antitrust law

The prevailing view seems to be that antitrust law is not the proper response to misconduct in standard setting. Courts have imposed robust standards that would be difficult for antitrust plaintiffs to meet. For example under D.C. Circuit jurisprudence in *Rambus*, antitrust plaintiffs need to show, that but for the patentees' deception, the SSO would have selected a different technology.[20] This may be difficult to do when the patentees' deception itself has created uncertainty about what course the SSO would have taken if disclosure had occurred. Standards battles are generally unpredictable and it is difficult to reconstruct a counterfactual situation where an SSO had chosen no standard, or to be confident in speculating whether the

---

[19] See ibid. at 10 ("A patent holdup can occur when a standard owner unexpectedly increases the cost, which we call bait-and-switch, or when some third party unexpectedly asserts a patent, which we call snake-in-the-grass").

[20] See *Rambus Inc. v. Fed. Trade Comm'n*, 522 F.3d 456, 461 (D.C. Cir. 2008) (holding that the Federal Trade Commission (FTC) was unable to prove the counterfactual that Rambus' disclosure would have resulted in standardization around a different technology). The court thus held that the FTC had not proven its case even assuming that deceiving the SSO would have been an antitrust violation (ibid. at 467). The court also concluded that Rambus' ability to charge a higher royalty for its patents was not an antitrust violation, even if such opportunity arose through deceptive conduct because a higher royalty would be more likely to encourage alternatives to emerge.

market would have adopted the technology subject to patents even if the SSO had chosen another technology for the standard.[21] Consequently, it is often the case where a patentee does not violate antitrust law when refusing to license unless they receive their bounties in full.[22]

It may surprise some to note that under current law, even where patentees set prices substantially higher than industry norms, this is not considered an indication of anticompetitive effect.[23] A government official interviewed noted that the D.C. Circuit's requirement was very "robust," surmising that this result may have been influenced by the Federal Circuit's expansive view of patents, and the deference given to what can be done within its scope.[24] The official interviewed for this study offered

---

[21] See Joseph Farrell et al., *Standard Setting, Patents, and Hold-Ups*, 74 ANTITRUST L.J. 603, 653 (2007) ("It is inherently difficult to determine how an SSO *would have* behaved in a but-for world, and de facto standards battles are notoriously unstable and 'tippy'. Therefore, a burden of proof regarding what would have happened in the absence of deceptive conduct by the patent holder may be hard for either party to meet. What does economics tell us about how it should be assigned?").

[22] See *Hartford-Empire Co. v. United States*, 323 U.S. 386, 432 (1945) ("A patent owner is not in the position of a quasi-trustee for the public or under any obligation to see that the public acquires the free right to use the invention. He has no obligation either to use it or to grant its use to others").

[23] See *Rambus*, 522 F.3d at 464 (finding that nondisclosure preventing an extraction of a RAND commitment from Rambus when standardizing its technology would not involve an antitrust violation is an insufficient basis for liability); see also ibid. ("Deceptive conduct—like any other kind—must have an anticompetitive effect in order to form the basis of a monopolization claim"). The right to charge as high a price as the market can bear, provided that the patentees do not unlawfully acquire the monopoly or do not take improper actions to maintain or extend that monopoly is consistent with the tenor of the Supreme Court's opinion in *Trinko*. See *Verizon Commc'ns Inc. v. Curtis V. Trinko, LLP*, 540 U.S. 398, 407 (2004) ("The opportunity to charge monopoly prices—at least for a short period— is what attracts 'business acumen' in the first place; it induces risk taking that produces innovation and economic growth"); *Rambus*, 522 F.3d at 463–64 ("The critical question is whether Rambus engaged in exclusionary conduct, and thereby acquired its monopoly power in the relevant markets unlawfully . . . even if deception raises the price secured by a seller, but does so without harming competition, it is beyond antitrust laws' reach").

[24] On file with the author. ("Similarly, the approach taken by the D.C. Circuit in Rambus I think is also one that I would characterize as demanding a very powerful causation standard, and I sense an insistence that proof of misrepresentation be very robust, perhaps a skepticism about accepting a theory that treats nondisclosure as a form of fraud or infers duties to reveal the nature of one's ownership rights or anticipated ownership rights. So if I were to describe the state of the law at the moment and the direction of the law in both areas, the standard of proof is

as an example the generous deference given under antitrust to patentees in the form of pharmaceutical settlements. A judge interviewed for this study opined that the Federal Trade Commission failed in Rambus because the facts did not support the theory, and not that the theory was wrong.[25] However, the Supreme Court's denial of certiorari may suggest that antitrust is not the right tool to respond to deceptive conduct by patentees.[26]

Others courts appear more willing to consider the applicability of antitrust laws. For example in the Federal Circuit case of *Broadcom v. Qualcomm*, Judge Sharon Prost observed that:

> in a consensus-oriented private standard-setting environment ... a patent holder's intentionally false promise to license essential proprietary technology on FRAND terms ... coupled with [a standard setting group's] reliance on that promise when including the technology in a standard, and ... the patent holder's subsequent breach of that promise, is actionable anticompetitive conduct.[27]

The right of patentees to refuse to license their technology under §271d(4) of the Patent Act is central to antitrust analysis of patent holdups.[28] Federal case law points to a high threshold that antitrust plaintiffs must meet in order to prove actionable anticompetitive injury. As discussed in Chapter 2, under Federal Circuit jurisprudence, patentees are effectively immune from antitrust liability except in cases involving tying patented and non-patented products, fraud on the PTO, or engaging in sham litigation.[29] Absent the ability of opposing parties to meet this high

---

a very demanding one. I think the role of the public institutions, in particular, is going to be a very difficult one").

[25]   On file with the author. ("I think the problem that has led to the FTC's lack of success has been an indefiniteness in the standard setting court's rules and practices, so that it wasn't as clear as perhaps the FTC felt it was. Therefore, the actions failed not because the theory was wrong but because the facts didn't support it as well as the FTC alleged.")

[26]   *Fed. Trade Comm'n v. Rambus Inc.*, 129 S. Ct. 1318 (2009) (denying cert.).

[27]   *Broadcom Corp. v. Qualcomm Inc.*, 501 F.3d 297, 314 (3d Cir. 2007).

[28]   See 35 U.S.C. §271d(4) (2006); U.S. Dep't Justice & Fed. Trade Comm'n, ANTITRUST ENFORCEMENT AND INTELLECTUAL PROPERTY RIGHTS: PROMOTING INNOVATION AND COMPETITION 30, 32 (2007) ("[The] unilateral right to decline the grant of a license is a core part of the patent grant ... antitrust liability for mere unilateral, unconditional refusals to license patents will not play a meaningful part in the interface between patent rights and antitrust protections").

[29]   See *In re Indep. Serv. Orgs.*, 203 F.3d 1322, 1326 (Fed. Cir. 2000) (stating that antitrust doctrine preserves a patentee's immunity from antitrust liability for enforcing its patent rights unless the accused infringer establishes either that: (i) the patent was obtained from the USPTO through knowing and willful fraud within the meaning of *Walker Process Equipment, Inc. v. Food Machinery & Chemical*

threshold, patentees enforcing their statutory rights enjoy presumptive immunity from antitrust liability, even if the suit would otherwise have an anticompetitive effect.[30]

A lawyer interviewed for this study observed that antitrust does not work because antitrust plaintiffs fail to prove that the patentee possesses the level of market power required to rise to the level of an antitrust concern.[31] According to the lawyer, courts will consider the presence of substitutes and do not give much regard to the costs of re-design.[32] It is notable in this regard, that a government official interviewed also acknowledged that antitrust law was the "second best solution."[33]

Corp., or (ii) the infringement suit is a "mere sham" to cover what is in reality "an attempt to interfere directly with the business relationships of a competitor.").

[30]   See James R. Atwood, *Securing and Enforcing Patents: The Role of Noerr/ Pennington*, 83 J. Pat. & Trademark Off. Soc'y 651, 659 (2001) (noting that in view of the heightened requirements of Professional Real Estate Investors for claiming an exception to Noerr, "absent classic *Walker Process* facts—few [patent] infringement suits will fail to qualify for Noerr immunity"); Dan L. Burk, *Anticircumvention Misuse*, 50 UCLA L. Rev. 1095, 1117–18 (2003) ("This patent fervor has, in part, been fueled by the creation of the U.S. Court of Appeals for the Federal Circuit, a body invested by Congress with exclusive appellate jurisdiction over patent cases, and with a perceived mandate to produce a uniform body of U.S. patent law").

[31]   On file with the author.

[32]   Ibid.

[33]   Ibid. (" . . . making the rights-granting more robust, more effective, would be a useful step towards resolving a variety of questions that arise either under patent law or under competition law, by making it less likely that defective applications or faulty claims would be recognized, and by doing that diminishing the inclination of some courts, or at times enforcement agencies, to use competition law as a second-best solution to what are fundamentally problems of the rights-granting process"). He continues: "In the competition area, the concern that it's just using traditional competition law concepts, the concern on the part of our courts about over-deterrence and overreaching by the litigation mechanism, has had the effect of causing courts to raise liability standards, to make them more demanding. The courts—I trace this back to the mid-1970s—began to look at the private litigant as being a dangerous influence in the tendency to bring exaggerated claims and, if successful, to immediately get treble damages, and in some instances through a simple class action [inaudible] increase leverage. The matters are tried in front of juries, rather than judges, which is a concern. Again, many features of that system are immutable. A judge can't change it. The trebling is statutory. Jury trials are also a matter of statute, the Constitutional principle. Class actions can be policed, but they are hard to police. I think many courts have looked at that and said, 'I'm afraid that if I flip the liability switch on all these bad things are going to happen. I can't control those features, but there is one thing I can control, and that's doctrine. I can screen out these private suits by raising the bar that must be cleared to establish the fact of liability'. That has been a significant trend in U.S.

2. Section 5

In theory, Section 5 of the FTC Act offers the advantage of being able to sidestep the quagmire of antitrust jurisprudence. Recent work by Professor William Kovacic and Marc Winerman make the case that Section 5 could be employed more robustly than is currently the case. They suggest that this effort should focus on competitive dangers of concern to antitrust statutes, but evade effective control because these dangers lack characteristics required by antitrust law.[34] Elaborating, they note that:

> Through repeated exposure to competition policy problems, the FTC would use distinctive research and data collection powers to develop, apply, and assess doctrine. Expert commissioners would determine the appropriate standards of liability. Business over time would conform to those standards, and courts would eventually look to the Commission for guidance about how to frame and apply antitrust rules. By this design, there was the possibility that the Department of Justice would gravitate toward focusing on the prosecution of offenses deemed suitable for criminal punishment, along with some monopolization cases. Other civil law enforcement would become the province of the FTC, and the flexibility inherent in Section 5 and the Commission's other institutional features would be a major reason for its specialized role.[35]

Reflecting on the FTC's loss in Rambus, FTC Commissioner Rosch concurred with the development of Section 5.

> As our loss in *Rambus* underscores, antitrust courts are not likely to be receptive to marrying claims of deception with Sherman Act violations. I suspect this

---

jurisprudence with respect to agreement issues or with respect to monopolization and abuse-of-dominance issues. Standards set in the private cases or by the government. In Schering and Rambus, for example, the jurisprudence that the courts relied on, all of it developed in private cases where the express concern of the court was over-deterrence by the private litigant. Either we continue on a path where standards become more and more demanding as a second-best solution to put the private litigant in a confined area, with the effect that it spills over onto the public prosecutors and limits them too, and we throw up our hands and do nothing about it; or we start thinking about whether the public litigant ought to stand on a different footing, whether when the FTC brings administrative proceedings those should be seen in a different light," ibid.

[34] William E. Kovacic & Marc Winerman, *Competition Policy and the Application of Section 5 of the Federal Trade Commission Act*, 76 ANTITRUST L.J. 929, 935 (2009–2010) (giving examples of prohibiting invitations to collude that neither constituted unlawful agreements within the reach of Section 1 of the Sherman Act nor violated the Sherman Act Section 2 ban on attempted monopolization and exclusive dealing).

[35] Ibid. at 932–33.

is because proving that a party was deceived is not the type of evidence that is normally sufficient to show harm to the competitive process. In some cases, however, such as when there is a gatekeeper (like a standard setting organization), deceiving that entity can cause a breakdown in the competitive process because it prohibits the market from making well-informed decisions in the first place. The FTC with its dual expertise in consumer protection and competition law is well equipped to make the hard decisions about the unique circumstances where such deception can trigger an antitrust violation.[36]

In theory, Section 5 could be used to bridge the gap between patent and antitrust laws, rather than invoking misuse. There are, however, several problems with this potential approach. First, as Professor Kovacic and Winerman note, Section 5 has an "uninspiring" record in appellate litigation.[37] The FTC's difficulty in reaching an unanimous opinion in *N-Data* under § 5, despite clearly anticompetitive behavior, underscores the difficulty of using it to sidestep the roadblocks set up by antitrust case law.[38] A government official interviewed for this study also acknowledged that there were no cases where appellate courts had vindicated Section 5 in the last 40 years. Professor Kovacic and Mr Winerman suggest that to change this trend, courts need to be persuaded that the FTC "knows where it is going and has a sound conceptual and empirical basis for the steps it wishes to take."[39]

Secondly, as in misuse, Section 5 itself has difficulty maintaining an existence independent of the other antitrust laws.[40] In the absence of FTC

---

[36]   J. Thomas Rosch, Comm'r Fed. Trade Comm'n, Promoting Innovation: Just How 'Dynamic' Should Antitrust Law Be?, Remarks at USC Gould School of Law 2010 Intellectual Property Institute 17 (Mar 23, 2010), available at: http://www.ftc.gov/speeches/rosch/100323uscremarks.pdf.

[37]   William E. Kovacic and & Marc Winerman, *supra* note 34, at 941.

[38]   See *Negotiated Data Solutions LLC*, FTC File No. 051-0094 (2008), available at: http://www.ftc.gov/os/caselist/0510094/080122do.pdf. N-Data's patent claim was anticompetitive for several reasons: (1) N-Data was aware that National had committed before they purchased the patents; (2) N-Data's demand for higher-than-market royalties after switching costs rose shows that they exploited industry lock-in; and (3) N-Data's actions may result in higher prices for consumers. Fed. Trade Comm'n, *FTC Challenges Patent Holder's Refusal to Meet Commitment to License Patents Covering 'Ethernet' Standard Used in Virtually All Personal Computers in U.S.* (Jan. 28, 2008), available at: http://www.ftc.gov/opa/2008/01/ethernet.shtm.

[39]   Kovacic & Winerman, *supra* note 34, at 942.

[40]   Ibid. at 93–94 ("In practice, the FTC's application of Section 5 has played a comparatively insignificant role in shaping U.S. competition policy. Since enactment of the FTC Act in 1914, the adjudication of cases premised on the Sherman Act, rather than upon the FTC Act, has provided the main vehicle for

guidelines or policy statements, courts are concerned that the apparent absence of limiting principles has led Section 5 cases to be subsumed, *à la* patent misuse, into "standards familiar to them from Sherman Act and Clayton Act cases. The cost-benefit concepts devised in rule of reason cases supply the courts with natural default rules in the absence of something better."[41] As discussed in the previous chapter, even if Section 5 forges an independent existence from the other antitrust statutes, its role may be limited to regulation of economic performance, market indicators which from the FTC's expertise, rather than dealing with innovation policy levers that animate just about every opinion in patent law.[42]

Thirdly, Professor Robert Merges and Jeffrey Kuhn suggest that "strategic behavior like this should not require antitrust enforcement; patent law can deal with it more directly and judiciously."[43] Commissioner Rosch too notes that antitrust may be too unwieldy a vehicle for high tech markets. He vividly illustrated this using the example of the FTC's investigation of Intel for alleged violations of Section 5.[44] Accordingly,

---

setting boundaries for business behavior. The treatment of dominant firm conduct illustrates the point. The Supreme Court last examined the FTC's application of Section 5 to address allegations of improper exclusion by a dominant firm in 1927 (when it ruled against the Commission). Dominant firm cases litigated under Sherman Act theories overwhelmingly provide the frame of reference by which courts assess firm conduct, attorneys advise clients, and antitrust professors teach students. One would be hard-pressed to come up with a list of ten adjudicated decisions that involved the FTC's application of Section 5 in which the FTC prevailed and the case can be said to have had a notable impact, either in terms of doctrine or economic effects").

41 Ibid. at 942.

42 Ibid. at 945 ("We believe that UMC should be a competition-based concept, in the modern sense of fostering improvements in economic performance rather than equating the health of the competitive process with the well-being of individual competitors, per se. . . . It should not, moreover, rely on the assertion in *S&H* that the Commission could use its UMC authority to reach practices outside both the letter and spirit of the antitrust laws"); see ibid. at 949, n.87 ("To this end, we note that, to the extent an argument relies on the FTC's expertise (as opposed to the more limited consequences of a Section 5 violation), such an argument will be more persuasive when the Commission uses it to consider issues that draw on the Commission's core expertise in analyzing competition issues, rather than to require the Commission to balance competition concerns against values outside its core expertise in competition (or consumer protection) matters").

43 See Merges & Kuhn, *supra* note 6, at 12.

44 J. Thomas Rosch, Comm'r, Fed. Trade Comm'n, Intel, Apple, Google, Microsoft, and Facebook: Observations on Antitrust and the High-Tech Sector, Remarks at the ABA Antitrust Section Fall Forum 4 (Nov. 18, 2010), available at: http://www.ftc.gov/speeches/rosch/101118fallforum.pdf ("For one, the constant innovation in fast-moving markets means the market at issue in a case or investiga-

patent misuse may fill a gap where antitrust law is inappropriate because it is considered as part of an infringement trial and allegations of misuse may be more easily resolved.

3.   Implied waiver and equitable estoppel

The doctrines of equitable estoppel and implied waiver have also been raised to address the issue of patent holdups. In *Qualcomm*, the Federal Circuit denied Qualcomm's allegations of actionable infringement against Broadcom because Qualcomm knew that the asserted patents reasonably might be necessary to practice that standard, and that it intentionally did not disclose them.[45] The fact that the patents eventually were not necessary to practice the standard was irrelevant.[46] The Federal Circuit held that forcing a party to accept a license and pay whatever fee the licensor demands, or to undergo the uncertainty and cost of litigation, are significant and relevant burdens in determining whether the patentee should be allowed to enforce its patent.[47] The Federal Circuit found detrimental reliance by Broadcomm based on Qualcomm's silence in the face of its disclosure duty.[48]

---

tion can literally change. One moment we may be claiming Intel is a monopolist in the market for the x86 processor (the only major processor that most of us use for daily computing) and is seeking to take control of the entire computing platform, but the advent of tablets and smartphones may mean that the market tips such that ARM or some other processor is the dominant processor. In other instances it may be that when we start an investigation, mobile advertising is offered through one means (such as cost-per-click), but that some new, better technology (be it developed by Apple, Google, Microsoft, or a startup we've never heard of) comes up with a better means to deliver targeted advertising. This can make market definition very challenging – [in] particular when these events occur (as they sometimes have) during our investigations. Indeed, one can argue that the more thorough the agencies are in their investigations (or, to put it bluntly, the longer the investigations drag on), the more we risk having events overtake us").

[45]   See *Qualcomm Inc. v. Broadcom Corp.*, 548 F.3d 1004, 1027 (Fed. Cir. 2008).

[46]   See ibid. at 1018.

[47]   Ibid. at 1021 ("Even if Qualcomm agreed not to pursue an injunction in this case, injunctions are not the only type of harm. Forcing a party to accept a license and pay whatever fee the licensor demands, or to undergo the uncertainty and cost of litigation (which in this case was substantial), are significant burdens").

[48]   *Qualcomm Inc.*, 548 F.3d at 1018 ("[W]e agree with the district court that the language requires JVT participants to disclose patents that 'reasonably might be necessary' to practice the H.264 standard. This is an objective standard, which applies when a reasonable competitor would not expect to practice the H.264 standard without a license under the undisclosed claims. This formulation does not require that the patents ultimately must 'actually be necessary' to practice the H.264 standard").

Nonetheless, the district court's opinion in *Openwave Systems, Inc. v. 724 Solutions, Inc*, shows that some courts still undertake patent misuse analysis in their analyses.[49] While the Federal Circuit's general reluctance toward a robust application of patent misuse may have prompted Judge Prost in *Qualcomm* to prefer the implied waiver/estoppel solution.[50] Later courts such as *Openwave Systems* have read the Federal Circuit's holding as advocating a form of implied waiver rather than patent misuse.[51]

There is a view that "[estoppel] is a subset of patent misuse. No matter what you call it—patent misuse or standards estoppels—the beneficial result is much the same."[52] But there are important differences between the two. Equitable estoppel requires an alleged infringer to prove three things by a preponderance of the evidence. First, through misleading conduct, the patentee led users to reasonably infer that it did not intend to enforce its patent against them. Second, users relied on this conduct.

---

[49] *Openwave Sys. v. 724 Solutions* (US) Inc., No. C 09-3511 RS, 2010 U.S. Dist. LEXIS 20502, at *1–2 (N.D. Cal. Mar. 8, 2010) ("The more important teaching of *Qualcomm*, however, is that the *scope* of an unenforceability remedy must be 'fashioned to give a fair, just, and equitable response reflective of the offending conduct'. Notably, in reaching this conclusion, the *Qualcomm* court even *analogized* to the limitations on the scope of the remedy in patent misuse cases. Thus, in the event 724 were to prevail on the merits of its 'failure to disclose to an SSO' defense in this action, patent misuse concepts could be at least relevant in evaluating the appropriate scope of any remedy to be imposed. Additionally, as Openwave acknowledges, *Qualcomm* makes clear that under some circumstances breach of a duty to disclose to an SSO can render patents unenforceable under the doctrines of waiver or estoppel").

[50] See Ibid. at *4–5 ("Openwave lays heavy emphasis on its argument that the Federal Circuit has *never* recognized the failure of a patentee to disclose its patents to an SSO to be a basis for applying patent misuse doctrine. Openwave cites *Qualcomm Inc. v. Broadcom Corp.* for the proposition that when faced with the question, the Federal Circuit instead found that a failure to disclose to an SSO warranted equitable remedies under the doctrines of waiver or estoppel. The *Qualcomm* court, however, was not asked to consider whether a failure to disclose to an SSO could ever constitute patent misuse, and therefore cannot be said to have held squarely that it cannot. Nevertheless, Openwave is correct that the *Qualcomm* analysis is persuasive that patent misuse may not be the most appropriate label or framework that should be applied to an alleged breach of a duty to disclose to an SSO").

[51] *Qualcomm Inc.*, 548 F.3d at 1018 (holding that the doctrine of implied waiver was applicable in the present case based on the district court's findings that "JVT participants understood the JVT IPR policies as imposing a disclosure duty, that Qualcomm participated in the JVT prior to release of the H.264 standard, and that Qualcomm was silent in the face of its disclosure duty").

[52] Marshall Leaffer, *Patent Misuse and Innovation*, 10 J. HIGH TECH. L. 142, 167 (2010).

Third, due to the reliance, users will be materially prejudiced if the patentee is allowed to proceed on its claims. The court will consider other evidence and facts respecting the equities of the parties in exercising its discretion and deciding whether to allow the defense of equitable estoppel.[53] Unlike misuse, which allows unrelated parties to the infringement suit to raise the issue with the court, both implied waiver and equitable estoppel deal with promises made in the context of a direct relationship. In both instances, the remedy is an implied license that benefits only those to whom patentees made a representation. Neither covers instances without a direct relationship between the parties. With technological standards, all present and future adopters of a standard must have predictable access to the technology. These doctrines therefore have limited application, because those parties had not participated in the standard setting. Without contact with the patentee, they would be unable to establish the required detrimental reliance.

One solution may be legislation requiring SSOs to expressly provide in their agreements that any SSO member can bring an action against the patentee, both for themselves and on behalf of downstream users of that technology. In addition, in order to provide meaningful protection to good-faith standards adopters, the remedy must be able to ride on the patent. In other words, good faith users should be able to continue to use a patented technology as long as they were compliant with standards established by the SSOs. Otherwise, patentees could entirely circumvent the defense by assigning the patent to a third party who could then choose to enforce the patent despite the reliance interest established by standards adopters, as was the case in *N-Data*.[54] The reality, however, is

---

[53] See *Wang Labs., Inc. v. Mitsubishi Elecs. Am., Inc.*, 103 F.3d 1571, 1582 (Fed. Cir. 1997).

[54] In *N-Data*, National assigned the NWay patents to Vertical Networks, Inc. (Vertical), a corporate spin-off run by former National employees. After a successor standard for networking known as "Gigabit Ethernet" had taken root, Vertical sought licenses on every device operating within the affected network. Given the billions of dollars worth of equipment already in place, and the rate at which new equipment was being manufactured and installed, Vertical's royalty demands had enormous implications. Vertical announced that, in order to "further its intellectual property initiatives," it would be assigning the NWay patents to N-Data, a company controlled by Vertical's outside patent counsel. N-Data thereafter continued to demand exorbitant royalties from network device manufacturers while at the same time disclaiming any obligation to respect National's express agreement to license the NWay technology for a flat $1,000 fee. See Complaint at 5, *Negotiated Data Solutions LLC (N-Data)*, FTC File No. 051-0094 (2008), available at: http://www.ftc.gov/os/caselist/0510094/080923ndscomplaint.pdf.

that SSO members are rational economic actors who are understandably driven more by the desire to maximize private profits than to further the public interest.[55] Even if SSO members could be persuaded into a crusade for the public benefit, the inclusion of such a broad and undefined class of users into a contract could result in the term's being unenforceable for uncertainty.[56] Furthermore, estoppel is based on the reasonable expectations of standards adopters. The sophistication of the parties and their access to relevant information are key considerations for determining whether reliance is reasonable. The majority of SSO participants are highly sophisticated parties, a factor that weakens claims of reasonable reliance.

4. Patent misuse

Professor Janice Mueller has been a vocal proponent of applying patent misuse to deceptive conduct in the standard setting context,[57] arguing that a patentee's refusal to license its patent on RAND terms should be considered misuse if it induced the industry to adopt the technology covered by that patent as an industry standard without first disclosing the patent's existence. This position is complicated by the fact that courts have summarily rejected patent misuse on the same basis "[b]ecause a complete refusal to license does not constitute patent misuse, [the] lesser act of proposing a set of licensing terms (even though perceived by the defendants as commercially unreasonable) cannot constitute patent misuse."[58]

Commentators have suggested that this analysis may stem from the statutory limitations imposed by the Patent Misuse Reform Act of 1988,

---

[55] See *supra* discussion at Part II.B.2.

[56] See *Tincher v. Arnold*, 147 F. 665, 675 (7th Cir. 1906) ("When a definite function or duty is to be performed, and it cannot be done in exact conformity to the scheme of the donor, it must be performed with as close an approximation to that scheme as reasonably practicable, and thus enforced. It is the doctrine of approximation. It is not confined to the administration of charities, but is equally applicable to all devises and contracts wherein the future is provided for; and it is an essential element of equity jurisprudence").

[57] See Mueller, *supra* note 8, at 671 (noting that nonenforcement of patent rights based on patent misuse may be applicable in "cases in which the patent owner participated in the standards-setting activity and intentionally or willfully failed to disclose its relevant patent or pending patent application").

[58] See *Townshend v. Rockwell Int'l Corp.*, 55 U.S.P.Q.2d (BNA) 1011, 46–47 (N.D. Cal. 2000).

including § 271(d)(4).[59] Under § 271(d)(4), patentees are immune from liability for an unconditional unilateral refusal to license.[60] At one end of the spectrum lie patentees who wish to simply exploit their inventions themselves without licensing them. Further down the spectrum are patentees who are willing to license, whether for RAND royalties, or taking another step down that spectrum—for exhorbitant sums after a patent hold-up. The more egregious a patentees' conduct becomes, the less convincing their protestations that their refusals are "unconditional." Of course, patentees may nonetheless argue that the ability to extort the industry came about because they enticed the SSO into adopting the standard, and were still acting within the scope of its rights by bringing the infringement suit.

Patent hold-ups are unlike post-expiration royalty demands or tying claims that have characterized patent misuse, where the physical or temporal scope of the patent was exceeded, which are perhaps more obvious and clear forms of misuse.[61] However, the stranglehold that patentees enjoy does not derive from the patent, but comes from the adoption of the standard owing to a patentees' deceit in concealing their patents and ambushing later adopters locked into the standard. This deceit brings the patentees' conduct outside the scope of the patent. Thus Professor Mueller has suggested that:

> Moreover, the prefatory "otherwise entitled to relief" qualifier of section 271(d) indicates that Congress envisioned newly-arising factual scenarios where a patentee should be excluded from the section's protections for public policy reasons not envisioned at the time of passage of the 1952 Patent Act. The problem of standards capture by refusal to license a non-disclosed standards technology presents exactly this type of newly-arising scenario. The sensitivity of the patent misuse doctrine to these public policy concerns permits courts to consider whether a patentee's refusal to license a patent on standards technology extends the anti-competitive effect of the refusal beyond

---

[59] See Mark A. Lemley, *Antitrust and the Internet Standardization Problem*, 28 Conn. L. Rev. 1041, 1061 n. 69 (1996) ("One might interpret the patent misuse doctrine as a rule compelling interoperability [of IP law and industry standards] in limited circumstances. The problem with this approach is that Congress appears to have foreclosed it in 1988, when it passed the Patent Misuse Reform Act. That Act added 35 U.S.C. § 271(d)(4), which provides that refusal to license a patent does not constitute patent misuse").

[60] The text of § 271(d)(4) does not state that the refusal must be unconditional. However, it has come to be regarded as such. See, e.g., R. Hewitt Pate, *Refusals to Deal and Intellectual Property Rights*, 10 Geo. Mason L. Rev. 429, 441 (2001–2002).

[61] See, e.g., *Brulotte v. Thys Co.*, 379 U.S. 29 (1964).

the statutory patent grant and propels the refusal into the realm of actionable patent misuse.[62]

An attorney interviewed for the study remarked "I would have thought that in the *Rambus* situation patent misuse would come into play simply because of the unfairness of the patent ambush that was created by Rambus' conduct."[63] Another attorney agreed, that this was "a potential growth area."[64] An academic noted that patent misuse could play a useful role with respect to strategic non-disclosure cases, and was attractive especially in light of the *Rambus* view that refusals to license on RAND terms previously agreed to would violate antitrust law if a workable test could be found.[65] A government official saw misuse as one way to solve the problem of putting "the evaluation of these agreements on a better footing.[66]

Patent misuse has, however, never been successfully applied to the context of standards opportunism, and it remains to be seen whether

---

[62] Mueller, *supra* note 9, at 683.

[63] On file with the author.

[64] Ibid. ("Yes, I think that's certainly a potential growth area. There could be in individual cases a decision that a patent owner has acted inequitably vis-à-vis the SSO . . . I think the question then is how broad is the penumbra, if you will, of patent misuse beyond what would be considered an antitrust violation").

[65] Ibid. ("I think standard setting is a potential place it could be used, primarily in the case of strategic nondisclosure, so a Rambus-style situation. It might be that my failure to disclose the existence of a patent to a standard setting organization as part of a strategic effort to jack up royalty rates could be considered misuse of that patent, an effort to expand the rights or the power given under the patent. That might be an attractive theory, given the D.C. Circuit's decision in *FTC v. Rambus*, which short-circuits any prospect that just proving that I would have had to license unreasonable and nondiscriminatory terms had I disclosed prevented the antitrust laws. Now, the problem there, as I see it, is that the Federal Circuit's formulation of the tests, which is expansion beyond the lawful scope of the patents, isn't implicated in the standard setting case. The problem is not that I'm trying to reach the patent beyond its scope; the problem is that I'm trying to get more market control within the scope of that patent by misrepresenting to the standards body. I think misuse might be a plausible claim, but we would have to rethink a little bit what it means to be misuse for that to work. . . . That said, at least in the D.C. Circuit after the *FTC-Rambus* case, there's an antitrust gap. There's a place where there is clear competitive harm that can't be remedied under the antitrust laws. In that circumstance, having a misuse remedy might be a second-best solution").

[66] Ibid. ("Whether it's in the context of the patent misuse doctrine, the acceptance of a patent misuse-like framework, or by an explicit rethink of the antitrust approach, I think that would put the evaluation of these agreements on a better footing").

either argument would find traction with the courts.[67] The view that patentees must be found to have violated antitrust law before they can be found guilty of patent misuse was shared by only a few of this study's interviewees. While acknowledging a role for patent misuse, one academic had difficulty seeing its applicability because there were already other recognized avenues of equitable remedies, such as equitable estoppel.[68] To him, the policy difference between "misuse" and "misrepresentation" was semantic, and "another doctrinal hook" was unnecessary.[69] Another lawyer responded to this point by noting that estoppel and implied licenses do not work well because there is a need to show detrimental reliance, and if the alleged infringer was not a member of the SSO at the time the standard was adopted, then reliance would be hard to show.[70] One judge interviewed suggested that courts were reaching in different directions because defenses such as antitrust violations, estoppel and misuse overlapped substantially.[71] He commented further that the Federal Circuit in *Qualcomm* should have characterized the defense as one of equitable estoppel rather than implied waiver.[72] He reasoned that waivers were the voluntary and intentional giving up of a known right, and that it was difficult to see how Qualcomm was doing so.[73] Commenting on the *Qualcomm* case, an academic remarked that while waiver was the right response in *Qualcomm*, anticompetitive harm may warrant the concurrent application of antitrust laws or patent misuse, which because of its resultant unenforceability, offers a mid-way point of deterrence between the two.[74]

---

[67] See Mueller, *supra* note 8, at 699 ("[F]ew courts have even considered the applicability of the patent misuse doctrine to the problem of industry standards capture via patenting, and no court has yet found patent misuse in this context").

[68] On file with the author.

[69] Ibid.

[70] Ibid.

[71] Ibid.

[72] Ibid.

[73] Ibid.

[74] Ibid. ("I don't think it's a substitute for antitrust enforcement. It's not enough, in all cases, to say, 'Okay, now that you have been found to have done something inconsistent with your promise to a standard setting organization, you have to stop. You can't enforce the patent and demand injunctive relief anymore'. There may still be substantial competitive harm that has occurred in the interim, and a waiver defense to a patent infringement suit isn't going to compensate the public or competitors for any of that harm.

Now, patent misuse doesn't directly compensate either, though it does have a deterrence effect, because the effect of a finding of misuse is stronger than the effect of a finding of waiver, and not just 'you've already pre-committed to license on these terms. You can't enforce the patent beyond those terms', but 'you can't

Another judge observed that the cases before him were not seeking to render the patentee's patents unenforceable.[75] Rather, the parties opposing the patentees sought to "kill them", that is the patents, through invalidation challenges and thereby eliminate the impediment to unrestricted access to the use of the patent technology by competing companies.[76] In this regard, the judge posited that patent misuse may be more useful because it allowed a more careful tailoring of the remedy, rather than a "wiping out" of the patent.[77] Ultimately, as one lawyer opined, the relevance of patent misuse may depend on the continued irrelevance of antitrust in this area, as case law appears to continue to shrink its penumbra.[78]

An academic commented that equitable doctrines were not a substitute for antitrust enforcement because there may still be competitive harm, and that failing to stop bad conduct did not compensate for that harm.[79] However, he noted that while patent misuse did not compensate injured parties, unlike implied waiver, it does have a deterrent effect because patentees will not merely be unable to enforce the contractual terms against an SSO member and the patent as a whole will be unenforceable against the world at large.[80] This may discourage entities like Rambus from "gaming the SSO system."[81] However, patent misuse will likely be more applicable to hold-ups resulting from patent ambush situations like *Rambus* rather than RAND disagreements as in *Qualcomm* because of the Supreme Court's decision in *Trinko*, expressing reticence at interfering with the quantum of royalties charged for access.[82]

Perhaps a combined dose of antitrust law and patent misuse may

---

enforce the patent at all, even against someone who is not in a standard setting organization who is clearly infringing'. So misuse might have a role to play there as a deterrent, a bit of a stronger weapon, which discourages companies like Qualcomm from gaming the standards in existence").

[75]   Ibid.

[76]   Ibid. ("don't know whether there's a role for patent misuse there or not. The attention I have paid where I have had occasion to see it, I don't recall patent misuse being the focus of the party's efforts. They weren't just trying to keep it from being enforced for a while. The defendants were trying to kill the patent altogether").

[77]   Ibid.

[78]   Ibid.

[79]   Ibid.

[80]   Ibid.

[81]   Ibid.

[82]   See *Verizon Commc'ns Inc. v. Curtis V. Trinko*, LLP, 540 U.S. 398, 407 (2004) ("The opportunity to charge monopoly prices—at least for a short period—is what attracts 'business acumen' in the first place; it induces risk taking that produces innovation and economic growth").

provide the necessary deterrence for arresting opportunistic behavior in standard setting organizations. Misuse allows adopters of the technology not privy to the standards setting process to insulate themselves from infringement, while availing themselves of judicial aid in seeking antitrust damages for any loss sustained from the patentee's misconduct. However, patent misuse and antitrust laws are only symptomatic remedies.

Features inherent in American patent law contribute to, and perpetuate opportunistic behavior in standard setting.[83] Professors Hovenkamp and Bohannan note that "[c]ases such as *Rambus, Inc.* . . . arise because it is too easy for patentees surreptitiously to file retroactively enforceable continuation applications on the technology of rivals."[84] Rambus participated in the standard setting process while filing continuation applications to modify an earlier application it had to cover the standard promulgated. After members of the organization had implemented the standards and were locked into the technology, Rambus asserted its patent against them.[85] And the current system tolerated such actions, thus validating a patentee's participation in the standard setting process, inherently validating and perhaps even shielding its actions against claims of misuse or anticompetitive behavior.

Another feature of patent law that may contribute to opportunisitc behavior is that it allows applicants to add and amend claims during the application process, so long as the originally filed application supports the new claim language and the amendments introduce no "new matter" into the application.[86] Continuation applications are used for a number of reasons. First, the applicant might not have foreseen the claim at the time of filing. Second, the applicant might have decided to delay to extend the

---

[83]   Christina Bohannan & Herbert Hovenkamp, *IP and Antitrust: Reformation and Harm*, 51 B.C. L. REV. 905, 935 (2010) ("Much of the problem of priority and holdup in the patent system results from 'late claiming', or patent claims that are submitted to the PTO and approved subsequent to the filing of the original application").

[84]   Ibid. at 940.

[85]   *Rambus Inc. v. Fed. Trade Comm'n*, 522 F.3d 456, 459 (D.C. Cir. 2008).

[86]   35 U.S.C. § 132(a) (2006); Mueller, *supra* note 8, at 638 n. 71 ("providing that claims may be amended and specifying that '[n]o amendment shall introduce new matter into the disclosure of the invention'"); see 1-Glos Donald S. Chisum, CHISUM ON PATENTS (2012) ("New matter includes any alteration or addition to the matter originally disclosed. It does not include amendments that merely clarify or make definite matter originally disclosed"); Mark A. Lemley & Kimberly A. Moore, *Ending Abuse of Patent Continuations*, 84 B.U. L. REV. 63, 78–79 (2004) ("Strategic claim changes may hold up legitimate improvers or independent inventors, reducing their ability and incentive to innovate").

claim to cover new technological developments. Third, the claim may be narrowed in response to an office action by the patent examiner.[87]

Employing the continuation application process to their advantage, patentees amend pending patent claims to resemble technology under the standard, and some do so blatantly.[88] The Federal Circuit's position is that "there is nothing improper, illegal or inequitable in filing a patent application for the purpose of obtaining a right to exclude a known competitor's product from the market; nor is it in any manner improper to amend or insert claims intended to cover a competitor's product the applicant's attorney has learned about during the prosecution of a patent application."[89] One blog reported that as much as 70 percent of issued patents claim priority to at least one previously filed patent.[90]

Professors Hovenkamp and Bohannan argue, however, that such retroactive claims lead to third parties "whose technological development actually preceded approval and publication of the claim that they have allegedly infringed. These parties become infringers even though they could not have had notice of the patent claims at the time of their own investment."[91] Misconduct of this form, creates disincentives for the innocent infringer by increasing the risks of development, while doing little to incentivize the patentee and derogates from the Constitution's IP Clause which "clearly mandates that the purpose of the patent system is to incentivize invention, and the only things that create incentives are those

---

[87] Tun-Jen Chiang, *Fixing Patent Boundaries*, 108 MICH. L. REV. 523, 530 (2009–2010).

[88] *Rambus Inc. v. Infineon Techs.*, AG, 318 F.3d 1081, 1084–85 (Fed. Cir. 2003) (describing how Rambus had filed patent applications that related to a proposed standard for DRAM devices, waited until the standard was adopted, and then modified its patent applications so that the claims covered the standards); see Lemley & Moore, *supra* note 86, at 80 ("There is no social benefit whatsoever to submarine patents. They extend the effective life of patents, permit patentees to hold up competitors who have made investments in plant capacity, and upset the settled expectations of manufacturers in a variety of industries. They do nothing to encourage innovation and indeed, on balance, they probably discourage it. Abolishing continuations would make it far more difficult to engage in submarine patenting").

[89] *Kingsdown Med. Consultants, Ltd. v. Hollister Inc.*, 863 F.2d 867, 874 (Fed. Cir. 1988).

[90] See Dennis Crouch & Jason Rantanen, *Priority Claims in Issued Patents*, PATENTLYO (July 26, 2009 at 06:26 PM), http://www.patentlyo.com/patent/2009/07/priority-claims-in-issued-patents.html?cid=6a00d8341c588553ef0115723c298e970b.

[91] Bohannan & Hovenkamp, *supra* note 83, at 935.

that are anticipated at the time invention takes place."[92] If cases such as *Morton Salt* and the Federal Circuit's jurisprudence in *Mallinckrodt* point to misuse "to restrain practices that *did not in themselves violate any law*, but that drew anticompetitive strength from the patent right, and thus were deemed to be contrary to public policy," such instances of misconduct conceivably fall within the ambit of misuse.[93]

American patent law also currently evaluates novelty and nonobviousness as of the earlier invention date, rather than the later patent application filing date. This means that the universe of potentially invalidating prior art is comparatively smaller than foreign patent rules. Further, some secrecy continues to exist. Thus, it is relatively more likely that the technology of industry standards will not be available as prior art to defeat patents on the technology involved in those standards. Standard setting activity such as oral communications or documentation that might have been available as prior art under foreign patent regimes is often not available to invalidate an American patent.[94] In contrast, in many other countries disclosures of technology prior to a patent application's filing date, even those made through purely oral divulgation, count as anticipatory prior art.[95] With the recent patent reform legislation, America is moving to a modified first-to-file system. This should expand the amount of available prior art available, but its full impact remains to be seen.

As long as these features remain, patent misuse and antitrust are only symptomatic remedies. It has been observed that any lasting solution must come from the industry and PTO. In response to this issue, Professor Mark Lemley has offered a number of proposals. For one, members could cap the total royalty charged for a standard between all members, impose penalty defaults for nondisclosure of essential patents, and innovative means of determining royalty rates.[96] Lemley has also proposed that the

---

[92]   Ibid. at 942.

[93]   *Mallinckrodt, Inc. v Medipart, Inc.*, 976 F.2d 700, 704 (Fed.Cir. 1992) (emphasis added).

[94]   Patentees may antedate such standards and remove them as prior art references, a strategy not available in foreign patent systems. 37 C.F.R. § 1.131 (2001).

[95]   See, e.g., Convention on the Grant of European Patents, Oct 5, 1973, art. 54, 13 Int'l Legal Mats 271, 286, available at: http://www.epo.org/law-practice/legal-texts/html/epc/2010/e/ma1.html ("An invention shall be considered to be new if it does not form part of the state of the art," where "state of the art" is defined as "everything made available to the public by means of a written or oral description, by use, or in any other way, before the date of filing of the European patent application").

[96]   See Lemley, *supra* note 11, at 161 ("Although a step-down royalty rate would be a logical way of both encouraging disclosure and resolving the Cournot

PTO should limit abuse of continuation practice, while courts should limit findings of wilfulness,[97] and further should calculate reasonable royalty rates and damages in a way that accounts for the fact that many patents may read on a single standard.[98] More fundamentally, PTO reform must come from a more robust process of granting quality patents and administering effective post-grant reviews.[99] Inadequate attention to both aspects has been recognized as a reason for harmful patents.[100] These proposals

---

complements problem, it raises antitrust red flags because it involves buyers in the technology market collectively setting a maximum price they will pay for IP rights. This is especially true if the SSO sets a total royalty cap rather than just a declining rate").

[97] See ibid. at 164 ("Right now, willfulness is mostly used in circumstances where the technology has been in existence for four or five years before the patent owner sends a letter to the developer alleging infringement. Suddenly, a company that independently developed the technology becomes a willful infringer, and potentially liable for treble damages. The result is another way that a patent owner can hold up an independent developer").

[98] See ibid. at 166 ("the data suggest that courts don't calculate damages taking full account of the contributions that other people besides the patent owner have made to a defendant's product. But they could. H.R. 2795 once again takes steps in this direction, requiring that a patent owner seeking damages based on the sale of a multicomponent invention demonstrate that the royalty is attributable to the patentee's inventive contribution, as distinguished from all the other aspects of the product being sold. That requirement would help alleviate some of the holdup problem by reducing patent royalty rates in litigation, and therefore in licensing, to something approximating what it is that the patentee actually contributes").

[99] See Bronwyn H. Hall & Dietmar Harhoff, *Post-Grant Reviews in the U.S. Patent System—Design Choices and Expected Impact*, 19 BERKELEY TECH. L.J. 989, 993 (2004) ("On the incumbent side, problems may also arise if a proliferation of patents with dubious validity or uncertain breadth are granted because incumbents with sunk investments, especially investments involving technological standards, are highly vulnerable to hold-up or patent predation by firms who have not sunk investments"); Doug Lichtman & Mark A. Lemley, *Rethinking Patent Law's Presumption of Validity*, 60 STAN. L. REV. 45, 70 (2007–2008) ("the primary beneficiaries are the countless firms who, in the course of putting out some product or service, might inadvertently infringe a patent. These firms need the patent system to exercise due care to ensure that only genuine inventions are awarded patent protection because these firms are the ones who will end up paying royalties, having to redesign their products, or in other ways having their businesses disrupted if some obvious idea is patented").

[100] Fed. Trade Comm'n, TO PROMOTE INNOVATION: THE PROPER BALANCE OF COMPETITION AND PATENT LAW AND POLICY 5 (2003), available at: http://www.ftc.gov/os/2003/10/innovationrpt.pdf ("Questionable patents are a significant competitive concern and can harm innovation") (recommending for patent reform including: greater funding for PTO; "second-pair-of-eyes" review to improve patent quality; post-grant review; "preponderance of the evidence" for validity

involve interlocking modyfing components of a complex patent regime and, understandably, any meaningful change requires time. In the meanwhile, litigants and courts operating in fast moving industries, where much of the standard setting activity occurs, may find the equitable doctrine of patent misuse to be a workable and fruitful recourse yet.

C. Collusive Conduct

The second form of misconduct in standard setting relates to the suppression of competing technology, as exemplified in the Federal Circuit's *Princo* decision. In *Princo*, Philips obtained patents on technology to create blank storage media known as CD-Rs and CD-RWs and with others created a "Recordable CD Standard," informally dubbed the "Orange Book" standard.[101] Sony was a principal Orange Book collaborator. It also secured patents in the field but did not contribute to Orange Book.[102] Faced with a technical problem during development, the engineers of both companies agreed to use Philips' Raaymakers technology instead of Sony's Lagadec technology.[103] Both the Lagadec and Raaymakers technologies were licensed as a package license to manufacture Orange Book compliant storage media, and Philips exclusively administered it.[104]

Princo, like other manufacturers, obtained the package license from Philips.[105] When Princo and others stopped paying licensing fees, Philips filed a complaint with the International Trade Commission (ITC) to prevent Princo from importing CDs into the United States that were manufactured under the Orange Book standard.[106] Philips also separately sued Princo in the Southern District of New York for patent infringement.[107]

---

challenges; tighter standards for "obviousness," considering harm to competition in patent decisions).

[101]   *Princo Corp. v Int'l Trade Comm'n*, 616 F3d 1318, 1322 (Fed. Cir. 2010).

[102]   Ibid. at 1345. ("Philips' employees conceded that Sony employees 'were more observers than real active developers of' the CD-RW format. . . . The situation was not much different with respect to the CD-R pool . . .").

[103]   Ibid. at 1322.

[104]   Ibid.

[105]   Ibid. at 1323.

[106]   Ibid.

[107]   *In re Princo*, 478 F.3d 1345, 1356 (Fed. Cir. 2007); see also Brief of Petitioners' Reply at 10, *Princo Corp. v. Int'l Trade Com'n*, 131 S. Ct. 2480 (2011) (No. 10-898) ("Moreover, parallel pending litigation between the same parties and arising from the same conduct remains pending in the Southern District of New York, but has been stayed pursuant to 28 U.S.C. § 1659 pending resolution of this case").

This bifurcated route has significant implications for defendants. First, the ITC, unlike the federal courts, is not bound by the higher threshold under *eBay*, and according to the Federal Trade Commission's 2011 study on patent remedies and notice, it routinely grants injunctions upon a finding of infringement.[108] Second, the ITC lacks jurisdiction over antitrust counterclaims, and the delay involved in filing a separate antitrust action in a federal court may result in the ITC investigation being resolved long before such an action.[109]

The ITC's administrative law judge (ALJ) found that while Princo infringed Philips' patents, these patents were unenforceable for misuse because of price fixing, price discrimination, tying of non-essential patents in the package license and an anticompetitive royalty-rate structure.[110] The ALJ did not determine whether Philips and Sony agreed not to license the Lagadec technology for non-Orange Book uses. The ITC upheld the ALJ's finding of misuse by tying, and expressed no view on the other findings of misuse.[111] The Federal Circuit panel found that the ITC erred in finding anticompetitive effect in the tied market since the evidence did not show that the package license was unjustified.[112] On remand, the ITC found that none of the other allegations of patent misuse were properly grounded.[113] A divided Federal Circuit Panel affirmed the ITC's finding of misuse by tying, noting that the Lagadec technology was included because it was a potentially blocking patent.[114] This exonerated Philips from Princo's charges of misuse by tying the license of the Lagadec technology with other patents in the package license.[115] However, the Commission

---

[108]   See Fed. Trade Comm'n, THE EVOLVING IP MARKETPLACE: ALIGNING PATENT NOTICE AND REMEDIES WITH COMPETITION 29–30 (March 2011).

[109]   28 U.S.C. § 1337(c) (1980); see also Geoffrey D. Oliver, *Princo v. International Trade Commission: Antitrust Law and the Patent Misuse Doctrine Part Company*, 25 ANTITRUST 62, 67 (2010–2011).

[110]   *Princo Corp.*, 616 F.3d at 1323.

[111]   Ibid.

[112]   Ibid. at 1323–24.

[113]   Ibid.

[114]   The panel majority found that Claim 6 could be potentially blocking because it lacks a digital limitation and may cover the Orange Book standard. However, Claim 6 was never interpreted by any of the administrative or judicial panels.

[115]   The panel preferred a looser definition of essentiality given the nascent nature of the technology. *U.S. Philips Corp. v. Int'l Trade Comm'n*, 424 F.3d 1179, at 1198 (2005) ("package licensing agreements in which the royalty was based on the number of units produced, not the number of patents used to produce them, can resolve in all potential patent disputes between the licensor and licensee, whereas licensing patent rights on a patent by patent basis can result in continuing

"did not determine that Lagadec was fundamentally incapable of being commercialized as part of an alternative standard, but merely that it was not workable while within the context of the existing Orange Book technology."[116] The panel remanded the case for the ITC to determine the legal standard for invoking misuse and whether that standard was satisfied, as well as whether Philips and Sony agreed to suppress Lagadec as an alternative to the Orange Book.[117] All parties petitioned for rehearing *en banc*.[118]

The majority held that the alleged agreement restricting the availability of the Lagadec technology was not a misuse of Philips' patents.[119] It determined that misuse rested on "leverage," a connection between the patent-in-suit and the wrongful act, rather than a contributing factor, regardless of its purpose or effect. Philips thus did not "leverage the power of a patent to exact concessions from a licensee that are not fairly within the ambit of the patent right."[120] The majority also found no anticompetitive effect in Philips and Sony's alleged suppression of the Lagadec technology.[121] While the existence of the agreement was never determined by the ITC, the majority found that the Lagadec technology would not have been a viable alternative to the Raaymakers technology; hence there could be no anticompetitive effect even if such an agreement existed.[122] The majority also found that the pooling arrangement was not designed to allow Philips to share royalties with Sony in exchange for not competing against the Orange Book standard.

The concurrence affirmed the ITC because Princo had failed to prove anticompetitive effects but "reserve[d] judgment on the precise metes

---

disputes over whether the licensee's technology infringes certain ancillary patents owned by the licensor that are not part of the group elected by the licensee"); but see Mark A. Lemley & Christopher R. Leslie, *Categorical Analysis in Antitrust Jurisprudence*, 93 Iowa L. Rev. 1207, 1243 n. 174 (2008) ("This was a mistake. Limiting a pool to essential patents serves the useful purpose of permitting competition where it is possible").

[116]   *Princo Corp. v. Int'l Trade Comm'n*, 563 F.3d 1301 n. 2 (Fed. Cir. 2009) (Bryson concurring). The panel majority also found that expert evidence that Lagadec was defective had to be discounted since the testimony was directed to the validity of the Raaymakers solution.

[117]   *Princo Corp.*, 616 F.3d. at 1326.

[118]   Ibid. The Federal Circuit granted the petition for rehearing *en banc* filed by ITC and Philips, denied Princo's petition for rehearing and vacated the panel's decision.

[119]   Ibid. at 1332.

[120]   Ibid. at 1333.

[121]   Ibid.

[122]   Ibid. at 1334.

and bounds of the patent misuse doctrine."[123] The dissent found that the majority's opinion "emasculate[d] the doctrine [of patent misuse] so that it will not provide a meaningful obstacle to patent enforcement."[124] The dissent would have treated the collateral agreements between Sony and Philips on one hand, and Philips and Princo on the other as "inherently suspect" with Philips failing to carry the burden of showing that there was a lack of anticompetitive effect.[125]

1. Facts and procedural history

In the standard setting context, package licensing arrangements found in *Princo* are commonly used to reduce transaction costs and hold-ups.[126] However, these licenses can also foreclose competition and harm innovation when "patents are unavailable for individual licensing outside of the package bundle and the package contains competing patents."[127] The majority emphasized the "narrow scope" of misuse and held that the defendant failed to prove that two parties in a joint venture had leveraged patents owned by one of them with anticompetitive effect when it prohibited the licensing of an alternative technology for uses outside the industry standard it had helped to establish.[128] Misuse, according to the majority, rested on "anticompetitive conduct by patentees who leverage their patents to obtain economic advantages outside the legitimate scope of the patent grant."[129] Beyond that, there is no misuse even if parties shut off alternative technologies through horizontal non-compete agreements, since Philips "did not place any conditions on the availability of Philips's

---

[123] Ibid. at1340 ("Princo failed to meet its burden of showing that any agreement regarding the Lagadec patent had anticompetitive effects").

[124] Ibid. at 1342.

[125] Ibid. at 1354.

[126] See Phillip W. Goter, *Princo, Patent Pools, and the Risk of Foreclosure*, 96 Iowa L. Rev. 699, 712 (2011) (package licensing "reduces transactions costs otherwise associated with separately licensing individual patents and adds further value to the licensee (and to the end-customer) by minimizing the risk of blocking patents and patent hold-up").

[127] Ibid.

[128] Applying the rule of reason to the record developed by the Commission, the Court concluded that "even if there was such an agreement, it did not have the effect of suppressing potentially viable technology that could have competed with the Orange Book standards. See *Princo Corp.*, 616 F.3d at 1337.

[129] See *Princo Corp.*, 616 F.3d at 1337 ("Princo's complaint is not that its license to the Raaymakers patents is unreasonably conditioned, but that the Lagadec patent has not been made available for non-Orange Book uses. And that is not patent misuse under any court's definition of the term").

patents and so did not misuse the power of the Philips patents at issue in the lawsuit."[130]

The concurring opinion in *Princo* would have disposed of the case based on the defendant's failure to show anticompetitive effect.[131] Remarkably, both the majority and dissent opted instead to lock horns in dicta over the scope of misuse and its relationship with antitrust law against the backdrop of standard setting. Finding misuse for suppression of competing technology would be a watershed in misuse jurisprudence, since cases traditionally revolved around restrictive licensing terms. Commentators quickly identified *Princo* as an important decision that illuminates the views of the Federal Circuit on misuse as well as the likely results that its panels will produce.[132]

Yet, a full discussion of *Princo* is beyond the scope of this study. It instead focuses on three main areas that saw a split in the Federal Circuit. The first is whether patent misuse is limited to those patentees who leverage their patents to obtain economic advantages outside the legitimate scope of the patent grant.[133] The practical effect in this matter is whether, if there had been an agreement between Philips and Sony to suppress the Lagadec patent, it could infect the agreement between Philips and its Orange Book licensees. The second issue is whether there is a need to demonstrate anticompetitive effects and, if so, which party bears the burden of proving or disproving those effects. In this matter, it would apply to whether allegedly suppressing nascent technology had anticompetitive effects and whether Princo or Philips would have the burden of proof.

---

[130]   See Oliver, *supra* note 109, at 66.

[131]   See *Princo Corp.*, 616 F.3d at 1341 ("Because we need not reach the issue, I would thus reserve judgment on the precise metes and bounds of the patent misuse doctrine").

[132]   See Charan Sandhu & Adam Hemlock, *Princo Corp. v. International Trade Commission and U.S. Philips Corp.*, METRO. CORP. COUNSEL, December 2010, at 24 ("Given the Federal Circuit's exclusive appellate jurisdiction over patent infringement cases, the decision will likely serve to limit the availability of misuse as a defense in such cases and have a significant impact on patent licensing practices going forward."); see also Oliver, *supra* note 109, at 62. (Noting that *Princo* has "significant implications for the doctrine of patent misuse and for antitrust law", and that "[b]y signaling a difference between antitrust law and the patent misuse doctrine, the decision marks a distinct shift in the Federal Circuit's approach to patent misuse in recent years").

[133]   See *Princo Corp.*, 616 F.3d at 1337 ("Princo's complaint is not that its license to the Raaymakers patents is unreasonably conditioned, but that the Lagadec patent has not been made available for non-Orange Book uses. And that is not patent misuse under any court's definition of the term").

The third area is whether misuse of a patent could amount to an antitrust violation and yet not amount to patent misuse.

2. Three points to consider

a. Collateral agreements On the first issue of the need for leveraging and its effect on collateral agreements, the majority found the Sony-Philips agreement irrelevant to the patent misuse inquiry, since it did not relate to the package license agreement between Philips and Princo, which prohibited using the Lagadec technology for non-Orange Book purposes.[134] Thus licensees of package licenses cannot rely on an agreement that their licensor had with its joint venture partner to suppress competing technology which the joint venture partner provided to the package of patents licensed.[135] The agreement with the joint venture partner was deemed separate from the license agreement between the licensor and licensees.[136] This distinction fails to take into account anticompetitive effects that such collateral agreements have on those who want to develop alternative platforms. It also insulates suppression of alternative technologies from a misuse challenge by all but the other joint venture partner, since the suppressed technology would never be the patent-in-suit asserted against an infringer. Other courts have echoed similar thoughts. The Sixth Circuit in *Kolene Corporation v. Motor City Metal Treating, Inc.* stated that "misuse must be of the patent in suit."[137]

---

[134] Ibid. at 1333 ("At bottom, Princo's complaint is not that its license to the Raaymakers patents is unreasonably conditioned, but that the Lagadec patent has not been made available for non-Orange-Book uses. And that is not patent misuse under any court's definition of the term. . . . If the purported agreement between Philips and Sony not to license the Lagadec technology is unlawful, that can only be under antitrust law, not patent misuse law; nothing about that agreement, if it exists, constitutes an exploitation of the Raaymakers patents against Philips's licensees").

[135] Ibid. (The majority found that "the use of funds from a lawful licensing program to support other, anticompetitive behavior is not the kind of 'leveraging' that the Supreme Court and this court have referred to in discussing the leveraging of a patent that constitutes patent misuse. . . . Even if such use of funds were to be deemed misconduct, it does not place any conditions on the availability of Philips's patents to any potential licensees, so it is not the power of Philips's patent right that is being misused").

[136] Ibid. at 1333 ("If the purported agreement between Philips and Sony not to license [Sony's] technology is unlawful, that can only be under antitrust law, not patent misuse law, [because] nothing about that agreement, if it exists, constitutes an exploitation of the Raaymakers patents against Philips's licensees").

[137] *Kolene Corp. v. Motor City Metal Treating, Inc.*, 440 F.2d 77 (6th Cir.), *cert. denied*, 404 U.S. 886 (1971).

Other courts have held that "any conduct that effectively extends the patentee's statutory rights with anticompetitive effect can qualify as misuse if the patentee sought to use the patent to secure more protection from competition than patent law intended to provide."[138] The Supreme Court early on indicated that patent misuse was tied to the inherent limitations on patent law contained in the Patent and Copyright clause of the Constitution,[139] and "necessarily gives wide range to the equity court's use of discretion . . . not bound by formula . . ."[140] Rather, "[i]n construing and applying the patent law so as to give effect to the public policy which limits the granted monopoly strictly to the terms of the statutory grant, the particular form or method by which the monopoly is sought to be extended is immaterial."[141] In *Morton Salt*, there were no license agreements and the leases did not refer to the patents at issue.[142] In *Kobe, Inc. v. Dempsey Pump Co.*, the Tenth Circuit found that the patentee had engaged in a series of acts amounting to a scheme of misuse which prevented the patentee from recovery for infringement of its patents.[143] Antitrust law also recognizes that because patents affect the public interest, courts scrutinize the entire course of dealings between licensors and licensees to determine whether or not a conspiracy in violation has occurred.[144]

The dissent found the two agreements were "part and parcel of the same course of conduct," and that "the effect of these agreements was to protect the Philips Raaymakers technology from any actual or potential

---

[138]   *In re Gabapentin*, 648 F. Supp. 2d 641, 655 (D.N.J. 2009) citing *Blonder-Tongue Labs., Inc. v. Univ. of Ill. Found.*, 402 U.S. 313, 344 (1971); *Virginia Panel Corp. v. MAC Panel Co.*, 133 F.3d 860, 869 (Fed. Cir. 1997); *SmithKline Beecham Corp. v. Apotex Corp.*, 247 F. Supp. 2d 1011, 1046–47 (N.D. Ill. 2003).

[139]   U.S. CONST, art. I, § 8, cl. 8 (expressing the Constitutional mandate to "Promote the Progress of Science and the useful Arts").

[140]   *Morton Salt Co. v. G.S. Suppiger Co.*, 314 U.S. 488, 492, 494 (1942) ("courts . . . may appropriately withhold their aid where the plaintiff is using the right asserted contrary to the public interest").

[141]   *Anderson Co. v. Trico Prods. Corp.*, 237 F. Supp. 834, 837 (W.D.N.Y. 1964); see also *United States v. Univis Lens Co., Inc.*, 316 U.S. 241, 251–52 (1942) ("Nor does it matter what form or method the patentee selects to attempt to extend his patent").

[142]   Ibid.

[143]   *Kobe, Inc. v Dempsey Pump Co.*, 198 F2d 416 (10th Cir 1952). See also Joel R. Bennett, *Patent Misuse: Must an Alleged Infringer Prove an Antitrust Violation?*, 17 AIPLA Q.J. 1, 16 (1989) ("The misuse scheme in *Kobe* involved the accumulation of patents relating to hydraulic pumps; obtaining covenants not to compete from those from which it purchased the patents; publicizing its infringement suits throughout the industry, and threatening suit against anyone trading with the infringer").

[144]   *United States v. Singer Manufacturing Co.*, 374 US 174 (1963).

competition" from the Lagedec technology.[145] Since "no one could license the Lagadec patent outside of the Orange Book patent pool, the patent was rendered useless as an alternative technology."[146] The Lagadec patent was suppressed both because licensees were obligated not to use it to produce competing products and because Sony restricted itself under its agreement with Philips not to offer a separate license for it. This suppression was made possible by the royalty kickback it received from Philips' monopoly power, accrued from the fact that the Raaymakers technology was the only one available for licensees to use. The manifestation of anti-competitive effect attributable to the patentee's monopoly power, rather than a direct anticompetitive effect flowing from the exercise of the exclusionary rights of its patent-in-suit, is relevant to the antitrust inquiry. The concurrence agreed that "the challenged agreement could just as easily be framed as a [joint] decision to license [the Orange Book] patents . . . and an affirmative refusal to license [Lagadec]."[147]

The concurrence was concerned that the majority "unnecessarily narrowed the patent misuse enquiry" and ignored the anticompetitive effect of the Sony-Philips agreement that extended beyond the scope allowed by the Raaymakers patents.[148] The dissent echoed this concern.[149] In the dissent's view:

---

[145] *Princo Corp. v Int'l. Trade Comm'n*, 616 F3d 1318, 1346 (Fed. Cir. 2010). See Goter, *supra* note 126, at 725–26 (noting that the antitrust rule of reason framework required the court to identify restraints to determine whether they threatened to reduce price or output, and observing that "[t]he Federal Circuit in *Princo* departed from this established understanding by limiting the focus on agreements between a patent-pool licensee and the patent-pool administrator with respect to only the patents in suit").

[146] *Princo Corp.*, 616 F.3d. at 1345.

[147] Ibid. at 1341. The facts themselves raise an unrebutted suspicion that the Lagadec solution may have been more viable than the majority believed. As a matter of record, Sony was rewarded with 36% of the revenues from the CD-RW pool, in part due to agreeing not to separately license its CD-R/RW patents. Ironically, the less viable the Lagadec solution is made out to be, the more puzzling the quantum of royalties paid to Sony appears. Ibid. at 1345.

[148] Ibid. at 1341 ("the challenged agreement could just as easily be framed as a decision to license some patents (Raaymakers) and an affirmative refusal to license another (Lagadec). By asking only whether the Raaymakers patents has been 'leveraged', the majority may have unnecessarily narrowed the patent misuse inquiry—particularly when one can readily argue that the combined effect of an agreement to license the Raaymakers patents, but not license the Lagadec patent, enabled Philips to obtain the type of 'market benefit beyond that which inheres in the statutory patent right' of either patent, amounting to misuse").

[149] Ibid. at 1348–49 ("What the majority ignores is that the non-compete agreements here, as in *Gypsum* and the court of appeals misuse cases, are part and

[I]t is one thing for Philips and Sony to agree that Sony would not compete; it is quite another to use the patent monopoly to prevent anyone from utilizing a competitive technology to compete with the joint venture and thus to preserve Philips' virtual monopoly on recordable CD technology. Such agreements cannot be justified simply by relying on the legitimacy of non-compete agreements with the joint venture participant.[150]

---

parcel of the agreements governing the asserted patents (here, the Raaymakers patents). The agreement between Philips and Sony with respect to the suppression of the Lagadec technology appears in the same letter agreement between Philips and Sony that provided for the pooling of their patents, including the Raaymakers patents, and the division of royalties. The agreement between Philips and its licensees not to use the Lagadec technology in competition with the Raaymakers technology appears in the agreements licensing the Raaymakers technology. The overall effect of the two agreements was to prevent competitors from utilizing the alternative Lagadec technology and to protect the licensed Raaymakers patents from competition with the Lagadec technology. The licenses to the asserted patents were "condition[ed] . . . so as to control conduct by the licensee not embraced within the patent monopoly" of the asserted patents. The agreements with respect to Raaymakers and Lagadec cannot be treated separately, as the Supreme Court held in *Gypsum* and as the circuit courts held in the other cited cases. Nor is it significant that two separate agreements (the licensee agreements and the Philips/Sony agreement) are involved. In *Gypsum* itself, the agreements to suppress the competing open edge boards were in fact not even formally part of the license agreements, but were treated together because they were directed to the same course of conduct. Thus, the agreement to promote the Raaymakers patents cannot be separated from the agreement to suppress the Lagadec patent. This misconduct renders both the Raaymakers and Lagadec patents unenforceable").

[150]   In particular, the dissent found the significant royalties Sony accrued probative of both the significant value of the Lagadec patent as well as Sony's agreement to suppress it. To the dissent, it defied elementary business logic to pay Sony this amount unless the patent was significant and amounted to a competing technology whose potential threat Philips wanted eliminated through the agreement—a factual matrix reminiscent of reversing payments in pharmaceutical settlements between brand and generic companies. Ibid. at 1344 ("The rewards flowing to Sony from this series of agreements were considerable. In return for a minimal contribution to the Orange Book patent pool, Sony was rewarded a substantial portion of the royalties. For example, the Lagadec patent was the only essential Sony patent in the CD-RW pool. For this contribution Sony received 36% of the royalties under the CD-RW patent pool. Philips' employees conceded that Sony employees "were more observers than real active developers of" the CD-RW format"). The dissent also noted that misuse had been found in a number of cases involving similar non-compete agreements in copyright law. Ibid. at 1348 ("The same approach has been taken in copyright law where courts have found copyright misuse based on suppression of competing products. . . . These cases establish that, regardless of the form of intellectual property involved, a party's efforts to use its intellectual property to suppress a competitive product constitutes unacceptable misuse").

Along similar lines, the Court of Appeals for the Ninth Circuit held that:

> There is in fact a relationship and it seems to us to be a very practical one, for it may not be assumed that the contracts and the patent came into juxtaposition inadvertently or accidentally. The parties, their dealers, distributors and, indeed, their customers, are not living in a strange, non-commercial world where exclusive agreements are found under Christmas trees.[151]

The relevant test is "whether 'the patent itself significantly contributes' to the unlawful practice."[152] As a corollary, "the particular form or method by which the monopoly is sought to be extended is immaterial."[153] In *Ansul Co. v. Uniroyal, Inc.*, the Second Circuit affirmed the trial court's refusal to enforce the patent against the infringing party because it found that the form of the agreement was less material than whether the patent itself significantly contributes to the unlawful practice.[154] The court found that "the only reason that Uniroyal was able to impose the restraints it did with any degree of success was that it owned the patent . . . and thus had a monopoly on its sale. This is by itself enough of a significant connection between the patent and the restraints . . . "[155] The fact that most of the anticompetitive behavior occurred prior to the alleged infringement was irrelevant. The patentee's anticompetitive conduct in enforcing its price and territorial

---

[151] *Berlenbach v. Anderson & Thompson Ski Co.*, 329 F.2d 782, 785 (9th Cir. 1964).

[152] *Ansul Co. v. Uniroyal, Inc.*, 306 F. Supp. 541, 557–58 (S.D.N.Y. 1969) *aff'd* in part, *rev'd* in part and remanded, 448 F.2d 872 (2d Cir. 1971), quoting Rpt. of the Atty. Gen.'s Committee to Study the Antitrust Laws 251 (1955); see Antitrust Developments 1955–1968: A Supplement to the Rpt. of the Atty. Gen's Nat'l Comm. to Study the Antitrust Laws, 1955181 (1968).

[153] *United States v. Univis Lens Co.*, 316 U.S. 241, 251–52 (1942). See also *Berlenbach*, 329 F.2d 782 (holding that the patentee who entered into a sales agreement which precluded the other party from manufacturing or distributing any equipment competitive to that manufactured by the patentee, was guilty of misuse while the provision remained in effect, even though the clause was not yet enforced).

[154] *Ansul Co. v. Uniroyal, Inc.*, 448 F.2d 872, 879-81 (2d Cir. 1971). On the facts, the court agreed with the trial court that the patent played an important role in Uniroyal's marketing program, since "[w]ithout the patent Uniroyal would not have been able to impose upon distributors its resale price maintenance and territorial restrictions, since the [invention], in the absence of the patent, would have been available to distributors from alternative sources and Uniroyal would have been relegated to the same type of price and market competition that had existed before it initiated its 'orderly market' program. The key to the success of the latter program was the 916 patent," ibid.

[155] Ibid. at 880.

restrictions continued during the infringement period, and the effects of its prior restraint of trade had not been dissipated. The court approved the proposition that "[w]here the patent plays a major role in enabling its holder unlawfully to restrain trade, public policy against abuse of the limited lawful monopoly requires that its enforcement against infringers be stayed until the effects of the restraint have been purged or dissipated."[156]

Reflecting on *Ansul*, Joel Bennett comments "the fact that the patent played a role in the success of the product provided the only nexus required."[157] In particular he notes that "[i]t is not necessary, to establish the defense of patent misuse, that the conduct pertain[s] *solely* to the patent at issue. ... The alleged infringer need only establish that the antitrust violation is sufficiently related to the patent in suit."[158] Instead, what is relevant is whether "[s]uch an arrangement in purpose and effect increased the area of the patent monopoly".[159] The Sixth Circuit in *Kolene Corp. v. Motor City Metal Treating, Inc.* offered a possible reason for this:

> Where the patent is used as a means of restraining competition with the patentee's sale of an unpatented product, the successful prosecution of an infringement suit even against one who is not a competitor in such sale is a powerful aid to the maintenance of the attempted monopoly of the unpatented article, and is thus a contributing factor in thwarting the public policy underlying the grant of the patent. Maintenance and enlargement of the attempted monopoly of the unpatented article are dependent to some extent upon persuading the public of the validity of the patent, which the infringement suit is intended to establish. Equity may rightly withhold its assistance from such a use of the patent by declining to entertain a suit for infringement, and should do so at least until it is made to appear that the improper practice has been abandoned and that the consequences of the misuse of the patent have been dissipated.[160]

Courts are therefore wary of patentees who use infringement suits to protect their market positions in violation of patent policy. Competitors

---

[156] Ibid. at 872.

[157] Bennett, *supra* note 143, at 17.

[158] Ibid., at 15–17.

[159] *United States v. U.S. Gypsum Co.*, 333 U.S. 364, 397 (1948). See also *Hartford-Empire Co. v. United States*, 323 U.S. 386, 399–400 (1945) (finding misuse based on suppression of competition and not the form it took.). Commentators support misuse to address suppression of technology resulting from foreclosure. As Phillip Goter notes: "Recognition that foreclosure-based patent misuse initially arises out of innovation policy rather than competition policy allows foreclosure to focus primarily on protecting intellectual property policy goals while also promoting competition among innovators," Goter, *supra* note 126 at 711.

[160] *Kolene Corp. v. Motor City Metal Treating, Inc.*, 440 F.2d 77, 84 (6th Cir. 1971).

who pool their patents and split revenues from licensing arrangements also risk attracting scrutiny when done in conjunction with price fixing or benefit sharing arrangements. The Fifth Circuit noted that:

> competition is restricted to a greater degree where two or more patent holders fix prices than where one patent holder does so even though there was little potential for competition between the blocking patents . . . [because] the potential for the development of competitive alternative technology is restricted by the cooperative exploitation of patents in combination with fixing sale prices. This rationale applies in equal, if not greater, measure where non-patent holder competitors are also allowed to share the benefits of the patent . . . because the non-patentee machinery manufacturers are left with less incentive to patronize alternative technology as well as the reduced incentive to do so on the part of the patent holders.[161]

The Federal Circuit's formalism seems selective. In *Rite-Hite Corp. v. Kelley Co., Inc.*, it had to determine whether a patent owner was entitled to lost profits related to invention not covered by its patent but which competed with the infringing product.[162] The panel had no trouble finding that it was so entitled, reasoning that "[b]eing responsible for lost sales of a competitive product is surely foreseeable; such losses constitute the full compensation set forth by Congress, as interpreted by the Supreme Court, while staying well within the traditional meaning of proximate cause. Such lost sales should therefore clearly be compensable"[163] because "the patentee would have made no profits from the patented invention by additional sales of the unprotected [device]."[164] More recently in *Akamai Technologies, Inc. v. Limelight Networks, Inc.* the Federal Circuit held that inducement does not require a single direct infringer—merely knowingly inducing the performance of each claim limitation, regardless of who is performing that limitation.[165] It was the effect on the patentee that

---

[161]   *In re Yarn Proc.*, 541 F.2d 1127, 1141–42 (5th Cir. 1976).

[162]   *Rite-Hite Corp. v. Kelley Co., Inc.*, 56 F.3d 1538 (Fed. Cir. 1995).

[163]   Ibid. at 1546. The dissent criticized the majority's reasoning because the patentee had "obtained indirectly what it may or may not be entitled to recover directly by suit" and "without putting the [collateral] patents at risk to a challenge of invalidity," Ibid. at 1573. In doing so, it turned patent infringement into a form of unfair competition. Ibid. at 1570.

[164]   Ibid. 1572.

[165]   *Akamai Techs., Inc. v. Limelight Networks, Inc.*, 692 F.3d 1301, 1309 (Fed. Cir. 2012) ("A party who knowingly induces others to engage in acts that collectively practice the steps of the patented method—and those others perform those acts—has had precisely the same impact on the patentee as a party who induces the same infringement by a single direct infringer; there is no reason, either in the text of the statute or in the policy underlying it, to treat the two inducers differently. In

mattered more than the form it took.[166] This begs the question why patentees are not likewise penalized under the misuse doctrine if the effect of their conduct prejudices innovation and competition regardless of whether they had directly leveraged on their rights of the patent in suit.[167]

In the context of *Princo*, Professor Hovenkamp et al. explain that "the effect of the unused Lagadec patent would be to restrain the developing of any digital CD technology that competed with the analog technology that Philips and Sony employed unless the developer could invent around the claims contained in the Lagadec patent."[168] This is because "the effect of the patent plus the nonuse and nonlicensing agreements could have been very considerably to increase the cost of developing competing technology and perhaps even to prevent such technology from being developed during the lifetime of the Lagadec patent."[169] Can a patentee in *Princo* then raise section 271(d) as a shield against allegations of misuse? Camille Barr argues that they cannot, because "the statute's licensing exemption to patent misuse should not imply an exemption for technology suppression."[170]

The majority's position could create a number of unintended loopholes

---

particular, there is no reason to hold that the second inducer is liable for infringement but the first is not").

[166] Ibid.

[167] See *United States v. Univis Lens Co., Inc.*, 316 U.S. 241, 251–52 (1942) ("Nor does it matter what form or method the patentee selects to attempt to extend his patent").

[168] 10 Phillip E. Areeda & Herbert Hovenkamp, Antitrust Law ¶1781 (2004). See also Christopher A. Suarez, *Look Before You "Lock": Standards, Tipping, and the Future of Patent Misuse After* Princo, 13 Colum. Sci. & Tech. L. Rev. 371, 375 (2012) ("consumers should be accorded the possibility of variety in emergent markets for new technological standards. While the market may not produce optimal outcomes in a given standards war, enabling natural market forces is more desirable from both a patent misuse and antitrust standpoint than a regime that allows for suppression. Suppression, in and of itself, does not seem to provide any procompetitive benefits to consumers, especially in industries where the procompetitive benefits of 'network effects' in those industries are minimal or unknown").

[169] Ibid.

[170] Camille Barr, *License to Collude: Patent Pools, the Patent Misuse Doctrine, and* Princo, 45 U.C. Davis L. Rev. 629, 639–40 (2011) ("Because § 271(d) of the Patent Act is a list of items, it can invoke the canon of *expressio unius est exclusio alterius*, or negative implication. This canon states that expressly including one thing implies the exclusion of the other. For example, when Congress explicitly enumerates certain exemptions to a general prohibition, one should not imply additional exemptions—inclusion of the exemptions implies exclusion of others. As applied to patent law, the statute's licensing exemption to patent misuse should not imply an exemption for technology suppression").

for patentees in the standard setting context and "[u]ncertainties could arise in particular from the complexity of determining whether the patent-in-suit is the subject of misuse."[171] One effect of restricting patent misuse to the leveraging of the patent-in-suit is that it will allow patentees to leverage on related patents to immunize themselves from a finding of patent misuse. An example is a broad grantback license provision that gives the patentee a *de jure* right to its own patented technology as well as a *de facto* right to its licensee's patented technology.[172] The patentee could also hold multiple related patents, and the misuse may be attributed to the patent family rather than one patent in that group asserted as patent-in-suit. As Geoffrey Oliver notes, "[a]ntitrust law may be less likely to differentiate between these two situations if the economic result is identical."[173] Ignoring the effect of the patentee's conduct on the marketplace, leads some to conclude that "[u]nder *Princo*, it appears that a patentee's unilateral conduct, including misleading an [SSO], would not constitute misuse."[174] It is plausible that in some instances patentees may hide behind the veil of patent pools or licensing clauses to defeat misuse allegations under the holding in *Princo*. At the same time cases such as *Rambus* and *Qualcomm* show that patents asserted in patent hold-ups are the same ones accused of being misused, and defendants in such cases should be able to establish the leveraging nexus even under *Princo*.

b. Anticompetitive effect and burden of proof On the second issue of whether anticompetitive effect is required and who has the burden of proof, the majority required Princo to show that the Lagadec technology "would have matured into a competitive force in the [relevant] market,"[175] since otherwise no anticompetitive effects would result even if it were sup-

---

[171]   Oliver, *supra* note 109, at 66.

[172]   See, e.g., Second Amended Answer, Defenses, and Counterclaims, *Nokia Corp. v. Apple, Inc., Apple Inc.*, 2011 WL 495957 (D. Del., February 11, 2011) (No. 09-791-GMS) ("Nokia's demand for a reciprocal 'grantback' license to Apple's non-standards-essential patents as a condition for licensing Nokia's purported essential patents at a F/RAND royalty rate constitutes misuse of Nokia's purported essential patents"). See also Oliver, *supra* note 109, at 67 ("It would appear that neither subsequent enforcement of patent A minus the grantback obligation nor subsequent enforcement of patent B would constitute patent misuse under *Princo*, although the conduct might constitute an antitrust violation").

[173]   Ibid.

[174]   Daniel J. Matheson, *Patent Misuse: The Questions That Linger Post-Princo*, A.B.A. SECTION OF ANTITRUST LAW INTELLECTUAL PROPERTY COMMITTEE, April–May 2011, at 3.

[175]   *Princo Corp. v Int'l. Trade Comm'n*, 616 F.3d 1318, 1351 (Fed. Cir. 2010).

pressed.[176] It further opined that a "quick look" analysis of a non-compete agreement was unwarranted in joint venture agreements unless there was a sham or a restraint unnecessary "to achieve efficiency-enhancing benefits of the joint venture."[177] As the dissent noted, the majority's requirement that Princo show the Lagadec technology's probable commercial viability "finds no support in the case law or antitrust policy."[178] Innovation markets for technologies like the one the Lagadec patent represents is treated with skepticism by courts.[179]

The general rule under the rule of reason approach is for the party alleging an adverse effect on competition in the relevant market to prove its actual existence.[180] At the same time, antitrust law also recognizes that a "quick look" approach may be applied to inherently suspect practices, including those that limited price, output or consumer choice.[181] Under the "quick look" approach, the burden falls on the patentee to "come . . . forward with some plausible (and legally cognizable) competitive justification for the restraint . . . "[182] These justifications "may consist of plausible

---

[176] Ibid.

[177] Ibid. at 1335.

[178] Ibid. at 1356.

[179] J. Thomas Rosch, Comm'r, Fed. Trade Comm'n, Some Thoughts on the Role of Intellectual Property in Innovation Market Cases and Refusals to License, Conference on Antitrust and Digital Enforcement in the Technology Sector (January 31, 2011) ("[I]t cannot be ignored that, in the 35 years since the Commission first challenged a merger under an innovation market theory when it contested the Rank-Xerox merger in 1974, there still has not been a successful antitrust challenge (public or private) based on the theory that a defendant stifled or threatened competition in a pure innovation market (i.e., when there is no product market at the time that the patent is acquired"); Jonathan M. Jacobson, ABA Section of Antitrust Law, Antitrust Law Developments 587 (6th ed. 2007) ("To date, no court has invalidated a transaction solely because it reduced competition in an innovation market").

[180] *Geneva Pharm. Tech. Corp. v. Barr Labs. Inc.*, 386 F.3d 485, 506–507 (2d Cir. 2004) ("Under the rule of reason, the plaintiffs bear an initial burden to demonstrate the defendants' challenged behavior had an *actual* adverse effect on competition as a whole in the relevant market").

[181] See *Polygram Holding Inc. v. Fed. Trade Comm'n*, 416 F.3d 29, 36 (D.C. Cir. 2005) (noting that an agreement is inherently suspect "[i]f, based upon economic learning and the experience of the market, it is obvious that a restraint of trade likely impairs competition").

[182] Ibid. at 36; see *Nat'l Collegiate Athletic Ass'n v. Bd. of Regents of Univ. of Ok.*, 468 U.S. 85, 111 (1984) ("these hallmarks of anticompetitive behavior place upon petitioner a heavy burden of establishing an affirmative defense which competitively justifies this apparent deviation from the operations of a free market"); Brief of Amicus Curiae Federal Trade Commission on Rehearing En Banc Supporting Neither Party at 26, *Princo Corp. v. Int'l Trade Comm'n*, 616 F.3d 1318

reasons why practices that are competitively suspect as a general matter may not be expected to have adverse consequences in the context of the particular market in question, or . . . may consist of reasons why the practices are likely to have beneficial effects for consumers."[183] The dissent in *Princo* thus argued that "[g]iven the inherently suspect nature of the agreements to suppress the Lagadec technology, Princo has satisfied its burden, and Philips has the burden to establish a justification or lack of anticompetitive effects."[184]

The countervailing view may be presented in three parts: (1) the danger of horizontal agreements; (2) the danger of refusals to license; and (3) what happens when competitors refuse to license nascent technology, as was the case in *Princo*.

The danger of horizontal agreements was articulated by the Fifth Circuit in *In re Yarn Processing*.[185] In affirming the finding of misuse by the lower court, The Fifth Circuit held that where competing patentees agree to a non-compete agreement, "competition is restricted to a greater degree," "even though there was little potential for competition between the blocking patents."[186] It examined a prior Supreme Court decision where payments "shared among the patent holders were clearly identified as royalty income which was split in a fashion to reward patent holders for their technological contribution."[187] The Supreme Court found that this amounted to a price-fixing agreement involving "royalty kickbacks" and it was condemned on antitrust grounds on the principle that "[i]t is only necessary that benefits arising from any one or more patents be shared among patentees in the same patent field to establish the price fixing prohibition."[188] The Fifth Circuit explained that "[t]he rationale for the distinction was that the potential for development of competing alternative technology is restricted by the cooperative exploitation of patents in combination with fixing sale prices."[189] It held that "[t]his rationale applies in equal, if not greater, measure where non-patent holder competitors are allowed to share the benefits of the patent."[190] With such practices, "no

---

(No. 337-TA-474) (Fed. Cir. 2010) (explaining that because the agreement with Sony to suppress the Lagadec patent was inherently suspect, the burden would be on Philips to show that the agreement was not anticompetitive).

[183]   *Polygram*, 416 F.3d at 36.
[184]   *Princo*, 616 F.3d at 1354.
[185]   *In re Yarn Proc.*, 541 F.2d 1127, 1141 (5th Cir. 1976).
[186]   Ibid.
[187]   *In re Yarn Proc.*, 541 F.2d at 1141.
[188]   Ibid.
[189]   Ibid. at 1142.
[190]   Ibid.

elaborate industry analysis is required to demonstrate the anticompetitive character of such an agreement."[191] Instead, the party denying anticompetitive effect or asserting precompetitive benefits bears the burden of proof.[192] Antitrust precedent is clear that the burden is on the patentee to show that it was not suppressing that technology. The same reasoning is applied in determining anticompetitive effects in misuse cases.[193] The *Princo* dissent cited with approval argued that the "quick look" approach was "particularly salient" where "the gravamen of the claimed restraint is that it has squelched development of a nascent, alternative technology."[194]

---

[191] *Nat'l Collegiate Athletic Ass'n v. Bd. of Regents of Univ. of Ok.*, 468 U.S. 85, 109 (1984); *United States v. Microsoft Corp.*, 253 F.3d 34, 79 (D.C. Cir. 2001) (*en banc*) (quoting 3 Philip E. Areeda & Herbert Hovenkamp, ANTITRUST LAW ¶651c, at 78 (1996)) ("To require that §2 liability turn on a plaintiff's ability or inability to reconstruct the hypothetical marketplace absent a defendant's anticompetitive conduct would only encourage monopolists to take more and earlier anticompetitive action. We may infer causation when exclusionary conduct is aimed at producers of nascent competitive technologies as well as when it is aimed at producers of established substitutes . . . [N]either plaintiffs nor the court can confidently reconstruct a product's hypothetical technological development in a world absent the defendant's exclusionary conduct. To some degree, 'the defendant is made to suffer the uncertain consequences of its own undesirable conduct'").

[192] See *Polygram Holding Inc. v. Fed. Trade Comm'n*, 416 F.3d 29, 36 (D.C. Cir. 2005) (noting that such justifications "may consist of plausible reasons why practices that are competitively suspect as a general matter may not be expected to have adverse consequences in the context of the particular market in question, or . . . may consist of reasons why the practices are likely to have beneficial effects for consumers").

[193] See *Krampe v. Ideal Indus.*, 347 F. Supp. 1384, 1387 (N.D. Ill. 1972) (holding a non-competition clause in a patent licensing agreement binding the licensee not to sell competing products constitutes patent misuse); see also 6 Chisum, *supra* note 86, at § 19.04[3], [3][B] ("If an agreement to suppress competition in an unpatented product to protect a patented product constitutes misuse, it is clearly misuse where the agreement involves the suppression of one patented technology to protect another patented technology from competition, as is the case here").

[194] Brief for Fed. Trade Comm'n as Amicus Curiae on Rehearing En Banc Supporting Neither Party at 23, *Princo Corp v. Int'l Trade Comm'n*, 616 F.3d 1318 (D.C. Cir. 2005) (No. 2007-1376), 2010 WL 804423. See also *Standard Oil Co. of California v. United States*, 337 U.S. 293, 309–10 (1949) ("to demand that bare inference be supported by evidence as to what would have happened but for the adoption of the practice that was in fact adopted . . . would be a standard of proof, if not virtually impossible to meet, at least most ill-suited for ascertainment by courts"); see *United States v. Microsoft Corp.*, 253 F.3d 34, 79 (D.C. Cir. 2001) (placing the burden on antitrust plaintiffs "to reconstruct the hypothetical marketplace absent a defendant's anticompetitive conduct would only encourage monopolists to take more and earlier anticompetitive action . . . to allow monopolists free reign to squash nascent, albeit unproven, competitors at will").

Commentators have observed that a refusal to license is more harmful than a refusal to deal in other assets. When firms refuse to share a physical asset,[195] those denied access have an incentive to develop these independently. In contrast, a patent blocks all technologies that violate its claims even if the patent is not used or where the technology is independently developed. In *Princo*, the two sets of agreements go much further than a simple refusal to deal.[196] Not having access to Sony's alternative technology means that no one could ever develop a competing technology unless the developer could work around both Sony's digital technology and Philips' analog one. The record shows that even after Philips' technology was chosen and Sony's was not, Sony continued to develop its technology and applied for a patent which showed improvements in the technology.[197] These suggest that while Sony's technology may have been inferior to Philips' at the point of adoption, a number of reasons expose the fact that Philips was concerned that others in the future would be more successful in developing it.

Commentators have argued that if Sony's technology had no commercial prospects, then there was no need to restrain the development of the technology. According to this view, such an agreement has no other reason than to forestall the development of the nascent technology by others.[198] It would have been a simple decision, given the confidence that Philips had in its technology, for it to then decouple the Lagadec

---

[195] 10 Areeda & Hovenkamp, *supra* note 168, at ¶1781 ("The effect of permitting concerted refusals to license a patent can be significantly more harmful to competition than the effect of concerted refusals to share other assets").

[196] Ibid. at ¶1781 ("Once subject to this agreement, the effect of the unused Lagadec patent would be to restrain the developing of any digital CD technology that competed with the analog technology that Philips and Sony employed unless the developer could invent around the claims contained in the Lagadec patent. That is to say, the effect of the patent plus the nonuse and nonlicensing agreements could have been very considerably to increase the cost of developing competing technology and perhaps even to prevent such technology from being developed during the lifetime of the Lagadec patent").

[197] *Princo Corp.*, 616 F.3d at 1355 ("Even after the Lagadec technology was rejected for the Orange Book standard, Sony continued to pursue the technology, and applied for a U.S. patent over seven months after the Raaymakers technology was adopted for the Orange Book and the Lagadec technology was rejected. As noted . . . the U.S. patent reflected improvements in the Lagadec technology").

[198] 10 Areeda & Hovenkamp, *supra* note 168, at ¶1781 ("Of course, if the Lagadec patent had no commercial "prospects," then an agreement to restrain the development of the technology it described would not have been necessary. Further, such an agreement has no obvious utility except to forestall the development of as yet nascent technology by others").

patent and license it to Princo. This would have allayed any color-able concerns of misuse. As early on as in 1931, the Supreme Court highlighted this in *Standard Oil Co., Ind. v. United States*.[199] The Court found probative the fact that the license agreements did not restrain the individual patentees from licensing third parties.[200] Similarly, the Court of Appeals for the Ninth Circuit counseled that: "[p]robably the best way for an owner of such a patent to protect himself from a charge of misuse would be to offer or stand ready to offer the patented item alone."[201] More recently, the District Court for the Northern District of Illinois agreed that patentees could preempt or exculpate themselves from allegations of misuse by accommodating at least one request to license the patents individually.[202]

Providing an alternative to users and competitors has always been a central tenet of American IP law in order to fulfill its constitutional man-date.[203] The fact that the technology in question is in its nascent stages adds a layer of complication to the issue. FTC Commissioner Rosch observed that:

> determining what conduct in its nascent stage is likely to lead to conduct that is more anticompetitive than procompetitive is a challenging task—one that private plaintiffs, generalist judges, and lay juries are arguably ill-suited to

---

[199]   *Standard Oil Co., Ind. v. United States*, 283 U.S. 163 (1931).

[200]   Ibid. at 170 ("There is no provision in any of the agreements which restricts the freedom of the primary defendants individually to issue licenses under their own patents alone or under the patents of all the others").

[201]   *Stearns v. Tinker & Rasor*, 252 F.2d 589, 604 (9th Cir. 1957).

[202]   *Semiconductor Energy Lab. Co. v. Chi Mei Optoelectronics Corp.*, 531 F. Supp. 2d 1084, 1101 (N.D. Cal. 2007) ("Furthermore, SEL has cited unrefuted evidence showing that it has accommodated at least one request to license an indi-vidual patent. Even if package-licensing constituted patent misuse, therefore, SEL has shown a willingness to refrain from the practice").

[203]   In Rosch, Intel, Apple, Google, Microsoft, and Facebook, *supra* note 44, at 8, Commissioner Rosch, discussing the difficult balance between access and protection, noted that: "As a threshold matter, it would be irresponsible of us to treat any transaction or conduct by an inventor as per se legal. That would be like creating a super-immunity for patent holders. To be sure, patent law grants a period of exclusivity to an inventor who lawfully obtains a patent from the PTO. But even determining the bounds of that exclusivity is not easy. On the one hand, we must be sensitive—as Justice Scalia noted in Trinko—to the fact that monopoly profits are often what incentivize a firm to innovate in the first place. On the other hand, however, as the FTC acknowledged in its amicus brief to the Federal Circuit in the TiVo v. Echostar litigation (which dealt with incentives for work around innovators), we must also protect the incentives of parties to compete with the original innovaton."

attempt. Moreover, the cost of them getting it wrong—creating liability for procompetitive conduct – is far too high.[204]

Further, not all agree with that shuttering of inchoate alternatives. As Professors Hovenkamp and Bohannan argue "protecting inchoate innovation is precisely what patent law should be about."[205] While requiring Princo to demonstrate that Lagadec would have become a viable competitive force is appropriate as a matter of antitrust law, they further argue, that "it completely submerges the IP concern with preserving all forms of innovation (particularly that which is not immediately foreseeable) under the antitrust concern of predictability."[206] The patent system is engineered to promote innovation often still nascent at the time protection is given. Commentators have thus noted that "the great majority of patents are subsequently proven to have no economic value, not because we have a policy of rewarding useless inventions without patents, but rather because at the time the patenting decision is made, the future of that particular patent's technology is uncertain. If the patent examiner insisted on the proof of commercial success that the antitrust tribunal requires of plaintiffs, very few patents will ever be issued."[207]

Commentators have also cited the browser wars which dominated much of the IP-antitrust interface during the 1990s, when Microsoft tied its internet browser to its operating system in order to thwart the nascent Java-threat. The advent of browsers as the basis for our mobile communications experience today indicates how much "browser competition may have been suppressed."[208] Commentators have also spoken out stridently against requiring "evidence that the rival's technology or product was ready to be commercialized in order for the courts to find that a package license constitutes misuse . . . "[209] On the facts, commentators have argued that the *Princo* majority "failed to appreciate the importance of protecting nascent innovation. The unlicensed digital technology may not have been commercially feasible in its present form, but Philips and Sony's agreement not to license it also prevented others from building on that technology to develop a viable or even superior digital technology."[210]

---

[204] Rosch, Promoting Innovation, *supra* note 36, at 17.
[205] Christina Bohannan & Herbrt Hovenkamp, CREATION WITHOUT RESTRAINT 274 (2012).
[206] Bohannan & Hovenkamp, *IP and Antitrust, supra* note 83, at [276].
[207] –10 Areeda & Hovenkamp, *supra* note 168, at ¶1781.
[208] Bohannan & Hovenkamp, *IP and Antitrust, supra* note 83, at 276.
[209] Ibid. at 279.
[210] Ibid. at 281.

Joseph Noferi argues that "because it is a nascent technology that is in question, the patent owner is in the best place to disclose its reasoning for refus[ing] to license it."[211] Since the innovation trajectories are unpredictable and path-breaking technology unappreciated until commercialization, the rival producer often will not be able to show the new product or technology will not have succeeded in the market but for the patentee's conduct. In such cases, commentators argue, the correct threshold is that "some appreciable harm to innovation is likely and that the conduct is not justified in offsetting efficiencies."[212]

Additionally, Charan Sandhu and Adam Hemlock have noted that as a result of the majority's view in *Princo*, motions to strike the defense may become more common as patentees "seek to avoid the diversion and discovery involved in litigating a misuse defense," since the actual competitive harm from patent leveraging and commercial viability of suppressed technology "may be difficult to prove in cases of nascent or developing technologies where the required evidence may not yet be present."[213] As a result, "[a]lleged infringers may only be able to challenge certain patent-related conduct by filing a separate antitrust claim or a counterclaim (assuming the additional elements of an antitrust claim are satisfied)."[214] More fundamentally, others have criticized the Federal Circuit for "fail[ing] to provide guidance where competitive effects are more complex—e.g., a situation in which *some* competition appears to be foreclosed, or the evidence suggests that a marginal or nascent competitor *might* be impacted." In this regard, the applicable analysis in the case of nascent technology, which is characteristic of standard setting cases, is likely to be less certain post-*Princo*.

c.   *A patent misuse "plus" standard?*   On the third issue, whether an antitrust violation of a patent right might escape liability under patent misuse, the *Princo* majority's answer is "yes."[215] If there was no leverage

---

211   See Joseph Noferi, Comment, *A Wholistic Approach to Antitrust Law and Patent Misuse*, 28 (2011) (on file with the author).

212   Ibid. at 282.

213   See Sandhu & Hemlock *supra* note 132, at 24.

214   See Oliver, *supra* note 109, at 67 (suggesting the likelihood that courts might stay the antitrust claim pending resolution of the infringement claim and the added cost of filing a counterclaim or separate suit as factors).

215   See *Princo Corp. v. Int'l Trade Comm'n*, 616 F.3d 1318, 1332 (Fed. Cir. 2010) ("That agreement might be vulnerable to challenge under the antitrust laws, but it could not reasonably be characterized as misuse of the Raaymakers patents. Thus, it does not follow from the possible existence of an antitrust violation with respect to Sony's Lagadec patent that Philips is guilty of patent misuse with respect to the Raaymakers patents").

of the patent in suit, the patentees' conduct would not be misuse even if it amounted to an antitrust violation. It is not an isolated view. This view, according to the dissent however, was contrary to Supreme Court precedent and to conventional wisdom.[216] In observing that antitrust was "inadequate for the task," the dissent was concerned that misconduct which impedes "the Progress of Science and the useful Arts" may become unrestrainable by misuse.[217] Sharing the dissent's concern, the concurrence distanced itself from the majority because "[w]hether use of a patent runs afoul of antitrust law seems in itself probative of whether the patent owner has also abused, or 'misused', the limited monopoly granted by Congress."[218] The concurrence also noted that:

> By asking only whether the Raaymakers patents [have] been 'leveraged', . . . the majority may have unnecessarily narrowed the patent misuse inquiry— particularly when one can readily argue that the combined effect of an agreement to license the Raaymakers patents, but not the Lagadec patent, enabled Philips to obtain the type of 'market benefit beyond that which inheres the statutory patent right' of either patent, amounting to misuse.[219]

There is a significant vein of commentary arguing for the development of misuse along channels distinct from antitrust law, because the latter

---

[216] *Princo Corp.*, 616 F.3d at 1341 ("The critical question is whether the existence of an antitrust violation—in the form of an agreement to suppress an alternative technology designed to protect a patented technology from competition—constitutes misuse of the protected patents. The majority holds that it does not").

[217] See Petition for Writ of Certiorari to the United States Court of Appeals for the Federal Circuit at 31, *Princo Corp. v. Int'l Trade Comm'n*, (No. 10-898) (Jan 5, 2011) ("due to the stringent standing requirements for an antitrust claim, the difficulty of proving causation and damages from an agreement to suppress nascent technology, and the complete unavailability of an antitrust counterclaim in the increasingly important ITC forum, the antitrust laws provide only minimal deterrence in this setting"). *Princo Corp.*, 616 F.3d, at 1357 ("The majority's strict standard fails to provide adequate protection against the suppression of nascent technology, and allows patent holders free rein to prevent the development of potentially competitive technologies except in the most extreme and unlikely circumstances"); *Dawson Chem. Co. v. Rohm & Haas Co.*, 448 U.S.176, 221 (1980) ("The policy of free competition . . . underlies . . . the doctrine of patent misuse . . . [b]ut the policy of stimulating invention that underlies the entire patent system runs no less deep").

[218] In *Princo*, Judge Prost in her concurrence noted that patent misuse was not "as narrow or expansive as" either the *en banc* majority or minority suggested. Antitrust considerations were relevant to a finding of patent misuse, and "thus reserve[d] judgment on the precise metes and bounds of the patent misuse doctrine," *Princo Corp.*, 616 F.3d., at 1340.

[219] Ibid. at 1341.

does not address conduct stemming from the patentee's bad faith or abuse of the patent system.[220] Geoffrey Oliver observes that "[b]y divorcing patent misuse from antitrust law, the *Princo* decision significantly alters the relationship between them."[221] According to Oliver, "[p]rior Supreme Court and Federal Circuit decisions established patent-related conduct may constitute patent misuse without giving rise to antitrust liability. *Princo* establishes the converse as well: patent-related conduct may create antitrust liability without amounting to patent misuse."[222]

The *Princo* majority's assertion that a proven antitrust violation could not in certain circumstances amount to misuse has no empirical or anecdotal support. Indeed, this study reveals no such rule. On the contrary, case law both at the Supreme Court level as well as in the district courts reflects the rule that "[i]f a practice does rise to the level of an antitrust violation, it will also constitute misuse."[223] As the Supreme Court noted,

---

[220] See Bohannan & Hovenkamp, *supra* note 83, at 514 (arguing that *Princo* "highlights the problem with basing misuse exclusively on foreclosure of competition and failing to consider foreclosure of innovation as a potential basis for IP misuse. If it is true that Philips and Sony's agreement restrained development of a rival technology, then it might be an appropriate case for finding misuse even if it cannot be shown that the restraint ultimately resulted in foreclosure of a competing product"); Matheson, *supra* note 174 at 7 (such notions of fairness find little support in modern antitrust doctrine, which focuses on maximizing consumer welfare rather than restraining bad actors. Thus, under antitrust law, "[e]ven an act of pure malice by one business competitor against another does not, without more, state a claim under the federal antitrust laws," and the fact that dominant firms "may impose painful losses on [their competitors] is of no moment to the antitrust laws if competition is not injured") (quoting *Brooke Group Ltd. v. Brown & Williamson Tobacco Corp.*, 509 U.S. 209, 224–25 (1993)).

[221] Oliver, *supra* note 109, at 66.

[222] Ibid.

[223] See 6 Chisum, *supra* note 86, at §§ 19.04 [3], [3][b]. See also *Hartford Empire Co. v. U.S.*, 323 U.S. 386, 415 (1945) ("so long as the patent owner is using his patent in violation of the antitrust laws, he cannot restrain infringement of it by others"). See, e.g., *Van Well Nursery, Inc. v. Mony Life Ins. Co.*, No. CV-04-0245-LRS, 2007 U.S. Dist. LEXIS 15694 (E.D. Wash. March 7, 2007) ("While one who misuses a patent does not also necessarily violate antitrust laws, one who violates antitrust laws by inappropriate use of a patent is necessarily guilty of patent misuse"); *Jack Winter, Inc. v. Koratron Co.*, 375 F. Supp. 1, 71 (N.D. Cal. 1974) ("Although an antitrust violation involving a patent comes clearly within the patent misuse doctrine, a showing of such a violation and actual lessening of competition is not required"); *Hear-Wear Techs., LLC v. Phonak, LLC*, No. 07-CV-0212-CVE-SAJ, 2008 U.S. Dist. LEXIS 21048, at *23 (N.D. Okla. Mar. 18, 2008) ("Out of an abundance of caution, the Court finds that Phonak's claim sufficiently crosses 'some threshold of plausibility' and thus this 'patent antitrust case should be permitted to go into its inevitably costly and protracted discovery phase'. [quoting *Twombly*].

"[i]t would be absurd to assume that Congress intended to provide that the use of a patent that merited punishment as a felony [under the Sherman Act] would not constitute 'misuse'."[224] Other courts have similarly noted that "a patentee who uses a patent to violate the antitrust laws is guilty of patent misuse."[225] Commentators similarly agree that "[i]f a patentee's conduct rises to the level of an antitrust violation, it will constitute patent misuse."[226]

D. Concluding Thoughts

Princo reached the correct outcome on the facts. The facts of *Princo* made it a suitable vehicle for the majority to narrow the doctrine of patent misuse. First, there was scant evidence of anticompetitive effect. The industry had also moved on by then, and by 2010 the use of CD-RWs to store data was superseded by more advanced storage alternatives. Second, the settled expectations of the industry were at risk. Had Princo won, Philips would have lost control over the industry standard and its secondary markets, a major sore point for those decrying the disproportionate punishment inflicted on patent owners for their misuse of a single patent, however trivial the misuse might be. To Eugene Chang, the dissent's argument implied "that a patent holder may be guilty of misuse for agreeing not to license its patent outside the pool, even if there is no evidence that anyone wanted such a non-pool license."[227] Had the *en banc* court decided otherwise, patent holders collaborating in licensing patents would have to second-guess the legality of any restrictions they imposed in this regard for fear of patent misuse allegations.

Further, because Phonak also asserts the affirmative defense of patent misuse, which is broader than its antitrust counterclaim [quoting *C.R. Bard*], discovery over the sham litigation issue will occur regardless of the Court's ruling here").

[224] *Illinois Tool Works Inc. v. Indep. Ink., Inc.*, 547 U.S. 28, 42 (2006). The majority attempts to parry this argument by asserting that "the Court was simply making the point that Congress's decision to require proof of market power to establish patent misuse was powerful evidence that Congress intended proof of market power to be similarly required to establish a criminal antitrust violation for the same conduct. The Court was not suggesting that every antitrust violation committed by a patentee constitutes patent misuse." *See* Princo 616 F.3d, at n. 3. However conventional wisdom suggests otherwise.

[225] *Hunter Douglas, Inc. v. Comfortex Corp.*, 44 F. Supp. 2d 145, 156 (N.D.N.Y 1999); see also *Rohm & Haas Co. v. Dawson Chem. Co., Inc.*, No. 74-H-790, 1976 WL 21292 (S.D. Tex. Aug. 10, 1976) ("conduct of a patent owner which constitutes a violation of the antitrust laws would usually, if not always, constitute patent misuse as a matter of law").

[226] Bennett, *supra* note 143, at 9. See also Chisum, *supra* note 86.

[227] Eugene L. Chang et al., *Princo Corp. V. ITC*, Law360, at 4 (2010).

Third, as the majority recognized, suppression of competing technology was necessary in order to induce competitors to participate and agree on a common standard in the context of a patent pool.[228] Any joint venture agreement necessarily requires parties in the agreement to agree to refrain from competing against the venture in order to avoid having one party "free ride" on the others. At the same time, none of this exonerates deficiencies in the majority's reasoning nor do they preclude in more appropriate cases.

Perhaps haunted by the plague of inequitable conduct, the majority was determined to provide greater commercial certainty and bolster the position of patentees in infringement litigation.[229] To the majority, strong patent rights and agreements between patentees bring private and public benefit. High profits and a lack of challengers to the standard, contrary to being signs of misuse, indicate that the system is working to produce good technology, and reward those who create and disseminate it. Indeed, the majority flirts with the idea that patent misuse is an obsolete doctrine that should be abolished altogether.[230] At the same time, however, smothering a doctrine created by the Supreme Court and acknowledged by Congress dilutes the credibility of the majority's analysis. In the standard setting context, *Princo* also further muddies the relationship between antitrust and misuse, and "adds to the challenge of evaluating whether and how certain antitrust principles apply to patent-related conduct."[231] It "also raises the possibility that an alleged infringer might not be able to raise certain patent-related exclusionary conduct under the patent laws, which

---

[228]   Brief of Intervenor U.S. Philips Corporation on Rehearing En Banc at 19, *Princo Corp. v. ITC*, 616 F.3d 1318 (Fed. Cir. 2010) (No. 337-TA-474) (aligning interests of competitors through suppression of technology okay. As Philips noted: "Given, however, Lagadec's collaborative origins, any agreement not to allow it to be used to compete *against the venture from which it arose* would be a classic example of a facially reasonable ancillary restraint, adopted to facilitate a highly procompetitive joint venture by aligning the interests of the collaborators and reducing the likelihood that one participant might use the fruits of the collaboration to harm either another participant or the joint enterprise itself").

[229]   See Matheson, *supra* note 174 at 2–3 ("This standard should be easier for lower courts to apply than the pre-*Princo* articulations, which condemned attempts to 'broaden' the scope of a patent grant – a standard that proved so vague that even the panel opinion in *Princo* failed to interpret it correctly").

[230]   *Princo Corp.*, 616 F.3d at 1329 n. 2. The Federal Circuit recognized that the "Supreme Court's patent misuse cases have not been overruled, however, and we therefore apply the principles of patent misuse as that Court's decisions and our own prior precedents direct," ibid.

[231]   See Oliver, *supra* note 109, at 62 ("[*Princo*] requires that certain patent-related conduct be considered separately under the patent and antitrust laws because the results may differ").

would force greater reliance on antitrust counterclaims or separate antitrust lawsuits as appropriate."[232]

The dissent was equally convinced that it was incumbent upon the Federal Circuit as *de facto* promulgator of patent policy to reinvigorate a policy lever that could address misconduct by standards owners. Unfortunately, the dissent stopped short of providing a framework for patent misuse in exclusionary abuses of the patent right. As the concurrence lamented, "the dissent does not address how a patent owner's right to *exclude* others from using the invention could, and possibly should, affect the calculus in the antitrust and patent misuse contexts."[233] Had the dissent succeeded in doing so, it might have won more support from the *en banc* panel and *Princo* may well have been a watershed in reinvigorating patent misuse jurisprudence. More fundamentally, the dissent's retro-like opinion seems driven by a view reflecting the *Mercoid* Court's suspicion that patents risk conferring rights and providing patentees with rewards that do not reflect the market value of the patentees' technology. Its ideologically-charged analysis opens it to accusations of selective fact-finding to fit its ideology, as well as a return to *per se* misuse or a "rule of reason-lite" analysis based on its "quick-look" approach. It fails to provide a clear basis for a patent misuse doctrine that is broad enough but not so broad as to be easily misused. Ironically, the dissent's sometimes emotional diatribe feeds the majority's concern that misuse becomes commandeered by ideological judges willing to find misuse without proper factual support.

The majority and dissenting opinions reflect two polar opposite ideologies on patent misuse. By going beyond the usual practice of *en banc* courts, *Princo* shows how strongly both felt the need to shape a doctrine that they viewed as critically affecting the proper functioning of the patent system. It is a division so strong that the split will likely ripple across the patent litigation landscape even as new cases emerge to test the boundaries of *Princo*.[234] On May 16, 2011 the Supreme Court

---

[232] Ibid. at 67.

[233] See *Princo* Corp., 616 F.3d. at 1341.

[234] See, e.g, Fourth Amended Answer, Defenses, and Counterclaims at 29, *Nokia Corp. v. Apple, Inc.*, No. 2011 WL 495957 (D. Del., February 11, 2011) (No. C 09-3511 RS) ("Nokia's deliberate and deceptive non-disclosure of purported essential IPR during the standards-setting process, its false representations to SSOs that it would license on F/RAND terms the patents it belatedly declared essential, and Nokia's assertion of its wrongfully obtained monopoly power against Apple in demanding non-F/RAND license terms from Apple and then suing Apple for patent infringement when Apple refused to accede to those unreasonable demands even though Apple had a license as a matter of

denied Princo's petition for certiorari.[235] Patent misuse is ultimately a judge-made doctrine, and its vitality rests upon the will of those shaping it. Without competing appellate circuits, the Federal Circuit's jurisdiction of patent law in general, and patent misuse in particular, is near absolute, and its influence on their respective contours is tremendous.[236] The majority in *Princo* placed its thumb on commercial certainty, seen by some as narrowing misuse jurisprudence beyond its previous threshold in *Windsurfing*. Whether the faith they share with those like Thomas Friedman in patentees to deliver and develop the fire of genius to the nation is justified remains yet to be seen.

III. MISCONDUCT IN THE PHARMACEUTICAL INDUSTRY

A. Reverse Payments

The key controversy in the area of pharmaceutical settlements is whether the patentee and its potential generic competitors should have the prerogative to agree that the latter remain outside of the former's market in

---

law, constitute patent misuse and render the Nokia Asserted Patents unenforceable. Nokia's acts of patent misuse have had anticompetitive effects, including the unlawful and unfair exclusion of alternative technologies from various Input Technologies Markets defined below, as well as the threat of increased prices to consumers in downstream markets for mobile wireless communications devices"); *Openwave Sys. v. 724 Solutions (US) Inc.*, 2010 U.S. Dist. LEXIS 20502, at *5 (N.D. Cal. Mar. 8, 2010) (asserting that Openwave engaged in patent misuse through vexatious or sham litigation); *Microsoft Corp v. Barnes & Noble Inc.*, No. 2:11-cv-00485 RAJ (W.D. Wash. Apr 25, 2011) (arguing that Microsoft is attempting to exclude competition from the Android Operating System by bundling patents that should not have the effect of excluding competition, and that it has engaged in a pattern and practice of saber rattling with patents it never intends to assert, and instead actually asserts patents with a much weaker position, thereby attempting to extend the scope of its asserted patents well beyond their limited reach).

[235] *Princo Corp. v. Int'l Trade Comm'n*, 131 S. Ct. 2480 (U.S. May 16, 2011).

[236] As Princo pointed out in its Petition, "The vast majority of antitrust claims involving patent pools will be heard by the Federal Circuit, because they will be brought as counterclaims in patent infringement suits against those refusing to take licenses at monopoly rates; potential consumers of an alternative product based on an alternative product based on the suppressed patent will lack standing to sue. Thus, unless this Court intervenes, the legal regime of this case will immediately become the national law of antitrust as well as patent misuse," *Princo Corp.*, Petition for Writ of Certiorari, *supra* note 217 at 34–35.

return for compensation. The typical situation arises when the generic company files an Abbreviated New Drug Application (ANDA) under the Hatch-Waxman Act, claiming either that the owner's patent was invalid or that the generic company did not infringe the valid patent.[237] The Hatch-Waxman Act was intended to encourage the introduction of generic alternatives to brand name products by giving the successful generic challenger 180 days of exclusivity if it could show that the patent was invalid or not infringed. While the purpose of the Act was to encourage patent challenges, the 180-day period has allowed brand pharmaceutical companies to block challenges by settling with the first generic challenger by paying it to delay entering the market. Other generics are prohibited because of the 180-day exclusivity period awarded to the first generic challenger. Both parties benefit from the monopoly because each receives more economic rent than they would have with a competitive market created by the duopolistic market. Patentees in such cases typically point to the guaranteed years of competition before the end of the patent term.[238]

By keeping the challenger out, the branded company remains a monopolist and can charge monopoly prices. The Sixth Circuit in *re Cardizen CD* held that such a pay-for-delay agreement "was, at its core, a horizontal agreement to eliminate competition in the market for Cardizem CD throughout the entire United States, a classic example of a *per se*

---

[237] See Drug Price Competition and Patent Term Restoration Act of 1984, Pub. L. No. 98-417, 98 Stat. 1585; Yee Wah Chin, *The Growing Interplay of Patent and Competition Law: Antitrust Pitfalls in Licensing*, 877 PLI/PAT 439, 471 (2006) ("The Hatch-Waxman Act allows generic drug makers to avoid the strict requirements of a new drug application (NDA) through an abbreviated new drug application (ANDA). In an ANDA, the generic applicant relies on the safety and efficacy information that supported the NDA for the brand name drug. The ANDA must also include a 'Paragraph IV' certification, that either the generic drug applicant is not infringing any patent covering the branded drug that is listed in the FDA's 'Orange Book' or the branded drug's patent is invalid. The branded drug maker can challenge that certification by suing for patent infringement within 45 days. Once this suit is filed, the generic applicant may not sell its drug until the earlier of 30 months or the final resolution of the lawsuit. In addition, when approved by the FDA, the first generic drug applicant has an 180-day exclusivity against all other generics that made the same certification. Under the Hatch-Waxman Act as originally enacted, if the generic applicant never markets its generic version of the drug, and thus never triggers the 180-day period, all other generic applicants are blocked").

[238] See, e.g., Defendant's Motion to Dismiss at 26, *FTC v. Cephalon, Inc.*, 2008 U.S. Dist. LEXIS 34390 (D.D.C. 2008) (No. 08-cv-00244 (JDB)) (where Cephalon noted that the settlement, which allowed entry in 2012, "resulted in generic entry years earlier than patent expiration" in 2015).

illegal restraint of trade."[239] As such, the agreement was *per se* illegal.[240] Michael Carrier argues that such settlements raise "severe anticompetitive dangers" and "frequently offer the best evidence of patent invalidity or noninfringement . . . the longer the generic firm agrees to refrain from entering the market, the greater the anticompetitive concern in some of the early reverse-payment settlements, the generic agreed to stay out of the market for all or nearly all of the patent term."[241] The Federal Circuit in *In re Ciprofloxacin Hydrochloride* rejected the Sixth Circuit's view and held such agreements to be *per se* legal.[242] The Federal Circuit adopted a narrow interpretation of the instances where the scope of the rights would be subject to antitrust scrutiny, holding that "in the absence of evidence of fraud before the PTO or sham litigation, the court need not consider the validity of the patent in the antitrust analysis of a settlement agreement involving a reverse payment."[243]

---

[239] *In re Cardizem CD*, 332 F.3d 896, 908 (6th Cir. 2003).

[240] H.R. 3962, 111th Cong § 2573 (2009) (Legislative efforts include a provision barring agreements that prohibit the generic company receiving anything of value and agreeing to limit or forego production or marketing its generic drug); J. Thomas Rosch, The Antitrust/Intellectual Property Interface: Thoughts on How to Best Wade Through the Thicket in the Pharmaceutical Context, World Generic Medicine Congress (Nov 17, 2010) ("In July 2010, the House passed legislation that would give the FTC authority to initiate proceedings against any party that enters into a pay-for-delay deal, which the legislation defines as a circumstance in which the filer of an abbreviated new drug application challenging the validity of a patent for a brand-name drug agrees to 'anything of value' in exchange for forgoing research, development, manufacturing, marketing or selling the new generic alternative. The legislation would not ban pay-for-delay settlements, but would make them presumptively anti-competitive. The parties could then overcome that presumption by demonstrating by 'clear and convincing evidence' that the procompetitive benefits of the deal outweigh any potential anticompetitive effects").

[241] Michael A. Carrier, *Provigil: A Case Study of Anticompetitive Behavior*, 3 Hastings Sci. & Tech. L.J. 441, 445 (Summer 2011) ("For example, in *In re Tamoxifen Citrate Antitrust Litigation*, generic firm Barr agreed in 1993 not to enter the market with a generic breast cancer treatment until brand firm Zeneca's patent expired in 2002. And in *In re Ciprofloxacin Hydrochloride Antitrust Litigation*, brand firm Bayer in 1997 paid generic firm Barr to stay out of the market until six months before Bayer's patent on Cipro, a drug treating bacterial illnesses, was set to expire in 2003").

[242] *In re Ciprofloxacin Hydrochloride*, 544 F.3d 1323 (Fed. Cir. 2008) (holding that it was "well within Bayer's rights as the patentee" to "exclude the defendants from profiting from the patented invention. . . . [T]he mere fact that the Agreements insulated Bayer from patent invalidity challenges by the generic defendants was not in itself an antitrust violation").

[243] Ibid.

The Eleventh Circuit was similarly deferential in *Schering-Plough v. FTC*.[244] According to the Eleventh Circuit, the correct view is to examine "the extent to which antitrust liability might undermine the encouragement of innovation and disclosure,"[245] a view bearing striking shades of patent law's mandate to "promote the Progress of Science and the useful Arts." Proceeding to echo the analytical matrix under the Federal Circuit's *Windsurfing* case, the court held that the settlement agreement's legality rested on whether the patent owner had exceeded the scope of its patent rights with anticompetitive effects.[246] The Second Circuit applied *Schering-Plough* in *In re Tamoxifen Citrate*, noting that the settled litigation was a sham or fraudulent procurement, indicative but not necessary to show that the scope of the patent had been exceeded.[247] In *FTC v. Watson Pharmaceuticals*, the Eleventh Circuit reiterated that reverse payments do not violate antitrust laws as long as they do not expand the scope of the patent.[248] The FTC argued that the generic challenger would likely have successfully proven that the patent was invalid or not infringed. The court rejected this argument, refusing to decide an antitrust case based on the likelihood of a successful Paragraph IV challenge. It held that allowing that "would be deciding a patent case within an antitrust case about the settlement of the patent case, a turducken task."[249] Instead, the court simply looked to the term that the patent grant had as the touch stone of whether the settlement had had anticompetitive effects. It found that since generics could in fact enter the market five years before the patent expired, there was no violation of antitrust laws.[250]

---

[244] *Schering-Plough v. Fed. Trade Comm'n*, 402 F.3d 1056 (11th Cir. 2005) (rejecting the FTC's argument that the settlement eliminated competition, since "[b]y their nature, patents create an environment of exclusion, and consequently, cripple competition").

[245] Ibid. at 1066.

[246] Ibid.

[247] *In re Tamoxifen Citrate*, 466 F.3d 187 (2d Cir. 2006) ("we do not . . . think there is a 'requirement' that 'antitrust plaintiffs must show that the settled litigation was a sham, i.e. objectively baseless before the settlement can be considered an antitrust violation . . .' There is no such requirement. . . . A plaintiff need not allege or prove sham litigation in order to succeed in establishing that a settlement has provided defendants 'with benefits exceeding the scope of the tamoxifen patent'. Whether there is fraud or baseless litigation may be relevant to the inquiry, but it is hardly, we think, 'the standard', as the dissent posits in order to take issue with it").

[248] *Fed. Trade Comm'n v. Watson Pharmaceuticals, Inc.*, 677 F.3d 1298 (11th Cir. 2012) *cert. granted*, 12 U.S.416 (2012)

[249] Ibid. at 39.

[250] Ibid.

Recently, the Third Circuit in *re K-Dur Antitrust Litigation* rejected the position taken by the Second, Eleventh and Federal Circuits that as long as the reverse payments settlements between branded and generic pharmaceutical companies restrained competition within the scope of the underlying patent, and the underlying patent lawsuits were not objectively baseless, the defendants were entitled to summary judgment on the anti-trust claims.[251] It reasoned that the scope-of-the-patent test "improperly restricts the application of antitrust law and is contrary to the policies underlying the Hatch-Waxman Act and a long line of Supreme Court precedent on patent litigation and competition."[252] In its view, the test created an "almost unrebuttable presumption of patent validity", even though many patents issued by the Patent Office were later found to be invalid or not infringed.[253] It also questioned an assumption supporting the presumption of legality that subsequent challenges by other generic manufacturers would suffice to eliminate weak patents preserved through a reverse payment to the initial challenger.[254]

One fundamental reason that theories of antitrust harm have not been favorably received by some courts lies with the judicial attitude toward settlements. According to the Ninth Circuit, "[i]t is well recognized that settlement agreements are judicially favored as a matter of sound public policy. Settlement agreements conserve judicial time and limit expensive litigation."[255] It disagreed with the defendant's argument that "the equitable doctrine of patent misuse prevails over the policy of favoring the settlement of disputes."[256] It found no evidence "to allow a subversion of the deeply-instilled policy of settlement of disputes by applying the doctrine of inequitable conduct, in the manner contended for by the defendants, would have the effect of stripping good-faith settlements of any meaning".[257] Judge Posner in *Asahi Glass Co. Ltd v. Pentech Pharms., Inc*, voiced a similar opinion, noting that condemning settlement agreements would limit the generic company's incentive to challenge the brand company's patent, since once it embarked on that course it had no real

---

[251]   *In re K-Dur Antitrust Litig.*, 686 F.3d 197 (3d Cir. 2012). See also In re Tamoxifen Citrate Antitrust Litig., 466 F.3d 187 (2d Cir. 2006); *Schering-Plough Corp. v. Fed. Trade Comm'n*, 402 F.3d 1056 (11th Cir. 2005), *In re Ciprofloxacin Hydrochloride Antitrust Litig.*, 544 F.3d 1323 (Fed. Cir. 2008).
[252]   *In re K-Dur Antitrust Litig.*, 686 F.3d 197 (3d Cir. 2012).
[253]   Ibid. at 214.
[254]   Ibid. at 215.
[255]   *Speed Shore Corp. v. Denda*, 605 F.2d 469, 473–74 (9th Cir. 1979) citing *Williams v. First Nat'l Bank*, 216 U.S. 582 (1910).
[256]   *Speed Shore Corp. v. Denda*, 605 F.2d at 473.
[257]   Ibid. at 473–74.

option to settle.[258] Courts have also taken a similar view in misuse cases. In *W. L. Gore & Assoc., Inc. v. Carlisle Corp.*, the patentee had threatened to discontinue purchasing goods from the defendant.[259] The Court found that:

> Where such a statement is made in the context of settlement negotiations in which the patent holder has also offered the infringer a license by which to legalize his infringing activities and assure the patent holder the royalties to which he is entitled under the patent, the patent has not been misused. And where, in addition, one of the patent holder's proposed terms of settlement is the termination of the infringement suit, there is no patent misuse. Essentially, the purpose of settlement negotiations is the termination of the suit involved. There is, therefore, little significance to be attached to its inclusion as an express term of the settlement by either of the parties.[260]

Interviewees offered a mixed response to the role of misuse in reverse payments. One lawyer interviewed considered reverse payments a "pure antitrust situation," and that patent misuse had no role to play.[261] A second lawyer agreed, noting that generic settlements were an "artifact of poor policy," citing the *Tamoxifen* case as an example of precedent entrenching bad policy.[262] Indeed, the Federal Trade Commission has indicated that it would consider challenging a pharmaceutical settlement agreement if a patent holder were to compensate a generic manufacturer

---

[258] *Asahi Glass Co. Ltd v. Pentech Pharms., Inc.*, 289 F. Supp.2d 986, 994 (N.D. Ill. 2003) ("A ban on reverse-payment settlements would reduce the incentive to challenge patents by reducing the challenger's settlement options should he be sued for infringement, and so might well be thought anticompetitive").

[259] *W. L. Gore & Assoc., Inc. v. Carlisle Corp.*, 529 F.2d 614, 623–25 (3d Cir. 1976).

[260] Ibid.

[261] On file with the author. ("I don't see it other than conceivably in circumstances where there is some tie. But that wouldn't really be related to the nature of the settlement. That would be something else going on.")

[262] *See In re Tamoxifen Citrate*, 466 F.3d 187, 213 (2d Cir. 2006) (noting that settlements, even with large reverse payments, are in the public interest and will violate the antitrust laws only if the terms of the settlement "extend[ed] . . . the monopoly beyond the patent's scope (or) . . . the patent was procured by 'fraud' or the underlying infringement lawsuit was 'objectively baseless'"); see also *Valley Drug Co. v. Geneva Pharm., Inc.*, 344 F.3d 1294, 1304–11 (11th Cir. 2003) (agreements were not *per se* unlawful to the extent that they had no broader exclusionary effect than that provided by patent for brand name drug; rejecting Sixth Circuit's *per se* analysis because, at this early stage of litigation, it did not appear that the "exclusionary effect[s] of the Agreements were bolstered by the exit payments to a degree that exceeds the potential exclusionary power of the patent").

to stay off the market beyond the expiry of the underlying patent.[263] However, as an academic who was interviewed pointed out, it would be difficult to rely on antitrust law, given the narrow reading of the instances where the settlement would be scrutinized under those rules.[264] He saw patent misuse as an alternative to correct what he viewed as an abuse of process—where the parties use the out-of-court settlement agreements to essentially divide and share the market for the drug, reducing the incentive to innovate in those markets due to the artificially high entry barriers.[265] A government official remarked:

> Settlements are seen as sacred. The firms gravitate in the direction of using set-tlements as a way to avoid possible criminal liability for horizontal price fixing. We know that if we have a conversation and I simply say, "I won't sell in your territory if you don't sell in mine," in the United States we'd both go to jail for it if we say yes. Change the scenario. You have a plant in Asia and I have a plant in North America. We both sell in each other's geographic areas. I'd say, "You're infringing." You'd say, "No, actually you're infringing." We say, "Oh, let's settle this dispute. You license your patent to me and I can sell only in North America, and I license a patent to you and you can only sell in Asia" in the context of what is said to be a resolution and settlement of an IP dispute with a geographic limitation built in. At a minimum, what I think that does, if Tamoxifen means what I think it means and Schering means, there won't be a grand jury for that. There will not be a criminal process. As a business decision-maker, that's a great relief. And maybe there won't be any civil liability either if the courts could say, "Oh, my goodness, it's an IP dispute. We can't decide unless we know whether the claims are valid and whether there was actual infringement. Come back to us when you figure that out."[266]

As with misconduct in the standard setting context, patent misuse has been raised in the reverse payment context. Professors Dan Burk and Mark Lemley observed that "one policy lever that will likely take on greater importance in the pharmaceutical industry than in biotechnology is patent misuse."[267] According to them, "[p]harmaceutical companies have gone to great lengths to try to extend the lawful scope of their patents, by collusively settling disputes with generic companies, strategically delaying

---

[263] See J. Thomas Rosch, FTC Litigation at the Antitrust/Intellectual Property Interface, Remarks of J. Thomas Rosch, Commissioner, Federal Trade Commission, at Law Seminars International, Pharmaceutical Antitrust (Apr. 26, 2007), available at: http://www.ftc.gov/speeches/rosch.shtm.

[264] On file with the author.

[265] Ibid.

[266] On file with the author.

[267] Dan L. Burk & Mark A. Lemley, *Biotechnology's Uncertainty Principle*, 54 CASE W. RES. L. REV. 691, 741 (2004).

prosecution of patents, and obtaining multiple patents covering the same invention."[268] In these situations, "[t]he patent misuse doctrine can play a powerful role in deterring anticompetitive efforts to extend patent rights beyond the scope a rational pharmaceutical patent policy would give."[269]

Courts have applied misuse to the pharmaceutical industry. *In re Gabapentin Patent Litigation*, the district court proposed a rule of reason framework to determine when delayed entry of lower priced pharmaceuticals could amount to misuse "where the patentee's conduct violates the public policies addressed by the patent laws." In particular, "policy interests favor the prompt issuance and expiration of patents so that the public's free access to inventions, and, more specifically, to lower-priced generic pharmaceuticals, is not further delayed."[270] In *Pfizer v. Apotex*, Pfizer owned a patent used to produce a drug prescribed to treat cardiovascular disease and prevent hypercholesterolemia.[271] It sued its competitor, Apotex, alleging patent infringement related to competitor's

---

[268]   Ibid.

[269]   More recently, commentators have proposed specific frameworks to apply misuse to pharmaceutical settlements. See Alyssa L. Brown, *Modest Proposals for A Complex Problem: Patent Misuse and Incremental Changes to the Hatch-Waxman Act as Solutions to the Problem of Reverse Payment Settlements*, 41 U. BALT. L. REV. 583, 606 (2012) ("Under this approach, a subsequent ANDA filer being sued by the innovator patent owner for infringement can respond with the defense that the brand-name manufacturer misused its patent. If successful, the innovator patent is invalidated, and the first ANDA filer would thus effectively forfeit its 180-day exclusivity period"); Cory J. Ingle, *Reverse Payment Settlements: a Patent Approach to Defending the Argument for Illegality*, 7 I/S: J. L. & POL'Y FOR INFO. SOC'Y 503, 538 (2012) ("First, a government agency such as the FDA, DOJ, FTC, or a private party, such as a class action group or an organization such as AARP, could charge the settling parties with a claim of misuse. Standing for these groups would be appropriate within the patent policy framework of misuse since the Court has explicitly stated that the public interest is critical as a policy lever. Next, a court would examine the reverse payment settlement and identify whether the settlement is suspicious and presumptively illegal. . . . If the settlement was found to fall into the presumptively illegal group, the patent would become unenforceable under misuse. The burden of showing that the brand name pharmaceutical company's patent was infringed would fall to the settling parties (misuse defendants)").

[270]   Finding that "Warner-Lambert's alleged efforts to delay the issuance of the '482 Patent in order to delay its expiration, thereby effectively broadening the temporal scope of the series of gabapentin patents held by Warner-Lambert and preserving an exclusive hold on the gabapentin market, may be found to contravene such policy," *In re Gabapentin*, 648 F.Supp.2d 641, 655 (D.N.J. 2009).

[271]   *Pfizer Inc. v. Apotex Inc.*, 2010 WL 3087458 (No. 08 C 7231) (N.D.Ill. 2010).

ANDA filing for production of a generic version of the drug.[272] Apotex argued that the settlement agreements Pfizer entered into with a potential generic competitor could amount to patent misuse.[273] The court, in granting discovery of Pfizer's documents in spite of Pfizer's protest that misuse allegations were speculative, recognized that:

> Pfizer cannot merely assert that no patent misuse occurred and direct Apotex to publicly available documents and press releases to confirm that. Apotex needn't take Pfizer's or Ranbaxy's word on whether Pfizer misused a patent. No sane defendant would. Because the settlement documents may be relevant to patent misuse, they are discoverable.[274]

The importance of misuse has been underscored by the cases which have refused to find reverse payments to be an antitrust violation because the conduct was within the scope of the patent. Commentators note that "[c]ourts have been extremely deferential to settling parties, even to the point of tolerating naked antitrust restraints."[275] Professors Hovenkamp and Bohannan observe that "[t]his deferential attitude toward anticompetitive patent settlements may reflect judges' eagerness to encourage parties to resolve their disputes privately."[276] However, they identify the "real source of the problem" as "the complete indeterminacy that the patent system creates with respect to ownership and priority of patent rights" and conclude that "if patent boundaries were clearer, we would almost certainly have many fewer anticompetitive settlement agreements."[277]

There are at least two further reasons why keeping misuse as a judicial safeguard should be explored. First, as with misconduct in standard setting, while competitors are normally the parties best placed and with the most incentive to challenge the validity of the patent, failure to do so results in a "sealed vacuum" because no second comer generic company can challenge the validity of the brand's patent. Second, the view that anticompetitive

---

[272] Ibid.

[273] Ibid. at *4.

[274] Ibid.

[275] Bohannan & Hovenkamp, *supra* note 83, at 992 (referring to the Federal Circuit's decision in *In re Ciprofloxacin Hydrochloride*, 544 F.3d at 1334–35).

[276] Bohannan & Hovenkamp, *supra* note 83, at 934.

[277] Ibid. ("No court would think twice about investigating the land tide records, determining that there was no property dispute here, and concluding that the whole charade was a cover for unlawful collusion. The difference in the pharmaceutical situation has nothing to do with any kind of deference to settlements generally. Rather, the reason is that the state of the 'title records' in patent law is so abysmal that courts are inclined to defer to the parties' judgments about them").

harm within the scope of the patent makes a misuse inquiry moot ignores the fact that misuse also safeguards abuses to the patent system. Patentees who seek to prevent challenges to potentially invalid patents they own by paying off their generic competitors prevent courts from weeding out the kind of blockages the Supreme Court in *Prometheus* warned about when it talked of monopolies that rewarded patentees beyond the contribution of the inventor which "might tend to impede innovation more than it would tend to promote it."[278]

B. Product Hopping

In addition to pay-for-delay settlements, brand firms at the end of a patent term have also engaged in "product hopping" by switching from one formulation of a drug to another. In *Provigil*, the patentee sought to switch consumers from Provigil, its branded drug, to Nuvigil, a reformulated version of Provigil, before generic Provigil reached the market.[279] The patentee projected that that generic entry would lead to up to a 90 percent price reduction and would lower revenues by more than $400 million, or nearly 75 percent of the annual sales within one year.[280] It sought to maintain its market share through a successor product offering modest improvements by allowing patients to take a pill once a day instead of two times daily.[281] State laws allow and often require pharmacists to substitute generic versions of brand name drugs. These laws allow pharmacists, who are more sensitive to drug prices than doctors to offer cheaper drugs to consumers. According to Professor Michael Carrier, product hopping limits price competition by avoiding these state laws and making it difficult to compare the quality of the reformulated drug with the old version.[282] The brand then promotes the new drug rather than the old one, and "evidence shows that patients who switch to the new drug are unlikely to switch back."[283] Both pay for delay settlements and product hopping rest on similar concerns, and it is likely that the applicability of misuse in

---

[278] *Mayo Collaborative Services v. Prometheus Laboratories, Inc.*, 132 S. Ct. 1289, 1293, 1303 (2012).

[279] Carrier, *supra* note 241, at 445–49.

[280] Ibid. at 443.

[281] Ibid.

[282] Ibid. at 446.

[283] Ibid. ("For example, in a product-hopping case involving the cholesterol drug TriCor, brand firm Fournier switched from a once-daily tablet taken with food to one taken without food. It conceded that such a change would not have "an expansive effect [on sales] on its own" but would have "a substantial benefit in avoiding losses of sales due to generics." Such a change would allow Fournier to

one area will determine its fate in other. Whether courts will allow patent misuse to play a meaningful role in these areas remains to be seen. One judge remarked that the "the defense is an important defense and given the right faces, it has some potential to be powerful."[284]

IV.   BEYOND PATENT MISUSE

While misconduct in standard setting and reverse payments in pharmaceutical settlements provide two possible forums for judges to expand the applicability of misuse, the doctrine of misuse is also found in the neighboring fields of copyright and trademark law. On one level, the issues facing the courts are the same: does such a doctrine exist within trademark or copyright law, and if so, which policies inform the doctrine and its development? On another level, how should courts approach rights that are also clearly distinct from patent rights?

A.   Copyright Misuse

Conventional wisdom points to the Fourth Circuit case of *Lasercomb America, Inc. v. Reynolds*, as the genesis of copyright misuse.[285] Lasercomb owned the copyright to a software program and licensed four copies of the software to Reynolds. Reynolds copied the software without Lasercomb's permission in order to develop a competing program. When Lasercomb sued, Reynolds argued that Lasercomb misused its copyright because the licensing agreement Lasercomb entered into with its licensees restricted

---

"sell more than ten times as many TriCor tablets than if the reformulated product competed head-to-head with the generic with simultaneous market entry").

[284]   Ibid. ("I think the defense is an important defense, and given the right facts, it has some potential to be powerful").

[285]   *Lasercomb Am., Inc. v. Reynolds*, 911 F.2d 970 (4th Cir, 1990). Karen E. Georgenson, *Reverse Engineering of Copyrighted Software: Fair Use or Misuse?*, 5 ALB. L.J. SCI. & TECH. 291, 315 (1996) ("Copyright misuse was not clearly defined until the Fourth Circuit case, Lasercomb America, Inc. v. Reynolds"); Jonas P. Herrell, *The Copyright Misuse Doctrine's Role in Open and Closed Technology Platforms*, 26 BERKELEY TECH. L.J. 441, 464 (2011) ("Copyright misuse was first successfully used in Lasercomb America, Inc. v. Reynolds"). Copyright misuse in fact antedates *Lasercomb*, and has been recognized as early as 1979 by the Court of Appeals for the Fifth Circuit in *Mitchell Bros. Film Group v. Cinema Adult Theater*, 604 F.2d 852, 865 (5th Cir. 1979), *cert. denied*, 445 U.S. 917(1980) ("In an appropriate case a misuse of the copyright statute that in some way subverts the purpose of the statute—the promotion of originality—might constitute a bar to judicial relief").

them from creating competing products. The Fourth Circuit, in a landmark decision, imported the principles of patent misuse into copyright law. This decision is remarkable for at least four reasons.

1. Patent misuse as the basis for copyright misuse

The *Lasercomb* court built copyright misuse upon patent misuse's doctrinal foundations.[286] The panel remarked that copyright law and patent law are symbiotically linked because both "seek to increase the store of human knowledge and arts by rewarding inventors and authors with the exclusive rights to their works for a limited time. At the same time, the granted monopoly power does not extend to property not covered by the patent or copyright."[287] It followed that the copyright misuse was a valid defense, "analogous to the misuse of patent defense."[288] Similar to patent misuse, an antitrust violation provides a successful basis for asserting a copyright misuse defense.[289] And as with patent misuse, the panel affirmed that copyright misuse could be raised by third parties not directly harmed by the misuse.[290] The panel also affirmed the view that misuse does not invalidate the right to the monopoly but only temporarily divests the owner of the right to legal remedy for vindication of his rights.[291] Once the misuse is purged, the right is restored.[292]

Subsequent cases have recognized the separate vein of copyright misuse jurisprudence carved out by *Lasercomb*. In *Assessment Technologies*,

---

[286]   *DSC Comm'cns Corp. v. DGI Techns.*, Inc., 81 F.3d 597 (5th Cir. 1996) ("In *Lasercomb*, the Fourth Circuit extended the rationale behind *Morton Salt* to copyright misuse. . . .We concur with the Fourth Circuit's characterization of the copyright misuse defense").

[287]   *Lasercomb Am., Inc.*, 911 F.2d at 976; see also *Atari Games Corp. v. Nintendo of Am. Inc.*, 975 F.2d 832, 846 (Fed. Cir. 1992) ("Numerous cases suggest that the purpose and policy of patent misuse apply as well to copyright. *See, e.g., Sony Corp.*, 464 U.S. 417, 439 (1984); *United States v. Paramount Pictures*, 334 U.S. 131, 157–59 (1948); *Mitchell Bros.*, 604 F.2d, 852, 865 (5th Cir. 1979); *Bellsouth*, 933 F.2d, 952, 960–61 (11th Cir. 1991)").

[288]   *Lasercomb Am., Inc.*, 911 F.2d at 976.

[289]   *F.E.L. Publications, Ltd. v. Catholic Bishop*, 506 F. Supp. 1127 (N.D.Ill.1981), *rev'd*, 214 U.S.P.Q. 409 (7th Cir.), *cert. denied*, 459 U.S. 859 (1982) (recognizing that misuse of a copyright, in violation of the antitrust laws, may be asserted as a defense in copyright infringement cases).

[290]   Reynolds was the owner of the defendant business corporation and not privy to the license agreement. He was, however, the one being sued, and it seemed reasonable to the court that that legal technicality should not pose an obstacle to him raising the misuse defense. Ibid. at 979.

[291]   *F.E.L. Publications, Ltd*, 506 F. Supp. at 1136.

[292]   Ibid.

LLC v. WIREdata. Inc., the Court of Appeals for the Seventh Circuit held that market power "by virtue of its having a copyright on one system for compiling valuation data for real estate tax assessment purposes" was irrelevant in determining whether there was misuse.[293] On the facts, the copyright plaintiff was the sole source of public domain tax assessment data, which was entered into the copyrighted database. The plaintiff's use of its copyright in the database prevented access to the uncopyrighted data with the effect that public domain data is foreclosed in violation of copyright policy.[294] In the Court's opinion, "[c]ases such as *Lasercomb*, however, cut misuse free from antitrust, pointing out that the cognate doctrine of patent misuse is not so limited."[295]

2.   Intellectual property policy animates copyright misuse

The *Lasercomb* court held that "misuse need not be a violation of antitrust law in order to comprise an equitable defense to an infringement action" because "the question is not whether the copyright is being used in a manner violative of antitrust law . . . but whether the copyright is being used in a manner violative of the public policy embodied in the grant of a copyright."[296] It recognized that "copyright law seek[s] to increase the store of human knowledge and arts by awarding . . . authors with the exclusive rights to their works for a limited time . . . the granted monopoly power does not extend to property not covered by the . . . copyright."[297]

---

[293]   *Assessment Tech., LLC v. WIREdata, Inc.*, 350 F.3d 640, 647 (7th Cir. 2003).

[294]   Ibid.

[295]   Ibid. The court explained: "The argument for applying copyright misuse beyond the bounds of antitrust, besides the fact that confined to antitrust the doctrine would be redundant, is that for a copyright owner to use an infringement suit to obtain property protection, here in data, that copyright law clearly does not confer, hoping to force a settlement or even achieve an outright victory over an opponent that may lack the resources or the legal sophistication to resist effectively, is an abuse of process," ibid.

[296]   See *Lasercomb Am., Inc.*, 911 F.2d at 978; see also *M. Witmark & Sons v. Jensen*, 80 F. Supp. 843, 849–50 (D. Minn. 1948), *appeal dismissed*, 177 F.2d 515 (8th Cir. 1949) (*per curiam*) (holding that ASCAP violated the Sherman Act and committed copyright misuse by fixing prices and monopolizing the market for musical works integrated into motion pictures).

[297]   *Lasercomb Am., Inc.*, 911 F.2d at 976. Paraphrasing Morton Salt, the Fourth Circuit in *Lasercomb* stated that the Constitutional mandate underpinning copyright law precluded protection "not embraced in the original expression [and] . . . equally forbids the use of the copyright to secure an exclusive right or limited monopoly not granted by the Copyright Office and which it is contrary to public policy to grant," ibid. at 977. See also *DSC Comm. Corp v. DGI Tech.*, Inc

The Supreme Court in *United States v. Paramount Pictures, Inc.*, explained that copyrights reward authors for market power stemming from "the products of [their] creative genius,"[298] and once inferior works are bundled with superior ones, this artificially props it up and inflates the reward accruing to the copyright owner.[299] Recently, the First Circuit, while noting that it has not recognized copyright misuse, acknowledged *Lasercomb's* formulation based on "(1) a violation of the antitrust laws or (2) that [the copyright owner] otherwise illegally extended its copyright monopoly or violated the public policies underlying the copyright laws."[300] It is remarkable that courts today do so in spite of the dominance of the Federal Circuit's misuse jurisprudence and the waning of *Morton Salt* over the years.[301]

Remarkable also is the fact that the copyright owner's conduct manifests itself as anticompetitive conduct, which continues to make it a relevant inquiry under misuse rather than antitrust law, as where the Seventh Circuit noted that "[m]isuse of copyright in pursuit of an anticompetitive end may be a defense to a suit for infringement, along the lines of the patent-misuse doctrine in antitrust."[302] In *DSC Communications Corp v. DGI Technologies*, the Fifth Circuit found that the copyright owner attempted to use its copyright in its software to obtain "a patent-like

---

81 F.3d 597 (5th Cir. 1996) ("We concur with the Fourth Circuit's characterization of the copyright misuse defense"); *Alcatel Inc. v. DGI Tech., Inc.*, 166 F.3d 772, 792 (5th Cir. 1999) ("The copyright misuse defense is analogous to the patent misuse defense, which was originally recognized by the Supreme Court in Morton Salt Co. v. G.S. Suppiger").

[298]   *United States v. Paramount Pictures*, 334 U.S. 131, 158 (1948).

[299]   Ibid., at 158 ("Where a high quality film greatly desired is licensed only if an inferior one is taken, the latter borrows quality from the former and strengthens its monopoly by drawing on the other. The practice tends to equalize rather than differentiate the reward for individual copyrights. Even where all the films included in the package are of equal quality, the requirement that all be taken if one is desired increases the market for some. Each stands not on its own footing but in whole or in part on the appeal which another film may have. As the District Court said, the result is to add to the monopoly of the copyright in violation of the principle of the patent cases involving tying clauses").

[300]   *Soc'y of the Holy Transfiguration Monastery, Inc. v. Gregory*, 689 F.3d 29, 65–66 (1st Cir. 2012), citing *Broad. Music Inc.*, 1995 WL 803576, at *5 (citing *Lasercomb*, 911 F.2d at 978).

[301]   See, e.g., *DSC Comm. Corp v. DGI Tech., Inc.*, 81 F.3d at 601 (noting that "[t]he copyright misuse defense is analogous to the patent misuse defense. The patent misuse defense was recognized by the Supreme Court in *Morton Salt Co. v. G.S. Suppiger*.")

[302]   *Reed-Union Corp. v. Turtle Wax, Inc.*, 77 F.3d 909, 913 (7th Cir. 1996).

monopoly over unpatented microprocessor cards" based on the need for compatibility.[303] Since reverse engineering is lawful even if the protected expression is copied as an intermediate process, a restriction forbidding it clearly contradicts it. In a later related case, *Alcatel USA, Inc. v. DGI Technologies, Inc.*, the software license agreement provided that the software was "licensed to customers to be used only in conjunction with DSC-manufactured hardware," and such hardware included expansion cards.[304] To develop compatible cards, the defendant had to download and copy the software for testing and development purposes.[305] This would, however, breach the licensing agreement. The Fifth Circuit held that the restrictive terms of the licensing agreement constituted copyright misuse.

In *Apple Inc. v. Psystar Corp.*, the Ninth Circuit distinguished *Alcatal*.[306] The Court found that "[t]he copyright misuse doctrine does not prohibit using conditions to control use of copyrighted material, but it does prevent copyright holders from using the conditions to stifle competition."[307] The copyright owner did not prevent licensees from developing their own software or it precluded customers from using third party components with its computers and "effectively prohibited the licensee from using any competing expansion cards."[308] In *Apple*, the license agreement "merely restricts the use of [the copyright owner's] own software to its own hardware" and "represents the legitimate exercise of a copyright holder's right to conditionally transfer works of authorship . . ."[309] Accordingly, the licensee was not allowed to copy the copyright owner's operating software to run competing hardware.

More recently, copyright misuse has been considered in the context of takedown notifications under the Digital Millennium Copyright Act

---

[303]   *DSC Comm. Corp.*, 81 F.3d at 601. (The court explained that "[a]ny competing microprocessor card developed for use on DSC phone switches must be compatible with DSC's copyrighted operating system software. In order to ensure that its card is compatible, a competitor such as DGI must test the card on a DSC phone switch. Such a test necessarily involves making a copy of DSC's copyrighted operating system, which copy is downloaded into the card's memory when the card is booted up. If DSC is allowed to prevent such copying, then it can prevent anyone from developing a competing microprocessor card, even though it has not patented the card.")

[304]   *Alcatel Inc.*, 166 F.3d at 793.

[305]   Ibid. at 779.

[306]   *Apple Inc. v. Psystar Corp.*, 658 F.3d 1150, 1159–60 (9th Cir. 2011).

[307]   Ibid. at 1159.

[308]   Ibid. at 1160.

[309]   Ibid.

(DMCA) in *Amaretto Ranch Breedables, LLC v. Ozimals, Inc.*[310] The copyright owner and infringer were competitors selling virtual animals to online gamers in an online universe known as Second Life for real-world money. The copyright owner, Ozimals, filed a DMCA Takedown Notice accusing Amaretto's virtual horses copyright of infringement of its virtual bunnies, and required Linden Research Inc., who administered Second Life, to empty Amaretto's virtual feed troughs and water, which would result in Amaretto's virtual animals starving and disrupting Amaretto's business "during a critical selling season."[311] Both parties agree that there was no literal copying, but disagree as to whether there was non-literal copying of traits using different source code. Amaretto alleged, amongst other things, copyright misuse.[312] The court's misuse rubric was based on the idea that "[t]he doctrine 'forbids the use of the [copyright] to secure an exclusive right or limited monopoly not granted by the [Copyright] Office and which is contrary to public policy to grant'."[313] While noting that "[t]here is no consensus on whether copyright misuse can be brought as an independent claim (as opposed to as an affirmative defense) and district courts come down on both sides of the issue,"[314] the court was prepared to deny Ozimals' Motion to Dismiss on the basis that "an independent claim for copyright misuse [was] proper".[315]

These cases show that copyright misuse is intimately tied to copyright policy. Its continued presence in the evolving media that copyright cases appear in suggests that its relevance will remain a part of the landscape for the foreseeable future. This last observation leads to the next remarkable feature of copyright misuse.

3.   Copyright misuse is more established today than patent misuse

Despite the Supreme Court never formally recognizing copyright misuse, it has outpaced patent misuse in garnering recognition as an equitable defense to infringement. As Professor Thomas Cotter noted, "[w]hatever the current state of patent misuse may be, it is clear that copyright misuse, as currently understood by several circuit courts, goes well beyond the

---

[310]   *Amaretto Ranch Breedables, LLC v. Ozimals, Inc.*, 790 F. Supp. 2d 1024 (N.D. Cal. 2011).
[311]   Ibid. at 1027.
[312]   Ibid. at 1027–28.
[313]   Ibid. at 1033, citing *Altera Corp. v. Clear Logic, Inc.*, 424 F.3d 1079, 1090 (9th Cir. 2005) (quoting *Alcatel USA, Inc. v. DGI Techs., Inc.*, 166 F.3d 772, 792 (5th Cir. 1999)).
[314]   Ibid.
[315]   Ibid. at n. 7.

contours of antitrust law."[316] One reason that copyright misuse might enjoy wider acceptance than patent misuse could be because it exists to protect the public domain and implicates the free speech interest enshrined in the Constitution. The additional mix of the constitutional right and free speech makes the nature of copyright misuse different from patent misuse. It is more than simply one based on the utilitarian justifications purportedly driving American IP law. Nor does it merely accommodate the reality that copyright is increasingly viewed as a form of misappropriation or unfair competition, to regulate interstate or international commerce.[317] Justice Steven Breyer explained that both seek to create and disseminate information by being an "engine of free expression" and "assuring that government throws up no obstacle to its dissemination."[318]

Interviewees who had a view on this issue agreed and observed that there was more justification for developing copyright misuse compared to patent misuse both because copyright implicates free speech interests and because they saw the expansion of copyright in recent years as warranting a counterbalance.[319] This was interesting given the fact that copyright

---

[316] Thomas F. Cotter, *Misuse*, 44 Hous. L. Rev. 901, 925 (2007). See Raymond T. Nimmer & Murali Santhanam, *The Concept of Misuse in Copyright and Trademark Law: Searching for a Concept of Restraint*, 524 PLI/PAT 397, 418–19 (Practicing Law Institute ed., 1998) (noting that *Lasercomb* held that to constitute a misuse, the impugned practice should seek to achieve an object or employ means that are against the policy objectives of the copyright law).

[317] *Eldred v. Ashcroft*, 537 U.S. 186, 263 (U.S. 2003) (Breyer, dissenting) ("I recognize that Congress has sometimes found that suppression of competition will help Americans sell abroad—though it has simultaneously taken care to protect American buyers from higher domestic prices. In doing so, however, Congress has exercised its commerce, not its copyright, power. I can find nothing in the Copyright Clause that would authorize Congress to enhance the copyright grant's monopoly power, likely leading to higher prices both at home and abroad, solely in order to produce higher foreign earnings. That objective is not a copyright objective. Nor, standing alone, is it related to any other objective more closely tied to the Clause itself. Neither can higher corporate profits alone justify the grant's enhancement. The Clause seeks public, not private, benefits").

[318] Ibid. at 244.

[319] On file with the author. See also Daryl Lim, *Copyright Under Siege: An Economic Analysis of the Essential Facilities Doctrine and the Compulsory Licensing of Copyrighted Works*, 17 ALB. L.J. SCI. & TECH. 481, 555–56 (2007) ("There is no retreat from the growth of copyright over functional works. Business needs shape the law. As economies become more technology dependent, the case for exclusive rights in database and software industries will be more compelling. To reduce the commercial risks from misappropriation in already risky ventures, businesses appreciate and, in some cases, demand the security that copyright provides in safeguarding their investments. This is not ideal, as it trades one form of risk for

law has a safety valve in the form of the fair use doctrine, which has no parallel in patent law. On the other hand, functional works such as software more closely approximate the subject matter typically protected under patent law. Yet paradoxically Professor Raymond Nimmer and Santhanam observe that "[t]he decisions show that the misuse defense has received more acceptance in copyright relating to computer software products."[320] One reason for this is because "the commercial life of the copyrighted work is fleeting in proportion to the term of the copyright." Another is that "the market for the work is also not so pervasive as in the case of other copyrighted works. The cost of development of such works is also comparatively high."[321] These cumulatively "combine to impel the holder to adopt measures that would ensure recouping of the investment, stabilizing market presence and reaping rewards. These measures may present the aura of misuse to a court applying vague concepts of equity in light of its own views of what scope of leverage a property rights owner should have."[322] With the expansion of copyright into functional works like software, copyright misuse will likely be asserted more generally by copyright defendants and received with greater receptiveness by courts. This is because functional or informational works such as computer programs and databases, unlike expressive ones such as traditional forms of literary and artistic works, cut close to the bone of the idea/expression dichotomy. Since the purpose of conferring copyright protection is to incentivize the dissemination of ideas for "the Progress of Science and the useful Arts," that objective will be frustrated if others cannot use or build upon those ideas.[323]

Another reason for the difference between copyright and patent misuse may be the inherent differences between the nature of the rights concerned and how they are obtained. Unlike patents, copyrighted works requires no

---

another—the risk that information gets balkanised by copyright owners control-ling access to interface information or raw data").

[320] See Nimmer & Santhanam, *supra* note 316.

[321] Ibid.

[322] Ibid.

[323] See *Sony Corp. v. Universal City Studios*, 464 U.S. 417, 431–32 (1984) (explaining that "the limited scope of the copyright holder's statutory monopoly . . . reflects a balance of competing claims upon the public interest: Creative work is to be encouraged and rewarded, but private motivation must ultimately serve the cause of promoting broad public availability of literature, music, and the other arts," and therefore, the "ultimate aim" of copyright law is "to stimulate artistic creativity for the general public good").

substantive examination.[324] On the other hand, the scope of the exclusive right is thinner in copyright. For example, copyright extends only to the expression of the idea and not to the idea itself; patent rights cover the idea itself.[325] The copyright defendant is exculpated if he can show independent creation. In the same situation, the patent defendant remains liable. The fair use defense provides use of the copyrighted work to create "transformative works" which may use a substantial portion of the work itself to produce a work which competes directly with the original.[326] Patent rights not only bar identical inventions, but extend under the doctrine of equivalents to bar inventions with insubstantial differences, or which perform the same function in the same way to achieve the same result. Scott Miskimon, an attorney, noted that for some of these reasons—in particular the 'economic power' afforded by a patent—"the danger to the public interest is greater when a patentee seeks to enlarge his monopoly than when a copyright holder acts similarly".[327] This observation begs the question why patent misuse should be any less robust than copyright misuse, particularly given that the nearly identical contours of the fair use defense arguably serve to check anticompetitive abuses of the copyright owner's exclusive rights. In this regard Professors Peter Yu and John Cross have identified four types of copyright misuse: "(1) the use of copyright to exact concessions from the licensee; (2) restriction of the licensee's ability to deal with the copyright owner's competitors; (3) dealings that limit others' ability to compete; and (4) the anticompetitive use of the judicial system."[328] As to the last type of misuse, the case of *Assessment Technologies of WI, LLC v. WIREdata, Inc.*

---

[324]   See Donald W. King et al., COST-BENEFIT ANALYSIS OF U.S. COPYRIGHT FORMALITIES 35 (1987) ("[the] Copyright Office does not generally examine works for artistic merit or newness, nor (as misperceived by individuals in the US) does it 'examine' works to determine if the work is in fact an 'original' work.).

[325]   *Baker v. Selden*, 101 U.S. 99 (1879) (holding that while exclusive rights to the bookkeeping described in a book might be available by patent, only the expression of the method of bookkeeping was protectable by copyright).

[326]   *Campbell v. Acuff-Rose Music, Inc.*, 510 U.S. 569, 579 (1994) ("the goal of copyright, to promote science and the arts, is generally furthered by the creation of transformative works. Such works thus lie at the heart of the fair use doctrine's guarantee of breathing space within the confines of copyright, and the more transformative the new work, the less will be the significance of other factors, like commercialism, that may weigh against a finding of fair use").

[327]   Scott A. Miskimon, *Divorcing Public Policy From Economic Reality: The Fourth Circuit's Copyright Misuse Doctrine In Lasercomb America, Inc. v. Reynolds*, 69 N.C. L. REV. 1672, 1689 (1990).

[328]   John T. Cross & Peter K. Yu, *Competition Law and Copyright Misuse* (Mich. St. U. College of Law Legal Studies Research, Research Paper No. 04-29, 2007), available at: http://ssrn.com/abstract=986891.

provides an illustration. In that case, the Court of Appeals for the Seventh Circuit acknowledged that "for a copyright owner to use an infringement suit to obtain property protection, here in data, that copyright law clearly does not confer, hoping to force a settlement or even achieve an outright victory over an opponent that may lack the resources or the legal sophistication to resist effectively, is an abuse of process."[329]

At the same time declaratory judgments are less controversial in a case involving patent misuse than copyright misuse. In *Shirokov v. Dunlap, Grubb & Weaver PLLC*, the District Court for the District of Massachusetts observed that courts were divided on whether defendants could assert copyright misuse as a declaratory judgment.[330] However, because the First Circuit did not yet "recognize the doctrine even as a defense," it found it more prudent to hold that copyright misuse could not be brought as an independent course of action.[331]

4. Opponents of copyright misuse

Like patent misuse, the *Lasercomb* decision roused its share of opponents. Some, like attorney James Kobak Jr., point out that determining the scope of a copyright is even more difficult to discern than patent misuse because there is nothing analogous to a patent claim that defines the outer limits of the work of authorship.[332] Judge Richard Posner, drawing upon his earlier opinion in *USM Corp v. SPS Technologies*, rejected creating "a federal common law rule that would jostle uncomfortably with the Sherman Act."[333] He cautioned that copyright misuse was even more redundant than patent misuse since "the danger of monopoly is less," and held the contested licensing clause valid "unless shown to violate antitrust law."[334]

---

[329] *Assessment Tech., LLC v. WIREdata, Inc.*, 350 F.3d 640, 647 (7th Cir. 2003).

[330] *Shirokov v. Dunlap, Grubb & Weaver PLLC*, 2012 U.S. Dist. LEXIS 42787, at *99 (D. Mass. Mar. 1, 2012).

[331] Ibid. at 100.

[332] See James B. Kobak, Jr., *A Sensible Doctrine of Misuse for Intellectual Property Cases*, 2 ALB. L.J. SCI. & TECH. 1, 33 (1992) (noting that copyright has "no comparable system of examination and public disclosure of precise, carefully defined claims").

[333] See *Saturday Evening Post Co. v. Rumbleseat Press, Inc.*, 816 F.2d 1191, 1200 (7th Cir. 1987).

[334] Ibid.; see *also* James A.D. White, *Misuse or Fair Use: That is the Software Copyright Question*, 12 BERKELEY TECH. L.J. 251, 260–63 (1997) (discussing the debate between proponents of the antitrust-based and public policy-based approaches). See also Aaron Xavier Fellmeth, *Copyright Misuse and the Limits of the Intellectual Property Monopoly*, 6 J. INTELL. PROP. L. 1, 39 (1998) ("The patent misuse defense, upon which the copyright misuse defense is partially based,

Work done by Professors Brett Frischmann and Dan Moylan confirm that "[m]ost of the opinions rejecting the copyright misuse defense on the facts have applied antitrust principles. The Seventh and Eighth Circuits have employed a rule of reason analysis to assess the anticompetitive effects of alleged misuse."[335]

Thus while copyright misuse has been better received than patent misuse, it continues to face the challenge of justifying its existence. This may be because, as Professor Nimmer and Santhanam suggest, "[t]he nature of the right and the limitations on the right built into the statute combine together to reduce the opportunities for use of the doctrine," and consequently, "[t]he cases in copyright law on misuse doctrine shows a far less aggressive use of the doctrine."[336] The Supreme Court in *Eldred v. Ashcroft* also signaled a shift from its earlier position in *Paramount Pictures* where analysis was based on a utilitarian reward sufficient to induce authorial creativity for the public good toward a copyright regime more closely resembling a blend between foreign trade policy and a misappropriation doctrine where "what is worth copying is worth protecting."[337] According to Professor Thomas Cotter, in order to provide useful jurisprudential guidance for determining whether misuse

---

is itself a confused doctrine. Courts have been unable to agree exactly how the defense differs from an antitrust claim. The patent misuse doctrine should be reformed before the copyright misuse doctrine proceeds further along the same incoherent lines of development").

[335]   Brett Frischmann, & Dan Moylan, *The Evolving Common Law Doctrine of Copyright Misuse: A Unified Theory and Its Application to Software*, 15 BERKELEY TECH. L.J. 865, 897 (2000).

[336]   See Nimmer & Santhanam, *supra* note 316, at 403.

[337]   *Univ. of London Press v. Univ. Tutorial Press* [1916] 2 Ch 601, 610. *Eldred v. Ashcroft*, 537 U.S. 186, 242 (2003) (holding that the Copyright Term Extension Act was a rational exercise of the legislative authority conferred by the Copyright Clause. The majority's views may be contrasted with the voices in the dissent) ("By failing to protect the public interest in free access to the products of inventive and artistic genius—indeed, by virtually ignoring the central purpose of the Copyright/Patent Clause—the Court has quitclaimed to Congress its principal responsibility in this area of the law" (Stevens J., dissenting)); ibid. 254, 262 ("What copyright-related benefits might justify the statute's extension of copyright protection? First, no one could reasonably conclude that copyright's traditional economic rationale applies here. The extension will not act as an economic spur encouraging authors to create new works. . . . I recognize that Congress has sometimes found that suppression of competition will help Americans sell abroad—though it has simultaneously taken care to protect American buyers from higher domestic prices. In doing so, however, Congress has exercised its commerce, not its copyright, power. I can find nothing in the Copyright Clause that would authorize Congress to enhance the copyright grant's monopoly power, likely leading to higher prices both at home

has taken place, cases need to go beyond "focusing attention on a relative handful of recurring situations such as contractual restrictions on reverse engineering or fair use."[338] As with patent misuse precedent, advocates of copyright misuse must also deal with prior decisions that may be dubious in light of contemporary economic theory.[339] In both respects, it appears that getting patent misuse straightened out will be a crucial first step.

B. Trademark Misuse

It is intriguing that of the three misuse doctrines found in each main artery of IP law, trademark misuse is the oldest and yet perhaps the least known and used.[340] In 1883, the Supreme Court in *Manhattan Medicine Co. v. Wood* held that:

> [A] court of equity will extend no aid to sustain a claim to a trade-mark of an article which is put forth with a misrepresentation to the public as to the manufacturer of the article, and as to the place where it is manufactured, both of which particulars were originally circumstances to guide the purchaser of the medicine.[341]

---

and abroad, *solely* in order to produce higher foreign earnings. That objective is not a *copyright* objective" (Breyer J., dissenting)).

[338] Cotter, *supra* note 316 at 963 ("In addition, courts should work towards developing a more predictable set of criteria for determining whether misuse has occurred, focusing attention on a relative handful of recurring situations such as contractual restrictions on reverse engineering or fair use").

[339] In reference to *Brulotte*, Tom Cotter notes that "[s]imilar critiques might be raised against arguments that restraints conditioning access to an IPR upon the user's agreement to buy or license some aftermarket product or service expand the scope of the copyright grant, despite the fact that they do so only in a very formalistic sense and are anticompetitive only in the (most likely) uncommon setting in which monopoly leveraging is a plausible outcome. To the extent such restraints facilitate price discrimination their enforceability should turn on the desirability (or not) of enabling such discrimination," Cotter, *supra* note 316, at n. 169.

[340] See Nimmer & Santhanam, *supra* note 316, at 424 (stating that trademark misuse existed before patent of copyright misuse and that equity would not allow a claim to trademark if that claim misrepresented to the public); William E. Ridgway, *Revitalizing the Doctrine of Trademark Misuse*, 21 BERKELEY TECH. L.J. 1547, 1553 (2006) ("Courts first applied the doctrine of misuse to a trademark dispute in 1883, long before its application to other intellectual property").

[341] *Manhattan Medicine Co. v. Wood*, 108 U.S. 218, 222 (1883); Nimmer & Santhanam, *supra* note 316, at 424 (stating that trademark misuse existed before patent or copyright misuse and that equity would not allow a claim to trademark if that claim misrepresented to the public).

Today, trademark misuse is still discussed and a case for its revitalization has been trenchantly made by true believers.[342] Like patent and copyright misuse, trademark misuse has been used in a variety of settings, including post-expiration royalties,[343] vexatious litigation,[344] and use of internet domain names to exclude competition.[345] Generally, trademarks are seen to give rise to fewer anticompetitive concerns than copyright or patents. The Court in *Clorox Co. v. Sterling Winthrop, Inc.* wrote that "[a] trademark, unlike other intellectual property rights, does not confer a legal monopoly on any good or idea; it confers rights to a name only."[346] It observed that because a trademark prevents others from using the mark "as distinguished from competitive manufacture and sale of identical goods bearing another mark," "effective antitrust misuse of a trademark" was limited compared to patent misuse.[347]

---

[342] William E. Ridgway, *Revitalizing the Doctrine of Trademark Misuse*, 21 BERKELEY TECH. L.J. 1547 (2006) (arguing that "trademarks protect society rather than creators and that the boundaries of the right depend more upon fairness-based factors—render trademark law more amenable to an equitable doctrine of misuse than patent and copyright law, especially if the doctrine monitors enforcement decisions and curbs overprotection"); Charles E. Colman, Trademark Misuse: Crafting a Safety Valve for a Normatively Deficient Body of Law (Oct. 8, 2012) (unpublished manuscript), available at: http://papers.ssrn.com/sol3/papers.cfm?abstract_id=2158863 (arguing that "the federal courts must welcome into the fold this long neglected defense").

[343] See *Leviton Mfg. Co. v. Universal Sec. Instruments, Inc.*, 304 F. Supp. 2d 726 (D.Md. 2004) (alleging that the trademark owner sued to induce the defendant to "pay large royalties in perpetuity" for use of Leviton's trade dress).

[344] See *U.S. Jaycees v. Cedar Rapids Jaycees*, 794 F.2d 379 (8th Cir. 1986) (detailing a local affiliate who alleged that a service mark owner's revocation of a license because the affiliate admitted women with full voting rights against the affiliate's own by-laws was misuse and the mark owner later amended their own laws but persisted with a suit against the local affiliate).

[345] *Juno Online Servs. v. Juno Lighting, Inc.*, 979 F. Supp. 684, 690 (N.D. Ill. 1997) ("While, Juno Online does claim that Juno Lighting tried to use its government granted marks to put Juno Online out of business, there is no factual allegation backing up this conclusory statement. Plaintiff does not allege that defendant's purpose in asserting its rights under the NSI policy was to derive a competitive advantage over Juno Online, which, on its face, would be an absurd allegation considering that the two entities are involved in completely different businesses. Furthermore, while defendant did obtain the domain name 'juno-online.com', there is no evidence that would lead a reasonable trier of fact to conclude that Juno Lighting attempted to confuse Internet users by using the domain name 'juno-online.com'.... Therefore, the only remedy sought via plaintiff's affirmative claim for trademark misuse that it could not receive otherwise is compensatory damages").

[346] *Clorox Co. v. Sterling Winthrop, Inc.*, 117 F.3d 50, 56 (2d Cir. 1997).

[347] Ibid.

Courts have, however, been reluctant to apply the trademark misuse doctrine even to conduct that contravenes trademark policy's goal of preventing the monopolization of words and symbols. One example is the case of *Whirlpool Props. v. LG Elecs. U.S.A.*[348] The Court in that case agreed with the defendants that the trademark owner was attempting "to suppress all use of the words Whisper Quiet in connection with any household appliances, even uses that are descriptive only and would fall under the fair use doctrine."[349] The Court, however, finding no authority "that would grant an alleged infringer a claim or defense based on a trademark owner's attempts to expand the use of its trademark beyond its legal bounds" candidly concluded that "[a]lthough the concept of patent misuse is well developed, the doctrine of trademark misuse is nonexistent."[350] It explained that:

> This is undoubtedly attributable to the fundamental differences between patent rights and trademark rights. A patent represents a limited monopoly created by law. A trademark, by contrast, creates no monopoly or property rights. Unlike overly aggressive assertion of patent rights, which can curtail production and stifle competition, assertion of trademark rights where they do not exist excludes no one from the market. For whatever reason, the courts have not recognized an inequitable defense for trademark misuse, and this court will not be the first one to innovate in this area.[351]

Even where courts are willing to recognize the doctrine of trademark misuse, they do so in a limited fashion. One reason fueling this reluctance is the view that trademark misuse exists only to prevent misrepresentations rather than to correct anticompetitive conduct. The District Court for the Northern District of Illinois in *Northwestern Corp. v. Gabriel Mfg. Co.* wrote that "the policy underpinning trademark protection is not a constitutional mandate, such as the one which creates patents."[352] Since trademarks distinguish between competing products, it was "inappropriate to predicate trademark misuse upon the same anticompetitive practices which comprise patent misuse."[353] Instead, it was based on the policy of

---

[348] *Whirlpool Props. v. LG Elecs. U.S.A.*, No. 1:03-cv-414, 2005 U.S. Dist. LEXIS 30311 (W.D. Mich. Nov. 17, 2005).

[349] Ibid. at *90–92 ("As the court has noted above, Whirlpool's enforcement efforts have clearly been overly aggressive").

[350] Ibid. at *91.

[351] Ibid. at *91–92.

[352] *Nw. Corp. v. Gabriel Mfg. Co.*, No. 95 C 2004, 1998 U.S. Dist. LEXIS 12763, at *25–26 (N.D. Ill. Aug. 14, 1998).

[353] Ibid.

"providing consumers with clear product identifiers."[354] In such situations, "trademark misuse defense will permit the court to exercise its equitable powers and deny enforcement of the trademark."[355] To support this view, the court in *Northwestern Corp.* turned to a 1903 Supreme Court decision of *Clinton E. Worden & Co v. California Fig Syrup Co.*[356] In that case, the Court found that the trademark owner misrepresented his product "Syrup of Figs," because it contained no figs. It held that:

> when the owner of a trade-mark applies for an injunction to restrain the defend-ant from injuring his property . . . it is essential that the plaintiff should not in his trade-mark, or in his advertisements and business, be himself guilty of any false or misleading representation; that if the plaintiff makes any material false statement in connection with the property which he seeks to protect, he loses his right to claim the assistance of a court of equity . . .[357]

However, other courts have recognized antitrust analysis applies as equally in trademark cases as they do in patent and copyright misuse cases. In *Juno Online Services*, a case decided by the Northern District of Illinois, the court recognized that while "[t]he misuse defense has also enjoyed a substantial history in the field of trademarks. However, courts have taken different approaches in applying the defense in this field."[358] Referring to *Clinton E. Worden & Co.*, the court recognized that "[s]ome courts have applied trademark misuse in situations where the mark is being used to violate the antitrust laws,"[359] while "[o]ther courts have relied on the 'clean hands' doctrine and found misuse even where there was no antitrust violation."[360] As to a case in the first category, a Missouri district court in *Phi Delta Theta Fraternity v. J.A. Buchroeder & Co.* applied trademark misuse and found sufficient basis for trademark misuse under § 33(b)(7) of the Lanham Act, which provides as one of the defects or defenses to a trademark becoming incontestable the use of the mark to violate antitrust

---

[354] Ibid.

[355] Ibid.

[356] *Clinton E. Worden & Co. v. California Fig Syrup Co.*, 187 U.S. 516 (1903).

[357] Ibid. at 528.

[358] *Juno Online Servs., L.P. v. Juno Lighting*, 979 F. Supp. 684, 688 (N.D. Ill. 1997).

[359] Ibid.; see *Carl Zeiss Stiftung v. V.E.B. Carl Zeiss, Jena*, 298 F. Supp. 1309, 1315 (S.D.N.Y. 1969) ("An essential element of the antitrust misuse defense in a trademark case is proof that the mark itself has been the basic and fundamental vehicle required and used to accomplish the violation").

[360] Ibid.; see *Clinton E. Worden & Co.*, 187 U.S. at 539–40.

laws.[361] However, in *Carl Zeiss Stiftung v. N.E.B. Zeiss*, the district court recognized that trademarks did not give a monopoly over the goods and services sold,[362] and consequently that:

> Since denial of a plaintiff's exclusive right to the use of his trademark is not essential to the restoration of competition, it is not enough merely to prove that merchandise bearing a trademark, however valuable the trademark, has been used in furtherance of antitrust violations. If this is all that were required, any antitrust violation in the distribution of such merchandise would result in a forfeiture of the trademark with a consequent unnecessary frustration of the policy underlying trademark enforcement. An essential element of the antitrust misuse defense in a trademark case is proof that the mark itself has been the basic and fundamental vehicle required and used to accomplish the violation.[363]

Might there be a better explanation for why courts like the one in *Carl Zeiss Stiftung* prefer to raise the bar for trademark misuse claims? It seems that the reason compelling a narrower view of trademark misuse than patent or copyright misuse may lie in trademark policy itself. Professor Thomas McCarthy explains that since trademark law exists to protect the public from consumer confusion, the effect of courts liberally upholding misuse defenses would be to risk introducing more confusingly similar marks into the marketplace.[364] Hovenkamp et al. describe the policy conflict that lies at the heart of trademark misuse: "a trademark as a cover for a scheme among competitors to divide up markets" through a franchise

---

[361] *Phi Delta Theta Fraternity v. J.A. Buchroeder & Co.*, 251 F. Supp. 968, 975–80 (W.D. Mo. 1966) (holding that if the defendant could prove that a group of fraternities had conspired with certain companies to restrain trade, it would have shown a valid misuse defense to infringement). In ruling, the court relied significantly on 15 U.S.C. § 1115(b)(7), which explicitly states that a defense to the presumption granted to incontestable marks is "that the mark has been or is being used to violate the antitrust laws of the United States,." ibid. at 978–80.

[362] *Carl Zeiss Stiftung*, 298 F. Supp. at 1314 ("A valid trademark, on the other hand, merely enables the owner to bar others from use of the mark, as distinguished from competitive manufacture and sale of identical goods bearing another mark, or even no mark at all, since the purpose of trademark enforcement is to avoid public confusion that might result from imitation or similar unfair competitive practices rather than to authorize restraints upon trade").

[363] Ibid. at 1315.

[364] 6 J. Thomas McCarthy, McCarthy on Trademarks and Unfair Competition §31:91 (4th ed. 2012) ("an additional policy pointing toward reluctance to uphold an antitrust misuse defense in trademark litigation is the necessity of protecting customers from confusion"); see also Thomas F. Cotter, *supra* note 316, at 904 n. 6 ("Applications of the doctrine to trademarks in particular might harm consumers by enabling infringers to continue using trademarks in a confusing manner").

tying arrangement, but that dividing markets may be "a perfectly rational solution to the problem of consumer confusion resulting from overlapping marks."[365] Professor Nimmer and Santhanam note that courts have invoked patent and copyright misuse both to prevent anticompetitive practices and to protect IP policies underlying the laws, and conclude that "the premise that misuse doctrine will be applicable only where the competition is threatened is flawed."[366]

Beyond the species of copyright and trademark misuse, other species of misuse lurk within the dicta of courts who perhaps spurred on the equity's guiding hand in preventing outcomes which are formalistically correct but nonetheless unjust, remain alert to developing the doctrine of misuse as the justice of the case calls for.[367] Ultimately, equitable doctrines will be employed by judges who prefer the occasional uncertainties of rough justice rather than those with a greater proclivity to cling to certainty "with something akin to religious passion, to the defense of what they have so laboriously learned."[368]

V. THE INTERNATIONAL DIMENSION

A discussion on potential growth would not be complete without at least briefly considering the international dimension. A government official expressed that patent misuse has never formally been part of U.S. foreign trade policy, either bilaterally or multilaterally.[369] One reason is the dif-

---

[365] 1 Herbert Hovenkamp et al., IP AND ANTITRUST §3.5 (2d ed. 2010).

[366] See Nimmer & Santhanam, *supra* note 316, at 428 ("The misuse doctrine has been upheld in patent and copyright law not merely when they 'attempt to destroy the competitors through the use of' the patent or copyright. It has been invoked in those cases where the practices seek to achieve something that is abhorrent to the objectives or the policies behind the controlling statutes").

[367] See also Cotter, *supra* note 316, at 904 n. 6 ("There is also a smattering of decisions hinting at a trademark and even trade secret misuse doctrine as well, but the case law remains sketchy").

[368] John Kenneth Galbraith, THE AFFLUENT SOCIETY 7 (1998).

[369] On file with the author. ("It's not something that we look to export. It's not something we have looked to export in the past. I would compare it in some ways to fair use under the copyright law. In both of those you have a typically, if not American, at least Anglo-American or Anglo-Saxon kind of common-law approach, having [inaudible] this doctrine over a long time and sussed all its nooks and crannies through very complex case law. Whether you are talking about IP misuse or talking about fair use, it is very difficult to wrap that into a package and put it into something like a trade agreement and say, 'All right, there will be this'. Common-law doctrine just doesn't admit of that very easily").

ficulty of defining every nuance of the doctrine.[370] Foreign countries have been interested in patent misuse to the extent that they could learn how patent abuses are corrected within the U.S. system, and how they might incorporate similar checks into their own patent regimes. It could therefore play a useful role in encouraging the strengthening of intellectual property regimes abroad and thereby protecting American technology exports. However, the interviewee observed that U.S. laws, particularly case law, tend to be taken to such a high level of abstraction overseas that by the time they are applied locally, they become oversimplified and under- or over-inclusive.[371] This may end up hurting, rather than helping U.S. commercial interests. He cited the copyright defense of fair use as an example of common law doctrines that are not easily incorporated into

---

[370] Ibid. ("Q: So would it be fair to say that if patent misuse were ever exported, it would have to be similarly converted into some kind of a statutory form so that foreign countries would find it easier and more tractable to apply? A: The question there is always, how can you do that? It's like modeling courage, in a way. If you take something that is a case-law doctrine, as you no doubt discovered from your research, as you get to the margins of case-law doctrine like that, it becomes increasingly difficult to say that the law is here or there. It's like the Heisenberg uncertainty principle applied to law. At some point, at the margins, we're not really sure exactly what the law would be. Courts have found this way and courts have found that way. This hasn't been definitively settled yet. As you then consider whether and how to shape an outward-looking policy in the U.S. government based on something like that, it's then a question of whether you go with an approach something like the three-step test, for example, where you draw some broad boundaries that you are confident of falling within, without getting in and trying to define every nuance, since that would be too difficult to do").

[371] Ibid. ("I think that if we were thinking about doing that as a matter of trade policy, you would have to make a real risk/reward calculation about whether you were bringing significant benefits by doing that or whether you were just injecting a great deal of uncertainty. You would also have to bear in mind that there are defensive considerations. Of course, we would want to maintain doctrines that already exist in U.S. law. You wouldn't want to define things in a way that was too restrictive. If the courts take this doctrine in a different direction in twenty years or thirty years or forty years, if it evolves more toward that or toward that, whatever lines you draw in terms of trade policy would have to be drawn in a way that anticipated the different boundaries. The three-step test is a good example of that setting of some boundary principles without getting into all the nuances. I have to say, not having thought about it in any great detail, it would take a lot to persuade me that it was a good idea to translate patent misuse into an element of U.S. trade policy. My instinct is that that would be used against U.S. interests more often than it would be used to benefit U.S. interests. But that's just strictly a personal reaction to something I've never had to—as far as I know, I have never had any stakeholder come in and say that was something we should do.")

trade policy.[372] On the suggestion that it might be more easily exported if it could be codified, the interviewee said it was difficult to do that with common law because case law gets to the margins of doctrine, "like bottling courage."[373] However, he acknowledged that the U.S. would be willing to enter into bilateral or multilateral negotiations with countries with comparable patent regimes.[374]

A lawyer interviewed noted that while the U.S. appeared to be the only country with an equitable doctrine like patent misuse, many countries had misuse-like provisions within their patent laws.[375] He cited the U.K. Patent Act's tying provisions as an example.[376] More broadly, he noted that E.U. competition law has addressed the sort of conduct traditionally recognized as falling within the fold of anticompetitive conduct, such as tying and restrictive or oppressive licensing terms imposed by a dominant undertaking.[377] In addition, E.U. competition law has also developed to address newer forms of misuse such as deceptive conduct and generic drug settlements in a way that is more robust than antitrust law does.[378] He elaborated that this was so because it was easier to show an abuse of a dominant position under E.U. competition law than monopolization or attempted monopolization under U.S. antitrust law.[379] A government official noted that the lack of private rights mechanism in Europe could account for a greater willingness to use competition law to address misuse issues than antitrust law has.[380] Yet a judge commented that while it made

---

[372] Ibid.

[373] Ibid.

[374] Ibid.

[375] Ibid.

[376] See The Patents Act 1977, ch. 37 § 45 (Oct. 1, 2011).

[377] On file with the author. For a recent application of EU competition law by the Court of Justice for the European Union (CJEU) to patent abuses, see Case C-457/10, *AstraZeneca v. Commission* (6 December 2012). The patentee submitted misleading statements to regulatory authorities to extend patent protection for its blockbuster drug. The CJEU held that each wrong representation made to a patent authority will not automatically constitute an abuse. In that case, the CJEU looked at the deliberateness and duration of the misrepresentations to establish their abusive character and concluded that they could harm competition, even though some were detected and corrected before any competitor had been misled.

[378] Ibid.

[379] Ibid.

[380] On file with the author. ("I think the biggest difference is the absence of the private rights mechanism in Europe. I think when the Court of First Instance or the Court of Justice look at DG COMP, there is more trust that DG COMP is the real conservator of the public interest than a private litigant would be. Because the spillover effects into private litigation to this point don't exist, and because

sense to use competition law to deal with competition-related issues in the exploitation of patent rights, it was "silly" to use competition law to deal with non-competition considerations, and that matters such as innovation policy were more properly dealt with under patent law.[381] In response to the same question, a lawyer noted that other countries without patent misuse face similar problems and the legal system will devise ways to prohibit inappropriate uses of patent rights, as the E.U. had done through its competition law.[382]

VI. CONCLUSION

Whatever one may think of patent misuse, it is indisputable that courts and commentators see a future for misuse, whether along the same stream of patent law in areas such as reverse payments and misconduct in standard setting, or in a parallel stream of copyright law. While the Federal Circuit plays an extremely significant role in determining that future, the role of district courts cannot be understated either. The Supreme Court has long recognized the deference appellate courts should give to district courts when they "model their judgments to fit the exigencies of the

---

the consequences of finding an infringement are not as powerful, I think courts have more confidence that a finding of infringement will not have significant adverse effects. One way to put it, to explain the difference in EU and U.S. abuse-of-dominance doctrine, I think a major explanation is the fact that U.S. doctrine in the last thirty or so years has been shaped in large measure out of a fear of over-deterrence by private suits and the way in which judges have achieved an equilibration to deal with this.")

[381] On file with the author.

[382] Daryl Lim, *Beyond Microsoft: Intellectual Property, Peer Production and the Law's Concern with Market Dominance*, 18 FORDHAM INTELL. PROP. MEDIA & ENT. L.J. 291, 297–98 (2007–2008) ("In December 2005, the European Commission initiated a public consultation to review the application of Article 82 of the E.C. Treaty to exclusionary abuses and treatment of refusals to license, followed by a public hearing on June 14, 2006. It adopted an effects-based analysis grounded on economic principles rather than per se prohibitions, which was roundly welcomed. However, respondents were also concerned that an effects-based analysis would be hard to implement. There were numerous requests for clearer rules to assist businesses in self-assessments of lawful conduct, including 'white areas'. DG Competition has indicated that IPRs and their effects will be carefully evaluated. However, as in the U.S., a concern has also been expressed that economic theory in this area had not developed to an extent where the impact of such refusals can be sufficiently understood for regulators to intervene with confidence").

particular case."[383] As the first port of call by parties in patent litigation cases, district courts can do justice to the parties before it by distinguishing ill-reasoned appellate precedent. Progress sometimes depends on little acts of treason.[384] At the same time, the exercise of discretion must be grounded in defensible precedent and facts. In the realm of misuse, no study has yet been undertaken to provide a comprehensive survey of the landscape of misuse. This landscape exists on two levels. The first is the physical dimension, where one can observe the nature of industries in which misuse cases take place, the distribution of cases by circuit and the outcomes of these cases. The second, more elusive level is a metaphysical inquiry into how misuse cases are decided within the minds of judges. The key to this inquiry is a systematic deconstruction of what the "scope" of a patent means to the cases this study looks at. It is to these two dimensions that we now turn.

---

[383]   *United States v. Glaxo Group Ltd.*, 410 U.S. 52, 64 (1973) ("This Court has repeatedly recognized that '(t)he framing of decrees should take place in the District rather than in Appellate Courts' and has generally followed the principle that district courts 'are invested with large discretion to model their judgments to fit the exigencies of the particular case'. International Salt Co. v. United States, supra, 332 U.S., at 400-401, 68 S.Ct., at 17; accord, Ford Motor Co. v. United States, 405 U.S. 562, 573, 92 S.Ct. 1142, 1149, 31 L.Ed.2d 492 (1972)").

[384]   See Cotter, supra note 316 at 936–37 ("To be sure, a decision to consider the doctrine anew need not entail fealty to these existing decisions. But perhaps this common feature provides a useful starting point for trying to sketch out what a rational version of (transactional) misuse that goes beyond antitrust strictures might resemble. In other words, let us consider provisionally a regime under which misuse exists when the IP owner uses its IP to extract concessions that we believe, on policy grounds, should not be extracted. Why might we wish to restrict IP owners from extracting some concessions from their purchasers and licensees?").

6. The empirical landscape of misuse

I. FREQUENCY AND CASE DISTRIBUTION

A. Courts

This study coded every case substantively discussing patent misuse that was decided by a federal district and appellate court in each of the 12 circuits, as well as the Federal Circuit and the Supreme Court. The dataset consisted of four Supreme Court opinions, 70 court of appeals opinions and 294 district court opinions between January 1, 1953 and December 31, 2012.[1] It is noteworthy that no Supreme Court opinions have been rendered since 1982, the year the Federal Circuit came into being. This was not due to a lack of petitions for certiorari filed. In 55 cases, petitions were filed but only four were granted. *Dawson Chemical Co. v. Rohm & Haas Co.*[2] and *Zenith Radio Corp. v. Hazeltine Research Inc.*[3] were appeals from the Fifth Circuit and Seventh Circuit respectively, while *Brulotte v. Thys Co.*[4] was an appeal from the Washington State Supreme Court. The last case, *United States Gypsum Co. v. National Gypsum Co,*[5] the appeal was directly from the district court and expedited because it related to a matter of "general public importance."[6] Figure 6.1 shows

---

[1]   Except for *United States Gypsum Co. v. Nat'l Gypsum Co.*, 352 U.S. 457 (1957), each Supreme Court opinion produced one dissent. *Dawson Chem. Co. v. Rohm & Haas Co.*, 448 U.S. 176 (1980) (Opinion by: Blackmun; with Burger, Stewart, Powell, and Rehnquist. Dissent by: White; with Brennan, Marshall, and Stevens; Dissent by: Stevens). *Zenith Radio Corp. v. Hazeltine Research, Inc.*, 395 U.S. 100 (1969) (Opinion by: White; Concurrence by: Warren, Black, Douglas, Harlan, Brennan, Stewart, and Marshall. Partial dissent by: Harlan). *Brulotte v. Thys Co.*, 379 U.S. 29 (1964) (Opinion by: Douglas with Warren, Black, Clark, Brennan, Stewart, White, and Goldberg. Dissent by: Harlan).

[2]   *Dawson Chem. Co.*, 448 U.S. 176.

[3]   *Zenith Radio Corp.*, 395 U.S. 100.

[4]   *Brulotte*, 379 U.S. 29.

[5]   *United States Gypsum Co.*, 352 U.S. 457.

[6]   See 15 U.S.C. § 28 (1984) ("§ 28 repealed by Pub. L. No. 98-620, title IV, § 402(11), 98 Stat. 3358 (1984). Section, acts Feb. 11, 1903, ch. 544, §1, 32 Stat. 823; June 25, 1910, ch. 428, 36 Stat. 854; Mar. 3, 1911, ch. 231, §291, 36 Stat. 1167; Apr. 6, 1942,

the distribution of appeals. Most came from the Federal Circuit. None were granted. The study remains agnostic, however, as to whether there was simply no proper vehicle for the Supreme Court to take certiorari or whether by its silence the Supreme Court has implictly endorsed the Federal Circuit's vein of misuse jurisprudence.

B.   Cases per year: Fair Use and Inequitable Conduct

In the 60 years from January 1, 1953 to the conclusion of 2012, the federal courts produced 368 reported opinions that discussed misuse. This averages out to six opinions per year. By way of comparison, there were 11 opinions per year deciding fair use under copyright law between January 1, 1978 and December 31, 2007.[7] A comparison with the number of misuse cases to inequitable conduct cases shows an even starker difference. The Federal Circuit alone decided over 300 inequitable conduct cases between 1983 and 2008, giving an average of about 13 cases a year.[8] Whatever one might wish to think about misuse, it is not a "plague" deserving of radical surgical intervention as the Federal Circuit has described inequitable conduct in the *Therasense* case.[9]

---

ch. 210, §1, 56 Stat. 198; June 25, 1948, ch. 646, §32(a), 62 Stat. 991; May 24, 1949, ch. 139, §127, 63 Stat. 107; Dec. 21, 1974, Pub. L. 93–528, §4, 88 Stat. 1708, related to expedition of actions by the United States involving general public importance").

[7]   See Barton Beebe, *An Empirical Study Of U.S. Copyright Fair Use Opinions, 1978–2005*, 156 U. Pa. L. Rev. 549, 565 (2007–2008).

[8]   Christian E. Mammen, *Controlling the "Plague": Reforming the Doctrine of Inequitable Conduct*, 24 Berkeley Tech L.J. 1329, 1348 (2009).

[9]   See *Therasense, Inc. v. Becton, Dickinson & Co.*, 649 F.3d 1276 (Fed. Cir. 2011) (*en banc*). See Lee Petherbridge et al., *The Federal Circuit and Inequitable Conduct: An Empirical Assessment*, 84 S. Cal L. Rev. 1293, 1349–50 (2010–2011) (". . . Federal Circuit judges do not very much like the doctrine, the majority used the case as a vehicle for radically redefining the doctrine of inequitable conduct. The majority was not shy about its goal: it deliberately sought to make it more difficult to successfully pursue inequitable conduct claims, a change that it predicted would improve both patent quality and litigation"). The court describes reasons why the incidence of inequitable conduct claims are high: "Most prominently, inequitable conduct has become a significant litigation strategy. A charge of inequitable conduct conveniently expands discovery into corporate practices before patent filing and disqualifies the prosecuting attorney from the patentee's litigation team. Moreover, inequitable conduct charges cast a dark cloud over the patent's validity and paint the patentee as a bad actor. Because the doctrine focuses on the moral turpitude of the patentee with ruinous consequences for the reputation of his patent attorney, it discourages settlement and deflects attention from the merits of validity and infringement issues. Inequitable conduct disputes also 'increas[e] the complexity, duration and cost of patent infringement litigation

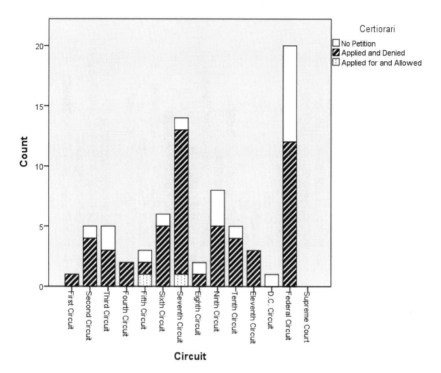

Figure 6.1   Petition for writ of certiorari by circuit

Comparing the longitudinal studies between inequitable conduct and misuse at the appellate level (Figures 6.2 and 6.3), a couple of observations

that is already notorious for its complexity and high cost'. Perhaps most importantly, the remedy for inequitable conduct is the 'atomic bomb' of patent law. Unlike validity defenses, which are claim specific, inequitable conduct regarding any single claim renders the entire patent unenforceable. Unlike other deficiencies, inequitable conduct cannot be cured by reissue, or reexamination. Moreover, the taint of a finding of inequitable conduct can spread from a single patent to render unenforceable other related patents and applications in the same technology family. Thus, a finding of inequitable conduct may endanger a substantial portion of a company's patent portfolio. A finding of inequitable conduct may also spawn antitrust and unfair competition claims. Further, prevailing on a claim of inequitable conduct often makes a case 'exceptional', leading potentially to an award of attorneys' fees under 35 U.S.C. § 286. A finding of inequitable conduct may also prove the crime or fraud exception to the attorney-client privilege. With these far-reaching consequences, it is no wonder that charging inequitable conduct has become a common litigation tactic"); *Therasense, Inc.*, 649 F.3d at 1288–90.

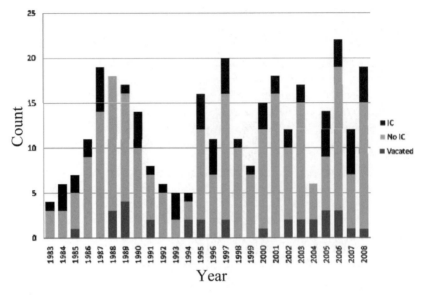

Source: Christian E. Mammen, *Controlling the "Plague": Reforming the Doctrine of Inequitable Conduct*, 24 BERKELEY TECH. L.J. 1329 (2009), at 1353.

Figure 6.2   Outcomes over time (inequitable conduct)

emerge. First, the count of misuse cases has largely remained low despite a spike in cases between 2006 and 2010. Inequitable conduct cases in contrast show much more consistency, with clusters of high frequency occurences between the late 1980s and early 1990s, and then consistently from the mid-1990s onwards. Second, the misuse appears to be generally less successful than inequitable conduct claims. Third, there appears to be a sudden dearth of both inequitable conduct and misuse cases in the early 1980s followed by a common peak in 1997. Such parallel trends may provide interesting avenues for further research.

C.   Outcomes over Time

Looking at misuse outcomes over time between 1953 and 2011 in Figure 6.4, it is readily apparent that the early success enjoyed by defendants in asserting misuse between 1953 and 1982 dipped dramatically from 1983 onwards, reaching an all time low in the 2003–2012 period. The peak success rate for defendants was in the initial 1953–1962 period, where 40 percent of defendants succeeded in an allegation of misuse. One reason for this may be because it was easier to allege misuse under a *per se* standard

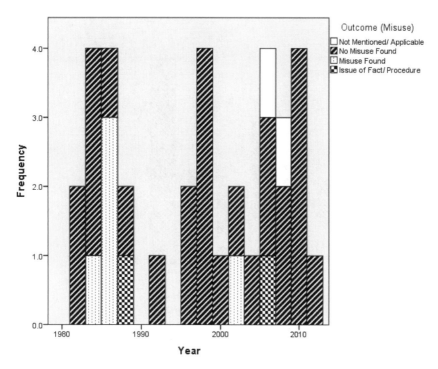

Figure 6.3   Misuse outcomes over time (appellate level)[10]

than a rule of reason standard where anticompetitive effects had to be shown.[11] Another reason is the reccurring theme that the Federal Circuit has done much to raise the threshold needed to sucessfully allege misuse.

Apart from a spike in cases observed between 1953 and 1972, where the

---

[10]   The frequency numbers on the y-axis of graphs in this book presenting the outcome of misuse and antitrust cases reflect individual counts of alleged misuse and antitrust violation rather than individual cases. These give a more accurate representation of case outcomes, as courts make separate determinations for each count of misuse. Simply reflecting the number of cases would understate the activity during a particular time period, circuit or industry. At the same time, readers may be interested in the number of misuse cases in each time period, circuit or industry. For this reason, an additional set of graphs based on unique case counts rather than unique misuse or antitrust counts may be found online at http://goo.gl/hUcly.

[11]   *Illinois Tool Works Inc. v. Indep. Ink, Inc.*, 547 U.S. 28, 45 (2006) ("It is no doubt the virtual consensus among economists that has persuaded the enforcement agencies to reject the position that the Government took when it supported the *per se* rule that the Court adopted in the 1940's").

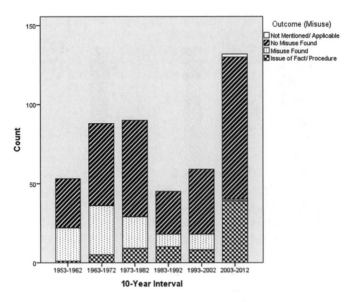

Figure 6.4   Overall win rates (over 10-year interval)

number of patent misuse cases doubled, and a dip observed from 1983 to 2002, the number of cases over time has gradually risen. The district court count saw the most radical swing, from a low of 29 in the 1953–1962 period to an all time high of 96 cases in the 2003–2012 period. This indicates that despite the Federal Circuit's tightening up of the misuse doctrine following the *Windsurfing* decision, more parties than before are bringing misuse claims before the courts. Anecdotal evidence is consistent with this result. Judges and lawyers interviewed noted that they encountered patent misuse with greater frequency at the lower courts in recent years.[12] One judge interviewed attributed the rise in the number of misuse cases to two factors. First, that the patent bar had the "cream of the crop" of attorneys, second, that the stakes are usually high and "and so they've got plenty of money generally to assert every possible claim or defense they have."[13] Another judge interviewed remarked that:

---

[12]   For example, a judge remarked that "One patent attorney analogized misuse to inequitable conduct allegations, which he said were roughly raised "98% of the time." On file with the author.

[13]   On file with the author. ("The patent bar, particularly the patent bar, I think is the cream of the crop as far as being the brightest lawyers and the most imaginative, and the stakes are high so they've got plenty of money generally to assert every possible claim or defense that they have. And it's not like other areas, where

people aren't inclined to bring stuff they don't think has some chance of success. The courts have done a good job of bringing some of the rigor of antitrust analysis to the patent misuse defense. You don't get to just throw junk around and stop them with the misuse. You actually have to, typically, show some anticompetitive effect associated with impermissible effort to broaden the scope of the patent grant. Because of that, rational litigants aren't inclined to waste their money by hiring experts to try to make the claim of anticompetitive effect if they can't make it stick.[14]

The only appellate case that has found misuse in recent times is *Scheiber v. Dolby Labs., Inc.*, where Judge Richard Posner, writing for the Seventh Circuit found that a licensing agreement that extended beyond patent term was unenforceable.[15] In the same period, the only district court case to find misuse was *SmithKline Beecham Corp. v. Apotex Corp.*[16] In that case, Judge Posner, sitting by designation, found misuse because the infringement was inevitable, incidental, and injurious to the infringer's business.[17]

Looking at the distribution of cases over time by level in Figure 6.5, the first striking feature is the rise in the number of misuse cases over time. District court cases have also formed a larger proportion of cases in the 2003–2012 period compared to any other period. In contrast, appellate court cases in the 1953–1962 period formed the largest proportion of cases in the study. This trend may indicate that parties are better able to satisfactorily resolve their differences without seeking review in a higher court. It could also show a stabilization of misuse law over the years, therefore requiring less error correction by an appellate court. If this is so, then it some indication that the Federal Circuit's harmonizing of patent law may be a positive thing insofar as achieving this stability.

---

maybe you'd say, 'Well, I won't bother with this because, although I can assert it, it's too expensive'. They're going to do it in a patent case. So I just think that leads to more issues being raised and asserted.")

[14]   On file with the author.

[15]   293 F.3d 1014 (7th Cir. 2002).

[16]   247 F. Supp. 2d 1011 (N.D. Ill. 2003).

[17]   Ibid., at 1046–48 ("Another way to explain SmithKline's disentitlement to an injunction is in terms of the doctrine, classically equitable—an aspect of the historic doctrine of 'unclean hands'—of patent misuse . . . the efficacy of Apotex's generic competition with Paxil will gain nothing from the fact that Apotex cannot eliminate minuscule quantities of the hemihydrate from its anhydrate product. The infiltration of Apotex's production process by hemihydrate is merely a pretext for an infringement suit designed to prevent competition from a product that is in the public domain").

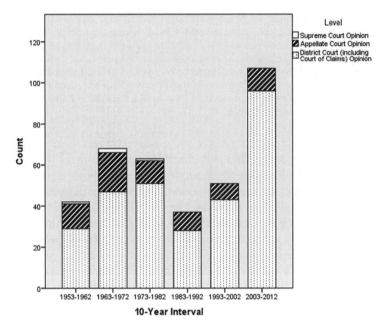

Figure 6.5   Distribution over time by level

D.   Circuit Dominance as a Whole

Looking at both cases from all levels as a whole in Figure 6.6, it appears that misuse juriprudence is dominanted by cases from the Seventh Circuit, followed by the Ninth Circuit and then the Second Circuit. As popular venues for patent litigation, it is unsurprising that misuse should also appear with a higher frequences in those Circuits. Over time, it appears that the Ninth and Second Cirucit have risen in prominence as the venue of choice in misuse cases to take the number one and three spots in the 2003–2012 period, with the Seventh Circuit taking the number two spot (Figure 6.7). In the case of both the Second and Ninth Circuit, the number of cases has increased from their respective heights in earlier years between twice to three times. The Seventh Circuit was clearly the venue of choice in the 1960s and 1970s but diminished in popularity between 1981 and 2000, before regaining some of its earlier popularity in recent years.

District Court Level: A more accurate picture of the landscape emerges when the cases are differentiated based on whether they are district or appellate court (excluding Supreme Court) cases. Figure 6.8 shows the frequency and distribution of district court cases over time. Here, the dominance of the Seventh and Ninth Circuit becomes clearer. District courts in

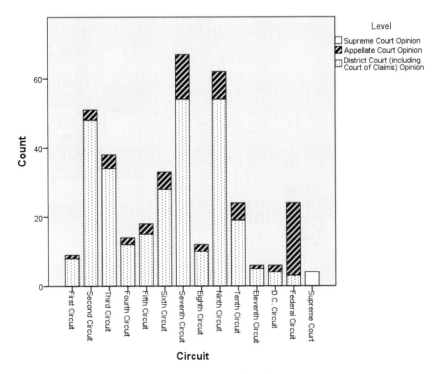

Figure 6.6 Distribution over circuits by level

the Seventh Circuit dominanted in the 1970s and 1980s, with most Seventh Circuit cases coming from the Northern District of Illinois. District courts in the Ninth Circuit took over the dominant role from the 1990s to the present, with most Ninth Circuit cases coming from the Northern District of California, perhaps corresponding to the rise of technological markets in Silicon Valley. In this instance, cases appearing under the "Federal Circuit" tab refers to Court of Claims opinons rendered between 1963 and 1972.

Federal Circuit dominant post-1982: Looking at the decisions rendered at the circuit appellate level in Figure 6.9, the dominance of the Federal Circuit is obvious. Since its formation in 1982, the Federal Circuit has decided almost all patent misuse appeals. The Federal Circuit has addressed patent misuse in 24 opinions since its inception in 1982. This data is consistent with conventional wisdom. Professor Martin Adelman et al. notes that "[t]he Federal Circuit does not have exclusive jurisdiction over patent-antitrust cases. They can be heard in any of the regional circuits. However, since misuse is an equitable defense to a charge of patent

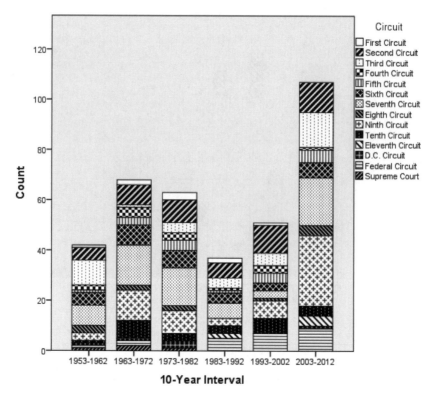

Figure 6.7   Distribution of circuits over time

infringement, what constitutes substantive misuse is ordinarily a matter within the control of the Federal Circuit."[18]

Interviewees were surprised that misuse cases continued to arise in circuits other than the Federal Circuit after 1982. For example in a 1985 opinion, the Sixth Circuit had to determine "whether the terms of

---

[18]   Martin J. Adelman et al., CASES AND MATERIALS ON PATENT LAW 814 (3d ed. 2009). See also *Holmes Group, Inc. v. Vornado Air Circulation Sys., Inc.*, 535 U.S. 826, 832-34 (2002) ("Not all cases involving a patent-law claim fall within the Federal Circuit's jurisdiction. By limiting the Federal Circuit's jurisdiction to cases in which district courts would have jurisdiction under § 1338, Congress referred to a well-established body of law that requires courts to consider whether a patent-law claim appears on the face of the plaintiff's well-pleaded complaint. Because petitioner's complaint did not include any claim based on patent law, we vacate the judgment of the Federal Circuit and remand the case with instructions to transfer the case to the Court of Appeals for the Tenth Circuit. *See* 28 U.S.C. § 1631.")

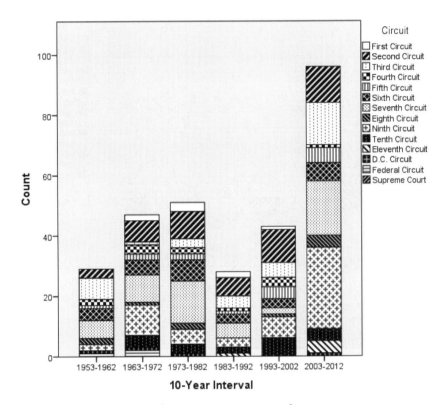

Figure 6.8   Distribution by circuits over time in district courts

a licensing agreement, which the parties entered into prior to application for or issuance of anticipated but subsequently issued patents, can be enforced beyond the expiration dates of the patents."[19] Between 2003 and 2012 three federal appellate cases have discussed misuse, one from the Ninth Circuit and two from the Seventh Circuit. In one of the Seventh Circuit cases, the court had to decide whether a covenant not to compete in a patent licensing agreement was unenforceable.[20] In the other, the patentee sought to enforce its licensing agreement against its licensee.[21] The patentee appealed from a lower court's decision that the agreement was unenforceable even though the agreement extended

---

[19]   *Boggild v. Kenner Prods.*, 776 F.2d 1315, 1316 (6th Cir. 1985).
[20]   *County Materials Corp. v. Allan Block Corp.*, 502 F.3d 730, 732 (7th Cir. 2007).
[21]   *Scheiber v. Dolby Labs., Inc.*, 293 F.3d 1014, 1016 (7th Cir. 2002).

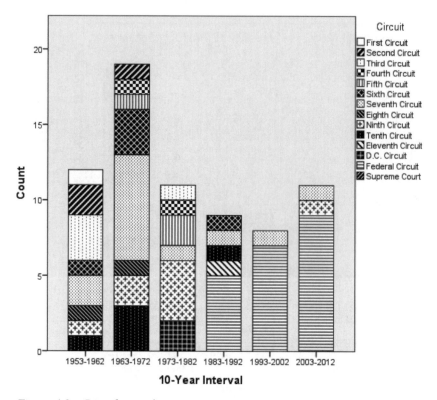

Figure 6.9   Distribution by circuits over time at intermediate appellate
courts

beyond the patent term. In all these instances, it can be seen that misuse
cases may arise outside of the Federal Circuit despite its monopoly
over patent appeals in the case of licensing agreements which, as will be
seen, form the bulk of misuse cases. Thus, misuse may be one of the few
aspects of patent law in which other circuits may yet play a proactive
part in shaping misuse doctrine if provided with an appropriate vehicle
on the facts of the case before it. Robert Hoerner offers an explanation
for this phenomenon:

> Patent misuse can be asserted not only in defense against a suit for patent
> infringement but also against a suit for royalties due on a license agreement.
> Accordingly, the regional circuits and, indeed, state courts, as well as the
> Federal Circuit, will have a hand in shaping the future of the doctrine of patent
> misuse, subject, of course, to existing relevant United States Supreme Court
> holdings and ongoing supervision by the United States Supreme Court by way
> of the grant, or not, of petitions for a writ of certiorari. Nevertheless, the future

contours of the patent misuse doctrine will most likely be sculpted by the Court of Appeals for the Federal Circuit . . .[22]

A Ninth Circuit case involved a suit between an insured and insurer and whether the former alleged a violation of the latter's duty to defend it against underlying defamation claim.[23] Misuse was raised in the context of whether it fell within the intellectual property clause in the agreement.[24] This and other cases like this were included because the court expressed a substantive view on misuse, though the outcome was naturally recorded as not applicable for the purposes of this study.

II. OUTCOMES

A. Outcomes by Circuit

Looking first at the overall picture (Figure 6.10), it is clear that patentees are most successful at the Federal Circuit (82%), followed by Seventh Circuit (69%), the Ninth Circuit (69%) and the Second Circuit (67%). There is a clear correlation with patentees win rates and the dominance of the respective circuits in misuse cases. However this correlation does not hold for patentees win rates in the Tenth Circuit (73%) which ranks second

---

[22]   Robert J. Hoerner, *Patent Misuse: Portents for the 1990s*, 59 ANTITRUST L.J. 687, 688–89 (1990–1991). See also Christopher Leslie, ANTITRUST LAW AND INTELLECTUAL PROPERTY RIGHTS 586 (2011) ("the order in which litigants file their claims may determine which court will hear any appeals. If the patentee files an infringement action and the alleged infringer files an antitrust counterclaim, the Federal Circuit will hear the appeal. Conversely, if an antitrust plaintiff brings a claim and the defendant brings a patent infringement counterclaim, the regional circuit in which the district court sits will hear the appeal. This matters because some litigants perceive the Federal Circuit to be relatively hostile to antitrust claims. This means that an antitrust plaintiff who wants to avoid having the Federal Circuit decide its case could either file its antitrust claim *before* the patentee files an infringement action or, at least, decline to file its antitrust claim as a counterclaim in an infringement suit (and instead file it as a separate case). The first strategy is not possible when the antitrust claim is based on the patentee's infringement suit. Patentees have tried to eliminate the second strategy by arguing that antitrust claims are compulsory counterclaims. Consequently, they assert that if the infringement defendant does not file their antitrust lawsuit as a counterclaim (whose appeal would be heard by the Federal Circuit), then the antitrust claim is barred.")

[23]   *Aurafin-OroAmerica, LLC v. Fed. Ins. Co.*, 188 F. App'x 565 (9th Cir. 2006).

[24]   Ibid. at 566–67.

Patent misuse and antitrust law

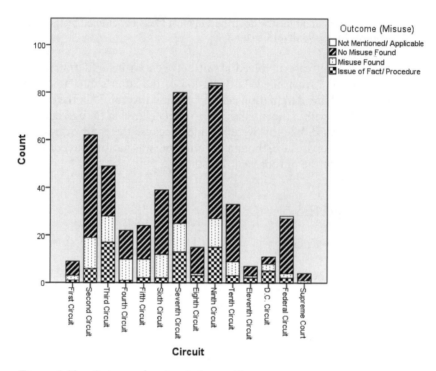

Figure 6.10 Outcome by circuit (overall)

only to the Federal Circuit in terms of overall win rates yet lags a distant sixth in terms of being the choice venue for misuse cases.

B. Appellate Outcomes

Zooming into the federal appellate outcomes, patentees maintained the same win rate at the Federal Circuit (89%). The win rate on appeal at the Seventh Circuit was slightly higher at 76 percent (Figure 6.11). The win rate on appeal at the Ninth Circuit fell dramatically to 30 percent. Defendants won a significant 67 percent of the time at Third and Sixth Circuits, followed by 60 percent at the Fifth Circuit, winning 50 percent of the time at the Fourth Circuit. At the district court level, patentees won 72 percent at the Ninth Circuit, 67 percent at the Seventh Circuit, 70 percent at the Second Circuit. Defendants did much more poorly at the district court level winning 39 percent of the time in the Fourth Circuit, 26 percent of the time at the Fifth Circuit and 14 percent at the Seventh Circuit (Figure 6.12).

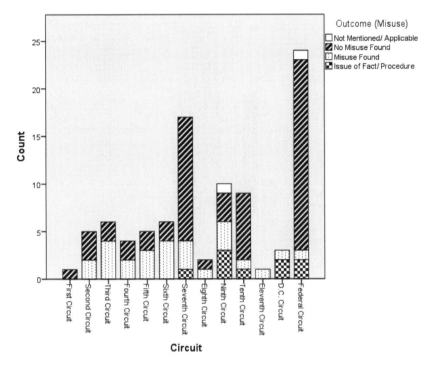

Figure 6.11   Outcome by circuit (appellate court)

III.   PROCEDURAL POSTURE

A.   Introduction

The study's coding instrument identified 15 different postures taken in patent misuse cases covering the entire spectrum of the litigation process. The 15 postures and their corresponding codes are as follows:

1   Preliminary Injunction
2   Summary Judgment Patentee/Licensor
3   Summary Judgment Infringer/Licensee
4   Summary Judgment Cross
5   Bench Trial
6   Jury Trial
7   Motion to Dismiss/Strike
8   Declaratory Judgment
9   Certified Question

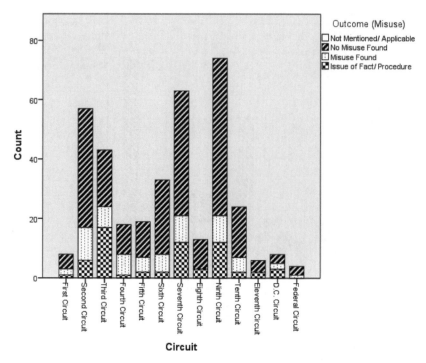

Figure 6.12   Outcome by circuit (district court)

10   Motion for Reconsideration
11   Post-trial Motions
12   Motion for Contempt
13   Interlocutory Motions
14   Appellate Panel Review
15   *En Banc*

Figure 6.13 shows the trends in procedural postures over time. It is clear that there have been marked swings with bench trials being the dominant form of trials between 1953 and 1990, thereafter shrinking significantly from 1991 onwards. Summary judgments and motions to strike or dismiss, once nearly nonexistent in the 1953–1962 period have grown most recently to be the most dominant procedural postures taken in misuse cases. Declaratory judgments have also fallen after a rise through 1970, though the quality of such judgments has remained fairly consistent throughout the period studied. Appellate reviews rose through 1980 and remained fairly constant between 1981 and 2012, coinciding with the Federal Circuit's establishment in 1982. *En banc* reviews are decidedly rare, con-

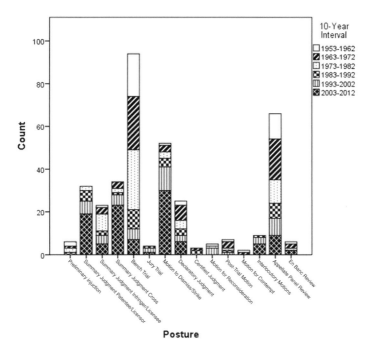

Figure 6.13 Postures (overall)

sisting of Supreme Court opinions and one Federal Circuit opinion. The following discussion focuses on these postures.

Looking at Figure 6.14, bench trials at the district court level formed the bulk of the cases surveyed (26%), followed distantly by appellate reviews (18%) and Motions to Dismiss/Strike (14%).

B. Bench v. Jury Trials

As indicated in a PricewaterhouseCoopers report ("PWC Report"), juries have been central to the patent litigation landscape, rising from 14 percent of cases in the 1980s to 56 percent of cases since 2000 (see Figure 6.15).[25] The PWC Report found that the widening disparity between jury and bench awards likely contributed to this increased use.[26] In contrast,

---

[25] Chris Barry et al., *2012 Patent Litigation Study: Patent Litigation Trends as the "America Invents Act" becomes Law*, PRICEWATERHOUSECOOPERS LLP, 9 (2012), http://www.pwc.com/en_US/us/forensic-services/publications/assets/2012-patent-litigation-study.pdf (hereinafter "PWC Report").

[26] Ibid.

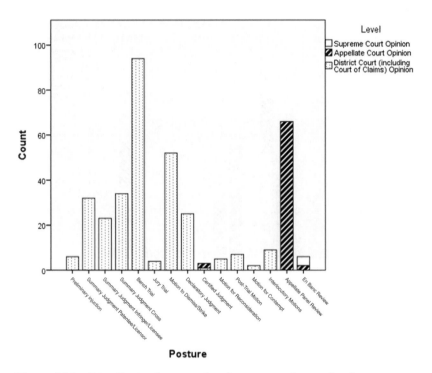

Figure 6.14   Distribution by procedural posture and court level

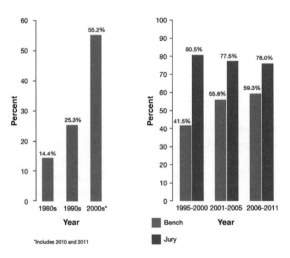

Source: PWC Report 2012.

Figure 6.15   Use of jury trials by decade (left) and success rates (right)

this study found that there were only four cases with jury verdicts out of the 368 patent misuse cases.[27] This seems remarkably low and may be explained by the fact that the role of juries in misuse cases is unclear. The opinions reveal a split in how courts view the role of the jury in determining misuse. Some courts regard issues of equity to be outside the purview of the jury. As the Fifth Circuit in *Alcatel v. D.G.I. Tech.* noted, "[i]t is well established that the right to trial by jury does not extend matters historically cognizable in equity."[28] Other courts, such as the Seventh Circuit in *Beckman Instruments, Inc. v. Technical Dev. Corp.*, opined diametrically that "[q]uestions of patent misuse are for the trier of fact to determine."[29] While it may seem strange that questions of equity should be determined by a jury, this position is not without precedent. The doctrine of equivalents, like patent misuse, finds its roots in equity. Yet, as the Supreme Court in *Graver Tank* held, "[a] finding of equivalence is a determination of fact."[30]

Other courts take a more paternalistic view. In *Cordance Corp. v. Amazon*, the U.S. District Court for the District of Delaware evaluated the issues with jury involvement in such cases by first determining that "[a]s an equitable defense, the right to trial to a jury on a claim for patent misuse is not automatic."[31] It reasoned that judges should decide the issue of misuse since the facts involved in determining misuse were "fraught with potential abuse, including 'unfair prejudice, confusion of issues, or misleading the jury,' resulting in the loss of 'fundamental fairness of the adjudication.'"[32] The court thus took a stance reminiscent of the Supreme Court in *Markman* which relinquished juries from claim construction issues where the court found that "the trained ability to evaluate the testimony in

---

[27] See, e.g., *Arcade, Inc. v. Minnesota Mining & Mfg. Co.*, 24 U.S.P.Q.2d 1578 (E.D. Tenn. 1991); *Virginia Panel Corp. v. MAC Panel Co.*, No. 93-0006-H, 1996 WL 335381 (W.D. Va. May 29, 1996); *Bausch & Lomb, Inc. v. Allergan, Inc.*, 136 F. Supp. 2d 166 (W.D.N.Y. 2001); and *Pace Int'l, LLC v. Indus. Ventilation, Inc.*, No. C08-1822RSL, 2009 U.S. Dist. LEXIS 73847 (W.D. Wa. Aug. 6, 2009).

[28] *Alcatel v. D.G.I. Tech., Inc.*, 166 F.3d 772, 795 (5th Cir. 1999); see also *GFI, Inc. v. Franklin Corp.*, 265 F.3d 1268, 1272 (Fed. Cir. 2001) ("The defenses of inequitable conduct, obviousness, laches, equitable estoppel, and patent misuse were tried to the court in a non-jury trial").

[29] *Laser Alignment, Inc. v. Woodruff & Sons*, 491 F.2d 866 (1974), citing *Beckman Instruments, Inc. v. Technical Dev. Corp.*, 433 F.2d 55 (7th Cir. 1970), *cert. denied*, 401 U.S. 976 (1971).

[30] *Graver Tank & Mfg. Co. v. Linde Air Prods. Co.*, 339 U.S. 605, 609 (1950).

[31] *Cordance Corp. v. Amazon, Inc.*, No. 06-491-MPT, 2009 U.S. Dist. LEXIS 64986 (D. Del. July 28, 2009).

[32] Ibid.

relation to the overall structure of the patent" made claim construction a task better suited for judges since document interpretation is what "judges often do and are likely to do better than jurors unburdened by training in exegesis."[33] Similarly, the *Cordance* court decided that since the jury was already burdened with "the Einsteinian analysis and Herculean" of determining infringement and invalidity, it "will not further burden (and potentially further confuse) the jury with patent misuse."[34]

The opinions studied also show where juries feature during the trial. In *Virginia Panel Corp. v. MAC Panel Co.*, the U.S. District Court for the Western District of Virginia noted that "[a]t the second phase of the trial, the jury returned a verdict in favor of MPC on the issue of patent misuse."[35]

Where the predominately factual nature of the dispute meant an inevitable delay and difficulty in severing some issues for determination by the court, this could militate in favor of submitting the entire case to the jury.[36] The *Virginia Panel* court observed that the Federal Rules of Civil Procedure allows the trial court to submit a determination of an equitable matter to a jury if all parties consented. Otherwise, the court was obliged to treat the jury's findings as advisory and must provide its own findings of fact and conclusions of law with respect to the equitable issue.[37] On appeal, the Federal Circuit expressly noted the jury instructions relating to misuse and upheld its verdict.[38] In the face of the defendant's objection to

---

[33]   *Markman v. Westview Instruments, Inc.*, 517 U.S. 370, 388, 390 (1996).

[34]   *Cordance Corp.*, 2009 U.S. Dist. LEXIS 64986 at *5–6.

[35]   *Virginia Panel Corp. v. MAC Panel Co.*, No. 93-0006-H, 1996 U.S. Dist. LEXIS 8514, at *11–12 (W.D. Va. May 29, 1996). See also *Hunter Douglas, Inc. v. Comfortex Corp.*, 44 F. Supp. 2d 145, 157 (N.D.N.Y. 1999) ("It is not unusual for a jury to make a finding as to patent infringement independent of a finding of patent enforceability. A jury may in any given case find that a party has infringed another's patent but that the subject patent is unenforceable. Under the trial plan herein devised, one aspect of the enforceability determination is merely delayed.")

[36]   *Malbon v. Pennsylvania Millers Mutual Insur. Co.*, 636 F.2d 936, 940 n.11 (4th Cir. 1980).

[37]   *Virginia Panel Corp.*, 1996 U.S. Dist. LEXIS 8514 at *7; see also *Alcatel USA, Inc. DGI Techs., Inc.*, 166 F.3d 772, 795 (5th Cir. 1999) ("Fed. R. Civ. P. 39(c) provides that 'in all actions not triable of right by a jury[,] the court upon motion or of its own initiative may try any issue with an advisory jury or . . . the court, with consent of parties, may order a trial with a jury whose verdict has the same effect as if trial by jury had been a matter of right'").

[38]   *B. Braun Med., Inc. v. Abbott Labs.*, 124 F.3d 1419, 1426 (Fed. Cir. 1997) ("The jury also found Braun guilty of patent misuse based on the following instruction from the district court (emphasis added): '[A] patent holder is not allowed to place restrictions on customers which prohibit resale of the patented

a jury trial in *B. Braun Med. v. Abbott Lab.*, the Federal Circuit responded that "Braun cites no authority for the proposition that these issues may never be submitted to a jury. Fed. R. Civ. P. 39(b) clearly allows that 'the court in its discretion upon motion may order a trial by jury of any or all issues.'"[39] *Virginia Panel* also gave guidance on how appellate courts review the trial court's decision. It instructed that:

> When reviewing a jury finding on an equitable issue normally reserved for the court such as patent misuse, we will first presume that the jury resolved the underlying factual disputes in favor of the verdict winner and leave those presumed findings undisturbed if they are supported by substantial evidence. Then, in a manner analogous to our review of legal conclusions, we examine the conclusion *de novo* to see whether it is correct in light of the jury fact findings.[40]

Patentees were much more likely to succeed in jury trials than bench trials, with jury trials consistently outperforming bench trials between 1995 and 2008 (Figure 6.16).[41] In 2012, however, the overall success rates for bench and jury trials were similar at 67 percent and 66 percent respectively.[42] A 2009 version of the report also noted that jury awards have

---

product, or allow the customer to resell the patented product only in connection with certain products. . . . If you find, by a preponderance of the evidence, that Braun placed such restrictions on its customers, including Abbott, you *must* find that Braun is guilty of patent misuse'. Braun contends that this jury instruction is legally erroneous because it essentially creates *per se* liability for any conditions that Braun placed on its sales. We agree."); see also *C.R. Bard v. M3 Sys.*, 157 F.3d 1340, 1372 (Fed. Cir. 1998) ("The jury returned special verdicts that Bard had misused both the '056 and '308 patents.").

[39] *B. Braun Med., Inc. v. Abbott Lab.*, 892 F. Supp. 112, 114–115 (E.D. Pa. 1995) (Noting that "[t]he factors which bear on the decision to exercise the discretion authorized by Rule 39(b) and grant a jury trial include: (1) whether the issues are more appropriate for determination by a jury or a judge . . . (2) any prejudice that granting a jury trial would cause the opposing party . . . (3) the timing of the motion . . . (4) any effect a jury trial would have had on the court's docket and the orderly administration of justice . . . ").

[40] *Virginia Panel Corp.*, 133 F.3d at 868.

[41] Aron Levko et al., *A Closer Look: Patent Litigation Trends and the Increasing Impact of Nonpracticing Entities*, PRICEWATERHOUSECOOPERS, LLP. 6–7 (August 2009), http://www.pwc.com/us/en/forensic-services/publications/assets/2009-patent-litigation-study.pdf ("Adjusting for inflation using the Consumer Price Index, the annual median damage award has ranged from $2.2 million to $10.6 million, with a median award of $4.4 million over the last 14 years. In the aggregate, there is no discernable trend over this period. . . . Landmark damages awards continue to make corporate management keenly aware of the risks and rewards for enforcing their patent rights. Since 2005, at least 10 significant federal district court decisions have awarded damages exceeding $100 million . . .").

[42] PWC Report *supra* note 25, at 12.

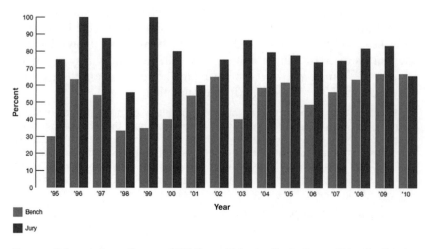

Source: PricewaterhouseCoopers, *2011 Patent Litigation Study: Patent Litigation Trends as the "America Invents Act" becomes Law* (October 2011). Available at: http://www.pwc. com/us/en/forensic-services/publications/2011-patent-litigation-study.jhtml

Figure 6.16   Bench v. jury trials success rate over time (percentage wins between 1995 and 2010)

been significantly greater than bench awards since 2000, due to factors such as self-selection bias by plaintiffs who believe that juries are swayed by the disclosed worth of defendants or by the visceral desire to punish perceived wrongdoing, rather than merely to compensate the plaintiff for infringement of its patent.[43]

The success which patentees enjoyed in bench trials based on the PWC study between 2001 and 2010 was approximately 58 percent and 76 percent

---

[43]   Aron Levko et al., *supra* note 41, at 10 ("A number of reasons may account for the decrease in bench awards, including an increase in the number of Abbreviated New Drug Application pharmaceutical cases (which do not have damages and are tried by the bench), as well as the possibility that plaintiffs with larger envisioned damages may believe juries will look more favorably upon them than judges; thus, introducing self-selection bias in the results. The increase in damages awarded by juries in patent cases may be due to juries' reduced sensitivity to large dollar awards with public disclosures of larger profits and net worth from major company defendants. Greater outrage at a finding of liability to punish the infringer rather than merely compensate the patent holder may also be a factor in increased damages awards. Self-selection bias could also play a part, as plaintiffs may believe juries will look more favorably upon them than judges, especially when seeking large monetary awards.")

in jury trials. Their success in misuse cases in that same period was 92 percent. However, it is doubtful that this comparison has any significance, because of the difference in proving infringement and refuting an allegation of misuse in the form of an equitable defense. The dataset provided too few cases to draw any meaningful conclusion on the success rate of jury trials in misuse cases.

C.   Motion to Strike/Dismiss

Misuse arises in Motions to Strike or Dismiss a case. In *Altana Pharma AG v. Teva Pharms., USA, Inc.* the defendants alleged that the patentees engaged in patent misuse by amending their existing patent license agreement to treat the patent as if it were in force six months beyond the expiration date.[44] In denying the patentees' motion to strike, the District Court for the District of New Jersey found that:

> Defendants' theory of the case is predicated on their contention that the relevant case law supports the conclusion the Plaintiff's alleged conduct is patent misuse under Brulotte. Defendants should be allowed to test this theory and, as such, this Plaintiff['s] challenge is more properly decided at the summary judgment stage.[45]

It also observed that "[t]o the extent that leveraging need be shown in a per se case, as alleged here, merely pleading extension [of] the temporal scope of the patent by charging post-expiration royalties would constitute 'patent leverage' for the purpose of surviving a motion to strike."[46]

Motions to Strike/Dismiss appear in 14 percent of cases overall, and 18 percent of cases at the district court level over the years.[47] It has risen from 3 percent between 1953 and 1962 to 31 percent between 2003 and

---

[44]   *Altana Pharma AG v. Teva Pharms.*, USA, Inc., 2012 U.S. Dist. LEXIS 79166, 8 (D.N.J. June 7, 2012).

[45]   Ibid. at 11.

[46]   Ibid.

[47]   "Motions to strike under Federal Rule 12(f) is the appropriate remedy for the elimination of redundant, immaterial, impertinent, or scandalous matter in any pleading, and is the primary procedure for objecting to an insufficient defense," 5C FED. PRAC. & PROC. CIV. § 1380 (3d ed. 2010). Motions to dismiss are "most frequently aimed at a petition or complaint on the grounds that it fails to state a cause of action, or a claim upon which relief can be granted. A motion to dismiss is designed to test the legal sufficiency of the complaint, not to determine factual issues," ibid. The Federal Rules of Civil Procedure allows a District Court to strike "any insufficient defense," Fed. R. Civ. P. 12(f) (providing that a motion to strike be brought within 21 days after the service of the pleading).

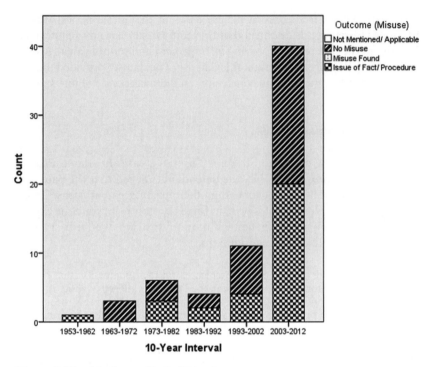

Figure 6.17   Motion to Strike/Dismiss

2012 (Figure 6.17). By contrast, bench trials have fallen from 69 percent to 7 percent during those two same periods. The literature notes that "[b]oth because striking a portion of a pleading is a drastic remedy and because it often is sought by the movant simply as a dilatory or harassing tactic, numerous judicial decisions make it clear that motions . . . are viewed with disfavor by the federal courts and are infrequently granted."[48] Thus, in order to succeed on a "motion to strike surplus matter from an answer, the federal courts have established a standard under which it must be shown that the allegations being challenged are so unrelated to the plaintiff's claims as to be unworthy of any consideration as a defense and that their presence in the pleading throughout the proceeding will be prejudicial to the moving party."[49] Yet the fact that Motions to Strike/Dismiss feature prominently indicate that patentees desire a quick resolution of misuse

---

[48]   5C FED. PRAC. & PROC. § 1380 (3d ed. 2010).
[49]   Ibid.

issues. Few misuse cases have been fully considered during a bench trial in recent years.

Motions to Strike/Dismiss did not feature in the 1953–1962 period (Figure 6.17). They did, however, feature in every subsequent period, with a 100 percent success rate in 30 instances, and 35 instances decided on a matter of fact or procedure that did not favor either party. One reason for this one-sided outcome is revealed by a survey of the cases. The survey showed an astounding lack of awareness by infringers or their legal advisors on what is required to successfully allow a claim of misuse to survive motions to strike by patentees. As an initial matter, infringers need to plead the minimum threshold of notice pleadings.[50] Yet, merely parroting elements of a misuse claim without facts to support that claim is a recipe for disaster.[51] What then is required? Some courts have required infringers to state how patentees have attempted to provide some description of how the patent scope was exceeded with some anticompetitive effect.[52] Another requirement outlined is that "a patent misuse defense must be plead with the specificity required under Rule 9(b)."[53]

---

[50] *Takeda Chem. Indus., Ltd. v. Alphapharm Pty., Ltd.*, No. 04 Civ. 1966, 2004 U.S. Dist. LEXIS 16584, at *4–5 (S.D.N.Y. Aug. 19, 2004).

[51] Ibid. ("The parties dispute whether the defendants' allegations of patent misuse are governed by the liberal pleading standards of Rule 8(a), Fed. R. Civ. P., or by the particularized pleading requirements set forth in Rule 9(b), Fed. R. Civ. P. It is unnecessary to reach this issue, since the defendants' allegations fail to meet even the minimal requirements of notice pleading. The defendants merely parrot the elements of a claim for patent misuse, without alleging even general facts to support that claim. Conclusory references to an 'anti-competitive effect' and 'improper restraint on competition' contained in the defendants' pleadings are not sufficient to give Takeda notice of the misconduct alleged"); see also *Network Caching Tech., LLC v. Novell, Inc.*, No. C-01-2079-VRW, 2001 U.S. Dist. LEXIS 26211, at *11–12 (N.D. Cal. Dec. 31, 2001) (finding "conclusory allegation, with reference only to [patentee's] licensing practices, does not provide fair notice of [infringer's] defense", and proceeded to strike it off.).

[52] *Advanced Cardiovascular Sys., Inc. v. Scimed Sys., Inc.*, C-96-0950 DLJ, 1996 WL 467277, at *4 (N.D. Cal. July 24, 1996) ("plaintiff has attempted to overbroadly and impermissibly construe its patent such as to cause an anticompetitive effect. . . ."); *County Materials Corp. v. Allan*, 502 F.3d 730, 736 (7th Cir. 2007) (citing *Windsurfing*) ("at the summary judgment stage, some evidence tending to show an adverse effect in an economically sound relevant market is essential for any claim governed by the rule of reason").

[53] *Ortho-Tain, Inc. v. Rocky Mountain Orthodontics, Inc.*, No. 05 C 6656, 2007 WL 1238917, at *3 (N.D. Ill. April 25, 2007) (citing *Advanced Cardiovascular Sys., Inc. v. Medtronic, Inc.*, No. C-95-3577 DLJ, 1996 WL 467293, at *13 (N.D. Cal. July 24, 1996) (holding that the affirmative defence for unclean hands and patent misuse rested on allegations of inequitable conduct before the PTO).

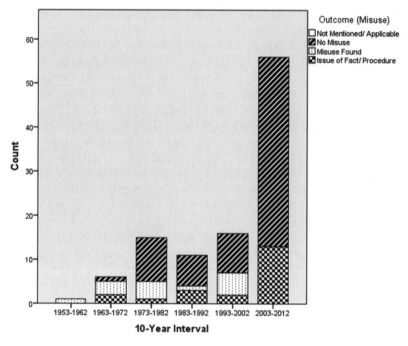

Figure 6.18   Summary judgments (overall)

D. Summary Judgments

Summary judgment proceedings determine whether there are any triable issues of fact requiring a formal trial on the merits rather than the deciding factual disputes "thus putting a swift end to meritless litigation . . . because it allows the court to move beyond the allegations in the pleadings and analyze the evidence to ascertain whether there is a need for a trial."[54] A motion for summary judgment, compared to a motion on the pleadings, typically allows matters outside the pleadings, specifically affidavits, to be presented and considered.[55]

This study distinguished between three types of summary judgments: (1) those initiated by the patentee, (2) those initiated by the defendant, and (3) those initiated by both in the form of a cross motion for summary judgment.

---

[54]   73 Karl Oakes, AMERICAN JURISPURDENCE 2D § 1 (2012).
[55]   Ibid. at § 6.

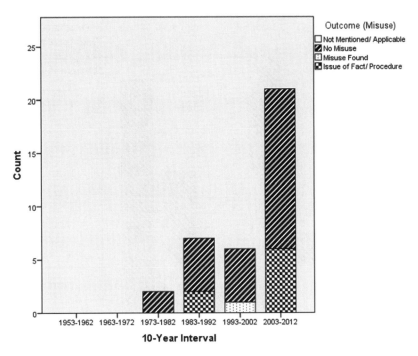

Figure 6.19   Summary judgments (patentee)

Looking at summary judgments as a whole (Figure 6.18), it is clear that as with Motions To Strike/Dismiss, there is a marked rise in recent years, with the most number of motions for summary judgment brought between 2003 and 2012. This period saw a staggering rise from the three previous decades, where the numbers remain relatively constant before nearly tripling. Notably, the proportion of patentee wins also increased from 67 percent in the 1973–1982 period to 95 percent in the 2003–2012 period.

Breaking the data down into the three categories of summary judgments, more interesting trends emerge (Figures 6.19–6.21). A spike in summary judgments during 2003–2012 was observed in all three categories with cross motions as well as motions initiated by patentees accounting for about 75 percent of the overall figure during that time period. This is consistent with the notion that patentees are more inclined to have misuse resolved prior to a full hearing on the merits. Indeed, if one looks at Figure 6.19, which shows motions initiated by the patentee alone, summary judgments do not even feature between 1953 and 1972. Defendants also appeared tentatively in the early years, with only two cases featuring summary judgments initiated by them between 1953 and

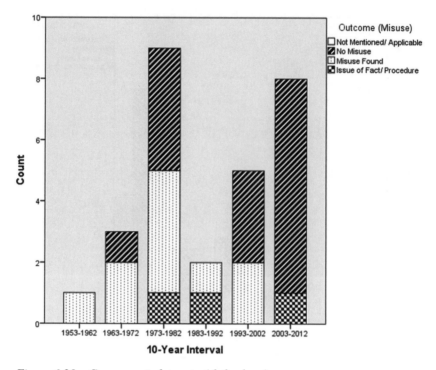

Figure 6.20   Summary judgments (defendant)

1972. The 1973–1982 period, however, saw a spike followed by a fall for another twenty years, before the recent spike in the 2003–2012 period. That spike in the 1972–1981 period correlates to the success which infringers had in summary judgment motions—a remarkable 63 percent success rate which fell to a zero in the 2003–2012 period (Figure 6.21). In terms of cross motions, the trend follows that of patentees, as seen in Figure 6.19 with similar rates of success. As with fair use under U.S. copyright law, the parties' win rates were sharply lower for cross motions for summary judgment.[56] At the same time, however, it is possible that the rise in misuse appearing in pre-trial motions simply reflects a broader trend towards pre-trial actions, as Figure 6.22 shows.

---

[56]   See Beebe, *supra* note 7, at 575–76 ("Among summary judgment opinions, 86.4% of the opinions that addressed a plaintiff's uncrossed motion for summary judgment granted that motion, while 76.7% of the opinions that addressed a defendant's uncrossed motion for summary judgment granted that motion. The parties' win rates were sharply lower for cross-motions for summary judgment").

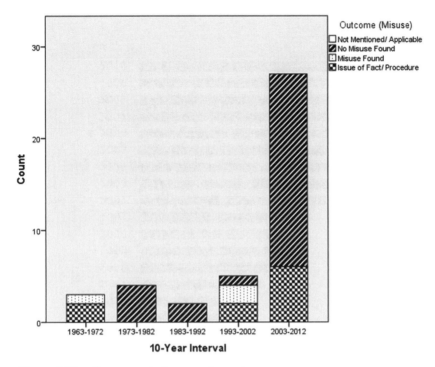

Figure 6.21   Summary judgments (cross)

E.   Declaratory Judgments

Cases in recent times have recognized that "parties may raise patent misuse through an action for declaratory relief".[57] It may be used "solely to enjoin defendant from asserting a patent infringement claim against plaintiff" and any "must limit its effect to rendering the patent unenforceable only until the misuse is purged."[58] While "monetary damages may not be awarded 'under a declaratory judgment counterclaim based on patent misuse,' because patent misuse simply renders the patent unenforceable," after such

---

[57]   *Powertech Tech., Inc. v. Tessera, Inc.*, 2012 U.S. Dist. LEXIS 113194, at *13–18 (N.D. Cal. Aug. 10, 2012), citing *B. Braun Medical, Inc. v. Abbott Laboratories*, 124 F.3d 1419, 1428 (Fed. Cir. 1997) (noting that the district court could enter a declaratory judgment that the patent was unenforceable due to misuse); *Inamed Corp. v. Kuzmak*, 275 F. Supp. 2d 1100, 1124 (C.D. Cal. 2002).

[58]   *Rosenthal Collins Group, LLC v. Trading Tech. Int'l*, 2005 U.S. Dist. LEXIS 37504, at *23–24 (N.D. Ill.) (citing *B. Braun Medical, Inc. v. Abbott Laboratories*, 124 F.3d 1419, 1427 (1997)).

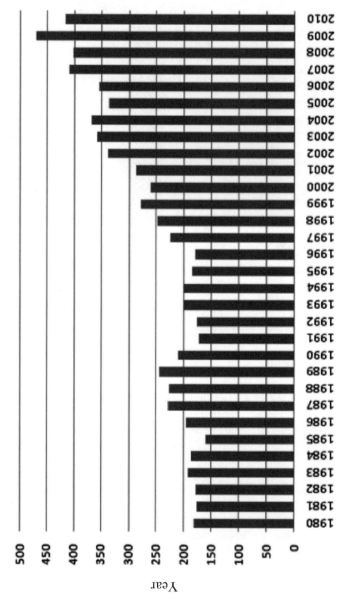

Source: IP WATCHDOG (2010).

Figure 6.22 Termination of patent cases

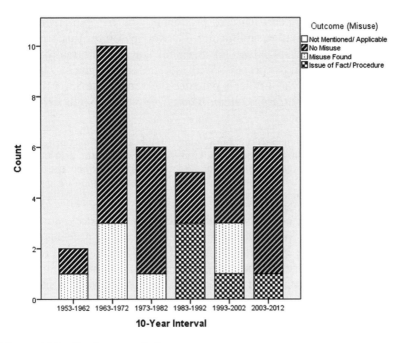

Figure 6.23   Declaratory judgments

a finding, the court may consider whether the plaintiff has stated another "substantive claim upon which it is entitled to recover damages," such as "through an antitrust or breach of contract theory".[59] Declaratory judgments did not feature significantly in the data (6.8%), featuring about as often as individual motions for summary judgment (or a third as frequently if one were to aggregate summary judgments). By way of comparison with general patent litigation trends, the PWC report found that declaratory judgments represent 8 percent of patent cases.[60] The two spikes observed in Figure 6.23 were in the 1963–1972 and the 2003–2012 periods. The latter period further confirms the use of pre-trial motions by patentees to resolve issues of misuse. The former period, however, raises more questions. Infringers were also the most successful during that period, succeeding in showing misuse 75 percent of the time, compared to about 20 percent of the time in the 1973–1982 and the 2003–2012 periods, where they were next most successful. Indeed, infringers did not win in any other period.

---

[59] *Powertech Tech., Inc. v. Tessera, Inc.*, 2012 U.S. Dist. LEXIS 113194, at *15, citing *B. Braun*, 124 F.3d at 1428.

[60] Aron Levko et al., *supra* note 41, at 14.

Declaratory judgments featured prominently in the opinions reviewed as a matter of qualitative significance. The key reason for this is probably because defendants in patent infringement suits are normally reactive parties in the litigation process. With declaratory judgments, however, they can proactively neutralize a patentee's advance. The Seventh Circuit in *County Materials Corp. v. Allan Block Corp* vividly paints declaratory judgments in action:

> Allan Block threatened to sue, but County Line beat it to the courthouse with this suit for a declaratory judgment. County Line wanted the district court to declare that the covenant not to compete was unenforceable because it violated federal patent policy, essentially raising an anticipatory patent misuse defense to its planned breach of the Agreement.[61]

Indeed, patent literature recognizes the strategy in declaratory judgments, noting that "[i]n addition to being interposed as a defense, patent misuse can also be affirmatively asserted in an action or counterclaim seeking a declaratory judgment of patent unenforceability, and may even be the basis for an action or counterclaim for unfair competition."[62] The Second Circuit, in barring a plaintiff's complaint on the ground that its antitrust claims were counterclaims and should have been raised in a previous patent infringement suit, distinguished counterclaims based on patent invalidity from those based on patent misuse, "thus implicitly recognizing that a counterclaim for patent misuse is a valid action."[63] Similarly, the Federal Circuit, citing as precedent the Supreme Court's *Mercoid* decision, held in *Glitsch Inc. v. Koch Engineering Co.* that a "party that did not raise the issue of patent misuse in one action may raise that issue in another action based on a separate assertion of infringement, whether as a defense against the claim of infringement or in a request for declaratory relief."[64]

---

[61] *County Materials Corp. v. Allan Block Corp*, 502 F.3d 730, 732 (7th Cir. 2007).

[62] 1 Louis Altman & Malla Pollack, CALLMANN ON UNFAIR COMPETITION., TR. & MONO. § 4:57 (4th ed. 2010).

[63] *Marchon Eyewear, Inc. v. Tura LP*, No. 98-CV-1932, 2002 U.S. Dist. LEXIS 19628, at *27–29 (E.D.N.Y. Sept. 30, 2002) (discussing *Critical-Vac Filtration Corp. v. Minuteman Int'l, Inc.*, 233 F.3d 697, 703–04 (2d Cir. 2000) ("On the other hand, counterclaims related to *misuse* and other more economically oriented antitrust claims would seem generally to be distinct in nature and substance from patent validity and infringement issues"); see also *Affymetrix, Inc. v. PE Corp.*, 219 F. Supp. 2d 390 (S.D.N.Y. 2002) (denying defendants' motion to dismiss plaintiff's patent misuse claim); see also *Moore U.S.A., Inc. v. Std. Register Co.*, 139 F. Supp. 2d 348, 362 (W.D.N.Y. 2001) ("[The Counterclaimant] can state a patent misuse claim to the extent that it alleges that [counterdefendants] have engaged in sham litigation").

[64] *Glitsch Inc. v. Koch Eng'g Co.*, 216 F.3d 1382, 1386 (Fed. Cir. 2000); see also *Linzer Products Corp. v. Sekar*, 499 F. Supp. 2d 540, 552–53 (S.D.N.Y. 2007)

However, the U.S. District Court for the Northern District of Ohio in *Semco, Inc. v. Exco Techs. Ltd.* remarked that "[a]lthough courts have allowed patent misuse claims to be presented as counterclaims, these have been limited to circumstances where patent infringement claims were also involved."[65] Courts have also drawn the line on allowing defendants to claim damages in the event misuse is shown.[66]

F. Appellate Reviews

Appellate reviews form a substantial proportion of all the cases, at about a fifth of all the cases studied (Figure 6.24). The most appeals were taken between 1953 and 1982, which saw a year on year increase before halving and remaining fairly constant at about 10 appeals every decade between 1983 and 2012. This consistency in appeal numbers between those years may suggest that the Federal Circuit's establishment plays a role in controlling the number of misuse appeals. Infringers were most successful between 1953 and 1982. Indeed, they were equally successful in those three decades, winning 42 percent of the time. In succeeding decades, they saw a fall in success rates, such that in 2003–2012, infringers won only 14 percent of the time. Overall, infringers were successful about 37 percent of the time. On appeal, 67.4 percent of appeals are upheld and 26.7 percent reversed (Figure 6.25). By way of comparison, infringers during 1983–2008 were successful in allegations of inequitable conduct on appeal about 24 percent of the time,[67] whereas they were successful in allegations of misuse about 18 percent of the time. The Federal Circuit on appeal affirms almost all inequitable conduct decisions rendered by district courts.[68] Findings of no inequitable conduct are affirmed 92 percent of the time, and affirmed findings of inequitable conduct 41 percent of the time. In misuse cases, district court opinions finding misuse are affirmed 77.8 percent of the time, and findings of no misuse are affirmed 72.7 percent of the time.

The data also confirms that patent misuse has only been considered

---

(observing that "*Braun* did not proscribe claims seeking a declaratory judgment of patent misuse. Indeed, in later actions, the Federal Circuit has allowed such claims without comment").

[65] *Semco, Inc. v. Exco Techs. Ltd.*, No. 3:06 CV 2045, 2007 U.S. Dist. LEXIS 67425, at *4 (N.D. Ohio Sept. 11, 2007).

[66] *Shuffle Master, Inc. v. Awada*, No. 2:05-CV-1112-RCJ, 2006 U.S. Dist. LEXIS 71748, at *10 (D. Nev. Sept. 26, 2006) ("Most courts . . . have held that a defense of patent misuse 'may not be converted to an affirmative claim for damages simply by restyling it as a declaratory judgment counterclaim'").

[67] Petherbridge, *supra* note 9, at 1309.

[68] Mammen, *supra* note 8, at 1354.

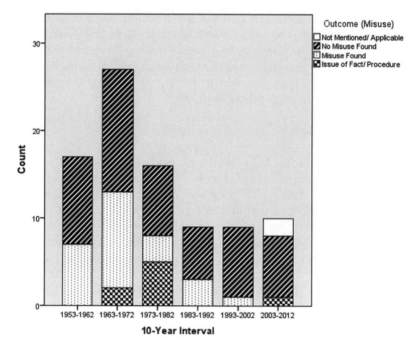

Figure 6.24   Appellate panel review

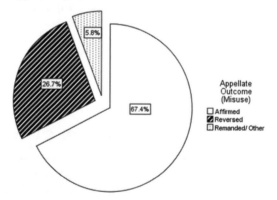

Figure 6.25   Outcome on appeal

en banc by the Federal Circuit in *Princo*. At the appellate level, there appears to be a lack of judicial interest in clarifying the boundaries of the doctrine—whether to reinvigorate or eliminate the doctrine. With the Supreme Court regaining its interest in reviewing patent cases from the Federal Circuit and correcting its doctrinal position in many cases, it

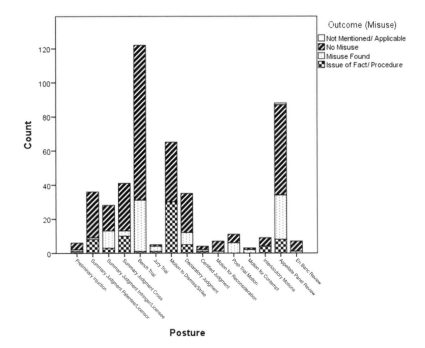

Figure 6.26   Outcomes by posture

may be timely to tee up misuse for a fresh reconsideration by the Supreme Court. The Supreme Court has granted petitions for certiorari in 12 Federal Circuit decisions between 2003 and 2012.[69] In seven of those cases, the Supreme Court reversed and/or vacated the Federal Circuit's decision. In two of the five decisions it affirmed it changed the applicable legal standard[70] (Figure 6.26).

---

[69]   See *J.E.M. Ag Supply v. Pioneer Hi-Bred Int'l, Inc.*, 534 U.S. 124 (2001); *Festo Corp. v. Shoketsu Kinzoku Kogyo Kabushiki Co.*, 535 U.S. 722 (2002); *Merck KGaA v. Integra Lifesciences I, Ltd.*, 545 U.S. 193 (2005); *Lab. Corp. of Am. Holdings v. Metabolite Labs., Inc.* 548 U.S. 124 (2006); *eBay Inc. v. MercExchange*, L.L.C., 547 U.S. 388 (2006); *MedImmune, Inc. v. Genentech, Inc.*, 549 U.S. 118 (2007); *KSR Int'l Co. v. Teleflex, Inc.*, 550 U.S. 398 (2007); *Microsoft Corp. v. AT&T Corp.*, 550 U.S. 437 (2007); *Quanta Computer, Inc. v. LG Elecs.*, 553 U.S. 617 (2008); *Bilski v. Kappos*, 130 S. Ct. 3218 (2010); *Global-Tech Appliances, Inc. v. SEB S.A.*, 131 S. Ct. 2060 (2011); *Bd. of Trs. of Leland Stanford Junior Univ. v. Roche Molecular Sys., Inc.*, 131 S. Ct. 2188 (2011); *Microsoft Corp. v. i4i Ltd. P'ship*, 131 S. Ct. 2238 (2011).

[70]   See *Festo Corp.*, 535 U.S. at 737–38 (The U.S. Court of Appeals for the Federal Circuit failed to apply the proper standard. It was an error to adopt a

IV. JUDGES RESPONSIBLE FOR SHAPING THE MISUSE DOCTRINE

That the Federal Circuit is responsible for shaping current conventional wisdom on patent misuse begs the question of who within the "Secret Circuit" shaped patent misuse as we know it today. It is precisely this kind of question that this empirical study was created to answer. The first step in the inquiry is to identify all the patent misuse cases decided by the Federal Circuit from its inception to the end period of the study in December 2012. The results are presented in Table 6.1.

The second step involves using the data from Table 6.1 and combining that data with information about each judge's position in the relevant case. This gives the table displayed in Table 6.2.

A. Three Judges

A number of conclusions are apparent from Tables 6.1 and 6.2. First, the cases which shape conventional wisdom of patent misuse—the *Windsurfing* case, the *Senza-Gel* case, the *Mallinkrodt* case, the *C. R. Bard* case and two cases involving Monsanto were authored by just three judges – Judges Bryson, Newman and former Chief Judge Markey. Judge Newman's pro-patent view is apparent from the earlier discussion. As Chris Mammen noted in the context of inequitable conduct, Judge Newman has also been lukewarm at best to inequitable conduct, another doctrine which risks eroding legitimately exercised patent rights.

> Perhaps the most striking feature of this graph is that, despite her long tenure and many opinions, Judge Newman has *never* written a majority opinion supporting a finding of inequitable conduct. When this fact is considered, it should come as no surprise that, although she did not originally coin the 'plague'

complete bar. The reach of prosecution estoppel "requires an examination of the subject matter surrendered by the narrowing amendment. The complete bar avoids this inquiry"); *Merck KGaA*, 545 U.S. at 193 (the Federal Circuit applied an incorrect standard and interpretation of the statute. The Court held that "the use of patented compounds in preclinical studies was protected under [35 U.S.C.A.] § 271(e)(1) at least as long as there was a reasonable basis to believe that the compound tested could be the subject of an FDA submission and the experiments would produce the types of information relevant to [drug applications under 21 U.S.C.S. § 355]"); *KSR Int'l Co.*, 550 U.S. 398 (altering the standard for §103 nonobviousness determination.); *eBay Inc.*, 547 U.S. at 393–94 (stating that the Federal Circuit applied an incorrect standard for assessing the grant of permanent injunction. The Supreme Court held that the traditional four-factor test should be employed in instances of permanent injunction determination).

Table 6.1   Case and panel details

No.	Case name	Cite	Year	Cir.	Panel*	Outcome
1	*Sanofi-Aventis v. Apotex Inc.*	659 F.3d 1171	2011	13	**Moore**, Schall, Newman Dissent in part: Newman	No misuse
2	*Princo Corp. v. ITC*	616 F.3d 1318	2010	13	Bryson, Rader, Newman, Lourie, Linn, Moore Concur.: Prost, Mayer Dissent: Dyk, Gajarsa	No misuse
3	*Princo Corp. v. International Trade Com'n*	563 F.3d 1301	2009	13	**Dyk**, Bryson, Gajarsa Dissent in part: Bryson	No misuse
4	*Qualcomm Inc. v. Broadcom Corp.*	548 F.3d 1004	2008	13	**Prost**, Mayer, Lourie Lourie	Not applic-able
5	*Monsanto Co. v. McFarling*	488 F.3d 973	2007	13	**Bryson**, Lourie, Rader	No misuse
6	*Monsanto Co. v. Scruggs*	459 F.3d 1328	2006	13	**Mayer**, Bryson, Concur.: in part and dissent in Part: **Dyk**	No misuse
7	*United States Philips Corp. v. Princo Corp.*	173 Fed. Appx. 832	2006	13	Bryson, Linn, Dyk (per curiam)	Vacated
8	*U.S. Philips Corp. v. ITC*	424 F.3d 1179	2005	13	**Bryson**, Gajarsa, Linn	No misuse
9	*Monsanto Co. v. McFarling*	363 F.3d 1336	2004	13	**Clevenger**, Lourie, Plager	No misuse
10	*Monsanto Co. v. McFarling*	302 F.3d 1291	2002	13	**Newman**, Clevenger, Bryson	No misuse
11	*Ricoh Co. v. Nashua Corp.*	1999 U.S. App. LEXIS 2672	1999	13	Plager, Bryson, Gajarsa (per curiam)	No misuse
12	*C.R. Bard v. M3 Sys.*	157 F.3d 1340	1998	13	**Newman**, Mayer, Bryson	No misuse
13	*Virginia Panel Corp. v. MAC Panel Co.*	133 F.3d 860	1997	13	**Lourie**, Archer, Rader	No misuse

Patent misuse and antitrust law

Table 6.1   (continued)

No.	Case name	Cite	Year	Cir.	Panel*	Outcome
14	B. Braun Med., Inc. v. Abbott Labs.	124 F.3d 1419	1997	13	**Clevenger**, Michel, Plager	No misuse
15	Engel Indus. V. Lockformer Co.	96 F.3d 1398	1996	13	**Rich**, Mayer, Bryson	No misuse
16	Glaverbel Societe Anonyme v. Northlake Mktg. & Supply	45 F.3d 1550	1995	13	**Newman**, Mayer, Clevenger	No misuse
17	Mallinckrodt, Inc. V. Medipart, Inc.	976 F.2d 700	1992	13	**Newman**, Lourie, Clevenger	No misuse
18	Hodosh v. Block Drug Co.	833 F.2d 1575	1987	13	**Markey**, Davis, Baldwin	Vacated
19	Allen Archery, Inc. v. Browning Mfg. Co.	819 F.2d 1087	1987	13	**Friedman**, Davis, Bennett	No misuse
20	Senza-Gel Corp. v. Seiffhart	803 F.2d 661	1986	13	**Markey**, Bennett, Nies,	Misuse found
24	Windsurfing Int'l v. AMF, Inc.	782 F.2d 995	1986	13	**Markey**, Smith, Newman	No misuse

Note: *Author of opinion indicated in bold.

label, she is responsible for nine of the twelve subsequent characterizations of inequitable conduct as a 'plague' in Federal Circuit opinions. Judges Lourie and Rader together are responsible for the remaining three opinions. The six most recent invocations of 'plague' have appeared in dissenting opinions, five of which were written by Judge Newman.

Mammen continues, "Among those judges who have expressed concern about inequitable conduct as a 'plague,' Judge Newman stands out as particularly vocal on the issue. But are her protestations warranted? The statistical data is suggestive that the prevalence of inequitable conduct cases is expanding, especially at the pleading stage."[71]

Judge Bryson's involvement in patent misuse cases is perhaps the most interesting analysis of the three. While, like the other two judges, he has authored three opinions, he has also sat on 11 panels out of the 23 that heard patent misuse cases—nearly half—and far more than Chief Judge

---

[71]   Mammen *supra* note 8, at 1357–58, 1361.

Table 6.2   Data breakdown by judge

Judge	No. of opinions authored	No. of panels judge was part of	No. of dissents	No. of concurrences
Bryson	3	11	1	0
Newman	3	5	1	0
Markey	3	3	0	0
Rich	1	2	0	0
Clevenger	2	4	0	0
Mayer	1	6	0	1
Lourie	1	5	0	0
Dyk	1	4	2	1
Prost	1	2	0	0
Friedman	1	0	0	0
Gajarsa	0	4	1	0
Linn	0	3	0	1
Rader	0	3	0	0
Plager	0	3	0	0
Moore	1	2	0	0
Schall	0	1	0	0
Total	**18**	**58**	**5**	**3**

Mayer who, as the next in line in terms of case count, sat on six panels. Judge Bryson was also involved in every one of the four *Philips/Princo* cases, and wrote the only *en banc* opinion on patent misuse in the twenty or so years since the last Supreme Court case in *Dawson Chem. Co. v. Rohm & Haas Co.* in 1980. It is safe to say that the Federal Circuit's patent misuse doctrine was primarily conceived by then-Chief Judge Markey, nurtured by Judge Newman and matured under Judge Bryson. Given that Judge Bryson has taken senior status at the time of writing, the future shape of patent misuse may be left to other members of the Federal Circuit. For example, Judge Lourie, who wrote *Virginia Panel*, cited interchangeably with *Windsurfing*, and sat on five panels, making him the third in line after Bryson and Mayer. Mammen notes that Judge Lourie shared Judge Newman's concern for inequitable conduct.[72] While not conclusive, one might wonder if this concern also extends to patent misuse, which shares many of the key characteristics of inequitable conduct, such as the vagueness in their equitable nature and their non-enforceability until all offending elements are purged. Judge Rich wrote the opinion for one misuse case, *Engel Industries, Inc v. Lockformer Co.*, and sat on three panels.

---

[72]   Ibid.

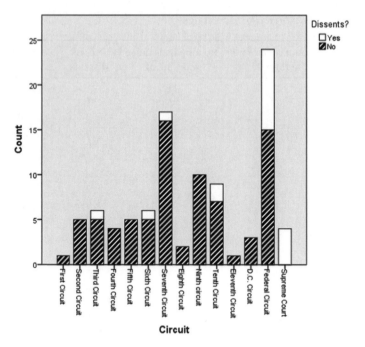

Figure 6.27   Dissents by circuit

B.   Dissents

It is remarkable that the number of dissents appears to be fairly high. Nearly one in five appellate opinions studied have one dissent. This suggests that misuse is controversial among the judiciary. At the Supreme Court level, every misuse case has a dissenting opinion (Figures 6.27 and 6.28). Even at the Federal Circuit level, 30% of the cases have dissents. Of course, one would recall that the history of misuse in Chapter 2 was marked by dissents, with the majority view often becoming subsumed into a minority one as the attitudes toward patents oscillated over time.

V.   CONTROLLING PRECEDENT

A.   Introduction

Controlling precedents are important because they both point to the origin of a body of case law as well as trace its development. The cases surveyed were grouped according to ten categories of controlling precedents.

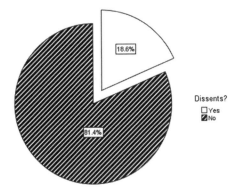

Figure 6.28 Dissents (overall)

A controlling precedent was identified as the case that the court regarded as having been instructive in determining how misuse as to be viewed.[73] Where two or more cases are consecutively cited, the one case that most clearly and authoritatively governs the case is identified as the controlling precedent.[74] Courts also sometimes cited different cases to stand for the same precedent. In these instances the cases will be coded under a single header. For example, *Windsurfing* stands for the proposition that to prove misuse, infringers must show that patentees exceeded the physical or temporal scope of their patents with anticompetitive effect. So do *Virginia Panel, Philips*, and *Monsanto*. Some cases cite *Windsurfing*. Others cite *Virginia Panel* or one of the others. However, since the proposition remains the same, they are all coded under the *Windsurfing* header, since *Windsurfing* was the case most often cited for that proposition. In such cases, they were coded by their label.

Where two cases stand for a similar proposition but are applied to different categories of misuse, or if they do not strictly flow from the same view of misuse, the two cases were separately coded. For example,

[73] See, e.g., *F.C. Russell Co. v. Consumers Insulation Co.*, 226 F.2d 373, 373 (3d Cir. 1955) ("The answer to the first question turns on our decision in National Lockwasher Co. v. George K. Garrett Co., 3 Cir., 1943, 137 F.2d 255, 256").

[74] For example, in *Applera Corp. v. MJ Research, Inc.*, 349 F. Supp. 2d 321, 333–38 (D. Conn. 2004), the court held that "[i]n the absence of this tie, the prospect of paying more than once for the right to use a thermal cycler to perform PCR amounts to no more than an increased royalty fee, which is within the scope of Applera's lawful patent monopoly. *See Brulotte*, 379 U.S. at 33, 85 S. Ct. 176; *Monsanto Co. v. McFarling*, 302 F.3d 1291, 1299 (Fed. Cir. 2002)." Since *Brulotte* is more specifically relates to royalty extensions rather than *Monsanto*, it was chosen as the controlling precedent.

Morton Salt and *Brulotte* both take a strict view of patent misuse in favor of defendants, but while the former adopts a more flexible patent policy focus in assessing the improper expansion of patent scope, the latter takes a more formalistic assessment of patent scope by looking at the length of the patent. These are coded differently. Finally, some cases such as *Broadcom* were not specifically misuse cases but still discussed misuse and were cited by later misuse cases for their views. These were also captured in the data-table. The details are presented in Table 6.3.

B. Precedent Trends as a Whole

One can see the resulting trends of controlling precedent in Figure 6.29. Looking at trends over the last 60 years as a whole, it is clear that the dominant case precedents over time are *Windsurfing* (31.5%), *Morton Salt* (17.9%) and *Mercoid* (16.2%). These three groups of precedents are far more dominant than any other precedent group—the next more dominant precedent group being *Brulotte* (6.0%).

C. Dominant Precedents over Time

Morton Salt was the precedent cited most often between 1953 and 1982 (Figure 6.30). Between 1983 and 1992 courts turned to *Zenith Radio* and *USM Corp.* Between 1993 and 2012 the *Windsurfing* line of cases became the standard cited by the courts, and was cited more frequently than any other line of precedent. This is consistent with conventional wisdom that patent misuse is premised on an extension of patent scope with anticompetitive effects—the golden nugget from *Windsurfing*.

By the 1990s, the *Windsurfing* jurisprudence was commonly applied misuse analysis in the district courts.[75] Robert Hoerner observed that: "most trial judges are not vastly knowledgeable or strongly opinionated on questions concerning patent misuse. They will likely attempt conscientiously to apply the precedents which the lawyers appearing before them urge with reason to be controlling; most are not likely to be innovators."[76] As Hoerner noted:

---

[75] See, e.g., *Raychem Corp. v. PSI Telcomms., Inc.*, No. C-93-20920, 1995 U.S. Dist. LEXIS 22325, at *9–11 (N.D. Cal. Mar. 6, 1995) ("PSI's 'inequitable conduct' allegation is too vague to support a claim of patent misuse. PSI provides no supporting facts explaining what this unspecified 'inequitable conduct' is, let alone how it is anticompetitive in nature").

[76] Hoerner, *supra* note 22, at 714–16.

Table 6.3   Controlling precedent (details)

No.	Case	Year	Circuit	Remarks
1	*Morton Salt Co. v. G.S. Suppiger Co.*[a]	1942	Supreme Court	Public policy requires limitation to patent grant; not limited to antitrust policy
2	*Mercoid Corp. v. Mid-Continent Inv. Co & Mercoid Corp. v. Minneapolis–Honeywell Regulator Co.*[b]	1944	Supreme Court	Patentee prohibited from restraining competition in all items outside the scope of the patent grant, whether staple or not
3	*Brulotte v. Thys Co.*[c]	1964	Supreme Court	Extension beyond period of patent; per se illegal
4	*Walker Proc. Equipment, Inc. v. Food Mach. & Chem.*	1965	Supreme Court	Fraud on patent office amounting to antitrust violation by filing infringement claim based on an invalid patent
5	*Well Surveys, Inc. v. McCullough Tool*[d]	1965	10th Circuit	Misconduct must be connected with the matter in litigation, and not available to a party with whom the misconduct is of no concern
6	*Glaverbel Societe Anonyme v. Northlake Mktg. & Supply*[e]	1995	Federal Circuit	Sham litigation: bad faith and improper purpose required
7	*USM Corp. v. SPS Techs., Inc.*	1982	7th Circuit	Analyzed under antitrust principles
8	*Senza-Gel Corp. v. Seiffhart*	1986	Federal Circuit	Tying analysis based on physical product; market power requirement
9	*Windsurfing Int'l., Inc. v. AMF*[f]	1986	Federal Circuit	Outside physical or temporal scope with anticompetitive effect
10	*Dawson Chem. Co. v. Rohm & Haas Co.*	1980	Supreme Court	Applies 271(d)'s market power requirement to tying cases

Notes: [a] *Motion Picture Patents Co. v. Universal Film Mfg. Co.*, 243 U.S. 502 (1917); *National Lockwasher Co.*,137 F.2d at 256.; *United States v. Paramount Pictures*, 334 U.S. 131 (1948); *Standard Sanitary Mfg. Co. v. United States*, 226 U.S. 20 (1912); *Carbice Corp. of Am. v. Am. Patents Dev. Corp.*, 283 U.S. 27 (1931); [b] *United States v. United States Gypsum Co.*, 333 U.S. 364 (1948); *Automatic Radio Mfg. Co. v. Hazeltine Research, Inc.*, 339 U.S. 827 (1950); *United States v. Loew's Inc.*, 368 U.S. 973 (1962); *Transparent-Wrap Machine Corp. v. Stokes & Smith Co.*, 329 U.S. 637 (1947); *Zenith Radio Corp. v. Hazeltine Research, Inc.*, 395 U.S. 100 (1969); *Univ. of Ill. Found. v. Blonder-Tongue Labs., Inc.*, 334

Table 6.3   (continued)

F. Supp. 47 (N.D. Ill. 1971); *Leitch Mfg. Co. v. Barber Co.*, 302 U.S. 458 (1938); *Congoleum Industries, Inc. v. Armstrong Cork Co.*, 366 F. Supp. 220 (E.D. Pa. 1973); *Am. Securit Co. v. Shatterproof Glass Corp.*, 268 F.2d 769 (3d Cir. 1959); ᶜ *Meehan v. PPG Indus.*, 802 F.2d 881 (7th Cir. 1986); *Aronson v. Quick Point Pencil Co.*, 440 U.S. 257 (1979); *Mestre v. Pitney Bowes, Inc.*, 464 U.S. 893 (1983); *Boggild v. Kenner Prods.*, 776 F.2d 1315 (6th Cir. 1985); *In re Yarn Proc.*, 541 F.2d 1127 (5th Cir. 1976); ᵈ *Kolene Corp. v. Motor City Metal Treating, Inc.*, 440 F.2d 77 (6th Cir. 1971); *Binks Mfg. Co. v. Ransburg Electro-Coating Corp.*, 366 U.S. 211 (1961); *Apex Elec. Mfg. Co. v. Altorfer Bros. Co.*, 238 F.2d 867 (7th Cir. 1956); ᵉ *Prof'l Real Estate Investors, Inc. v. Columbia Pictures Indus., Inc.*, 508 U.S. 49 (1993); ᶠ *C.R. Bard v. M3 Sys.*, 157 F.3d 1340 (Fed. Cir. 1998); *Mallinckrodt, Inc. v. Medipart, Inc.*, 976 F.2d 700 (Fed. Cir. 1992); *B. Braun Med., Inc. v. Abbott Lab.*, 892 F. Supp. 112 (E.D. Pa. 1995); *Virginia Panel Corp. v. MAC Panel Co.*, No. 93-0006-H,1996 U.S. Dist. LEXIS 8514 (W.D. Va. May 29, 1996); *County Materials Corp. v. Allan Block Corp.*, 502 F.3d 730 (7th Cir. 2007); *U.S. Philips Corp. v. Int'l Trade Comm'n*, 424 F.3d 1179 (Fed. Cir. 2005); *Monsanto Co. v. McFarling*, 302 F.3d 1291 (Fed. Cir. 2002).

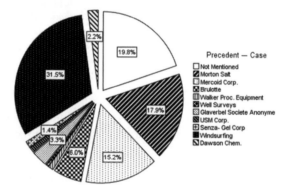

Figure 6.29   Distribution of precedent cases (overall)

[A]n alleged infringer in a patent case of financial importance should have a record to stand on which goes beyond the narrow requirements of extension of the monopoly-type patent misuse. If he does not, he may risk denial of his defense by a judge not familiar with the doctrine, who feels he is overreaching. He could, instead, face a knowledgeable judge who would take the bull by the horns and abolish the doctrine in his courtroom until a higher court said him "nay." Such a judge, without any record showing alleged harm, could reason that the doctrine unfairly diminishes the rights of patentees, rights which are crucial in our world battle for competitiveness, which include a constant struggle to keep American jobs in America.[77]

---

[77]   Ibid. at 714.

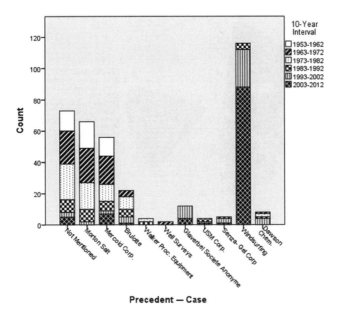

Figure 6.30   Distribution by precedent over time

Indeed, one court even went so far as to state that:

> In a striking display of chutzpah, CMO relies exclusively on cases decided in other circuits and districts before the establishment of the Federal Circuit and before a critical amendment to the patent statute for the proposition that such package-licensing constitutes patent misuse. While this may have been the law of the land in times past, the legal landscape of today is somewhat different.[78]

That legal landscape, according to the Middle District of Florida in *Diamond Heads, LLC v. Everingham* is one where "[a]nticompetitive effects are a critical element of any patent misuse case that is evaluated under this 'rule of reason' approach."[79]

D.   District Courts not Citing Precedent

District court opinions comprised all the cases in the "Not Mentioned" category, that is, where no precedent was cited. In fact, a staggering

---

[78]   *Semiconductor Energy Lab. Co. v. Chi Mei Optoelectronics Corp.*, 531 F. Supp. 2d 1084, 1100 (N.D. Cal. 2007).

[79]   *Diamond Heads, LLC v. Everingham*, No. 8:07-CV-462-T-33TBM, 2009 WL 1046067, at *7 (M.D. Fla. Apr. 20, 2009).

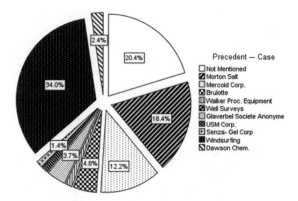

Figure 6.31   Precedent cases (district court level)

20.4 percent of cases, or more than one in five, do not cite any precedent (Figure 6.31). An example of this occurred in *Novo Industri A/S v. Travenol Lab., Inc*, a case arising in the Northern District of Illinois in 1981 and affirmed by the Seventh Circuit.[80] The defendant alleged that Novo had misused its patent rights by entering into a licensing agreement with a third party which extended Novo's monopoly power to control the sale of unpatented products in countries where Novo had no patent protection.[81] The court found the agreement ambiguous and that the record lacked the evidence to support Travenol's view of the restrictive nature of the contract terms.[82] On the basis that the defendant failed to carry its burden of proof, the court deemed it unnecessary to reach the question whether the agreement would constitute misuse of Novo's patent if construed as the defendant asserted it should be.[83]

An academic interviewee offered an explanation for the high frequency, suggesting that district court judges may not have firm grasp of patent misuse.[84] Those judges could have decided to simply dismiss the allegations based on their factual findings, which they have greater expertise at doing, without mention of precedent. Decisions based primarily on facts rather than law may also limit the grounds on which disgruntled parties may rely upon if they appeal. Many opinions merely regurgitated a few

---

[80]   See, e.g., *Novo Industri A/S v. Travenol Labs., Inc*, No. 77 C 2778, 1981 U.S. Dist. LEXIS 15707 (N.D. Ill. Mar. 25, 1981).

[81]   Ibid. at *22.

[82]   Ibid.

[83]   Ibid.

[84]   On file with the author.

facial statements of law on misuse and proceeded to do a cursory overview of the facts before rushing toward a conclusion of no misuse.

Sometime even appellate courts would recite facts and rush to a conclusion that there was or was not misuse. A typical example is the Eighth Circuit decision in *Automated Building Components, Inc. v. Hydro-Air Engineering, Inc.*, which simply held that "[a] viewing of the record as a whole can yield no logical or reasonable inference that Hydro-Air's damage, if any, was caused by patent misuse or antitrust violations, if any, on the part of Automated."[85] It is interesting that even the Federal Circuit has, on at least one instance done the same. In upholding the lower court's finding of no misuse, it simply stated that "[w]ith respect to the misuse allegation, the administrative judge found that Roysol did not meet its burden in establishing the elements of patent misuse by Alloc. This court affirms those rulings."[86] It is possible that the appellate court found the district court's judgment strikingly clear and convincing and was comfortable upholding the latter's decision without a more lengthy analysis of the misuse issue.

In contrast, one example of where a district court did an outstanding job of analyzing misuse was the District Court for the District of Columbia in *Minebea Co. v. Papst*.[87] In that case Minebea sought a declaratory judgment alleging that Papst "improperly collected double royalties on its patents and that it engaged in improper 'package licensing.'"[88] Minebea argued that Minebea and its customers each paid for the same rights and/or that Minebea has paid indirectly for its customers' drive rights because Minebea's motor sales have exhausted the drive patents.[89] Since the motor patents are the same as the drive patents from an exhaustion standpoint, the assertion of Papst's patents constituted misuse.[90] The collection of double royalties is a form of misuse recognized by the courts. For example, in *PSC Inc. v. Symbol Technologies, Inc.*, the court found that "it has the effect of suppressing competition by increasing the manufacturing cost" of products embodying the invention and "unfairly restrains competition in a market that is essentially controlled" by the patentee.[91]

In *Minebea*, the court determined that Minebea paid for rights to

---

[85]   *Automated Bldg. Components, Inc. v. Hydro-Air Eng'g, Inc.*, 362 F.2d 989, 992 (8th Cir. 1955).
[86]   *Alloc, Inc. v. Int'l Trade Comm'n*, 342 F.3d 1361, 1375 (Fed. Cir. 2003).
[87]   *Minebea Co. v. Papst*, 444 F. Supp. 2d 68, 210 (D.D.C. 2006).
[88]   Ibid. at 209.
[89]   Ibid. at 210.
[90]   Ibid.
[91]   *PSC Inc. v. Symbol Techs., Inc.*, 26 F. Supp. 2d 505, 511 (W.D.N.Y. 1998).

engage in the manufacture, use and sale of hard disk drive motors only and not for a complete product license on hard disk drives.[92] It was therefore entitled to transfer only that right to its customers. Minebea's customers had to enter into separate licensing agreements with Papst and pay a royalty for the rights to directly infringe the drive patents.[93] Thus, even though Papst collected two sets of royalties on its drive patents, one directly from Minebea, and one directly from Minebea's customers, those royalties paid for different sets of rights applying to different products.

Minebea also asserted that Papst has engaged in misuse by refusing to license individual patents and instead required potential licensees to take package licenses, which included patents that the licensees did not want.[94] Such package-licensing, according to Minebea, was a form of tying.[95] The court distinguished patent-to-product tying arrangements from patent-to-patent tying arrangements. In patent-to-product tying, the patentee uses the market power conferred by a patent to compel customers to purchase a product in a separate market.[96] This constituted patent misuse. By contrast, a patent-to-patent tying includes both essential and non-essential patents and is evaluated under a rule of reason analysis. Licensees could use alternative technologies offered by competitors of the licensor.[97] The court concluded that Papst did not coerce or condition its license upon the licensee's acceptance of other patents.[98] An example of what amounts to coercion may be seen in the Seventh Circuit's opinion in *Hazeltine Research, Inc. v. Zenith Radio Corp.* There, the court upheld the district courts findings that:

> The demands upon Zenith were unlawful economic coercion which, coupled with this suit and threats of other suits, constituted an illegal attempt to force acceptance of the standard package and a misuse of patents to unlawfully extend HRI's patent monopoly, and awarded damages based on Zenith's expenses in defending this suit and in investigating other patents asserted.[99]

---

[92] *Minebea Co.*, 444 F. Supp. 2d at 212.
[93] Ibid. at 212.
[94] Ibid. at 213.
[95] Ibid.
[96] Ibid. at 213–14.
[97] Ibid. at 214.
[98] Ibid. at 214.
[99] *Hazeltine Research, Inc. v. Zenith Radio Corp.*, 388 F.2d 25, 34 (7th Cir. 1967), *aff'd in part, rev'd in part*, 395 U.S. 100 (1969) ("We think there is substantial evidence in the record to support the findings with regard to the misuse inherent in HRI's 1962 licensing offer").

The licensees in *Minebea*, in contrast, simply preferred to get a license under all of the Papst patents but were unwilling to pay for it.

Despite not having proven either count of misuse, the court proceeded to examine if there was any anticompetitive effect from either the alleged package licensing or double royalties.[100] The court found that Papst did not have market power in the market for hard disk drives or the market for motors.[101] Papst does not make or sell either hard disk drives or motors. It licensed patents. Nor was there evidence that Papst competed with Minebea or its customers in any market.[102] Papst sold no products that were interchangeable with products sold by Minebea or its customers. The court also considered whether Papst had market power in a "technology market" consisting of the intellectual property necessary to produce hard disk drives.[103] After noting that the concept of defining a market consisting of one party's patents has never been adopted by the Supreme Court, by the Federal Circuit, or by any other court of appeals, and had been expressly rejected by courts that have considered the issue, the court concluded that a patent was not and did not define a competitive market.[104]

Remarkably, the court took its analysis one step further and assumed that even if Papst had market power in a "technology market" solely on its patents, Minebea failed to prove that Papst had market power in this purported "technology market."[105] The court found that there was no basis to find market power in the relevant technology market.[106] With respect to the double royalty argument, the court found that the HDD market had been and remained highly competitive.[107] Price competition was intense and resulted in "a number of firms" exiting the market in recent years, "those that remain have struggled to earn profits," because "[t]here is very little product differentiation across different firms, and drives with the same characteristics (form factor, capacity, and speed) are very close substitutes for customers."[108] To the extent that Papst's licensing efforts increased the costs associated with the manufacture of hard disk drives, the court found that any such "costs" would just get passed through to the

---

[100] *Minebea Co.*, 444 F. Supp. 2d at 215–16.
[101] Ibid. at 216.
[102] Ibid.
[103] Ibid. at 217.
[104] Ibid.
[105] Ibid.
[106] Ibid. at 218.
[107] Ibid. at 219.
[108] Ibid.

customers, thus keeping the competitive balance intact.[109] Therefore, even if Papst had intended to cause anticompetitive effects, none had actually occurred. Moreover, there was no logical reason—business, economic or otherwise—for Papst to try to cause any anticompetitive effect. Because Papst was not a competitor, it had no motivation to try to upset the market. Indeed, Papst benefited from the market being competitive and market players being successful in that market.

E.   Circular Reasoning

Courts have also fallen into the trap of using circular reasoning in patent misuse analysis. For example, in *A.G. Design & Associates, LLC v. Trainman Lantern Co.*the court held that "[a] patent is unenforceable for misuse when its owner attempts to use it to exclude competition knowing that the patent is invalid or unenforceable. For a patent to become unenforceable, the patent owner must both have an unenforceable patent and know the patent is unenforceable."[110] But such a proposition finds no support in precedent. Courts using *Windsurfing* have found misuse based on a broadening of patent scope with anticompetitive effect. Courts using *Morton Salt* have found misuse based on extension of scope in violation of patent policy. Courts such as *Arcade Inc. v. Minnesota Min. & Mfg. Co,* have found misuse based on bad faith.[111] But none have required such an odd combination of knowledge and enforceability in order to render a patent unenforceable.

F.   Trends over Time

A breakdown of the data into two time periods shows more clearly the movement toward Federal Circuit jurisprudence in general, and the *Windsurfing* line of cases in particular (Figures 6.32 and 6.33). Before 1988, Supreme Court precedent features most prominently, cited in nearly 65 percent of cases.

Post-1988, the graph undergoes a dramatic transformation (Figures 6.34 and Figure 6.35).The frequency of Supreme Court precedents and overall cases without precedential values falls dramatically, and is dwarfed by the

---

[109]   Ibid.

[110]   *A.G. Design & Assocs. v. Trainman Lantern Co.*, 630 F. Supp. 2d 1275, 1279 (W.D. Wash. 2008).

[111]   *Arcade Inc. v. Minnesota Min. & Mfg. Co.*, No. CIV-1-88-141, 1991 WL 429344 (E.D. Tenn. June 7, 1991), *aff'd sub nom.* 1 F.3d 1253 (Fed. Cir. 1993); See *infra* Chapter 7.

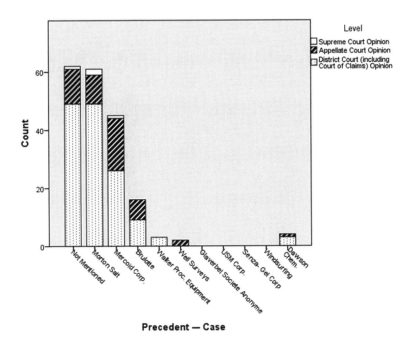

Figure 6.32   Distribution by precedent by level (pre-1988)

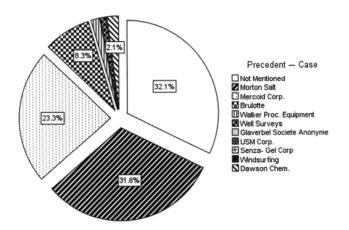

Figure 6.33   Distribution of precedent (pre-1988)

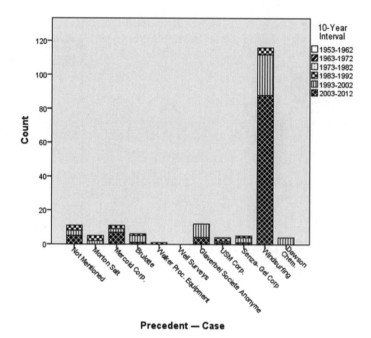

Figure 6.34   Distribution by precedent over level (post-1988)

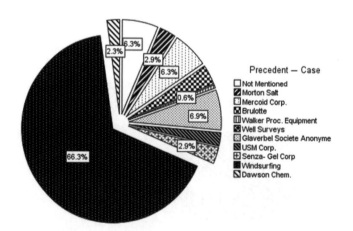

Figure 6.35   Distribution by precedent (post-1988)

surge of Federal Circuit cases—by far the most dominant source of precedent, with the *Windsurfing* case and its progeny as the most prominent example. Indeed, 66.3 percent of post-1988 cases cite to the *Windsurfing* line of cases.[112] As the nation's forum for patent infringement disputes, it is not surprising that the Federal Circuit should feature so prominently. However, this observation also underscores the tremendous influence Federal Circuit jurisprudence has had on shaping our attitudes towards patent misuse. As one court noted, "[i]n evaluating the practice of turning Regular cartridges into Prebate cartridges during the remanufacturing process, the Court relies upon a body of patent misuse law that the Court of Appeals for the Federal Circuit has largely defined."[113]

Windsurfing has also been embraced by other Circuits when hearing cases involving misuse for the proposition that "[a]nticompetitive effects, in short, are a critical element of any patent misuse case that is evaluated under a rule of reason approach."[114] In *County Materials Corp. v. Allan Block Corp.*, the Seventh Circuit noted that "*Windsurfing* was one of the first cases to recognize this; it required 'a factual determination [that] . . . reveal[s] that the overall effect of the license *tends to* restrain competition unlawfully in an appropriately defined relevant market.'"[115] In doing so, the Seventh Circuit court distanced itself from Supreme Court precedent:

> Most of the cases on which County Materials relies come from an era before the Supreme Court recognized the efficiencies that might flow from vertical restrictions, which is the type of restriction we have when a patent owner (which does not compete in the manufacturing sector) imposes restraints on a manufacturing licensee. . . . This is not the assumption that would govern today, either in the courts or in the federal enforcement agencies.[116]

County Materials is also interesting because it is one of the cases that illustrates that other Circuits may still play a role in shaping misuse despite the

---

[112]   See, e.g., *Keystone Retaining Wall Sys., Inc. v. Westrock, Inc.*, 792 F. Supp. 1552, 1560 (D. Or. 1991) ("I conclude that the *Windsurfing* rule is applicable. . . . Under *Windsurfing*, a finding of overall harm to competition is a necessary predicate to establishing patent misuse").

[113]   *Static Control Components, Inc. v. Lexmark Int'l, Inc.*, 487 F. Supp. 2d 830, 853 (E.D. Ky. 2007).

[114]   *County Materials Corp. v. Allan Block Corp.*, 502 F.3d 730, 736 (7th Cir. 2007).

[115]   Ibid. (quoting *Windsurfing Int'l Inc. v. AMF, Inc.*, 782 F.2d 995, 1001–1002 (Fed. Cir. 1986)).

[116]   Ibid.

Federal Circuit's virtual monopoly of patent matters, an issue discussed earlier in this chapter.[117]

G. Influence of the Seventh Circuit

Seventh Circuit jurisprudence experienced a minor upsurge post-1988, with four cases citing *USM*,[118] which required misuse to be tested by antitrust principles.[119] While numerically insignificant, the influence of *USM* on the Federal Circuit should not be underestimated, because it informed the analysis in *Windsurfing* and other notable precedents that created streams of jurisprudence of their own.[120] Thus it would be reasonable to say that while Judge Bryson is the key architect of contemporary patent misuse, its foundations were laid by Chief Judge Markey in *Windsurfing*

---

[117] Ibid. at 732–33 ("The district court granted summary judgment to Allan Block, finding no violation of federal patent policy or Minnesota law. We agree with the district court's conclusions and affirm").

[118] *Wuxi Multimedia, Ltd. v. Koninklijke Philips Elecs.*, No. 04cv1136 DMS (BLM), 2006 U.S. Dist. LEXIS 9160, at *17–18 (S.D. Cal. Jan. 5, 2006); *Raychem Corp. v. PSI Telcoms.*, No. C-93-20920 RPA, 1995 U.S. Dist. LEXIS 22325, at *9 (N.D. Cal. Mar. 6, 1995); *Rohm & Haas Co. v. Brotech Corp.*, 770 F. Supp. 928, 931 (D. Del. 1991); *Amgen, Inc. v. Chugai Pharm. Co.*, 706 F. Supp. 94, 104–105 (D. Mass. 1989).

[119] See *USM Corp. v. SPS Techs., Inc.*, 694 F.2d 505, 511–12 (7th Cir. 1982) ("If misuse claims are not tested by conventional antitrust principles, by what principles shall they be tested? Our law is not rich in alternative concepts of monopolistic abuse; and it is rather late in the day to try to develop one without in the process subjecting the rights of patent holders to debilitating uncertainty").

[120] *Windsurfing Int'l., Inc. v. AMF, Inc.*, 782 F.2d 995, 1001 n. 9 (Fed. Cir. 1986) ("Recent economic analysis questions the rationale behind holding any licensing practice per se anticompetitive. *See, e.g.*, USM Corp. v. SPS Technologies, Inc., 694 F.2d 505, 510-14(7th Cir. 1982), *cert. denied*, 462 U.S. 1107, 103 S. Ct. 2455, 77 L. Ed.2d 1334 (1983)"); see also *Princo Corp. v. Int'l Trade Comm'n*, 616 F.3d 1318, n. 2 (Fed. Cir. 2010) ("Some courts and commentators have questioned the continuing need for the doctrine of patent misuse, which had its origins before the development of modern antitrust doctrine. See *USM Corp.*, 694 F.2d at 511 ('Since the antitrust laws as currently interpreted reach every practice that could impair competition substantially, it is not easy to define a separate role for a doctrine also designed to prevent an anticompetitive practice—the abuse of a patent monopoly'.)"); *Scheiber v. Dolby Labs. Licensing Corp.*, 293 F.3d 1014, 1017 (7th Cir. 2002) ("Brulotte involved an agreement licensing patents that expired at different dates, just like this case; the two cases are indistinguishable. The decision has, it is true, been severely, and as it seems to us, with all due respect, justly, criticized, beginning with Justice Harlan's dissent, 379 U.S. at 34, and continuing with our opinion in *USM Corp. v. SPS Technologies, Inc.*, 694 F.2d 505, 510–11 (7thCir. 1982)").

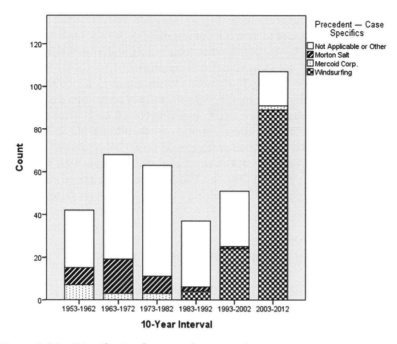

Figure 6.36   Distribution by precedent over time

under the inspiration of Judge Posner, the author of the *USM* opinion. It may, however, also be said that the notion of requiring anticompetitive effects for misuse predates even *USM*. In a district court opinion originating from the Northern District of Oklahoma, the court held that "[a]fter the said date the refusal of WSI to sell its apparatus to others than its research and service licensees was reasonable and did not tend to eliminate competition and did not have an anticompetitive effect."[121]

While the data were consistent with these perceptions, which were shared by most interviewees, some interviewees expressed surprise at the high number of Supreme Court case citations as a whole (Figure 6.36).[122] One academic suggested that this might have been due to cases that merely mention patent misuse without discussing it.[123] However, this is not the situation. The precedents were coded based on cases that cited precedents

---

[121]   *Well Surveys, Inc. v. McCullough Tool Co.*, 199 F. Supp. 374, 394 (N.D. Okla. 1961), *aff'd*, 343 F.2d 381 (10th Cir. 1965).
[122]   On file with the author.
[123]   Ibid.

that influenced the analysis of the facts. Cases that merely cited a precedent for the bare existence of misuse but did not mention how it understood that precedent, such as the relationship between misuse and antitrust, are coded as "Not Mentioned". As stated earlier, a significant proportion of the opinions (19.8%) do not cite legal precedents when undertaking patent misuse analysis. Instead, they base their conclusions solely on factual findings.

Looking at the distribution of the main precedent cases over time, it is clear that *Windsurfing* has almost exclusively dominated the cases across all levels since 1992. This change happened remarkably quickly. *Morton Salt* was on the wane between 1953 and 1982, falling from 40.5 percent of cases to 27 percent. By the time the Federal Circuit began to take cases, *Morton Salt* formed a mere 21.6 percent of cases before vanishing from the 1990s onwards.

VI. OUTCOMES: MISUSE V. ANTITRUST

About two-thirds of cases studied pleaded misuse alone and about one-third pleaded both misuse and antitrust (Figure 6.37).

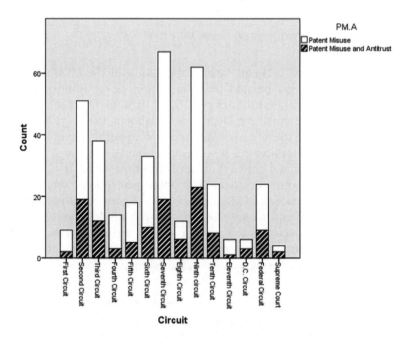

Figure 6.37   *Proportion of pure misuse cases v. misuse cases based on antitrust claims (by circuit)*

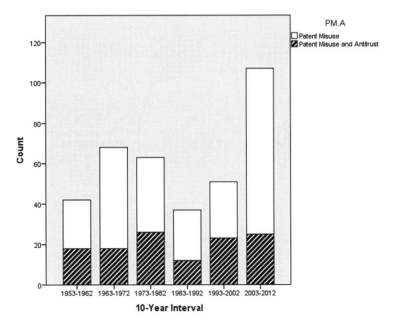

Figure 6.38   Proportion of pure misuse cases v. misuse cases based on antitrust claims (over time)

Judge Posner's observed that:

> The doctrine arose before there was any significant body of federal antitrust law, and reached maturity long before that law (a product very largely of free interpretation of unclear statutory language) attained its present broad scope. Since the antitrust laws as currently interpreted reach every practice that could impair competition substantially, it is not easy to define a separate role for a doctrine also designed to prevent an anticompetitive practice—the abuse of a patent monopoly.[124]

If this observation is true, one should expect to see misuse and antitrust cases rise over time, and cases where misuse is pleaded alone fall over time. Looking at Figure 6.38, however, misuse cases not only continue to feature but take up an increasing proportion of patent cases involving an abuse of patent rights.

Across circuits, misuse cases were more dominant, except in the Supreme Court and Eighth Circuit where both types of cases appeared half of the

---

[124]   *USM Corp.*, 694 F.2d at 511.

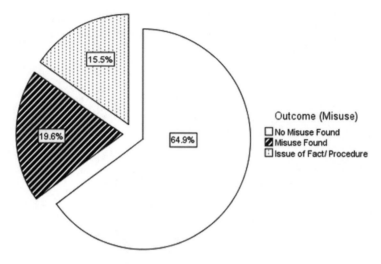

Figure 6.39   Wins (misuse)

time. Over time, there has also been more misuse than antitrust cases, although the difference was appreciably less between 1953 and 1962, as well as between 1993 and 2002. Interestingly, those were the two time periods that immediately followed from the 1952 Patent Act and the 1988 Patent Misuse Reform Act. However, this study recognizes that any conclusions on whether these legislative developments actually impacted the decision of parties to proceed on one ground rather than the other would be speculative.

A.   Win Rates

Of the opinions, 19.6 percent found misuse compared with 20.6 percent of the opinions finding an antitrust violation (Figures 6.39 and 6.40). Most interviewees were unsurprised that the win rate for alleged patent defendants was small, especially in recent years.[125] The interviewees commented on the relative win rate of patent misuse cases compared to antitrust violations, noting that they had expected patent misuse to be significantly lower than antitrust wins.[126] However, a few interviewees maintained that the difference between the win rates was sufficiently insignificant to alter their perceptions.[127]

---

[125]   On file with the author.
[126]   Ibid.
[127]   Ibid.

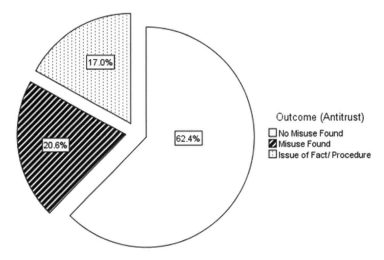

Figure 6.40   Wins (antitrust)

One academic interviewed explained that patent misuse was easier to assert successfully because of laxer standing requirements.[128] This comment appears to be borne out of a misapprehension of standing, which simply allows a wider variety of people to come before the court. Standing, be it stringent or lax, has nothing to do with the substantive legal requirements that need to be satisfied to prove misuse, and therefore has nothing to do with the outcome.

The low patent misuse win rate may be due to a few factors. First, defendants bear a significant portion of the responsibility in influencing the outcome where losses were due to poorly substantiated assertions of misuse. Many of the results on Lexis and Westlaw had to be discarded because, while the facts were similar to cases where patent misuse was considered more substantively, the defendants did themselves the disservice of making allegations "so meritless as to be unworthy of discussion".[129] One

---

[128]   On file with the author.

[129]   See *Am. Photocopy Equip. Co. v. Rovico, Inc.*, 384 F.2d 813, 818 (7th Cir. 1967) ("We have considered other points raised by Rovico which we deem so meritless as to be unworthy of discussion"); *Kolene Corp. v. Motor City Metal Treating, Inc.*, 307 F. Supp. 1251, 1263-64 (E.D. Mich. 1969) ("The argument by defendants that Kolene has misused the patent comes to us with very skimpy proofs. We know very little about Kolene's quantitative use of the patents in the industry, this arising from defendant's disclaimer of any anti-trust violation though it relies heavily upon anti-trust cases by way of analogy, should analogy there be. Much of

judge interviewed remarked that "[u]sually if it's argued, it's argued in an extremely brief fashion, maybe just a few paragraphs at the tail-end of the brief, and not even mentioned in the oral arguments. We rarely grapple with interesting or close cases of alleged patent misuse."

That this observation has been expressly noted by courts in their written opinions shows that it is of significant concern. It was interesting that two lawyers and one government official viewed the reduction of patent misuse as a result of better counseling, whereas most judges refused to take a view on the issue.[130] One judge suggested that the fact that defendants had to prove anticompetitive effect brought a rigor and corresponding rise in legal costs to the analysis, and that those defendants had to be fairly certain that their theories of harm would "stick".[131] An academic suggested that with the alignment of patent misuse to antitrust, the decline in patent misuse cases was to be expected.[132] This was either because litigants preferred immediately proceeding with antitrust claims or found that, despite the more lax standing requirements in patent misuse, the elements needed for an antitrust claim would not make it possible or worthwhile to pursue the patent misuse claim.

A second factor concerns the other actor in the trial—the courts. In the context of the Federal Circuit, Bruce Abramson wrote critically about the Federal Circuit, noting that: "A court unable to find a single instance of patent misuse, or a single example of a patentee wielding a valid patent in an anticompetitive manner, must either believe that patent rights are incorruptible (or at least nearly so) or be delinquent in identifying their

---

defendant's 'misuse' case rests squarely upon argument and speculation. Very few hard facts are presented"); *Linzer Prods. Corp. v. Sekar*, 499 F. Supp. 2d 540, 554 (S.D.N.Y. 2007) ("Linzer's definition of its relevant market is unclear. . . . Under any of these three definitions, Linzer's Sherman Act claims fail.")

[130] On file with the author. ("We live in an economy now where technology has become more important rather than less. Having a patent is extremely valuable. I think most people, looking at the prospect of losing their ability to enforce a patent versus some short-term tactical gain from something that would be considered misuse, would forgo the misuse. That's just common sense. Maybe there's better counseling now. Those of us who were out there counseling—maybe there's better education.") One judge did remark "I think that reflects the rationality of litigants, looking at that and also reading the case law that began to emerge. I recognize that it's not an easy go to make a misuse case stick. If I have limited resources and opportunity to mount defenses, I'm not going to do one that I think there's a bit of a steeper hill on. I wasn't surprised to see that, but I was interested to see the data bearing that out".

[131] Ibid.

[132] Ibid.

abuse."[133] He continued that "If the former is true, the Federal Circuit should announce it, solicit support from scholars, and encourage the Supreme Court and Congress to address the issue. If the latter is true, the Federal Circuit must remedy this serious deficiency in its work."[134]

B. Appeals

Of the 70 appellate opinions reviewed for this study, slightly more than a quarter reversed the district court's holding. By comparison, this is lower than the reversal rate of 33.1 percent for fair use in copyright.[135] The affirmance rate at the Federal Circuit is 60.0 percent, significantly lower than the overall average of 70.6 percent, though higher than the Ninth Circuit at 71.4 percent (Figure 6.41). The Seventh Circuit has a much higher affirmance rate of 70.6 percent, and the Second Circuit has the highest, with an affirmance rate of 100 percent. Over time, the affirmance rate fluctuated. Between 1953 and 1972 the affirmance rate was above 70 percent, plunging to just over 60 percent between 1973 and 1992, and dipping even further to an all-time low of 62.5 percent between 1993 and 2002, before making a dramatic recovery between 2003 and 2012 to 70.0 percent (Figure 6.42). Given that the Federal Circuit was the main appellate court between 1982 and 2003 deciding misuse cases, coupled with the low overall affirmance rate by the Federal Circuit it is conceivable that many of the reversals were of district courts who had found misuse.

C. Reversals

Since there were no post-1982 Supreme Court cases, this evidence suggests both the stabilizing role that the Federal Circuit has had on patent misuse jurisprudence, as well as the effective trickling of the Federal Circuit's views towards misuse downward to the district court level. Thus, district court judges reached outcomes that were more consistent with the result that the Federal Circuit would have arrived at on the facts of the case. It is notable that all Federal Circuit reversals were of district court misuse findings, and all affirmances were of district court findings of no misuse. This striking result has led commentators such as Bruce Abramson to observe:

---

[133] Bruce D. Abramson, THE SECRET CIRCUIT: THE LITTLE KNOWN COURT WHERE THE RULES OF THE INFORMATION AGE UNFOLD 334 (2007).

[134] Ibid.

[135] See Beebe, *supra* note 7, at 574 (noting also that "[t]hese results are not substantially different from recent estimates of overall circuit court reversal rates (for example, 32% across all circuits for the period 1980–2002).")

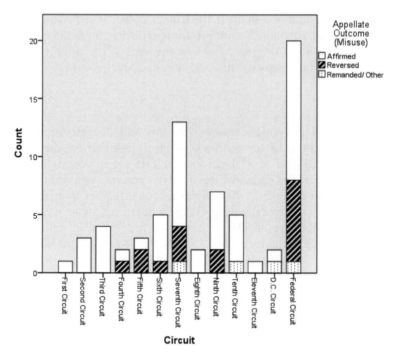

Figure 6.41   Misuse outcome (by circuit)

According to the Federal Circuit, during a twenty-year period in which the Patent and Trademark Office has granted almost two and a half million patents, numerous companies have leveraged patents to commercial success, and thousands of patent disputes have made their way to Lafayette Park, *no one* has 'draw[n] anticompetitive strength from the patent right' in a manner that the court would 'deem to be contrary to public policy.' Such a track record boggles the mind. There is only one possible way for it to make sense. The Federal Circuit *must* believe that no one has misused a patent in a manner contrary to public policy because it is impossible (or at least nearly impossible) to do so. No other explanation is even remotely plausible.[136]

The study also drew correlations between case outcomes and a number of other variables used in the coding instrument. These include: the category of misuse alleged; the industry where the alleged misuse occured; the circuit in which the case was heard; the level at which the case was heard, that is, the district court level, circuit appellate level or at the

---

[136]   Bruce D. Abramson, *supra* note 133, at 318.

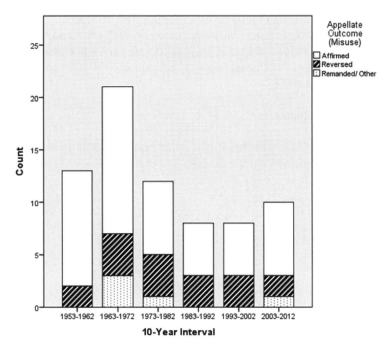

Figure 6.42   Misuse outcome over time

Supreme Court; outcomes over time; and outcomes based on the procedural posture of the case. These will be considered in later sections.

VII.   INDUSTRY

A.   Correlation between Innovation and Patent Protection

The correlation between innovation and patent protection varies between
industries. In 2002, the American Bar Association Section on Antitrust
Law surveyed a number of empirical studies. The survey noted that patents
correlated positively with innovation, but only in selected industries such
as pharmaceuticals.[137] In contrast with the high-tech industry, "the advantages that come with a head start, including setting up production, sales,
and service structures and moving down the learning curve, were judged

---

[137]   *The Economics of Innovation: A Survey*, 2002 A.B.A. Sec. Antitrust L. 19,
available at http://www.ftc.gov/opp/intellect/0207salabasrvy.pdf.

much more effective than patents as an inducement to R&D".[138] As FTC Commissioner Rosch noted, this was "not entirely surprising, given the large upfront costs and degree of risk [in] developing a new product and the relative ease of developing copycat products."[139] Patent misuse too, varies among industries.

B. Categories (Industry)

The coding instrument identified 14 distinct and occasionally overlapping industries. Categories for the industries and their codes are as follows:

0   Not Mentioned
1   Construction
2   Print & Media
3   Services
4   Software
5   Textiles
6   Agriculture & Food
7   Communications & Entertainment
8   Medical Devices, Measurement, Instrumentation, Optics
9   Semiconductor, Electrical & Computers
10 Sports & Games
11 Chemicals, Materials & Biopharma
12 Machinery
13 Manufacturing
14 Articles of Manufacture

C. Method of Selecting Industry Categories

In settling on the categories a number of sources were referred to. The natural choice was to use the USPTO classification. However, this classification system proved too detailed and complicated to be feasibly used in this study, while it was not suitable for the broad categorization of industries required for any meaningful number of cases to fall into the discrete categories. Information from the patents also did not necessarily point to

---

[138]   Ibid.
[139]   J. Thomas Rosch, Comm'r, Fed. Trade Comm'n, The Role of Static and Dynamic Analysis in Pharmaceutical Antitrust, Remarks at the Fifth Annual In-House Counsel Forum on Pharmaceutical Antitrust 10 (Feb 18, 2010), *available at* http://www.ftc.gov/speeches/rosch/100218pharmaantitrust.pdf.

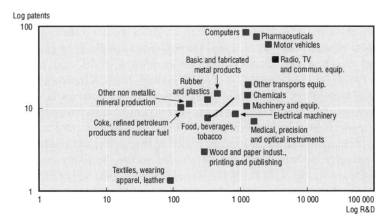

Source: OECD (2009), OECD Patent Statistics Manual, OECD Publishing.

Figure 6.43   The 17 OECD technology groups

the economic sectors to which the technologies were associated, but rather pointed to the utility areas.

Another official source referred to was the OECD Patent Statistics Manual (Figure 6.43).[140] The Manual provided an interesting insight into the classification process. It described two different criteria in designating the industry affiliation: according to the economic sector where the inventor belongs; or according to the sector which the product incorporating the technology was used.[141] The manual noted that "[n]early all available concordance tables have taken the first approach."[142] It also noted the limitation with this approach: that "not all inventions can be allocated to a sector or, as in most cases, they can be pertinent to different industries at the same time."[143] The problem with the second approach is that "large firms in particular patent in a variety of fields which do not necessarily correspond to their main economic activity. While small companies are likely to be more specialised, their field of activity might not be accessible from any database."[144]

The OECD Manual classified the various technologies into 17 groups, as shown in Figure 6.43.

---

140   OECD, Patent Statistics Manual (2009).
141   Ibid. at 91.
142   Ibid.
143   Ibid.
144   Ibid.

Academic literature also provided another reference point. For example, Professors John Allison and Mark Lemley did a study on the industries in which a random sample of 1,000 patents were sought over a two-year period.[145] They identified 14 technology groups.[146] In evaluating this aspect of the coding process, it is worth noting that any attempt to define areas of technology, as the Allison-Lemley study reminds us, is "as much art as it is science" and that "it is possible to devise an almost endless list of categories and subcategories".[147] Indeed, categories may overlap.[148] As with many of the narratives contained in this study, reasonable people may disagree on whether these definitions most effectively capture the industry landscape. This study has chosen 14 areas custom defined for the purposes of this study, just as the Allison-Lemley study did after finding the PTO's classification "inadequate"[149] and "suspect" (Table 6.4).[150]

D. Correlation between Misuse and Industry

Beyond these matrices, we can glean still other aspects of misuse for example, market concentration, the interconnection between different products and the rate of change in the industry. These have important

---

[145] See John R. Allison & Mark A. Lemley, *Who's Patenting What? An Empirical Exploration of Patent Prosecution*, 53 VAND. L. REV. 2099, 2100 (2000).

[146] See ibid. at 2110–12 (noting groups: (1) Pharmaceutical; (2) Medical device; (3) Biotechnology; (4) Computer-Related; (5) Software; (6) Semiconductor; (7) Electronics; (8) Chemistry; (9) Mechanics; (10) Acoustics; (11) Optics; (12) Automotive-related (13) Energy-Related; (14) Communications-Related).

[147] Ibid. at 2109.

[148] See, e.g., ibid. at 2010–11 ("A pure software invention is also placed in the Computer-Related classification. The instructions embodied in software code can often be embodied in semiconductor chips in a device; this is done in the obvious instances of modern consumer electronic devices, automobiles, and other devices in which the instructions are very specific to a particular function of the device and the use of software for logic instructions simply is not practically feasible. Another researcher might include within the Software classification those inventions in which the algorithms are embodied in chips, but we have chosen to include within our definition of Software only those inventions that consist purely of software that is not embodied in hardware"); ("[A] technology classified as Pharmaceutical will also be within either the Chemistry or Biotechnology areas"); ("An invention classified as a medical device will normally fall within at least one other classification, such as computer-related, electronics, mechanics, acoustics, or optics").

[149] Ibid. at 2109.

[150] Ibid. at 2109 n. 35 (". . . we believe the PTO classifications themselves are sometimes suspect"). This study relies on the definitions of the Allison-Lemley study for the following areas: software, communications, medical devices, optics, semiconductor, electrical, computers, chemical, biotechnology, and machinery.

Table 6.4   Details of industries

No.	Industry	Description
1	Construction	Construction and Home Improvement related technologies
2	Print & Media	Print, Media, Paper, Wood, Publishing
3	Services	Post sales services
4	Software	This includes any set of instructions embodied in software
5	Textiles	Textiles, Clothing, Cloth, Apparel
6	Agriculture & Food	Agricultural Machinery & Chemicals, Food, and anything related
7	Communications & Entertainment	Radio TV, Entertainment, and other Communications related fields
8	Medical Devices, Measurement, Instrumentation, Optics	Medical Devices, Precision Instrumentation, Measurement Devices, and any invention that could be used for diagnosis, disease treatment, and precision measurements
9	Semiconductor, Electrical & Computers	Computers, Electrical, Hardware, Semiconductors, Computer related Chips, Traditional Electronic Circuitry
10	Sports & Games	Sporting Goods, Games, Toys, and General Recreation
11	Chemicals & Biopharma	Chemicals, Pharmaceuticals, Biotech, Rubber, Plastics, Metals. (Does not include agricultural chemicals which can better be classified under Agriculture)
12	Machinery	Catchall—related to machines and machinery not otherwise classified
13	Manufacturing	Technologies used in factory/manufacturing setting
14	Articles of Manufacture	Single Items of Manufacture including tools, Furniture, Containers, Lids, etc.
15	Not Mentioned	Not mentioned and unascertainable technologies

implications as "courts could use patent misuse to enforce a conception of the proper scope of a patent in a given industry in the face of efforts by patentees in different industries to change that scope."[151] Professors Dan Burk and Mark Lemley explain that "whether conduct gives rise to misuse is likely to vary from industry to industry"[152] and list three factors which they argue are determinative:

---

[151]   Dan L. Burk & Mark A. Lemley, *Policy Levers in Patent Law*, 89 VA. L. REV. 1575, 1664 (2003).
[152]   Burk and Lemley argue that "Highly concentrated industries or those dominated by a single firm are more amenable to patent misuse claims," ibid.

(1) *Concentration of market power in an industry.* This could affect whether the licensing practices alleged to constitute patent misuse have anticompetitive effect.[153]

(2) *The importance of interconnection between different products and the need to cross-license different patents.* This determines the prevalence of practices like tying, patent pooling, and cross-licensing. In particular, they argue that "[i]ndustries with overlapping and conflicting patents, like software and semiconductors, are more likely to see efforts to use a patent to gain control of an adjacent product market."[154]

(3) *The rate of change in an industry determines whether patentees have much to gain by seeking to extend patents beyond their temporal scope.* In this regard, they argue that "[p]harmaceutical companies have strong incentives to extend the life of their patents, which are most valuable years after the invention. Software companies, by contrast, have no similar incentive."[155]

Claim #1: Industry Concentration: The first claim Professors Burk and Lemley make is that highly concentrated industries are more susceptible to patent misuse. Biotechnology and pharmaceutical industries are examples of where the high start-up costs and specificity of assets limit the number of market actors. The study reveals that biopharma and related industries featured prominently in the population of misuse cases throughout the entire period of study. Indeed, as noted earlier, biopharma cases are the only category of cases which see an increased level of findings of misuse post-1988.

Figure 6.44 shows the overall distribution of misuse cases. It is clear that the most dominant industry group is "Chemical, Materials & Biopharma" (14.7%), followed by "Construction" (9.8%) and "Agriculture & Food" (8.7%). On the whole, the industries were fairly evenly distributed over the entire period. Pre-1988, the most dominant industry was "Construction" (13.0%), followed by "Chemical & Biopharma" (10.9%), and "Medical Devices" (8.3%). Post-1988, "Chemicals & Biopharma" took on a more prominent role (18.9%), followed by "Semiconductor" (12.6%) and then "Software" (9.1%).

The biopharma industry has consistently been a hotbed for misuse allegations through the 1953–2012 period. Indeed, as Figure 6.45 shows,

---

[153] Ibid.
[154] Ibid.
[155] Ibid.

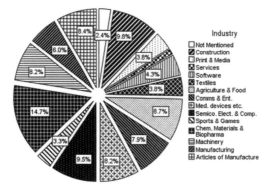

Figure 6.44   Distribution of misuse cases by industry

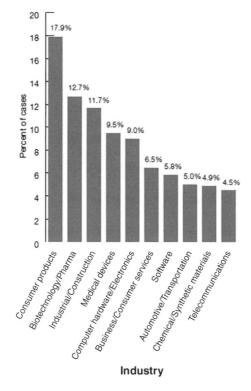

Source: PricewaterhouseCoopers, 2012 *Patent Litigation Study: Litigation continues to Rise Amid Growing awareness of Patent Value* (September 2012). Available at: http://www.pwc.com/en_US/us/forensic-services/publications/assets/2012-patent-litigation-study.pdf

Figure 6.45   Distribution of cases by industry: 1995–2011

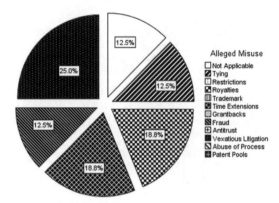

Figure 6.46   Industry—types of misuse (software)

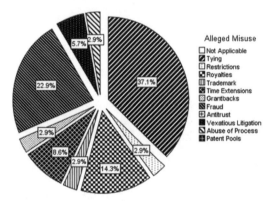

Figure 6.47   Industry—types of misuse (semiconductor)

the biopharma industry was a hot bed for litigation as a whole between 1995 and 2011.

Claim #2: Licensing: The second claim Professors Burke and Lemley make is that industries with interconnected technologies see more licensing-type abuses, citing software and semiconductor industries as examples. Figure 6.46 shows the categories of misuse in the software industry, and licensing-type abuses make up 50% of abuse cases. These include: tying, restrictions, royalties, trademark-related abuses, time extensions and grantbacks, all clearly licensing related abuses. Antitrust cases may or may not involve misuse and were excluded. Figure 6.47 shows the categories of misuse in the semiconductor industry. These same categories of misuse aggregated to 67.1 percent.

Table 6.5   *Breakdown of industries by percentage of licensing abuses*

Industry	Percentage of licensing-type abuses (%)
Construction	78.0
Print & Media	78.5
Services	76.0
Software	50.1
Textiles	64.2
Agriculture & Food	81.3
Communications & Entertainment	62.0
Medical Devices	63.3
Semiconductor	68.7
Sports & Games	66.7
Chemicals & Biopharma	56.7
Machinery	80.1
Manufacturing	72.8
Articles of Manufacture	54.9

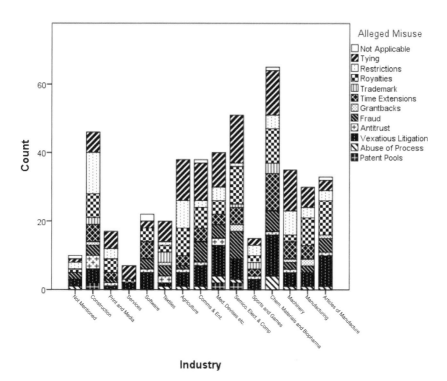

Figure 6.48   Distribution of alleged misuse by industry

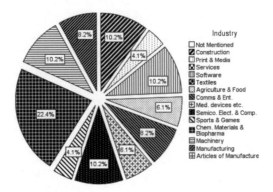

Figure 6.49   Industries (extension of temporal scope only)

Repeating the exercise for the other 12 industries, Table 6.5 reflects the percentage of licensing-type abuses out of total abuses for each of the other industries (see Figure 6.48 for a graphical representation).

As the table indicates, the percentages of licensing-type abuses are high. Indeed, this confirms conventional wisdom that misuse is largely concerned with licensing-type abuses. From comparing these high figures, it is apparent that software and semiconductor industries do not stand out as having more of these types of abuses than other industries. In fact, the highest percentages of licensing type abuses are seen in the agriculture and food industry, followed by print and media and then sports and games. And perhaps counterintuitively, software has the lowest incidence of licensing-type misuses amongst all the industries studied. While the semiconductor industry has the fourth lowest. This result does not necessarily show that Professors Burk and Lemley are wrong about the nature of abuses. For one can easily imagine that the number of patents involved in the industry has direct bearing on the mathematical probability that more licensing agreements may be accused of being a vehicle for misuse. What these results do show is that misuse may not be the response of choice by those alleging an abuse of the patent right. Indeed, as Chapter 3 shows, in cases involving standard setting organizations, where many semiconductor and software cases arise, litigants turn to antitrust law as well as estoppel and implied licenses to remedy findings of patent abuses.

Claim #3: Rate of change: The last category of misuse allegations resonates with Burk and Lemley's third claim that fast changing industries such as the software industry have less incentive to use royalty extensions than slower-developing ones such as pharmaceuticals. Figure 6.49 shows that allegations of time extensions in chemical and biopharma industry occur twice as much as in the next highest industry categories: machinery, software and semiconductors.

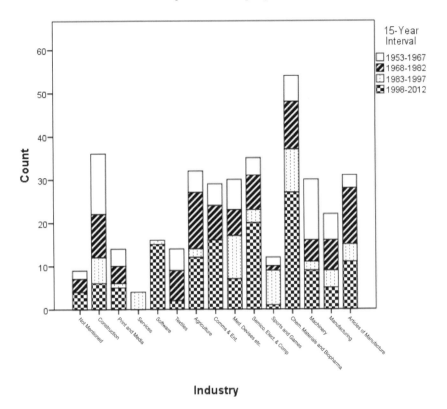

Figure 6.50   Trends over 15-year period

E.   Trends over Time

Looking at trends over 15-year periods, it is clear that the dominant industries in terms of number of patent misuse cases have shifted gradually over time (Figure 6.50). Construction remained dominant from 1953 to 1996. Machinery and Medical Devices, which were dominant in the 1950s and 60s were replaced by Agriculture & Food, and Articles of Manufacture by the end of 1980, although Medical Devices made a comeback in the 1980s and 1990s. Between 1996 and 2011 the landscape changed entirely, becoming dominated by Chemicals & Biopharma, Communications & Entertainment, Semiconductors, Electronics and Computers.

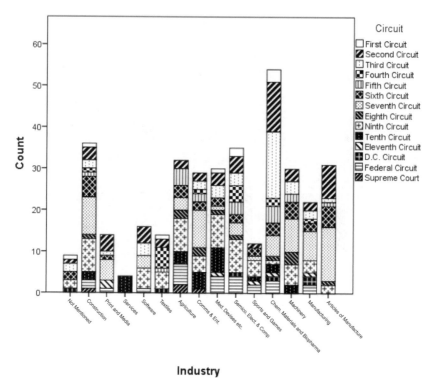

Figure 6.51   Distribution by circuit and industry

F. Dominance by Circuit

Certain industries feature more prominently in certain circuits
(Figure 6.51). For example, the Ninth Circuit has the dominant share of
software and technology patent misuse cases. The Second Circuit has the
lion's share of Chemical and Biopharma cases, a trend consistent with
Professor Fromer's study which showed that technology cases tended
to go to the Northern District of California while pharmaceutical cases
tended to go to the District of New Jersey.[156] This is understandable, given
that these form a major part of the industries there. However, it is less

---

[156]   Jeanne C. Fromer, *Patentography*, 85 N.Y.U. L. Rev. 1444, 1481 (2010)
("When patent disputes arise, having the case adjudicated by a district court at
the principal place of business of a defendant will tend to cluster patent litigation by technology or industry. There will likely be, say, much litigation about
software patents centered in the Northern District of California, the District of

Table 6.6   Success rates in different industries

Industry	Pre-88 (%)	Post-88 (%)
Construction	32.3	0
Print & Media	26.0	0
Services	–	28.6
Software	–	4.5
Textiles	50.0	0
Agriculture & Food	47.8	0
Communications & Entertainment	10.5	6.3
Medical Devices	22.7	6.6
Semiconductor	16.8	6.2
Sports & Games	26.0	0
Chemicals & Biopharma	14.3	13.5
Machinery	38.1	7.7
Manufacturing	39.1	14.3
Articles of Manufacture	26.3	7.1

clear why for example, the Seventh Circuit has a remarkably high number of Construction and Articles of Manufacturing cases. Unlike the conclusions of Frommer's study, however, the Third Circuit has a high incidence of pharmaceutical cases and a low incidence of software cases.

G.   Success in Different Industries

The industries in which infringers were most successful in asserting misuse were the "old world" industries of textiles (46.0%), machinery (26.7%), manufacturing (33.3%), construction (23.9%), and articles of manufacture (18.2%). It was striking that patentees were more successful in defending post-1988 misuse allegations in every industry compared to their pre-1988 predecessors (see Table 6.6).

Misuse has therefore become a much diminished defense in the last 22 years. One notable exception was in the Chemicals & Biopharma industry where defendant win rates actually went up and indeed nearly doubled (see Figures 6.52–6.54).

The PWC Report reveals that the success rate for patentees and patent holders in technology areas associated with Consumer products, Biotechnology/Pharma, Medical devices, and Computer hardware/

Massachusetts, and the Western District of Washington and about pharmaceutical patents in the District of New Jersey").

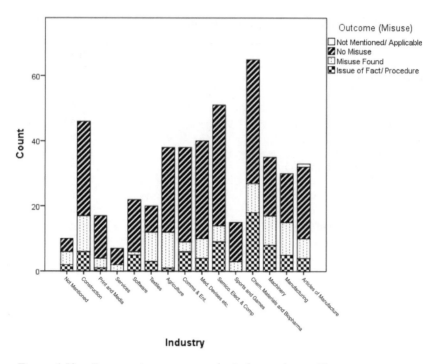

Figure 6.52   Patent misuse outcome by industry (overall)

Electronics industries was higher than the overall average (see Figure 6.55). In contrast, patentees with technology associated with the Software, Telecommunications, and Chemicals/Synthetic materials industries, in particular, experienced significantly lower success rates than the overall rate for all industries. One academic interviewee remarked that:

> One of the things, I think, that actually is quite interesting is industry categorization. Obviously, post-1988 there are more software cases and more chemical cases, but we're still talking mostly about a doctrine that is applied in traditional mechanical or manufacturing industries, which I think doesn't reflect patent litigation overall. I think it's an interesting thing to explore there. Why is it that we don't see misuse claims nearly as often in the software industry in proportion to the number of software cases there are? That's a curious fact.[157]

Another interviewee focusing on another aspect of the pre-and post-1988 trends observed that "there were more successful assertions of misuse [in machine and manufacturing] than I thought there would be. ...

---

[157]   On file with the author.

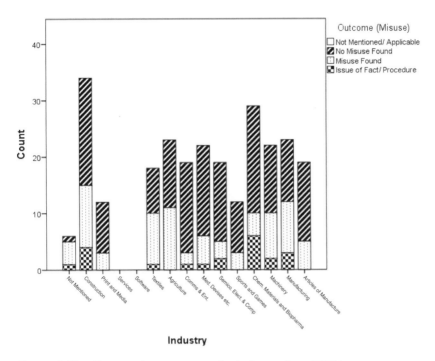

Figure 6.53   Patent misuse outcome by industry (pre-1988)

[which] . . . confirms what I just said, which is that pre-1988 has a much higher success rate for misuse than post-1988."[158]

VIII.   LITERATURE AND LEGISLATIVE HISTORY

Literature, both from academic and governmental sources, featured in the cases studied. Courts generally cited them for restatements of the law.[159]

---

[158]   Ibid.

[159]   See, e.g., *Riker Lab., Inc. v. Gist-Brocades*, 636 F.2d 772, 777 (D.C. Cir. 1980), abrogated on other grounds by *Nat'l Patent Dev. Corp. v. T.J. Smith & Nephew Ltd.*, 877 F.2d 1003 (D.C. Cir. 1989) ("While the parameters of the doctrine are indistinct (Report of the President's Commission on the Patent System, *To Promote the Progress of the Useful Arts in an Age of Exploding Technology* (1966)) and fluid, *Report of the Attorney General's Committee to Study the Antitrust Laws* 251 (1955) ('The outer reach of the misuse doctrine has not yet been fully defined'), we need not attempt to define its precise limits to resolve the issue presented here").

Patent misuse and antitrust law

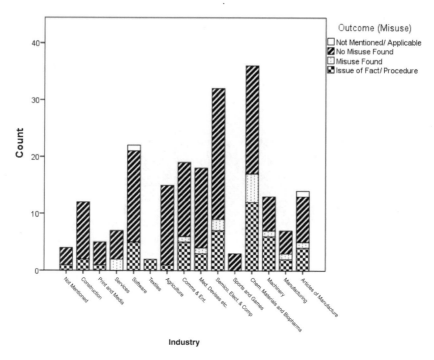

Figure 6.54   Patent misuse outcome by industry (post-1988)

The perceptions that interviewees had of patent misuse came from a variety of sources. Most understood misuse from reading Federal Circuit cases. Judges interviewed had decided patent misuse cases. Interviewees who were academics were informed by academic articles and treatises. It was remarkable that few non-academics were aware of academic writings, a fact borne out in the findings in this study which indicated that 13.3 percent or about an eighth of all cases made any reference to academic literature or policy papers (Figure 6.56). The period where courts referred most frequently to literature was between 1968 and 1982 (20.9%), with the frequency of cases referring to literature taking a sharp plunge thereafter to 9.1 percent between 1983 and 1997 and 9.3 percent between 1998 and 2012 (Figure 6.57). Studying trends by circuit (Figures 6.58 and 6.59), it is interesting to note that the Fifth Circuit has the highest incidence of referring to literature, though the Federal Circuit and Seventh Circuit dominate by absolute numbers. Overall, as expected, appellate courts refer to literature much more frequently than district courts.

Looking at cases that refer to legislative history, about 10.9 percent of cases refer to it (Figure 6.60). It is interesting to note that more courts

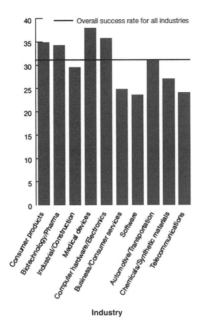

Source: PricewaterhouseCoopers, 2012 *Patent Litigation Study: Litigation continues to Rise Amid Growing awareness of Patent Value* (September 2012). Available at: http://www. pwc.com/en_US/us/forensic-services/publications/assets/2012-patent-litigation-study.pdf

Figure 6.55   Patent holder success rate: top ten industries, 1995–2011

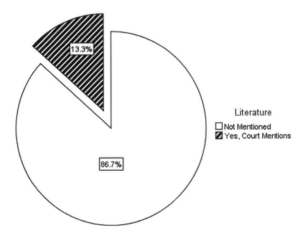

Figure 6.56   Percentage of cases that refer to literature

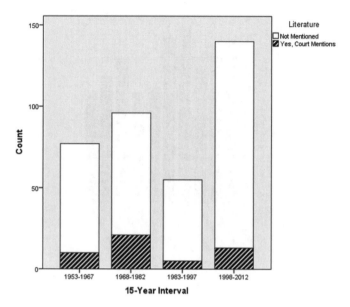

Figure 6.57   Distribution by time and whether literature was cited

have referred to legislative history in the period 1998–2012 (9.29%), than in any other previous period (Figure 6.61). The key reason for this may be because of the 1988 Patent Misuse Reform Act, which 6.9 percent of those cases referred to.

As with reference to literature, appellate courts clearly referenced legislative history with greater frequency, although the difference between the two court levels was less stark in this instance (Figure 6.62). The D.C. Circuit and Supreme Court most frequently reference legislative history, though the Federal Circuit once again dominates in absolute numbers (Figure 6.63).

IX.   CATEGORIES OF MISUSE

A.   Conventional Wisdom

One branch of conventional wisdom holds that categories of misuse are confined to "a relatively limited number of specific acts of the patent owner, often in the context of patent licensing."[160] Yet another source notes that:

---

[160]   Marshall Leaffer, *Patent Misuse and Innovation*, 10 J. HIGH TECH. L. 142, 147 (2010); *Princo Corp. v. Int'l Trade Comm'n*, 616 F.3d 1318, 1329 (Fed. Cir.

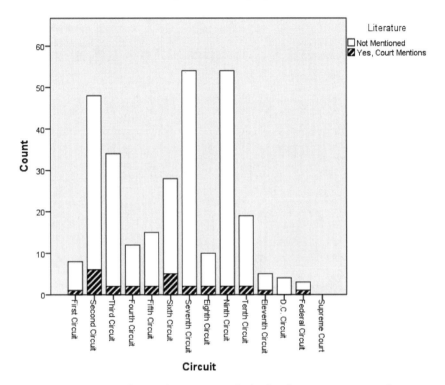

Figure 6.58   Distribution by circuit and whether literature was cited (district courts)

Tying is by far the most common basis for a patent misuse allegation. Depending on how broadly tying is defined, roughly half of the Supreme Court cases dealing with misuse have involved tying. Congress has twice spoken specifically to the proper scope of patent misuse law dealing with ties. And the only Federal Circuit opinion ever to find misuse was a tying case.[161]

2010) ("Given that the patent grant entitles the patentee to impose a broad range of conditions in licensing the right to practice the patent, the doctrine of patent misuse 'has largely been confined to a handful of specific practices by which the patentee seemed to be trying to "extend" his patent grant beyond its statutory limits'."); see, e.g., *Nat'l Lockwasher Co. v. George K. Garrett Co.*, 137 F.2d 255, 256 (3d Cir. 1943) (finding the patentee used its patent to "suppress the manufacture of possible competing goods not covered by its patent."); see also *Berlenbach v. Anderson & Thompson Ski Co.*, 329 F.2d 782, 784 (9th Cir. 1964) (holding "that a clause prohibiting a licensee from selling articles in competition with the patented articles likewise constitutes patent misuse").

[161]   1 Hovenkamp et al., IP & ANTITRUST §3.3 (2010).

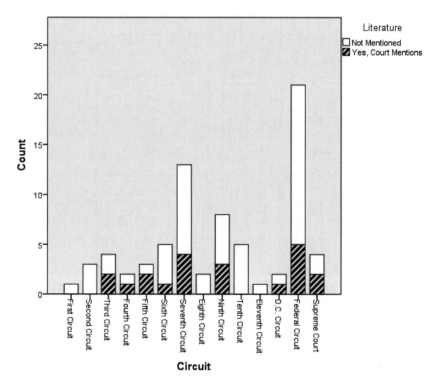

Figure 6.59   Distribution by circuit and whether literature was cited (appellate courts)

This leads to three propositions: first, that there are only a limited number of categories of misuse; second, that these categories revolve around patent licensing; and third that the most common form of misuse is tying. With respect to the first proposition, many interviewees identified patent licensing terms as most often being at issue in patent misuse cases, particularly in the form of tying arrangements.[162] The other classic type of misuse that featured involves a patent owner's use of a royalty agreement that projects beyond the expiration date of the patent, which is unlawful *per se*.[163] With respect to the second proposition, a leading

---

[162]   On file with the author.

[163]   See *Brulotte v. Thys Co.*, 379 U.S. 29 (1964). However, it should be noted that *Brulotte* was not a misuse case. The Court did not hold the patent at issue to be unenforceable since it had already expired. Instead, the plaintiff was suing for breach of the agreement to pay post-patent termination royalties, and it was this agreement that the Court held to be unenforceable on the ground that it violated

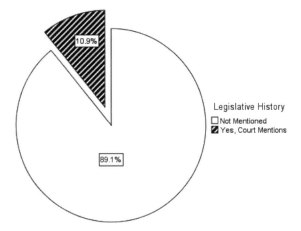

Figure 6.60   Proportion of cases citing legislative history

treatise has identified six further examples of misuse, all related to licensing.[164]

This study vindicates the third proposition. It also shows the first two propositions to be generally true, though inaccurate. There is a surprising degree of diversity in the species of patent misuse that exist. Contrary to the first two propositions, 11 discrete categories with little or no overlap were identified, which took into account the full array of patent misuses pled and decided by the federal courts, many which have little to do with licensing.[165] For example, *Revlon, Inc. v. Carson Prods. Co.* concerned a continuation-in-part application, which was characterized as inequitable conduct giving rise to patent misuse.[166] The court declined to find misuse

federal patent policy, ibid. at 30, 32–34. However, subsequent courts have interpreted *Brulotte* as representing the principle that conditioning a patent license on the agreement to pay post-termination royalties does constitute patent misuse. See, e.g., *Virginia Panel Corp. v. MAC Panel Co.*, 133 F.3d 860, 869-71 (Fed. Cir. 1997).

[164]   See 1 Hovenkamp et al., *supra* note 161, at §3.3 (providing a comprehensive taxonomy of misuse categorized by conduct and statutory restrictions: package licensing and non-metered royalties; grantback clauses; field-of-use restrictions; horizontal agreements; and price discrimination).

[165]   Less well-known examples but no less prevalent examples where the court has found misuse include the treatment of royalties based on net sale prices in *Leesona Corp. v. Varta Batteries, Inc.*, 522 F. Supp. 1304 (S.D.N.Y. 1981), and the use of collateral pressure in *Analytichem Int'l, Inc. v. Har-Len Assoc.*, 490 F. Supp. 271 (W.D. Pa. 1980).

[166]   Revlon, Inc. v. Carson Prods. Co., 602 F. Supp. 1071, 1100 (S.D.N.Y. Feb. 27, 1985).

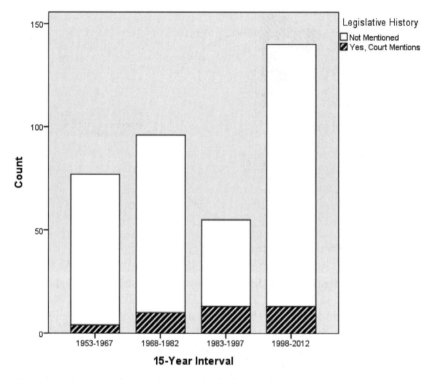

Figure 6.61   Distribution by time and whether legislative history was cited

on the basis that "defendants were exercising their legal rights in filing a continuation application, even if the purpose of the application may have been in part to broaden the patent."[167] Other examples involve fraudulent conduct such as mismarking patents, misrepresentations and vexatious litigation. The 11 categories are presented below.

B.   Categories of Misuse

1   *Tying*. Including: tying non-patented products to a patented product; package licensing; block booking; lock-outs; refusals to license a patent

2   *Restrictions*. Including: field of use limitations; restrictions after sale; territorial restrictions; non-compete clauses; post-expiry no challenge;

---

[167]   Ibid.

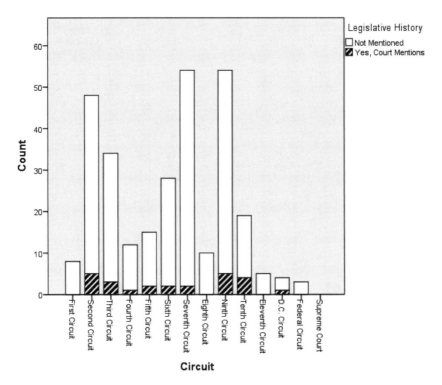

Figure 6.62   Reference to legislative history (district court)

exclusive dealerships; non-disclosure agreements; non-termination clause; granting exclusive right to sell product; no-challenge clause

3   *Royalties*. Including: royalties based on total sales; royalties based on non-patented goods; claim for damages on non-patented goods; extension to post-grant patents; pre-grant royalties; excessive royalties; excessive pricing; price restraints; price fixing; double royalties; resale price maintenance (to change the rest later); discriminatory pricing; punitive contractual penalties

4   *Trademark related abuses*

5   *Time extensions*. Including: post-expiration royalties (with or without reduction in royalty rate); post-expiry supply and marking; pre-issuance royalties

6   *Grantbacks*. Including: grantback clauses; tie-ins

7   *Fraud*. Including: fraudulent procurement; misrepresentation on

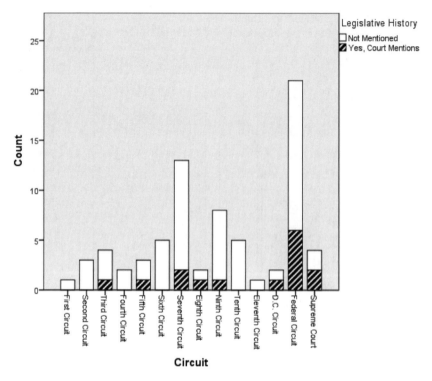

Figure 6.63   Reference to legislative history (appellate courts)

expiry dates; patent mismarking; misrepresentation in standard
setting

8   *Antitrust.* Including: improper use of patents contributing to an antitrust violation; market sharing

9   *Vexatious litigation.* Including: vexatious litigation; collateral pressure; group boycott; bad faith enforcement

10   *Abuse of process.* Including: procedural delays; filing continuations;
collusive settlements

11   *Patent pools.* Including: patent pooling, accumulation

C.   Findings

Skeptics of these expanded forms of misuse might dismiss the expanded
categories as flowing from the creative or desperate minds of defendants. Consistent with the low win rates for misuse discussed earlier, it
may be reasonable to presume that a number of categories of misuse

are dud-defenses raised by desperate defendants.[168] Some categories of misuse, such as those relating to field-of-use restrictions on propagation of patented plants, were considered on the merits and rejected in favor of patentees.[169] Other forms of misuse, however, have withstood judicial scrutiny and indeed have proven quite robust. For example, courts have found that a refusal to license combined with patent pooling and an agreement to assert pooled patents against third parties suppresses competition and constitutes patent misuse.[170]

---

[168] *Delano Farms Co. v. California Table Grape Comm'n.*, 623 F. Supp. 2d 1144, 1179 (E.D. Cal. 2009) ("there is no viable claim for the 'amnesty program' as the Commission could not have misused patents that did not exist and at most were inventions in the pre-issuance stage. . . . Pre-issuance, there is no patent right to impermissibly broaden"); *Am. Medical Sys., Inc. v. Laser Peripherals*, LLC, 712 F. Supp. 2d 885, 923 (D. Minn. 2010) ("LP discerns a sinister motive in AMS's amendment of claims during the reexamination to cover the accused devices. There is nothing improper in AMS's amendment of its claims. . . . [A]cquisition of patent rights for the purpose of enforcing them, without more, does not constitute patent misuse").

[169] *Delano Farms Co.*, 623 F. Supp. 2d at 1180 ("Here, it is not misuse of a plant patent to prevent the plant's disclosure to prevent its reproduction"); *Monsanto Co. v. McFarling*, 363 F.3d 1336, 1341 (Fed. Cir. 2004) ("In the cases in which the restriction is reasonably within the patent grant, the patent misuse defense can never succeed"). The background to cases involving Monsanto have been succinctly summarized by Professor Cotter. See Thomas F. Cotter, *Misuse*, 44 HOUS. L. REV. 901, 915–16 (2007) ("The two Monsanto cases both involved patents that claim, among other things, the insertion of genetically modified enzymes into seeds. A farmer who plants the modified seed can then spray her crops with specified insecticides or herbicides; the insecticide or herbicide will kill pests or other plants (such as weeds), respectively, but it does not affect the genetically modified organism grown from the seed. Monsanto licenses seed companies to incorporate its technology into their seed, but only on condition that the seed companies in turn license farmers to use the seed subject to certain restraints. In particular, Monsanto requires the seed companies to distribute seed to farmers only on condition that the farmers use the seed for only one growing season and not to save any seed or crop for replanting. In both cases, Monsanto filed suit against a farmer who ignored these restrictions, alleging patent infringement and (*in McFarling*) breach of contract").

[170] *M-B-W Inc. v. Multiquip, Inc.*, No. 07-CV-390, 2009 U.S. Dist. LEXIS 90418, at *35, 38–39 (E.D. Wis. Sept. 29, 2009) (citing for this proposition, but rejecting the defendant's patent misuse defense because there was no evidence that, on the facts, such an agreement existed).

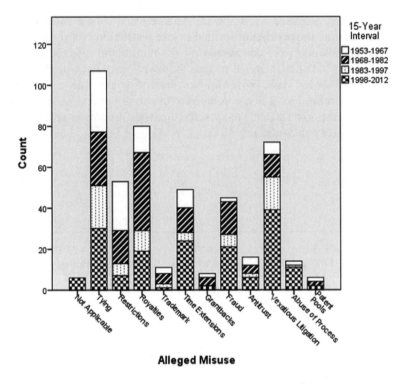

Figure 6.64   Alleged misuse over time (15-year intervals)

D.   Analysis

The prominent appearance of tying in Figure 6.64 among the various categories of misuse in every time period bears out the perception of it as the classic form of misuse.[171] Between 1998 and 2012 however, vexatious litigation has overtaken tying as the dominant category of misuse, perhaps in response to the raised threshold following from *Windsurfing*. Academics interviewed cite the impact of the Federal Circuit opinion in *U.S. Philips Corp. v. International Trade Commission* in 2003, holding that package licensing that ties essential and non-essential patents is not *per se* patent

---

[171]   One attorney interviewed remarked "[t]he classic examples, of course, have been tying." Another said "patent legislation has taken care of some of those in terms of tying claims. I think traditionally that was the largest area of misuse claims." On file with the author.

misuse and has to be tested by a rule of reason.[172] Possibly reflecting this point, there appears to have been a sharp rise in the number of tying cases between 1998 and 2012 compared to the previous period. In contrast to this, an attorney interviewed for this study reflected the conventional wisdom discussed in Chapter 2 when he noted that the 1988 amendments together with the Supreme Court's decision in *Illinois Tool Works* "largely removed" tying from the patent litigation landscape.[173]

The frequency with which licensing restrictions are alleged to be patent misuse have diminished by half between the 1953–1982 period and the 1983–2012 period. Like licensing restrictions, royalty obligations under licensing agreements have seen a crushing drop in the last 20 years. Patentees are now generally given a great deal of latitude in deciding how to structure agreements. The parties may decide to base royalties on "any convenient measure of the business value of a patent license, even if it includes royalties on items not embodying the patented invention or royalties on a percentage of the licensee's total sales."[174] Misuse arises by virtue of the purpose and effect of the royalty provision rather than the fact that royalties are paid on unpatented goods.[175] If mutual convenience or efficiency results in a royalty base which includes the licensee's total sales

---

[172] *U.S. Philips Corp. v. Int'l Trade Comm'n*, 424 F.3d 1179, 1190, 1197–98 (Fed. Cir. 2005) ("[A] package licensing agreement that includes both essential and nonessential patents does not impose any requirement on the licensee. . . . [I]t merely puts [a competing licensor] in the same position he would be in if he were competing with unpatented technology").

[173] On file with the author. ("I think that if you look at the case law, patent misuse was most frequently alleged as part of a tying claim. The amendment to the patent law has kind of knocked that out, coupled with the Independent Ink [inaudible], which says you can't presume market power from the existence of a patent. If you are going to be an antitrust plaintiff claiming tying, you are going to have to demonstrate that there is sufficient market power in the relevant market to tie. So I would say that that has largely removed an area of patent misuse claims from the litigation landscape.")

[174] *Magnavox Co. v. Mattel, Inc.*, No. 80 C 4124, 1982 U.S. Dist. LEXIS 13773, at *109–10 (N.D. Ill. July 29, 1982) (citing *Automatic Radio Mfg. Co. v. Hazeltine Research, Inc.*, 339 U.S. 827 (1950); *Zenith Radio Corp. v. Hazeltine Research, Inc.*, 395 U.S. 100 (1969); *Am. Photocopy Equip. Co. v. Rovico, Inc.*, 384 F.2d 813 (7th Cir. 1967), *cert. denied*, 390 U.S. 945 (1968); *Ohio-Sealy Mattress Mfg. Co. v. Sealy, Inc.*, 585 F.2d 821, 839 (7th Cir. 1978), *cert. denied*, 440 U.S. 930 (1979)).

[175] *Zenith Radio Corp.*, 395 U.S. at 135, 138, 139; *Automatic Radio Mfg. Co.*, 339 U.S. at 833; *General Tire & Rubber Co. v. Firestone Tire & Rubber Co.*, 349 F. Supp. 333, 343 (N.D. Ohio 1970), *appeal dismissed*, 431 F.2d 1199 (6th Cir. 1970), *cert. denied*, 401 U.S. 975 (1971).

or sales of non-patented items, courts will not find misuse.[176] However, patentees may not condition the grant of a patent license upon payment of royalties on products which do not use the teaching of the patent[177]. Thus the patentee may not refuse to license on any other basis, leaving potential licensees with the choice between a license with those terms and no license at all.[178]

Courts have also upheld licenses which reach through into future generations of the invention. Interesting implications arise in the context of living inventions. In *Monsanto Co. v. Swann*, the court found:

> Although plaintiff's Technology Agreement in effect compels a grower to re-purchase seeds in the subsequent growing seasons, it does not require the purchase of plaintiff's patented seed. Without more, a prohibition on saving and replanting a certain brand of seed, does not create an obligation to purchase that same seed in subsequent growing seasons.[179]

One can imagine the flurry of counterarguments as to why the patent right should be exhausted on first sale. However, even the most recent pronouncements from the Federal Circuit uphold this rule.

Another interesting finding was that the industry concerned may have a direct impact on the outcome of the same category of misuse. For example, in *Glen Mfg., Inc. v. Perfect Fit Indus., Inc.*, the defendant argued that a royalty structure based on a percentage of licensee's total sales of its product was permitted under Supreme Court precedent.[180] The court, however distinguished *Hazeltine*, because the licensor there

> possessed over 570 patents and 200 patent applications for electronic apparatus used in radios, televisions and phonographs, and a royalty structure based on a percentage of the licensee's total sales was devised to avoid the difficulty of determining whether each type of the licensee's product embodied any of the patents or patent applications. Because of the complexities involved in the patents and the alleged difficulty in determining whether the patented devices

---

[176]   *Zenith Radio Corp.*, 395 U.S. at 138; *Automatic Radio Mfg. Co.*, 339 U.S. at 834; *Ohio-Sealy Mattress Mfg. Co.*, 585 F.2d at 839.

[177]   *Zenith Radio Corp.*, 395 U.S. at 136.

[178]   Ibid.

[179]   *Monsanto Co. v. Swann*, 308 F. Supp. 2d 937, 942 (E.D. Mo. 2003) (citing *Monsanto Co. v. McFarling*, 302 F.3d 1291, 1298 (Fed. Cir. 2002)) (rejecting the defendant's contention that Monsanto's prohibition on seed saving and replanting constitutes patent misuse).

[180]   *Glen Mfg., Inc. v. Perfect Fit Indus., Inc.*, 299 F. Supp. 278, 282 (S.D.N.Y. 1969) (citing *Automatic Radio Mfg. Co.*, 339 U.S. at 827).

were used in the licensee's products, the court permitted the royalty structure in question.[181]

In contrast, in *Glen Manufacturing* the patentee's patent was "a single, relatively uncomplicated object, a toilet tank cover, and it would be possible to determine readily whether plaintiff's patent was been utilized." Hence, a royalty structure based on a percentage of defendant's total sales of toilet tank covers was unnecessary because of minimal difficulty in ascertaining whether its patent is utilized.

The proportion of patent misuse allegations involving time-extension misuse has increased over the last 15 years (Figure 6.64). At first sight, this is surprising, given that *Brulotte* has fallen out of favor with courts more attuned to contemporary economic analysis. This may have given rise to a cottage industry devoted to crafting agreements in such a way that the post-termination royalties can plausibly be attributed to something other than the patented invention,[182] or parties may have structured their agreements so that all royalties attributable to the patent are paid before the end of the patent term. This is also consistent with jurisprudence in other areas of patent law.[183] Interviewees were surprised that time extension abuses have increased.[184] One academic surmised that there was little that the lower courts could do about *Brulotte*, and that it was not surprising that defendants would see that as basis for alleging misuse.[185] Most courts and commentators would disapprove of *Brulotte* today.[186]

---

[181]   Ibid. at 282.

[182]   See, e.g., *Boggild v. Kenner Prods.*, 776 F.2d 1315, 1318 (6th Cir. 1985) (declining to find a "hybrid" agreement even though the agreement was entered into before the patent issued because the agreement required royalty payments based on patent rights beyond the term of the patent).

[183]   E.g. in *MedImmune, Inc. v. Genentech, Inc.*, 427 F.3d 958 (Fed. Cir. 2005), *rev'd* 549 U.S. 118 (2007), the Federal Circuit allowed the parties to contract away the right to future challenges of the validity of the patent at issue.

[184]   On file with the author.

[185]   On file with the author.

[186]   See, e.g., *Scheiber v. Dolby Labs., Inc.*, 293 F.3d 1014 (7th Cir. 2002); see, e.g., Hovenkamp et al., *supra* note 161, at 3-3 ("If a patent gives its owner power in a relevant economic market, a long-term royalty agreement may effectively 'lock in' licensees to use the patented technology even after the patent expires. . . . Such circumstances do not justify a per se prohibition on term extensions, however. Rather, the categorical treatment of term extensions under patent misuse seems to be driven by noneconomic concerns about the use of patent law to gain some perceived economic advantage"); Ian Ayres & Paul Klemperer, *Limiting Patentees' Market Power Without Reducing Innovation Incentives: The Perverse Benefits of Uncertainty and Non-Injunctive Remedies*, 97 MICH. L. REV. 985, 1026–27

Still, *Brulotte* has also been applied in cases involving hybrid forms of misuse categories. For example, in *Well Surveys, Inc. v. Perfo-Log, Inc.* the court found that:

> a package license agreement which provides that that agreement shall continue in full force and effect until the expiration date of the last patent to expire under which the license is granted, constitutes patent misuse because it extends the payment of royalties under patents which will expire to the expiration date of patents which will expire later.[187]

This, together with the *per se* status of such claims may explain the increase in the frequency of "time extension" opinions in recent years. As a final note, trademark-related allegations have remained consistently low over time.

E.   Bad Faith Litigation: Vexatious Litigation, Fraud and Abuse of Process

The fact that the two instances of misuse which do not require the fulfillment of the *Windsurfing* test have increased in the last 15 years shows that legal actors may increasingly see misuse in non-licensing terms, a conclusion which only buttresses the relevance of the issues discussed in Chapter 3. These are the three categories of misuse which have grown over the years: fraud, vexatious litigation, and antitrust.

Figures 6.65 and 6.66 provide some clue as to why vexatious litigation and fraud seem to buck the trend of declining cases of misuse over the years. It appears that in both instances, infringers are winning more often at the district court level. This is remarkable in itself. However, what is perhaps even more baffling is that patentees do not appeal in most cases, as seen by the low count of appeals for these two categories of misuse at the appellate level. Given the strict requirements imposed by the courts, it is difficult to demonstrate that litigation is vexatious, and one academic expressed surprise at the number of vexatious litigation claims that continue to be brought.[188]

(1998–1999) (arguing "the Court's concern with leverage was misplaced" because constant royalty payments spread beyond the life of the patent are economically reasonable for both parties).

[187]   *Well Surveys, Inc. v. Perfo-Log, Inc.*, 154 U.S.P.Q. 313, 319 (W.D. Okla. 1967) *rev'd*, 396 F.2d 15 (10th Cir. 1968).

[188]   On file with the author. ("I am a little surprised at how many vexatious litigation cases you found, given, as I said, the difficulties in 271(d) with bringing such a claim and the fact that if you have a successful one, you have probably

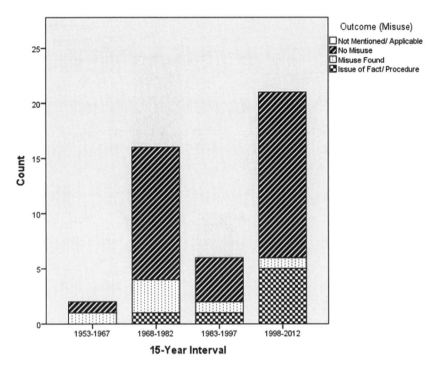

Figure 6.65 Fraud outcomes

F. Antitrust

A look at the trend in antitrust-related misuse cases over time in Figure 6.67 shows its peak to be between 1968 and 1982, with a dramatic fall to a historic low between 1983 and 1997. This period coincides with the formation of the Federal Circuit, and it may be that its ability to resolve patent abuses endogenously by other policy levers such as criteria for patentability or nonobviousness may have reduced the need for misuse. The surge in cases between 1998 and 2012 may be explained by the need for defendants to buttress their patent misuse allegations with more favorably perceived arguments under antitrust law. Looking at the specific types of antitrust allegations raised, one notices from Figure 6.68 that most cases either are Section 2 Sherman Act cases or else

---

already beaten the case on other grounds. So I'm kind of curious. It's not clear what explains that.")

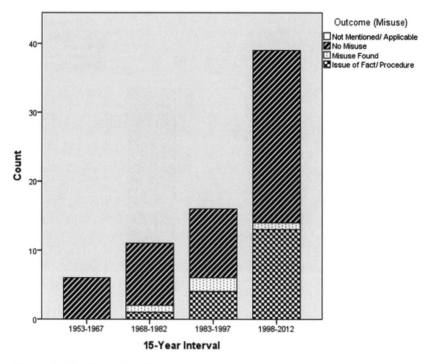

Figure 6.66   Vexatious litigation outcomes

combinations of Sections 1 and 2 of the Sherman Act. These instances together account for 30 percent of the cases, with another 31.2 percent coming from Section 1 Sherman Act cases. Infringers were most successful with Section 1 Sherman Act cases, winning 40.9 percent of the time, compared with Section 2 Sherman Act cases (16.2%) or a combination of the two (20.5%) (Figure 6.69).

G.   Variations by Circuit

While tying is the most prevalent type of misuse conduct as a whole across circuits, it is interesting that different circuits dominate on specific types of misuse cases (Figures 6.70). Cases from courts in the Seventh Circuit are dominated by misuse related to restrictions and royalties. Those from the Ninth Circuit are dominated by fraud and vexatious litigation cases, which constitute the overwhelming bulk of "bad faith" cases.

Once the district court level cases are filtered away, however, an interesting finding emerges (Figure 6.71). The prevalence of "bad faith" claims

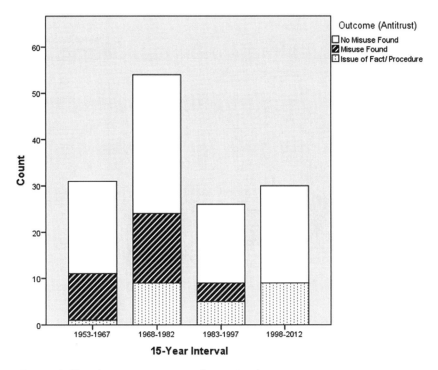

Figure 6.67   Antitrust outcomes (over time)

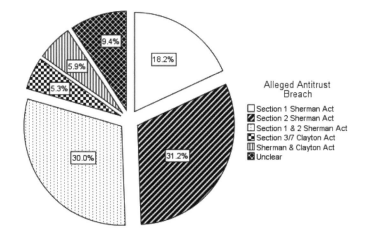

Figure 6.68   Antitrust categories

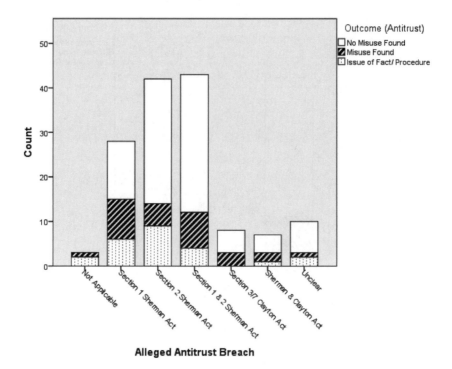

Figure 6.69   Antitrust outcomes by specific antitrust law provisions

seen earlier melts away, leaving an overwhelming dominance of tying-related cases, followed distantly by restrictions, royalty and time extension cases. This suggests that few infringers or patentees appeal a finding of the district courts on bad faith matters.

Types of misuse are not uniform across the circuits. For example, courts disagree whether pre-issued patents can form the basis for a misuse claim. The Eastern District of California, for example, has held that:

> License agreements entered into after a patent application has been filed but before the patent issues are not necessarily unenforceable. . . . Pre-issuance, there is no patent right to impermissibly broaden. The doctrine of patent misuse could not be brought into play in *Aronson*, which concerned a license agreement entered into before issuance of the patent, but after patent application submitted.[189]

---

[189]   *Delano Farms Co. v. California Table Grape Comm'n*, 623 F. Supp. 2d 1144, 1179 (E.D. Cal. 2009).

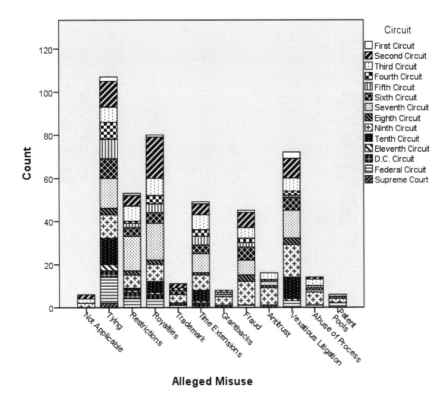

Figure 6.70   Variations by circuit (as a whole)

Other courts have held that pre-issued patents can still be leveraged in a way that gives rise to actionable misuse on the basis that *Morton Salt* "determined that the maintenance as well as the procuring of such a restriction constituted misuse."[190] As the Seventh Circuit in *Meehan v. PPG Industries, Inc.*, explained: "[e]ven when an inventor has not yet applied for a patent, the right to apply for and obtain those protections is valuable. Such a right places the inventor in a strong bargaining position."[191] Other courts, however, have found misuse in instances where

[190]   *Krampe v. Ideal Indus., Inc.*, 347 F. Supp. 1384, 1387 (N.D. Ill. 1972) ("Finally, even if plaintiff could be said to have no protective rights in the cable stripper at the time he entered into the contract, the fact that that agreement is in effect concurrently [sic] with the patent compels this Court to conclude that plaintiff's patent is now being misused").

[191]   *Meehan v. PPG Indus., Inc.*, 802 F.2d 881, 884–86 (7th Cir. 1986); see also *Boggild v. Kenner Prods.*, 776 F.2d 1315, 1320 (6th Cir. 1985) ("the same violations

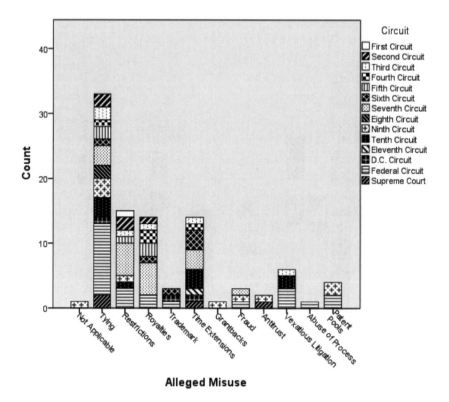

Figure 6.71　Variations by circuit (appellate level)

the offending terms of a license remained unenforced.[192] Another example, as Professor Cotter observed is when two district court decisions have taken different approaches and are in disagreement as to whether vexatious litigation can be a form of misuse.[193]

---

of patent law arising from abuse of the leverage attached to a pending or issued patent can arise from abuse of the leverage afforded by an expressly anticipated application for a patent").

[192]　See *Stewart v. Mo-trim, Inc.*, 192 U.S.P.Q. 410, 412 (S.D. Ohio 1975) ("These and other cases make it abundantly clear that paragraph 19, the anti-competitive clause of the license agreement before this Court, is an example of patent misuse. This is true even though the clause may never have been enforced").

[193]　Cotter, *supra* note 169, at 929 n. 149 ("*Compare* Adv. Magnetic Closures, Inc. v. Rome Fasteners, Inc., No. 98-CV-7766 (PAC), 2006 WL 3342655, at *3 (S.D.N.Y. Nov. 16, 2006) (holding that enforcement of a patent knowing it to be invalid or not infringed does not constitute misuse), *with* Huthwaite, Inc. v. Randstad Gen. Partner (US), L.L.C., No. 06-C-1548, 2006 WL 3065470, at *8-9

H. Categories of Misuse Not Closed

Courts have noted that the categories of patent misuse are not closed.[194] Some courts have advocated a global view of the patent owner's conduct and business practices in determining whether misuse has occurred.[195] In *Zenith*, for example the Supreme Court extended the notion of misuse to include setting of royalty rates based on the licensee's sale of unpatented products.[196] More recently *Princo*, concerned pooling agreements between competing patent owners where, upon the establishment of a standard, competing technologies owned by those in the pool would not be licensed.[197]

Whether because of the 1988 amendments to the Act alone, or because there was a pre-existing trend toward applying antitrust principles to

---

(N.D. Ill. Oct. 24, 2006) (stating that 'mere filing of a copyright infringement lawsuit is not grounds for a copyright misuse claim', but that an allegation that the plaintiff 'is attempting to use its copyrighted books to cover the unprotectible [sic] ideas within those books by filing copyright infringement lawsuits and forcing companies such as Randstad to either settle or incur litigation expenses' properly raises the misuse defense)").

[194] See *Analytichem Int'l, Inc. v. Har-Len Assoc.*, 490 F. Supp. 271, 273 (W.D. Pa. 1980) ("While the most common mode of attempting to extend the impact of a patent beyond its proper scope is by means of a tying clause requiring use of unpatented articles as a condition of using the patented article, misuse of a patent can occur in other ways").

[195] *United States v. Telectronics Proprietary, Ltd.*, 607 F. Supp. 753, 754 (D. Colo. 1983) ("There are no 'classic' acts of patent misuse alleged in this case, e.g. (1) requiring the purchase of unpatented goods for use with patented apparatus or processes, (2) prohibiting production or sale of competing goods, or (3) conditioning the granting of a license under one patent upon the acceptance of another and different license. Misuse of a patent, however, may be inferred from the totality of a licensor's conduct and business practices").

[196] See *Zenith Radio Corp. v. Hazeltine Research, Inc.*, 395 U.S. 100, 139 (1969) ("There is nothing in the right granted the patentee . . . which empowers him to insist on payment not only for use but also for producing products which do not employ his discoveries at all"). As Tom Cotter notes, this view may be controversial. Cotter, supra note 161, at 909 n. 32 (quoting *Engel Indus., Inc. v. Lockformer Co.*, 96 F.3d 1398, 1408–409 (Fed. Cir. 1996) (observing that "'voluntary' package licensing does not constitute misuse, and distinguishing *Zenith* on the ground that the licensing arrangement there was coerced)").

[197] *Princo Corp. v. Int'l Trade Comm'n*, 616 F.3d 1318, 1341 (Fed. Cir. 2010) (Dyk Dissenting), *cert. denied*, 131 S. Ct. 2480, (2011). The dissent in Princo phrased it differently: "The critical question is whether the existence of an antitrust violation—in the form of an agreement to suppress an alternative technology designed to protect a patented technology from competition—constitutes misuse of the protected patents," ibid.

patent misuse, cases and commentary soon adopted the tenor of antitrust policy and categories of cases—essentially frozen in time since 1988.[198] Case data studying trends over time reveal that courts have generally been reluctant to expand the categories of misuse. It is, however, striking that proportionately more opinions expressly deny expansion and find no misuse following from the 1988 amendments than compared to the preceding period.[199] Some commentators observed a corresponding hostility toward misuse,[200] with only one case finding patent misuse since 1982.[201]

Novel cases of misuse have appeared before the courts consistently over the years for which no precedent exists. In *Kolene Corp. v. Motor City Metal Treating, Inc*, the Sixth Circuit had to consider whether a combined use of patent and servicemark could amount to misuse.[202] In *Bela Seating Co. v. Poloron Products, Inc*, the Seventh Circuit had to determine "whether injunctive relief against future infringement should be 'withheld from a patent owner who seeks to discriminate in royalty rates charged to undifferentiable competitors under the patent.'"[203]

In 13.0 percent of the cases, litigants argued for an expansion of the scope of patent misuse (Figure 6.72). However, in only 1.9 percent of the cases did the court agree to expand it. Most of the expansion occurred at the appellate level (4.1%), compared to (1.4%) at the district court level

---

[198] See Janice M. Mueller, *Patent Misuse Through the Capture of Industry Standards*, 17 BERKELEY TECH. L.J. 623, 673 (2002) ("In practice, determinations of patent misuse have been based upon a fairly narrow range of specific acts or practices of the patent owner, often (but not exclusively) in the context of patent licensing. The key inquiry is whether, by imposing a challenged condition (e.g., the imposition of an onerous term in a license granted under the patent), the patent owner has 'impermissibly broadened the "physical or temporal scope" of the patent grant with anticompetitive effect'").

[199] See Figure 6.70.

[200] See Tyler J. Gee, *Illinois Tool Works v. Independent Ink: Inking out Limits of the Patent Grant*, 41 U.S.F. L. REV. 261, 271–72 (2006–2007) ("The Federal Circuit, created primarily to enforce the patent codes, has been extremely hostile to the defense. The Federal Circuit has introduced new requirements and generally limited its findings of misuse to conduct that also violated the antitrust laws").

[201] See *Senza-Gel Corp. v. Seiffhart*, 803 F.2d 661, 669 (Fed. Cir. 1986).

[202] *Kolene Corp. v. Motor City Metal Treating, Inc.*, 440 F.2d 77, 84 (6th Cir. 1971) ("Motor City urges on appeal, however, that the patent and servicemark are so interrelated that, even accepting the finding of the District Court, there is still patent misuse. This theory presents a novel issue for which we can find no case directly on point").

[203] *Bela Seating Co. v. Poloron Prods.*, Inc., 438 F.2d 733, 738 (7th Cir. 1971).

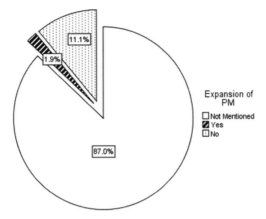

Figure 6.72   Whether courts were willing to expand the categories of misuse

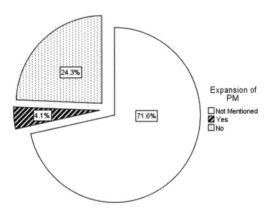

Figure 6.73   Whether courts were willing to expand the categories of misuse (appellate level)

(Figures 6.73 and 6.74). The smaller figure for district courts might well be expected given that they are expected to toe the line in terms of precedent set by the appellate courts. However, the fact is that the specific nature of misuse allows district courts more flexibility than many other areas of patent law, and it may be questioned why a judge might not exercise his discretion in appropriate cases to find misuse even though there is no ready precedent for it. At the appellate level, nearly a quarter of cases in which the court was invited to expand misuse, the court responded in the negative, perhaps an indication that either infringers are desperate or

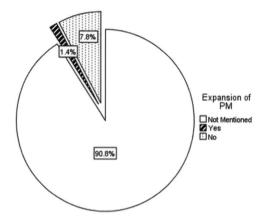

*Figure 6.74   Whether courts were willing to expand the categories of
misuse (district court level)*

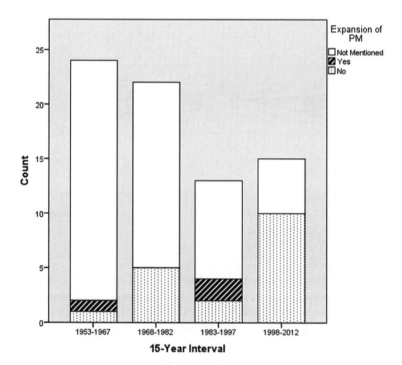

*Figure 6.75   Whether courts were willing to expand the categories of
misuse (appellate level)*

courts are too closed minded. The latter might be more plausible than it initially appears, given that there has also been a higher frequency of cases expressing unwillingness to expand the categories of misuse in recent years (Figures 6.75).

I. Expansion

One judge interviewed emphasized that there was no judicial hostility toward misuse. He noted that while patent misuse has potential "given the right facts and evidence," it was difficult for him to "sense vigor beyond antitrust case law."[204] The concurrence in *Princo* may provide a clue to this reluctance. Judge Prost, in commenting on the dissenting view that misuse includes suppression of technology, noted that "the dissent does not address how a patent owner's right to *exclude* others from using the invention could, and possibly should, affect the calculus in the antitrust and patent misuse contexts."[205]

However, precedent seems to suggest that far from stultifying the growth of the categories of misuse, courts should be more willing to explore new avenues where application of the doctrine may be appropriate. As the Supreme Court in *Univis Lens Co.* explained, "the particular form or method by which the monopoly is sought to be extended is immaterial. The first vending of any article manufactured under a patent puts the article beyond the reach of the monopoly which that patent confers."[206] Litigants have added that "[n]or is there any reason to expand the misuse defense to reach alleged collateral anticompetitive conduct, when the antitrust laws already provide any party that suffers competitive injury with powerful means of redress."[207]

The stultification in the growth of patent misuse categories may also

---

[204]   On file with the author. ("The important point that I want to be clear about—if people assume that judges on this court or any court are hostile to the patent misuse defense, I think that's quite wrong. If people assume that judges on the court are just dying to expand it greatly, I think that's also wrong. . . . Given the right facts and the right evidence, we might be expected to reverse a finding of no misuse or to affirm a finding of misuse where that's made in a strong, clear case. I don't think the doctrine is dead or totally redundant of antitrust case law. But, on the other hand, it's hard to have any sense of how much vigor it might have, beyond antitrust case law.")

[205]   *Princo Corp. v. Int'l Trade Comm'n*, 616 F.3d 1318, 1340-41 (Fed. Cir. 2010).

[206]   *United States v. Univis Lens Co.*, 314 U.S. 241, 249–52 (1942).

[207]   Brief for Intervenor U.S. Philips Corporation on Rehearing *En Banc, Princo Corp. v. Int'l Trade Comm'n*, 616 F.3d 1318 (Fed. Cir. 2010) (No. 2007-1386).

be due to defendants' perception that courts are generally not receptive to calls to expand the scope of misuse. It may also be that new forms of misuse may be classified as permuatations of existing forms and are therefore classified within the existing categories.[208] However, few courts have exercised any degree of boldness in venturing to suggest the form that new categories might take and to point the way for future litigants to explore. Indeed, in statements that suggest a fallacious circularity, some courts have blamed the parties for failing to cite cases or theories in support of their invitation for the court to expand the categories of misuse.[209]

Sir Henry Maine cautioned against this sort of closed-mindedness. He noted that "[s]ocial necessities and social opinion are always more or less in advance of law. We may come indefinitely near to the tendency to re-open ... The greater or less happiness of a people depends on the degree of promptitude with which the gap is narrowed."[210] In this respect, English jurist Lord Denning wrote:

> This argument about the novelty of action does not appeal to me in the least. It has been put forward in all the great cases which have been milestones of progress in our law. In each of these cases the judges were divided in opinion. On the one side there were timorous souls who were fearful of allowing a new cause of action. On the other side there were the bold spirits who were ready

---

[208]   See *Nat'l Presto Indus., Inc. v. Black & Decker, Inc.*, 760 F. Supp. 699, 702–703 (N.D. Ill. 1991) ("As should be apparent, the traditional examples of patent misuse bear very little if any resemblance to what has been alleged here— 'suppressing or concealing' an invention before filing and sending threatening letters to competitors and retailers"); *Lucent Techs., Inc. v. Microsoft Corp.*, 544 F. Supp. 2d 1080, 1102 (S.D. Cal. 2008) (in which summary judgment was granted, in part, and denied, in part, concerning *Lucent Techs., Inc. v. Microsoft Corp.*, 2008 U.S. Dist. LEXIS 93392 (S.D. Cal., Feb. 28, 2008). "The Court concludes that these additional theories are insufficient to support patent misuse. Other than the general characterization of the test from *Virginia Panel Corp.*, cites no authority that these particular actions constitute patent misuse").

[209]   See *Nat'l Presto Indus., Inc.*, 760 F. Supp. at 703 ("Black & Decker has not cited a patent misuse case involving conduct similar to Presto's mail campaign or suppression and concealment, and we are not persuaded that the doctrine of misuse reaches the misconduct Black & Decker has alleged"); *Congoleum Indus., Inc. v. Armstrong Cork Co.*, 366 F. Supp. 220, 233 (E.D. Pa. 1973) ("Armstrong has not cited legal authority which supports the proposition that the existence of such a clause in a patent license agreement amounts to misuse, and the Court is not persuaded of possible anticompetitive effects resulting from the inclusion of this provision in this case").

[210]   Henry Maine, ANCIENT LAW: ITS CONNECTIONS WITH THE HISTORY OF SOCIETY AND ITS RELATION TO MODERN IDEAS 24 (10th ed. 1920).

to allow it if justice so required. It was fortunate for the common law that the progressive view prevailed.[211]

One court that has heeded the call for expanding the categories of misuse was the Seventh Circuit in *Meehan v. PPG Industries*.[212] The panel was invited to consider the Sixth Circuit's decision in *Boggild v. Kenner Products*, which had earlier extended the "*Brulotte* rule of *per se* invalidity precluded enforcement of license terms that were entered into in anticipation of patent protection and that required royalty payments beyond the life of the patent."[213] Chief Judge Cummings, in writing for a unanimous panel agreed "with the Sixth Circuit's holding that the *Brulotte* rule should be extended to agreements entered into in anticipation of applying for patents."[214] Remarkably, Chief Judge Cumming noted that "*Brulotte* is not concerned with restrictions on the sale of patent rights but rather the impact of such arrangements on the policies and purposes of the federal patent laws."[215] This statement echoed the *Morton Salt* opinion some forty years earlier, which considered the policies and purposes of the "special privilege of a patent monopoly."[216]

Further, as Professor Mark Lemley notes, "[s]ince the patent misuse doctrine has a policy foundation separate from the antitrust laws, there is no theoretical bar to the creation of non-antitrust classes of patent misuse."[217] Misuse has been raised as a possible solution to prevent the circumvention of the doctrine of exhaustion[218] and open source

---

[211] *Candler v. Crane, Christmas and Co.* [1952] 2 K.B. 164, 178 (Eng.).

[212] *Meehan v. PPG Indus., Inc.*, 802 F.2d 881, 884–86 (7th Cir. 1986).

[213] Ibid. at 884 (citing *Boggild v. Kenner Prods.*, 776 F.2d 1315, 1319 (6th Cir. 1985)).

[214] Ibid. at 884.

[215] Ibid. at 886.

[216] *Morton Salt Co. v. G. S. Suppiger Co.*, 314 U.S. 488, 492, (1942) ("The grant to the inventor of the special privilege of a patent monopoly carries out a public policy adopted by the Constitution and laws of the United States, 'to promote the Progress of Science and useful Arts, by securing for limited Times to . . . Inventors the exclusive Right . . .' to their 'new and useful' inventions. But the public policy which includes inventions within the granted monopoly excludes from it all that is not embraced in the invention. It equally forbids the use of the patent to secure an exclusive right or limited monopoly not granted by the Patent Office and which it is contrary to public policy to grant").

[217] See Mark A. Lemley, *The Economic Irrationality of Patent Misuse*, 78 CAL. L. REV. 1599, 1611–12 (1990).

[218] See Paul J. Heald & James Charles Smith, *The Problem of Social Cost in a Genetically Modified Age*, 58 HASTINGS L.J. 87, 148 (2006–2007) ("When the patent owner acts wrongfully, however, in advocating a proprietary standard,

restrictions.[219] Professor Leaffer suggests another possible area for the expansion of misuse doctrine is in the area of exclusive grant-backs in patent pooling agreements.[220]

Recently the dissent in *Princo* highlighted the need to employ misuse where patentees upset the Constitutional bargain or violate competition policy, but where they remain beyond the reach of antitrust.[221] This issue was previously examined in Chapter 4.

---

the patent misuse doctrine may render the patent unenforceable against putative infringers who must conform with the standard. In the standard settings cases, the key factor is the unilateral imposition of legal duties on unwitting parties, just as in the case of the patentee and the bystanding farmer. But the case of the farmer is even more compelling. Sometimes firms can avoid a standard or design around it, but the bystanding farmer who discovers that his fields are full of allegedly infringing plants has been completely captured by the patent owner. He has no choice but to plow under his fields or pay a licensing fee").

[219] See Robin Feldman, *The Open Source Biotechnology Movement: Is It Patent Misuse?*, 6 MINN. J.L. SCI. & TECH. 117, 118–19 (2004–2005) ("Improvements in the core technology may not be within the teachings of the original patent. Thus, when open source biotechnology licenses require that advances in the technology must be made available to others on the same open terms as the original technology, the open source group may be using the power of the patent grant to reach an invention outside the original patent. When a patent holder appears to expand the scope of the patent beyond the patent grant, the question is whether the behavior is impermissible, as measured by the tests within the patent misuse doctrine").

[220] See Leaffer, *supra* note 160, at 161–62. ("The exclusivity of a license agreement, particularly a pattern of exclusive licenses in patent-pooling arrangements undermines the incentive to innovate even for non-licensees as well as potential innovators in the same technological field. It may discourage non-licensees from remaining in the technological field, much less their continued investment in innovation. This occurs with greater force when the number of patents in a pool increases. Facing an accumulated set of pooled patents, and bolstered by exclusive grant-back agreements, the cost of remaining outside the pool increases with the omnipresent threat of litigation. In sum, grant-backs in a patent pool context not only create disincentives to innovate by licensees, they may equally have a negative impact on third parties in the same technological field and both active participants and potential innovators who experience increased barriers to entry. For this reason, grant-back clauses bear directly on patent policy and its scrutiny under the doctrine of patent misuse").

[221] *Princo Corp. v. Int'l Trade Comm'n*, 616 F.3d 1318, 1342 (Fed. Cir. 2010) ("The majority declines to give the patent misuse doctrine significant scope because it 'is in derogation of statutory patent rights against infringement'. Evidently the majority thinks it appropriate to emasculate the doctrine so that it will not provide a meaningful obstacle to patent enforcement. Outside of unlawful tying arrangements and agreements extending the patent term, the majority would hold that antitrust violations are not patent misuse and would leave to private and government antitrust proceedings the task of preventing abuse of

With respect to case outcomes, it is notable that no post-1988 defend-ants successfully raised patent misuse on licensing and royalty related restrictions, consistent with the high standard of proof—the requirement of an anticompetitive effect. One judge opined that this reflected the rationality of litigants, who realized that it was "not easy to make a patent misuse case stick."[222] Interviewees also noted that even though Congress was targeting two specific types of misuse, it reflected a broader concern that misuse not be invoked like a magical incantation.[223]

Finally, parties seeking to invite a court to expand the categories of misuse might take a leaf from *Technology Licensing Corp. v. Gennum Corp.* The court noted:

> Because patent misuse is an equitable doctrine, [defendant] would not neces-sarily need to show that the facts here fit precisely into the mold of situations in which it has been previously applied. Nevertheless, because the *type of harm* that patent misuse doctrine is designed to prevent is not present here even under [defendant's] characterization of what occurred, its patent misuse defense fails.[224]

Thus, at least for some courts, the policy goals underlying misuse become an important part of the inquiry. At the same time, the wisdom of conflat-ing antitrust mechanics with patent policy has been called into question, citing systematic overdeterrance as a possible outcome.[225] Professor Vincent Chiappetta commented that:

---

patent monopolies, enforcement that is likely inadequate to the task. Indeed, the majority goes so far as to suggest that the misuse doctrine be eliminated entirely. I read the relevant Supreme Court cases and congressional legislation as supporting a vigorous misuse defense, clearly applicable to agreements to suppress alternative technology. The majority cabins the doctrine in contravention of this Supreme Court authority").

[222] On file with the author.

[223] Ibid.

[224] *Tech. Licensing Corp. v. Gennum Corp.*, No. C 01-04204 RS, 2007 U.S. Dist. LEXIS 35521, at *81 (N.D. Cal. May 4, 2007).

[225] See Note, *Is the Patent Misuse Doctrine Obsolete?*, 110 HARV. L. REV. 1922, 1931 (1997) ("Although considering patent scope is necessary to maximize 'economic efficiency', courts should, in theory, be able to take account of it under the rule of reason. In practice, however, a misuse doctrine that is distinct from the rule of reason may better focus courts' attention on how a patent restriction affects innovation and ultimately economic efficiency"). In the copyright context, see Aaron Xavier Fellmeth, *Copyright Misuse and the Limits of the Intellectual Property Monopoly*, 6 J. INTELL. PROP. L. 1, 37–38 (1998) ("Why not simply apply antitrust law and supplement it with equity where the plaintiff has committed no antitrust violation but has violated public policy? Unless the anticompetitive

[t]he internal balances analysis reinforces the fundamental difficulty with misuse's 'scope of the patent' test. Because it does not accurately reflect the crucial difference between inherent costs from refusing to deal and the potential harms arising from *any* term imposed on access, it will both over-react (the beyond the term and claims per se violations) and under-react (failing to consider conditions on access found to be within the patent's scope).[226]

Every court invoking misuse from *Motion* Picture *Patents* to *Princo* turns to the scope of a patent as being the lodestone of misconduct. The cases mention the scope of a patent as if it that were a clear measure of what is permissible and what is not. But is that truly the case? That is the subject of the next chapter.

---

behavior is obviously unrelated to the copyright owner's monopoly, there is a risk that the copyright owner will be subjected to antitrust liability for behavior that borders on proper use of the copyright monopoly. Antitrust and intellectual property law may in some cases be too inherently contradictory for this approach to work reliably. Courts should be able to punish borderline anticompetitive licensing practices by negating the copyright monopoly without adjudicating a true antitrust claim that requires both market power and intent to monopolize. A successful antitrust defense in a borderline case would expose the copyright owner to the risk of estoppel in an affirmative antitrust claim, with accompanying treble damages (or even a criminal investigation), even though the real purpose of the adjudication was not to punish willfully anticompetitive conduct, but to discourage questionable licensing practices").

[226] Vincent Chiappetta, *Living With Patents: Insights From Patent Misuse*, 15 MARQ. INTELL. PROP. L. REV. 1, 45 n. 197 (2011).

7. Charting the scope of patent misuse

I. INTRODUCTION

Understanding the scope of a patent is central to deciphering whether a patentee's conduct amounts to misuse. Courts have been relatively consistent in defining misuse based on some notion of patent "scope". Looking at Figure 7.1, over 80 percent of cases overall defined misuse according to "scope." From Figure 7.2, it was calculated that about 86 percent of courts identified misuse according to some definition of "scope" between 1953 and 1962. This figure rose to 87 percent between 1963 and 1972, briefly falling by a remarkably significant margin to 72 percent between 1973 and 1992, before rising again to 91 percent between 2003 and 2012.

Looking through the cases studied by their level of judicial hierarchy, it is clear that most of the cases where scope was not defined came from the district courts. One in five cases did not define the scope of a patent for misuse purposes (Figure 7.3), compared to one in ten at the appellate level (Figure 7.4). In particular, district courts cases between 1983 and 1992, contributed the most to this phenomenon, with more than one in four

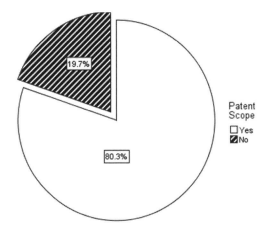

Figure 7.1   Proportion of cases defining "scope" (overall)

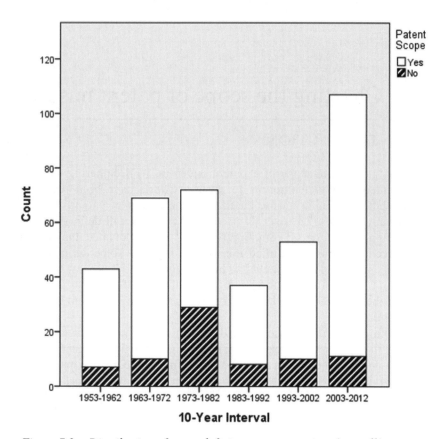

Figure 7.2   Distribution of cases defining scope over time (overall)

cases failing to base their analysis of misuse on any cognizable "scope." This practice has not passed unnoticed at the appellate level. For example in *Carpet Seaming Tape Licensing Corp. v. Best Seam, Inc.*, the Ninth Circuit noted that the lower court's "legal conclusions are so summary that it is virtually impossible to ascertain what legal standards were in fact applied, and the factual record and findings are so sparse in some essential areas that independent assessment of the presence of the elements of the named violations is impossible." [1] As a matter of judicial practice, this is undesirable. As Lord Denning explained:

---

[1]   *Carpet Seaming Tape Licensing Corp. v. Best Seam Inc.*, 616 F.2d 1133, 1141 (9th Cir. 1980).

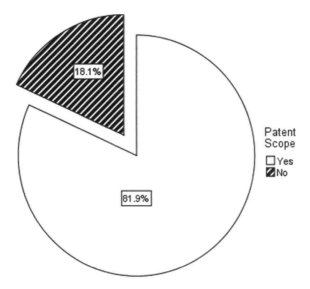

Figure 7.3   Proportion of cases defining "scope" (district courts)

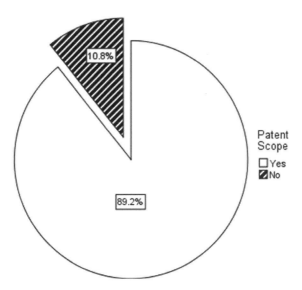

Figure 7.4   Proportion of cases defining "scope" (appellate courts)

[A] judge must give his reasons for his decision: for, by doing so, he gives proof that he has heard and considered the evidence and arguments that have been addressed before him on each side: and also that he has not taken extraneous considerations into account. It is of course true that his decision may be correct even though he should give no reason for it or even give a wrong reason: but, in order that a trial should be fair, it is necessary, not only that a correct decision should be reached, but also that it should be seen to be based on reason; and that can only be seen, if the judge himself states his reasons. Furthermore, if his reasons are at fault, then they afford a basis on which the party aggrieved by his decision can appeal to a higher court.[2]

Where an equitable doctrine such as misuse has been invoked, that holds even truer still. Misuse cases are animated by the facts that arise from the alleged abuse of patent rights. If these findings are to be useful as a basis for forming legal precedent in the American common law system, they must be properly described, analyzed and justified. This is a trend that appears to have been reversed by the establishment of the Federal Circuit. Figure 7.5 shows the distribution of district court cases defining scope over time, the number of opinions which described misuse according to some measure of "scope" rose from 75 percent to 91 percent between 1983 and 2012. By way of comparison, appellate courts have consistently defined misuse according to the scope of the patent. Other than a low of 77 percent during the initial period between 1953 and 1962, the average was 92 percent between 1962 to 2012 (see Figure 7.6).

It is interesting that where the courts defined the scope of misuse, 25 percent were willing to find for the defendant, compared to just 16 percent when the scope was not defined (Figure 7.7). This could suggest that where defendants took more time to brief judges on misuse and on how the patentee's conduct exceeded the scope of its claims, courts were more willing to find for them. This data could also suggest that when judges took more care to perform a thorough analysis, those judges may also have been more sympathetic to the defendant's arguments.

While most opinions do include some discussion of the scope of patent in determining misuse, courts did not simply rely on one standard measure of "scope," but eight different measures. These measures are not completely distinct. While in some cases they may overlap, the eight can be discretely plotted along three dimensions: the absolute dimension, the relative dimension and the policy dimension (see Figure 7.8).

The physical dimension comprises the patent claims, the patent's temporal length or the patented product. Also examined was the way in

---

[2]   Alfred Denning, THE ROAD TO JUSTICE 29 (1955).

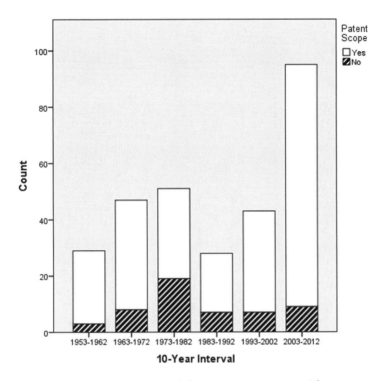

Figure 7.5   Distribution of cases defining scope over time (district courts)

which misuse was treated with respect to antitrust. A category was made to indicate whether the court viewed the two bodies of law as coexisting. Another was created to indicate more specifically their relationship, whether they are coextensive, broader, or just different. The policy dimension examined what sort of policy-based principles were informing the court, what principles were guiding the outcome of the case, and what policy objectives were trying to be achieved. "Patent Policy" refers to those policies related to the proper functioning of the patent system as discussed in earlier chapters. Similarly, "Antitrust Policy" refers to policies dealing with the proper functioning of the market. "Bad faith" captured cases animated by issues relating to fraud, vexatious litigation and abuse of process, where the court applied a legal rubric different from the other cases.

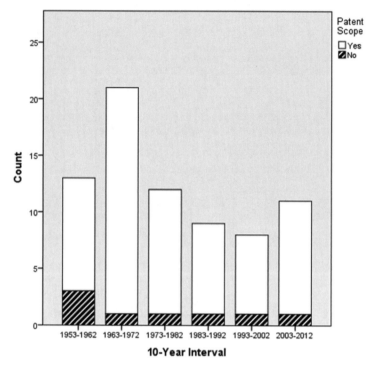

Figure 7.6   Distribution of cases defining scope over time (appellate courts)

II.   THE ABSOLUTE DIMENSION

A.   "Scope" as Claims

It is hornbook law that the scope of a patent is defined by its claims.[3] Patentees must prove that their claims are valid and infringed. If the

---

[3]   See *Dawson Chem. Co. v. Rohm & Haas Co.*, 448 U.S. 176, 221 (1980) ("The boundary of a patent monopoly is to be limited by the literal scope of the patent claims"); Martin J. Adelman et al., CASES AND MATERIALS ON PATENT LAW 459 (3d ed. 2009) ("The essence of the patent right is the right to exclude others from making, using, selling or offering to sell the claimed invention. The claims define the bounds of that right to exclude. Accordingly, the claims are the most significant part of the entire patent instrument. As such, they are the principal focus of the dialogue the patent drafter will have with an inventor, of the entire process, and ultimately of any licensing activity or infringement suit to enforce patent rights").

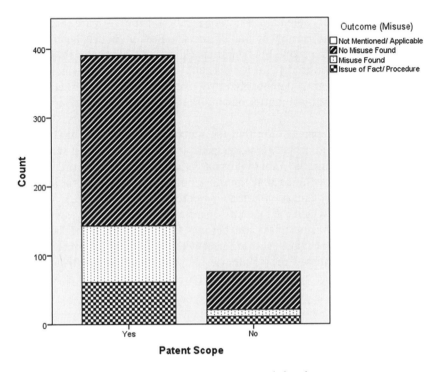

Figure 7.7   Outcome where patent scope was defined

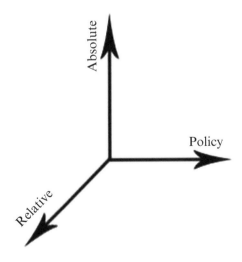

Figure 7.8   The three dimensions of misuse

accused device or defendant's actions fall outside of patent claims, courts will not find infringement.[4] By the same token, courts have found conduct outside the scope of the patent claims can support a finding of misuse. For example, the Supreme Court in *Motion Pictures* held that patent legislation gives patentees control over the invention defined in the claim, but not in subject matter beyond that because it would contravene public policy.[5]

From the basic proposition that the scope of a patent is limited to the invention described in its claims, coupled with the rule that the statutory policy of benefitting the public outweighs the policy of benefitting inventors, the Court concluded that the monopoly granted by law should not extend to, and thus cannot sanction a patentee's control of, mere materials with which or on which the machine operates.[6]

A quarter of misuse cases are defined by this measure of "scope." This view of "scope" has also been accepted in the antitrust context, and courts have determined the boundaries of patent monopoly through the "literal scope of the patent claims."[7] As patent attorneys also know claim

---

[4] See William J. Nicoson, *Misuse of the Misuse Doctrine in Infringement Suits*, 9 UCLA L. REV. 76, 109–10 (1962).

[5] *Motion Picture Patents Co. v. Universal Film Mfg. Co.*, 243 U.S. 502, 513 (1917) ("Whatever the right of the owner may be to control by restriction the materials to be used in operating the machine, it must be derived through the general law from the ownership of the property in the machine, and it cannot be derived from or protected by the patent law, which allows a grant only of the right to an exclusive use of the new and useful discovery which has been made,—this and nothing more"); see also *Mallinckrodt, Inc. v. Medipart, Inc.*, 976 F.2d 700, 708 (Fed. Cir. 1992) (holding that for a practice not alleged to be *per se* patent misuse, a court must determine if the practice is "reasonably within the patent grant, *i.e.*, that it relates to the subject matter within the scope of the patent claims"); *Bausch & Lomb, Inc. v. Allergan, Inc.*, 136 F. Supp. 2d 166, 170 (W.D.N.Y. 2001) ("When a practice alleged to constitute patent misuse is neither per se patent misuse nor specifically from a misuse analysis by § 271(d), a court must determine if that practice is reasonably within the patent grant, i.e., *that it relates to subject matter within the scope of the patent claims*") (emphasis added); *Ansul Co. v. Uniroyal, Inc.*, 306 F. Supp. 541, 556–57 (S.D.N.Y. 1969) ("Ansul's various contentions of patent misuse are governed by certain basic principles. The first of these is that a patentee's lawful monopoly 'must be limited to the invention described in the claims of his patent'").

[6] *Rohm & Haas Co. v. Dawson Chemical Co.*, 599 F.2d 685, 693 (5th Cir. 1979) (quoting *Motion Picture Patents Co.*, 243 U.S. at 509–13).

[7] *In re Indep. Serv. Orgs.*, 989 F. Supp. 1131, 1135 (D. Kan. 1997) ("The scope of a 'patent monopoly' is defined by the claims of the patent, not by the limits of what a court determines is the most analogous antitrust market").

construction is a matter of considerable complication and controversy.[8] In *Autogiro Co. of America v. United States*, the U.S. Court of Claims explained how the difficult process in determining that scope is exacerbated by the technology that patents protect:

> The inability of words to achieve precision is none the less extant with patent claims than it is with statutes. The problem is likely more acute with claims. Statutes by definition are the reduction of ideas to print. Since the ability to verbalize is crucial in statutory enactment, legislators develop a facility with words not equally developed in inventors. An invention exists most importantly as a tangible structure or a series of drawings. A verbal portrayal is usually an afterthought written to satisfy the requirements of patent law. This conversion of machine to words allows for unintended idea gaps which cannot be satisfactorily filled. Often the invention is novel and words do not exist to describe it. The dictionary does not always keep abreast of the inventor. It cannot. Things are not made for the sake of words, but words for things. To overcome this lag, patent law allows the inventor to be his own lexicographer.
>
> Allowing the patentee verbal license only augments the difficulty of understanding the claims. The sanction of new words or hybrids from old ones not only leaves one unsure what a rose is, but also unsure whether a rose is a rose. Thus we find that a claim cannot be interpreted without going beyond the claim itself. No matter how clear a claim appears to be, lurking in the background are documents that may completely disrupt initial views on its meaning.[9]

---

[8] See Thomas F. Cotter, *Misuse*, 44 Hous. L. Rev. 901, 938 (2007) ("Although the claims of a patent are often described as the 'metes and bounds' of the invention, IPRs don't come with metes and bounds in any literal sense; determining whether a given invention falls within the literal scope of those claims is often a difficult task, as any patent lawyer will attest"). For a chequered history of claim interpretation, see generally Craig Allen Nard, The Law of Patents 394–430 (Aspen, 2008).

[9] *Autogiro Co. of Am. v. United States*, 384 F.2d 391, 396–97 (Ct. Cl. 1967), see Thomas F. Cotter, *supra* note 8, at 938 ("misuse occurs when the patent or copyright owner attempts to transgress these boundaries, i.e., to assert patent or copyright rights beyond the limits the law has set. Notice that, under this definition, it may not matter whether the 'broadening' of the IPR results in any anticompetitive result—that is, in some result (such as increase in price or reduction in output) that would be of concern to antitrust enforcers. The preceding definition is far from perfect, however, for several reasons. Most obviously, it begs the question of what the relevant boundaries are. Although there are a few relatively clear boundaries set forth in the applicable statutes—patent and copyright terms, for example, are usually not hard to calculate—there is more frequently a substantial gray area within which it is unclear whether one's IPRs extend. Although the claims of a patent are often described as the 'metes and bounds' of the invention, IPRs don't come with metes and bounds in any literal sense; determining whether a given invention falls within the literal scope of those claims is often a difficult task, as any patent lawyer will attest").

Interviewees stated that the reliance on patent scope as a basis for finding misuse was consistent with their views.[10] Some were surprised that a third of the cases did not treat "scope" as relating to the claims of the patent, and appeared also surprised that nearly a third of the courts did not discuss the patent claims in question when defining "scope" for the purposes of analyzing patent misuse.[11] It is interesting that courts adopt a different measure for patent scope for infringement purposes compared to determining misuse. And this may be a good thing for patentees. Given that nearly half of claim constructions by district courts are reversed on appeal, it seems unreasonable to impute misuse when the patentees could reasonably have relied on the perceived breadth of their patent claims only to find that they were guilty of misuse because those claims were exceeded.[12] The fact remains, however, that patentees through the years have been found guilty of misuse despite being found to have their claims tread upon by the defendant's conduct.[13] A monopoly defined by patent claims alone does not explain why a patentee's attempt to extend royalties beyond the patent's term constitute misuse. Nor do claims explain why vexatious litigation has been found to be a form of misuse when the exercise of patent rights is—at least formalistically speaking—unimpeachable.

B.   "Scope" as Physical and Temporal

An academic interviewed pointed out that while claims formed the normal understanding of the metes and bounds of a patentee's rights, scope could also refer to the *rights* that the patentee has with respect to those claims.[14] Under this view, "scope" must include claims as well as the physical or temporal rights that come with the patent grant. Contemporary Federal Circuit jurisprudence recognizes patent misuse as encompassing situations where the patent owner has improperly expanded the physical or temporal scope of the patent grant with anticompetitive effect.[15] The physical scope defines "whether a product is a necessary concomitant of the invention or

---

[10]   On file with the author.

[11]   Ibid.

[12]   Christian A. Chu, *Empirical Analysis of the Federal Circuit's Claim Construction Trends*, 16 Berk. Tech. L.J. 1075, 1090 (2001).

[13]   See, e.g., *Morton Salt Co. v. G.S. Suppiger Co.*, 314 U.S. 488 (1942); *Brulotte v. Thys Co.*, 379 U.S. 29 (1964); *Senza-Gel Corp v. Seiffihart*, 803 F.2d 661 (Fed. Cir 1986); *Princo Corp. v. Int'l Trade Comm'n*, 563 F.3d 1301 (Fed. Cir. 2009).

[14]   On file with the author.

[15]   *Windsurfing Int'l Inc. v. AMF, Inc.*, 782 F.2d 995, 1001 (Fed. Cir. 1986) ("The doctrine of patent misuse is an affirmative defense to a suit for patent infringement, and requires that the alleged infringer show that the patentee has

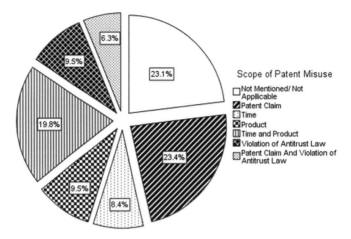

Figure 7.9   How courts define the scope of patent misuse

an entirely separate product."[16] The Federal Circuit in *Senza-Gel Corp. v. Seiffhart* explained that "the nature of the claimed invention [is] the basis for determining whether a product is a necessary concomitant of the invention or an entirely separate product."[17] The temporal boundaries looks to the period of the grant, which is most vividly illustrated in cases involving an extension of licensing obligations beyond the lifetime of a patent.[18] Cases such as *Brulotte* and *Scheiber* in Chapter 3 discuss these cases in more detail.

Thus, in addition to patent claims, the coding instrument used by this study incorporated these two additional measures of "scope," taking care to distinguish between cases which equated "scope" with patent claims from those which understood it to mean time or product embodying the invention. It also took into account cases that found misuse based on a pure violation of antitrust law without taking account of whether the patentee exceeded the scope of its patent claims. In each of these cases, the coding instrument attempted to identify an absolute dimension of patent misuse. Nineteen percent of cases (or 11% and 8.6%) defined misuse exclusively by either a patent's physical or temporal scope. Twenty percent defined misuse in terms of both its physical and temporal scope (Figure 7.9).

---

impermissibly broadened the "physical or temporal scope" of the patent grant with anticompetitive effect").

[16]   *Senza-Gel Corp.*, 803 F.2d at 670 n. 14.

[17]   Ibid.

[18]   *Brulotte*, 379 U.S. at 33–34 ("[A] patentee's use of a royalty agreement that projects beyond the expiration date of the patent is unlawful per se").

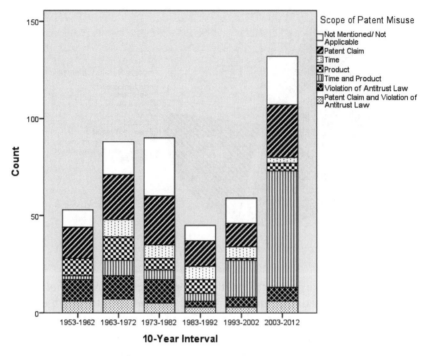

Figure 7.10   Scope of patent misuse over time

Figure 7.10 shows that during the initial period of 1953–1962, courts primarily dealt with misuse allegations premised on antitrust violations or patentees exceeding the scope of their claims. This phenomenon continued for much of the next four decades. From 2001 to 2012, however, the study observed a dramatic tipping in favor of defining misuse by time and product. This trend is consistent with *Windsurfing*'s formula of misuse, and with its rise as the dominant controlling precedent in that same period.[19] Given the low frequency of "antitrust" only claims, it seems reasonable to surmise that throughout each period, courts have generally viewed misuse as coexisting with antitrust rather than being coextensive with it.

In looking closer at the way that courts analyzed the scope of misuse, it is apparent from Figure 7.11 that defendants succeeded most often when the court defined the scope either by time (55%) or product (33%) alone. They were least likely to succeed when the court looked solely at time and product (10%). This figure may also be affected by different judicial

---

[19]   See *supra* Chapter 6.

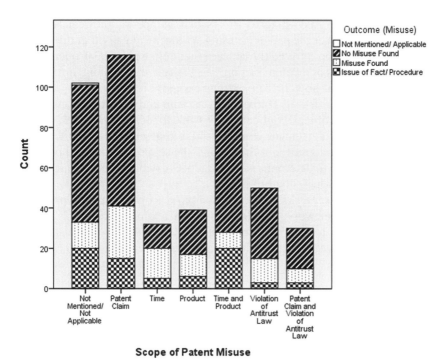

Figure 7.11   Distribution of outcome by scope

philosophies prevalent at each period, since the earlier discussion shows that definition of scope by time and product corresponds with a more pro-patentee period in the history of misuse.

The foregoing inquiry shows that determining the "scope" of a patent is no straightforward enterprise. Focusing on areas beyond the absolute and relative dimensions of a patent provides a framework to begin to think about misuse in a systematic fashion. Yet to some, the question of what the "scope" of a patent is for antitrust or misuse purposes is the wrong place to begin. Professor Vincent Chiappetta argued that "[f]orcing courts to engage in a distracting and ultimately meaningless scope of the patent debate only makes an already complicated inquiry more difficult."[20] Instead, he proposed that the focus should be on "assessing the efficiency effects of licensing terms, rather than going through the charade of labeling those which are found permissible as 'within the scope

---

[20]   Vincent Chiappetta, *Living with Patents: Insights from Patent Misuse*, 15 MARQ. INTELL. PROP. L. REV. 1, 29 n. 121 (2011).

of the patent.'"[21] According to Professor Chiappetta, the real issue in *Princo* was "whether the patent licensing arrangement caused undue social harm."[22] Others have voiced the concern that unlike physical property, the metes and bounds of a patent can only be vaguely traced along notions of preventing "patent holders from earning excessive rewards."[23]

According to Professors Herbert Hovenkamp and Christina Bohannan, the "boundaries" of an IP right are impossible to locate. They explain that "[e]very licensing agreement contains terms that are not express in the patent or copyright grant, but the beyond-the-scope test does not provide a meaningful way to determine which practices extend beyond the scope of the IP grant and which do not."[24]

If neither claims nor the physical or temporal scope of a patent provides a satisfactory framework, could looking at a relative measure of misuse or its policy goals to determine its parameters provide a more satisfactory and comprehensive solution to the concerns raised?

III. THE RELATIVE DIMENSION

A. "Scope" in Relation to Antitrust

The second important dimension that the study examined was the relative one—how misuse relates to antitrust law. This second dimension of "scope" is accordingly labeled the "relative" dimension. The overlap in policies in the two bodies of law, as well as their intertwining histories sometimes makes it difficult to place meaningful markers delineating one from the other. One court considering the two regimes noted that "[a]lthough the patent misuse doctrine and the antitrust doctrine are independent bodies of law, many of the same public policy considerations

---

[21] Ibid.

[22] Ibid.

[23] Note, *Is the Patent Misuse Doctrine Obsolete?*, 110 HARV. L. REV. 1922, 1932 (1996–1997). See 6 Donald S. Chisum, CHISUM ON PATENTS § 19.04 n. 1 (2012) (noting the difficulty of determining what constitutes overreaching beyond the scope of the grant, calling it "vague"); Note, *Clarifying the Copyright Misuse Defense: The Role of Antitrust Standards and First Amendment Values*, 104 HARV. L. REV. 1289, 1295 (1990–1991) (criticizing the "scope-of-the-grant-test" noting that "[the test] presupposes some transcendent notion of what constitutes 'natural' or 'proper' patent or copyright exploitation and thus fails to identify any legal rules or standards for fixing the boundaries of legitimate conduct").

[24] Herbert Hovenkamp & Christina Bohannan, CREATION WITHOUT RESTRAINT: PROMOTING LIBERTY AND RIVALRY IN INNOVATION 260 (2011).

underlie both misuse and antitrust cases, so that in an action where improprieties in the use of intellectual property are alleged, either or both doctrines may apply."[25] Perhaps the best characterization of misuse in its triumvirate form—the absolute, relative and policy dimensions—was expressed by the Third Circuit in *W. L. Gore & Associates, Inc. v. Carlisle Corp.*[26] There the court observed that:

> Where a patent has been used in violation of the antitrust laws, the holder cannot then restrain infringement of the patent by others. And even if an antitrust violation has not been proved, as where it is not shown that use of the patent substantially lessened competition or tended to create a monopoly, the courts will not protect a patent monopoly which is being used to restrain competition contrary to the policy of the antitrust laws. Moreover, misuse may be a violation of the public policy embodied in the patent law itself.[27] Courts adopting this view analyze misuse not as an antitrust violation but within the framework of the Constitution's IP Clause "to promote the Progress of Science and useful Arts."[28]

The following discussion first looks at how courts have articulated the doctrine misuse along lines that are coextensive with antitrust, broader than antitrust, and different from antitrust. It then looks at trends over time and the distribution of cases falling into each relative measure of misuse in relation to antitrust.

B. "Coextensive" with Antitrust

Where misuse is regarded as coextensive with antitrust, courts require defendants to show that patentees violated the antitrust laws. Even in

---

[25] *Van Well Nursery, Inc. v. Mony Life Ins. Co.*, No. CV-04-0245-LRS, 2007 U.S. Dist. LEXIS 15694, at *17 (E.D. Wash. Mar. 7, 2007).

[26] *W.L. Gore & Assocs., Inc. v. Carlisle Corp.*, 529 F.2d 614 (3d Cir. 1976).

[27] Ibid at 622; see also Note, *supra* note 23, at 1927–28 ("if courts applying the misuse doctrine were to consider patent policy in addition to antitrust principles to determine the legality of a particular practice, then the misuse doctrine would have a greater scope than the antitrust laws. Under the misuse doctrine, courts might condemn patent practices that they would permit under the antitrust laws, and as with position two above, the courts would hear more allegations of patent misuse than antitrust violations. *Morton Salt* manifests this third approach").

[28] *Preformed Line Prods. Co. v. Fanner Mfg. Co.*, 328 F.2d 265, 276 (6th Cir. 1964); see also *Keystone Retaining Wall Sys., Inc. v. Westrock, Inc.*, 792 F. Supp. 1552, 1559 (D. Or. 1991) ("Under the patent misuse doctrine, holders of patents granted in furtherance of the public policy of promoting invention are denied enforcement of their patents if they misuse them to extend the scope of their patent monopoly").

such instances, however, the remedy imposed by the antitrust court mirrors misuse.[29] While the analytics of cases in this category are staunchly antitrust in nature, some courts nonetheless base that intervention in equity.[30] Courts characterizing misuse as an equitable doctrine apart from antitrust law brings with it remedies which more fairly fit the wrong done. For example, in *Ansul Co. v. Uniroyal, Inc.*, the court found that denying the patentee "recovery on the ground of misuse is a sufficient vindication of antitrust policy, at least where the patentee is no longer actively engaging in antitrust violations at the time he brings his suit."[31] The court further found that while the effects of former violations had not been dissipated by the time of the defendant's infringement, the patentee had ceased actively engaging in at least its most objectionable antitrust violations. These circumstances meant that "Ansul, as a proven infringer, should not be permitted to recover treble damages for the costs of defending the patentee's nonfrivolous infringement suits."[32] An academic noted that these findings were consistent with his view that patent misuse was largely limited to antitrust violations.[33] The difference here is that patent misuse is used as a defense rather an affirmative cause of action.

This "first approximation" to an antitrust violation, as Professor Thomas Cotter noted, could be due to its "frequent invocation in cases involving purported threats to competition".[34] For example, the Second Circuit reviewed the patentee's licensing program to determine if it "constituted a tying arrangement, *per se* violative of s 1 of the Sherman Act,

---

[29]   *See In re Indep. Serv. Orgs.*, 964 F. Supp. 1454, 1460 (D. Kan. 1997) ("A finding of antitrust liability against Xerox would support CSU's patent misuse defense, which in turn would preclude Xerox's recovery on its patent infringement counterclaims").

[30]   *Gasswint v. Clapper*, 17 F.R.D. 309, 312–13 (W.D. Mo. 1955) ("[A] patentee makes use of his patent monopoly so as to violate the anti-trust laws, that is cause for equity to withhold its assistance from such a use of the patent by declining to entertain a suit for infringement until it is made to appear that the improper practice has been abandoned and that the consequences of the misuse of the patent have been dissipated"); see also *Georgia-Pac. Plywood Co. v. U.S. Plywood Corp.*, 139 F. Supp. 234, 234 (S.D.N.Y. 1956) ("Misuse of patent rights in suit by granting licenses by the defendant in violation of antitrust laws. Such misuse of patent rights operates only to suspend and temporarily deprive an owner of patent of his right to invoke the aid of court, and especially of an equity court, in protecting his property therein; it does not affect validity of patent itself").

[31]   *Ansul Co. v. Uniroyal, Inc.*, 448 F.2d 872, 883 (2d Cir. 1971).

[32]   Ibid at 883.

[33]   On file with the author.

[34]   See Cotter, *supra* note 8 at 934.

and consequently, a misuse of its patent."[35] Similarly, the Sixth Circuit held that the tying question it was asked to consider was "the principal question on the issue of misuse."[36] In some cases the distinction between the two is nonexistent. They note that "[t]he fullest reasoning in favor of converging misuse and antitrust tests was that of the Seventh Circuit in *USM*," because in that case "[t]he court denied that there could be misuse without market power or anticompetitive effect (except when antitrust law itself does not require them). Because there was no antitrust violation, there could be no patent misuse either, at least when misuse was based on competitive concerns."[37] At times litigating parties have also embraced this view.[38] However, one commentator rather grimly noted that "if a showing of patent misuse required a showing that the patent holder violated the antitrust laws, then the misuse doctrine would have the same scope as the antitrust laws. Such a relationship would end the misuse doctrine."[39]

While misuse was predicated on an antitrust violation in these cases, in others, it was the antitrust claim which rode upon the outcome of a misuse

---

[35] *Rex Chainbelt Inc. v. Harco Prods.*, Inc., 512 F.2d 993, 1000 (9th Cir. 1975); see also *Bellsouth Adver. & Pub. Corp. v. Donnelley Info. Pub., Inc.*, 933 F.2d 952, 960–61 (11th Cir. 1991) ("The antitrust misuse defense is an established defense to patent infringement. The policy supporting the patent misuse defense lies in the equitable clean hands doctrine. A patentee who comes into court, praying that defendant's patent infringement be enjoined will not be gratified if he is guilty of abusing his patent rights"); see also *Carter-Wallace, Inc. v. Davis-Edwards Pharm. Corp.*, 443 F.2d 867, 870 (2d Cir. 1971) ("Davis-Edwards attacked the patent on three general grounds. . . patent misuse predicated on violations of the antitrust laws"); *Ansul Co. v. Uniroyal, Inc.*, 448 F.2d 872, 875 (2d Cir. 1971) ("Ansul . . . interposed several affirmative defenses including Uniroyal's misuse of the patent through antitrust violations").

[36] *Preformed Line Prods. Co. v. Fanner Mfg. Co.*, 328 F.2d 265, 276 (6th Cir. 1964).

[37] Ibid. See also *Linzer Prods. Corp. v. Sekar*, 499 F. Supp. 2d 540, 552 (S.D.N.Y. 2007) ("Patent misuse, which developed long before the advent of antitrust law, has largely merged with antitrust law. 'Misuse is closely intertwined with antitrust law, and most findings of misuse are conditioned on conduct that would also violate the antitrust laws'").

[38] See, e.g., *Ansul*, 448 F.2d at 875 ("Uniroyal counterclaimed for infringement of the same patent; and Ansul denied such infringement and interposed several affirmative defenses including Uniroyal's misuse of the patent through antitrust violations"); *Carter-Wallace, Inc. v. Davis-Edwards Pharm. Corp.*, 443 F.2d 867, 870 (2d Cir. 1971) ("Davis-Edwards attacked the patent on three general grounds, the first two of which have some tendency to merge: invalidity over prior art, most of which was not previously cited; inequitable conduct of the applicants before the Patent Office; and patent misuse predicated on violations of the antitrust laws").

[39] See Note, *supra* note 23, at 1927.

defense. The Federal Circuit in *Monsanto Co. v. McFarling* found that the alleged infringer's "antitrust counterclaim was simply a repackaged version of his patent misuse defense, and [the court] affirmed the dismissal of the antitrust counterclaim on the same grounds."[40] In *Rex Chainbelt Inc. v. Harco Products, Inc.*, the Ninth Circuit affirmed the district court's determination that a label licensing program constituted a tying arrangement, which was *per se* violative of §1 of the Sherman Act, and consequently, a misuse of its patent.[41] The reason why this category of cases exists was explained by *Hunter Douglas, Inc. v. Comfortex Corp.*, which noted that "a party claiming patent misuse predicated on alleged antitrust violations will present its most forceful case which will entail showing the patentee to be a violator of the antitrust laws. Thus, one missing the primary target of establishing antitrust liability may nonetheless meet the lesser burden of showing misuse."[42]

Sometimes even an antitrust violation might not be enough. The Federal Circuit recently "came close to so holding in the *Princo* case" according to a leading antitrust treatise. [43] It noted that "[w]hile the court did not state conclusively that misuse could never be found in the absence of an antitrust violation, it clearly limited misuse in that direction, perhaps even going further to the point of immunizing a concerted refusal to license that would be presumptively unlawful if naked."[44]

C.   "Broader" than Antitrust

Cases have also tacked the antitrust rubric onto misuse without requiring defendants to meet the same requirements such as showing antitrust injury or market power. Such cases were regarded as being "broader" than antitrust law. The Supreme Court and the appellate circuit precedent take the position that misuse does not require a breach of the antitrust laws.[45] For example, in *C.R. Bard v. M3 System* the Federal Circuit noted that "patent

---

[40]   *Monsanto Co. v. McFarling*, 488 F.3d 973, 978 (Fed. Cir. 2007).

[41]   *Rex Chainbelt, Inc. v. Harco Prods., Inc.*, 512 F.2d 993, 1000 (9th Cir. 1975).

[42]   *Hunter Douglas, Inc. v. Comfortex Corp.*, 44 F. Supp. 2d 145, 157 (N.D.N.Y 1999).

[43]   10 Phillip E. Areeda & Herbert Hovenkamp, Antitrust Law ¶1781 (3d ed. 2012).

[44]   Ibid.

[45]   *Zenith Radio Corp. v. Hazeltine Research, Inc.*, 395 U.S. 100, 140 (1969) ("And if there was such patent misuse, it does not necessarily follow that the misuse embodies the ingredients of a violation of either §1 or §2 of the Sherman Act"); *Berlenbach v. Anderson & Thompson Ski Co.*, 329 F.2d 782, 784 (9th Cir. 1964) ("In view of the history and policy of the defense of patent misuse we find no

misuse is viewed as a broader wrong than antitrust violation because of the economic power that may be derived from the patentee's right to exclude. Thus misuse may arise when the conditions of antitrust violation are not met."[46] What are these conditions? The antitrust plaintiff must show that it has suffered antitrust injury as well as showing all of the elements of the substantive antitrust claim.[47]

The Federal Circuit has also identified more specific doctrinal differences between the two. For example Joel Bennett observed that "[t]he law of patent misuse in licensing need not look to consumer demand (which may be non-existent) but need look only to the nature of the claimed invention as the basis for determining whether a product is a necessary concomitant of the invention or an entirely separate product. The law of antitrust violation, tailored for situations that may or may not involve a patent, looks to a consumer demand test for determining product separability."[48]

This separation between misuse and antitrust law acknowledges the roots of misuse in preventing anticompetitive abuses of the patent grant while protecting patentees from punitive treble damages that result from a finding of an antitrust violation. This view has enjoyed support from the majority of the Federal Circuit bench over the years, and from commentators who observe that the "effect on competition is the only legitimate concern

---

merit in appellant's contentions that the proof of substantial lessening of competition is a prerequisite to finding patent misuse").

[46] See *C.R. Bard, Inc. v. M3 Sys., Inc.*, 157 F.3d 1340, 1372 (Fed. Cir. 1998); see also *Transitron Elec. Corp. v. Hughes Aircraft Co.*, 487 F. Supp. 885, 892–93 (D. Mass. 1980) (the Massachusetts district court noted that "patent misuse may be seen as having a less stringent standing requirement and a lesser burden of proof than an antitrust claim"); see also Note, *supra* note 23, at 1927 ("if courts were to decide patent misuse allegations by using only an antitrust inquiry (and not referring to patent policy) and if the patent misuse doctrine were to retain some of its distinctive characteristics (especially the more lenient standing requirements), then the misuse doctrine would have a greater scope than the antitrust laws. The legal status of any patent practice would be the same under either doctrine, because courts would look to antitrust principles to judge a restriction under both doctrines. However, courts would review a greater number of patent practices for patent misuse, because more alleged infringers would have standing to assert patent misuse than antitrust violations. The Court's language in *Transparent-Wrap Machine Corp.* evinces this view").

[47] Christopher Leslie, ANTITRUST LAW AND INTELLECTUAL PROPERTY RIGHTS 61 (2011).

[48] Joel R. Bennett, *Patent Misuse: Must an Alleged Infringer Prove an Antitrust Violation?*, 17 AIPLA Q.J. 1, 14 (1989).

of [the] patent misuse doctrine."[49] Some interviewees opined that while misuse requirements were less stringent than those of antitrust, it was really addressing the same issue, that is, abuse of monopoly power.[50] Other interviewees disagreed with this view, pointing out that post-expiration payment of royalties, as well as patent abuses asserted by parties that were not direct victims of those abuses, indicated distinct roles for patent misuse.[51]

D. "Different" from Antitrust

This third view of misuse is that it is neither co-extensive with nor broader than an antitrust violation, but rather that the two doctrines are different in focus and purpose. Despite the antitrust fixtures in Federal Circuit precedent, some commentators note that "viewing Federal Circuit precedent in light of the early Supreme Court decisions that addressed claims of patent misuse, it becomes clear that the Federal Circuit is attempting to stay true to these equitable origins of the doctrine and its roots in differing policy considerations between patent and antitrust law."[52] Katherine White elaborates on the distinction between the "broader" and "different" categories, explaining that "[p]atent misuse differs from antitrust theory because the purpose of misuse is to avoid extending the patent monopoly, while antitrust law weighs the effect of acts on competition."[53] Pointing to double royalties as an example, Geoffrey Oliver notes that collecting "royalties from both a licensee and a purchaser of the licensee's product under the same patent violates the principle of patent exhaustion under the patent laws, and does not find any counterpart in antitrust law."[54]

---

[49]   1 Hovenkamp et al., IP AND ANTITRUST, §§ 3.2c, 3-9 (2d ed. 2010); see also *Raychem Corp. v. PSI Telecomms.*, No. C-93-20920 RPA, 1995 U.S. Dist. LEXIS 22325, at *9 ("Although the contours of this doctrine are vague, patent misuse claims are generally tested by conventional antitrust principles. Application of the doctrine has been confined to a small number of specific anticompetitive acts, such as tying arrangements coupled with market power, covenants not to deal, and mandatory package licensing"). See also *Motorola, Inc. v. Kimball Int'l, Inc.*, 601 F. Supp. 62, 65 (N.D. Ill. 1984) (noting that "patent misuse may be established much more easily than an antitrust violation. Moreover no allegation of specific injury . . . is necessary in a claim of patent misuse").

[50]   On file with the author.

[51]   Ibid.

[52]   See Joe Potenza et al., *Patent Misuse—The Critical Balance, A Patent Lawyer's View*, 15 FED. CIR. B.J. 69, 97 (2005/2006).

[53]   Katherine E. White, *A Rule for Determining When Patent Misuse Should be Applied*, 11 FORDHAM INTELL. PROP. MEDIA & ENT. L.J. 671, 672 (2000–2001).

[54]   Geoffrey D. Oliver, *Princo v. International Trade Commission: Antitrust Law and the Patent Misuse Doctrine Part Company*, 25 ANTITRUST 62, 63–64

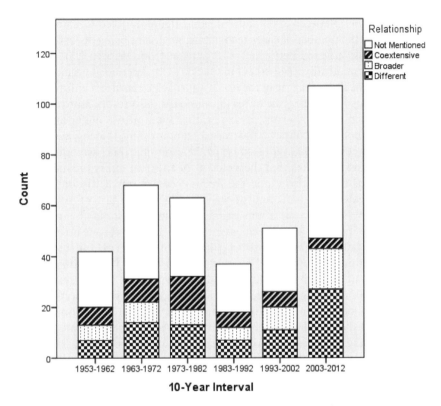

Figure 7.12   How cases are regarded between misuse and antitrust over time

E.   Shift from "Broader" to "Different"

Looking at trends over time in Figure 7.12, a number of features are note-worthy. First, both the proportion and absolute number of cases which recognize misuse as being "different" from antitrust has increased. Between 1953 and 1992, the proportion of cases recognizing misuse as "different" hovered around 12 percent before dipping slightly to 22 percent between

(2010–2011). This articles cites two cases which reached opposite conclusions, *PSC v. Symbol Techs. Inc.*, 26 F. Supp. 2d 505 (W.D.N.Y. 1998) (holding that the patentee could not claim royalties on both scanners used to read bar codes and the central computer used in connect with the scanner), and *Minebea Co. v. Papst*, 444 F. Supp. 2d 68 (D.D.C. 2006) (holding that the patentee was allowed to charge double royalties because the defendant had failed to prove anticompetitive effects).

1992 and 2002. Between 2003 and 2012 that figure doubled to 25 percent. In contrast, the number of cases recognizing misuse as being "coextensive" with antitrust hovered between 15–21 percent from 1953 to 2002 before dropping dramatically to 4 percent in the 2003–2012 period. This may have to do with the shift away from the *per se* approach to antitrust enforcement over the years to a higher rule of reason standard. As a result, more defendants turn to misuse under patent law, rather than misuse under antitrust law to attempt to circumvent this raised standard and thereby avoid the high litigation costs incurred because of the economic analysis required to define markets and show that the elements of antitrust injury are met.

The trends shown also erode the force of conventional wisdom that a misuse "coextensive" with antitrust is an established part of American patent law.[55] A better view of misuse may be that while it may be true that the origins of patent misuse are in patent policy, its present state is rooted in an antitrust policy that is still distinct from the application of antitrust law.[56] The proportion of cases regarding misuse as "broader" than antitrust was fairly constant through the entire period, between 14–18 percent, except in the 1993–2002 period where it increased to 30 percent, possibly in response to *Windsurfing*, decided in 1986. It is curious, however, that the proportion of cases regarded as "broader" did not maintain its foothold after that period.

Second, the proportion and number of cases where the relationship between misuse and antitrust was not mentioned has remained consistently high over the period studied, hovering around 50 percent. This suggests that in a significant proportion of cases courts do not think about both regimes but simply apply misuse formulaically to the facts of the case. A judge observed that in the early 1980s, his perception of patent misuse was that the doctrine was limited to antitrust-like conduct.[57] He was not aware of other categories of conduct at that time.[58] To the extent that those decisions stated that misuse should be subsumed into antitrust, those decisions may be understood in that light.[59] Patent misuse today,

---

[55] See *BellSouth Advert. & Pub. Corp. v. Donnelley Info. Pub., Inc.*, 933 F.2d 952, 960–61 (11th Cir. 1991) ("The antitrust misuse defense is an established defense to patent infringement").

[56] See Joe Potenza, *supra* note 52, at 81–82. ("Later cases have similarly addressed these extensions as potential forms of misuse based on whether they violate the policies underlying the patent right by impermissibly extending the scope of the patent grant. One point remains clear: both the courts (including the Supreme Court and the Federal Circuit) and Congress have specifically rejected attempts to make patent misuse commensurate with antitrust").

[57] On file with the author.

[58] Ibid.

[59] Ibid.

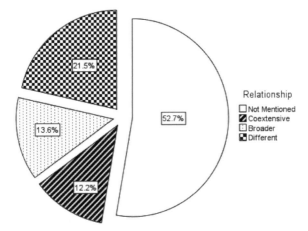

Figure 7.13   Distribution of cases discussing the relationship between misuse and antitrust

he noted, is broader than antitrust, but is nonetheless animated by anti-trust principles.[60] He cautioned that more recent appellate level decisions articulating a possible revitalized role for patent misuse should not be read as a *carte blanche* for exploding the categories of misuse.[61] In this regard, he cited abuse of process and vexatious litigation brought in bad faith as examples of conduct which, though it may not give rise to antitrust viola-tions owing to patentees' lack of significant market power, nonetheless violated patent policy and could be construed as a form of misuse.[62]

F.   How Courts Perceived the Relationship Between Patent Misuse and Antitrust

The observation in the previous section that there is a trend to see misuse as "different" is buttressed when one looks at the Figures 7.13 and 7.14. Figure 7.13 shows the absolute proportion between the three categorizations as well as where "scope" was not mentioned. It is readily apparent that most of the cases do not consider the relationship between the two. Also apparent is the fact that most cases consider the two as

---

60   Ibid.
61   Ibid.
62   Ibid.

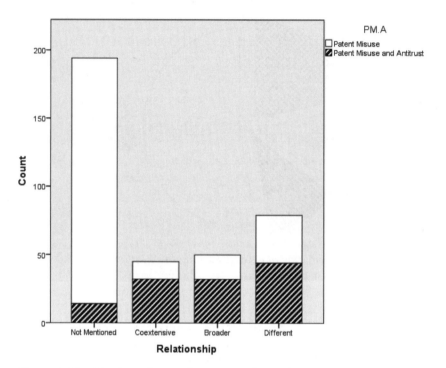

*Figure 7.14   Number of cases discussing relationship between misuse and
            antitrust according to whether the case featured misuse or
            misuse and antitrust*

being "different", with the remaining portion quite evenly split between
"broader" and "coextensive".

Figure 7.14, a histogram, shows the correlation between (1) whether
courts looked at misuse only or whether they looked at it together with
antitrust and (2) the nature of the relative relationship between the two.
The most striking feature of the graph is how many cases do not consider
the relationship between the two at all. Looking more closely at the graph
an interesting finding emerges. When the court considers misuse alone, it
does not consider the relationship between the two 73 percent of the time.
It should follow then that if the court considers both misuse and antitrust
together, the proportion should be high as well. That is certainly true for
cases in which misuse is found to be "coextensive" (71%) and "broader"
(64%) when compared to antitrust. Where misuse is regarded as "different," however, that figure is much lower (55%). This confirms that such
cases fall under a different rubric altogether and have much less relationship with antitrust, instead featuring as stand-alone misuse cases. Finally,

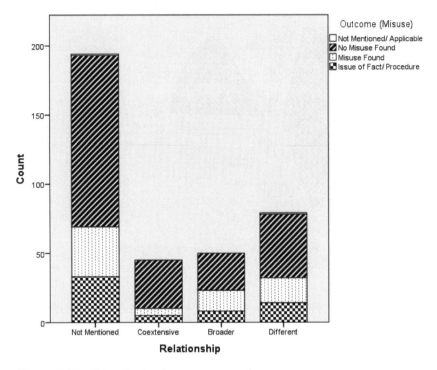

Figure 7.15   Distribution by outcomes and scope

despite the rhetoric that misuse tracks antitrust standards, only 33 percent of the cases that expressed an opinion specifically decided cases based on antitrust analysis being "coextensive" or "broader" than antitrust. A relatively high proportion (45%) stated that misuse was "different".

Defendant win rates are defined along the relative dimension as follows: coextensive (14%), broader (30%), and different (29%) (Figure 7.15). Two points of interest arise. First, defendants are not significantly better off when the courts considered misuse as "different" from antitrust, than when they considered misuse as being "coextensive" with antitrust. This is surprising because one would normally expect antitrust offenses to be more difficult to prove than asserting an affirmative defense. One explanation for that could be the presence of *per se* violations in antitrust law, which, at least in theory, makes it easier for the antitrust plaintiff to allege an offense. Another explanation is that defendants who frame their misuse defense under an antitrust rubric may succeed because courts are more comfortable finding misuse based on principles established by antitrust

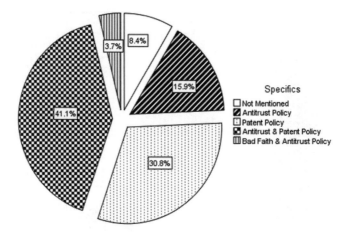

*Figure 7.16   Distribution by policy (where misuse was regarded as
                "different" from antitrust)*

cases, than if misuse were "different" and based on more amorphorous
patent policy considerations.

Second, looking at the specific policy components of cases where misuse
was treated as 'different' than antitrust (Figure 7.16), one sees that a combination of patent and antitrust policy dominate (41.1%). Here courts are
concerned with both market competition and incentivizing innovation.
Patent policy was also a prominent driver in many cases (30.8%).Where
misuse was treated as being 'coextensive' with antitrust (Figure 7.17),
antitrust policy dominates (81.4%), perhaps unsurprisingly, while patent
policy (5.1%) and a combination of the two policies (6.8%) are much
diminshed. Where misuse was treated as 'broader', antitrust policy (53.0%)
and a combination of the two (27.3%) dominate, with patent policy featuring only occassionally by itself (9.1%) (Figure 7.18). Additionally, bad
faith and antitrust policy concerns also feature in all three classfications of
the relationship between antitrust and misuse, though never prominantly.
Bad faith will be discussed in more detail later in the chapter. These findings confirm the conventioal wisdom that misuse is very much driven by
competitive concerns. At the same time, it also shows that the view that
misuse is simply an early protoype of antitrust law as applied to patents is
oversimplified.

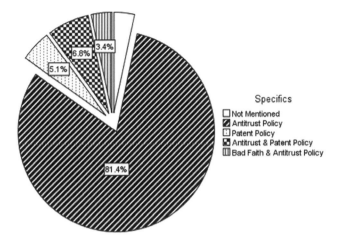

Figure 7.17   Distribution by policy (where misuse was regarded as "coextensive" with antitrust)

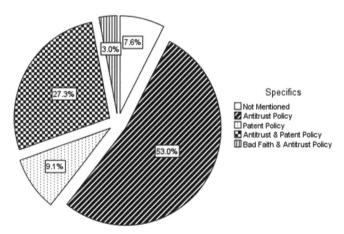

Figure 7.18   Distribution by policy (where misuse was regarded as "broader" than antitrust)

IV.   THE POLICY DIMENSION

The absolute and relative dimensions are valuable perspectives on misuse but they provide an incomplete picture. As the discussion in earlier chapters show, misuse has a dual nature. On the one hand, it seeks to promote competition and efficient functioning of markets. In those instances, it closely relates and sometimes commingles with antitrust law.[63] On the other hand, misuse retains an identity separate from the antitrust laws.[64] In *Laitram Corp. v. King Crab, Inc.*, the court remarked that "the doctrine of misuse rests upon the principle that the holder of an exclusive patent privilege granted in furtherance of public policy may not claim protection of his grant by the Court when such patent privilege is being used to subvert that policy."[65] The policy was explained by the D.C. Circuit, as "embedded in the Constitutional provision authorizing patent protection."[66] To comprehensively understand patent misuse, it is therefore necessary to also consider the policy dimension animating these cases if the analysis is to avoid the risk of elevating form over substance. Professor Thomas Cotter explains that misuse analysis "should focus less on appearances and more on the substantive question of whether, for example, enforcing a given contractual restriction would defeat *the purposes* of the patent or copyright laws—in which case, however, one needs first to define those purposes."[67]

Professor Cotter's observation is an important one. Because one of the key criticisms of misuse is its vagueness, it follows that identifying clear and cognizable goals makes the task of achieving those goals in a more principled and predictable fashion easier. Looking to policy goals to guide the application of the law is certainly not confined to patent misuse alone. It is critical to unraveling the competing interests underlying cases that lie at the interface between patent and antitrust law. As the Eleventh Circuit noted in *Valley Drug Co. v. Geneva Pharmaceuticals*, the key to resolving the tension at the interface between innovation and competition lies in

---

[63]   *Princo Corp. v. Int'l Trade Comm'n*, 616 F.3d 1318, 1334 (Fed. Cir. 2010) ("At the outset, Princo urges us to overrule the line of authority in this court holding that patent misuse requires a showing that the patentee's conduct had anticompetitive effects. We decline to do so").

[64]   *Columbus Auto. Corp. v. Oldberg Mfg. Co.*, 264 F. Supp. 779, 785 (D. Colo. 1967) ("[the] doctrine of patent misuse has been applied in both equity suits and actions for royalties and . . . its basis is not only the 'clean hands' doctrine, but is also in furtherance of a public policy against enforcement of an agreement which is contrary to the public interest by reason of its unlawful tendency to suppress competition and unreasonably extend the patent monopoly").

[65]   *Laitram Corp. v. King Crap, Inc.*, 245 F. Supp. 1019, 1020–21 (D. Alaska 1965).

[66]   *Riker Labs., Inc. v. Gist-Brocades N. V.*, 636 F.2d 772, 776 (D.C. Cir. 1980).

[67]   See Cotter, *supra* note 8, at 939; see also Robin C. Feldman, *The Insufficiency of Antitrust Analysis for Patent Misuse*, 55 HASTINGS L.J. 399, 399 (2003) ("Patent misuse lies at the intersection of patent and antitrust law. The history and conceptual overlap of patent law and antitrust law have left the doctrine of misuse hopelessly entangled with antitrust doctrines").

"achieving a suitable accommodation between the differing policies."[68] Elaborating on this observation, FTC Commissioner Thomas Rosch wrote that "the patent's exclusionary potential is a function of whether the patent holder employs the patent in ways that are inconsistent with the objectives of the patent and antitrust laws—and not simply a function of the patent's text and duration."[69]

In studying the policies animating misuse cases, the variables are as follows. First, the case could have been informed by antitrust policy. Cases such as *Windsurfing* that base misuse on a finding of anticompetitive effects fall in this category. Second, the case could have been informed by patent policy. An example is *Prestole Corp. v. Tinnerman Products*, where the court, in finding misuse, based its reasoning on the "unrestricted exploitation" of the patent.[70] Third, it could have been informed by a finding of bad faith on the part of the patentee in cases involving fraudulent procurement of a patent, vexatious litigation or abuse of process.

Figure 7.19 shows each of the different policies featured in misuse decisions. Most cases did not mention any policy (44%). Where they did, the most dominant policy was antitrust policy (26%) or antitrust policy featuring bad faith. This finding is consistent with conventional wisdom

---

[68] *Valley Drug Co. v. Geneva Pharms.*, 344 F.3d 1294, 1311 (11th Cir. 2003) (quoting *Walker Process Equip., Inc. v. Food Machinery & Chem. Corp.*, 382 U.S. 172, 179 (1965) (Harlan, J., concurring)). The antitrust analysis hinges on whether subjecting agreements that implicate a patent's exclusionary power would undermine the patent system's "incentive to induce investment in innovation and the public disclosure of inventions," ibid at 1304. *See also Motion Picture Patents Co. v. Universal Film Mfg. Co.*, 243 U.S. 502, 511, 519 (1917) ("this court has consistently held that the primary purpose of our patent laws . . . is 'to promote the progress of science and useful arts.' (U.S. Const. art I § 8, cl.8. . . a restriction which would give to the plaintiff such a potential power for evil over an industry, which must be recognized as an important element in the amusement of life of the nation, under the conclusions we have stated in this opinion, is plainly void, because [it is] wholly without the scope and purpose of patent laws").

[69] J. Thomas Rosch, Comm'r, Fed. Trade Comm'n, The Antitrust/Intellectual Property Interface: Thoughts on How to Best Wade Through the Thicket in the Pharmaceutical Context, Remarks at World Generic Medicine Congress 4 (Nov 17, 2010), available at: http://www.ftc.gov/speeches/rosch/101117roschworldspeech. pdf.

[70] See *Prestole Corp v. Tinnerman Prods., Inc.*, 271 F.2d 146, 155 (1959); see also *Senza-Gel Corp. v. Seiffhart*, 803 F.2d 661, 668 (Fed. Cir. 1986) (finding that violation of public policy underlying patent law could constitute patent misuse absent antitrust violation).

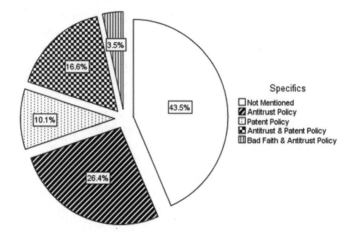

Figure 7.19   Distribution by time and policy

that misuse is rooted in the concern for anticompetitive abuses of a patent right.[71] Patent policy featured in 10 percent of opinions.

Antitrust policy was the dominant policy category in each period (Figure 7.20). Patent policy did not feature prominently in most periods, hovering between 5 and 10 percent of cases, except between 1973 and 1982 when it accounted for 16 percent of the cases. While this may seem inconsistent with an earlier observation that a significant proportion of cases found misuse to be "different" from antitrust, that difference may have been based not just on patent policy, but other cases where bad faith features or where patent and antitrust policy are considered together. The 2003–2012 period shows the emergence of bad faith (10%), which budded in the 1993–2002 period, perhaps in response to the higher bar set by the Federal Circuit for those attempting to prove misuse under *Windsurfing* (Figure 7.21). At the same time, both the number and proportion of cases featuring antitrust and patent policy also reached an all-time high in that period (42%). Both could have led to an eschewing of patent policy as the basis for misuse analysis. Another observation is that courts appear to be more comfortable articulating the policy basis for their decisions over time, with the proportion of cases where no mention was made of the policy falling from about 50 percent during the five decades between 1953 and 2002 to 36 percent between 2003 and 2012.

Interesting trends also emerge when comparing two specific time

---

[71]   See *supra* Chapters 2 and 6.

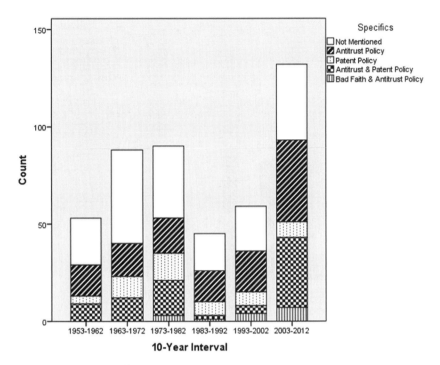

Figure 7.20   Specifics over time

periods: pre- and post-1988. Pre-1988, the Second, Seventh and Ninth Circuits were the dominant circuits for misuse cases (Figure 7.21). Antitrust policy was most dominant in Seventh Circuit jurisprudence, and patent policy most dominant in D.C. Circuit and Sixth Circuit jurisprudence. Ninth Circuit jurisprudence looked evenly split between the two policies. Both the sheer number of cases flowing from the Seventh Circuit, as well as its influential role in shaping antitrust policy, however, would have played an important role during those years in exporting its version of misuse to the other circuits. Pre-1988, defendants fared best when the court framed misuse as a matter of patent policy, winning in as many as 66 percent of cases in that category. In contrast, they won only about 30 percent of the time when misuse was framed under antitrust policy. When misuse was framed as patent and antitrust policy defendants still fared well, winning 37 percent of the time. It is interesting that during this time only one case featured bad faith (Figure 7.22).

Post-1988, bad faith arguments become featured in more than half of all the circuits, although in relatively small numbers. Antitrust policy remains the *de rigor* form of policy in misuse cases, although a mix of

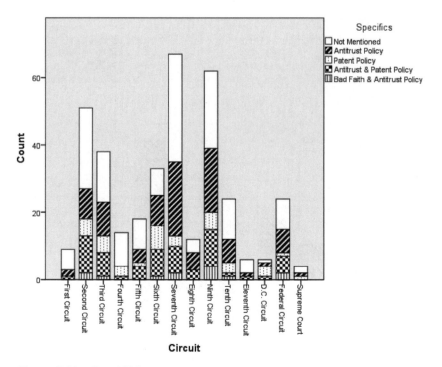

Figure 7.21   Pre-1988

patent and antitrust policy appears to have risen significantly in the Ninth and Federal Circuits (Figure 7.23). Following a line of Seventh Circuit and Federal Circuit jurisprudence, academics have observed a trend in which later cases pack misuse as a whole into the antitrust rubric.[72]

Interviewees were unsurprised that the win rate for defendants as a whole went down following the 1988 amendments (Figure 7.24). This in itself was a surprising finding, since the 1988 legislative amendments were confined to tying and refusals to license, in addition to which legislative history specifically rejected patent misuse based exclusively on antitrust law. This is one instance where conventional wisdom presents an accurate

---

[72]   See Sean Michael Aylward, *Copyright Law: The Fourth Circuit's Extension of the Misuse Doctrine to the Area of Copyright: A Misuse of The Misuse Doctrine?—Lasercomb America, Inc. v. Reynolds,* 17 U. DAYTON L. REV. 661, 670 (1991–1992) ("The decisions in *Senza-Gel, Windsurfing International* and *USM,* however, suggest that in cases involving claims of misuse in areas not within traditional misuse categories, antitrust analysis is appropriate to determine patent misuse").

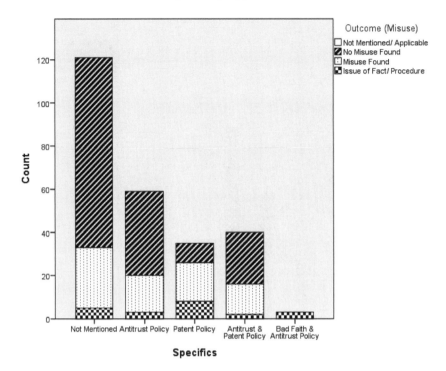

Figure 7.22   Case outcomes according to policy (pre-1988)

gauge of reality. An academic observed that in the post-1988 period, more cases articulated antitrust policy considerations in a way that was not expressly seen before the amendments. This was certainly borne out by the data, which shows an 11 percent increase (from 23% to 34% between the two periods). The proportion of cases relying on patent policy also shrunk dramatically during that period by 7 percent (from 15% to 8%).

Most cases did not mention bad faith (83.2%) (Figure 7.25). However, bad faith has played a decisive role in patent misuse litigation. As Figure 7.26 below shows where the court made a finding that a patentee displayed bad faith, the outcome was in the defendant's favor.

Where the court made a finding that there was no bad faith, the result was always in the patentees' favor. Three examples illustrate the circumstances from which these cases arise. In *Koratron Co. v. Lion Uniform*, the patentee owned a patent over a patented process for the manufacture of press garments.[73] The patentee and a competitor avoided potential

---

[73]   *Koratron Co. v. Lion Unif., Inc.*, 409 F. Supp. 1019, 1021 (N.D. Cal. 1976).

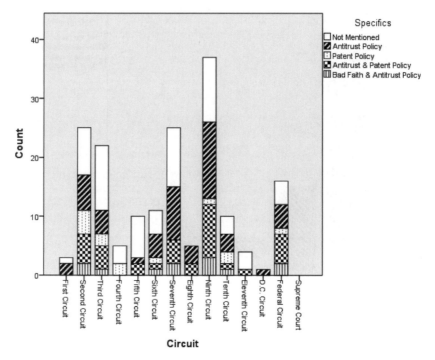

Figure 7.23   Post-1988

infringement litigation by entering into a consent decree.[74] The patentee placed a press release in *Time* magazine which misrepresented that its competitor acknowledged its patent and confessed to infringing that patent.[75] The court found that "[t]he patentee must itself maintain high standards of conduct and candor if it is to use its patent properly."[76] It found that "had [the patentee] acted in good faith to make a full and meaningful disclosure, it could have done so by letter or press release. Instead, [the patentee] elected to do nothing, for reasons known only to

---

[74]   Ibid. at 1025.
[75]   Ibid at 1026–27 ("While the press release purports to describe the Dan River agreement, it does so in a plainly inaccurate and misleading fashion. The press release reflects Koratron's continuing claim to royalties based on garments made from all bone dry fabrics save 'a limited type of Dan River fabric'. Koratron thus created a climate of uncertainty and confusion regarding the relationship between the '432 patent and the Dan Press process in the very document in which the 'arrangement' was revealed to the public").
[76]   Ibid at 1028.

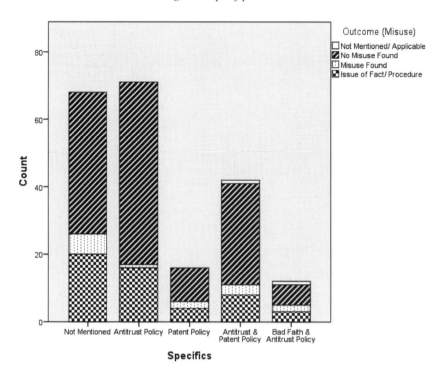

Figure 7.24   Case outcomes according to policy (post-1988)

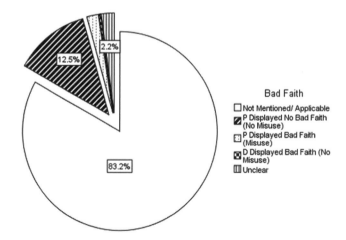

Figure 7.25   Proportion of bad faith cases

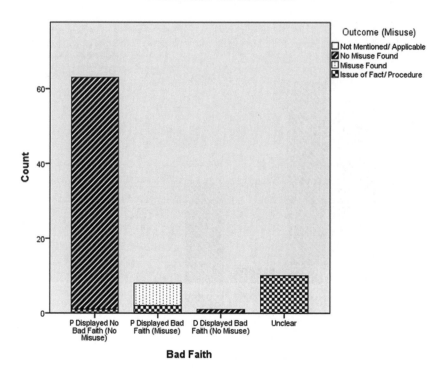

Figure 7.26   Outcomes (bad faith)

it," and was thus barred from enforcing its patent.[77] In *Barry Wright Corp. v. ITT Grinnell Corp.*, the patentee threatened patent litigation against any company who purchased a mechanical snubber used in nuclear power plants from anyone other than the patentee.[78] The Court found that the threatened litigation gave rise to a finding of bad faith, particularly in light of other exclusionary activities including contractual interference, a preferential discounting scheme and tie-in agreements.[79] In *Arcade Inc. v. Minnesota Min. & Mfg. Co*, the patentee sent out letters to the defendant's customers coercing them to do business only with the patentee.[80]

---

[77]   Ibid at 1027.

[78]   *Barry Wright Corp. v. ITT Grinnell Corp.*, No. 78-485-S, 1981 U.S. Dist. LEXIS 9432, at *6 (D. Mass. Feb. 26, 1981).

[79]   Ibid at *29 ("There is evidence, however, which suggest that Pacific's alleged threats of patent litigation were made in bad faith. This is particularly true where these threats were coupled with other alleged exclusionary activities").

[80]   *Arcade Inc. v. Minnesota Min. & Mfg. Co.*, 24 U.S.P.Q.2d 1578, 1591 (E.D. Tenn. 1991) ("What the evidence showed was that after the '417 Patent

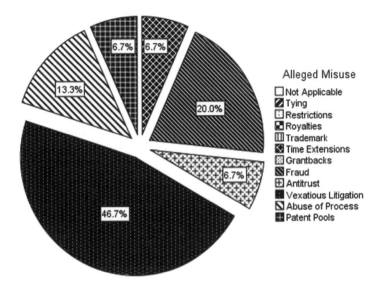

Figure 7.27   Distribution by alleged misuse (bad faith)

Concurrently, the court also found that the patentee was guilty of inequitable conduct and *Walker Process* fraud with respect to the patent at issue.[81] In evaluating the patentee's course of conduct, the court found that "prior to this suit [patentee] sent letters to [defendant's] customers, ostensibly to notify them of their patent, but in reality to acquire [defendant's] business with an implied threat of litigation."[82]

The data also reveals that most bad faith cases involved vexatious litigation (46.7%), fraud (20.0%) and abuse of process (13.3%). The other three categories of misuse which featured included patent pools, time extensions and violations of antitrust law (Figure 7.27).

Bad faith on the part of the defendant appears irrelevant to misuse analysis, and courts have held it to be so. In *Rocform Corp. v. Acitelli-Standard Concrete Wall, Inc.*, the court held that "[i]f defendant's hands be unclean in that it made no bona fide application to plaintiff for licensing, or for

---

was obtained, Raymond D. Sayers, 3M's manager of encapsulated products, sent a number of letters to fragrance advertisers announcing that 3M had obtained the '417 Patent; that other companies (Arcade not specifically mentioned, but certainly implied) were producing infringing products; that 3M may take steps to enforce the patent; and encouraging them to do business only with 3M").

[81]   Ibid at 1592.
[82]   Ibid.

any other reason indicated by the facts in this case, such uncleanliness will not render plaintiff's hands clean if it is attempting to unlawfully extend its patent monopoly."[83] This fact is important in rebutting the criticism that patent misuse is overbroad in its lack of statutory requirements.

Interviewees had a number of views on bad faith. A government official remarked that:

> a lot of cases are not ultimately about this doctrinal protection of the law. They are about the facts that come before the judge in that case. If there is bad faith or if there is a particular set of facts that is a good fit for one line of cases or another, then the judge is going to put it in that box that looks the safest for holding up on appeal.[84]

A lawyer interviewed noted that equity was a useful tool to address egregious conduct in patent cases in changing circumstances without the need to undertake expensive or complex economic analysis.[85] While bad faith was expressly discussed in the context of vexatious litigation, he opined that it was an undercurrent in all patent misuse cases where courts have been candid about articulating its findings of bad faith, even though it was not expressly pleaded.[86] A judge interviewed took special interest in the findings of bad faith, noting that he was encouraged that this was an important aspect of patent misuse's role in preventing nefarious conduct.[87] Indeed, this seemed to be one area in which most interviewees saw patent misuse as having an enduring role.[88] An academic reviewing the findings confirmed that this was consistent with his view.[89] In particular, he noted that courts were more willing to impute bad faith to litigation-related misuse than to transaction-related misuse.[90] Controversially, some courts

---

[83]   *Rocform Corp. v. Acitelli-Standard Concrete Wall, Inc.*, 237 F. Supp. 34, 43 (E.D. Mich. 1964).

[84]   On file with the author.

[85]   Ibid.

[86]   On file with the author. See *Reid-Ashman Mfg. v. Swanson Semiconductor Serv.*, No. C-06-4693 JCS, 2007 U.S. Dist. LEXIS 37665, at *23 (N.D. Cal. May 10, 2007) ("The Court concludes that this is what Swanson is alleging as the basis for its unclean hands affirmative defense, although the various 'magic words' of 'bad faith,' 'improper purpose,' and 'objectively baseless' do not appear in the defense itself. As discussed below, the Court concludes that Swanson has adequately alleged that Reid-Ashman's lawsuit was brought in bad faith and is objectively baseless").

[87]   On file with the author.

[88]   See discussion in Chapter 5.

[89]   On file with the author.

[90]   Ibid.

have held that bad faith plays second fiddle to anticompetitive conduct, and they will not find misuse unless the latter is found to be present.[91]

V. CONCLUSION

Reflecting on the development of misuse jurisprudence post-1988, commentators noted several important principles. First, while Congress confined its amendments to the Patent Act they "in no way *forbade* courts from employing antitrust principles in developing patent misuse doctrine in these areas where the statute is silent."[92] Second, as Chapter 6 shows, most of the misuse cases involve tying. In these cases a form of misuse that is coextensive with antitrust law should prevail over the other two forms since "the underlying rationale for patent misuse in cases involving patent ties, particularly of unpatented goods, is that these practices might impair competition. In such cases the antitrust laws provide plenty of definition, and with over-deterrence to spare."[93] Third, the forms of misuse that are "broader" and "different" from antitrust should continue having a separate existence because "misuse is fundamentally a question of intellectual property policy and not of antitrust policy. As a result it has its own purposes, which include promotion of innovation and protection of the public domain . . . even if the technical requirements for an antitrust violation are not met." [94]

---

[91]   See, e.g., *Static Control Components, Inc. v. Lexmark Int'l, Inc.*, 487 F. Supp. 2d 830, 855 (E.D. Ky. 2007) ("To wit, 'a factual determination must reveal that the overall effect of the license tends to restrain competition unlawfully in an appropriately defined relevant market.' Lexmark merely doing something 'wrong' in a vague sense is not grounds for a successful assertion of the misuse defense, an equitable defense, to patent infringement"), *rev'd* 615 F. Supp. 2d 575 (E.D. Ky. 2009) (first sale doctrine exhausted the patent rights).

[92]   10 Areeda & Hovenkamp, *supra* note 43, at ¶1781e.

[93]   Ibid.

[94]   Ibid.

8. Conclusion

I. MISUSE AND ANTITRUST

From its early roots in patent law's doctrine of contributory infringement of *A.B. Dick* and *Motion Picture Patents*, misuse became intertwined with the antitrust laws in the *Mercoid* cases. The Supreme Court in *Morton Salt* returned misuse to its roots and patent policy. As the antitrust laws became shaped by the Chicago School, so did it seep into misuse. That approach was carried from the Seventh Circuit's *USM Corp* decision to the Federal Circuit in *Windsurfing* and *Princo*. And under a crust of Supreme Court precedent which remains good law, we have a sea change initiated by the Federal Circuit. Now, courts routinely order patent litigation to be bifurcated, with issues of validity and infringement decided in one trial and antitrust and misuse decided in the other.[1]

It is incontrovertible that patent misuse overlaps with antitrust, and in some instances antitrust violations have formed the basis for a finding of misuse.[2] The antitrust bridle placed upon patent misuse provides a principled and robust means of developing the doctrine as a means to curb

---

[1] See, e.g., *Magnavox Co. v. APF Elecs., Inc.*, No. 77 C 3159, 1981 U.S. Dist. LEXIS 11209 (N.D. Ill. Mar. 18, 1981) ("Further, the fact that the issues of patent misuse and antitrust claims overlap the patent issues militates in favor of one trial. It is significant that courts which have granted separate trials have done so in situations where there was little likelihood of overlapping issues or duplication of proof"). Factors considered include whether "(1) Economy is served because in the trial of the patent issues the validity of the patent and Innotron's affirmative defenses will be determined and will become law of the case and thus removed from trial on the original antitrust issues; (2) Convenience of all is served in trying the less complex patent issues first; (3) Expedition is served because the patent issues on the present schedule will be ready for trial more than a year before the antitrust issue can be made ready; (4) Avoidance of prejudice and confusion is served in trying first the patent issues, without injecting the different counterclaim issues which require different proof and different witnesses." See *In re Innotron Diagnostics*, 800 F.2d 1077, 1085 (Fed. Cir. 1986).

[2] See David W. Van Etten, Note, *Everyone in the Patent Pool: U.S. Philips Corp. v. International Trade Commission*, 22 BERKELEY TECH. L.J. 241, 247 (2007) ("The rationale behind patent misuse doctrine, generally, is to prevent unfair

anticompetitive conduct according to contemporary economic analysis. Some view this development as providing a more workable and predictable doctrine.[3]

If, however, antitrust law has truly developed to a point where it can satisfactorily subsume misuse, then Congress or the Supreme Court should eliminate misuse. If not, they should say what misuse is and what it does. The uncertainty as to the nature of misuse is undesirable. With the marked increase in patent litigation, patentees and defendants will benefit from further clarification of the doctrine of patent misuse.

Less commented upon, is the important point that misuse law has also served to create concepts that were picked up in antitrust law. For example, the District Court for the Northern District of California recently reflected on the interface between misuse and antitrust law.[4] It began by observing that "[w]hile the patent system serves to encourage innovation, the antitrust laws serve to foster competition,"[5] noting that "the Supreme Court has cautioned that even if patent misuse exists, 'it does not necessarily follow that the misuse embodies the ingredients of a violation of either § 1 or § 2 of the Sherman Act,' before concluding that "[t]he intersection between these two competing concepts continues to develop."[6] This suggests that the relationship is not unidirectional, with misuse providing the rudimentary foundation for the evolution of the antitrust–IP interface, to be ultimately discarded now that antitrust is better developed.[7] Instead, this *lack* of a one-way relationship shows that the interface between patent misuse and antitrust is dynamic: just as antitrust

---

market behavior, barring patentees from leveraging their patent rights to obtain unrelated market benefits").

[3] *C.R. Bard, Inc. v. M3 Sys., Inc.*, 157 F.3d 1340, 1373 (Fed. Cir. 1998) ("Although the defense of patent misuse indeed evolved to protect against 'wrongful' use of patents, the catalog of practices labelled 'patent misuse' does not include a general notion of 'wrongful' use"); see also Herbert Hovenkamp et al., IP AND ANTITRUST § 3.2 (2010) ("Notwithstanding these differences, antitrust principles provide a useful check on misuse doctrine. If misuse doctrine departs from antitrust doctrine, it is useful to ask why. Departures from accepted principles of competition must be justified by reference to some specific patent policy, and not merely by unsupported assumptions that certain conduct is 'bad' for competition").

[4] *PNY Techs., Inc. v. SanDisk Corp.*, 2012 U.S. Dist. LEXIS 55965 (N.D. Cal. Apr. 20, 2012).

[5] Ibid. at 16.

[6] Ibid. (quoting *Zenith Radio Corp. v. Hazeltine Research, Inc.*, 395 U.S. 100, 140 (1969)).

[7] As was arguably the view in *USM Corp. v. SPS Techs., Inc.*, 694 F.2d 505, 511–12 (7th Cir. 1982).

continues to shape the boundaries of antitrust,[8] patent misuse refines the understanding of nuances in antitrust law.[9]

How would one articulate a statement explaining what misuse really is? *Morton Salt* outlined three basic pillars: (1) courts possessed equitable powers to restrain conduct contrary to public policy; (2) this policy includes whether the useful arts were being promoted or harmed; and (3) whether the patentee's actions had anticompetitive effects.[10] Misuse exists within the double helix of patent and antitrust laws, and is rooted in both antitrust and patent policy.[11] Which policy dominates a judicial inquiry depends on the type of misconduct at issue.[12] It is concerned both with

---

[8] See *Illinois Tool Works Inc. v. Indep. Ink, Inc.*, 547 U.S. 28 (2006) (holding, based on patent misuse doctrine, there should be no presumption of market power under the Sherman Act when the sale of a patented product is conditioned on the sale of a second product in a tying arrangement—a plaintiff alleging an antitrust violation must instead establish the defendant's market power in the patented product through evidence).

[9] Ramsey Hanna in commenting on the interface between antitrust law and copyright misuse, noted that: "This continued reliance on antitrust analysis ignores the fact that antitrust doctrine looks to copyright law to determine whether a product is sufficiently unique and desirable to allow the copyright owner to restrict competition to his advantage, and whether conditioning the sale or license of the protected product on the purchase of other products or on accepting use restrictions involves an abuse of economic power," Ramsey Hanna, *Misusing Antitrust: The Search for Functional Copyright Misuse Standards*, 46 STAN. L. REV. 401, 417–18 (1993–1994).

[10] *Morton Salt Co. v. G. S. Suppiger Co.*, 314 U.S. 488, 492–93 (1942); see also Jere M. Webb & Lawrence A. Locke, *Intellectual Property Misuse: Developments in the Misuse Doctrine*, 4 HARV. J.L. & TECH. 257, 266–67 (1991) ("Supporters of the misuse doctrine argue that it should remain a viable equitable doctrine, distinct from antitrust principles and analysis, because antitrust and misuse principles address different policy considerations. Antitrust laws are said to be concerned with injury to the market environment. . . . [A]s an equitable doctrine preventing unfair extensions of patents, the misuse defense offsets other pro-patentee doctrines that effectively extend patents, such as the 'doctrine of equivalents' and the provisions of 35 U.S.C. § 271 (1982) relating to contributory infringement").

[11] Robert J. Hoerner, *The Decline (and Fall?) of the Patent Misuse Doctrine in the Federal Circuit*, 69 ANTITRUST L.J. 669, 671 (2001) (describing "two species" of patent misuse: "use of a patent to violate the antitrust law and so-called extension of the monopoly-type misuse"). Hoerner cites *Hartford-Empire* as exemplifying the first type and *Morton Salt* as the progenitor of the second. Ibid. at 669–70.

[12] 10 Phillip E. Areeda & Herbert Hovenkamp, ANTITRUST LAW ¶1781 (2d ed. 2004) ("in cases involving patent ties and related practices where the perceived threat is output or pricing, which are the traditional concerns of antitrust policy, misuse is best addressed by antitrust-like principles. However, the policy of the intellectual property laws necessarily protects more than price competition, and

providing socially optimal incentives for the creation and dissemination of technology and with competition concerns underpinning the doctrine.[13]

II. DECONSTRUCTING EQUITY

The interaction of Congress, the courts, and litigants over the history of patent misuse and antitrust in this study reveals a shared sense that there is more at stake than the transfer of wealth or the generation of innovation.[14] Like many other areas of the law, patent misuse seeks to put right what was done wrong. In that sense, Lord Atkin's observation so many years ago continues to resonate in misuse cases today:

> The rule that you are to love your neighbour becomes in law you must not injure your neighbour: and the lawyer's question 'Who is my neighbour' receives a restricted reply. You must take reasonable care to avoid acts or omissions which you can reasonably foresee would be likely to injure your neighbour. Who then in law is my neighbour? The answer seems to be—persons who are so closely and directly affected by my act that I ought reasonably to have them in my contemplation as being so affected when I am directing my mind to the acts or omissions which are called in question.[15]

The law's desire to keep patentees acting justly toward others while gaining a fair reward for their investment is at the heart of the equitable doctrine of misuse. Yet equity is an emotive, and an almost spiritual concept. This may deter those with a penchant for rationality or commercial certainty from buying into reinvigorating misuse as a robust defense. The study has shown that some of those interviewed regard the malleability of misuse as an asset, its broad standing requirements allow courts to use defendants as proxies to arrest harm to the public while retaining discretion to mold and withhold relief to the defendants in appropriate cases. Others are less convinced. They prefer to bottle misuse within the decanter of antitrust law. Conduct which cannot meet the high thresholds required

---

these concerns are often not captured by antitrust, given its strictness of proof for competitive effects, causation, and damages").

[13]   See, e.g., Case T-69/89, *Radio Telefis Eireann v. Comm'n*, 1991 E.C.R. II-489.

[14]   See *Biotech. Indus. Org. v. Dist. of Columbia*, 496 F.3d 1362, 1373 (Fed. Cir. 2007) ("Of course, the patent laws are not intended merely to shift wealth from the public to inventors. Their purpose is to 'promote the Progress of . . . useful Arts,' ultimately providing the public with the benefit of lower price through unfettered competition").

[15]   *Donoghue v. Stevenson* [1932] A.C. 562, 580.

to justify a claim of treble damages should instead look to invalidity and noninfringement as the appropriate response.

While the fact remains that Supreme Court precedent and congressional intent point to a doctrine of misuse that exists apart from antitrust law, there is no doubt that its parameters have to be more carefully marked out to address the valid concerns of its detractors. Those who advocate revitalizing misuse face a task whose definition is not simple and whose implementation is not easy. The antitrust laws exist parallel to as well as within misuse. They have also developed to embrace many innovation-related concerns traditionally within the ambit of patent law and policy. For misuse to thrive advocates must find avenues unreached or unreachable by the antitrust laws but which nonetheless threaten the central tenets of patent or antitrust policy.

III.   A FINAL WORD

From the 1930s through to 1970s the pendulum of the misuse doctrine swung in the direction of protecting rivalry and openness in the market. From the 1980s onward, the pendulum swung back in favor of patent owners, a position which remains to this day. That sentiment toward patents at the Supreme Court, however, seems to be changing. The Court's recent reversal of the Federal Circuit in *Prometheus* was accompanied by an expressed concern over "a danger that the grant of patents . . . will inhibit future innovation . . . or otherwise forecloses more future invention than the underlying discovery could reasonably justify."[16] Echoing *Morton Salt*, the Court expressed concern over the need to keep patent owners within the scope of the patent grant.[17] *Prometheus* follows a number of earlier decisions to reverse the standards put in place by the Federal Circuit which were contrary to earlier Supreme Court precedent.[18]

The doctrinal and policy aspects of misuse are important, but the researcher eventually comes to the point where abstract discourse must give way to the careful observation of concrete instances. Despite the deceptively simple rhetoric adorning the defense, the analytical process that judges undertake in misuse cases is surprisingly complex. This

---

[16]   *Mayo Collaborative Servs. v. Prometheus Labs., Inc.*, 132 S. Ct. 1289, 1301 (2012).

[17]   Ibid.

[18]   See, e.g., *KSR Int'l Co. v. Teleflex Inc.*, 550 U.S. 398 (2007); *eBay Inc. v. MercExchange, L.L.C.*, 547 U.S. 388 (2006).

imperfect attempt to deconstruct the judicial psyche is the first step in facilitating a more systematic analysis of this process. Hopefully it will lead to a better understanding of how equitable doctrines are applied, and, in time, provide greater predictability for litigants and their counselors.

The best that this study can do is to trace the doctrine of misuse, pointing out where the law has departed from precedent and looking forward to where the law might be headed. That is what the study has tried to do. The empirical data, in the form of case content analysis as well as insights from interviews, helped to better understand the development of the doctrine and its interplay with antitrust law and policy. Court opinions have been given their roles, both at once conflicting and complementary, an audible and, importantly for this study, a quantifiable voice. Through analyzing court opinions spanning 60 years, this study has attempted to focus on the most discernible and significant aspects of patent misuse in order to determine its vitality as a separate discourse to antitrust. Interviewees looking at the graphs and data often uncovered new insights not previously envisaged in earlier findings, and which could not be comprehensively explored.

Empirical research teases the earnest seeker as much as it rewards. The study is meant to be as provocative as informative. If this study has produced more questions than it answered, it has accomplished its goal—as a basis for spurring further thought in this important concern of patent law. One of the judges interviewed remarked that misuse "has potentially some very considerable value to stir more careful thinking by litigators and counselors and trial judges and appellate judges and other actors in the legal arena." Patent misuse certainly has done that. It is hoped that so has this book.

It would then have succeeded in its purpose of rousing those otherwise drifting blissfully along the streams of conventional wisdom and rhetoric out of inertia or ignorance. For there is sometimes a temptation for things to be resolved and swept under the antitrust carpet for the sake of simplicity or convenience. That temptation must be resisted, unless future developments or research decisively reveals the irrelevance of patent misuse.[19]

The vitality of patent misuse apart from antitrust ultimately depends on those it was created by and for—the judges themselves. If the

---

[19]   Perhaps this is what prompted one judge interviewed for the study to remark that it "has potentially some very considerable value to stir more careful thinking by litigators and counselors and trial judges and appellate judges and other actors in the legal arena." On file with the author.

reinvigoration of patent misuse takes place, it will likely be a compromise: balancing innovation and fairness in dealing with competitors and consumers with commercial certainty and robust exclusionary rights and thus encourage the continued production and exploitation of inventions that enrich our daily lives.

Appendices

APPENDIX I—NOTES ON METHODOLOGY

Forming the Dataset

Case reports

Case reports were obtained from Lexis-Nexis. To collect the relevant opinions, the following was done.

a. A Lexis opinion search was conducted in the Lexis Federal Court Cases, Combined database: "patent misuse" or patent w/3 misuse and date (geq (1/1/1953) and leq (12/31/2012)).[1]

b. A countersearch was done in Westlaw to ensure that no reported cases had been omitted.

    i. The problems relating to single databases searches are described by Professor Jason Ratanen:

> Many empirical studies of Federal Circuit jurisprudence rely on searches of one of the leading legal databases such as Westlaw or Lexis. Relying on a search of a single database is potentially problematic, however, if the substantive content of the databases is not identical—in other words, if Lexis and Westlaw don't contain the same universe of cases, any claims about the results are necessarily limited by the dataset being used. . . . In order to avoid this problem in connection with an empirical study of inequitable conduct that I'm working on, I recently performed a comparison of results obtained by a keyword search on Westlaw versus an identical search on Lexis. This comparison revealed that although the data obtained from the two sources is largely comparable, small differences do exist that certain types of searchers may want to take into account.[2]

---

[1] The design format of this study was inspired by, and modelled after Professor Barton Beebe's paper on fair use in U.S. copyright law. Barton Beebe, *An Empirical Study of U.S. Copyright Fair Use Opinions, 1978–2005*, 156 U. Pa. L. Rev. 549 (2008).

[2] Jason Ratenen, *The Use of Online Databases for Legal Scholarship*, Patently-O (Jan. 11, 2011), http://www.patentlyo.com/patent/2011/01/search-differences-between-westlaw-and-lexis.html

    ii.   A Westlaw opinion search was run in the Westlaw All Federal Cases database: patent w/3 misuse or "patent misuse" & (aft 1/1953 & bef 1/2013). One example of a case found on Lexis but not Westlaw was *Apex Elec. Mfg. Co. v. Altorfer Bros. Co.*[3]

c.   These opinions were then reviewed to exclude those that did not involve in any way a substantive issue of patent misuse.

    i.   Procedural: Voluntary dismissal by court, discovery, withdrawal by one or both parties, bifurcation, contention interrogatories, jurisdictional dispute, failure to respond to summary judgment, motion *in limine*, dispute on attorney's fees, amending claims, matters decided under state law.[4]

    ii.   Substantive: Patent misuse was mentioned but not argued; consideration whether misuse was purged, patent invalid; antitrust case which discussed misuse but where the issue was not raised. An example of this is the Supreme Court's opinion in *Illinois Tool Works Inc. v. Independent Ink, Inc.*[5] It was an antitrust case which considered the presumption of market power in tying cases against the backdrop of amendments to the Patent Misuse Reform Act. The defense of patent misuse was not raised, nor did the Court express any opinion on how misuse was to be analyzed or applied in a way relevant to the variables listed.

    iii.   Not patent related: mandamus, repeated cases, copyright or trademark misuse.[6]

---

[3]   238 F.2d 867 (7th Cir. 1956).

[4]   See, e.g., *Symbol Techs., Inc. v. Lemelson Med* 277 F.3d 1361, 1385–86 (Fed. Cir. 2002) ("The doctrine 'may render a patent unenforceable when it has issued only after an unreasonable and unexplained delay in prosecution' that constitutes an egregious misuse of the statutory patent system under the totality of the circumstances").

[5]   547 U.S. 28, 29, 126 S. Ct. 1281, 1283, 164 L. Ed. 2d 26 (2006); see also *Aro Mfg. Co. v. Convertible Top Replacement Co.*, 365 U.S. 336, 380, 81 S. Ct. 599, 623, 5 L. Ed. 2d 592 (1961) ("Although the Mercoid cases involve the doctrine of patent misuse, which is not an issue in this case, they also specifically delimit the character of a combination patent monopoly and it is upon that matter that they are relevant here").

[6]   See, e.g., *N.L.R.B. v. Stevens Ford, Inc.* 773 F.2d 468, 472–73 (2d Cir. 1985) ("We believe the present case involves a patent misuse of what is known as the accretion doctrine. Under that doctrine, groups of new employees, or present employees in new jobs, can be added to an existing bargaining unit without holding a vote on their representation. . . . Essentially, the doctrine is designed to preserve industrial stability by allowing adjustments in bargaining units to conform to new industrial conditions without requiring an adversary election every time new jobs are created or other alterations in industrial routine are

d. Where the literature revealed that a federal case substantively discussed patent misuse but was not captured by the initial net of cases, they were manually added. An example is Brulotte v. Thys Co.[7]

e. Limitations

i. Under-reportedness: There is a natural limitation in trying to explain the state of the law through a small number of decisions that make their way into reports. A vast majority of cases are never litigated, and fewer of those find their way into law reports. For example, pre-1953 cases were excluded. These ante-dated the current Patent Act of 1952. The dataset also did not include cases which were settled or discontinued for other reasons as well as those otherwise unavailable on Lexis and Westlaw. A more complete picture of misuse would require an inclusion of cases which are found on PACER or the IP Litigation Clearinghouse database.

ii. Study based on 2009 work: This book is based on a thesis I did while enrolled in Stanford Law School's Masters in the Science of Law Program. The results in the book differ from the results in the thesis in two primary ways. The first change is that the number of cases coded has increased. The thesis covers cases reported up until December 31, 2008. This resulted in 264 cases. When a decision was made to expand the period to December 31, 2012, a decision was also made to relook at all the unfiltered cases to extract cases which did not go into as much depth as the earlier identified cases in discussing misuse but which nonetheless gave enough of a clue as to what the court's sense of misuse was. The 2012 study produced 368 cases. Because some interviews were conducted based on the earlier results, I was aware of the possibility that the expanded pool of cases might yield results which would make the earlier interview findings misleading and was prepared to redo all the interviews based on the new results. However, two facts made this step unnecessary. First, while the 2012 results produced slightly different proportions in the variables study, the trends observed were identical to those found earlier. Second, because the trends were identical, and as the interviews were conducted on the basis of those trends, as well as

---

made"); *Altmayer-Pizzorno v. L-Soft Int'l, Inc.*, 302 F. App'x. 148, 156 (4th Cir. 2008) ("L-Soft further contends that Pizzorno should not recover on his copyright infringement claim because the inclusion of the non-competition covenant in the IPDA constituted a misuse of copyright").

[7] 379 U.S. 29 (1964).

on the basis of the personal experiences of the interviewees apart
from the data, all that was said by the interviewees as reported in
this book remain accurate. The second change is that the number
of interviewees has increased. Since the 2009 study I added
three interviewees: Hon. Randall R. Rader, Chief Judge of the
Federal Circuit as well as Professors Martin Adelman and John
Thomas of the George Washington University and Georgetown
Law Center. The interviews were based on the results of the
2009 study. The new perspectives were added to the narratives
described in the 2009 study, but did not change any of the conclusions or findings contained therein.

iii.   Use in predicting case outcomes: One judge interviewed noted
that regional circuit case law antedating the Federal Circuit was
limited in its use for predicting what the Federal Circuit would
do in a given case.[8] Another lawyer interviewed echoed that the
data was of limited interest to him because what was relevant to
him were the facts before him, and whether someone else had
succeeded before gave him little comfort.[9] These reactions under-

---

[8]   On file with the author. ("I don't think it's terribly useful to focus on what
regional circuits said in the 1940s or 1950s or 1960s or 1970s, because that's not
very relevant anymore. Their cases are not binding precedent on the Federal
Circuit or its panels. Even less so is there any precedential force for statements
made by district court judges in cases that were not appealed. So it looks to me that
a very large portion of the universe of cases you looked at, while interesting, don't
tell you much of anything about what the Federal Circuit has done or what the
Federal Circuit might do in the future. It might actually lead you away from the
right guesses. I think it's interesting to look at them and I think it's relevant to look
at them. I just think it doesn't reveal nearly as much as you would think, because
a panel of this court is going to focus on what the record and briefs and trial court
opinions in a specific case contain; they're not going to focus on what some district
judge said thirty years ago in some case that apparently never got appealed.

It's just of very little relevance to us as we make decisions in cases. Even old
cases in regional circuits would have limited power, in general. A specific case
might be so well analyzed and well written that it would be impressive, but, in
general, I don't think, just speaking for myself, that I would be hugely moved in
a patent misuse-related appeal by what the Ninth Circuit said in 1957 in the so-
and-so case or what district judge so-and-so in Oregon said in 1962. It would be
of very little weight, I think, compared to the facts and the findings below and the
arguments and authorities provided by the lawyers.")

[9]   On file with the author. ("No, it wouldn't be interesting to me as a practitioner, because the statistics don't mean anything. What mean something to me are
the particular facts in front of me in a particular case. The fact that somebody else
succeeded somewhere else doesn't give me any comfort at all. Looking at statistics
like that is not very interesting, to be very candid with you.")

score two fundamental observations that this study makes. First, that the Federal Circuit sees itself as responsible for shaping the misuse doctrine independently of its evolutionary route. Second, misuse is perceived as being fact specific and general trends are consequently perceived to be of little value in determining the outcome of a case in the present. This second observation, however, could be broadly said of any new case. The fact remains, however, that other than an odd collection of district court cases prior to the 1980s, cases involving patent misuse, just like any other cases, turn to precedent to guide the outcome of the case. The more comprehensively one understands the field, the more one can understand the minute levers within the court's mind that lead to its final determination on those facts.

Coding

Coding provides a means of quantifying otherwise qualitative notions in misuse for comparison over indicia such as time and space. They also allow the results of the study to be examined and verified, as well as to be tailored to specific inquiries not considered by this study.

An initial set of variables were created based on the literature review. A sample number of cases were coded according to variables. The number of cases was expanded and the variables were refined along the way.

Each of the opinions was coded directly into an Excel 2010 SP2 spreadsheet according to a coding instrument consisting of 34 variables. The data from the case content analysis was analyzed using SPSS 20. The coding instrument recorded the following:

a. Reference Data: Case citation; date; caption.
b. Docket Data: Level of court deciding case; circuit case was decided in; court; case posture.
c. Facts of the Case: Industry case took place in; alleged misuse or antitrust breach; literature and governmental reports cited,[10] whether legislative history featured; whether the case concerned patent misuse, antitrust or both; the controlling precedent and the circuit it came from;[11] whether the court was willing to expand the preexisting

---

[10] See, e.g., *Kolene Corp. v. Motor City Metal Treating, Inc.*, 440 F.2d 77, 85 (6th Cir. 1971) ("Motor City is not a party to the allegedly illegal contracts, and a realistic analysis does not show that the patent in suit 'itself significantly contributes to the practice under attack'. See, Report of the Attorney General's Committee to Study the Antitrust Laws 251 (1955)").

[11] In some cases the court cited a precedent which generally stands for one

categories of misuse; the outcome of the case in that instance as well as on appeal; instances of application for certiorari to the Supreme Court; whether there were dissents. A marker was used to denote cases in which multiple accounts of misuse were alleged. When this occurred, each count was analyzed independent of the other counts.

d. Scope of the Patent: whether the court defined the "scope of the patent"; whether the court regarded misuse and antitrust as coexisting or not; whether coextensive, broader or different and the policies informing the decision-making;[12] the court's treatment of bad faith by one or both parties.

e. Policy Applied: the study distinguished between patent and antitrust policy. The distinction between the two can sometimes be easily

---

proposition but used it in the context of another. For example in *Cummins, Inc. v. TAS Distrib. Co.*, the court cited *Windsurfing* for the usual proposition that "the patentee has impermissibly broadened the 'physical or temporal scope' of the patent grant with anticompetitive effect." The case, however, concerned whether the license at issue required the defendant to pay royalties past the expiration of the patents, and one where *Brulotte* might have been expected to be a more natural choice. Such cases were coded as *Windsurfing* because the lens through which the court viewed misuse was still consistent with the rest of the cases in the dataset cited for that proposition. Where a case had more than one type as misuse, each type of misuse was individually coded while keeping the rest of the variables constant. For example in *Miller Insituform, Inc. v. Insituform of North America, Inc.*, the defendant alleged two counts of misuse: tying under Section 2 of the Sherman Act and Section 3 of the Clayton Act, as well as an exclusive agreement under Section 1. 605 F. Supp. 1125 (M.D. Tenn. 1985). The Court found misuse with respect to the Section 1 claim but not Section 2 or the claim under the Clayton Act. In this instance *Miller Insituform, Inc* would be coded three times, keeping variables other than type of antitrust and antitrust outcome constant. A column in the dataset codes for repeated cases to avoid inflating counts of the other variables.

12 See, e.g., *Hearing Components, Inc. v. Shure, Inc.*, 2009 U.S. Dist. LEXIS 25050, 2–3 (E.D. Tex. Mar. 26, 2009) ("The doctrine of patent misuse 'relates generally to the use of patent rights to obtain or to coerce an unfair commercial advantage. Patent misuse relates primarily to a patentee's actions that affect competition in unpatented goods or [*3] that otherwise extend the economic effect beyond the scope of the patent grant'. *C.R. Bard, Inc. v. M3 Sys., Inc.*, 157 F.3d 1340, 1372 (Fed. Cir. 1998). The patent misuse doctrine is an extension of the equitable doctrine of unclean hands, whereby a court of equity will not lend its support to enforcement of a patent that has been misused. Patent misuse arose, as an equitable defense available to the accused infringer, from the desire to restrain practices that did not in themselves violate any law, but that drew anticompetitive strength from the patent right, and thus were deemed to be contrary to public policy. When used successfully, this defense results in rendering the patent unenforceable until the misuse is purged").

missed.[13] Because much of the coding is subject to the bias of the coder, steps were taken to ensure greater objectivity, though it is acknowledged that complete objectivity may be impossible to attain. I was the primary coder, and coded the data initially as part of my thesis while at Stanford Law School twice. That dataset extended as far as 2008. In this version of the work, I coded the data twice more. In addition, a research fellow at Fordham Law School and two research assistants at the John Marshall Law School independently checked the datasets between 2010 and 2012. Discrepancies were noted and the dataset was refined along the way. Any discrepancies were case specific and the final version of the study reports the same overall trends observed in the initial version.

f. District court cases proved to be more challenging than the cases coming from a higher-level court. These cases tended not to be organized as well, sometimes having no distinct headings or separate sections for each issue discussed. Many of the district court cases addressed on findings of fact more so than legal analysis and precedent interpretation. Sometimes they cited cases for different propositions. Sometimes they would list a series of cases and it would not be clear which one they were specifically referring to. However, this was mitigated by systemically grouping cases together because the proposition was often cited in groups of cases. In one specific example, the court cited *Microsoft*. For the purposes of the coding key, *Senza Gel* was used instead of *Microsoft* because *Microsoft* is a district court case cited only once and the quotes were from *Senza Gel*.

g. Some cases contained multiple variables, such as the outcome for each count of misuse. In such cases the same case was coded twice. An additional column was created in the dataset to mark cases that are repeats so that they can be filtered out where the inquiry required that each case only be counted once, such as the number of cases featuring in each regional circuit court of appeals.

h. Given the small size of the dataset, calculations were rounded off to one decimal place where appropriate.

Interviews

a. A representative sample of each category of interviewees may have been desirable for purposes of generalizing the findings of the interviews. However, this was not done for the following reasons.

---

[13] See discussion in Chapters 1 and 2.

i. In-depth interviews complement and are not substituted by more generalizable quantitative or qualitative studies. The interviews are aimed at providing insights on real-world thinking, and illuminate new ways of approaching conventional wisdom. Through rich interaction focused interviews unearth perceptions and insights from the organic complexity of legal consciousness. These complex economic, legal and political issues are difficult to quantify. It is a good starting point for understanding the industry as well as generating issues, questions and potential hypotheses for further rigorous empirical enquiries. Once the respective background and assumptions are known, the interviews can easily hold lessons for future stakeholders. Second, for reasons of time, resources and project objectives, it was decided that surveys would not provide me with the information and data needed for this study.

ii. All were familiar with patent misuse, and were able to relate it to their respective areas of expertise. Strictly limiting my selection of interviewees to those familiar with misuse would compromise the comprehensiveness of the findings. For example, one interviewee gave a very valuable perspective on whether and to what extent misuse featured in international IP policy. Another shed light on how courts and litigants approach the misuse issue from a tactical perspective.

b. However, it is readily recognized that the interviews are not without their limitations. Information gathered may be incomplete due to issues of confidentiality and the fact that much of the information obtained is based on unstructured interviews with busy individuals. Generally, what was obtained from the interviews were opinions formulated through professional anecdotal experience. However, it is still possible to draw preliminary conclusions. In addition, although I did not have a large sample size, my sampling of individuals distinguished in this field should provide some indication of stakeholder perception.

c. An ideal approach combines the two, or tags back and forth between the dimensions of quantitative and qualitative methods, as well as in-depth studies and more generalizable data collection and analysis. However, a wider scope of empirical analysis can hardly be undertaken. It is hoped that the sixty years of case content analysis spanning all levels of the federal jurisprudence, combined with carefully selected interviewees would mitigate any the shortcomings of the methods adopted by this study, be they perceived or real.

APPENDIX II—LIST OF INTERVIEWEES

Here follows a list of interviewees with their designations when interviewed.

Judiciary

Hon. Ellis, T.S. District Judge, U.S. District Court for the Eastern District of Virginia

Hon. Jordan, Kent A. District Judge, U.S. Court of Appeals for the Third Circuit

Hon. Michel, Paul R., Chief Judge, U.S. Court of Appeals for the Federal Circuit (until May 31, 2010)

Hon. Posner, Richard A, Circuit Judge, U.S. Court of Appeals for the Seventh Circuit

Hon. Rader, Randall R. Chief Judge, U.S. Court of Appeals for the Federal Circuit (from June 1, 2010)

Hon. Whyte, Ronald M. District Judge, U.S. District Court for the Northern District of California

Government

McCoy, Stanford, Assistant U.S. Trade Representative (Intellectual Property)

Kovacic, William E., Commissioner, U.S. Federal Trade Commission

Toupin, James, General Counsel, U.S. Patent and Trademark Office

Law Firms

Groombridge, Nicholas, Partner, Paul, Weiss, Rifkind, Wharton & Garrison LLP (New York)

Lipstein, Robert, Partner, Crowell & Moring (Washington D.C)

Kipnis, Jason D., Partner, Weil, Gotshel & Manges (California)

Richards, John, Partner, Ladas & Perry (New York)

Weinschel, Alan, Partner, Weil, Gotshel & Manges (New York)

Academia

Adelman, Martin, Professor of Law, George Washington University School of Law

Cotter, Thomas, Professor of Law, University of Minnesota Law School

Hansen, Hugh, Professor of Law, Fordham University School of Law

Hovenkamp, Herbert, Professor of Law, University of Iowa College of Law

Lemley, Mark A., Professor of Law, Stanford Law School

Thomas, John R., Professor of Law, Georgetown Law Center

APPENDIX III—SAMPLE INTERVIEW PROTOCOL

1. Prior to reading the findings
    1.1   Did you have a view of patent misuse and/or antitrust law constraints on commercial use of patents? If so, what is it?
    1.2   Does this view come from court opinions? Academic literature? Economic policy papers? Personal litigation experience? Knowledge of others' litigation experience?
    1.3   What, if any, professional experiences have you had with patent misuse and/or antitrust law constraints on commercial use of patents? Have you written or conducted research on the subject?
    1.4   How do you perceive patent misuse changing over time?
2. Personal reflections on the findings
    2.1   Have any of your prior views changed, and if so, to what extent have they changed?
    2.2   What are your thoughts on the following aspects of the findings:
    2.3   Case distribution
    2.4   The relationship between patent misuse and antitrust
    2.5   The scope of patent misuse
    2.6   Outcomes
    2.7   Alleged misuse
    2.8   Case law
    2.9   The role of bad faith
    2.10 Effect of 1988 federal amendments
    2.11 Generally
3. Do you think that patent misuse has vitality apart from antitrust law in placing constraints on commercial use of patents? If so, in what situations? Do you see patent misuse playing a more significant role than antitrust law constraints? In not, why not?

APPENDIX IV—STATUTES

Table A.1   United States of America

Patent Act

35 U.S.C. § 154; Contents and term of patent; provisional rights	(a)	In General—
	(1)	Contents.—Every patent shall contain a short title of the invention and a grant to the patentee, his heirs or assigns, of the right to exclude others from making, using, offering for sale, or selling the invention throughout the United States or importing the invention into the United States, and, if the invention is a process, of the right to exclude others from using, offering for sale or selling throughout the United States, or importing into the United States, products made by that process, referring to the specification for the particulars thereof.
	(2)	Term.—Subject to the payment of fees under this title, such grant shall be for a term beginning on the date on which the patent issues and ending 20 years from the date on which the application for the patent was filed in the United States or, if the application contains a specific reference to an earlier filed application or applications under section 120, 121, or 365(c) of this title, from the date on which the earliest such application was filed.
35 U.S.C. § 271 Infringement of patent	(a)	Except as otherwise provided in this title, whoever without authority makes, uses, offers to sell, or sells any patented invention, within the United States or imports into the United States any patented invention during the term of the patent therefor, infringes the patent.
	(b)	Whoever actively induces infringement of a patent shall be liable as an infringer.
	(c)	Whoever offers to sell or sells within the United States or imports into the United States a component of a patented machine, manufacture, combination or composition, or a material or apparatus for use in practicing a patented process, constituting a material part of the invention, knowing the same to be especially made or especially adapted for use in an infringement of such patent, and not a staple article or commodity of commerce suitable for substantial noninfringing use, shall be liable as a contributory infringer.
	(d)	No patent owner otherwise entitled to relief for infringement or contributory infringement of a patent shall be denied relief or deemed guilty of misuse or illegal extension of the patent right by reason of his having done one or more of the following:

Table A.1   (continued)

Patent Act

- (1) derived revenue from acts which if performed by another without his consent would constitute contributory infringement of the patent;
- (2) licensed or authorized another to perform acts which if performed without his consent would constitute contributory infringement of the patent;
- (3) sought to enforce his patent rights against infringement or contributory infringement;
- (4) refused to license or use any rights to the patent; or
- (5) conditioned the license of any rights to the patent or the sale of the patented product on the acquisition of a license to rights in another patent or purchase of a separate product, unless, in view of the circumstances, the patent owner has market power in the relevant market for the patent or patented product on which the license or sale is conditioned.

- (e)
- (1) It shall not be an act of infringement to make, use, offer to sell, or sell within the United States or import into the United States a patented invention (other than a new animal drug or veterinary biological product (as those terms are used in the Federal Food, Drug, and Cosmetic Act and the Act of March 4, 1913) which is primarily manufactured using recombinant DNA, recombinant RNA, hybridoma technology, or other processes involving site specific genetic manipulation techniques) solely for uses reasonably related to the development and submission of information under a Federal law which regulates the manufacture, use, or sale of drugs or veterinary biological products.
- (2) It shall be an act of infringement to submit—
- (A) an application under section 505(j) of the Federal Food, Drug, and Cosmetic Act or described in section 505(b)(2) of such Act for a drug claimed in a patent or the use of which is claimed in a patent,
- (B) an application under section 512 of such Act or under the Act of March 4, 1913 (21 U.S.C. 151–158) for a drug or veterinary biological product which is not primarily manufactured using recombinant DNA, recombinant RNA, hybridoma technology, or other processes involving site specific genetic manipulation techniques and which is claimed in a patent or the use of which is claimed in a patent, or

Table A.1   (continued)

Patent Act

    (C)

    (i)   with respect to a patent that is identified in the list of patents described in section 351(l)(3) of the Public Health Service Act (including as provided under section 351(l)(7) of such Act), an application seeking approval of a biological product, or

    (ii)   if the applicant for the application fails to provide the application and information required under section 351(l)(2)(A) of such Act, an application seeking approval of a biological product for a patent that could be identified pursuant to section 351(l)(3)(A)(i) of such Act, if the purpose of such submission is to obtain approval under such Act to engage in the commercial manufacture, use, or sale of a drug, veterinary biological product, or biological product claimed in a patent or the use of which is claimed in a patent before the expiration of such patent.

    (3)   In any action for patent infringement brought under this section, no injunctive or other relief may be granted which would prohibit the making, using, offering to sell, or selling within the United States or importing into the United States of a patented invention under paragraph (1).

    (4)   For an act of infringement described in paragraph (2)—

    (A)   the court shall order the effective date of any approval of the drug or veterinary biological product involved in the infringement to be a date which is not earlier than the date of the expiration of the patent which has been infringed,

    (B)   injunctive relief may be granted against an infringer to prevent the commercial manufacture, use, offer to sell, or sale within the United States or importation into the United States of an approved drug, veterinary biological product, or biological product,

    (C)   damages or other monetary relief may be awarded against an infringer only if there has been commercial manufacture, use, offer to sell, or sale within the United States or importation into the United States of an approved drug, veterinary biological product, or biological product, and

    (D)   the court shall order a permanent injunction prohibiting any infringement of the patent by the biological product involved in the infringement until a date which is not earlier than the date of the expiration of the patent that has been infringed under paragraph (2)(C), provided the

Table A.1   (continued)

Patent Act

patent is the subject of a final court decision, as defined in section 351(k)(6) of the Public Health Service Act, in an action for infringement of the patent under section 351(l)(6) of such Act, and the biological product has not yet been approved because of section 351(k)(7) of such Act.

The remedies prescribed by subparagraphs (A), (B), (C), and (D) are the only remedies which may be granted by a court for an act of infringement described in paragraph (2), except that a court may award attorney fees under section 285.

(5)   Where a person has filed an application described in paragraph (2) that includes a certification under subsection (b)(2)(A)(iv) or (j)(2)(A)(vii)(IV) of section 505 of the Federal Food, Drug, and Cosmetic Act (21 U.S.C. 355), and neither the owner of the patent that is the subject of the certification nor the holder of the approved application under subsection (b) of such section for the drug that is claimed by the patent or a use of which is claimed by the patent brought an action for infringement of such patent before the expiration of 45 days after the date on which the notice given under subsection (b)(3) or (j)(2)(B) of such section was received, the courts of the United States shall, to the extent consistent with the Constitution, have subject matter jurisdiction in any action brought by such person under section 2201 of title 28 for a declaratory judgment that such patent is invalid or not infringed.

(6)
(A)   Subparagraph (B) applies, in lieu of paragraph (4), in the case of a patent—
(i)   that is identified, as applicable, in the list of patents described in section 351(l)(4) of the Public Health Service Act or the lists of patents described in section 351(l)(5)(B) of such Act with respect to a biological product; and
(ii)   for which an action for infringement of the patent with respect to the biological product—
(I)   was brought after the expiration of the 30-day period described in subparagraph (A) or (B), as applicable, of section 351(l)(6) of such Act; or
(II)   was brought before the expiration of the 30-day period described in subclause (I), but which was dismissed without prejudice or was not prosecuted to judgment in good faith.

Table A.1 (continued)

Patent Act

(B) In an action for infringement of a patent described in subparagraph (A), the sole and exclusive remedy that may be granted by a court, upon a finding that the making, using, offering to sell, selling, or importation into the United States of the biological product that is the subject of the action infringed the patent, shall be a reasonable royalty.

(C) The owner of a patent that should have been included in the list described in section 351(l)(3)(A) of the Public Health Service Act, including as provided under section 351(l)(7) of such Act for a biological product, but was not timely included in such list, may not bring an action under this section for infringement of the patent with respect to the biological product.

(f)

(1) Whoever without authority supplies or causes to be supplied in or from the United States all or a substantial portion of the components of a patented invention, where such components are uncombined in whole or in part, in such manner as to actively induce the combination of such components outside of the United States in a manner that would infringe the patent if such combination occurred within the United States, shall be liable as an infringer.

(2) Whoever without authority supplies or causes to be supplied in or from the United States any component of a patented invention that is especially made or especially adapted for use in the invention and not a staple article or commodity of commerce suitable for substantial noninfringing use, where such component is uncombined in whole or in part, knowing that such component is so made or adapted and intending that such component will be combined outside of the United States in a manner that would infringe the patent if such combination occurred within the United States, shall be liable as an infringer.

(g) Whoever without authority imports into the United States or offers to sell, sells, or uses within the United States a product which is made by a process patented in the United States shall be liable as an infringer, if the importation, offer to sell, sale, or use of the product occurs during the term of such process patent. In an action for infringement of a process patent, no remedy may be granted for infringement on account of the noncommercial use or retail sale of a product

Table A.1   (continued)

Patent Act	
	unless there is no adequate remedy under this title for infringement on account of the importation or other use, offer to sell, or sale of that product. A product which is made by a patented process will, for purposes of this title, not be considered to be so made after—
	(1) it is materially changed by subsequent processes; or
	(2) it becomes a trivial and nonessential component of another product.
	(h) As used in this section, the term "whoever" includes any State, any instrumentality of a State, and any officer or employee of a State or instrumentality of a State acting in his official capacity. Any State, and any such instrumentality, officer, or employee, shall be subject to the provisions of this title in the same manner and to the same extent as any nongovernmental entity.
	(i) As used in this section, an "offer for sale" or an "offer to sell" by a person other than the patentee, or any designee of the patentee, is that in which the sale will occur before the expiration of the term of the patent.
Sherman Act	
Section 1, 15 U.S.C. § 1 (2000); Trusts, etc., in restraint of trade illegal; penalty	Every contract, combination in the form of trust or otherwise, in restraint of trade or commerce among the several States, or with foreign nations, is declared to be illegal. Every person who shall make any contract or engage in any combination or conspiracy hereby declared to be illegal shall be deemed guilty of a felony, on conviction thereof, shall be punished by fine not exceeding $10,000,000 if a corporation, or, if any other person, $350,000, or by imprisonment not exceeding three years, or by both said punishments, in the discretion of the court.
Section 2, 15 U.S.C. § 2 (2000); Monopolizing trade a felony; penalty	Every person who shall monopolize, or attempt to monopolize, or combine or conspire with any other person or persons, to monopolize any part of the trade or commerce among the several States, or with foreign nations, shall be deemed guilty of a felony, and, on conviction thereof, shall be punished by fine not exceeding $10,000,000 if a corporation, or, if any other person, $350,000, or by imprisonment not exceeding three years, or by both said punishments, in the discretion of the court.

Table A.1 (continued)

Sherman Act

Clayton Act[14]

Section 3, 15 U.S.C. § 14 (2000); Sale, etc., on agreement not to use goods of competitor	It shall be unlawful for any person engaged in commerce, in the course of such commerce, to lease or make a sale or contract for sale of goods, wares, merchandise, machinery, supplies, or other commodities, whether patented or unpatented, for use, consumption, or resale within the United States or any Territory thereof or the District of Columbia or any insular possession or other place under the jurisdiction of the United States, or fix a price charged therefor, or discount from, or rebate upon, such price, on the condition, agreement, or understanding that the lessee or purchaser thereof shall not use or deal in the goods, wares, merchandise, machinery, supplies, or other commodities of a competitor or competitors of the lessor or seller, where the effect of such lease, sale, or contract for sale or such condition, agreement, or understanding may be to substantially lessen competition or tend to create a monopoly in any line of commerce.

Federal Trade
 Commission Act

Section 5, 15 U.S.C. § 45 (a)(1) (2000); Unfair methods of competition unlawful; prevention by Commission	(a)	Declaration of unlawfulness; power to prohibit unfair practices; inapplicability to foreign trade
	(1)	Unfair methods of competition in or affecting commerce, and unfair or deceptive acts or practices in or affecting commerce, are hereby declared unlawful.

---

[14] Wikipedia provides a useful comparison of the Sherman and Clayton Acts: "The Clayton Act made both substantive and procedural modifications to federal antitrust law. Substantively, the act seeks to capture anticompetitive practices in their incipiency by prohibiting particular types of conduct, not deemed in the best interest of a competitive market. There are 4 sections of the bill that proposed substantive changes in the antitrust laws by way of supplementing the Sherman Act of 1890. In those sections, the Act thoroughly discusses the following four principles of economic trade and business: (1) price discrimination between different purchasers if such a discrimination substantially lessens competition or tends to create a monopoly in any line of commerce (Act Section 2, codified at 15 U.S.C. § 13; (2) sales on the condition that (A) the buyer or lessee not deal with the competitors of the seller or lessor ('exclusive dealings') or (B) the buyer also purchase another different product ('tying') but only when these acts substantially lessen competition (Act Section 3, codified at 15 U.S.C. § 14) . . ." http://en.wikipedia.org/wiki/Clayton_Antitrust_Act.

Table A.2   The European Union

Treating for the Functioning of the European Union Article 101	(1)	The following shall be prohibited as incompatible with the common market: all agreements between undertakings, decisions by associations of undertakings and concerted practices which may affect trade between Member States and which have as their object or effect the prevention, restriction or distortion of competition within the common market, and in particular those which:
	(a)	directly or indirectly fix purchase or selling prices or any other trading conditions;
	(b)	limit or control production, markets, technical development, or investment;
	(c)	share markets or sources of supply;
	(d)	apply dissimilar conditions to equivalent transactions with other trading parties, thereby placing them at a competitive disadvantage;
	(e)	make the conclusion of contracts subject to acceptance by the other parties of supplementary obligations which, by their nature or according to commercial usage, have no connection with the subject of such contracts.
	(2)	Any agreements or decisions prohibited pursuant to this Article shall be automatically void.
	(3)	The provisions of paragraph 1 may, however, be declared inapplicable in the case of:
	–	any agreement or category of agreements between undertakings;
	–	any decision or category of decisions by associations of undertakings;
	–	any concerted practice or category of concerted practices, which contributes to improving the production or distribution of goods or to promoting technical or economic progress, while allowing consumers a fair share of the resulting benefit, and which does not:
	(a)	impose on the undertakings concerned restrictions which are not indispensable to the attainment of these objectives;
	(b)	afford such undertakings the possibility of eliminating competition in respect of a substantial part of the products in question.

Table A.2   The European Union

Treating for the
   Functioning of the
   European Union

Article 102   Any abuse by one or more undertakings of a dominant position within the common market or in a substantial part of it shall be prohibited as incompatible with the common market in so far as it may affect trade between Member States. Such abuse may, in particular, consist in:

(a) directly or indirectly imposing unfair purchase or selling prices or other unfair trading conditions;

(b) limiting production, markets or technical development to the prejudice of consumers;

(c) applying dissimilar conditions to equivalent transactions with other trading parties, thereby placing them at a competitive disadvantage;

(d) making the conclusion of contracts subject to acceptance by the other parties of supplementary obligations which, by their nature or according to commercial usage, have no connection with the subject of such contracts.

APPENDIX V—CODING KEY

Caption	Case Name
Citation	Citation of the Opinion
Date	Date of the Decision
Pre-88	Was the case decided prior to 1988 (when the Patent Misuse Reform Act was enacted)?
	1 Yes
	2 No
Last 15 years?	Which 15-year period was the case decided?
	1 1953–1967
	2 1968–1982
	3 1983–1997
	4 1998–2012
Last 10 years?	Which 10-year period was the case decided?
	1 1953–1962
	2 1963–1972
	3 1973–1982
	4 1983–1992
	5 1993–2002
	6 2003–2012
Level	Level of court writing the opinion
	1 Supreme Court opinion
	2 Appellate Court opinion
	3 District Court (including Court of Claims) opinion
D.C.	Alphabetical Abbreviation of District Court
	NA Not applicable (0)
	DAla District of Alabama (11)
	DAlas District of Alaska (9)
	DAr District of Arkansas (8)
	DCol District of Colorado (10)

DC District of Columbia (12)

DCon District of Connecticut (2)

DDel District of Delaware (3)

DHaw District of Hawai'i (9)

DKan District of Kansas (10)

DMd District of Maryland (4)

DMas District of Massachusetts (1)

DMin District of Minnesota (8)

DNDa District of North Dakota (8)

DNeb District of Nebraska (8)

DNJ District of New Jersey (3)

DOr District of Oregon (9)

DRI District of Rhode Island (1)

DSCa District of South Carolina (4)

DTex District of Texas (5)

DUt District of Utah (10)

EDKy Eastern District of Kentucky (6)

EDLa Eastern District of Louisiana (5)

EDMic Eastern District of Michigan (6)

EDMis Eastern District of Missouri (8)

EDNCa Eastern District of Northern Carolina (4)

EDNY Eastern District of New York (2)

EDPa Eastern District of Pennsylvania (3)

EDTen Eastern District of Tennessee (6)

EDTex Eastern District of Texas (5)

EDVir Eastern District of Virginia (4)

EDWis Eastern District of Wisconsin (7)

MDNC Middle District of North Carolina (4)

MDTen Middle District of Tennessee (6)

NDCa Northern District of Carolina (4)

NDCal Northern District of California (9)

NDGeo Northern District of Georgia (4)

NDIll Northern District of Illinois (7)

NDInd Northern District of Indiana (7)

NDIo Northern District of Iowa (8)

NDMiss Northern District of Mississippi (5)

NDNY Northern District of New York (2)

NDOh Northern District of Ohio (6)

NDOre Northern District of Oregon (9)

NDOk Northern District of Oklahoma (10)

NDTex Northern District of Texas (5)

SDCal Southern District of California (9)

SDFla Southern District of Florida (11)

SDIll Southern District of Illinois (7)

SDIo Southern District of Iowa (8)

SDNY Southern District of New York (2)

SDOh Southern District of Ohio (6)

SDTex Southern District of Texas (5)

WDKy Western District of Kentucky (6)

WDMi Western District of Michigan (6)

WDMis Western District of Missouri (8)

WDNCa Western District of North Carolina (4)

WDNY Western District of New York (2)

WDPen Western District of Pennsylvania (3)

WDOk Western District of Oklahoma (10)

WDVir Western District of Virginia (4)

WDWas Western District of Washington (9)

Circuit	Circuit of the Appellate Court/ District Court
	1 First Circuit
	2 Second Circuit
	3 Third Circuit
	4 Fourth Circuit

5	Fifth Circuit
6	Sixth Circuit
7	Seventh Circuit
8	Eight Circuit
9	Ninth Circuit
10	Tenth Circuit
11	Eleventh Circuit
12	D.C. Circuit
13	Federal Circuit
14	Supreme Court

Posture   Procedural Posture

1	Preliminary Injunction
2	Summary Judgment Patentee/Licensor
3	Summary Judgment Infringer/Licensee
4	Summary Judgment Cross
5	Bench Trial
6	Jury Trial
7	Motion to Dismiss/Strike
8	Declaratory Judgment
9	Certified Question
10	Motion for Reconsideration
11	Post-trial motions
12	Motion for Contempt
13	Interlocutory Motions
14	Appellate Panel Review
15	*En Banc* Review

Repeated Case   (Case contained more than one type of misuse)

1	Marker for Case
2	Marker for Repeat of Same Case

PM/A   Whether allegations were based on patent misuse (PM) or antitrust (A) grounds

	1	Patent Misuse
	2	Both Patent Misuse and Antitrust
Alleged Patent Misuse	0	Unclear

1 Tying. *Including: Tying non-patented products to a patented product; Package licensing; Block booking; Lock-outs; Refusals to license a patent*

2 Restrictions. *Including: Field of use limitations; Restrictions after sale; territorial restrictions; Non-compete clauses; Post-expiry no challenge; Exclusive dealerships; Non-disclosure agreements; Non-termination clause; Granting exclusive right to sell product; No-challenge clause*

3 Royalties. *Including: Royalties based on total sales; royalties based on non-patented goods; Claim for damages on non-patented goods; Extension to post-grant patents; Pre-grant royalties; Excessive royalties; Excessive pricing; Price restraints; Price fixing; Double royalties; Resale price maintenance (to change the rest later); Discriminatory pricing; Punitive contractual penalties; Reneging on RAND obligations*

4 Trademark-related abuses

5 Time Extensions. *Including: Post-expiration royalties (with or without reduction in royalty rate); post-expiry supply and marking; Pre-issuance royalties*

6 Grantbacks. *Including: Grantback clauses; Tie-ins*

7 Fraud. *Including: Fraudulent Procurement; Misrepresentation on expiry dates; Patent mismarking; Misrepresentation in standard setting*

8 Antitrust. *Including: Improper use of patents contributing to an antitrust violation; Market sharing*

9 Vexatious Litigation. *Including: Vexatious litigation; Collateral pressure; Group boycott; Bad faith enforcement*

10 Abuse of Process. *Including: Procedural delays; Filing continuations; False marking; Collusive settlements; Mislisting of Patent in Orange Book; Failure to disclose and false Certification to obtain regulatory approval*

11 Patent Pools. *Including: Patent pooling, Accumulation*

Alleged Antitrust Breach — Conduct by patent owner accused of antitrust breach

0 Not applicable

1 Breach of Section 1 Sherman Act (Anticompetitive Agreements)

2 Breach of Section 2 Sherman Act (Monopolization)

3 Breach of Sections 1 and 2 Sherman Act

4 Breach of Section 3/7 Clayton Act

5 Breach of Section 1 and 2 Sherman Act, Section 3/7 Clayton Act

6 Unclear

Industry — What industry the subject patent was to be used in or the type of industry it was from

0 Not Mentioned

1 Construction

2 Print & Media

3 Service

4 Software

5 Textiles

6 Agriculture and Food

7 Communications & Entertainment

8 Medical Devices, Measurement, Instrumentation, Optics

	9	Semiconductor, Electrical, and Computers
	10	Sports & Games
	11	Chemicals & Biopharma
	12	Machinery
	13	Manufacturing
	14	Articles of Manufacture

Patent Scope   Whether patent scope was mentioned

    1   Yes

    2   No

Scope of Patent   How patent misuse was regarded
Misuse

    0   Not mentioned/Not applicable

    1   Patent claim

    2   Time

    3   Product

    4   Time and Product

    5   Violation of antitrust law

    6   Patent claim and violation of antitrust law

Co-existing?   Whether patent misuse is treated as co-existing with antitrust law

    0   Not mentioned

    1   Yes

    2   No

Relationship   Relationship of patent misuse with antitrust law

    0   Not mentioned

    1   Co-extensive

    2   Broader

    3   Different

Specifics   How was patent misuse perceived?

    0   Not mentioned

    1   Antitrust policy

2　Patent policy

3　Antitrust and patent policy

4　Bad faith and antitrust policy

Expansion of
PM

Was the court willing to consider expanding the
scope of patent misuse?

0　Not mentioned

1　Yes

2　No

Precedent Case

What did the court cite as the precedent case?

0　Not mentioned

1　Public policy requires limitation to patent grant;
not limited to antitrust policy

Morton Salt Co. v. G.S. Suppiger Co.

Motion Picture Patents Co. v. Universal Film Mfg.

National Lockwasher Co. v. George K. Garrett

United States v. Paramount Pictures

Standard Sanitary Mfg. Co. v. United States;

*Carbice Corporation of America v. American
Patents Corp*

2　Equity based prohibition against exploitation
contrary to public policy; focus on physical scope
of invention

Mercoid Corp. v. Mid-Continent Inv.

Mercoid Corp. v. Minneapolis-Honeywell

United States v. United States Gypsum Co.

Automatic Radio Mfg. Co. v. Hazeltine Research

United States v. Loew's

*Transparent-Wrap Machine Corp. v. Stokes &
Smith Co.*

Zenith Radio Corp. v. Hazeltine Research

Blonder-Tongue Lab. v. Univ. of Ill. Found.

Leitch Mfg. Co. v. Barber Co.

> *Congoleum Industries, Inc. v. Armstrong Cork*
>
> *American Securit Co. v. Shatterproof Glass Corp.*

3   Extension beyond period of patent; *per se* illegal

> *Brulotte v. Thys Co.*
>
> *Meehan v. PPG Indus., Inc.*
>
> *Aronson v. Quick Point Pencil Co.*
>
> *Pitney Bowe's, Inc. v. Mestre*
>
> *Boggild v. Kenner Products*
>
> *In re Yarn Processing Patent Validity Litigation*

4   Fraud on patent office amounting to antitrust violation

> *Walker Proc. Equipment, Inc. v. Food Mach. & Chem.*

5   Misuse doctrine, it can be stated generally that the misconduct must be connected with the matter in litigation, and the defense is not available to a party with whom the misconduct is of no concern

> *Well Surveys, Inc. v. McCullough Tool*
>
> *Kolene Corp. v. Motor City Metal Treating*
>
> *Binks Mfg. Co. v. Ransburg Electro-Coating*
>
> *Apex Electrical Mfg. Co. v. Altorfer Bros. Co.*

6   Sham litigation; bad faith and improper purpose required

> *Glaverbel Societe Anonyme v. Northlake Mktg. & Supply*
>
> *Prof'l Real Estate Investors v. Columbia Pictures Indus.*

7   Analyzed with antitrust law (except standing requirements)

> *USM Corp. v. SPS Techs., Inc.*

8   Framework for tying analysis based on physical product; market power requirement.

> *Senza-Gel Corp. v. Seiffhart*

9   Outside scope with anticompetitive effect

Windsurfing Int'l., Inc. v. AMF

C.R. Bard v. M3 Sys.

Mallinckrodt, Inc. v. Medipart, Inc.

B. Braun Med., Inc. v. Abbott Lab.

Virginia Panel Corp. v. MAC Panel Co.

County Materials Corp. v. Allan Block Corp.

U.S. Philips Corp. v. ITC

Monsanto Co. v. McFarling

Princo v. ITC

10   Altering the holding of the Mercoid case to the extent of exempting from the misuse doctrine the assertion by a patent owner of exclusive control over an unpatented nonstaple item useful only in practicing a patent process

Dawson Chem. Co. v. Rohm & Haas Co.

Precedent Case—Specifics	What did the court cite as the specific precedent case?

0   Not applicable or other

1   *Morton Salt Co. v. G.S. Suppiger Co.*

2   *Mercoid Corp. v. Mid-Continent Inv*

3   *Windsurfing Int'l., Inc. v. AMF*

Precedent— Circuit	Which circuit/court did the Precedent case belong to?

0   Not mentioned/not applicable

1   Supreme Court

2   Federal Circuit

3   Seventh Circuit

4   Ninth Circuit

5   Tenth Circuit

Precedent Circuit Level	What level was the Precedent from?

0   Not applicable

	1	Supreme Court
	2	Appellate Court

Legislative
History

Does Court refer to the legislative amendments of the Patent Act?

0   Not mentioned

1   Yes, Court directly refers to the legislative history

Literature

Does Court refer to academic literature/ policy papers?

0   Not mentioned

1   Yes, Court directly refers to academic literature/ policy papers

Bad Faith

Bad faith supports:

0   Not mentioned/applicable

1   P displayed no bad faith (No misuse)

2   P displayed bad faith (Misuse)

3   D displayed bad faith (No misuse)

4   Unclear

Outcome
(Misuse)

Disposition of the Patent Misuse Defense

0   Not mentioned/Applicable

1   No misuse

2   Misuse found

3   Issue of Fact/Procedure

Outcome
(Antitrust)

Disposition of the Antitrust Counterclaim

0   Not mentioned/Applicable

1   Patentee wins (Court finds no antitrust violation)

2   Infringer wins (Court finds antitrust violation)

3   Issue of fact/Procedure

Appeal

Misuse Ruling on Appeal

0   District court opinion/not applicable

1   Affirmed

	2 Reversed
	3 Remanded/Other
Dissent	Was there a Dissenting Opinion?
	1 Yes
	2 No
	3 Not applicable
Certiorari	Was certiorari applied for and what was the outcome?
	0 Not available/applicable
	1 No Petition
	2 Applied and Denied
	3 Applied for and Allowed
Relationship between Parties	What was the relationship between the Patentee and Infringer?
	0 Unclear
	1 Competitor
	2 Licensee
	3 Both
	4 Seeking License
	5 Third Party

APPENDIX VI—LIST OF SUPREME COURT AND FEDERAL CIRCUIT JUDGES IN PATENT MISUSE CASES

Table A.3   Patent misuse cases: Federal Circuit (1982–2012)

Patent Misuse Cases	Year	Seat 1	Seat 2	Seat 3	Seat 4
	Markey Court				
	1982	Baldwin	Bennet	Davis	Kashiwa
	1983	Baldwin	Bennet	Davis	Kashiwa
	1984	Baldwin	Bennet	Davis	Kashiwa
	1985	Baldwin	Bennet	Davis	Kashiwa
Windsurfing Int'l v. AMF, Inc., 782 F.2d 995 (1986)	1986	Baldwin	Bennet	Davis	Kashiwa
Senza-Gel Corp. v. Seiffhart, 803 F.2d 661 (1986)					
Hodosh v. Block Drug Co., 833 F.2d 1575 (1987)	1987	–	Mayer	Davis	–
Allen Archery, Inc. v.	1988	Michel	Mayer	Davis	–
Browning Mfg. Co., 819	1989	Michel	Mayer	–	Plager
F.2d 1087 (1987)	1990	Michel	Mayer	Clevenger	Plager
	Nies Court				
	1991	Michel	Mayer	Clevenger	Plager
Mallinckrodt, Inc. v. Medipart, Inc., 976 F.2d 700 (1992)	1992	Michel	Mayer	Clevenger	Plager
	1993	Michel	Mayer	Clevenger	Plager
	1994	Michel	Mayer	Clevenger	Plager
	Archer Court				
Glaverbel Societe Anonyme v. Northlake Mktg. & Supply, 45 F.3d 1550 (1995)	1995	Michel	Mayer	Clevenger	Plager
Engel Indus. v. Lockformer Co., 96 F.3d 1398 (1996)	1996	Michel	Mayer	Clevenger	Plager
Virginia Panel Corp. v. MAC Panel Co., 133 F.3d 860 (1997)	1997	Michel	Mayer	Clevenger	Plager
B. Braun Med., Inc. v. Abbott Labs., 124 F.3d 1419 (1997)					

Seat 5	Seat 6	Seat 7	Seat 8	Seat 9	Seat 10	Seat 11	Seat 12
Friedman	Markey	Miller	Nichols	Nies	Rich	Smith	–
Friedman	Markey	Miller	Nichols	Nies	Rich	Smith	–
Friedman	Markey	Miller	Newman	Nies	Rich	Smith	Bissell
Friedman	Markey	Miller/ Archer	Newman	Nies	Rich	Smith	Bissell
Friedman	Markey	Archer	Newman	Nies	Rich	Smith	Bissell
Friedman	Markey	Archer	Newman	Nies	Rich	Smith	Bissell
Friedman	Markey	Archer	Newman	Nies	Rich	Smith	Bissell
Friedman	Markey	Archer	Newman	Nies	Rich	Smith	Bissell
Lourie	Markey	Archer	Newman	Nies	Rich	–	Bissell/ Rader
Lourie	–	Archer	Newman	Nies	Rich	–	Rader
Lourie	–	Archer	Newman	Nies	Rich	Schall	Rader
Lourie		Archer	Newman	Nies	Rich	Schall	Rader
Lourie	Bryson	Archer	Newman	Nies	Rich	Schall	Rader
Lourie	Bryson	Archer	Newman	Nies	Rich	Schall	Rader
Lourie	Bryson	Archer	Newman	–	Rich	Schall	Rader
Lourie	Bryson	Archer	Newman	Gajarsa	Rich	Schall	Rader

Table A.3   (continued)

Patent Misuse Cases	Year	Seat 1	Seat 2	Seat 3	Seat 4
Mayer Court					
C.R. Bard v. M3 Sys., 157 F.3d 1340 (1998)	1998	Michel	Mayer	Clevenger	Plager
Ricoh Co. v. Nashua Corp., 185 F.3d 884 (1999)	1999	Michel	Mayer	Clevenger	Plager
	2000	Michel	Mayer	Clevenger	Plager
	2001	Michel	Mayer	Clevenger	Prost
Monsanto Co. v. McFarling, 302 F.3d 1291 (2002)	2002	Michel	Mayer	Clevenger	Prost
	2003	Michel	Mayer	Clevenger	Prost
Monsanto Co. v. McFarling, 363 F.3d 1336 (2004)	2004	Michel	Mayer	Clevenger	Prost
Michel Court					
U.S. Philips Corp. v. ITC, 424 F.3d 1179 (2005)	2005	Michel	Mayer	Clevenger	Prost
United States Philips Corp. v. Princo Corp., 173 Fed. Appx. 832 (2006)	2006	Michel	Mayer	Clevenger	Prost
Monsanto Co. v. Scruggs, 459 F.3d 1328 (2006)		Michel	Mayer	Clevenger/ Moore	Prost
Monsanto Co. v. McFarling, 488 F.3d 973 (2007)	2007	Michel	Mayer	Moore	Prost
Qualcomm Inc. v. Broadcom Corp., 548 F.3d 1004 (2008)	2008	Michel	Mayer	Moore	Prost
Princo Corp. v. Int'l Trade Com'n, 563 F.3d 1301 (2009)	2009	Michel	Mayer	Moore	Prost
Princo Corp. v. ITC, 616 F.3d 1318 (2010)	2010	Michel	Mayer	Moore	Prost
Rader Court					
Sanofi-Aventis v. Apotex Inc., 659 F.3d 1171 (2011)	2011	–	Reyna	Moore	Prost
	2012	–	Reyna	Moore	Prost

Note: Individuals who have held the office of Chief Judge are shaded.

Seat 5	Seat 6	Seat 7	Seat 8	Seat 9	Seat 10	Seat 11	Seat 12
Lourie	Bryson	–	Newman	Gajarsa	Rich	Schall	Rader
Lourie	Bryson	–	Newman	Gajarsa	Rich/ Linn	Schall	Rader
Lourie	Bryson	Dyk	Newman	Gajarsa	Linn	Schall	Rader
Lourie	Bryson	Dyk	Newman	Gajarsa	Linn	Schall	Rader
Lourie	Bryson	Dyk	Newman	Gajarsa	Linn	Schall	Rader
Lourie	Bryson	Dyk	Newman	Gajarsa	Linn	Schall	Rader
Lourie	Bryson	Dyk	Newman	Gajarsa	Linn	Schall	Rader
Lourie	Bryson	Dyk	Newman	Gajarsa	Linn	Schall	Rader
Lourie	Bryson	Dyk	Newman	Gajarsa	Linn	Schall	Rader
Lourie	Bryson	Dyk	Newman	Gajarsa	Linn	Schall	Rader
Lourie	Bryson	Dyk	Newman	Gajarsa	Linn	Schall	Rader
Lourie	Bryson	Dyk	Newman	Gajarsa	Linn	Schall	Rader
Lourie	Bryson	Dyk	Newman	Gajarsa	Linn	Schall	Rader
Lourie	Bryson	Dyk	Newman	Gajarsa	Linn	O'Malley	Rader
Lourie	Bryson	Dyk	Newman	Gajarsa/ Wallach	Linn	O'Malley	Rader
Lourie	Bryson	Dyk	Newman	Wallach	Linn	O'Malley	Rader

Patent misuse and antitrust law

Table A.4   Patent misuse cases: Supreme Court (1789–2012)

Patent Misuse Cases

The Jay Court

1789–1792	J. Blair	Wm. Cushing	J. Wilson	J.Jay
1792–1793	J. Blair	Wm. Cushing	J. Wilson	J.Jay
1793–1795	J. Blair	Wm. Cushing	J. Wilson	J.Jay
The Rutledge Court				
1795	J. Blair	Wm. Cushing	J. Wilson	
The Ellsworth Court				
1796–1798	O. Ellsworth	Wm. Cushing	J. Wilson	S. Chase
1798–Feb 1799	O. Ellsworth	Wm. Cushing		S. Chase
Feb–Oct 1799	O. Ellsworth	Wm. Cushing	B. Washington	S. Chase
Oct 1799–Apr 1800	O. Ellsworth	Wm. Cushing	B. Washington	S. Chase
Apr–Dec 1800	O. Ellsworth	Wm. Cushing	B. Washington	S. Chase
The Marshall Court				
1801–1804	B. Washington	Wm. Cushing	J. Marshall	S. Chase
1804–1806	B. Washington	Wm. Cushing	J. Marshall	S. Chase
1807–1810	B. Washington	Wm. Cushing	J. Marshall	S. Chase
1810–1811	B. Washington		J. Marshall	S. Chase
1811–1812	B. Washington		J. Marshall	G. Duvall
1812–1823	B. Washington	J. Story	J. Marshall	G. Duvall
1823–1826	B. Washington	J. Story	J. Marshall	G. Duvall
1826–1828	B. Washington	J. Story	J. Marshall	G. Duvall
1828–1829	B. Washington	J. Story	J. Marshall	G. Duvall
1830–1834	J. McLean	J. Story	J. Marshall	G. Duvall
1835	J. McLean	J. Story	J. Marshall	G. Duvall
The Taney Court				
1836–1837	J. McLean	P.P. Barbour	R.B. Taney	
1837–1838	J. McLean	P.P. Barbour	R.B. Taney	
1838–1841	J. McLean	P.P. Barbour	R.B. Taney	J. McKinley
1842–1843	J. McLean	P.V. Daniel	R.B. Taney	J. McKinley
1843–1844	J. McLean	P.V. Daniel	R.B. Taney	J. McKinley
1845–1846	J. McLean	P.V. Daniel	R.B. Taney	J. McKinley
1846–1851	J. McLean	P.V. Daniel	R.B. Taney	J. McKinley
1851–1852	J. McLean	P.V. Daniel	R.B. Taney	J. McKinley
1853–1857	J. McLean	P.V. Daniel	R.B. Taney	J.A. Campbell
1858–1860	J. McLean	P.V. Daniel	R.B. Taney	J.A. Campbell
1860–1861	J. McLean		R.B. Taney	J.A. Campbell

J. Iredell		J. Rutledge			
J. Iredell	Th. Johnson				
J. Iredell	Wm. Paterson				
J. Iredell	Wm. Paterson	J. Rutledge			
J. Iredell	Wm. Paterson				
J. Iredell	Wm. Paterson				
J. Iredell	Wm. Paterson				
	Wm. Paterson				
A. Moore	Wm. Paterson				
A. Moore	Wm. Paterson				
	Wm. Paterson	Wm. Johnson			
H.B. Livingston	Th. Todd	Wm. Johnson			
H.B. Livingston	Th. Todd	Wm. Johnson			
H.B. Livingston	Th. Todd	Wm. Johnson			
H.B. Livingston	Th. Todd	Wm. Johnson			
S. Thompson	Th. Todd	Wm. Johnson			
S. Thompson	R. Trimble	Wm. Johnson			
S. Thompson		Wm. Johnson			
S. Thompson	H. Baldwin	Wm. Johnson			
S. Thompson	H. Baldwin			J. M. Wayne	
S. Thompson	J. Story	H. Baldwin		J.M. Wayne	
S. Thompson	J. Story	H. Baldwin		J.M. Wayne	J. Catron
S. Thompson	J. Story	H. Baldwin		J.M. Wayne	J. Catron
S. Thompson	J. Story	H. Baldwin		J.M. Wayne	J. Catron
	J. Story	H. Baldwin		J.M. Wayne	J. Catron
	S. Nelson	L. Woodbury		J.M. Wayne	J. Catron
	S. Nelson	L. Woodbury	R.C. Grier	J.M. Wayne	J. Catron
	S. Nelson	B.R. Curtis	R.C. Grier	J.M. Wayne	J. Catron
	S. Nelson	B.R. Curtis	R.C. Grier	J.M. Wayne	J. Catron
N. Clifford	S. Nelson		R.C. Grier	J.M. Wayne	J. Catron
N. Clifford	S. Nelson		R.C. Grier	J.M. Wayne	J. Catron

Table A.4   (continued)

Patent Misuse Cases					
	The Taney Court				
	1862–1863		N.H. Swayne	R.B. Taney	S.F. Miller
	1863–1864	S.J. Field	N.H. Swayne	R.B. Taney	S.F. Miller
	The Chase Court				
	1864–1865	S.J. Field	N.H. Swayne	S.P. Chase	S.F. Miller
	1865–1867	S.J. Field	N.H. Swayne	S.P. Chase	S.F. Miller
	1867–1870	S.J. Field	N.H. Swayne	S.P. Chase	S.F. Miller
	1870–1872	S.J. Field	N.H. Swayne	S.P. Chase	S.F. Miller
	1973	S.J. Field	N.H. Swayne	S.P. Chase	S.F. Miller
	The Waite Court				
	1874–1877	S.J. Field	N.H. Swayne	M. Waite	S.F. Miller
	1877–1880	S.J. Field	N.H. Swayne	M. Waite	S.F. Miller
	1881	S.J. Field	S. Matthews	M. Waite	S.F. Miller
	1882–1887	S.J. Field	S. Matthews	M. Waite	S.F. Miller
	1888	S.J. Field	S. Matthews	M. Waite	S.F. Miller
	The Fuller Court				
	1888–1889	S.J. Field	S. Matthews	MelvilleFuller	S.F. Miller
	1890–1891	S.J. Field		MelvilleFuller	D.J. Brewer
	1891–1892	S.J. Field	H.B. Brown	MelvilleFuller	D.J. Brewer
	1892–1893	S.J. Field	H.B. Brown	MelvilleFuller	D.J. Brewer
	1893	S.J. Field	H.B. Brown	MelvilleFuller	D.J. Brewer
	1894–1895	S.J. Field	H.B. Brown	MelvilleFuller	D.J. Brewer
	1896–1897	S.J. Field	H.B. Brown	MelvilleFuller	D.J. Brewer
	1898–1902	J. McKenna	H.B. Brown	MelvilleFuller	D.J. Brewer
	1902–1903	J. McKenna	H.B. Brown	MelvilleFuller	D.J. Brewer
	1903–1906	J. McKenna	H.B. Brown	MelvilleFuller	D.J. Brewer
Paper Bag Co. v. Eastern Paper Bag Co., 210 U.S. 405 (1908)	1906–1909	J. McKenna	Wm. H. Moody	MelvilleFuller	D.J. Brewer
Leeds & Catlin Co v. Victor Talking Mach Co., 213 US 325 (1909)	Jan– Mar 1910	J. McKenna	Wm. H. Moody	MelvilleFuller	D.J. Brewer
	Mar– Jul 1910	J. McKenna	Wm. H. Moody	MelvilleFuller	

N. Clifford	S. Nelson	D. Davis	R.C. Grier	J.M. Wayne	J. Catron
N. Clifford	S. Nelson	D. Davis	R.C. Grier	J.M. Wayne	J. Catron
N. Clifford	S. Nelson	D. Davis	R.C. Grier	J.M. Wayne	J. Catron
N. Clifford	S. Nelson	D. Davis	R.C. Grier	J.M. Wayne	
N. Clifford	S. Nelson	D. Davis	R.C. Grier		
N. Clifford	S. Nelson	D. Davis	Wm. Strong	J.P. Bradley	
N. Clifford	W. Hunt	D. Davis	Wm. Strong	J.P. Bradley	
N. Clifford	W. Hunt	D. Davis	Wm. Strong	J.P. Bradley	
N. Clifford	W. Hunt	J.M. Harlan	Wm. Strong	J.P. Bradley	
N. Clifford	W. Hunt	J.M. Harlan	Wm. B. Woods	J.P. Bradley	
S. Blatchford	H. Gray	J.M. Harlan	Wm. B. Woods	J.P. Bradley	
S. Blatchford	H. Gray	J.M. Harlan	L.Q.C. LamarII	J.P. Bradley	
S. Blatchford	H. Gray	J.M. Harlan	L.Q.C. LamarII	J.P. Bradley	
S. Blatchford	H. Gray	J.M. Harlan	L.Q.C. LamarII	J.P. Bradley	
S. Blatchford	H. Gray	J.M. Harlan	L.Q.C. LamarII	J.P. Bradley	
S. Blatchford	H. Gray	J.M. Harlan	L.Q.C. LamarII	Geo. Shiras, Jr.	
S. Blatchford	H. Gray	J.M. Harlan	H.E. Jackson	Geo. Shiras, Jr.	
E.D. White	H. Gray	J.M. Harlan	H.E. Jackson	Geo. Shiras, Jr.	
E.D. White	H. Gray	J.M. Harlan	R.W. Peckham	Geo. Shiras, Jr.	
E.D. White	H. Gray	J.M. Harlan	R.W. Peckham	Geo. Shiras, Jr.	
E.D. White	O.W. Holmes	J.M. Harlan	R.W. Peckham	Geo. Shiras, Jr.	
E.D. White	O.W. Holmes	J.M. Harlan	R.W. Peckham	Wm. R. Day	
E.D. White	O.W. Holmes	J.M. Harlan	R.W. Peckham	Wm. R. Day	
E.D. White	O.W. Holmes	J.M. Harlan	H.H. Lurton	Wm. R. Day	
E.D. White	O.W. Holmes	J.M. Harlan	H.H. Lurton	Wm. R. Day	

Table A.4 (continued)

Patent Misuse Cases	Year				
The White Court					
	1910	J. McKenna	Wm. H. Moody	C.E. Hughes	
Henry v. A.B. Dick Co., 224 U.S. 1 (1912)	1911	J. McKenna	W. VanDevanter	C.E. Hughes	J.R. Lamar
Bauer & Cie v. O'Donnell, 229 U.S. 1 (1913)	1912–1914	J. McKenna	W. VanDevanter	C.E. Hughes	J.R. Lamar
Motion Pictures Patents Co. v. Universal Film Mfg. Co., 243 U.S. 502 (1917)	1914–1916	J. McKenna	W. VanDevanter	C.E. Hughes	J.R. Lamar
Fed. Trade Comm'n v. Gratz, 253 U.S. 421 (1920)	1916–1921	J. McKenna	W. VanDevanter	J.H. Clarke	L.D. Brandeis
The Taft Court					
	1921–1922	J. McKenna	W. VanDevanter	J.H. Clarke	L.D. Brandeis
	1922	J. McKenna	W. VanDevanter	Geo. Sutherland	L.D. Brandeis
	1923–1925	J. McKenna	W. VanDevanter	Geo. Sutherland	L.D. Brandeis
	1925–1930	H.F. Stone	W. VanDevanter	Geo. Sutherland	L.D. Brandeis
The Hughes Court					
	Feb–Mar 1930	H.F. Stone	W. VanDevanter	Geo. Sutherland	L.D. Brandeis
Carbide Corporation of America v. American Patents Development	Jun 1930–1932	H.F. Stone	W. VanDevanter	Geo. Sutherland	L.D. Brandeis

E.D. White	O.W. Holmes	J.M. Harlan	H.H. Lurton	Wm. R. Day
E.D. White	O.W. Holmes	J.M. Harlan	H.H. Lurton	Wm. R. Day
E.D. White	O.W. Holmes	M. Pitney	H.H. Lurton	Wm. R. Day
E.D. White	O.W. Holmes	M. Pitney	J.C. McReynolds	Wm. R. Day
E.D. White	O.W. Holmes	M. Pitney	J.C. McReynolds	Wm. R. Day
W.H. Taft	O.W. Holmes	M. Pitney	J.C. McReynolds	Wm. R. Day
W.H. Taft	O.W. Holmes	M. Pitney	J.C. McReynolds	Wm. R. Day
W.H. Taft	O.W. Holmes	P. Butler	J.C. McReynolds	E.T. Sanford
W.H. Taft	O.W. Holmes	P. Butler	J.C. McReynolds	E.T. Sanford
C.E. Hughes	O.W. Holmes	P. Butler	J.C. McReynolds	E.T. Sanford
C.E. Hughes	O.W. Holmes	P. Butler	J.C. McReynolds	O.J. Roberts

Table A.4   (continued)

Patent Misuse Cases	**The Hughes Court**				
Corporation, 283 U.S. 7 (1931)					
International Business Machines Corp. v. United States, 298 U.S. 131 (1936)	1932–1937	H.F. Stone	W. VanDevanter	Geo. Sutherland	L.D. Brandeis
	1937–1938	H.F. Stone	H. Black	Geo. Sutherland	L.D. Brandeis
Leitch Mfg. Co. v. Barber Co., 302 US 458 (1938)	1938	H.F. Stone	H. Black	S.F. Reed	L.D. Brandeis
	1939	H.F. Stone	H. Black	S.F. Reed	F. Frankfurter
	1940–1941	H.F. Stone	H. Black	S.F. Reed	F. Frankfurter
	Feb–Jul 1941	H.F. Stone	H. Black	S.F. Reed	F. Frankfurter
	The Stone Court				
B.B. Chemical Co. v. Ellis, 314 U.S. 495 (1942)	1941–1942	H.F. Stone	H. Black	S.F. Reed	F. Frankfurter
Morton Salt Co. v. G. S. Suppiger Co., 314 U.S. 488 (1942)	1943–1945	H.F. Stone	H. Black	S.F. Reed	F. Frankfurter
Mercoid Corp. v. Minneapolis-Honeywell Regulator Co., 320 U.S. 680 (1944)	1945–1946	H.F. Stone	H. Black	S.F. Reed	F. Frankfurter

C.E. Hughes	B.N. Cardozo	P. Butler	J.C. McReynolds	O.J. Roberts
C.E. Hughes	B.N. Cardozo	P. Butler	J.C. McReynolds	O.J. Roberts
C.E. Hughes	B.N. Cardozo	P. Butler	J.C. McReynolds	O.J. Roberts
C.E. Hughes	Wm. O. Douglas	P. Butler	J.C. McReynolds	O.J. Roberts
C.E. Hughes	Wm. O. Douglas	F. Murphy	J.C. McReynolds	O.J. Roberts
C.E. Hughes	Wm. O. Douglas	F. Murphy		O.J. Roberts
J.F. Byrnes	Wm. O. Douglas	F. Murphy	R.H. Jackson	O.J. Roberts
W.B. Rutledge	Wm. O. Douglas	F. Murphy	R.H. Jackson	O.J. Roberts
W.B. Rutledge	Wm. O. Douglas	F. Murphy	R.H. Jackson	H.H. Burton

Table A.4   (continued)

Patent Misuse Cases	The Stone Court			
Mercoid Corp. v. Mid-Continent Inv. Co., 320 U.S. 661 (1944)				
	The Vinson Court			
Int'l Salt Co. v. United States, 332 U.S. 392 (1947)	1946–1949	F.M. Vinson	H. Black	S.F. Reed	F. Frankfurter
Transparent-Wrap Mach. Corp. v. Stokes & Smith Co., 329 U.S. 637 (1947)	1949–1953	F.M. Vinson	H. Black	S.F. Reed	F. Frankfurter
	The Warren Court			
	1953–1954	R.H. Jackson	H. Black	S.F. Reed	F. Frankfurter
	1955–1956	J.M. HarlanII	H. Black	S.F. Reed	F. Frankfurter
	1956–1957	J.M. HarlanII	H. Black	S.F. Reed	F. Frankfurter
United States Gypsum Co. v. National Gypsum Co., 352 U.S. 457 (1957)	1957–1958	J.M. HarlanII	H. Black	C.E. Whittaker	F. Frankfurter
	1958–1962	J.M. HarlanII	H. Black	C.E. Whittaker	F. Frankfurter
Brulotte v. Thys Co., 379 U.S. 29 (1964)	1962–1965	J.M. HarlanII	H. Black	A.J. Goldberg	T.C. Clark
	1965–1967	J.M. HarlanII	H. Black	A. Fortas	T.C. Clark

W.B. Rutledge	Wm. O. Douglas	F. Murphy	R.H. Jackson	H.H. Burton
S. Minton	Wm. O. Douglas	T.C. Clark	R.H. Jackson	H.H. Burton
S. Minton	Wm. O. Douglas	T.C. Clark	E. Warren	H.H. Burton
S. Minton	Wm. O. Douglas	T.C. Clark	E. Warren	H.H. Burton
Wm. J. Brennan	Wm. O. Douglas	T.C. Clark	E. Warren	H.H. Burton
Wm. J. Brennan	Wm. O. Douglas	T.C. Clark	E. Warren	H.H. Burton
Wm. J. Brennan	Wm. O. Douglas	T.C. Clark	E. Warren	P. Stewart
Wm. J. Brennan	Wm. O. Douglas	B. White	E. Warren	P. Stewart
Wm. J. Brennan	Wm. O. Douglas	B. White	E. Warren	P. Stewart

Table A.4 (continued)

Patent Misuse Cases	The Warren Court				
Zenith Radio Corp. v. Hazeltine Research, 395 U.S. 100 (1969)	1967–1969	J.M. HarlanII	H. Black	A. Fortas	T. Marshall
	The Burger Court				
	1969–1970	J.M. HarlanII	H. Black	W.E. Burger	T. Marshall
	1970–1971	J.M. HarlanII	H. Black	W.E. Burger	T. Marshall
	1972–1975	Wm. Rehnquist	L.F. Powell,Jr.	W.E. Burger	T. Marshall
Dawson Chem. Co. v. Rohm & Haas Co., 448 U.S. 176 (1980)	1975–1981	Wm. Rehnquist	L.F. Powell,Jr.	W.E. Burger	T. Marshall
	1981–1986	Wm. Rehnquist	L.F. Powell,Jr.	W.E. Burger	T. Marshall
	The Rehnquist Court				
	1986–1987	Wm. Rehnquist	L.F. Powell,Jr.	A. Scalia	T. Marshall
	1988–1990	Wm. Rehnquist	A. Kennedy	A. Scalia	T. Marshall
	1990–1991	Wm. Rehnquist	A. Kennedy	A. Scalia	T. Marshall
	1991–1993	Wm. Rehnquist	A. Kennedy	A. Scalia	C. Thomas
	1993–1994	Wm. Rehnquist	A. Kennedy	A. Scalia	C. Thomas
	1994–2005	Wm. Rehnquist	A. Kennedy	A. Scalia	C. Thomas
	The Roberts Court				
	2005–2006	J. Roberts Jr.	A. Kennedy	A. Scalia	C. Thomas
	2006–2009	J. Roberts Jr.	A. Kennedy	A. Scalia	C. Thomas
	2009–2010	J. Roberts Jr.	A. Kennedy	A. Scalia	C. Thomas
	2010–2012	J. Roberts Jr.	A. Kennedy	A. Scalia	C. Thomas

Note: Individuals who have held the office of Chief Justice are shaded.

Wm. J. Brennan	Wm. O. Douglas	B. White	E. Warren	P. Stewart
Wm. J. Brennan	Wm. O. Douglas	B. White		P. Stewart
Wm. J. Brennan	Wm. O. Douglas	B. White	H. Blackmun	P. Stewart
Wm. J. Brennan	Wm. O. Douglas	B. White	H. Blackmun	P. Stewart
Wm. J. Brennan	J.P. Stevens	B. White	H. Blackmun	P. Stewart
Wm. J. Brennan	J.P. Stevens	B. White	H. Blackmun	S.D. O'Connor
Wm. J. Brennan	J.P. Stevens	B. White	H. Blackmun	S.D. O'Connor
Wm. J. Brennan	J.P. Stevens	B. White	H. Blackmun	S.D. O'Connor
D. Souter	J.P. Stevens	B. White	H. Blackmun	S.D. O'Connor
D. Souter	J.P. Stevens	B. White	H. Blackmun	S.D. O'Connor
D. Souter	J.P. Stevens	R.B. Ginsburg	H. Blackmun	S.D. O'Connor
D. Souter	J.P. Stevens	R.B. Ginsburg	S. Breyer	S.D. O'Connor
D. Souter	J.P. Stevens	R.B. Ginsburg	S. Breyer	S.D. O'Connor
D. Souter	J.P. Stevens	R.B. Ginsburg	S. Breyer	S. Alito
S. Sotomayor	J.P. Stevens	R.B. Ginsburg	S. Breyer	S. Alito
S. Sotomayor	E. Kagan	R.B. Ginsburg	S. Breyer	S. Alito

Index